The Nature of Hypnosis and Suggestion

Milton H. Erickson, MD
(1901–1980)

Ernest L. Rossi, PhD

The Nature
of Hypnosis
and Suggestion

by MILTON H. ERICKSON

*The Collected Papers of
    Milton H. Erickson on Hypnosis
        Volume I*

Edited by Ernest L. Rossi

IRVINGTON PUBLISHERS, INC.
551 FIFTH AVENUE NEW YORK, N.Y. 10017

Copyright © 1980 by Ernest L. Rossi, Ph.D.

All rights reserved. No part of this book may be may be reproduced in any manner whatever, including information storage or retrieval, in whole or in part (except for brief quotations in critical articles or reviews), without written permission from the publisher. For information, write to Irvington Publishers, Inc., 551 Fifth Avenue, New York, New York 10017.

Library of Congress Cataloging in Publication Data

Erickson, Milton H.
The nature of hypnosis and suggestion.

(The collected papers of Milton H. Erickson on hypnosis; v. 1)
Bibliography: p.
1. Hypnotism. 2. Mental suggestion. I. Rossi, Ernest Lawrence. II. Title.
RC495.E714 vol 1.   616.8'916'208s   [154.7'08]
                     79-15942
           ISBN 0-8290-0542-0

Printed in the United States of America

Foreword

This series of Milton Erickson's papers contains a fascinating array of original contributions related to every phase of hypnotic theory and practice. The papers contain stores of invaluable data that can be productively mined by researchers and clinicians for treasures useful in hypothetical structuring and experiment, as well as in catalyzing psychotherapy. Dr. Erickson is perhaps the most creative and imaginative contemporary worker in the area of hypnosis and his inspired writings in this series rank among the enduring classics in the field.

Lewis R. Wolberg, M.D.
Clinical Professor of Psychiatry,
New York University School of Medicine

Emeritus Dean, Postgraduate Center
for Mental Health

Acknowledgments

The Editor wishes to acknowledge the assistance and suggestions of many colleagues and members of the American Society of Clinical Hypnosis in the preparation of these volumes. In particular: Marian Moore, Robert Pearson, Florence Sharp, and Andre Weitzenhoffer. Significant editorial and secretarial skills have been contributed by Margaret Ryan.

The following journals and publishers have generously permitted the replication of papers in these volumes:

American Journal of Clinical Hypnosis, American Journal of Psychiatry, American Medical Association, American Psychiatric Association, American Psychological Association, Appleton-Century-Crofts, *Archives of Neurology and Psychiatry, British Journal of Medical Psychology, Bulletin of the Georgetown University Medical Center, Diseases of the Nervous System, Encyclopaedia Britannica,* Family Process, Harper and Row, Paul B. Hoeber, Inc., *Journal of Abnormal and Social Psychology, Journal of Clinical and Experimental Hypnosis, Journal of Experimental Psychology, Journal of General Psychology, Journal of Genetic Psychology, Journal of Nervous and Mental Disease, Journal of the American Society of Psychosomatic Dentistry and Medicine,* Journal Press, Julian Press, Macmillan Company, Medical Clinics of North America, Merck, Sharp and Dohme, *Perceptual and Motor Skills,* Physicians Postgraduate Press, *Psychiatry, Psychoanalytic Quarterly, Psychosomatic Medicine,* W. B. Saunders Company, Springer Verlag, William Alanson White Psychiatric Foundation, Williams and Wilkins, and Woodrow Press.

Contents

Editor's Preface ... xi
I. *On the Nature of Hypnosis* ... 1
   1. Initial experiments investigating the nature of hypnosis ... 3
   2. Further experimental investigation of hypnosis: Hypnotic and nonhypnotic realities ... 18
   3. A special inquiry with Aldous Huxley into the nature and character of various states of consciousness ... 83
   4. Autohypnotic experiences of Milton H. Erickson (written with E. L. Rossi) ... 108
II. *Approaches to Trance Induction* ... 133
   5. Historical note on the hand levitation and other ideomotor techniques ... 135
   6. Deep hypnosis and its induction ... 139
   7. Naturalistic techniques of hypnosis ... 168
   8. Further clinical techniques of hypnosis: utilization techniques ... 177
   9. A transcript of a trance induction with commentary (written with J. Haley and J. H. Weakland) ... 206
   10. The confusion technique in hypnosis ... 258
   11. The dynamics of visualization, levitation and confusion in trance induction ... 292
   12. Another example of confusion in trance induction ... 297
   13. An hypnotic technique for resistant patients: The patient, the technique, and its rationale and field experiments ... 299
   14. Pantomime techniques in hypnosis and the implications ... 331
   15. The "surprise" and "my-friend-John" techniques of hypnosis: Minimal cues and natural field experimentation ... 340
   16. Respiratory rhythm in trance induction: The role of minimal sensory cues in normal and trance behavior ... 360
   17. An indirect induction of trance: Simulation and the role of indirect suggestion and minimal cues ... 366
   18. Notes on minimal cues in vocal dynamics and memory ... 373
III. *On the Nature of Suggestion* ... 379
   19. Concerning the nature and character of posthypnotic behavior (written with E.M. Erickson) ... 381
   20. Varieties of double bind (written with E. L. Rossi) ... 412
   21. Two-level communication and the microdynamics of trance and suggestion (written with E. L. Rossi) ... 430
   22. The indirect forms of suggestion (written with E. L. Rossi) ... 452

23. Indirect forms of suggestion in hand levitation (written with E. L. Rossi)	478
IV. *On the Possible Dangers of Hypnosis*	491
24. Possible detrimental effects of experimental hypnosis	493
25. An experimental investigation of the possible antisocial use of hypnosis	498
26. An instance of potentially harmful misinterpretation of hypnosis	531
27. Stage hypnotist back syndrome	533
28. Editorial	536
29. Editorial	540
Appendix 1: Contents of future volumes in this series.	543
Appendix 2: Bibliography of writings not included in this series.	553
Bibliography of Volume I	556
Subject Index	561
Name Index	569

Editor's Preface

These four volumes of Milton H. Erickson's selected papers have been collected for clinicians and researchers who wish to explore in depth the work of one of the most seminal minds in the history of hypnosis and psychotherapy. When Erickson began publishing his studies in the early 1930s, hypnosis was in a curious position: most investigators agreed that hypnosis had played a central role in the early studies of psychopathology and our first efforts at psychotherapy, but the authoritative approaches associated with its use were supplanted on the one hand by the seemingly more sophisticated approaches of the psychoanalytic schools, and on the other hand by experimental psychology.

The situation might have continued in just this manner, with hypnosis regarded as nothing more significant than a colorful curiosity in our therapeutic past. Into this situation, however, came the accident that was Milton H. Erickson. He was an accident of nature born with a number of congenital sensory-perceptual problems that led him to experience the world in ways so different that his acute mind could survive only by realizing at a very early age the relativity of our human frames of reference. To these early problems was added the rare medical tragedy of being stricken by two different strains of polio at the ages of 17 and 51. His efforts to rehabilitate himself led to a personal rediscovery of many classical hypnotic phenomena and how they could be utilized therapeutically.

Erickson's experimental and therapeutic explorations with the hypnotic modality span more than 50 years. His successful rejuvenation of the entire field may be attributed to his development of the nonauthoritarian, indirect approaches to suggestion wherein subjects learn how to experience hypnotic phenomena and how to utilize their own potentials to solve problems in their own way. The contents of these four volumes can be best understood as working papers on a journey of discovery. There is little that is fixed, final, or permanently validated about them. Most of these papers are heuristics that can stimulate the mind of the reader and evoke the awe of discovery, the potentials for which are unlimited in the dimension of human consciousness.

The problem of how to present these papers in the best order could have been solved in many ways. A simple chronological order seemed unsatisfactory because the record of much of Erickson's earliest work was published only at a later date. Many papers dealing with the same theme which should obviously be grouped together were published in different phases of his career. Because of this the editor decided to make a balanced presentation wherein each volume identifies a major area of exploration with appropriate sections wherein the papers are presented in an approximation of chronological order.

Each of the first four volumes of this series contains a number of unpublished papers selected by the editor from several boxes of manuscripts entrusted to him by Erickson for this purpose. A companion volume, in preparation, will contain only previously unpublished lectures and hypnotic demonstrations by Erickson throughout his career. Many of these exist in various forms of neglect and deterioration all over the world wherever he gave his numerous presentations. The editor is currently assembling as many of these as can be accurately transcribed and reviewing them with Erickson for his elucidating commentaries. So subtle are his approaches that even a detailed study of his demonstrations often leaves the investigator without a full understanding of what Erickson is doing. Because of this the editor would like to take the occasion of the publication of these four volumes to make an appeal to whomever is in possession of previously unpublished records of Erickson's work to make them available to us for possible inclusion in this companion volume. It is only through such cooperation that we can all grow together.

Ernest L. Rossi

I. On the Nature of Hypnosis

The four papers of this first section provide a broad introduction to Erickson's lifelong quest for an understanding of the nature of the hypnotic experience. The first paper, "Initial experiments investigating the nature of hypnosis" (1964), is a retrospective report of Erickson's first studies of hypnosis as an undergraduate student during the 1923-24 seminar on hypnosis at the University of Wisconsin under the supervision of Clark L. Hull, Ph.D., one of the founding fathers of experimental psychology and learning theory in the United States. These studies as a student lay the groundwork for an understanding of hypnosis and trance as normal experiences that can develop naturally during periods of introspection. There is no need for mysterious manipulations of subjects. One does not really control subjects in hypnosis; rather, one provides them with stimuli and opportunities for an intense inner absorption that sometimes leads to recognizably different states of consciousness: what Erickson later calls hypnotic and nonhypnotic realities.

The next paper on Erickson's extended investigations of the nature of hypnotic and nonhypnotic realities yields extraordinary insights into deep trance (somnambulism) and the methodological problems involved in its study. One basic problem is that most workers in the field tend to confuse hypnosis and trance behavior with suggestibility. Because many hypnotized subjects tend to be complacent in accepting and carrying out suggestion, since the time of Liebeault and Bernheim there has been an uncritical acceptance of the view that hypnosis can be defined as a condition of heightened suggestibility (see the editor's discussion in *Hypnotic Realities*, Irvington Publishers, p. 19). In the studies of this paper Erickson devises approaches that enable us to eliminate or at least minimize the effects of suggestion in order to explore the nature of hypnotic reality. In the process of this quest he presents what some regard as one of the most provocative studies on the characteristics of hypnotic somnambulism ever published. He illustrates the approaches we can use to recognize somnambulism and how investigators may train themselves to better facilitate its development.

Because this report is so rambling and rich in its detailed examples, many readers may lose themselves as they breathlessly attempt to digest it in one or two sittings. Rest assured, that cannot be done! It requires an extended period of study. This paper is actually a report covering more than four decades of intensive reflection and research on the most subtle issues of evaluating the nature and alterations of human consciousness. Consciousness usually does not recognize when it is in an altered condition. Consider how infrequently we realize we are dreaming during a dream. The situation is even more confusing and complex when it is realized that hypnotic and nonhypnotic realities may apparently coexist and fluctuate in their mutual relations from moment to moment. As Erickson states in his final sentence, "... this author feels that a somnambulistic hypnotic subject spontaneously apprehends the surrounding environment of realities differently than does a subject in the ordinary state of waking consciousness, [but] the one type of reality apprehension does not preclude the other type of reality apprehension." Many of the illustrations in this report demonstrate how somnambulistic subjects tend to mask their conditions from the operator as well as from themselves. Because of this we could well ask just how often hypnotic subjects may be experiencing somnambulistic states without it being recognized. It is intriguing questions like these that may inspire current and future students with a fresh sense of exploratory wonder about their subject.

The next two papers on Erickson's own autohypnotic experiences and his hypnotic work with Aldous Huxley continue this intensive exploration of hypnotic realities. Huxley's description of his own state of "deep reflection" helps us gain a perspective on the utilization of hypnosis for facilitating creativity, while his independent discovery of the "timeless and spaceless void" of deep trance verifies Erickson's previous findings. This together with Huxley's experience with hallucinations in all sense modalities, as well as his experiences with hypermnesia, two-stage dissociative regression, time distortion, and posthypnotic amnesia, illustrate what a talented mind can accomplish with hypnosis.

The final paper on the autohypnotic experiences of Milton H. Erickson provides a fascinating account of how Erickson's sensory and constitutional difficulties were a formative influence in leading him as a puzzled young lad to an early discovery of the relativity of perception and mental frames of reference. He outlines the successful approaches he has used to train himself as well as others in somnambulistic activity and the exploration of hypnotic realities. His discussions of the relation between hallucinatory experience and creative moments of insight, the role of autohypnosis in life crises and identity problems, and his use of early memories to cope with pain and the facilitation of physical rehabilitation suggest important lines of hypnotherapeutic research. His poignant account of his struggles in learning to cope with his personal infirmities reminds us of the archetype of the wounded physician who, in healing himself, learns to heal others.

1. Initial Experiments Investigating the Nature of Hypnosis

Milton H. Erickson

INTRODUCTION

During the 1923-24 formal Seminar on Hypnosis at the University of Wisconsin under the supervision of Clark L. Hull, the author, then an undergraduate student, reported for the discussion by the postgraduate students of the psychology department upon his own many and varied experimental investigative findings during the previous six months of intensive work and on his current studies. There was much debate, argument and discussion about the nature of hypnosis, the psychological state it constituted, the respective roles of the operator and the subject, the values and significances of the processes employed in induction, the nature of the subjects' responses in developing trances, the possibility of transcendence of normal capabilities, the nature of regression, the evocation of previously learned patterns of response whether remote or recent, the processes involved in individual hypnotic phenomenon and in the maintenance of the trance state, and above all the identification of the primary figure in the development of the trance state, be it the operator or the subject. The weekly seminars were scheduled for two hours each, but usually lasted much longer, and frequently extra meetings were conducted informally in evenings and on weekends and holidays, with most of the group in attendance.

No consensus concerning the problems could be reached, as opinions and individual interpretations varied widely, and this finally led the author to undertake a special investigative project in October 1923. This special study has remained unpublished, although it was recorded in full at the time, as were many other studies. One of the reasons for the decision not to publish at that time was the author's dubiousness concerning Hull's strong conviction that the operator, through what he said and did to the subject, was much more important than any inner behavioral processes of the subject. This was a view Hull carried over into his work at Yale, one instance of which was his endeavor to establish a "standardized technique" for induction. By this term he meant the use of the

---

Reprinted with permission from *The American Journal of Clinical Hypnosis,* October, 1964, 7, 152–162.

same words, the same length of time, the same tone of voice, etc., which finally eventuated in an attempt to elicit comparable trance states by playing "induction phonograph records" without regard for individual differences among subjects, and for their varying degrees of interest, different motivations, and variations in the capacity to learn. Hull seemed thus to disregard subjects as persons, putting them on a par with inanimate laboratory apparatus, despite his awareness of such differences among subjects that could be demonstrated by tachistoscopic experiments. Even so, Hull did demonstrate that rigid laboratory procedures could be applied in the study of some hypnotic phenomena.

Recently published papers concerning the realities of hypnosis have led to a rereading and analysis of the author's notebooks in which numerous unpublished studies were fully recorded. (Credit for this practice should be given to Dr. Hull, and the author often wonders what happened to the bookshelves of notebooks which Dr. Hull himself maintained, full of his own unpublished studies.) The rereading of this material produced the data upon which this paper is based, permitting this report on experimental investigations into some of the apparent misunderstandings of hypnosis which are still variously accepted without careful critical thinking.

EXPERIMENTAL PLAN

As originally planned and executed, this early experiment to secure some of the answers to the intriguing questions confronting the seminar group was so organized that it did not involve the use of hypnosis. Rather, it was based upon a consideration of the concepts of introspection developed by E. B. Titchener, Wilhelm Wundt, W. B. Pillsbury, and others, and was organized as a direct inquiry into these concepts as a possible initial approach to a later identification of hypnosis or of some of its phenomena. A central consideration in the proposed experimental project was suggested by the well-known Biblical saying, "As a man thinketh in his heart, so is he," a point made in the seminar discussions by several of the discussants. Professor Joseph Jastrow, who was then head of the psychology department, aided and advised the author in his plan of experimentation. Jastrow himself was only slightly interested in hypnosis, but he was interested in the author as a student. Hull was not consulted, nor did he know of the experiment until it was completed.

SUBJECT SELECTION

The securing of subjects was relatively easy, since any college population offers a wealth of volunteers. Two elements of selectivity were employed. All students taking psychology were excluded. All students who were acquainted

Initial Experiments

with the author were excluded for the reason that they might know that he was interested in hypnosis. Both male and female undergraduates were employed, most of them by mere chance being sophomores. Among them there was a predominance of agricultural, home economics, enginneering, commerce, and liberal art students, with an approximately even distribution of sex, and of comparable ages.

To these students individually, using prepared typewritten material, a plausible, somewhat interesting, but definitely superficial explanation was given of the concept of "introspection." A comparably carefully worded invitation was extended to each of them to participate in an experiment; this embraced the idea that the experimenter proposed to do research consisting of "discovering the processes of thought in thinking through from beginning to end any specified task." As an illustrative example, it was pointed out that people know the alphabet and can recite it fluently. However, the majority of those same people cannot recite the alphabet backward correctly from Z to A except by a slow "back-and-forth process of thinking." To those who promptly demonstrated that they could recite the alphabet backward easily, a second example was offered, namely, the extreme difficulty that would be encountered in reciting backward the entire nursery rhyme of, "Mary had a little lamb —."

It was then explained that a much simpler task was in mind for them to do, and they were earnestly asked not to do any reading of Titchener's "work on thought processes" (Titchener's name was repeatedly mentioned to discover any previous awareness of his work, to emphasize "thought processes," and to distract their attention from the word "introspection").

They were individually apprised of the possibility that the task might take from one half to two hours, and a clock was indicated in full view, running silently, located directly in front of them on a shelf on the laboratory wall. The experimenter, it was explained, would sit quietly behind a screen some 12 feet to the rear and would not be visible; he could be spoken to or questioned if the desire or need arose, but it was preferred that the task once begun be done in complete silence, so that there would be no distractions or interferences.

What the subjects did not know or observe was that a mirror was so arranged carelessly among odds and ends in a jumble of laboratory apparatus so that the author had a full view of the subjects' faces by means of an obscure peephole concealed by the patterned design on the screen.

From a typewritten copy each subject was separately given the following instructions:

> "You are to seat yourself in this chair comfortably, just looking straight ahead. With your eyes open you are to imagine that there is a small table standing beside the right (left in the case of those left-handed) arm of the chair. Your arms are to be resting comfortably in your lap. On that imaginary small table you will imagine that there is a large fruit bowl filled with apples, pears, bananas, plums, oranges,

or any other kind of fruit you like, but do not turn your head to look in that direction. All of this imaginary fruit you can imagine as being in easy reach of your hand resting in your lap.

Next you are to imagine a table of normal height on the bare floor just in front of you, just far enough away so that you would have to lean a little forward to place anything on it.

Now the task to be done is for you to sit in the chair looking straight ahead and *mentally go through the processes step by step and in correct order* of thinking at a mental level only of the task of lifting your hand up from your lap, of reaching up over the arm of the chair, of feeling elbow and shoulder movements, the lateral extension of your arm, the slight lowering of your hand, the touching of the fruit, the feel of the fruit, the selection of any one piece, of closing your fingers on it, lifting it, sensing its weight, moving your hand with the fruit up, back over the arm of the chair and then placing it on that imaginary table in front of you. That is all you have to do, just imagine the whole thing. If your eyes get tired or if you can think your thought processes out more clearly with them shut, just close them. You should expect to make errors in getting each step in the right order, and you will have to pause and think back just as you would in trying to think the alphabet (or the nursery rhyme) backward, and it is only reasonable that you will make mistakes and have to go back and start over again. Just take your time, and do it carefully, silently, really noting each of your thought processes. If you wish, I will reread these instructions, and you may realize that perhaps you might have such a thought as first picking up an apple and then changing your mind and deciding to pick up an orange. [All subjects wanted a second reading, some a third.]

Now that the instructions are clear, let's look at the bulletin board on the wall over there, and when the minute hand of the clock is directly on one of the numerals of the clockface, we will both take our positions and the experiment will begin.

THE EXPERIMENTAL RESULTS

There were three general types of results obtained from a total of 63 subjects. These may be classified for the purpose of discussion into three general categories: none; fright reactions; and full participation.

Concerning the first category, which included 18 subjects, they became restless, demanded further repetitions of instructions, and finally declared their total disinterest in the entire project, declaring that they could not do it, that it did not seem to make any sense, or simply that they were no longer interested in participating. Engineering and agriculture students predominated in this group. The author's tentative conclusion was that such students preferred concrete real-

Initial Experiments

ities to abstract imagining.

The second category, including 13 students, was much more interesting. They became frightened even to a state of panic, interrupted the experiment to demand reassurance, and finally refused to continue. (Unfortunately no personality studies had been done on them, nor did the author then have enough clinical experience to appraise them as personalities.)

Their reactions were described variously by them, but usually concerned uncontrollable and involuntary upward movements of the dominant hand; peculiar numb sensations of the legs, a feeling of rigidity of the body, and a blurring or closing of the eyes that they felt they could not control. To all of this they reacted with a frightened feeling which alarmed them, this alarm then allowing a freedom of action which led to an emphatic demand to be excused. The experimenter accompanied his dismissal of them by elaborately expressed gratitude for the clarity of their demonstrations of "one of the aspects of intense mental concentration." This proved to be a most reassuring maneuver, so much so that three subjects then volunteered to repeat the experiment. The offers were not accepted, assurance being given that the experimenter was already satisfied with their contribution.

The third group, numbering 32, manifested to varying degrees some remarkably similar forms of behavior. These may be listed as (1) slow loss of the blink reflex; (2) altered respiratory rhythm; (3) loss of swallowing reflex; (4) development of ideomotor activity in the dominant hand; (5) exceedingly slow movement of the hand and arm up and over the arm of the chair; (6) slow closing of the eyes, usually at some point preceding or during the ideomotor movement of the hand and arm; (7) groping movements of the fingers, as if selecting an object at the site of the imaginary fruit bowl; (8) a lifting movement involved in picking up an object, and a slow leaning forward, seemingly placing the object upon the imaginary table; and (9) then leaning back in the chair and *continuing to rest quietly.*

The experimenter was at a loss as to how to proceed the first time that this succession of events occurred, which was with the third subject. The first two subjects had rejected the task. Intense study of the quietly resting subject's face indicated that a deep trance had been induced. Yet there had been no mention of hypnosis; the author's then naiveté and inexperience with human behavior in a rigid, circumscribed, experimental situation did not permit him to grasp the significance of the situation immediately. The entire purpose had been to study behavior in two *presumably* different circumscribed situations; in one of these, designated as a hypnotic situation, the author felt that it was distinctly possible that the operator was the dominant and effective active figure; and the second, presumably different form of behavior was characterized by the nonparticipation of the operation with the subject as the active person.

The subject passively waited, while the experimenter considered that there had been a foundation for genuine hypnotic rapport because the original joint participatory activity concerned in the giving and receiving of instructions, the looking at the bulletin board while awaiting the minute hand of the clock to reach a numeral, and the separate but joint taking of respective positions. Acting upon this tentative assumption, and still remaining behind the screen, he remarked, "I think you have certainly worked on this concentrating long enough now, so it will be all right if you leave, because I have to stay and write this up."

Slowly the subject awakened in the manner characteristic of the hypnotic arousal pattern of behavior, commented, as he looked at the clock, that the time had seemingly passed remarkably rapidly, and then departed.

The previous two subjects who had failed were engineering students; this one was an English major. It was reasoned again that the engineers were more interested in concrete realities, and that the student of literature was interested in abstractions of thought.

Despite this early significant experimental occurrence with the third subject, and thence the expectation of similar possibilities in the experimenter's mind thereafter, a total of 31 subjects failed in random order, three of them being among the final five, and the very last subject was a failure in a fashion similar to the first two subjects.

The 32 subjects who manifested hypnoticlike behavior showed various degrees of what could be regarded as trance states, and some spontaneously made comments aloud about their behavior. Thus one subject made the accurate observation, "I not only talk with my hands, I think with them." Another, a music student, remarked similarly, "Every time a little old melody runs through my head, I just can't help beating time to it with my foot, and now with thoughts running through my head, I'm moving my arm." Both appeared to be commenting only to themselves.

Even more noteworthy was the behavior of some other subjects. One such subject, judging from his finger movements "picked up" an apple or an orange which he "placed on the table" and then he deliberately "reached" again into the "fruit bowl," apparently selected and ate two hallucinatory bananas, going through the motions with both hands of peeling them, and then droping the "peelings" into an apparently hallucinated wastebasket on the other side of the chair. Another subject, after apparently "placing" a banana on the "table," asked the author if she might have an orange to eat. Consent was given; she leaned over and, with open eyes, selected an orange as if visually, went through the motions of picking it up, peeling it, and apparently putting the peelings on the arm of the chair, and eating it, and then, seemingly at a loss how to dispose of the peelings, finally leaned forward and placed them on the imaginary table slightly to one side of where she had previously placed the banana. When she had finished this hallucinatory activity, she opened her handbag and dried her mouth and hands with her handkerchief.

Another subject asked if he might take an apple home with him, specifying "that big red one there," explaining that he wanted to take it to his room to eat while be studied. Consent was given, and he went through the motions of picking it up and putting it in his jacket pocket.

The same procedure was followed in arousing these apparently hypnotized subjects as had been employed with the third subject. This unprovided-for variation in the planned procedure had of necessity been improvised by the experimenter with the third subject, and since the first two subjects were uncooperative and had been dismissed, its introduction was not considered to be an undue variation in procedure.

The same words of reassurance were used for each of the group manifesting "fright reactions," thus making that enforced alteration of experimental procedure a constant factor in the experiment.

A variation of procedure involved a half-dozen subjects who apparently did not completely arouse from the trance state immediately upon instruction. This situation was met by walking with these subjects out of the laboratory and outside the building through a nearby side-door, making the comment "Well, before I write up my report, I'll have a breath of fresh air." This proved to be a sufficient procedure to arouse the subjects completely.

Some subjects who revealed only a partial or no amnesia for what they had done were surprisingly noted to continue to hallucinate after awakening the fruit bowl and its contents and the large and small tables, as actual objects and some even commented with curiosity, remarking that they had not seen those objects when they first entered the room. These comments were always evaded by the expedient of pleading pressure of work in writing up immediately the account of the experiment.

But there were 12 subjects who demonstrated a total amnesia from the moment of sitting down in the chair as they looked at the clock until the close of the session. Several, upon arousing, were startled by the length of time that had passed, as noted by again regarding the clock. The passage of time was obviously a surprise to them, and this confused several, each of whom declared, "But I'm just ready to begin." Others looked bewildered, glanced at the clock, and asked what had happened. None of this group continued to hallucinate either the large or small tables or the bowl of fruit, but one subject remarked that his mouth felt and tasted as if he had eaten a banana.

In no instance was any explanation given to or by the subjects except to say that they had "really concentrated."

CONTINUATION OF EXPERIMENTAL STUDY

Some three months later the 31 subjects who did not complete the experiment—that is, the 18 who had not been willing or able to begin and the 13 who had been frightened away—were again approached individually with a new request.

This request was that they participate in a new experiment—namely, that of being hypnotized. All but one agreed, this one being in the first category of complete nonparticipation, and several agreed but seemingly reluctantly. (These included some of those who had been frightened.)

In a different room, but comparable to the first, subjects were met individually, and it was explained that they were to seat themselves comfortably with their hands in their lap in a chair before a writing table on which was a pad of paper and a pencil. They were to look continuously at the pencil until their hand picked it up and started to write involuntarily. They were to concentrate secondarily on the lifting of the hand and primarily on seeing the pencil begin to write, and to do nothing more.

Again the experimenter retired to watch through the peephole in the previously prepared screen at the full-face mirror view of the subject which was afforded by several mirrors spaced so as to give full views from different angles. These mirrors were all obscurely and inconspicuously placed in stacks of laboratory apparatus.

Of the 30 subjects, 10 gave up. These were again all agricultural and engineering students, and none was from the frightened group. The remaining 20 all developed trance states of varying depths. Of the 18 who had originally walked out during the first experiment without more than a semblance of cooperation, seven remained. Of these, three developed a somnambulistic trance, three a medium trance, and one a light trance. The criteria at that time employed to classify these subjects as somnambulistic were simply the presence of open eyes, automatic writing, and a total subsequent amnesia. The criteria for a medium trance were a partial or a selective, but not total, amnesia. Thus there might be a memory of reading what had been written, but it was regarded as the hand, not the subject, that picked up the pencil and wrote. Light trances were so classified when adequate ideomotor activity occurred, but when there was full recollection of the events and an expressed description, "I could feel and see it happening to me, but I couldn't help it. It didn't seem to be me doing the movements."

All of the previously frightened group, 13 in number, developed trance states, four of whom were somnambulistic, seven medium, and two light. Of significance was the fact that the seven medium- and the two light-trance subjects spontaneously volunteered the information that going into hypnosis was "exactly like introspection and concentration." They described in detail the terrifying sensations they had felt originally, and the reexperiencing of the same feelings again, but with the comforting knowledge that they had been told that they were to be hypnotized, an idea that had evidently reassured them and effectively abolished their fears. They expected to feel different when hypnotized, and this understanding was reassuring. It served to allow them to accept the experience, not to effect it.

The somnambulistic subjects were subsequently questioned directly in the trance state for their feelings as they had developed the hypnotic state. They all reported having the same subjective feelings that they had experienced in the "introspection and concentration experiment" and volunteered the information

Initial Experiments

that they now knew that they had then developed a trance state, but did not so realize it at the time. The four somnambulistic subjects, who had also previously reacted with alarm, explained that the "unexpectedness of strange feelings" had frightened them. Knowing now that hypnosis was being employed, they had available an understanding of their subjective experiences, and hence there had been no alarm.

The original experiment of "introspection" was again repeated with all of the previously successful subjects, with the result that all except seven developed somnambulistic trances, and those seven all developed medium trances. The subjects previously manifesting light trances now developed medium or somnambulistic trances.

The experiment with pencil and paper was then repeated with the subjects who had been successful in the "introspection experiments," this time as an experiment in hypnosis. Hypnotic trances were induced in all subjects very quickly, and practically all were somnambulistic.

All of these subjects were used by Clark L. Hull's graduate students and also by the author during the second semester's continuation of the seminar, particularly in the conduction of various studies for publication in Hull's book and elsewhere, in replicating the author's reports during the first semester, and in the demonstration of the elicitation of other hypnotic phenomena.

ADDITIONAL EXPERIMENTATION

When the above-described experiments were almost completed, a particular event occurred during a seminar meeting. Some of the graduate students had been pursuing the hypothesis that "suggestions" constituted no more than a *point of departure for responsive behavior,* but that the manner and fashion in which these hypnotic suggestions and commands served as *points of departure* for complex hypnotic phenomena which were not encompassed by either the apparent or implied meaningfulness of the words employed seemed to be inexplicable problems. Out of the unsatisfying and divergent views and the more or less relevant discussions the author seized upon, for an immediate experiment, the narration of her anger pattern by Miss O, whom he knew fairly well as a group member but not as a person, although he knew alot about her family history.

Miss O's long-established anger pattern was of a temper-tantrum character. Whenever angered or frustrated by her father or mother, she, an only child, would turn away suddenly, rush upstairs to her bedroom, slam the door, throw herself on her bed, and burst into angry sobbing. She consented to accept the following "suggestion": "Go down the flight of stairs just beyond this seminar room, step outside the building through the side door at the foot of the stairway, look over the campus briefly, come back inside the building, look about briefly, then rush upstairs with increasing speed, rush in here slamming the door behind you, and fling yourself into your seat at the conference table."

With obvious embarrassment she consented, and a few minutes later, while the group waited expectantly, Miss O could be heard running up the stairway. She rushed into the room, flushed of face, slammed the door behind her, threw herself into her chair, resting her face on her arms on the table, and to the bewilderment and amazement of the group including the experimenter, burst into uncontrollable sobbing.

After some minutes of sobbing Miss O straightened up and furiously berated the experimenter for his "outrageous suggestion," and then turned her wrath on the entire group for their "shameful conduct." Then, with equal suddenness, her anger left her, and in a bewildered and startled fashion she asked, "Why did I get so angry?"

There followed much excited discussion and questioning until someone asked Miss O at what point her anger had developed. To this she could reply only that she had no idea, and she then readily and interestedly agreed to repeat the experiment with the addition that this time she was "to note exactly where you are when you develop anger."

As she left the room, she remarked with calm interest that it seemed to her that she had become angry on the way upstairs, but that she was not certain.

There followed an exact repetition of her previous behavior but with the exception that when she again began to berate the experimenter and the group, she suddenly recognized her reality situation, stopped, laughed through her tears, and said, "Why, I did the same thing again." She then explained, "I was thinking that I had been about halfway upstairs before, but then I suddenly got so angry I couldn't think until just now. But please don't talk to me because I still feel angry and I can't help it." Her facial expression and tone of voice confirmed her statement.

Shortly, however, evidently recovering her composure, she joined in the discussion of her behavior with interest and without embarrassment.

Later in the discussion she was asked again by the experimenter if she were willing to repeat the experiment. She hesitated a moment and then agreed. As she walked toward the seminar room door, she commented that it would not be necessary to go through the entire procedure, but that she could just mentally review the whole task, step by step. As she completed this comment she opened the door to leave the room, but immediately slammed it shut and whirled on the experimenter screaming, "You—you—you!" She then burst into tears and collapsed in her chair, sobbing. Shortly she again composed herself and asked to be excused from further participation in such experimentation.

A few seminars later, when the experimenter had completed his study as described above, Miss O was asked again about her previous demonstrations. She manifested embarrassment but reluctantly expressed a willingness to discuss them.

At once the author explained, "I don't want you to go downstairs or to get

Initial Experiments 13

angry. All you need to do is sit right there, rest your head on your arms on the table and quietly, very quietly, and very comfortably, remember every step you made going downstairs, opening the side door, looking over the campus, coming back inside, and looking up and down the hallway as you did before you started for the stairway. *Then when you have got that far in your thinking, sit up straight and look at me.''*

Miss O readily acceded to the request, and shortly straightened up and looked at the author, who was sitting directly opposite her at the conference table. As she did so, it was apparent to everyone that she was in a deep somnambulistic trance, and she was found to be in rapport only with the experimenter, being completely out of touch with her actual surroundings. She did not respond in any way to the group members, was passively responsive to the experimenter, and catalepsy, ideosensory phenomena, dissociation, apparent regression, and anaesthesia could be demonstrated. When she was asked to develop hand levitation, she apparently failed. Previous experience with other subjects led the experimenter to suggest hand levitation with the other hand. Apparently again she failed.

The experimenter then carefully stated, "I want to start hand levitation with you again, *doing so from the very beginning.* When you are ready, nod your head to let me know." Shortly she nodded her head, whereupon the experimenter slowly and systematically suggested right-hand levitation to be continued to a level higher than her head. As the author gave his suggestions, the group watched her hand. There was no upward movement. The experimenter, watching her head and neck for muscle tension, finally remarked, "That's fine. Now place slowly and gently and deliberately your left hand on the back of your right hand." Slowly, she lifted her left hand upward above her head, slowly moving it across the midline, then lowering it slightly and letting it come to rest, while the rest of the group stared in silent wonderment. At the cessation of the movement of her left hand she was asked if it were on top of her right hand. She slowly nodded her head affirmatively. This was only the third time the experimenter had encountered hallucinatory hand levitation, and the first instance had bewildered him immensely. Comparable hallucinatory hypnotic behavior of other forms has since been encountered occasionally in the author's subjects and those of others. Unfortunately lack of critical observation or inexperience sometimes leads to the inference that the subjects are unresponsive rather than the realization that they are most responsive in a more complex fashion than was intended, and that the requested hypnotic behavior is being subjectively experienced on an hallucinatory level.

In this instance, in demonstrating hypnotic phenomena with Miss O, hand levitation had been left as the final demonstration for one certain reason. Miss O, in the previous experiment dealing with her anger reaction, had been asked to run *up* the stairway. Hence the experimenter was being very cautious about a renewed use of the word *up* or a word of similar meaning because of the possible association with the previous use of the word. He had expected only likelihood of anger development, but with the failure of beginning levitation he had visually checked her neck muscles for evidence of tension which had been noted in the two previous subjects who had hallucinated hand levitation.

Indicating silence to the group, he asked Miss O to rest her hands comfortably in her lap and indicate if she were willing to answer a few general questions about the time she manifested anger for the experimenter. She nodded her head affirmatively.

She was then asked, "Are you now just like you were then, or perhaps I should say, Are your present mental state and your mental state at that time the same or identical?" Her face developed a thoughtful expression, and then slowly she nodded her head affirmatively. She was asked, "Will it be all right for me to ask you now to feel those feelings that you then developed?" Her reply was a verbal, "Please don't." "Why not?" "I don't want to get angry." She was asked if she wanted to do anything more. After a few moments she replied, "No." Accordingly she was asked to put her arms on the conference table, to rest her head upon them, and then "straighten up, just like you were when I first asked you to do this same thing." This she did, becoming fully awake with a seemingly total amnesia for the entire trance experience.

One of the group asked her if she could be hypnotized, to which she answered that she never had been but thought she would like to be, and she expressed an immediate willingness to act as a subject.

She was asked by the author to place her hands palm down on her thighs and *to watch her right hand*. Essentially similar hand-levitation suggestions were given as before, but this time, because of the instruction to *watch* her right hand which actually remained immobile on her lap, her visual hallucinating of the slow continuous rise of her right hand was apparent, until the direction of her gaze indicated that the hand was above her head level. Several of the group tried to question her, but she proved to be in rapport only with the experimenter.

She was asked by him if she had ever been in a trance before, the intended meaning being only during that day. Her answer was a simple "Yes." "How many times?" Instead of the expected answer of "Once" she replied, "Four times." "When?" "Today, that other day." "What other day?" "When I got angry."

She was awakened, and an apparently total amnesia was demonstrated by the expedient of asking her again if she had ever ben hypnotized, which elicited the previous negative reply and offer to volunteer.

Instead of overtly accepting her offer, a member of the group asked her if she thought she could do hand levitation. She replied, "I don't know but I'd like to try," immediately settling herself in position and duplicating without any further remarks or suggestions her previous hallucinatory ideomotor behavior and trance development. The member of the group who had put the question proved to be the only person in rapport with her.

She was asked to awaken from the trance state. Again she manifested amnesia. The next few hours of the seminar were spent discussing her behavior to which was added a discussion of the author's private experimentation. The entire sequence of events was disturbing and obviously displeasing to Dr. Hull, since he felt that the importance of suggestions and suggestibility and the role of the operator in trance induction were being ignored and bypassed, with the result that this approach to a study of hypnosis was then abandoned in the University of Wisconsin seminars.

FURTHER CONSIDERATIONS

Since then, particularly after the author had received his doctoral degree and was finally officially permitted to resume experimental work at the Worcester State Hospital in Worcester, Massachusetts, much use was made of these learnings in developing the author's various techniques of indirect and permissive hypnotic induction.

In addition, and by way of contrasting their respective values, the author has done much experimentation on direct and authoritative techniques and on traditional, ritualistic, repetitive verbal techniques.

In general his findings, based upon experience with many thousands of subjects, have been that the simpler and more permissive and unobtrusive is the technique, the more effective it has proved to be, both experimentally and therapeutically, in the achievement of significant results. Also, his experience has been that the less the operator does and *the more he confidently and expectantly allows the subjects to do,* the easier and more effectively will the hypnotic state and hypnotic phenomena be elicited in accord with the subjects' own capabilities and uncolored by efforts to please the operator. However, it must be borne in mind that subjects differ as personalities, and that hypnotic techniques must be tailored to fit the individual needs and the needs of the specific situation. Therefore users of hypnosis should be fully cognizant with all types of hypnotic techniques and fully appreciative of the subjects as personalities. They should bear ever in mind that the role of the operator is no more than that of a source of intelligent guidance while the hypnotic subjects proceed with the work that demonstrates hypnotic phenomena, insofar as is permitted by the subjects' own endowment of capacities to behave in various ways. Thus the color-blind person can not be given visual receptors to receive color stimuli, but the person with normal color vision may be enabled to block the utilization of visual receptors of a specific type—just as happens in the common experience in ordinary everyday life, when a book with a certain clearly visible title cannot be found in the bookcase because it is blue-covered and the search has been made in a mistaken belief that it is red-covered, thereby utilizing a different frame of reference and thus defeating the effort to find the book.

It should also be kept in mind that moods, attitudes, and understandings often change in the subjects even as they are undergoing trance induction, and that there should be a fluidity of change in technique by the operator from one type of approach to another as indicated.

Unfortunately much experimentation is done in only rigid terms of the operator's limited understandings and abilities. Perhaps this may best be exemplified by such typical experiments as naively demonstrating such "antisocial behavior in hypnosis" as persuading a subject to open a new lipstick or to appropriate a dollar bill in a strict laboratory setting, in ignorance of the later demonstrated fact that the laboratory setting and the experimental situation alone, with no utlization of hypnosis whatsoever, may be so demanding as to elicit behavior contrary to the subjects' wishes, backgrounds, training, better judgments and even moral sense (Milgram, 1963). Further, such ignoring of the subjects' understandings in preference to the experimenter's belief that he is controlling conditions may lead to "experiments" in which the equivocation of waking and trance responses may actually be a product of the development of an identity of the subjects' supposedly different conscious states rather than the evocation of similar responses in genuinely different states.

This experimental work was done long before any studies were being done on so-called simulation of hypnosis, in which subjects are asked by the experimenter to "simulate" hypnotic behavior. Many such reports have been made by various authors, who seem to be unaware that the best simulation is an actualization. Additionally in these so-called controlled experimental studies the simulating subjects often have had hypnotic experience, have witnessed hypnosis, and certainly have some preconceptions of hypnosis. Hence experimentation with such subjects leads to a doubt of the experimenters's scientific sophistication or integrity.

The above experiments were not done to determine if there could be a simulation of hypnosis and the achievement of comparable behavior. Rather, the experiment was designed for the prupose of determining the role importance of operator and subject. However, quite unintentionally it was discovered that if a nonhypnotic subject is innocently (the author admits his naiveté at that period in his scientific career) asked to perform, at a waking level, the same sort of behavior that can be used to induce a hypnotic trance, although no mention of hypnosis is made, a hypnotic state can unmistakably result. There is no need to ask for simulation, since the task itself can lead to hypnosis. Hence one can only wonder at the scientific acumen of those who endeavor to demonstrate that requested "simulated hypnotic behavior" is otherwise than actual hypnotic behavior.

Additionally, the findings of this early experimentation have been confirmed throughout the years in the experience of this author and many of his colleagues. The operators or experimenters are unimportant in determining hypnotic results

Initial Experiments

regardless of their understandings and intentions. It is what the subjects understand and what the subjects do, not the operators' wishes, that determine what hypnotic phenomena shall be manifested. Hence hypnotic experimentation which is evaluated in terms of the experimenters' plans, wishes, intentions, and understandings is invalid unless communicated to the subjects' understandings and so accepted. Evaluation should be purely in terms of the subjects' performances, and it is behavior, not the experimenters' words, that should be the deciding factor in appraising experimental work. Many clinicians have had the experience of weighing the advisability of hypnosis for a patient who requiests it, only to find that the matter is entirely out of their hands because of a spontaneous trance. Not only this, the clinician may carefully suggest relaxation and have the patient respond with catalepsy and anaesthesia. Or the clinician may suggest anesthesia and discover that the patient is manifesting dissociation or even regression. At best operators can only offer intelligent guidance and then intelligently accept their subjects' behaviors.

2. Further Experimental Investigation of Hypnosis: Hypnotic and Nonhypnotic Realities

Milton H. Erickson

PRELIMINARY OBSERVATIONS

The rejective attitude of Clark L. Hull toward the author's first experimental study of the nature of hypnotic phenomena (Erickson, 1964b) stimulated still further investigation intended to discover what tasks could be accomplished by the use of hypnosis in such areas as conditioned responses, anaesthesia, sensory changes, ideomotor activity and regression, among other fields of inquiry. All of this latter served to form a background of experience in regard to the intriguing question of what hypnosis is and what the hypnotic state really constitutes.

Of significant importance to the author in furthering his awareness that waking state realities were quite different from the realities of the hypnotic state was the following startling occurrence. Miss O had volunteered for continued experimental work with the author, and various hypnotic phenomena had been studied with her aid. Then one afternoon the author endeavored to discover what could or would happen when the wording of a suggestion was changed without there being any seeming significance to the alteration of the wording. Experimentally Miss O had been trained to hallucinate visually by opening her eyes, seeing nothing, then to become aware of a visual haziness and fogginess in which lines and shadows would appear slowly, and then progressively become clearer and more definitive until a complete, even elaborate, visual hallucination would result. To this could be added a faint suggestion of sound properly graduated suggestions that would become progressively clearer until elaborate auditory hallucinations could be elicited. (At that time the author's experience had not taught him that hallucinations could be induced more rapidly and easily.) The author was much interested in the nature and wording of suggestions that would be most effective and was very much under the mistaken impression that all hypnotic phenomena depended upon the induction of a somnambulistic trance

---

Reprinted with permission from *The American Journal of Clinical Hypnosis*, October, 1967, *10*, 87–135.

state. (Undoubtedly this was a fortunate error, since it led the author to spend from four to 20 hours to train subjects to insure profoundly somnambulistic trance states for his experimental studies, especially those that involved possible extensive neurological and physiological alterations of bodily functioning, instead of the two to 10 minutes so frequently reported in the literature on hypnotic experiments, where if the work were to be done in the waking state, a much longer time would be allotted. Unfortunately even among those endeavoring to do scientific work, the attitude that hypnosis is miraculous and minimizes time requirements is still prevalent.)

Miss O had been worked with in the somnambulistic state so extensively that it was discovered that she could respond with a positive hallucination to the simple suggestion of "There is a nice pretty brown dog over there." She had learned to easily develop both negative and positive visual and auditory hallucinations to other comparable suggestions. On this particular occasion the author, intending to elaborate a complicated hallucinatory response, said with slow emphasis, *"THERE* is a nice pretty little *doggie* over there," and paused to elaborate further suggestions.

To his utter astonishment, during this pause Miss O replied in a childish tone of voice, "Uh huh, he's mine." Then as if speaking to the hallucinated dog, she spoke again in a definitely childish tone of voice, "Come to Alwis, doggie. Come here. Come here wight now."

For the next two hours the author bewilderedly and cautiously explored the situation and tried to correlate it with the suggestion given above and with previous comparable suggestions. The findings and conclusions reached were that:

1. Miss O had spontaneously regressed to a childhood state because of the childish implication of the word "doggie" instead of "dog."
2. The suggestion to induce a visual hallucination uttered in such a fashion may have been at a moment when a possible fortuitous train of thought in Miss O's mind served to evoke a revivification of childhood memories resulting in a spontaneous regression.
3. The author soon found that he had become transformed into a grown-up cousin of hers and that the laboratory had become the front yard of her home.
4. Further suggestions to "create" the rest of her environment were unnecessary, since she talked freely in a childish fashion and pointed out various things on the "lawn" and "acwoss the stweet."
5. She used a vocabulary befitting her "seven" years of age, and she maninfested typical childish failure to understand words beyond her vocabulary. Her behavior and manner and even movements were suggestive of a small child, and she seemed to see herself not as she was dressed at the moment, but presumably as she had been at the age of seven. (A wealth of data was easily secured, since she proved

to be a most sociable and talkative "little girl.")
6. Extreme efforts were made by the author to avoid offering suggestions, but this proved unnecessary, since apparently Miss O was reliving item by item the events of a day in her eighth year.
7. Finally the author realized that he was confronted by a technical problem of reestablishing the original hypnotic situation—a most frightening (to him then) problem.
8. Finally the idea occurred of reestablishing the situation as it had been when the hallucinatory dog was first visualized by Miss O. Much painful thought was given to this problem while Miss O sat on the laboratory floor "paying with the fowers." (Subsequent inquiry disclosed that her extremely indulgent mother had purposely encouraged a continuance of "baby talk" long after the time it is usually outgrown. This baby talk seemed most inconsistent with the regressed age of seven in the laboratory situation and had distressed the author greatly.)
9. Discovery was made, as time passed in the laboratory, that the "doggie" had wandered away. Miss O leaped to her feet, called to the dog, manifested a violent temper tantrum, childishly sobbing and stamping her feet and clenching her fits. In frightened desperation the author gently suggested that "maybe the doggie is coming now." She burst into happy smiles, squatted on the floor, and seemed to be hugging the dog. The moment seemed to be propitious for the suggestion, "And now, just remember how everything was just a few minutes before you saw the doggie the first time."
10. Miss O blinked her eyes, was obviously still in a somnambulistic state, but not regressed. Instead she was in good visual contact with the laboratory setting. Her immediate bewildered facial expression at finding herself sitting on the laboratory floor was followed by an angry, explanation-demanding look at the author, rendering the situation crystal-clear as betokening trouble for the author.
11. She was asked if she wanted a full explanation. Her emphatic "Yes" left no doubts. Previous experience in restoring memories enabled the author to effect a complete recollection by her while she was still in the trance state and while she was still sitting on the floor.
12. Miss O was obviously delighted and pleased with the whole course of events, going over them several times and affirming them as a revivification of a past reality.
13. Still sitting on the floor, she asked that she be awakened from the trance, "Just tell me to wake up." The author hurriedly and unthinkingly acceded to her request.
14. At once the author realized he was again in trouble. Miss O awakened at once, found herself sitting on the floor, glared angrily at the author, and demanded an explanation of the situation. However, her anger

was so great that she gave the author a thorough verbal excoriation before she got up off the floor, when she again emphatically demanded an explanation. It was painfully realized that a full memory in the trance state did not necessarily continue into the waking state.

15. Despite her angry demands, it became possible to relate bit by bit the events of that afternoon in their correct order, with the author repeatedly managing to throw in the suggestions of "And you remember, next—", "Remember how that led to," and "Now maybe you can remember the next thing—."

16. Finally Miss O dropped her hand on the author's wrist in a friendly fashion and said, "Be still—I'm getting it all now."

17. There followed, delightful for both the author and Miss O, a remarkably complete recall by her of all of the events of the afternoon, including the anger episodes.

18. Miss O made an extensive list of her memories, later queried her parents, alarmed them greatly, but subdued them with a temper tantrum, and confirmed to the author the validity of that afternoon's regression experience.

19. In further "regression experiments" both she and the author had a strong desire to tread carefully. Limits of time, place, situation, and circumstances were always placed on regression as a primary procedure. all of which, in the opinion of both Miss O and the author, tended to circumscribe and limit results, while spontaneity of behavior led to more extensive findings and even more reliable results.

20. Working together and testing possibilities, a general type of permissive technique was elaborated to give rise to spontaneity of behavior by the subject. This was found to lead to more informative, reliable, and extensive results, not only for Miss O, but for other subjects as well. During the course of this work Miss O asked to be allowed to write out instructions for regression to a specific time. These were not to be known by the author, but, she explained, after she had been hypnotized, she was to be handed the typewritten instructions enclosed in an envelope with the directions from the author to read them and to act upon them. Additionally she added verbally that if she manifested any emotional distress, she was to be told by the author to awaken in the current time. She was asked to type these additional understandings and directions as a concluding part of her secret instructions. The reason was that in a self-induced regression state, it was considered possible that there might be a loss of rapport.

She developed a trance readily, opened the envelope, read the contents, and then began yelling at the author, "Get out, get out" while she cowered and cringed. At once the author yelled at her, "Awaken, awaken." She did so, short of breath, panting, shuddering and trembling, greatly puzzled about her "peculiar frightened condition." She asked aid in finding out what was wrong with her. She was handed the secret instructions, read them, remarked, "Yes, I know I wrote them out and added to them those additional instructions you suggested. But what has that got to do with the awful way I'm feeling?" This question led to the conclusion by the author that she had an amnesia for her recent trance state and self-induced regression. Accordingly she was asked if the induction of a trance and the execution of those secret instructions for which she might have an amnesia could account for her "peculiar condition." Immediately she demanded, "Tell me to remember; hurry, tell me to remember." She was so instructed. Her response was to sit down weakly in a chair and to gasp, "It did happen, it really did happen, and I wasn't sure it could, and I wanted to find out how real things were. I'll never do that again." She then read the special typewritten instructions and nodded her head affirmatively. Not until months later did she disclose to the author what she had attempted experimentally with such startling results. She explained with much embarrassment that she had happened to recall two summers previously during a vacation trip her practice of going for a swim at a private beach and then removing her bathing suit and stepping into the enclosed bathhouse for a shower. She had decided to regress to one such occasion but "to interpolate" the author into it as present at the beach. Her success in her venture had appalled her and left no doubt in her mind about the subjective realities of hypnotic regression.

This particular work with Miss O was strongly influential in governing the course and development of the author's investigation of the hypnotic state and its phenomena, and rendered him exceedingly curious about the nature of the hypnotic state. The work with Miss O was repeated with variations added, with other subjects, both male and female. The results obtained from these other subjects were fully in accord with those obtained from Miss O.

PROBLEMS OF AWARENESS: INITIAL INVESTIGATIONS

In general the author tended to follow his own patterns of working with hypnosis, but in the privacy of his own personal experimentation, he followed more and more the understandings gained from Miss O (who did not return to the university the next year because of her marriage) and which were confirmed by the other various highly instructive special experiences with male and female subjects, with whom the author continued his studies of hypnotic phenomena. This in turn led to an ever-increasing interest in the nature of hypnosis, the methods by which the hypnotic state of awareness could be differentiated from ordinary waking awareness, and the possible methods of procedure by which

Further Experiments

such a study could be made.

It was soon realized that one could not ask a subject in an ordinary state of awareness to simulate hypnosis, nor could one use as a subject one with hypnotic experience to differentiate between hypnotic and waking awarenesses, since the better the simulation, the greater would be the actualization. Nor could one be certain that an entirely naive subject would not unpredictably develop hypnosis as had been so well learned in the initial experiment on the nature of hypnosis cited above.

At first it was thought a reliable inquiry could be done by the seminar group by having some volunteer who knew nothing at all about hypnosis to demonstrate how a hypnotic subject, in a deep trance, would walk around the table at which the members of the seminar were seated while his behavior was observed. Several such subjects were secured, and they were informed after they entered the seminar room of what was desired of them. The result was always the same. The subjects would say, "You want me to walk around this table like a hypnotic subject in a deep trance when I don't even know what a hypnotic subject acts like, while you watch me pretending to be a hypnotized subject? The only way I can walk around this table while you watch me is to walk my own way unless you tell me how a hypnotized subject walks. Does he walk fast? Slow? Does he keep still? Does he speak to each of you? What does he do?" Repeated urging resulted only in further requests for information. Finally it was decided that a simpler approach be made by asking the subjects possessed of no personal knowledge of hypnosis to walk around the table as if they were in a light trance. The results were entirely the same as with the first group of subjects. After much discussion, it was decided that some member of the seminar group who had not been hypnotized but who had seen hypnosis, as all of them had, be asked to perform specific acts to simulate a hypnotic performance—but *in so doing to remain in a state of conscious awareness,* giving his attention very carefully to the simulation of an agreed-upon list of tasks of which the subject would be unaware until he was asked to perform the acts. It was also agreed by the entire group that all the other members of the group would observe and note the adequacy of the simulation and the continuance of the waking state, and all agreed that any instructions to simulate hypnotic behavior would necessitate instructions for the maintenance of conscious awareness. Only in this way could there be any possibility of differentiating hypnotic behavior from simulated hypnotic behavior.

The first subject chosen was Miss O, who had demonstrated her capability to enter the hypnotic state spontaneously. She was asked to walk around the table simulating the somnambulistic state, since all the group knew she was capable of this behavior.

An unexpected development occurred. Miss O declared, "But I don't really remember how I moved or looked at things when I was in a somnambulistic state. I have seen other subjects in a somnambulistic state, and I know their pupils are dilated; I know they do not seem to hear anybody unless instructed to hear by the one who did the hypnosis; I have seen a detached manner, a dissociated way of behavior that indicated that they were out of touch with much of the surrounding reality. I don't know how to stay out of a trance and simulate that. I don't know how to dilate my pupils. I don't know how to hold my arm in an extended position and not feel a fatigue in my shoulder. I don't know how to inhibit my hearing so that I make no visible response to someone outside of the immediate hypnotic situation who is speaking to me. I don't even know how to freeze my face the way I see somnambulistic subjects do this kind of thing. From hearing the group discuss my somnambulistic behavior, I know that I can do all these things; but these things that are discussed do not seem real to me or even understandable unless I go into a trance."

At this point another member of the group who had been in a deep hypnotic trance and somnambulistic on several occasions stated, "I agree with Miss O. I can discuss somebody else's behavior objectively and observe it objectively, but when any of you start discussing what I did in the trance state, I lose my objectivity and drift into a trance state. I can feel what is being mentioned, but I am not then in the state of conscious awareness. I don't think it is possible to simulate without feeling the simulated behavior subjectively. I think it is like acting. Any good actor, whenever he acts out a scene of anger, feels angry. If he doesn't, he isn't a good actor. Poor actors just go through the motions, but they don't get another acting part because they haven't really sensed what they try to portray. I have taken part in various plays, and when I portray amusement, I feel it. When I portray interest in what another member of the cast is saying, I feel the interest. In fact the play becomes a reality to me, and I just don't think about the audience until the right time comes to be aware of the audience. I just simply get lost in the play, and it becomes very real to me. I don't think about what I am doing as portraying a part; I think of being that part. I know that if I tried to simulate hypnotic behavior in a real sort of way, I would go into a trance."

There was much discussion of Miss O's comments and the other speaker's remarks. (Digressive discussion of the various schools of thought concerning how one enacts a theatrical role were not considered pertinent to the question at hand.)

The question arose as to what observations would enable one to recognize hypnotic behavior. Various specific items of hypnotic behavior were discussed, one of them being automatic writing.

Miss O said, "Ordinarily I write like this [demonstrating], but if I tried to write automatic writing—." She ceased speaking at this point, and everybody in the group realized that she had unexpectedly developed a somnambulistic state of hypnosis.

The question arose at once about rapport. The author, who was out of Miss O's visual range, held up his hand and indicated that the entire group leave Miss O alone in the room and adjourn to an adjacent room to decide the order in which each of the group should speak to her. It was suggested that, since the author had hypnotized her repeatedly, he should be the last one. The group returned to the seminar room, where Miss O was still in the somnambulistic state. She made no response to anybody until the author asked her the same question everybody else had put to her, namely, "Would you like to awaken now?" She nodded her head affirmatively but remianed in the trance while the entire group waited silently for over five minutes. There was no change in her behavior, no alteration of her expression. She seemed to be totally unaware that anyone was waiting. After a lapse of that time the author said, "All right, wake up *now.*" She did so very promptly, with an amnesia for having been in the trance. She disclosed this by saying, "What I mean is I usually write like this, but if I tried to do automatic writing—." She repeated her previous behavior, and the author again awakened her with a continuing amnesia for her hypnotic behavior. Before she could say anything, the author asked her if she would like to hear some comments by the seminar member who had spoken about her feelings in playing dramatic roles, a comment expected by the author to be related to Miss O's behavior. However, the subject said, "I have been in a trance for three members of this group, and I wonder with which one of them I would show rapport if I developed a spontaneous trance while trying to simulate hypnosis and levitation." She paused, her hand slowly lifted, and she was observed to be in a trance. Beginning at the right, the first of the seminar group spoke to her without eliciting a response. The author, who was next in order, had the same results. The third person was found to be in rapport with her; so were the fifth and eighth persons. These three had been the ones who had hypnotized her previously.

PROBLEMS OF SIMULATION: INITIAL INVESTIGATIONS

There were many hours spent discussing the various evidences manifested by the subjects in the trance state. It was agreed finally that one could go through the motions of simulating hypnotic behavior and retain full conscious awareness, but any "real portrayal of hypnotic behavior" resulted in the spontaneous development of a trance. Additionally it was found that inexperienced, uninformed subjects could not simulate hypnotic behavior unless they were told directly or indirectly what to do. Of even greater importance it was discovered that experienced hypnotic subjects would simulate hypnotic behavior by going into a trance state, thereby manifesting actual hypnotic behavior, but that they could learn to simulate the behavior of the waking state. When this was done, an observant person could then point out minor discrepancies in behavior that betrayed the actual state of affairs. This was reported on in a much later experiment (Erickson, 1944).

As a result the author attempted a large number of experimental projects to secure simulated hypnotic behavior from both inexperienced and experienced subjects. The results obtained were always the same. The inexperienced, unsophisticated subjects simply did not know what to do but could easily learn to go into a trance state by being told how to simulate hypnosis. This has become a technique much used by this author, particularly with resistant subjects and patients who fear hypnotic states. Long experience has shown this author that it is a technique that can be used easily and quickly, especially with patients who respond to hypnotic psychotherapy but who are otherwise resistant to psychotherapy.

During these discussions of the simulation of hypnotic behavior, which took place during the scheduled and unscheduled meetings of the seminarians, there was also another type of occurrence which, to this author's knowledge, has not been reported in the literature. One such event, about which the author did not learn until later, concerned a graduate student in psychology who had been asked by a group of professors of biology and philosophy to give a private lecture-demonstration of hypnosis. This graduate student was not a member of the seminar group, but he had seen hypnosis demonstrated several times by the author. Accordingly he arranged with an experienced hypnotic subject to act as his subject for the evening demonstration. As was related to this author, there occurred a startling sequence of events. Approximately an hour before the lecture and demonstration the graduate student learned that his experienced subject would not appear, and he knew of no one else upon whom to call. He felt that he himself knew too little about hypnosis to undertake hypnotizing a novice, and he felt extremely distressed at the thought of disappointing this very special audience by failing to meet their wishes. In discussing this catastrophic (to him) development with his wife, in some way there arose the question of having someone pretend to be hypnotized. The graduate student refused this idea very strongly as being "scientifically dishonest," but he felt himself increasingly on the horns of a dilemma. Finally he decided to perpetrate this subterfuge on his audience, realizing that his honest discussion of hypnosis would not be invalidated by the subject's pretense of being hypnotized. The only pretense subject available was his wife, and the graduate student gave her a hurried description of the hypnotic phenomenon that she was supposed to pretend to develop. He was rather fearful that his own lack of experience might make it impossible for him to describe adequately the hypnotic behavior he wanted his wife to pretend to manifest. Furthermore he was most distressed by making his wife an "accessory" to "scientific dishonesty." His wife, who had never seen hypnosis nor had ever been hypnotized, assured him that she would put forth her very best efforts to enable him to give a satisfactory lecture and demonstration.

During the course of that rather long evening he was rather astonished and pleased with his wife's capability as an actress, but he was constantly fearful that he had not described the various phenomena correctly and hence that she might make a mistake. At the close of the lecture, when the last of the professors had left, he sat down, extremely fatigued, dried the perspiration on his face with a handkerchief, and expressed his relief that "the whole thing was over with."

He then made, half to himself and half to his wife, various statements about the inadvisability of "scientific dishonesty" for any purpose whatsoever. Receiving no comment from his wife, he looked up at her and slowly realized that she was still in a somnambulistic trance, since he had overlooked awakening her. This rather frightened him and led him to make cautious tests of his wife's hypnotic state, finally convincing himself that she was actually and unquestionably in a somnambulistic, hypnotic trance. Thereupon he asked her to awaken in accord with the procedures that he had seen demonstrated by this author.

He discovered that his wife had a total amnesia for all the events of the evening, that she still thought it was 7 P.M. and that they were awaiting the arrival of the professors. He tried to explain to her that she had been in a trance, had demonstrated hypnosis without his recognition of the fact that she had been in a trance, and that the lecture and demonstration had taken place. She disputed him and was convinced to the contrary only by looking at the clock, her watch, his watch, and the bedroom clock. (The lecture had been in his home.)

The narration of this event and of his wife's incredulity about what she had done that evening, and her amazement at her unawareness of having demonstrated hypnotic behavior to a group of professors toward whom she felt a feeling of awe, resulted in the conclusion that simulation of hypnotic behavior could not reliably be used as an objective test of hypnotic phenomena.

A member of the seminar group had had a similar but intentionally planned experience with similar results; whether this has been published is not known to this author, although it was privately related to him the next day and later to the seminar group. As in the first instance, despite the concerted, deliberate planning, the resulting trance had not been expected.

Another type of occurrence at about the same time as the above instances happened to the author. He was invited to demonstrate hypnosis to a group of undergraduates in psychology and to utilize as subjects volunteers from the group. Three members of the group, as a prank at the expense of the author and the others of the audience, arranged with a student who was studying drama and who had seen hypnotic demonstrations to perpetrate a fraud upon the author. The drama student was asked by the three students to be the first volunteer and to "fake going into hypnosis." During the demonstration one of them would ask the author if a hypnotic subject could respond in the trance state to a suggestion that he would sneeze. At this point the volunteer subject was to disclose to the audience how he had "faked the whole demonstration" and thus embarrass the author. This entire plan was based on the fact that the drama student could sneeze voluntarily and often developed episodes of sneezing to avoid answering questions in his classes.

Quite innocently the author instructed the subject to sneeze whenever the author tapped on the table with a pencil and to sneeze once, twice, or more times in accord to the number of taps. The subject responded as the author suggested. One of the three students called the subject by name and asked him to "do as planned." The subject made no response to that student, who angrily came up and demanded that the subject "make good for the five dollars paid you." The subject was obviously in a trance and made no response, since no rapport existed with that student.

In the resulting confusion the student embarrassedly disclosed the secret arrangement with the subject. With this clarification, the subject was awakened with a suggested amnesia for all trance events. It became immediately apparent that the subject was spontaneously reoriented to the moment when he had sat down in front of the audience as a volunteer subject. He was asked if he really wanted to be hypotized or if he wanted to "fake being hypnotized." With marked discomfort he asked the reason for "such an odd question." Reply was made that he was being paid five dollars to "fake hypnosis" and to disclose this fact when a request was made to him that he sneeze. After a resentful look at his fellow conspirators he ruefully remarked that apparently the plan was to embarrass him and not the author, and he started to return to his seat in the audience. Questioning of him by the audience soon disclosed his amnesia for trance events and the lapse of time.

He was rehypnotized and asked to recall, in slow chronological order, when aroused, the events of the first trance, the events of the state of conscious awareness following it, and then the experience and suggestions of this second trance, and to report upon them verbally to the audience. His report was most instructive both to the author and the audience.

SCOPE OF INVESTIGATION AND EXPERIMENTATION: NATURE, EXTENT, AND ILLUSTRATIVE MATERIAL

Various experiments were conducted with naive subjects, and the conclusion was repeatedly confirmed that neither the subjects nor the experimenter could be at all objective in such experiments. The attempts to investigate the nature and character of hypnotic phenomena would depend upon limiting such investigation to situations where undirected, unsuggested, completely spontaneous hypnotic behavior was manifested and where the unhypnotized subjects could respond with equally spontaneous waking behavior without any effort to alter or to falsify such spontaneous waking behavior. This discussion led the author into numerous experimental efforts to discover a possible situation in which reliable experimentation could be done. During the course of this experimentation it was realized that a "light trance" and a "medium trance" could not be employed for such experimentation, since both such states offer a possibility for some degree of ordinary waking behavior. Thereupon it was realized that only somnambulistic subjects could be employed to manifest their own natural, spontaneous, completely undirected (so far as the experimenter was concerned) behavior. Such spontaneous somnambulistic behavior could be manifested in situations where, unwittingly and unknowingly, hypnotic subjects would demonstrate their somnambulistic state and where unhypnotized subjects would make their own normal, natural, spontaneous behavior manifestations in accord with their own waking understandings. The experimenter would become merely an objective observer of the behavior of the somnambulistic hypnotic subjects, and the behavior manifested would be in relation to a reality situation to which both types of subjects could react without being directed or influenced in their behavior. In other words merely a simple, ordinary problem would have to be presented for an ordinary, simple solution to both types of subjects.

The various findings reported above led to the early realization that in the development of the proposed experiment it should not be constructed to be used as a method of defining the existence of a state of hypnosis, nor of detecting a simulation of the hypnotic state. It would have to be constructed solely to determine if there were differences in the apprehension of realities by subjects in the ordinary state of conscious awareness, and by subjects in the somnambulistic hypnotic state.

As a measure of recognizing somnambulistic hypnotic behavior there was a systematic appraisal by the group of the various manifestations that were likely to occur in the behavior of such subjects, but which could vary from subject to subject. However, they would be manifestly apparent to the experienced observer, but in varying degrees (from subject to subject). These criteria were:

> Pupillary dilation or altered eyeball behavior.
> Changes in muscle tone and altered patterns of body movements with a peculiar economy of movement.
> Literalness of response to verbal stimuli; a capacity to wait without effort and without seeming to experience the passage of time when a long pause was interjected into the middle of a situation.
> An absence of ordinary startle responses.
> An absence of physical adjustments to stimuli, such as the lack of a turning of the head toward the speaker, inattentiveness to distracting visual stimuli, and unresponsiveness to many physical stimuli.
> An apparent inability to perceive external stimuli included in the immediate situation, and the frequent spontaneous ability to misperceive the surrounding realities as the realities experienced or imagined possible in the past of the individual subject, often with peculiar restrictions or alterations in the actual perception of reality.

These criteria, it was agreed by the seminar group, were reasonably descriptive of the somnambulistic hypnotic trance; but it was also agreed that each subject could vary in an individual manner in meeting them. This has been the author's experience since his participation in that seminar of 1923-24.

It was finally decided, after much study and after recalling the fruit-eating episodes in a study previously reported (Erickson, 1964b), to attempt to differentiate between waking and hypnotic states of awareness by some type of behavior that could occur naturally and easily in either state of awareness. Such behavior, it was reasoned, could in no way be dependent upon the state of awareness, should in no way be hindered in its performance as such by the state of the subject's awareness, must be as easily elicited in the trance state as in the waking state, and yet in some way must be separately definitive of the nature, limits, attributes, or other not yet realized qualities of the two states of awareness.

When the problem was first considered, the question of sensory changes, ideosensory activity, memory changes, and transcendence of usual neurophysiological behavior and responses were all considered. However, the question of the experimental subjects knowing what was wanted at some level of awareness and responding complaisantly always came to mind and led to the discarding of such naive and profoundly unscientific approaches. The question was one in which the answer would have to be obtained without the knowledge of the subjects or any kind of intentional or knowing participation at any level of understanding. *In other words the differentiation of the waking and hypnotic states of awareness would have to derive from some quality or attribute of the performance inherent in the task but in no way specified to the subjects but which would be dependent wholly upon the experimental subjects' kind of awareness, whether waking or hypnotic.* Thus there could then be no invalidation of the experimental results so attendant upon the deliberate effort to have subjects offer counterfeit behavior as a means of differentiation, as so often has been done. (See numerous studies in the literature on "simulation behavior.")

The nature of such an experimentation was conceived as requiring no recognizable experimental procedure, as requiring an indefinite period of time with a multitude of subjects, a large variety of experimental situations, and an actual experimental procedure that would have to be, in most if not all instances, an incidental part of another formal or perhaps informal situation or experimental study. It was also recognized that it would also be essential to formulate some kind of a controlled experimental procedure in which the task could be done with a minimal, if any, risk involved of the possibility of the experimental subjects becoming aware of the experimentation. Extensive thought was given to this contingency as well as to others that were considered as possibly arising. Almost from the beginning it was recognized that the task would require long-continued study, experimentation, and extensive experience, probably extending over several years, before any attempt at a definitive study could be made, and then only out of the continued acquisition of a knowledge of hypnosis.

Throughout medical school, internship, and the first years of psychiatric practice the intriguing question of how to differentiate experimentally between hypnotic and waking states of awareness was kept in mind. Clinically the author felt certain that he experienced no great difficulty in differentiating between the two states of awareness. But how to establish such a differentiation objectively with no awareness of what was being done by the experimental subjects was a most difficult question to answer. Innumerable projects were begun, only to be abandoned as unsuitable for definitive results.

Further Experiments

Serving to affect the eventual experiment were a multitude of separate experiences in which subjects in somnambulistic states have interjected into the intended hypnotic situation items alien to the operator, but belonging either to their experiential past or their comprehension and understandings of possible occurrences.

Repeatedly, since this experiment was first considered, the author has encountered in teaching situations before university students, medical, nursing, social service, dental, and psychological groups a certain significant phenomenon upon which this experimental study was based, even though its full significance was not appreciated in formulating the experiment at that time, becoming clear only as the experimental studies progressed in the first dozen efforts. This finding will be summarized first, and then a detailed account of one such instance will be given.

In demonstrating hypnosis before professional groups, naive subjects have often been employed, the purpose being to illustrate the technique of hypnotic induction and to demonstrate various hypnotic phenomena of the deep trance. In using these naive subjects to demonstrate negative visual hallucinations, the author has asked such subjects, gesturing toward the audience, "What do you see there?" In reply he would be given the answer, "Your hand." "I mean back of my hand." "Oh, part of the ring on your finger is back of your hand." "I mean further back." "Nothing." Suggestion would be offered to them that they see the speaker's platform on which they sat, and they would be asked what they saw beyond that. In several hundred such instances the answer was that they saw nothing, that they "stopped seeing" where the platform ended. When instructed to see the audience, they would do so, and simple inquiry about what was behind the audience would elicit the reply of "nothing." When they were questioned why they saw nothing beyond the audience, they would explain that they had looked at the audience but had "stopped seeing farther." They could then be asked to see the persons standing in back of the audience. This they would do, but in several hundred cases they "stopped seeing" before they could see the back wall of the auditorium behind the persons standing behind the audience, as illustrated by the tape recording cited above—a manifestation which was expected by the author because of his understandings. Just what this "stoppage" of the linear extent of the vision means is difficult to comprehend. Yet naive subjects, ranging in education from the eighth grade to doctoral degrees in medicine, dentistry, or psychology, have given the remarkable reply signifying that there had occurred for them, from a trance induction resulting in somnabulism with the eyes open, definite linear limitations of vision.

Following is an almost verbatim account of one such completely unexpected occurrence. (The omitted material pertains to answered and unanswered inquiries and comments from the audience.)

At a lecture-demonstration before the staff of a psychiatric hospital a social service worker with an MSW degree in psychiatric social work volunteered as a demonstration subject. She had never seen hypnosis demonstrated, nor had she ever previously thought of volunteering as a subject. A simple direct eye fixation and a lifting of her right hand in the manner described previously (Erickson, 1964c) served to induce a somnambulistic trance within one-half minute.

Immediately the following series of questions was asked and answered:

> Do you think you can be hypnotized?
> I do not know. I want to find out.
> Will you know when you are hypnotized?
> I really don't know.
> Are you hypnotized right now?
> Oh no, I just volunteered.
> Why?
> I don't know, I just want to know what it is like.
> As you can see, you are sitting at my immediate left and facing me. Is there someone sitting to my right? [A nurse was sitting at my immediate right, facing toward me and toward her.]
> I don't know.
> Why?
> I haven't looked that far.
> Can you see my right arm? [Resting it across the arm of the chair in which the nurse was sitting]
> Yes.
> Do you see anything else?
> No.
> Why not?
> I haven't looked any farther.
> Is there anything to see if you look farther?
> I don't know, I haven't looked.
> Just review these questions I have been asking you and the answers you have given me and tell me what you think of the questions and the answers.
> [After a pause] I know I'm not in a trance because you didn't put me in one. You ask odd questions, and my answers are just as odd. I really don't understand.
> Why is your hand lifted up in the air?
> Why, [noticing it] what is it doing there? It's just staying there.
> Did you put it there?
> I'm not keeping it there, it's just staying there.
> Does that reply make sense to you?
> [Laughingly] No, it doesn't. This whole conversation doesn't make sense, and I don't know what's happened to my hand and arm.
> Oh, it's right there, isn't it?
> Yes, but why?

Further Experiments

Are you in a trance?

No. Are you going to put me in one?

Before I answer that question, may I ask you a few questions and secure your answers?

Yes.

What is your name? Your first name?

Lucy.

Where are you?

Here.

Where is "here"?

Right to your left and a little in front of you.

But in general, where are you?

Here in a chair.

Who owns the chair?

[She looked at the chair curiously] I don't know.

Where is the chair besides "here"?

Well, I'm on the chair and the chair is on the floor.

What floor is it?

I don't know.

Don't you recognize it?

No, I just see the floor the chair is on.

You say you are not hypnotized, and you give answers like the one you just offered, and your arm remains in the air—what does this all mean?

Well, I'm not hypnotized.

Well, in the ordinary, waking, nonhypnotized state a person asked, Where are you? replies with an informative answer. Hence I will ask you, Where are you?

I-I-I-I don't know.

Can you look around, and what do you see?

I see you, the chair I'm sitting in, and the floor the chair is on.

Can you see anything else?

No, that's as far as I can see. Do you want me to see farther?

Do you see farther?

No, I just see so far.

Would you say that your behavior is that of someone who is not hypnotized?

Well, it's very odd behavior when I think about it, but I know you didn't hypnotize me.

What about your seeing just "so far?"

Well, I look at you and my vision just stops. I can't explain it. It has never stopped before.

What do you see beside me or behind me, and what do you think of your answer?

I don't see anything beside you or behind you because I don't see that far, and I think that is a very queer answer. I don't understand it.
Is there anything else you don't understand?
Yes.
Much?
Yes.
Start telling me the things that are not understood.
Well, my hand. Why does it stay there without moving? I know it is my hand, but I don't understand why it doesn't seem like my hand. It's different in some way.
What else?
Well, there's you. I know you are a doctor and I know your last name, but I don't know why you are talking to me or what we are doing or even where we are.
What do you mean?
Well, usually when two people are together they have to be somewhere, and you are sitting there and I have to try hard to see the chair you are in. And I'm here in a chair and that is as far as I can see and there isn't anything around—nothing at all—just like in science fiction, just you and me and two chairs and a bit of wooden floor—oh, there is some floor under your chair too—just the two of us and empty space. There is something awfully different here that I don't understand. I feel comfortable. I'm not alarmed or worried. When I look at you, I see you, but my vision stops. It's very peculiar. Yet I have a comfortable feeling that you can explain everything.
Are you hypnotized?
I really don't know what that word means. It has something to do with one's mental state, and as I think about the way my hand behaves, the way my vision just stops, this just being alone with you in empty space with nothing around and still feeling comfortable, I would have to deduce that I am hypnotized. Am I?
You are, and how do you feel about it?
Well, it's a nice feeling but a strange feeling. I just can't understand my eyes or my hand. My eyes see you, but I don't look any farther, and that is my hand, but I don't feel it to be my hand.
Would you like to know the whole set of attendant circumstances accounting for you and me being here?
Well, yes, very much.
All right, remain in the trance, be responsive and aware of the immediate past and the current present.
Oh, my goodness! The whole staff is here—now I remember. But I'm in a trance, but how did you hypnotize me? I still can't move my hand. You did something to my hand and everything changed. Everything except you vanished. How is that possible? Somebody must have

> talked, but I didn't hear any sound except your voice. Did anybody talk, because they must have stayed right here. They couldn't really vanish, but they did, even the walls, everything. Please, could I do that again?
>
> Yes, if you watch the hand that is up slowly lower and the other hand slowly lift up to a comparable height, it will happen again.
>
> She watched her hands, and when the first was lowered and the other was fully lifted, she looked up in a puzzled fashion, apparently awaiting some remark. Accordingly she was asked:
>
> Do you think you can be hypnotized?
>
> I don't know. I want to find out.
>
> Thereupon various aspects of the previous procedure was repeated with the same results.

Privately the psychiatrist in charge of the course of lectures was told that the continuous tape recording that had been made should be released for those in attendance to discuss at their leisure but not in his presence nor in that of the author. This was done, and the social worker was completely astonished when she heard her voice responding to the author's inquiries. She was greatly amazed at her replies and could not understand their meanings. Neither did she have any conscious recollection of the experience. She was also astonished to discover from the tape recording that she had no full memory at the close of that experience of having been hypnotized. She was also amazed that in the state of conscious awareness she still had no conscious memories of the experience.

No recording was made of these discussions, but the author was assured that she had been subjected to many probing questions and that there had been much theorizing. On the morning of the day preceding the conclusion of the course, she was asked by the author how she felt about the experience of hearing the tape recording and thereby learning that she had been hypnotized. In summary her statement was:

> The most that I can say is that I apparently did not place any meaning upon stimuli other than those coming from you. I simply do not know how one can stop seeing or hearing, and it amazes me that I do not yet know of my own experience: that I was hypnotized and talked to you in the trance state. Neither do I remember having recalled, in the trance state, that I had been hypnotized and that I was talking to you in the trance state. Apparently I excluded any meaningful perceptual experiences other than those disclosed on the tape recording, which disclosed also that not only were you and I talking but others had talked and questions were asked. But I still have no memory of the experience.

I asked if she were aware that a tape recording was being made of the present conversation. She stated that everybody was aware that all sessions were being tape-recorded. She was asked if she would like to be hypnotized, and she asserted that she most certainly would and immediately came up and sat down in a chair beside the author. As the author asked her if she were sitting comfortably, he gently touched her wrist and "lifted" her hand as he had done several days previously. It was apparent to everybody that she had again developed a somnambulistic trance instantly. The same questions were put to her as reported above, and the same replies were given. Finally it was suggested that she remain in the trance state but become aware that she was in a trance state. She was again questioned in the same fashion that she had been on that previous day. Then the suggestion was offered that she recall in full the previous experience. She was greatly amazed to discover that she was repeating her behavior of several days previously. She compared it with her present behavior of going into a trance state. She did not know how she went into the trance, and she still could give no satisfactory explanation of why or how she "looked just so far and no farther." The suggestion was offered that she might be interested to recall her conscious experiences while listening to the tape recording and to comment upon what she experienced while listening. She stated that at first she found it difficult to believe that it was her voice on the tape recorder. She could not, in that separate conscious experience, understand the course of events. She stated that she had struggled hard to effect a conscious recovery of the entire experience, but had failed. She agreed that in some way unknown to her she "simply arrested the reception or perception of the stimuli that she undoubtedly had been receiving, and had limited her perceptual awareness and memories completely to the immediate situation of herself and the author. She was then gently awakened with a total amnesia, which included coming up to the front of the audience and returning to her seat. Later that day this new recording was played back. She was most astonished by it and began comparing it aloud with her conscious memories of the previous recording that she had discussed with her associates. She was again amazed to realize that she had no conscious memory of either experience. Again she offered the uninformative explanation comparing it aloud with her conscious memories of the previous recording that she had discussed with her associates. She was again amazed to realize that she had no conscious memory of either experience. Again she offered the uninfor- that she had in some peculiar way made no responses to the auditory stimuli recorded on the tape that had come from the audience and that she still could not understand how she could limit her reception and perception of visual stimuli by "not looking any farther, and being unaware of the sounds from the audience." Early that evening she and her associates listened to both tape recordings, and she found that she still lacked any conscious memories and understandings of the two experiences.

The next morning, at the beginning of the day's work, she was asked if she would like to volunteer to be a hypnotic subject. She replied, "I certainly would like to, but would it be possible for me to know that I am being hypnotized?" She was told that this was possible. As she sat expectantly in the chair, she became aware slowly of changes occurring within her. Her first statement was, "I still see everybody in the audience, but the walls have disappeared and everything is getting quieter. The audience is getting smaller. I don't know how I am doing this, but very slowly everything except you and me and your voice and my voice is leaving. Now here we are sitting on these chairs, with these chairs on the floor . . . we're all alone. In some way I know that this really isn't so, but this is the way I am experiencing everything. There is my hand up in the air. I know it's my hand, but I am not holding it there; I'm just letting it be there. It is something like being in a very real dream—swimming, socializing, driving a car, skating, skiing, and enjoying it all—with no knowledge about being sound asleep in bed. That is the best explanation I can give."

She was told that after awakening she could recall all three experiences in order that she could listen to and recognize *as her own experiences* the events of the first two tape recordings and then of the present tape recording, which would be played back to her; she would remember the present experience fully and be interested in and anticipating the next remarks that she would hear as the tape recording was played back.

She was awakened with full conscious memories of all three experiences and she declared her eager interest in listening to the present tape recording. She later reported how, upon listening to the first two tape recordings, each of them had suddenly been sensed as her own experience, as was the third experience.

This is but one of many such tape-recorded experiments. It was selected because the subject was so highly intelligent, sophisticated psychiatrically, and subjected to so much pressure by colleagues to break down her amnesias.

DEFINITION AND EXPLANATION OF PROBLEM TO BE INVESTIGATED

It was eventually realized that the fundamental problem centered around the intriguing question of *the significances of the reality situation in and out of the hypnotic trance: that is, Do hypnotized people apprehend or perceive or sense their surrounding realities in the same fashion as do people not in the trance state?* Hull was emphatic in his statement, even emotionally so, that a somnambulistic hypnotic subject who was told to look, for example, at Person A (actually present, not a hallucination), saw Person A in exactly the same way as he did in the ordinary state of awareness. The author, for reasons he had not clearly formulated at that time but which he related to the hypnotized subject's different attitudinal behaviors in the trance state, disagreed with Hull, but was puzzled by the question of how one's waking apprehension of a person might differ from one's trance state apprehension of the same person. The author regarded the trance state as colored by what is called "rapport," and as marked by such rigidities of behavior as those deriving from catalepsy and other alterations of physical behavior and by the reality detachment, dissociation, and ideomotor and ideosensory manifestations that appear to be important, but which are not always consistently present, characteristics of the somnambulistic state. Also characteristic of the trance state are the subjects' apparent unawareness of items of reality and stimuli which are not pertinent to their trance or to the potentiation of other mental frames of reference. Perhaps the best analogies can be found in the persistence of visual illusions in the waking state, as for example the well-known persistent recognition of a vase and the nondiscovery of the two facial profiles that form the outline of the vase. Another example employed for psychotherapeutic purposes for many years by the author has been to write plainly the number 710 on a piece of paper and to ask a patient to "read what I have put on the paper in all possible ways." There would be a persistence of the numerical frame of reference by *reading* the number by various permutations of the digits even when the paper was turned upside down. Sometimes the rigidity of the numerical frame of reference could not be altered by even the measure of printing the word S-O-I-L above, adding the letter *B* as a prefix to the "upside down number" of O-I-L, and then printing beneath it the word R-O-I-L. The author has encountered such rigidity of frames of reference that while the upper and lower words were recognized properly, the person, normally well-adjusted, would continue to read the middle word as "B, zero, one, and an upside-down seven."

Giving consideration to all the points just enumerated, the author considered it probable (Erickson, 1938) that the hypnotic subjects sensed reality objects and other stimuli which are out of context with the trance state in some different fashion than would be the case in the waking state; and (Erickson, 1943a) that this same phenomenon would also be true for all types of stimuli within the framework of the trance itself because of the ease with which hypnotic subjects can apparently vary their perceptions of objects or stimuli by substitution, at the hallucinatory level, of memory images for actualities. This process of substituting corresponding memory images for sensory stimuli in the trance state is both a possible and a frequent manifestation of hypnosis, but it certainly is not a part of the ordinary waking apprehension of reality, nor even an ordinary variation of it. It appears, however, to be remarkably characteristic that somnambulistic subjects who can, for example, readily see a reality object, can then subsequently hallucinate it vividly with appropriate physiological consequences (Erickson, 1943a). Hull strongly contended that all sensory stimuli continued to be constant in effect or conditional upon the degree of attention, but that a blocking occurred in hypnosis which affected only the communication of experience on the part of the subject to the experimenter but did not alter the subject's actual perception of reality experiences. In this same connection the author had done considerable work upon hypnotic deafness and conditioned responses in which an auditory stimulus was involved. The results of this study (Erickson, 1933) had made the author doubtful of the identity of hypnotic with waking realities. Discussion on this matter led to considerable estrangement

Further Experiments

between Hull and the author, since Hull regarded the author's views as unappreciative disloyalty and willful oversight of Hull's views. (It should not be forgotten that the author at the time of the original discussions was only a student and that Dr. Hull was a professor.)

In any case, as the outcome of these personal discussions with Dr. Hull, (sometimes acrimonious on the part of both), the author, bearing in mind his attempt to devise separately his own private experimental investigation of what constituted the hypnotic state, was aided in his understandings of scientific experimental procedure by Professor Joseph Jastrow, then head of the psychology department; by Dr. William F. Lorenz, professor of psychiatry; and by Dr. A. Loefenhart, professor of pharmacology and a most enthusiastic experimentalist extremely rigid in his insistence upon completely controlled scientific procedures. Later Dr. William Blackwenn of the psychiatric department and Dr. Hans Rees, professor of neurology, who had used hypnosis extensively in the German Army in World War I, offered much advice, encouragement, and instruction regarding the scientific procedure for this project to the author. These advisors all approved the need of extreme care in formulating concepts of procedural methodology and emphasized the importance of not attempting direct contrasts, but of letting experimental procedures be an incidental part of a larger framework of hypnotic work. They emphatically agreed that any discovery of a difference in behavior between nonhypnotic and hypnotic states, to be valid, would have to be a natural or spontaneous manifestation and not a response to direct intervention or suggestion. They could offer no suggestions of how to solve the problem, but they did discuss at great length the difficulties confronting the author, and their counsel has been kept in mind throughout the years.

The questions which continued to concern the author in this investigation centered around:

1. Do hypnotic subjects in the trance state perceive or apprehend a reality object in the same fashion as in the nonhypnotized state?
2. Do the hypnotized persons in some manner "abstract," "extract," and "remove from context" or "apprehend" in some different fashion reality items in the environment of which those items are a part when they are not a part of the hypnotic situation?
3. Is a specific reality object which is perceived by the hypnotized subjects apprehended, sensed, or understood in some fashion alien to or differing from their ordinary waking experience?
4. How does this perceived or apprehended reality object or the hypnotic subjects' reality environments become altered so that their relationships are lost or altered in some way, as is so often indicated by hypnotic subjects whose behavioral responses suggest most strongly such changes?
5. What is there about apprehended reality experience in hypnosis that allows or permits ready substitution of memory images of another kind or counterparts for environmental reality objects?

6. Is the actual environmental reality the same for a person in a hypnotic trance as it is in the waking state?
7. Is there some manner or kind of exclusion or alteration of reality actualities in the hypnotic state which consitutes a part of the state of being in hypnosis?

There were no expectations of securing answers to all of these questions nor even of securing a definitive answer to any one of them. These questions also led to the realization of the importance of an experiential situation wherein the subject could react in accord only with himself *uninfluenced by the responsive behavior of other experimental subjects, and without becoming complaisant in his responses*. Only thus would there be an actual opportunity to discover possible differences between the hypnotic state of awareness and that of waking awareness rather than learned or attempted similarities.

To illustrate roughly the considerations upon which these questions were based the following example may be given: Persons A and B in the ordinary state of awareness are sitting at a desk discussing a complex mathematical formula. However intent they may be on the significance of the mathematical formula, there is a full actual, and available, but secondary continuous knowledge and awareness of the desk at which they sit, the overhead light, the telephone on the desk, the four walls of the room, the day of the week, the approximate time of day, the impending conclusion of the discussion, knowledge of X's opinions, and so on. People in the nontrance state do not lose complete general awareness of the immediate reality surroundings nor of the general context of thinking and speaking; and should they do so in partial fashion, they "come to" with a start, explaining (usually without a request to do so), "For a moment or two there I absentmindedly forgot everything except what I was thinking," reorienting themselves as they so speak to their general environment. But it is to the actual reality environment that they orient themselves.

This is not so with deeply hypnotized somnambulistic subjects, even though it may be their first experience with hypnosis, and eyes may have been continuously wide open, and they may have been hypnotized by some ritualistic verbalized technique of suggestions, or by any other method that had been written out in full or recorded and that could then be examined for hidden or implied meanings of the words employed. Yet, without suggestions of any sort, as subjects sit quietly and passively in the chair in a somnambulistic state, they can be asked simply, "What are you looking at?" to which they can reply in terms of their own past experience, "The mountains" (trees, lake, dog, boat, etc.). Yet mountains have not been mentioned, there are no pictures suggestive of mountains on the walls, but the subjects not only readily describe them but disclose that they have in some manner oriented themselves to the environs of their hunting shack and that the laboratory is nonexistent. All sensory intake apparently has lost its value except the awareness of the presence of the experimenter as a part of the hypnotic situation; and the reality stimuli have been

Further Experiments

replaced in the subjets' experiential behavioral responses by memory images unreleated to the actual reality situation.

Similarly the nontrance state of concentration can be constrasted with a deep somnambulistic trance suddenly induced in willing subjects by measures not consciously recognizable by them. For example a woman intensely concentrating on her own understandings aggressively mounted the speaker's platform and interrupted the author's lecture by assertively declaring, "I dare you to put me into a trance because there is no such thing as hypnosis." The author replied with complete simplicity, "Oh, I wouldn't dare. *That's what you will have to do all by yourself,*" and turned back to the audience and continued his lecture, thereby rendering the woman completely vulnerable psychologically by virtue of the fact that his reply had left her with no target for her aggression except herself. As a result, in a few moments the woman developed a deep, recognizable, somnambulistic trance as was apparent to the various observant students of hypnosis present; it was apparent immediately that only the lecturer was aware of the audience, the podium, the pitcher of water on the table, sounds from the audience, etc. The woman, however, apparently did not perceive her surroundings except for the mere presence of the lecturer, nor did she seem to hear what the author was saying to the audience. Neither did she seem to be aware of the passage of time. As the author continued his lecture, she merely stood immobile, eyes unblinking, totally unresponsive until the author turned to her and asked her if she were willing to demonstrate hypnotic phenomena. She agreed readily and proved to be an excellent demonstration subject. When aroused from the trance, she expressed bewilderment at her presence on the speaker's platform, but added, "It doesn't matter, I just have some kind of an inner feeling; that I have learned a great deal and it is very satisfying." She was subsequently informed of the sequence of events by friends present at that lecture. She expressed simple unconcerened disbelief in their accounts, neither arguing nor protesting, not even asking for any further information. She simply dismissed their jointly proffered information by stating that she would like to be hypnotized some time.

During the demonstration of hypnotic phenomena for that audience, she appeared oblivious of everything until the author addressed her directly. He could then direct her attention to any reality item in that situation, and she could identify it as an isolated reality object, without associated reality significance, either temporal or physical. It would be identified at request in terms of the reality situation, if this were indicated, but spontaneously only in her own special hypnotic frame of reference, whatever that might have been. For example, she could see an indicated chair but could as easily identify it as a chair in her own home as she could see it as a lecture-room chair. What had become of the audience in her apprehension of reality was then and still is to this author a bewildering question. What had become of all the stimuli of which the author was so aware?

Numerous other comparable instances of the sudden development, neither expected nor intended, of profound hypnotic somnambulistic trance states have been observed since Miss O's hypnotic trance behavior in 1923 and the experience just recounted, which occurred in 1930. These events bewildered the author greatly, since they led him to the conclusion that their development signified inner processes of great portent to the subject. This conclusion led the author to the understanding that when he induced a trance, his purposes not being of great inner significance to the subject, it would require prolonged and intensive labor on the author's part to give the subject an awareness that the intended work possessed intrinsic value.

One particular instance seemed to confirm this understanding. A psychologist working for a doctoral degree had been laboriously trained to be a "good" somnambulistic subject. In 1932, in an informal group discussion about the nature of hypnosis interspersed with casual unrelated remarks, this subject had commented upon the coldness and disagreeableness of the weather and stated that she wished it were spring and that she were at home. The author remarked "If wishes were horses, beggars might ride." Almost instantly the group became aware that she had developed a profound trance and had assumed the position of resting her chin on her hands and her elbows on her knees.

It was immediately discovered that she was out of rapport with everybody and that she seemed to be communing with her own thoughts and deeply engrossed in them. Shortly she began to slap at various parts of her body, suggestive of the author's memories of his own spring experiences. Shortly she murmured to herself, "Damm mosquitoes—have to go inside," but there occurred only a lifting of her head and shoulders and a different appearance of her eyes, and the direction of her gaze seemed altered. Since the author was in direct range of her vision, he asked, "Mosquitoes bad?" "Uh huh! You waiting for my father? He's always a little late." She was answered, "What interests you at college?" She replied, "Hypnosis. . ." paused, looked puzzled, and stated "the thought of being at home on the backporch, sitting in the moonlight thinking, and the mosquitoes being so bad that I had to go in the house, and I saw one of my father's clients waiting for him—all that passed through my mind so vividly that I can still feel the mosquito bites."

Highly interested questioning by the group disclosed that she had no awareness of the entire experience as such, the passage of time, the various efforts to make contact with her until the author's fortuitous remark fitted into her own mental frame of reference she was experiencing.

The above examples of totally unexpected, unplanned, and not understood experiences with hypnosis have been encountered many times in the author's career, and the cumulative effect has been to make the author ever-increasingly aware that the hypnotic state is an experience that belongs to the subject, derives from the subject's own accumulated learnings and memories, not necessarily consciously recognized but possible of manifestation in a special state of non-waking awareness. Hence the hypnotic trance belongs only to the subject—the operator can do no more than learn how to proffer stimuli and suggestions that evoke responsive behavior based upon the subject's own experiential past.

This sort of experience, encountered so repeatedly from the very beginning of the author's hypnotic experimentation, led to much speculative thinking. What could be meant or what was implied when a deeply hypnotized somnambulistic subject with a Ph.D. degree in psychology, his eyes open, would reply simply, "Here," when asked "Where are you?" When asked, "What do you mean?" he would reply again simply, "Here, just here." "Elaborate further." "Here with you." "Where am I?" "Right in front of me." "Where is that?" "Here." If one then flicked his eyes at the subject's chair and again asked, "Where are you?" the answer might be, "Here in the chair." One could continue such futile questioning concerning the chair until a flick of the eyes, a tone of voice, or a more specific question indicated the expectation of more elaborate and comprehensive replies, but it would be truly necessary to do something to alter the somnambulistic state of reality. Only by specific instruction by words, tone of voice, manner, or behavior could the somnambulistic subject be led to include nonhypnotic realities, and this could be done only be recognizable intent on the part of the operator, as was so well illustrated by the tape recording given in detail in relationship to the psychiatric social worker.

Numerous such interrogations of highly educated subjects would elicit no comprehensive information from them if leading or suggestive questions were not asked. Yet the same questions in the waking state before or in the waking state after hypnosis would yield markedly different replies, including perhaps annoyance with the questioner and expostulatory responses such as, "Why tell you? You are here and know as well as I do. Your questions are senseless." It is true that somnambulistic subjects can include the opeator in their hallucinated reality and they may even suggest that the operator take a seat on the adjacent stump there beside their hunting shack. Both the nonhypnotic and the hypnotic subjects perceive the experimenter in their environment, but in the case of the nonhypnotic subjects it is a reality environment common to both and verifiable by others. With the somnambulistic subjects they may "insert" the experience of being in a trance into an environment compounded of memory images into which stimuli from surrounding reality are excluded or, if admitted, may be, but not necessarily, subject to transformation. Thus a knock on the laboratory door could be responded to by the subjects as footsteps on the pathway. (All of the illustrative examples cited and to be cited will be from actual instances.) The meaningfulness of numerous such experiences intrigued the author greatly but left Hull uninterested, since he was interested in laboratory procedures for the study of planned and deliberately elicited responses, and he did not have an interest in field observation and the study of spontaneous behavioral manifestations.

However, this type of behavior has continued to be one of challenging interest to the author in all of his experimental and clinical work to the present day, since this paper does not constitute a final explication of what and how and why hypnotic realities are so different from waking state realties.

In general as time passed it was recognized that any satisfactory experimental procedure formulated would have to involve the presentation of an item of reality to as many subjects as possible in both waking and somnambulistic trance states, as well as to a large number of subjects in the waking state who might or might not become hypnotic subjects; and that this item of reality would have to be perceptible to both somnambulistic and waking subjects, and the experimental results entirely dependent upon the understandings belonging to the subjects in special state of awareness, whether waking or somnambulistic.

This item of reality was to be dealt with in relation to the surrounding reality environment as experienced by each subject in his own manner, but this fact was not to be so specified. It was to be only inherent in the task proposed. The experimental procedure derived from understandings achieved from repeated hypnotic experiences observed over a period of 10 years, and which were apprehensible only as signifying a satisfactory somnambulistic trance state. A chance realization led to the recognition of the experimental potentialities which those observed manifestations offered for the differentiation of the realities of the hypnotic state and of those of the state of ordinary awareness.

FORMULATION OF EXPERIMENT

The experiment as finally formulated centered simply around the task of relating an item of reality to the surrounding reality of the experimental situation. No explicit instructions regarding the exact performance were offered. Instead, all subjects, hypnotic and nonhypnotic, were confronted with a simple task in which there was an implicit need to meet the reality of the experimental situation as it was apprehended by them at the time of execution of the task. The actual performance of the hypnotic subjects was not expectable to the experimenter nor even comprehensible for any of the experimenter's assistants. The performance of the subjects not in a state of hypnosis was fully expectable, and an entirely similar performance was at first fully expected of the hypnotic subjects. In no instance did the experimenter's expectations influence the hypnotic subjects, nor were the expectations of the experimenters influential for the nonhypnotic sybjects. The nature and simplicity of the task performance itself excluded the experimenters as factors having an influence upon the results.

All of the hypnotic training for the subjects employed for this study was entirely in connection with projects completely unrelated to this study. The other projects served only to disclose incidentally what subjects could spontaneously develop somnambulism or who could learn to develop the somnambulistic state.

In this study there was no difference in the results obtained from subjects who developed a somnambulistic state during the first experience of being hypnotized, those who developed the somnambulistic state spontaneously while observing hypnosis in other subjects without expectation of becoming hypnotized by their own intense interest in observing hypnosis, and those subjects who were repeatedly hypnotized with the purpose of being trained to learn to develop the hypnotic state.

Nor did results differ for this study obtained from somnambulistic subjects who were employed to perform the experiment central to this report by this author's assistants, who in turn were selected sometimes because of their inexperience with hypnosis, and did not know that some subjects with whom they were dealing were in a somnambulistic state.

As a further control of the experimental study the same subjects were tested by differently oriented assistants of the author to make certain that the various types of procedure were not influenced by the experimenters' knowledge or lack of knowledge of the experimental study or the psychological state of the subjects. These control study findings were not included as additional results in this experiment. Their purpose was to validate the similarity and common identity of the experimental results obtained from the same experiment despite changes and variations of procedure, personnel, and psychological states and orientations presumed not to be relevant to the experimental, and actually discovered not to be pertinent. The only significant or meaningful negative results are included in this report, and they were very few in number.

In all, the control studies were made on more than 260 subjects, many of whom were used repeatedly not only as a control measure of the experiment itself, but also as a control measure of the differently oriented experimenters employed by the author to assist him in conducting the experiment.

To perform the experiment successfully it was decided that not only should the author act as experimenter, but also that other persons should conduct similar experimentation as assistants of the author. Some of these assistants had knowledge of hypnosis and some were without knowledge of hypnosis, some with and some without knowledge that an experiment as such was being conducted. Additionally the actual task was to be varied in certain specific details, althouvh its meaningful significances would remain the same. The experiment was to be done on nonhypnotic subjects, on waking subjects with a history of previous hypnotic experience, on subjects in the somnambulistic trance, and on waking subjects who had never previously been hypnotized but who, it was hoped, could be trained, months or even a year or two later, to be hypnotic subjects for further exploration of the same problem. These subjects were all to be used at varying intervals and by various experimenters including the author, his colleagues, and even by friends of colleagues who did not know the author nor the purposes to be served.

A crucial instruction for all experimenters was that experimental results had to be accepted unquestioningly, without hesitation, without manifestation of astonishment or lack of understanding. In brief all experimenters were thoroughly instructed to ask a specific question in a matter-of-fact manner and to accept any answer whatsoever in a similar matter-of-fact manner.

The actual experiment was in itself of a rather simple, ordinary, and casual character, and the procedure was executed in accord with a rigidly simple formula but under a great variety of situational circumstances. The subjects varied greatly in their backgrounds. There were undergraduate and graduate university students, hospital attendants, secretaries, nurses, social service workers, undergraduate and graduate psychology students, medical students, interns, residents, medical staff members, nonprofessional people, and even psychotic patients. However, the results on psychotic patients were not included in the total results of this experiment. The author was simply interested to see if the experiment could also be done with hypnotizable psychotic patients.

Assistants who were employed to conduct the experiment were sometimes aware that the experiment was related to hypnosis, but some thought it was only a psychological experiment under way for some unknown psychology student. Some regarded it not as an experiment but only as a simple earnest inquiry, meaningless, possibly having some obscure significance, or possibly testing their judgment and critical abilities. Others regarded the task requested as a somewhat nonsensical and purposeless but harmless casual activity of the moment. Some actually were fully informed that it was a test of hypnotic and nonhypnotic realities but without being given precise information beyond that general statement. Even this degree of sophistication did not alter experimental results, even though it was employed on many clinical psychologists with Ph.D. degrees.

Some of the experimenters were fully aware that the subjects were in a profound hypnotic state; some, because of the extensive somnambulistic training of the subjects, did not realize they were dealing with hypnotic subjects (Erickson, 1944); a large number of the subjects had been trained to be somnambulistic in trance states before this experiment was formulated. Care was consistently taken to see that the experimenters did not intrude their understandings into the experimental situation, often by the simple measure of a posthypnotic suggestion to the subjects that when the assigned task was performed, they would develop a profound amnesia for their performance immediately upon the experimenter's saying "Thank you now," as the experimenters were rigidly instructed to do as a part of their task, and the peculiar wording of "Thank you now" made it highly specific.

However, *experimental results were found to be dependent not upon the experimenters' understanding of the task nor upon the subjects' attitude toward or understanding of the test. The results derived solely from the subjects' task performance itself.*

In other words the subjects were asked to perform a task calling for the exercise solely of their own abilities without there being any need for guidance, advice, or instruction from the experimenters. Only the task was the controlling force, and when it was completed, the individual performance was the result. Then it became an established and an unalterable fact because it consisted of a demonstrated expression of a personal evaluation and judgment.

The nonhypnotic subjects differed from the hypnotic subjects in accepting the

Further Experiments

task variously, ranging in attitude from serious interest to indifference, curiosity, puzzlement, boredom, scorn, questioning, etc. Even so the nature and character of responses were consistent unless resentment developed from having their "time wasted." On the other hand the hypnotic subjects invariably showed a consistent attitude of willing, earnest cooperativeness regardless of previous use as nonhypnotic subjects, or as first-time subjects with any of the task attitudes mentioned above. There appeared to be no spontaneous emotionally-tinged judgment of the task itself such as was shown by the waking subjects.

The experimental results found by the various experimenters, even though some of these assistants were not personally acquainted with the author, were consistently comparable. The simplicity of the experimenters' task and the ease with which they could avoid any share in the subjects' performance was probably the most important factor.

Whenever possible, there were from two to a dozen repetitions at different times of the experiment with many subjects, many times possible in both the waking and trance states. These repetitions were *not* counted as additional experiments. However, it was not always possible to secure repetitions of the experiment particularly with the waking subjects, and thus there was a larger number of one-time-only waking subjects, as well as fewer repetitions with the waking subjects. The purpose of the reptitions was to discover possible errors in the procedure.

There was available a much larger supply of waking subjects than of hypnotic subjects. Every effort was made to secure as many waking and trance subjects as possible, but the number of subjects who used it in the trance state was the lesser. Practically all of those who served as trance subjects served also as waking subjects, sometimes first in the waking state, sometimes first in the trance state. Careful effort was made to effect an equal and random distribution of these alternations.

Usually the experiments were done in a university or a hospital setting, occasionally in such a situation as a private group or in a medical or psychological or other lecture setting. The format of the experiment was exceedingly simple and consisted of no more than the simple question of:

"While we are waiting (thus indicating vaguely some delayed or delaying circumstance appropriate to the situation and definitely implying that the real purposes to be accomplished were something else) *where in this room if you had a three-by-four foot picture of* ———— (specifying one at a time each of these four items: person actually present, a small snapshot of someone known to the subject, an actual bowl of fruit, and an actual snapshot of a picture of a bowl of fruit), *where in this room would you hang it? Consider carefully, and when you have made up your mind, specify exactly.*

The question was read from a typed card. This card constituted a hint that an experiment was in progress, but the question did not seem to warrant fully that conclusion. Instead it seemed to indicate that the question was seriously intended.

In presenting the question, the reality object to be mentioned was previously always positioned carefully. For example the person present in reality might be sitting in a chair beside a window or might be leaning against the window in some casual position; this person might be squatting in front of a bookcase apparently searching for a book on the bottom shelf, or sitting or standing at a desk in the middle of the room or in front of a blackboard placed diagonally across a corner of the room, or in any other casual position. As for the snapshots, these were held in a slotted wooden base and were simply positioned in a similar casual fashion, such as on top of a bookcase, on the chalk tray at the bottom of the blackboard, on the arm of a chair next to a window, on the top of a desk in the middle of the room, or on a small stand in a corner of the room. The bowl of fruit was similarly placed in various positions. The subject and the experimenter always walked to a position about three feet to the side of the reality object, which would be indicated by a hand gesture.

With both nonhypnotic and hypnotic subjects it became apparent within 10 experiments with each type of subject that a multiple placement of the reality objects with repetitious putting of the question for each object could be done with no alteration of the meaningfulness of the results. For example the question could be asked in relation to the person standing casually at the window and then, when the person sauntered over to the bookcase, to the desk, or to the blackboard, the question could be asked for each new position. Similarly the snapshots and the bowl of fruit could be openly repositioned and the question asked for each new placement. Or all four reality objects could first be positioned and then the question could be put in succession for each item, and then a repositioning openly effected, and the questioning repeated. This multiple testing on a single occasion in no way altered the responsive behavior, except that if it were done too many times, the waking-state subjects were likely to become impatient or irritated. Repetitions did not distress subjects in the hypnotic state.

Another effect upon the nonhypnotic subjects was that the repetitions tended at first to intrigue their curiosity without changing the character of their replies. It led to their own questioning of their original reply and the offering of a second and sometimes a third answer the same character as the first. As for the hypnotic subjects there was no effect. Each position and inquiry was accepted as a unit complete in itself and unrelated to any other matter or inquiry. This discovery served to make possible many more tests with each hypnotic subject, although such repetitions were not included as additional experiments. The only experimental results discarded were those from nonhypnotic subjects who regarded the questioning as nonsensical and either rejected the question or, annoyed by it, gave purposely nonsensical answers such as, "Oh, hang it up for Santa Claus." However, there were few of these, since the overall tendency was to accept the task as a simple straightforward question with no special meaning.

Well over 2,000 persons participated in this experiment. Of these the opportunity did not arise to induce somnambulistic hypnotic trances in more than one-third, and this was always done in relationship to some other hypnotic work, this other hypnotic work sometimes being nothing more than systematic training for deep hypnosis.

This traning for deep hypnosis was the use of traditional ritualistic verbalizations of hypnotic-induction techniques continued for several hours at a time and often repeated for several days to be sure that the subjects were in a "deep hypnotic trance." The criteria for a "deep trance" were: complete posthypnotic amnesia for trance experiences; ready ideomotor activity such as automatic writing; and ideosensory activity such as visual and auditory hallucinations. Sometimes an effective hypnotic anaesthesia of the hands and arms as tested by sudden sharp electrical shocks was employed. Usually the subjects were asked to recall some long-forgotten memory, and this would be discussed with them posthypnotically as a test of their posthypnotic amnesia, and an effort would be made to verify the validity of the recollection. Additionally innumerable minor tests of startle responses would be made to determine any deliberate retention of environmental contact instead of "sleeping completely soundly, restfully, as soundly asleep as if you were in a deep profound sleep in the middle of the night when awfully tired." "I want you to sleep as deeply and soundly as a log," was an exceedingly frequent suggestion. (When the author now wishes somnambulistic trances, much briefer, more effortless methods are employed.)

Hypnotic subjects were used for this experimentation only when deep somnambulistic trances were developed. This was done for the following reasons: Those in a light trance found it difficult to maintain a trance state if they opened their eyes and performed a task in relation to external reality; they felt a need to arouse from the trance state in order to do the task; and they expressed the belief that they would "do it wrong" if they tried to stay in the trance. Those in a medium trance were also disinclined to cooperate, and questioning revealed as their reason that the opening of the eyes and the doing something not in relationship to themselves would disturb them and tend to awaken them; they were willing to do things that affected them as persons, but they felt that any manipulation of external objects by them placed an undue burden on them. They would accede unwillingly upon insistence, and were most likely either to lessen the trance state or to arouse from it. For those reasons only fully somnambulistic subjects were employed. This required an extensive amount of work and a long period of time to secure so many such subjects. However, there was an additional reward in that such somnambulistic subjects had been used for other experimental studies and for lecture demonstrations.

It was quite possible to secure negative results easily by overenthusiastic presentation of the instructions, adding unintentional emphases and unrealized misdirectioning of the subjects. The correction of this unintentional securing of results construed as those desired by the experimenter was easily done by utlizing a practice employed by the author very early in his hypnotic investigations. This was his regular practice of having highly intelligent hypnotic subjects who developed spontaneously the somnambulistic state during the first trance induction, act as critics of the author's induction techniques while they were in a somnambulistic state and in rapport with both the author and a new hypnotic subject who was unaware of the trance state of the other person present.

Perhaps the best illustration is the following experience. The author was presenting a lecture-demonstration to a small medical group using as his volunteer subject a member of another group to whom a similar lecture-demonstration was to be given two days later with this first group also in attendance. The subject appeared to develop a somnambulistic state, but the author noted a "new quality" in the hypnotic manifestations and soon realized that the volunteer subject was simulating a trance state. Care was taken not to put too much strain upon the simulator and to give every evidence of accepting his performance as valid. At the close of the meeting the "subject" was asked if he would aid in training some new subjects the next day. He agreed readily. Arrangements were made separately with five experienced somnambulistic subjects who had each on different occasions acted in the somnambulistic state as a critic of the author's techniques. They were told to meet with the author and to develop a somnambulistic state together with full rapport with each other as well as with the author, but they were not to disclose their trance state to a new somnambulistic subject who would arrive shortly. Instead they were to present an appraisal of his aptitude in reacting silently to positive and negative visual and auditory hallucinations, manifesting catalepsy, and doing automatic writing. Each was to appraise these items successively, and then they were free to make any additional comments they wished. Thereupon they would first ask the newcomer if he knew they were in a somnambulistic trance state, and then they would ask him if he could recognize their arousal from the trance state, which was to be in accord with the ordinal numbers of 1 to 5, which had been given to them separately so that each of them would await his own turn to arouse. Should he fail to recognize their trance state, he would be challenged as to which were the first of them to awaken, and if he failed to do so correctly, those still in the trance state were to inspect their group and to write down in a notebook the correct identity, adding to the name the existing state of awareness. Also, before verbalizing their appraisals, they were to write them down. Upon awakening, they would remember the situation but have an amnesia for the simulator's individual performances and for the appraisals, which were separate from each other and to be remembered separately.

The results were in accord with actual and expected possibilities. The simulator had immediately been recognized as such in every regard; he failed to realize that they were in a trance state, also to identify the arousal of each of them. Additionally the simulator was startled to discover their separate amnesias for each other's appraisals, and that they all had identified the same three instances where "he started to go into a trance and then drew back."

The author had been rather mystified when the five somnambules had had whispered conferences and then had written down a comment that they had apparently agreed upon unanimously. This comment was that the author had also recognized that the simulator had three times started to go into a trance state but that he had withdrawn from such entry, and that they were also aware that the author was maintaining an attitude of nonparticipation, that all of his suggestions were offered in such a way the simulator was allowed to make, without help from the author, the choice of going into a trance or to continue simulating, and that there was no effort made to utilize those three instances when the simulator started to go into a trance to induce a trance. Neither had the author tried to induce a continuance of the simulation. It was apparent to them that the author was interested only in what the simulator would do in the situation in which he found himself.

The attitude of the simulator toward this exposure of his simulation was recognized by him as a genuine scientific inquiry to see how well somnambulistic subjects recognize somnambulism, simulation, and any particular behavior that they might observe.

This instance served to induce the author at every possible opportunity to use somnambulistic subjects to check on other hypnotic subjects and to check on his own behavior. This has been found to be a very significant factor in the author's development of his own hypnotic procedures.

Over 300 of these somnambulistic subjects had been used previously to this study in other kinds of nonhypnotic, systematically organized experiments in the waking state, and in experiments investigating color vision, automatic writing, anaesthesia, recovery of lost memories, etc., in which they had manifested a satisfactory degree of somnambulism. Half of these subjects were first used for this experiment in the waking state, and the other half were first used in the trance state. In employing the remaining 350 hypnotic subjects, half of them underwent their first hypnotic experience in connection with this study, although they were deliberately given an impression that the purpose of the hypnosis was for some other unrelated activity. For example they were intentionally allowed to think that the simple training procedure of automatic writing was an experiment in itself, when the purpose of such a teaching session was that of inducing and maintaining a deep trance despite activity in relation to reality objects such as pencils and paper, or chalk and a blackboard. Similarly, teaching them to remain in a deep somnambulistic trance with their eyes wide open was another training task which actually had no other meaning than that of remaining in a deep trance. Those used first for this experiment were subsequently used for other experimental purposes as another check on their hypnotic abilities. A few subjects had had hypnotic experiences before meeting the author, and these gave responses similar to those undergoing hypnosis by the author only. There were also some 30 subjects trained in hypnosis by students of the author. These were as easily used for this experiment by the author's assistants as by the author himself, or by those who had first trained them. The results they gave were in full accord with findings on other subjects.

SUBJECTS

Although over 2,000 persons participated in this experiment, the original plan had called for only 300, of whom approximately 100 were to be somnambulistic subjects. Other work and experiments intervened and more subjects were added until it was realized that the original figure had been far surpassed. Difficulties of preparing the manuscript and some fortuitous circumstances resulting in a sudden acquisition of large numbers of new subjects through special teaching projects postponed the conclusion of the experiment repeatedly.

There also arose the question of finding an exception to the experimental results. This led to the enthusiastic securing of a large number of additional subjects in the desire to secure negative results, but all findings have been consistently positive. Every spontaneous negative result would lead to the discovery of a light or medium trance, whether the inquiry was made by the author or by other investigators. Invariably the subjects would explain *a feeling of contact with the environment and a need to lessen or to awaken from the trance so that they would not "give a wrong answer."* Careful questions failed to disclose what would be the "wrong answer." The usual response was, "Well, just wrong in some way I can't explain." This remarkable reply was obtained not only by the author but by his assistants, who did not know that the author and others had also received similarly meaningful replies, not always in the words quoted above, but words having a similar meaning.

And the past 16 years of private practice have added a large number of additional subjects. For example in the final week of 1964 three private patients—one seeking freedom from university examination panics, one seeking relief from headaches diagonosed as functional by three neurological clinics, and one woman pregnant for the first time and sent to the author by her obstetrician for hypnotic training for delivery—all developed somnambulistic hypnotic states and were used to review various statements made in this study. Nor was this specific week a remarkably unusual occurrence in the author's private practice of psychotherapy.

Classification of the subjects employed has been difficult because of the long period of years during which this experiment was in development. Undergraduate students used as either hypnotic-state subjects or waking-state subjects might not be retested until they were graduate students. Medical students might become interns, interns sometimes became residents, and residents sometimes became staff members before their contributions were completed. Student social service workers often became graduates and staff members. The only constant subjects were those at the noncollege level or were members of the medical staff of the hospital and the actually psychotic patients who were used but not included in the total results. These latter totalled 25, and despite their psychotic state, which was manifested in both the waking and the trance states, they were constant in their experimental performance. Their results agreed with those obtained from well-adjusted, highly educated subjects. Another class of subjects that remained constant was formed by those persons employed from the author's private practice where experimentation did not interfere with the psychotherapy for minor maladjustments. Often therapeutic goals did not permit a large number of experimental repetitions, but the experimental results obtained from such subjects were in harmony with results obtained from volunteer subjects obtained from a college population.

In all, four college populations contributed a large number of subjects. For example one three-hour lecture-demonstration to over 500 students yielded 137 somnambules who were trained *en masse* but used as experimental subjects separately by the author and his assistants on the next few weekends. One other such massive yield was 93 subjects from a single lecture-demonstration to a large audience of another university. As it was, the author's extensive lecture-demonstrations before medical and hospital groups, and the attendance of nurses and social service workers and hospital personnel rendered relatively easy large numbers of subjects who could be tested for this experiment over weekends.

PROCEDURE AND RESPONSES

In performing the experiment, immediately upon reading the card of instruction to the subject as given above, the experimenter fixated his gaze completely upon the card and awaited the subject's reply. If further instructions were wanted, the experimenter merely reread the typewritten instructions and patiently waited.

There were in essence *two kinds of responses—the nonhypnotic and the hypnotic. The age, sex, and history of previous hypnotic relationships with the experimenter, or previous hypnotic or nonhypnotic experience with the question, place, situation, or occasion had no altering significance upon the answers obtained.*

The nonhypnotic response was an answer in terms of a complete reality perception and an orientation to the total reality situation, while the hypnotic response was invariably in terms of a restricted, limited, and altered perception of the realities constituting the hypnotic situation.

To illustrate by an impromptu experiment from a lecture on and a demonstration of hypnosis to a medical society, a somnambulistic hypnotic subject manifesting negative visual hallucinations was told to see Dr. X, who was in the audience and who actually happened to be sitting in front of a midroom narrow supporting column. In that setting the subject was asked, in this first-time hypnotic experience for him, *"Where in this room, if you had a three-by-four-foot picture of Dr. X, where in this room would you hang it? Consider carefully, and when you have made up your mind, specify exactly."*

Slowly the subject surveyed the walls of the room, apparently continuing to be unaware of the audience of more than 200 physicians. Finally he turned gravely to the author and pointing with his finger at the column directly behind Dr. X, stated, "I would hang it right there." This was a familiar response to the author but most unfamiliar and mystifying to the audience. It served to impress upon them that hypnosis altered a person's behavior significantly.

The author continued his lecture and demonstration for the physicians and later repeated exactly the same question, this time first having the subject become aware of the presence of Dr. Y, who happened to be sitting on the steps of a wide staircase. Further complications were added by having the subject first question Dr. Y about the weather, then turn to the author to relay the replies actually made, and then, while the subject was facing the author, Dr. Y, in response to signals not visible to the subject, quietly moved to another part of the room. The purpose of this was to demonstrate to the audience that an orientation to a reality object once achieved could continue unimpaired by reality changes. When the subject had finished reporting upon Dr. Y's replies, he was asked to question Dr. Y in new regards. He turned back to where Dr. Y had originally been sitting and asked furhter questions, to which Dr. Y replied from his new position. The subject reacted with a startled response and commented to the author that Dr. Y had changed his voice in some "funny way" which he, the subject, could not understand. But, as the audience realized, the subject was obviously hallucinating visually, and he continued to so hallucinate Dr. Y as sitting in his original place. To continue the impromptu experiment the author again asked the subject the test question in relation to Dr. Y that he had previously asked in relation to Dr. X. Slowly, thoughtfully, the subject surveyed the entire room, then his eyes returned to the hallucinatory Dr. Y and he stated that he would place it "Right there." Cautious inquiry indicated that "right there" constituted a space approximately six feet above the hallucinatory Dr. Y's head, and approximately one foot to his rear, which would placed the picture in the empty space of the stairwell!

Still later in the discussion being offered to the audience the subject was asked to see Dr. Y's "identical twin brother sitting over there," indicating a seat in front of a window where Dr. Y was then actually sitting. The subject immediately recognized Dr. Y's features, turned to make what seemed to be a visual comparison of the actual Dr. Y with the hallucinatory figure, and freely commented that they enhanced their similarity by wearing the same kinds of suits, but that the second Dr. Y was smoking a cigarette while the first was not. (This was true. In his new position Dr. Y had lit a cigarette, but he had not been smoking in his original seat.) The subject was then asked the same questions about the "second Dr. Y" as he had been asked with Dr. X and the real Dr. Y. Again he thoughtfully surveyed the entire room, his gaze lingering most at the site of the place he had selected for the picture of Dr. Y. Finally he commented that the two pictures ought not to be hung side by side, and thereupon he indicated that the picture of the "second" Dr. Y should be hung directly above him at the place where he sat. This placed it squarely in front of the upper part of a window.

Further Experiments

The subject was reminded that three times he had asked *where he would hang three separate pictures* and he declared that, while the author had been speaking to him, *this had been done*. (This sort of spontaneous development was encountered many times during the experiment and in itself emphasizes the possibility that the hypnotized subject's apprehension of reality is markedly different from that of a subject in waking state. In other words the mere request of *where* he might hang the picture sufficed to have the subject mentally accomplish an actual hallucinatory positioning of the merely specified picture in the question asked. This sort of a spontaneous development was a fairly frequent occurrence during the entire course of the experimental work, not only in the author's experience but in that of the other experimenters employed. However, no special effort was made to elicit this particular item of information (that there had been an hallucinatory hanging of the pictures), since it seemed that such effort might constitute some form of influence upon the subjects' spontaneity of response. The most frequent form in which this development occurred would be the subjects' satisfied spontaneous approval of the "pictures" in the sites they had selected, but this was not a constant feature and hence no questions were asked. In relation to the nonhypnotic subjects comparable reactions would be, "Yes, I really believe that such a picture *would* fit very well there," or perhaps, "I believe it could be placed over there too," indicating another place on the same or a different wall.

Since the demonstration subject had volunteered the information that the hypothetical task of the picture hanging had been done, he was asked to examine all three pictures critically and to appriase the "fitness of their hanging, the appropriateness, the suitablity" and to offer freely any suggestions that might occur to him. Slowly, critically, the subject examined all three areas, and then expressed, with full satisfaction, the opinion that all was well except that the portrait of the "second Dr. Y" was hanging slightly askew. The author immediately noted that Dr. Y was actually leaning to one side with his chin in his palm and with his elbow resting on his knee. Such a comparable finding has been sought repeatedly by deliberately asking a waking subject to visualize on the wall a picture of someone present and having that person subsequently slump in his position. In no instance has a waking subject's visual projection been affected by the subsequent physical shifting of the reality object. The contrary is common only with hypnotic subjects in a somnambulistic trance. Remarking to the subject that this would be corrected shortly, the author proceeded with his lecture. (Dr. Y obligingly sat up straight, and some 15 minutes later the subject spontaneously observed that the picture had been "straightened out.")

No picture-positioning request was made of this subject in the waking state.

So far as the group was concerned, only the author knew that an experiment of special interest to the author was being conducted. The audience merely looked upon the proceedings as an impromptu development of the lecture-demonstration situation for their instruction, as indeed it was.

Many months later the author was asked to present another lecture-demonstration for the same group in the same meeting-place, perhaps using the same or other subjects, the particular purpose being a demonstration of the control of pain both directly and posthypnotically.

Advantage was taken of this opportunity to employ three subjects, the one who had been used as described above and two other subjects who had not been used in any relation to the experiment central to this study and who did not know the first subject. The two new subjects had previously been used in a separate experiment concerning an investigation of hypnotic deafness (Erickson, 1938).

To all three subjects, one at a time and separately (the other two were asked to stay in a waiting room), the original medical-lecture impromptu experiment was repeated with each subject *in the waking state* and with the rationalized explanation, "Since it is not yet time for the meeting to begin, let's pass time while the rest of the audience is coming. There sits Dr. X. *'Where in this room, if you had a three-by-four-foot picture of Dr. X, where in this room would you hang it? Consider carefully, and when you have made up your mind, specify exactly.'* " (The procedure was then repeated concerning Dr. Y.) The subject used previously apparently did not recall his previous execution of the task in the trance state, but no test was made of possible recollection. His behavior was highly suggestive of a total amnesia.

Each subject obligingly surveyed the walls of the room, and each one selected areas on the front wall behind the speaker's desk, actually a spatially appropriate place for hanging such a picture. As a departure from the original procedure each was asked separately for a second and third placing, repeating the wording of the original request. In all three instances second and third possible positionings of the pictures were proposed, each subject giving his own and actually good reasons for each proposed site but which did not necessarily agree with the choices and reasons of the other two subjects. All of this waking-state-positioning of the hypothetical pictures was done in relationship to the spatial area of the walls and the view afforded to the possible viewer of the picture. The physical presence of Drs. X and Y, obligingly occupying the same seats for the subject used originally and their changing of their positions to other spots of the room, had no bearing upon the selection of proposed picture sites. Yet the same three subjects later in a somnambulistic trance selected separately, as proper sites for pictures of Drs. X and Y, unlikely sites for the pictures but sites which were in direct relationship to the physical presence of the two men. They disclosed no awareness nor influence of the total general reality situation. Although "Where in this room" constituted the exact question, the replies received were invariably couched in the subjects' apparent *trance understandings* or apprehension of the physical reality, which was definitely not in accord with their ordinary waking understandings of reality. In fact, the subjects' reality apprehension appeared definitely to be another type of experience than that of their waking state. The subject who had been previously used gave hypnotic responses comparable to those of his original experiences. Sophistication did not alter his trance responses.

Further Experiments

In still further demonstration of hypnotic behavior, at another medical meeting before which the author had not previously appeared, the topic for presentation was "Induction Techniques." To make this presentation the medical group had secured 10 possible volunteer subjects for the author, with none of whom he was acquainted until each was brought separately from a waiting room and introduced to the author. The reason for this formality was to insure that each subject would have to be approached with no previous awareness of what the author had done with the preceding subjects, thus to preclude any imitation or possible collusion. It was the desire of the medical group to appraise hypnosis as a legitimate and significant phenomenon and to do so in a controlled fashion.

This intelligently critical atmosphere consituted an excellent setting for further impromptu experimentation, since no one present knew of the author's private experiment. Hence, as each subject was brought forward by the physician in charge of the subjects and introduced, supposedly only for the purpose of the demonstration of variations of techniques of hypnotic induction, an item of which all the subjects had been apprised, remarks were made to the effect, "I do not know if you are acquainted with that gentleman (pointing), the one with the (bow tie, striped four-in-hand time, long-stemmed pipe, flower-in-lapel, or any special easily identified item), but then neither do I know if you are acquainted with (and then other physicians would be designated by another series of minor individual identifications)." Thus two or three persons could be selected at random, apparently for the purpose of initiating a conversation with the volunteer subject. The actual purpose, however, was to select two or three people advantageously seated for experimental purposes.

To each volunteer subject, none of whom had seen or experienced hypnosis, the standard question was put, "Where in this room, if you had a three-by-four-foot picture of (that doctor with the bow tie or whatever the specific identification mark was), where in this room would you hang it? Consider it carefully, and when you have made up your mind, specify exactly." To the audience as well as to the subjects this was merely a casual, irrelevant question serving merely as pointless, more or less routine, introductory conversation.

In each instance the subjects surveyed the walls of the room and indicated a spot spatially appropriate, although the choices of such spatially appropriate places varied somewhat. For example one subject said, "I'd take down that picture there and put up the new one." Another siad, "The best place is already occupied, so it would have to go there," indicating another wall area.

Then, after each subject had developed a trance state, and several hypnotic techniques had been demonstrated and a discussion of the specific induction techniques used had been given, the subject, in a somnambulistic trance, was again asked the same question which had been originally put to him in the waking state. It was learned that it made no difference whether the subjects were unaware of the audience or were in full rapport with and able to answer questions from the audience responsively and adequately. Nor did it matter whether the special question was put by the author or by a member of the society placed in rapport with the subjects, or whether the question was read from a typewritten card or merely asked. The inquiry, "Where in this room, if you had a three-by-four-foot picture of (whomever had been picked out for that subject in the waking state), where in this room would you hang it? Consider it carefully, and when you have made up your mind, specify exactly."

Without fail *each subject in the trance state slowly, thoughtfully surveyed the room and then placed the picture above and slightly behind the selected person, regardless of the absurdity of the reality background.* This departure from their previous waking performance of the same task was readily appreciated, and it was most impressive to the audience. It served to illustrate to them that hypnosis could alter significantly a subject's response to stimuli, an item of fact of great medical interest to them.

For each of the last two of these 10 subjects, both of whom proved to be excellent somnambulistic subjects, a new procedure was devised and repeated with each of them separately. This new measure was that, as one subject separately entered the room and before he had mounted the speaker's platform, he was halted by the author's request that "Will the man with the rumpled hair and the heavy beard and the one with the bow tie and the white carnation in his coat lapel leave their seats in the audience and sit on the speaker's platform" in two indicated chairs which had been placed in front of a ten-by-twelve-foot oil painting of a historical scene. The physicians acceded to the request for each subject, both times with some embarrassment and self-consciousness, while each subject watched with curious interest. Then the subject, still in the waking state, was asked the crucial picture-positioning question in relation to these two selected physicians in their new positions. Each of the subjects freely surveyed the walls of the auditorium and gave the usual reasonable waking responses.

Then, after the two subjects had been used for a technique demonstration and discussion, each was asked, still in the somnambulistic trance and out of rapport with all except the author, the picture-positioning question about the two physicians actually on the platform with him but who were identified only verbally for him by the special descriptions offered when they had been seated in the audience. Slowly, thoughtfully, each subject surveyed all the walls of the room and then seemed to be hesitating, to the author's intense astonishment, over a choice between *the wall behind the two physicians,* which was occupied by the oil painting, and *positions in direct relationship to the seats where the men had originally sat.* Finally a choice was made of a spot slightly above and to the rear of each doctor as he sat before the oil painting. Immediately the author asked, "Will you please ask each doctor if he agrees with your selection of a spot to hang his picture?" Unhesitatingly, again to the author's astonishment, both subjects turned from looking at the hallucinated pictures toward the audience and looked at the places where the physicians had sat originally. Apparently their initial awareness of those physicians occasioned by the author's request that they change their seats had had the effect of identifying those physicians for both subjects *in relation to audience-position.* In other words the change of position that happened in response to the author's request of the physicians became unwittingly a part of the trance environment, while the first sight of

Further Experiments

those physicians remained an abiding item of waking audience-reality. As they looked at the physicians hallucinated as being in the audience, each declared that their picture-positioning was affirmed by an affirmative nodding of the head by both physicians as they apparently hallucinated them in the audience.

One may speculate that the original identification of the physicians as audience members and the question of picture-positioning of both became a part of the actual external waking reality. *Then in the trance state a new and different trance reality developed which included hallucinated pictures to be hung on walls apparently differently apprehended than in the waking state.* The question of the physicians' approval then introduced into the trance state a need for a part of the original audience-reality, which was met by substituting visual memories of the physicians-in-the-audience experience and yet maintaining intact their trance-reality apprehension. In further discussion of this matter there may be added the fact that this peculiar incorporation into the hypnotic state of reality apprehension of a part of the waking-state-reality-apprehension has been frequently encountered in somnambulistic subjects engaged in complex behavior. Of interest is the fact that, however contradictory the two different apprehensions of reality are, the subjects experience no sense of incongruity or conflict. In this instance the description-identification of the men before the subjects mounted the speaker's platform apparently remained a part of waking audience-reality. Their presence on the platform was apparently a part of the hypnotic-reality background. Hence they hung the pictures in relation to the hypnotic setting, but when asked to secure a waking-reality opinion, they turned to the originally established waking-audience-reality. The hesitation in hanging the pictures does not necessarily imply conflict but may simply imply a choice between the two seemingly equal (to them) reality values.

Of the 10 volunteer subjects for this lecture-demonstration, four had been found, so far as the author was concerned, to be unresponsive to hypnosis, and after the author's failure to hypnotize them, they were allowed to sit in the audience. One of them, at the close of the meeting, volunteered again to be a subject, an item of intense interest to the audience. He proved this time to be an excellent subject, and he, too, like the other subjects in the trance state, placed the picture of another man with a dotted bow tie in an impossible place and later in a likely place in the subsequent waking state, but with an amnesia for his trance behavior.

As for the other hypnotic subjects, they had one by one been sent into another room as each had finished his share in the lecture-demonstration, under the watchful eye of the building custodian, who had been instructed to allow no conversation among them. Actually this precaution proved to be unnecessary, since each subject had been dismissed posthypnotically in a trance state with instructions to rest comfortably and restfully until the author again needed him, and all had obeyed. This precaution was solely in the event that questions by the audience might require calling them back, and it was not desired that they exchange information.

As a closing part of the meeting these six subjects were aroused from their trance states and summoned separately into the lecture room. There each was asked, using the same procedure and question, to indicate where they would place a specified hypothetical picture. Again, despite their previous trance behavior and entirely in accord with waking reality behavior, they selected areas on the wall in relationship to suitable spatial requirements, nor did unwanted, suggestions from the audience influence them.

The above instances are cited in detail because, though they do not form a part of the data of this experimental report, they allow a more comprehensive understanding of how an experiment can be done as an incidental part of a larger activity and not appear to the subjects as a planned study. Also, they illustrate clearly and vividly the experimental behavior elicited in the experimental study itself.

RESULTS OF EXPERIMENTAL STUDY

Returning now to the experimental study, the results obtained from both the waking and the hypnotic groups were consistently comparable within each of the two groups and consistently different in character for the different groups. The waking subjects viewed each of the four reality objects with no interest in their position at the moment. It made no difference to them whether, for example, the snapshot was on a windowsill, a desk, or a bookcase. They merely surveyed all four walls, visually measuring wall space. They then indicated where they would hang such a picture *if there were such a picture*. Additionally many added to their wall-space-appraisal consideration of the vantage point for a person entering the room as possibly different from that of a person seated in the room. Consideration was given also to the lighting effects of the windows and the possible light reflections from the lighting fixtures. All of them ruled out as not meriting consideration certain wall areas either by direct statement or by their disregard after one appraising look. Some debated the suitability of one wall space as compared with another, and second and even third choices were given. But all choices were in terms of the external realities of wall space, lighting, the point of vantage for the viewer, and other esthetic considerations.

For the hypnotic subjects the problem was solved in a totally different way. The reality object of which a picture was to be hung was viewed with intensity. There was then a slow, careful visual searching of all the walls, apparently with emphasis equal to that of waking-state subjects, and then despite physical realities, the subject's gaze would return to the object and a slow, thoughtful positioning of the suppositional picture in direct relationship to the reality object and at varying heights above and behind the object itself would be carried out. This happened regardless of whether the selected areas were an empty space, a window, steampipes, a corner of the room, a ceiling-high bookcase, a blackboard, another picture, or an impossibly small space. Occasionally a subject

Further Experiments

would offer as a second choice a slightly higher or a slightly lower positioning of the picture. None gave any consideration to the external realities of actual wall space, lighting effects, vantage point, or any other external reality consideration.

Subjects who were first tested in the waking state gave the characteristic responses for that state. External realities governed their responses entirely. Yet, when they were subsequently tested in that same room in the somnambulistic hypnotic state, they gave the characteristic response of the somnambulistic hypnotic state. They were uninfluenced by their previous test behavior, and external realities were without effect. Subjects tested first in the somnambulistic hypnotic state gave the characteristic response of that state of awareness. Then, when tested in the waking state, they were uninfluenced by this previous hypnotic test behavior and gave the characteristic external-reality-determined responses of the waking state.

Only one of the test-reality-objects remained constant—the snapshot of the picture of the bowl of fruit. The bowl of fruit necessarily changed repeatedly, and retests done on both waking and hypnotic subjects with different bowls of fruit in no way affected the responses elicited. The person known to the subject and the snapshot of a person known to the subject necessarily varied with different subjects. The use of the same person and the same snapshot of a person for tests in both states yielded no variation in characteristic results. The use of different persons and different snapshots for each state and for separate retests had no effect upon the findings. In essence test-reality-objects were merely test objects for both types of subjects. The task requested constituted the governing factor in their responses, and the responses were in consistent accord with their state of awareness.

The subject behavior may be illustratively summarized as follows: The snapshot of a person known to the subject, whether placed on a desk, on top of the bookcase, on a windowsill, or in some other casual position, was viewed by the person in the waking state and then the walls of the room were speculatively scrutinized and different areas compared. A final judgment would then be offered matter-of-factly for the hanging of the three-by-four-foot picture of the snapshot. In the trance state the same general survey was made of the room but always with hesitant behavior as the wall or the space above the position of the snapshot was viewed. Then with increasing decisiveness the hypnotized subject would indicate an area above the snapshot regardless of its unsuitability for picture hanging—it might be a window, it might be occupied by steampipes, it might be in a corner where it would be impossible to hang such a picture, or it might be empty space.

Another item of significant interest to this experimenter concerned the use of light- and medium-trance subjects. With both of these types of subjects it was found that there persists a definite subjective contact with reality which is sufficient to be verifiable by objective tests such as involuntary reactions, avoidance responses, startle reactions, etc. When the experiment was first outlined, the decision was made that only somnambulistic subjects would be used for the reason that these subjects presented the clearest evidence of the hypnotic state as differing from the waking state. Since that was the experimental question, and not an investigation of the degrees of difference or kinds and variations of difference, but only the question of an existence of an identifiable difference, the author and his advisors and assistants felt that the use of only somnambulistic subjects would be appropriate for the proposed study. However, as the study progressed, a separate study was made employing variously light and medium-deep hypnotic subjects.

These, too, showed a different reality apprehension than they did in the waking state. This difference was primarily one of degree, ranging from slight to that approaching the reality apprehension of the somnambulistic trance subjects. In the lighter stages of hypnosis external reality seemed to remain constant, but "less important," "not so real." The task of hanging a picture had to be accomplished by envisioning the task with the eyes closed, since opening of the eyes tended to disrupt or terminate the trance. This in itself was a situation. Also the actual task seemed to be disturbing to the subjects' sense of mental and physical peace, and there was a tendency to consider the task unwillingly and then to forget it. As the trance depth progressed from the very light stage to the deeper and deeper levels, external realities became increasingly "unreal," "not there," or "I forgot them." Some of the medium-deep subjects could keep their eyes open, even see the specific snapshot, but their peripheral vision was subjectively unclear and reality objects were obscured. This latter phenomenon was tested by introducing alien objects into the range of peripheral vision, which could be done without the subjects seeming to perceive them. However, when the good medium-deep subjects attempted to appraise the walls of the room for picture hanging, their peripheral vision would return, the trance state would lessen or vanish, and alien objects introduced into the setting would be seen immediately. Hence it was reluctantly concluded after several hundred tests that adequate experimental measures had not yet been devised for light- and medium-trance subjects.

After a vast amount of data had been collected on somnambulistic hypnotic subjects, a variation was tried after experimental testing of other subjects disclosed no significant alteration of their behavior under comparable circumstances. This new procedure was to express a doubt as to the suitability of the trance-selected spot for hanging the picture. Responsively the subjects willingly selected a spot on the wall faced by the snapshot, regardless of any reality suitability. The same thing occurred with snapshots of a bowl of fruit, with one difference. While subjects tended to place the suppositional picture of the bowl of fruit on the wall nearest to it, if this were not accepted, they placed the picture on that wall immediately opposite. If the bowl of fruit were employed and they were standing in front of the bowl, or they were standing to one side of it, they would place the picture of it on the wall forming the general background of the bowl of fruit. The suitability of the wall position did not enter

Further Experiments

into the question of picture-positioning, either for the experimental subjects or these trial subjects, although rooms were sought where the walls, such as those of the library, would render the hanging of pictures a difficult problem. The physical dimensions of the bowl of fruit seemed to have no significance in positioning a suppositional picture of it.

As this experiment was being continued, several minor experiments were conducted. With the aid of colleagues a number of volunteer subjects unknown to the author were secured. Among these were subjects with whom the colleagues secretly arranged that they simulate in the true sense of the word the state of being in a trance. They were not apprised of what tests the author might make, since this had not been revealed.

They were hypnotized in a large group arranged in a circle, facing outward so that they could not watch each other, and they were under poor lighting conditions to preclude the author from scrutinizing them closely. When all of them seemed to be in a deep somnambulistic trance, they were told that, continuing in their deep trance state, they would be led separately into another room by an assistant to whom they would indicate, if they had a three-by-four-foot picture of a snapshot which they would see in the next room, the place where they would hang it. This place they were to specify to the assistant, who had been selected because she knew nothing about the purposes of the entire procedure.

The assistant reported that three of the subjects had positioned the suppositional picture "sensibly" and that seven had been "ridiculous" in their choices of position, but that she had accepted their statements uncritically as instructed and had duly recorded them. (The colleagues had intentionally actually chosen seven somnambulistic subjects and three subjects who had never previously been in a trance.)

The three "sensible" subjects were promptly apprised by the author that they were subjects who obviously had not been hypnotized and they were told that they had been asked to deceive the author. To their curious inquiries of how they had betrayed themselves, since they knew nothing of their performance of the real subjects, it was explained they would be given an opportunity to learn.

They were all taken to the test room, the picture-positioning question put to them, to which they responded by wall-reality-evaluation responses, and they were then told that their responses were waking responses, that actual hypnotic responses were otherwise. They were then asked, without discussion among themselves, to attempt to perform the task as if they were in a trance state, and to study the problem silently until they were certain they could do this. When ready to do the task the "right hypnotic way," they were each to take a pencil from their jacket pocket and to hold it quietly as a signal to the author. Thus, in achieving "proper hypnotic placement" by them, there was precluded any awareness of what the others were doing. After 15 minutes one subject signaled the author. Another 15 minutes were allowed to pass. Then, since the other two subjects seemed to be at a loss, the one who had signaled was asked the experimental question, and he selected a position in accord with the trance-state response. The other two subjects offered adverse critical comments until they suddenly realized that their colleague was obviously in a deep, somnambulistic trance and out of rapport with them, although in rapport with the author. They began studying his behavior and appearance with much interest. One was a medical student, the other was a graduate psychology student. Quite suddenly the latter lapsed into silent thought, studied the snapshot, the subject, the impossible place on the wall, and he was observed to narrow his eyes as if to form a new visual focus on the wall. Visibly he developed a trance state out of rapport with the others and out of rapport with the author. When this had been established, the author slowly moved the snapshot at which this subject had been seen to look closer and close to the subject's face; then he stood behind the snapshot and repeatedly moved it up and down to indicate the author's face. Shortly the puzzled look on the subject's face was replaced by an expression of recognition of the author, and rapport was thus established.

The second subject was instructed to awaken from the trance state with full memories and understandings of his behavior. These proved to be only partially satisfactory. In essence he explained:

> "When I realized the absurdity of his choice of a place to put the picture, I began thinking that it was probably a different way of seeing things in a trance. So I half-closed my eyes and tried to get them out of focus so I could see things differently. It reminded my of my childhood "pretend" games. And the next thing I knew I was all alone looking at that snapshot, which began moving queerly. The more I watched it, the more it seemed to move in a meaningful way, and all of a sudden I saw you and knew you wanted the picture hung, so I picked out a spot just back of you and above you, and *there I saw the picture hanging in what I know now was midair*. But everything was completely natural to me and nothing seemed different or unreal. I just don't understand.

Nor have other introspective accounts been any more informative.

The other subject immediately attempted to develop a trance but failed. The first of these three subjects who had developed a trance was awakened, and it was found that he had a complete posthypnotic amnesia. The three subjects were allowed to discuss what had happened. The first subject did not believe that he had been in a trance or that his fellow subject would position a picture in the manner that was described by the subject who had not gone into a trance. Neither would he believe the statements of his fellow subject who had been given a waking memory of his trance behavior. Such picture-positioning would be, this subject declared, "totally unreasonable." When informed that he had been in a deep trance and had similarly positioned a picture in a "totally unreasonable" manner, he disbelievingly denied such a possibility.

EXPERIMENTAL PROBLEMS

From the beginning of the experiment certain difficulties were encountered in relation to the experiement itself as well as the subjects. These problems, however, did not tend to invalidate the experiment, but in their significances they enhanced the findings.

The rooms in which the experiment was done constituted a problem, but only for waking state subjects. In formulating the experiment it was assumed that any room might be used for tests in both states of awareness. It was soon realized that since all subjects could not be tested in the hypnotic state, some rooms would be used only for waking subjects, especially since such subjects would be tested in various locations. However, the opportunity did arise frequently to test hypnotic state subjects in both waking and trance states in rooms where only waking state subjects had first been tested. This served as an actual control, since only in certain regards to be discussed immediately were rooms a significant factor.

This special significance of rooms occurred only in relation to waking state subjects. All rooms had to be "reasonable" to them. When a room such as a library with all walls completely covered from floor to ceiling with bookshelves was used as the experimental room, waking state subjects, wondering and unbelieving in their attitude toward the author's experimental sincerity, rejected the task as absurd. They simply could not believe that the experimenter was serious in his request, and special effort and persuasion had to be used to secure even a half-hearted response from them. Yet the hypnotic state subjects in a deep somnambulistic trance could be taken into such a room for the first experimental testing and they would indicate as a suitable space for hanging the suggested picture an area above and to the rear of the reality object, even if it were a person leaning against a floor-to-ceiling bookshelf, or a snapshot actually placed on the bookshelf, or a bowl of fruit placed on the floor at the base of the bookshelf. The only effect of such a floor placing was to cause the selection of a "wall" area at the subjects' eye level. Yet these same somnambulistic subjects would later in the waking state show the typical waking state behavior to such a room. These findings in themselves are of definite significance in confirming the experimental findings.

In relation to the subjects themselves the difficulties centered around two special types of subjects, (1) the argumentative, and (2) the overly conscientious. There were relatively few of these, and they enhanced rather than detracted from the experimental findings.

The argumentative subjects were those who took issue with both the experimental room and the experimental task. They were all waking state subjects, and they discredited the wall sapce and the room in relation to the picture or the picture in relation to the room size, the wall space, the use of the room, or the suitability of the pictures themselves. The task itself, as a mere *if* proposition, was completely disregarded and rejected. They wished to argue and to debate questions of "fittingness." Yet some of these subjects, who had to be rejected for this experiment because of their critical waking attitude, were subsequently used in other hypnotic work, and the excellence of their hypnotic behavior suggested that it would be of interest to test them for this experiment in the somnambulistic state. Fortunately 18 such subjects were used and tested, some by the author, some by his assistants. In the somnambulistic state, regardless of their previous adverse waking state behavior, they gave the typical hypnotic responses. Then later, when tested in rooms with which they could not take exception, they gave typical waking state responses, except that invariably they took issue with the hanging of at least one or two of the hypothetical pictures, usually the picture of the bowl of fruit or of the snapshot of a bowl of fruit. The original testing room, accepted so easily in the somnambulistic state, would again be rejected in the waking state. In all instances the hypnotic testing was done at least six months after the original waking state test. Another six months later a retesting was done on 11 of these subjects, with entirely comparable results except for an omission of the originally rejected room. Three months later only seven of these subjects were available. They were tested in the waking state in the original test room. Four said in effect that because of the author's persistence they would abide by the unreasonable request and indicated possible wall areas, but two voiced general adverse criticisms of the task, and all four speculated aloud about why the experimenter had ever considered choosing so unsuitable a room. The other three summarily rejected the task and reminded the author that they had once, many months before, rejected that room. These 18 subjects were included in the experimental findings for hypnotic state subjects but were not included among the waking state subjects because of their rejective and selective attitudes toward the task and the special care needed to secure waking state responses.

The over-conscientious subjects were troublesome in one or the other or both states of awareness. In the waking state they manifested much uncertainty, debated the suitability of the room, of the picture, of the wall space, of the vantage point for the viewer, the lighting effects, and changed their minds repeatedly for different reasons. Hence they were not considered suitable as waking state subjects. They were not accepting the experimental task but merely creating from it another task of troublesome decisions involving other considerations.

Thirteen of these subjects were trained to develop somnambulistic trances. However, even in the trance state their personality attributes interfered. There was no ready simple compliance with the task. For example, when asked where the picture of the person present should be placed (standing beside a desk in the middle of the room), they would view him from various points of view, would perhaps ask him to change his position, or even move the desk in order to view him differently. Then they would reconsider the problem in relationship to his immediate spatial surroundings, or in relationship to the spatial relations of the desk beside which he had originally been standing, and then perhaps they would position the picture on the wall to which the desk had been pushed. Also, they would request that the snapshot of the person or the bowl of fruit or the picture of the bowl of fruit be placed in new positions while they considered other possible positionings of the suggested picture. Briefly, even in the trance they created new tasks instead of executing the one requested.

Fortunately two of these obsessive-compulsive persons were encountered early; this led the author to seek out others deliberately and to determine if such subjects could be used. Whether in the trance or the waking state they invariably manifested a need to alter and to change the experimental situation. Hence these subjects were not included in this experiment, and such personalities were avoided as possible subjects. However, it was noted that in the trance state they very definitely tried to position the suppositional pictures in relation to the spatial relationships of the object rather than in relationship to reality wall space, even though they did not abide by the experiment as formulated.

Concerning the question of sex as an influencing factor in this experiment, it was of significance only in relationship to the above-described difficulties. More females than males took issue with room choice and picture suitability, or argued issues and were overly conscientious. Otherwise the sex of the subjects was unimportant so far as experimental findings were concerned, but women did volunteer more readily than did men, so that the distribution was about 60 percent female and 40 percent male.

Another type of expected experimental difficulty that occasioned much concern at first and later was found to be of little importance was the question of intercommunication between subjects. One measure of control was the suggestion of posthypnotic amnesia for all hypnotic work. This was found to be decidedly effective except for the overly conscientious subjects, who "worried for fear of remembering what was supposed to be forgotten." These subjects, as has been noted above, were eliminated as unsuitable for both states of awareness.

For waking state subjects the intercommunication was minimal and had no effect upon the experimental findings. Nor did subsequent rumination occur sufficiently to have any significant effect, although careful indirect inquiry was made, and later even direct inquiry was found to be without effect on task performances.

However, as insurance against intercommunication there were intensive efforts to effect a misdirection of attention. Thus, when extensive work was done in a single location with many subjects, there would be performed other and much more interesting attention-compelling tasks which were undertaken to insure that discussion would be on work not connected with this experiment. For example automatic writing as a possibility in both waking and hypnotic states distracted one large college group effectively from the minor, unimportant picture-positioning request of the author, which was regarded as an incidental measure by which the author appraised the personality for the automatic writing. Thus an experimental atmosphere could be created safely. Glove anaesthesia, hypnotic and nonhypnotic, was another absorbing topic. So was the question of regression as a dream experience, or as one hypnotically induced.

As an additional check on this matter of intercommunication by subjects or spontaneous recollections and ruminations by both types of subject, indirect questioning and direct casual remarks proved to be non-provocative.

Also, postexperimental disclosure in full of the experiment served only to remind the subjects that they had actually acted as experimental waking subjects without realizing the importance of that fact at the time. Disclosure that there had also been hypnotic experimentation by other subjects did not serve to awaken memories of their own hypnotic participation. Even when they were told that they had participated hypnotically, they did not recall spontaneously their memories. Not until hypnotic suggestions by the author, and sometimes only hypnotic suggestions by his assistants who had done the work with them, were given, would there be a recollection, and then a genuine interest would be manifested. Repeatedly the strong impression was gained that when subjects were first used hypnotically, the posthypnotic amnesia suggested about their task performance would radiate to their waking state experience.

Such postexperimental hypnotic recall was induced in scores of subjects, only to have them disclose bewilderment at the peculiar positioning of the picture they had done. They could not explain this, and if they endeavored seriously to understand, they were decidedly likely to develop a spontaneous trance. In this trance they would reaffirm the "rightness" of the position. If this were definitely debated with them, they would obediently position the picture (since the trance invariably was a revivification of the original trance) on the wall in accord with arguments offered. As they would spontaneously (usually) slowly come out of the trance, they would have a waking memory of the trance positioning, but would offer a "corrective" waking state position. But they would still be unable to explain their trance-positioning of the picture. "It seemed to be all right then." This tended to be the most imformative reply from about 150 subjects. Other replies were to the effect that "You see things differently in the trance," "Things get changed some way," "Things look different," and, "You just hang the picture the way things look, and it's right that way." Yet more than a score of subjects who were given a full postexperimental understanding of what they had done in both trance and waking states were used in another test to learn what positioning they would offer for actual landscape pictures. It was promptly learned that they would have to be tested first in the trance state, otherwise a waking state test first would be affected by their sophistication and this would carry over into a subsequent trance-state performance. But if they were tested first in the somnambulistic state, they would give a performance comparable to their response in the original experiment. Then, tested in the waking state, they would give a response in accord with their experimental waking state performance and expressed evidence of their sophistication.

If a long, persistent, searching inquiry is made before a sophistication of the subjects, they may lose their ability to develop a trance; or they may simply refuse to discuss the matter further; or they may refuse to do any more hypnotic work. This author has lost a number of excellent subjects by questioning them too searchingly about hypnotic work. Some of these subjects, months or even years later, again became friendly with the author and would explain their previous withdrawal of friendship as a sensing of a feeling of being unwarrantably imposed upon by the author for work performances, a feeling of being "just plain worked to death," or a feeling that the author was questioning their personal integrity. The reestablishment of the original friendship could result in further hypnotic work well done, but a searching inquiry would again promptly be rejected, sometimes again with the feeling that the author was unjustly questioning the earnestness and honesty of their work.

One other experimental difficulty arising not out of the experiment itself as a procedure came from undue interest by some subjects in what work the experimenter was doing, in relation to other work as well as to this experiment. They would seek to discover what work was being done with them, and they would question various persons whom they thought possibly might know. These subjects numbered less than 50, and they were discarded for both waking and hypnotic experimentation. This same "busybody" trait was noted in other regards, and it always became apparent before the author concluded his studies with them in either state of awareness. Hence such subjects were avoided after a few experiences.

EXPERIMENTAL CONTROLS

Originally it was intended to use 300 subjects, of whom 100 would be capable of developing a somnambulistic trance with the eyes open and of having posthypnotic amnesia. The experimental plan also included the use of assistant experimenters, some with knowledge of hypnosis, some without such knowledge, and some who could not recognize a somnambulistic trance state if the subjects were cued to conceal that fact and the assistant experimenter were limited in participation to the experiment iltelf. Some of the assistant experimenters were actually not known to the author, but their participation was monitored by others who knew what should be done. Sometimes they too were monitored in their task of monitoring other assistants. Some assistants knew that an experiment was being conducted, some did not. Some assistants thought that the actual experiment was no more than a preliminary "passing of time" in preparation for some "actual experiment." In brief every possible control was employed on experimenters, but it became evident progressively that very few controls were necessary. These were primarily that the experimental question be asked or read as a simple posing of a question in which the questioner had only the interest of knowing the subject's response, which was passively and unconcernedly accepted.

Concerning the controls necessary for the experimental subjects, the need was first to recognize hypnotic subjects who are capable of developing somnambulistic states in which various hallucinatory behaviors and posthypnotic amnesia can develop. Experience since medical school days has progressively emphasized to the author that personal needs are strongly correlated with the intensity of the hypnotic state development. Also the personality structure is of importance. To illustrate, a school-dropout, cancer-afflicted patient with a history of poor occupational, economic, and social adjustments may develop a good somnambulistic trance equal to that of another cancer-afflicted school-dropout patient who is, however, occupationally, economically, and socially well-adjusted. They differ significantly in that the first type of patients do not continue to maintain within themselves the willingness to put forth their own effort in maintaining responsive hypnotic behavior, while those of the second type can and do maintain their own effort to benefit from therapeutic or palliative hypnotic suggestions.

This same significant fact is true of normal experimental hypnotic subjects. Many more somnambulistic subjects develop better and deeper somnambulistic states if some inner motivation can be given to them, a motivation experienced by the subjects as belonging to them and important to them and not recognized by the subjects as important to the operators. To illustrate, at an annual meeting of a society of anaesthesiologists at Newport Beach, California, in August, 1966, the author was asked to demonstrate various hypnotic phenomena on five subjects unknown to him personally. As the subjects came up to the foreground of the audience, the author said;

> The girl in the white dress is to sit right there in the middle chair, and you sit right here in this chair, and you sit over there, and the girl in the white dress will sit right there in the middle chair, and you sit right there, and the girl in the white dress will sit right there in the middle chair, and you sit down own softly, gently, and you in the white dress just sit doing nothing. All you need to do is just sit there doing nothing, you do not need to see, to hear, not anything at all, just sit right there doing nothing at all, just sitting right there, and now I will go about my work while all of you sit in your chairs, even as the girl in the white dress sits in her chair, doing nothing at all until I ask her, and then she will do whatever needs to be done! And so will all of you as you sit softly, gently in your chair.

The above is not the verbatim wording, but it is the most informative possible for the reader since intonations, inflections, pauses, gestures, altered direction of gaze cannot be expressed in print. Redundant, repetitious, the wording of the statements made to them gave them some undefined, profound conviction that sitting in the designated chair was of great importance to them as persons. What that matter of personal importance to them was, was not indicated in any way. They merely sensed that it was obligatory for them to experience it, while the author went about "my work." And the girl in the white dress, instructed to sit in the chair doing nothing, not needing to hear or see or do anything at all but sit in the chair until told otherwise, was employed without further delay to demonstrate a spontaneous somnambulistic state marked by a saddle-block anaesthesia.

VALIDITY OF HYPNOTIC EXPERIMENTAL RESULTS

As every well-experienced psychotherapist knows, highly important and most extensive changes in a person's adjustments in life can be effected, even after failure of as much as seven years of rigid "orthodox" or "classical" psychoanalytical therapy six hours a week. There is no way of proving that a short period of psychotherapy employing hypnosis following prolonged psychoanalytic therapy did cause therapeutic result. Instead one can prove only that the previous seven years of psychotherapy had not yet effected the desired result. The only thing possible of proof is the time relationship. But long-continued psychiatric experience has disclosed many times that hypnotic psychotherapy has enabled psychotherapeutic results otherwise not achievable until hypnosis was employed.

This author knows of major surgery, including cholecystectomy, performed on patients in the somnambulistic state without any medication preoperatively or during the operation; and these patients made excellent and "uneventful" recoveries. While the author knows that this does not prove that an anaesthesia of the body tissues existed during the operation, he also does not know of any such operations done by choice on a patient who was in the ordinary waking state, nor does he know of any surgeons willing to do such surgery on a patient who is in the ordinary waking state, even though there are many physicians and dentists who willingly and successfully substitute hypnosis for drugs, sometimes in part, sometimes entirely, and with complete success.

In brief the validity of hypnotic trance states and hypnotic manifestations is not a matter of what the critics or questioners do not understand or want to understand in terms of their own choosing. The validity of hypnotic phenomena lies within the phenomena themselves, and is not to be measured by standards applicable to another category of phenomena. While both water and iron can be measured by a common standard of specific gravity, the floating of iron upon water depends upon the shape of the iron, and the shape cannot be given in terms of specific gravity, nor does it alter the specific gravity of either the water or the iron. Yet the shape relationships can keep iron from sinking in water, and the standards of measurement are of another type than those for measuring specific gravity. Science will ever be plagued by those who insist upon understanding that which they do not understand in terms of which they think they do understand.

That somnambulistic trance realities have a validity as genuine as the validity of waking state realities is not questioned by this author. He questions only what is the nature and character of that category of experimental behavior. He knows that dreams during sleep can be experienced as actualities which do not include the actuality of being sound asleep in bed but, instead, of socializing, of flying a plane, or a myriad of other experiences that may be most pleasing or actually evocative of states of extreme terror. The author also has full respect for the hallucinatory experiences of mentally ill patients despite the absence of any discoverable physical basis. The author recalls his startling experience of dealing with a patient, diagnosed as having developed a sudden, inexplicable, acute state of catatonic schizophrenia, tell him with utter bitterness that she smelled "foul, putrid, rotting fish smells" and that people more than 20 miles away were "cursing" her and calling her "vile, despicable names." He was even more startled when she asked him to sit on her left side and secured, in response to his detailed inquiries, the explanation that she could "smell good smells" only in her left nostril and "hear good voices" only in her left ear. The author tentatively postulated a tumor in the olfactory area of the temporal lobe of the brain. The patient's sudden death and the autopsy that followed confirming the existence of a carcinomatous growth in the left temporal lobe served only to confirm that there was a basis in actuality for the patient's disturbed mental state and sudden death. But there was no explanation of her complaints of olfactory and auditory hallucinations, nor of her ability to identify odors correctly with her left nostril—but not at all with her right nostril when an eye dropper containing an aromatic fluid was carefully inserted. Nor did the autopsy findings explain why the patient would scream imprecations at the author accusing him of vile language when he spoke to her from the right, but would converse agreeably if complainingly when he spoke to her from the left.

Dreams, too, have long been recognized as valid, subjective experiential phenomena for which many theoretical explanations have been offered and sometimes even forcibly thrust upon those attempting to achieve an understanding of them. The author carefully recorded a dream of his in the early 1930s. In that dream he found himself to be an adult, and he had the valid knowledge that he was a psychiatrist at the Worcester State Hospital in Worcester, Massachusetts and that he had a limp caused by anterior poliomyelitis. He was standing on the north side of a country road in Wisconsin, watching a small barefooted boy climbing up and down a freshly made cut through a hillside where a new road was being graded. He watched the boy with interest; he knew that he could see the boy but that the boy could not see him; he was pleased with the boy's interest in the tree roots that had been cut in the grading of the hillside as a part of the grading of the road; he was pleased that the boy was interested in trying to determine which of the roots belonged to the white oak tree and which belonged to the chokecherry tree. The boy doubted that any of the roots belonged to the hazelnut bush which was east of the oak tree. The author knew all the thoughts and feelings of that little barefoot boy and approved of all of them. He was amused by the thought that the little boy had no realization that he would grow up and be a psychiatrist at the Worcester State Hospital.

Further Experiments

Subsequently the author drove by automobile from Massachusetts to Wisconsin and sought out through the country highway department the year, location, and employees involved in grading various country roads. By this means he discovered that a road running east and west had been graded when he was eight years old, that a hillside had been cut through by the grading, that several of the workmen employed recalled that the "pesty Erickson kid always getting in the way and asking questions" had been present at the time of the grading, and that just behind a barbed wire fence, (not included in the dream), at the top of the cut in the hillside, were from east to west, a hazelnut bush, a white oak tree, and a chokecherry tree, the latter two at least 50 years old. Yet the author has only his dream memories, those obtained by his investigation in the 1930s, and the statements from the workmen. Comparable accounts from many other persons indicate that the author's experience is far from unique and that comparable somnambulistic hypnotic trance-state experiences are of a similar order. For example, a national athletic champion recalls clearly having met the author in a casual social situation in a hotel more than 1,500 miles from Phoenix and, with amusement, describes the "probable appearance" of the kind of an office the author was "likely to have." The athlete is certain he was never in that office, does not believe that he ever developed a somnambulistic trance in that office, nor that he ever sought hypnotic aid because of difficulties he was experiencing in his particular athletic area. Yet the author's schedule book and his record files disclose that the national champion had sought hypnotic aid in overcoming certain difficulties in his participation in athletic endeavors and that a somnambulistic trance had been employed to correct his problem. This fact is included in his income tax return of that year, but so far as his subsequent waking states of awareness are concerned, he had merely met the author casually, far from Phoenix and only on a casual basis. This is not an uncommon experience so far as somnambulistic patients and subjects are concerned.

DISCUSSION OF THE RESULTS

The actual experimental results obtained in the formal experiment were invariable and consistent in character. All 750 somnambulistic subjects gave cursory attention to the walls of the room and then hung the suppositious picture in a relationship to the object itself, with a disregard of the existing realities. Impossible spatial relationships of the walls, or even merely empty space, did not constitute any kind of difficulty. Uninfluenced by the experimenter, all of the somnambulistic subjects "hung" the picture described to them in direct relationship to the subject matter of the picture. The walls of the room, spatial areas, vantage points for viewing the supposed picture, lighting effects, had no significance for the task. The object which the picture represented was the only determining force.

Another item of marked significance, not expected and hence not provided for in the formal experiment, was the discovery that once the task was presented to them as a possible task, there was a marked tendency for the somnambulistic subjects to complete it and thereafter, when in a trance state, to see the picture as actually hanging in the selected place. Even as long as three years later a somnambulistic subject might be taken in a somnambulistic state into the room where he had previously entered only once to carry out the experiment and "see" the picture he had been asked about in the experiment. Yet he could enter the same room in the waking state and sense it as a first-time experience with no recollection of somnambulistic values.

None of the nonhypnotic subjects ever manifested comparable behavior. Even if they recognized the room as previously entered and recalled the task presented to them, it was in terms of, "Oh, this is the room where you asked me where I would hang some pictures," and they might again survey visually the wall spaces as offering possibilities. Often they had forgotten the picture described to them—a matter of marked contrast to what the somnambulistic subjects did in "seeing" in the selected place for the hanging, the supposed pictures described in the stereotyped instructions given to them. Such surprising statements were often made by the hypnotic subjects as, pointing to the "picture" of the person known to them, "He has grown a mustache since I hung that picture of him there."

Of great importance was the fact that without using words the experimenter could influence the behavior of the somnambulistic subjects very easily and usually unintentionally. An unbelieving, incredulous expression on the experimenter's face, a glance at an actually suitable place, would suffice to cause the somnambulistic subjects to accept the unspoken but actual communication, however unintentional it might be. An example follows: Some of the author's subjects were found to show results different from those of some other experimenters. These experimenters were then blindfolded and placed under guidance of someone unacquainted with the experiment who was asked to report upon what the subjects did when presented with the experimental question by the blindfolded experimenter. The same subjects and a different room were used, or sometimes the same room if it could be used unknown to the blindfolded experimenter. The results obtained and reported would then be in accord with those of less communicative experimenters. Repeated experiments employing blindfolded experimenters who merely asked the experimental question but who were guided to the experimental room by someone not in rapport with the experimental subject who was accompanying the experimenter yielded the same results as those secured by experimenters who limited communication only to the experimental question. Another variation was to have the experimental subjects out of rapport with the experimenters but able to hear a voice "coming from nowhere" posing a problem which was to be met by the subjects. In these instances, regardless of the communicativeness of the experimenters' behavior, the subjects behavioral respones to the experimental question were in accord with those obtained by experimenters who controlled their own behavior in

Further Experiments

conducting the experiment. Another variation was employed by having the experimenters turn away from the subjects, ask the question for each of the four objects, and then turn around and ask the subjects to point out the places selected. None of these results obtained was then included as a part of the experimental results, even though they could quite rightly have been. The fact that they had been secured by a variation from the original experimental plan was considered proper grounds for exclusion.

However, these results did further confirm the experimental findings demonstrating that the realities of the somnambulistic hypnotic state are different from those of the waking state.

Recently (August, 1967) a college student and patient of the author remarked spontaneously, while in a trance state which had been induced by right-hand levitation:

> "I know intellectually that that [pointing with his left hand] is my right arm. But right now all of my understandings and feelings tell me that it is not my right arm, that it is something alien, apart from me, different from me. It isn't even a part of me. It's something complete in itself, and I have no control over it because I don't even feel that it is attached to me. It is just some alien thing that I can recognize as an arm, but not as my own arm. I know that if I were not in a deep hypnotic trance but just awake in the ordinary way, I would know that it was my arm, and I know that I couldn't think of it any way except as my own arm. But right now I can't even feel that it is any part of me. Not even knowing what I would know if I were consciously awake helps me to do anything except to look upon that thing as something completely alien to me.

Another example (September, 1966) is that of a college student called to the front of an audience of professionally trained people who developed a trance state most readily. During the trance state her left hand was lifted upward and slightly forward, with her elbow bent. She was aroused rather slowly so that the audience could question her before she was in full reality contact. She had her eyes open, demonstrated an amnesia for the trance induction, found herself at a loss to explain how it came about that she was awakening since she had not been "asleep," but what was interestingly puzzling to her was that she saw a hand in midair to the left and slightly in front of her. She wondered where the arm was to which, quite reasonably to her, the hand was attached, and she wondered to what person the arm belonged. At the time, to the audience of professionally trained men, she appeared to be in a state of ordinary waking consciousness, nor did she herself perceive any unusual state of affairs. She could see everybody, hear them, answer questions readily, and at the same time wonder why that hand was in midair, to whose arm it was attached, and why that person was holding the hand in such a fashion. Wonderingly, she let her eyes' gaze extend from the hand, to the wrist, to the arm, still wondering about its identity. Suddenly she realized that it was her own arm, whereupon she lowered her arm to her side with no concern about not recognizing her hand as her own, nor her wrist, nor her arm, but accepting her sudden realization of the arm, wrist, and hand as her own as a simple matter of fact.

The above behavior is reminiscent of infants who see their own right hand as an interesting object and reach for it with that same right hand, only to be bewildered by the interesting object's apparent moving away. Thereupon the infants lean forward and make a more extensive reach for their right hand, only to experience again the unaccountable moving away of that interesting object for which they are reaching. A parallel can be drawn between those infants who have not yet learned the realities of life and the putting aside of learned realities that can be observed as an entirely spontaneous manifestation in the hypnotic trance, most clearly so in the somnambulistic state.

FURTHER EXAMPLES

Since the completion of the original experiment, the author has given hundreds of lectures and demonstrations of hypnosis throughout the United States, in Canada, Mexico, and Venezuela, as well as conducting a private practice in psychiatry emphasizing psychotherapy and the use of hypnosis. Repeatedly, in first-time meetings, the author has seen somnambulistic trances in volunteer subjects and patients wherein hypnotized people have perceived their reality surroundings in a manner entirely foreign to actualities but most real to themselves. He has had volunteer subjects demonstrate hypnosis to a medical audience and have them develop visual and auditory hallucinations, and then has discovered that members of the audience, never before experiencing hypnosis, have gone into a trance, taking issue with the subject on the speaker's platform concerning the identity of the volunteer subject's hallucinations because they, too, had developed somnambulistic trance states and also hallucinations but quite differently than had the actual subject. Additionally there were volunteered explanations by them to the effect that they had in some manner left the reality world in which they could be identified as members of the audience and had entered another world of reality belong only to their own personal life experiences. A most striking and thought-provoking unpublished example is that of a somnambulistic subject used in the teaching of medical group in Phoenix, Arizona, some years ago. She was in full rapport with the entire group so that she could answer questions put to her by any member of the group. At one point the author elaborated on the nature of suggestions most likely to produce hypnoanaesthesia. At the conclusion of his discussion he called the subject by name, and she replied, "Oh, excuse me. I've just come back from a swim in the lake at the camp in Maine where I used to go when I was a little girl. It was so

Further Experiments

delightful—the water was just right and it felt so good, [stretching her arms and legs]. The lack of humidity here in Phoenix certainly has dried my hair fast [feeling it]. What do you want to ask me about?'' The author immediately raised questions about other events of the session to prevent the group from intruding upon this remarkable statement. Shortly thereafter she was asked to listen, still in the trance state, to the tape recording of the more recent part of the evening's discussion. At the conclusion of her spontaneous remarks about taking a swim in Maine that tape recorder was stopped and a second tape recorder was started unobtrusively. Without being questioned, but apparently stimulated by the turning off of that first tape recorder, she stated very simply, "I believe that the last time I went to that camp I was only 15. Sometimes the water was rough and cold, and of course we were never allowed to swim at night nor to go alone. But tonight's swim was just perfect in every way.'' She was asked how far she swam. She answered "Oh, I even swam way out beyond the raft. Then I came back and sat on the log there on the shore, looking at the reflection of the moon in the water.'' She was asked what bathing suit she wore. Her reply was given most thoughtfully, "I don't remember, but I'm sure I was wearing one because I have never gone swimming in the nude even though I have wanted to.''

The conversation was immediately changed by the author to other matters to prevent the other members of the group from intruding upon this entire item of the subjective experience of that hypnotic subject.

Later she was awakened with a spontaneous amnesia—that is, an amnesia in no way known to be suggested by the author or others of the group. She was thanked for her help, whereupon she laughed, stating that if she had been of help, she certainly knew nothing about what she had done. She was asked if she recalled having developed anaesthesia or catalepsy. Her reply was that if she had done so, she was now manifesting an amnesia, since she could remember nothing, "Not even the passage of time, since I was so surprised when I looked at the clock.''

She was asked if she would like to listen to a part of the tape recording for that evening. She stated that she would, and the first tape recorder was started at a point about 15 minutes previous to her statement about swimming. At the same time the second tape recorder was started.

She listened attentively, interjected various pertinent comments expressive of astonishment, interest, and bewilderment. However, upon hearing her statement about swimming in Maine, she laughed with much amusement, declaring, "That's so completely ridiculous that it just doesn't make sense. How could anybody possibly say something like that, even in a trance. The whole thing just isn't real, and yet I know that's my own voice speaking. I just can't understand such a thing because I never try to fool myself or anybody else. I just don't understand. It's too complex for me, and it would give me a headache to try to make sense out of it.''

At this point the first tape recorder was turned off and the second one was adjusted for a replay. This did not astonish her, since she knew that even four or five tape recorders had been employed variously at previous teaching situations.

She was, however, greatly astonished to hear her voice elaborating still further upon that swimming experience, followed by the additional recording of further discussion of hypnosis. Then there followed the instructions for her to awaken, the general conversation, and then the playback of the first recorder. She was decidedly startled as she listened to her waking state comments on her first comments on her swimming. She listend most attentively, and at the conclusion of the recording she declared,

> I know as an absolute fact that I didn't go swimming in the lake in Maine. That is true, it has to be true. But when I hear my voice telling about it now, I know inside me that I really did go swimming. The first time when I listened to that other tape recorder, I was just listening to the words and ideas, but when I started listening to the second tape recorder, I heard what I said and I felt my feelings at the same time. Now, to me, in my own feelings, I did not go swimming and I did too go swimming. I knw those two thoughts are contradictory when I try to compare them. But when I look at just one set of ideas, I know it is true. Then when I look at the other set, I know equally well that it is true. It's like being in two different worlds of understanding and feeling. But I just want to leave them that way. I don't have any desire or even wish to fit them together. I'm just willing to be in Phoenix and willing to talk to you about being a camp in Maine. But if you put me in a deep trance, I know that I can be anywhere I want to be and the real place where I am won't interfere at all. The way I mean all of that is that I could go swimming in Maine with complete enjoyment and at the same time I could stay in Phoenix and be able to answer all your questions or do anything that you wished without its interfering with the whole experience of swimming. It's like something I often do. I sleep soundly and restfully all night, but I can wake up still tasting that trout I caught in my dream and so happily dressed and cooked and ate with pleasure. But I'm hungry for breakfast in spite of all the trout I dreamed I ate and still taste.

This is but one of many comparable accounts the author has been given spontaneously by simply creating a favorable situation for such communication. The very first such communication was received when the author was an undergraduate student at the University of Wisconsin. At that time he asked one of his experimental subjects, "Considering all the time you give me for hypnotic experimentation and the time you spend on the football field, how do you manage to keep up your grades?" The astounding reply given was, "That's easy. When I'm out practicing on the football field doing the things that I could be doing there, I just mentally lean back comfortably in my chair and review everything I have already read. The only time I have to get out of that mental chair is when I'm making a run and carrying the ball. But I return to the chair if I'm stopped or if I make a completed run."

Thirty years later a chance encounter with this former student, then a full professor of history, led to reminiscences of their former relationships as fellow students. During this he was asked about "leaning back mentally in a comfortable chair" while engaged in football games. He replied that he had continued that same practice but in a different way. For example, while delivering a lecture, he might "lean back in a chair in the den at home" and review previous lectures to determine the appropriate questions for the next test or final examination that he would give. He stated that this practice made his teaching much more interesting, more efficient, and much less laborious. He also utilized the practice in other activities but had very early learned that this was an item of experience he could discuss with very few people because of the general tendency of people to look upon such statements with misunderstanding and disfavor. However, he had encountered a few psychologists, some psychiatrists, and several well-established writers who were genuinely interested in this type of phenomenon as something of scientific interest and even as something of possible value to themselves. He also declared that in his study of history the course of historical events seemed often to have been a result of an unconscious appraisal of past events, a singling out of certain generally unrecognized, seemingly insignificant items of past occurrence, and a devising of a course of action by the leader who achieved the goal reached.

PURPOSE OF STUDY

The purpose of the study reported here is not that of defining or evaluating or measuring hypnotic realities. Rather its purpose is to discover if an appreciable number of somnambulistic hypnotic subjects could react to their hypnotic state in such fashion that their experience of physical realities could be contrasted to the waking subjects' awareness of physical realities. During the course of this study the author encounted many different kinds of hypnotic realities, such as the reestablishment of the location of a subject's first hypnotic trance, which became manifest in a trance 15 years later, and an encounter with a somnambulist who found himself in space and identified the operator only as a pleasant stranger. Some somnambulistic subjects effect rapport with anyone present, not realizing that they are in a trance, but easily transforming the reality situation, for example, into a restaurant, where they listen to music and have the inner experience of eating but with no physical evidence that they are eating or even making of movements suggestive of it. Some somnambulistic hypnotic subjects regress to a time when they wished to do certain things, and they experience themselves doing it. For example one subject created a problem during an experiment, other than the one reported here, by developing a somnambulistic trance, but he was always found to be in a theater watching the move, *Gone with the Wind*. He had seen it once, and he regretted that he had not gone back and seen it twice. Repeatedly over a four-year period this college graduate was used as a subject who readily developed a somnambulistic trance, and he hushed the author, explaining that he was enjoying the second viewing of *Gone with the Wind,* and it always became necessary for the author to suggest a mechanical breakdown of the projector so that the subject would leave the theater and perform in accord with the experimental design.

The author has described these various manifestations to elucidate the purpose of this study, which was to discover if there were a kind of hypnotic reality wherein a simple experimental question could be asked which could direct the subject's attention to the surrounding realities in the same fashion as the waking subject and to discover if there was an appreciable number of such subjects. This author does not know how to measure and how to define what happens to the physical realities that the hypnotic subject can see as clearly as the waking subject and yet make responses in terms of hypnotic realities.

In evaluating the experiments here described and in planning their possible replication, a certain precaution must be kept in mind. This is the fact that the realities to which the somnambulistic subjects relate may not correspond with the objective reality situation, and may or may not correspond with previous somnambulistic trance experiences, if any, which the subjects have had. These unusual orientations may be completely spontaneous on the part of the subjects and if the experimenter is unaware of that possibility, he may continue the experimentation not realizing that a new element has been introduced. Some subjects have been known to orient themselves spontaneously to the laboratory, to the classroom, or to any other location in which their first hypnotic experience took place, others to the location in which their first somnambulistic trance developed. Some subjects orient themselves to actual objective reality but may not recognize the location. It may remain a new and unknown experience or it may be misidentified. Not only does this relocation in place sometimes develop unexpectedly, but subjects may reorient themselves spontaneously in time. This commonly is a reorientation to the time of a previous trance state; however, subjects have been known to regress to an earlier time period, which may even be the childhood of the subject. Thus one subject always initiated the somnambulistic trance by a reorientation to a peaceful New England rural environment where an old, picturesque grist mill was located. Another subject spontaneously located himself on a seashore on which he had passed many pleasant hours. The experimenter may spontaneously be recognized as he actually is, being adopted into a scene in his own identity, or he may be identified as some previously known person, or perhaps as a character whose intrusion upon the scene would be natural and acceptable.

Only those subjects were used in the experimental work who either spontaneously oriented to the room in which the actual setting of the experiment was taking place, or who suspended recognition and realization of the location until guided by the information supplied by the experimenter.

NOT A TEST OF SIMULATION

In view of the uniformly consistent results obtained in this experimental work, the reader might reach the conclusion that a reliable test for the detection of simulation has been devised. It must be emphasized that this experiment was not designed or devised to be considered as meeting in any way the criteria for a test for the existence of a state of hypnosis.

Whereas the experimenter believes, and the results confirm, that hypnotic subjects behave in a basically different manner from waking subjects, false and misleading results could ensue if the procedure here described were used as a definitive test for the detection of simulation. Sophisticated subjects would certainly find no insuperable difficulty in imitating a hypnotic response, once they were aware of the nature of that response. The purpose of this work has not been to construct a test for simulation but to investigate the apprehension of reality in the states of consciousness known as the "hypnotic state" and the "waking state."

SUMMARY

The original experiment was intended to determine if external reality was apprehended differently in the somnambulistic hypnotic state than it was in the ordinary state of conscious awareness. It was based upon a procedure in which a definite task could be assigned to the subjects in either the waking or the somnambulistic state, with the nature of the assignment placing all responsibility for performance upon the subjects themselves. It was believed that the experimental task performance had to be one in which any wishes, hopes, expectations, or desires on the part of the experimenters would have no influence upon the subjects' responses. The experiment was devised so that the subjects' performances would have to be in their terms of evaluation of reality values as they themselves perceived the realities without even being made aware of that fact. The somnambulistic hypnotic subjects were to be tested by random selection, half in the waking state first, half in the somnambulistic state first.

As first planned, 300 subjects were to be used, of whom a third would be chosen because of a known capacity to develop somnambulistic hypnotic states. A fortunate series of events led to an increase of the number of subjects from 300 to over 2,000 and the number of somnambulistic hypnotic subjects to over 750. This of course led to an extension of the length of time required to complete the experiment. This in turn led to the opportunity to enlist the aid of variously sophisticated assistant experimenters. These were used as controls upon each other and upon the author himself as well as upon the separate identifications of environmental realities for subjects in both the ordinary state of conscious awareness and the state of hypnotic somnambulism.

Also, the extended period of time permitted retests of many subjects, especially those first used only as waking state subjects. Additionally the extended period of time permitted control tests on subjects as much as three years later and retests by different assistants to determine the reliability of the first-time results.

Clinical work and the teaching of hypnosis to professionally trained audiences gave additional opportunities for unexpected spontaneous manifestations of behavior fully comparable to that elicited under the planned experimental conditions as well as the intentional utilization of a teaching situation to effect meaningful behavior comparable or actually equivalent to the experimental results obtained in the experiment itself.

The reporting of the experimental findings was delayed for an extended period of time because of the continued accumulation of comparable instances of behavior in other situations, and it was hoped to discover some understandable definition of that behavior.

As a final statement, after extensive experimental work aided by independent work of others employing the author's procedures, and the findings achieved over the years in teaching and clinical situations, this author feels that a somnambulistic hypnotic subject spontaneously apprehends the surrounding environment of realities differently than does a subject in the ordinary state of waking consciousness, and that the one type of reality apprehension does not preclude the other type of reality apprehension.

3. A Special Inquiry with Aldous Huxley into the Nature and Character of Various States of Consciousness

Milton H. Erickson

INTRODUCTION

Over a period of nearly a year much time was spent by Aldous Huxley and the author, each planning separately for a joint inquiry into various states of psychological awareness. Special inquiries, possible methods of experimental approach, and investigations and various questions to be propounded were listed by each of us in our respective loose-leaf notebooks. The purpose was to prepare a general background for the proposed joint study, with this general background reflecting the thinking of both of us uninfluenced by another. It was hoped in this way to secure the widest possible coverage of ideas by such separate outlines prepared from the markedly different backgrounds of understanding that the two of us possessed.

Early in 1950 we met in Huxley's home in Los Angeles, there to spend an intensive day appraising the ideas recorded in our separate notebooks and to engage in any experimental inquiries that seemed feasible. I was particularly interested in Huxley's approach to psychological problems, his method of thinking, and his own unique use of his unconscious mind, which we had discussed only briefly sometime previously. Huxley was particularly interested in hypnosis, and previous exceedingly brief work with him had demonstrated his excellent competence as a deep somnambulistic subject.

It was realized that this meeting would be a preliminary or pilot study, and this was discussed by both of us. Hence we planned to make it as comprehensive and inclusive as possible without undue emphasis upon completion of any one particular item. Once the day's work had been evaluated, plans could then be made for future meetings and specific studies. Additionally we each had our individual purposes—Aldous having in mind future literary work, while my interest related to future psychological experimentation in the field of hypnosis.

Reprinted with permission from *The American Journal Journal of Clinical Hypnosis*, July, 1965, *8*, 14–33.

The day's work began at 8:00 A.M. and remained uninterrupted until 6:00 P.M. with some considerable review of our notebooks the next day to establish their general agreement, to remove any lack of clarity of meaning caused by the abbreviated notations we had entered into them during the previous day's work, and to correct any oversights. On the whole we found that our notebooks were reasonably in agreement, but that naturally certain of our entries were reflective of our special interests and of the fact that each of us had, by the nature of the situation, made separate notations bearing upon each other.

Our plan was to leave these notebooks with Huxley, since his phenomenal memory, often appearing to be total recall, and his superior literary ability would permit a more satisfactory writing of a joint article based upon our discussions and experimentations of that day's work. However, I did abstract from my notebook certain pages bearing notations upon Huxley's behavior at times when he, as an experimental subject, was unable to make comprehensive notations on himself, although postexperimentally he could and did do so, though less completely than I had. It was proposed that from these certain special pages I was to endeavor to develop an article which could be incorporated later in the longer study that Huxley was to write. Accordingly I abstracted a certain number of pages, intending to secure still more at a later date. These pages that I did remove Huxley rapidly copied into his own notebook to be sure of the completeness of his data.

Unfortunately a California brushfire later destroyed Huxley's home, his extensive library containing many rare volumes and manuscripts, besides numerous other treasures to say nothing of the manuscripts upon which Huxley was currently working as well as the respective notebooks of our special joint study. As a result the entire subject matter of our project was dropped as a topic too painful to discuss, but Huxley's recent death led to my perusal of these relatively few pages I had abstracted from my notebook. Examination of them suggested the possibility of presenting to the reader a small but informative part of that day's work. In this regard the reader must bear in mind that the quotations attributed to Huxley are not necessarily verbatim, since his more extensive utterances were noted in abbreviated form. However, in the essence of their meaning they are correct, and they are expressive of Huxley as I knew him. It is also to be borne in mind that Huxley had read my notations on the occasion of our joint study and had approved them.

PROJECT INITIATION

The project began with Huxley reviewing concepts and definitions of conscious awareness, primarily his and in part those of others, followed by a discussion with me of his understandings of hypnotic states of awareness. The purpose was to insure that we were both in accord or clear in our divergences of understanding, thus to make possible a more reliable inquiry into the subject matter of our interest.

There followed then a review in extensive detail of various of his psychedelic experiences with mescaline, later to be recorded in his book (*The Doors of Perception*. New York: Harper, 1954).

Huxley then proceeded with a detailed description of his very special practice of what he, for want of a better and less awkward term which he had not yet settled upon, called "Deep Reflection." He described this state (the author's description is not complete, since there seemed to be no good reason except interest for making full notations of his description) of Deep Reflection as one marked by physical relaxation with bowed head and closed eyes, a profound, progressive, psychological withdrawal from externalities but without any actual loss of physical realities nor any amnesias or loss of orientation, a "setting aside" of everything not pertinent, and then a state of complete mental absorption in matters of interest to him. Yet in that state of complete withdrawal and mental absorption Huxley stated that he was free to pick up a fresh pencil to replace a dulled one, to make notations on his thoughts "automatically," and to do all this without a recognizable realization on his part of what physical act he was performing. It was as if the physical act were "not an integral part of my thinking." In no way did such physical activity seem to impinge upon, to slow, or to impede "the train of thought so exclusively occupying my interest. It is associated but completely peripheral activity. . . . I might say activity barely contiguous to the periphery." To illustrate further Huxley cited an instance of another type of physical activity. He recalled having been in a state of Deep Reflection one day when his wife was shopping. He did not recall what thoughts or ideas he was examining, but he did recall that, when his wife returned that day, she had asked him if he had made a note of the special message she had given him over the telephone. He had been bewildered by her inquiry, could not recall anything about answering the telephone as his wife asserted, but together they found the special message recorded on a pad beside the telephone, which was placed within comfortable reaching distance from the chair in which he liked to develop Deep Reflection. Both he and his wife reached the conclusion that he had been in a state of Deep Reflection at the time of the telephone call, had lifted the receiver, and had said to her as usual, "I say there, hello," had listened to the message, had recorded it, all without any subsequent recollections of the experience. He recalled merely that he had been working on a manuscript that afternoon, one that had been absorbing all of his interest. He explained that it was quite common for him to initiate a day's work by entering a state of Deep Reflection as a preliminary process of marshalling his thoughts and putting into order the thinking that would enter into his writing later that day.

As still another illustrative incident Huxley cited an occasion when his wife returned home from a brief absence, found the door locked as was customary, entered the house, and discovered in plain view a special delivery letter on a hallway table reserved for mail, special messages, etc. She had found Huxley sitting quietly in his special chair, obviously in a state of deep thought. Later that day she had inquired about the time of arrival of the special delivery letter, only to learn that he had obviously no recollection of receiving any letter. Yet both knew that the mailman had undoubtedly rung the doorbell, that Huxley had heard the bell, had interrupted whatever he was doing, had gone to the door, opened it, received the letter, closed the door, placed the letter in its proper place, and returned to the chair where she had found him.

Both of these two special events had occurred fairly recently. He recalled them only as incidents related to him by his wife but with no feeling that those accounts constituted a description of actual meaningful physical behavior on his part. So far as he knew, he could only deduce that he must have been in a state of Deep Reflection when they occurred.

His wife subsequently confirmed the assumption that his behavior had been completely "automatic, like a machine moving precisely and accurately. It is a delightful pleasure to see him get a book out of the bookcase, sit down again, open the book slowly, pick up his reading glass, read a little, and then lay the book and glass aside. Then some time later, maybe a few days, he will notice the book and ask about it. The man just never remembers what he does or what he thinks about when he sits in that chair. All of a sudden you just find him in his study working very hard."

In other words, while in a state of Deep Reflection and seemingly totally withdrawn from external realities, the integrity of the task being done in that mental state was touched by external stimuli, but some peripheral part of awareness made it possible for him to receive external stimuli, to respond meaningfully to them but with no apparent recording of any memory of either the stimulus or his meaningful and adequate response. Inquiry of his wife later had disclosed that when she was at home, Aldous in a state of Deep Reflection paid no attention to the telephone, which might be beside him, or the doorbell. "He simply depends completely on me, but I can call out to him that I'll be away and he never fails to hear the telephone or the doorbell."

Huxley explained that he believed he could develop a state of Deep Reflection in about five minutes, but that in doing so he "simply cast aside all anchors" of any type of awareness. Just what he meant and sensed he could not describe. "It is a subjective experience quite" in which he apparently achieved a state of "orderly mental arrangement" premitting an orderly free flowing of his thoughts as he wrote. This was his final explanation. He had never considered any analysis of exactly what his Deep Reflection was, nor did he feel that he could analyze it, but he offered to attempt it as an experimental investigation for the day. It was promptly learned that as he began to absorb himself in his thoughts to achieve a state of Deep Reflection, he did indeed "cast off all anchors" and appeared to be completely out of touch with everything. On this attempt to experience subjectively and to remember the processes of entering into Deep Reflection, he developed the state within five minutes and emerged from it

States of Consciousness

within two, as closely as I could determine. His comment was, "I say, I'm deucedly sorry. I suddenly found myself all prepared to work with nothing to do, and I realized I had better come out of it." That was all the information he could offer. For the next attempt a signal to be given by me was agreed upon as a signal for him to "come out of it." A second attempt was made as easily as the first. Huxley sat quietly for some minutes, and the agreed-upon signal was given. Huxley's account was, "I found myself just waiting for something. I did not know what. It was just a 'something' that I seemed to feel would come in what seemed to be a timeless, spaceless void. I say, that's the first time I noted that feeling. Always I've had some thinking to do. But this time I seemed to have no work in hand. I was just completely disinterested, indifferent, just waiting for something, and then I felt a need to come out of it. I say, did you give me the signal?"

Inquiry disclosed that he had no apparent memory of the stimulus being given. He had had only the "feeling" that it was time to "come out of it."

Several more repetitions yielded similar results. A sense of a timeless, spaceless void, a placid, comfortable awaiting for an undefined "something," and a comfortable need to return to ordinary conscious awareness constituted the understandings achieved. Huxley summarized his findings briefly as "a total absence of everything on the way there and on the way back and an expected meaningless something for which one awaits in a state of Nirvana since there is nothing more to do." He asserted his intention to make a later intensive study of this practice he found so useful in his writing.

Further experiments were done after Huxley had explained that he could enter the state of deep reflection with the simple undefined understanding that he would respond to any "significant stimulus." Without informing him of my intentions, I asked him to "arouse" (this term is my own) when three taps of a pencil on a chair were given in close succession. He entered the sate of reflection readily, and after a brief wait I tapped the table with a pencil in varying fashions at distinct but irregular intervals. Thus I tapped once, paused, then twice in rapid succession, paused, tapped once, paused, tapped four times in rapid succession, paused, then five times in rapid succession. Numerous variations were tried but with an avoidance of the agreed-upon signal. A chair was knocked over with a crash while four taps were given. Not until the specified three taps were given did he make any response. His arousal occurred slowly with almost an immediate response to the signal. Huxley was questioned about his subjective experiences. He explained simply that they had been the same as previously with one exception, namely that several times he had a vague sensation that "something was coming," but he knew not what. He had no awareness of what had been done.

Further experimentation was done in which he was asked to enter Deep Reflection and to sense color, a prearranged signal for arousing being that of a handshake of his right hand. He complied readily, and when I judged that he was fully absorbed in his state of reflection, I shook his left hand vigorously, then followed this with a hard pinching of the back of both hands that left deep fingernail markings. Huxley made no response to this physical stimulation, although his eyes were watched for possible eyeball movements under the lids, and his respiratory and pulse rates were checked for any changes. However, after about a minute he slowly drew his arms back along the arms of the chair where he had placed them before beginning his reflection state. They moved slowly about an inch, and then all movement ceased. He was aroused easily and comfortably at the designated signal.

His subjective report was simply that he had "lost" himself in a "sea of color," of "sensing," "feeling," "being" color, of being "quite utterly involved in it with no identity of your own, you know." Then suddenly he had experienced a process of losing that color in a "meaningless void," only to open his eyes and to realize that he had "come out of it."

He remembered the agreed-upon stimulus but did not recall if it had been given. "I can only deduce it was given from the fact that I'm out of it," and indirect questioning disclosed no memories of the other physical stimuli administered. Neither was there an absent-minded looking at nor rubbing of the backs of his hands.

This same procedure in relation to color was repeated but to it was added, as he seemed to be reaching the state of deep reflection, a repeated, insistent urging that upon arousal he discuss a certain book which was carefully placed in full view. The results were comparable to the preceding findings. He became "lost," . . . "quite utterly involved in it," . . . "one can sense it but not describe it," . . . "I say, it's an utterly amazing, fascinating state of finding yourself a pleasant part of an endless vista of color that is soft and gentle and yielding and all-absorbing. Utterly extraordinary, most extraordinary." He had no recollection of my verbal insistences nor of the other physical stimuli. He remembered the agreed-upon signal but did not know if it had been given. He found himself only in a position of assuming that it had been given since he was again in a state of ordinary awareness. The presence of the book meant nothing to him. One added statement was that entering a state of Deep Reflection by absorbing himself in a sense of color was in a fashion comparable to, but not identical with, his psychedelic experiences.

As a final inquiry Huxley was asked to enter the reflection state for the purpose of recalling the telephone call and the special-delivery letter incidents. His comment was that such a project should be "quite fruitful." Despite repeated efforts he would "come out of it," explaining, "There I found myself without anything to do, so I came out of it." His memories were limited to the accounts given to him by his wife, and all details were associated with her and not with any inner feelings of experience on his part.

A final effort was made to discover whether or not Huxley could include another person in his state of Deep Reflection. This idea interested him at once, and it was suggested that he enter the reflection state to review some of his psychedelic experiences. This he did in a most intriguing fashion. As the reflection state developed, Huxley in an utterly detached dissociated fashion began making fragmentary remarks, chiefly in the form of self-addressed comments. Thus he would say, making fragmentary notes with a pencil and paper quickly supplied to him, "most extraordinary . . . I overlooked that . . . How? . . . Strange I should have forgotten that [making a notation]. . . . fascinating how different in appears . . . I must look. . . ."

When he aroused, he had a vague recollection of having reviewed a previous psychedelic experience, but what he had experienced then or on the immediate occasion he could not recall. Nor did he recall speaking aloud or making notations. When shown these, he found that they were so poorly written that they could not be read. I read mine to him without eliciting any memory traces.

A repetition yielded similar results, with one exception. This was an amazed expression of complete astonishment by Huxley suddenly declaring, "I say, Milton, this is quite utterly amazing, most extraordinary. I use Deep Reflection to summon my memories, to put into order all of my thinking, to explore the range, the extent of my mental existence, but I do it solely to let those realizations, the thinking, the understandings, the memories seep into the work I'm planning to do without my conscious awareness of them. Fascinating . . . never stopped to realize that my Deep Reflection always preceded a period of intensive work wherein I was completely absorbed. . . . I say, no wonder I have an amnesia."

Later, when we were examining each other's notebooks, Huxley manifested intense amazement and bewilderment at what I had recorded about the physical stimuli for which he had no memory of any sort. He knew that he had gone into Deep Reflection repeatedly at my request, had been both pleased and amazed at his subjective feelings of being lost in an all-absorbing sea of color, had sensed a certain timelessness and spacelessness, and had experienced a comfortable feeling of something meaningful about to happen. He reread my notations repeatedly in an endeavor to develop some kind of a feeling or at least a vague memory of subjective awareness of the various physical stimuli I had given him. He also looked at the backs of his hands to see the pinch marks, but they had vanished. His final comment was, ". . . extraordinary, most extraordinary, I say, utterly fascinating."

When we agreed that at least for the while further inquiry into Deep Reflection might be postponed until later, Huxley declared again that his sudden realization of how much he had used it and how little he knew about it made him resolve to investigate much further into his Deep Reflection. The manner and means by which he achieved it, how it constituted a form of preparation for absorbing himself in his writing, and in what way it caused him to lose unnecessary contact with reality were all problems of much interest to him.

Huxley then suggested that an investigation be made of hypnotic states of awareness by employing him as a subject. He asked permission to be allowed to interrupt his trance states at will for purposes of discussion. This was in full accord with my own wishes.

He asked that first a light trance be induced, perhaps repeatedly, to permit an exploration of his subjective experiences. Since he had briefly been a somnambulistic subject previously, he was carefully assured that this fact could serve to make him feel confident in arresting his trance states at any level he wished. He did not recognize this as a simple direct hypnotic suggestion. In reading my notebook later he was much amused at how easily he had accepted an obvious suggestion without recognizing its character at the time.

He found several repetitions of the light trance intersting but "too easily conceptualized." It is, he explained, "A simple withdrawal of interest from the outside to the inside." That is, one gives less and less attention to externalities and directs more and more attention to inner subjective sensations. Externalities become increasingly fainter and more obscure, inner subjective feelings more satisfying until a state of balance exists. In this state of balance he had the feeling that with motivation he could "reach out and seize upon reality," that there is a definite retention of a grasp upon external reality but with no motivation to deal with it. Neither did he feel a desire to deepen the trance. No particular change in this state of balance seemed necessary, and he noted that a feeling of contentment and relaxation accompanied it. He wondered if others experienced the same subjective reactions.

Huxley requested that the light trance be induced by a great variety of techniques, some of them nonverbal. The results in each instance, Huxley felt strongly, were dependent entirely upon his mental set. He found that he could accept "drifting along" (my phrase) in a light trance, receptive of suggestions involving primarily responses at a subjective level only. He found that an effort to behave in direct relationship to the physical environment taxed his efforts and made him desire either to arouse from the trance or to go still deeper. He also on his own initiative set up his own problems to test his trance states. Thus before entering the light trance he would privately resolve to discuss a certain topic, relevant or irrelevant, with me at the earliest possible time or even at a fairly remote time. In such instances Huxley found such unexpressed desires deleterious to the maintenance of the trance. Similarly any effort to include an item of reality not pertinent to his sense of subjective satisfaction lessened the trance.

At all times there persisted a "dim but ready" awareness that one could alter the state of awareness at will. Huxley, like others with whom I have done similar studies, felt an intense desire to explore his sense of subjective comfort and satisfaction but immediately realized that this would lead to a deeper trance state.

When Huxley was asked to formulate understandings of the means he could employ by which he could avoid going into more than a light trance, he stated that he did this by setting a given length of time during which he would remain in a light trance. This had the effect of making him more strongly aware that at any moment he could "reach out and seize external reality" and that his sense of subjective comfort and ease decreased. Discussion of this and repeated experimentation disclosed that carefully worded suggestions serving to emphasize the availability of external reality and to enhance subjective comfort could serve to deepen the trance, even though Huxley was fully cognizant of what was being said and why. Similar results have been obtained with other highly intelligent subjects.

In experimenting with medium-deep trances Huxley, like other subjects with whom I have worked, experienced much more difficulty in reacting to and maintaining a fairly constant trance level. He found that he had a subjective need to go deeper in the trance and an intellectual need to stay at the medium level. The result was that he found himself repeatedly "reaching out for awareness" of his environment, and this would initiate a light trance. He would then direct his attention to subjective comfort and find himself developing a deep trance. Finally, after repeated experiments, he was given both posthypnotic and direct hypnotic suggestion to remain in a medium deep trance. This he found he could do with very little concern. He described the medium trance as primarily characterized by a most pleasing subjective sense of comfort and a vague, dim, faulty awareness that there was an external reality for which he felt a need for considerable motivation to be able to examine it. However, if he attempted to examine even a single item of reality for its intrinsic value, the trance would immediately become increasingly lighter. On the other hand, when he examined an item of external reality for subjective values—for example the soft comfort of the chair cushions as contrasted to the intrinsic quiet of the room—the trance became deeper. But both light and deep trances were characterized by a need to sense external reality in some manner, not necessarily clearly but nevertheless to retain some recognizable awareness of it.

For both types of trance experiments were carried out to discover what hypnotic phenomena could be elicited in both light and medium-deep trances. This same experiment has been done with other good subjects, with subjects who consistently developed only a light trance, and with those who consistently did not seem to be able to go further than the medium trance. In all such studies the findings were the same, the most important seeming to be the need of light- and medium-deep hypnotic subjects to retain at least some grasp upon external reality and to orient their trance state as a state apart from external reality—but with the orientation to such reality, however tenuous in character, sensed as available for immediate utilization by the subject.

Another item which Huxley discovered by his own efforts, and of which I was fully aware through work with other subjects, was that the phenomena of deep hypnosis can be developed in both the light and the medium trances. Huxley, having observed deep hypnosis, wondered about the possibility of developing hallucinatory pehnomena in the light trance. He attempted this by the measure of enjoying his subjective state of physical comfort and adding to it an additional subjective quality—namely, a pleasant gustatory sensation. He found it quite easy to hallucinate vividly various taste sensations while wondering vaguely what I would think if I knew what he were doing. He was not aware of his increased swallowing when he did this. From gustatory sensations he branched out to olfactory hallucinations both pleasant and unpleasant. He did not realize the he betrayed this by the flaring of his nostrils. His thinking at the time, so he subsequently explained, was that he had the "feeling" that hallucinations of a completely "inner type of process"—that is, occurring within the body itself—would be easier than those in which the hallucination appeared to be external to the body. From olfactory hallucinations he progressed to kinesthetic, proprioceptive, and finally tactile sensations. In the kinesthetic hallucinatory sensation experience he hallucinated taking a long walk but remained constantly aware that I was present in some vaguely sensed room. Momentarily he would forget about me, and his hallucinated walking would become most vivid. He recognized this as an indication of the momentary development of a deeper trance state, which he felt obligated to remember to report to me during the discussion after his arousal. He was not aware of respiratory and pulse changes during the hallucinatory walk.

When he first tried for visual and auditory hallucinations, he found them much more difficult, and the effort tended to lighten and to abolish his trance state. He finally reasoned that if he could hallucinate rhythmical movements of his body, he could then "attach" an auditory hallucination to this hallucinated body sensation. The measure proved most successful, and again he caught himself wondering if I could hear the music. His breathing rate changed, and slight movements of his head were observed. From simple music he proceeded to a hallucination of opera singing and then finally a mumbling of words which eventually seemed to become my voice questioning him about Deep Reflection. I could not recognize what was occurring.

From this he proceeded to visual hallucinations. An attempt to open his eyes nearly aroused him from his trance state. Thereafter he kept his eyes closed for both light and medium-deep trance activities. His first visual hallucination was a vivid flooding of his mind with an intense sense of pastel colors of changing hues and with a wavelike motion. He related this experience to his Deep Reflection experiences with me and also to his previous psychedelic experiences. He did not consider this experience sufficiently valid for his purposes of the moment because he felt that vivid memories were playing too large a part. Hence he deliberately decided to visualize a flower, but the thought occurred to him that even as a sense of movement played a part in auditory hallucinations, he might employ a similar measure to develop a visual hallucination. At the moment, so he recalled after arousing from the trance and while discussing his experience, he wondered if I had ever built up hallucinations in my subjects by combining various sensory fields of experience. I told him that that was a standard procedure for me.

He proceeded with this visual hallucination by "feeling" his head turn from side to side and up and down to follow a barely visible, questionably visible, rhythmically moving object. Very shortly the object became increasingly more visible until he saw a giant rose, possibly three feet in diameter. This he did not expect, and thus he was certain at once that it was not a vivified memory but a satisfactory hallucination. With this realization came the insight that he might very well add to the hallucination by adding olfactory hallucinations of an intense, "unroselike," sickeningly sweet odor. This effort was also most successful. After experimenting with various hallucinations, Huxley aroused from his trance and discussed extensively what he had accomplished. He was pleased to learn that his experimental findings without any coaching or suggestions from me were in good accord with planned experimental findings with other subjects.

This discussion raised the question of anaesthesia, amnesia, dissociation, depersonalization, regression, time distortion, hypermnesia (an item difficult to test with Huxley because of his phenomenal memory), and an exploration of past repressed events.

Of these Huxley found that anaesthesia, amnesia, time distortion, and hypermnesia were possible in the light trance. The other phenomena were conducive to the development of a deep trance with any earnest effort to achieve them.

The anaesthesia he developed in the light trance was most effective for selective parts of the body. When generalized anaesthesia from the neck down was attempted, Huxley found himself "slipping" into a deep trance.

The amnesia, like the anaesthesia, was effective when selective in character. Any effort to have a total amnesia resulted in a progression toward a deep trance.

Time distortion was easily possible, and Huxley offered the statement that he was not certain but that he felt strongly that he had long employed time distortion in Deep Reflection, although his first formal introduction to the concept had been through me.

Hypermnesia, so difficult to test because of his extreme capacity to recall past events, was tested upon my suggestion by asking him in the light trance state to state promptly upon request on what page of various of his books certain paragraphs could be found. At the first request Huxley aroused from the light trance and explained, "Really now, Milton, I can't do that. I can with effort recite most of that book, but the page number for a paragraph is not exactly cricket." Nevertheless he went back into a light trance, the name of the volume was given, a few lines of a paragraph were read aloud to him, whereupon he was to give the page number on which it appeared. He succeeded in identifying better than 65 percent in an amazingly prompt fashion. Upon awakening from the light trance, he was instructed to remain in the state of conscious awareness and to execute the same task. To his immense astonishment he found that, while the page number "flashed" into his mind in the light trance state, in the waking state he had to follow a methodical procedure of completing the paragraph mentally, beginning the next, then turning back mentally to the preceding paragraph, and then "making a guess." When restricted to the same length of time he had employed in the light trance, he failed in each instance. When allowed to take whatever length of time he wished, he could reach an accuracy of about 40 per cent, but the books had to be ones more recently read than those used for the light trance state.

Huxley then proceeded to duplicate in the medium trance all that he had done in the light trance. He accomplished similar tasks much more easily but constantly experienced a feeling of "slipping" into a deeper trance.

Huxley and I discussed this hypnotic behavior of his at very considerable length, with Huxley making most of the notations since only he could record his own subjective experience in relation to the topics discussed. For this reason the discussion here is limited.

We then turned to the question of deep hypnosis. Huxley developed easily a profound somnambulistic trance in which he was completely disoriented spontaneously for time and place. He was able to open his eyes but described his field of vision as being a "well of light" which included me, the chair in which I sat, himself, and his chair. He remarked at once upon the remarkable spontaneous restriction of his vision and disclosed an awareness that, for some reason unknown to him, he was obligated to "explain things" to me. Careful questioning disclosed him to have an amnesia about what had been done previously, nor did he have any awareness of our joint venture. His feeling that he must explain things became a casual willingness as soon as he verbalized it. One of his first statements was, "Really, you know, I can't understand my situation or why you are here, wherever that may be, but I must explain things to you." He was assured that I understood the situation and that I was interested in receiving any explanation he wished to give me and told that I might make requests of him. Most casually, indifferently he acceded, but it was obvious that he was enjoying a state of physical comfort in a contented, passive manner.

He answered questions simply and briefly, giving literally and precisely no more and no less than the literal significance of the question implied. In other words he showed the same precise literalness found in other subjects, perhaps more so because of his knowledge of semantics.

He was asked, "What is to my right?" His answer was simply, "I don't know." "Why?" "I haven't looked." "Will you do so?" "Yes." "Now!" "How far do you want me to look?" This was not an unexpected inquiry since I have encountered it innumerable times. Huxley was simply manifesting a characteristic phenomenon of the deep somnambulistic trance in which visual awareness is restricted in some inexplicable manner to those items pertinent to the trance situation. For each chair, couch, footstool I wished him to see specific instructions were required. As Huxley explained later, "I had to look around until gradually it [the specified object] slowly came into view, not all at once, but slowly, as if it were materializing. I really believe that I felt completely at ease without a trace of wonderment as I watched things materialize. I accepted everything as a matter of course." Similar explanations have been received from hundreds of subjects. Yet experience has taught me the importance of my assumption of the role of a purely passive inquirer, one who asks a question solely to receive an answer regardless of its content. An intonation of interest in the meaning of the answer is likely to induce subjects to respond as if they had been given instructions concerning what answer to give. In therapeutic work I use intonations to influence more adequate personal responses by the patient.

With Huxley I tested this by enthusiastically asking, "What, tell me now, is that which is just about 15 feet in front of you?" The correct answser should have been, "A table." Instead, the answer received was "A table with a book and a vase on it." Both the book and the vase were on the table but on the far side of the table and hence more than 15 feet away. Later the same inquiry was made in a casual, indifferent fashion, "Tell me now, what is that just about 15 feet in front of you?" He replied, despite his previous answer, "A table." "Anything else?" "Yes." "What else?" "A book." [This was nearer to him than was the vase.] "Anything else?" "Yes." "Tell me now." "A vase." "Anything else?" "Yes." "Tell me now." "A spot." "Anything else?" "No."

This literalness and this peculiar restriction of awarness to those items of reality constituting the precise hypnotic situation is highly definitive of a satisfactory somnambulistic hypnotic trance. Along with the visual restriction there is also an auditory restriction of such character that sounds, even those originating between the operator and the subject, seem to be totally outside the hypnotic situation. Since there was no assistant present, this auditory restriction could not be tested. However, by means of a black thread not visible to the eye, a book was toppled from the table behind him against his back. Slowly, as if he had experienced an itch, Huxley raised his hand and scratched his shoulder. There was no startle reaction. This, too, is characteristic of the response made to many unexpected physical stimuli. They are interpreted in terms of past body experience. Quite frequently as a part of developing a deep somnambulistic trance subjects will concomitantly develop a selective general anaesthesia for physical stimuli not constituting a part of the hypnotic situation, physical stimuli in particular that do not permit interpretation in terms of past experience. This could not be tested in the situation with Huxley, since an assistant is necessary to make adequate tests without distorting the hypnotic situation. One illustrative measure I have used is to pass a threaded needle through the coat sleeve while positioning the arms, and then having an assistant saw back and forth on the thread from a place of concealment. Often a spontaneous anaesthesia would keep the subject unaware of the stimulus. Various simple measures are easily devised.

Huxley was then gently and indirectly awakened from the trance by the simple suggestion that he adjust himself in his chair to resume the exact physical and mental state he had had at the decision to discontinue until later any further experimental study of Deep Reflection.

Huxley's response was an immediate arousal, and he promptly stated that he was all set to enter deep hypnosis. While this statement in itself indicated profound posthypnotic amnesia, delaying tactics were employed in the guise of discussion of what might possibly be done. In this way it became possible to mention various items of his deep trance behavior. Such mention evoked no memories, and Huxley's discussion of the points raised showed no sophistication resulting from his deep trance behavior. He was as uninformed about the details of his deep trance behavior as he had been before the deep trance had been induced.

There followed more deep trances by Huxley in which, avoiding all personal significances, he was asked to develop partial, selective, and total posthypnotic amnesias (by partial is meant a part of the total experience, by selective amnesia is meant an amnesia for selected, perhaps interrelated items of experience), a recovery of the amnestic material, and a loss of the recovered material. He also developed catalepsy, tested by "arranging" him comfortably in a chair and then creating a situation constituting a direct command to rise from the chair ("take the book on that table there and place it on the desk over there and do it now"). By this means Huxley found himself inexplicably unable to arise from the chair and unable to understand why this was so. (The "comfortable arrangement" of his body had resulted in a positioning that would have to be corrected before he could arise from the chair, and no implied suggestions for such correction were to be found in the instructions given. Hence he sat helplessly, unable to stand and unable to recognize why. This same measure has been employed to demonstrate a saddle-block anaesthesia before medical groups. The subject in the deep trance is carefully positioned, a casual conversation is then conducted, the subject is then placed in rapport with another subject, who is asked to exchange seats with the first subject. The second subject steps over only to stand helplessly while the first subject discovers that she is (1) unable to move, and (2) that shortly the loss of inability to stand results in a loss of orientation to the lower part of her body and a resulting total anaesthesia without anaesthesia having been mentioned even in the preliminary discussion of hypnosis. This unnoticed use of catalepsy not recognized by the subject is a most effective measure in deepening trance states.

Huxley was amazed at his loss of mobility and became even more so when he discovered a loss of orientation to the lower part of his body, and he was most astonished when I demonstrated for him the presence of a profound anaesthesia. He was much at a loss to understand the entire sequence of events. He did not relate the comfortable positioning of his body to the unobtrusively induced catalepsy with its consequent anaesthesia.

He was aroused from the trance state with persistent catalepsy, anaesthesia, and a total amnesia for all deep trance experiences. He spontaneously enlarged the instruction to include all trance experiences, possibly because he did not hear my instructions sufficiently clearly. Immediately he reoriented himself to the time at which we had been working with Deep Reflection. He was much at a loss to explain his immobile state, and he expressed curious wonderment about what he had done in the Deep Reflection state, from which he assumed he had just emerged, and what had led to such inexplicable manifestations for the first time in all of his experience. He became greatly interested, kept murmuring such comments as "most extraordinary" while he explored the lower part of his body with his hands and eyes. He noted that he could tell the position of his feet only with his eyes, that there was a profound immobility from the waist down, and he discovered, while attempting futilely because of the catalepsy to move his leg with his hands, that a state of anaesthesia existed. This he tested variously, asking me to furnish him with various things in order to make his test. For example he asked that ice be applied to his bare ankle by me, since he could not bend sufficiently to do so. Finally after much study he turned to me, remarking, "I say, you look cool and most comfortable, while I am in a most extraordinary predicament. I deduce that in some subtle way you have distracted and disturbed my sense of body awareness. I say, is this state anything like hypnosis?"

Restoration of his memory delighted him, but he remained entirely at a loss concerning the genesis of his catalepsy and his anaesthesia. He realized, however, that some technique of communication had been employed to effect the results achieved, but he did not succeed in the association of the positioning of his body with the final results.

Further experimentation in the deep trance investigated visual, auditory, and other types of ideosensory hallucinations. One of the measures employed was to pantomime hearing a door open and then to appear to see someone entering the room, to arise in courtesy, and to indicate a chair, then to turn to Huxley to express the hope that he was comfortable. He replied that he was, and he expressed surprise at his wife's unexpected return, since he had expected her to be absent the entire day. (The chair I had indicated was one I knew his wife liked to occupy.) He conversed with her and apparently hallucinated replies. He was interrupted with the question of how he knew that it was his wife and not a hypnotic hallucination. He examined the question thoughtfully, then explained that I had not given him any suggestion to hallucinate his wife, that I had been as much surprised by her arrival as he had been, and that she was dressed as she had been just before her departure and not as I had seen her earlier. Hence it was reasonable to assume that she was a reality. After a brief, thoughtful pause he returned to his "conversation" with her, apparently continuing to hallucinate replies. Finally I attracted his attention and made a hand gesture suggestive of a disappearance toward the chair in which he "saw" his wife. To his complete astonishment he saw her slowly fade away. Then he turned to me and asked that I awaken him with a full memory of the experience. This I did, and he discussed the experience at some length, making many special notations in his notebook and elaborating them with the answers to questions he put to me. He was amazed to discover that when I asked him to awaken with a retention of the immobility and anaesthesia, he *thought* he had awakened but that the trance state had, to him, unrecognizably persisted.

He then urged further work on hypnotic hallucinatory experiences and a great variety (positive and negative visual, auditory, olfactory, gustatory, tactile, kinesthetic, temperature, hunger, satiety, fatigue, weakness, profound excited expectation, etc.) were explored. He proved to be most competent in all regards, and it was noted that his pulse rate would change as much as 20 points when he was asked to hallucinate the experience of mountain climbing in a profound state of weariness. He volunteered in his discussion of these varied experiences the information that while a negative hallucination could be achieved readily in a deep trance, it would be most difficult in a light or medium trance, because negative hallucinations were most destructive of reality values, even those of the hypnotic situation. That is, with induced negative hallucinations, he found that I was blurred in outline even though he could develop a deep trance with a negative hallucination inherent in that deep trance for all external reality except the realities of the hypnotic situation, which would remain clear and well defined unless suggestions to the contrary were offered. Subsequent work with other subjects confirmed this finding by Huxley. I had not previously explored this matter of negative hallucinations in light and medium trances.

At this point Huxley recalled his page number identification in the lighter trance states during the inquiry into hypermnesia, and he asked that he be subjected to similar tests in deep hypnosis. Together we searched the library shelves, finally selecting several books that Huxley was certain he must have read many years previously but which he had not touched for 20 or more years. (One, apparently, he had never read; the other five he had.)

In a deep trance, with his eyes closed, Huxley listened intently as I opened the book at random and read a half-dozen lines from a selected paragraph. For some, he identified the page number almost at once, and then he would hallucinate the page and "read" it from the point where I had stopped. Additionally he identified the occasion on which he read the book. Two of the books he recalled consulting 15 years previously. Another two he found it difficult to give the correct page number, and then only approximating the page number. He could not hallucinate the printing and could only give little more than a summary of the thought content; but this in essence was correct. He could not identify when he had read them but was certain it was more than 25 years previously.

Huxley, in the post-trance discussion was most amazed by his performance as a memory feat but commented upon the experience as primarily intellectual, with the recovered memories lacking in any emotional significances of belonging to him as a person. This led to a general discussion of hypnosis and Deep Reflection, with a general feeling of inadequacy on Huxley's part concerning proper conceptualization of his experiences for comparison of values. While Huxley was most delighted with his hypnotic experiences for their interest and the new understandings they offered him, he was also somewhat at a loss. He felt that as a purely personal experience he derived certain unidentifiable subjective values from Deep Reflection not actually obtainable from hypnosis, which offered only a wealth of new points of view. Deep Reflection, he declared, gave him certain inner enduring feelings that seemed to play some significant part in his pattern of living. During this discussion he suddenly asked if hypnosis could be employed to permit him to explore his psychedelic experiences. His request was met, but upon arousal from the trance he expressed the feeling that the hypnotic experience was quite different from a comparable "feeling through" by means of Deep Reflection. He explained that the hypnotic exploration did not give him an inner feeling—that is, a continuing subjective feeling—of just being in the midst of his psychedelic experience, that there was an ordered intellectual content paralleling the "feeling content," while Deep Reflection established a profound emotional background of a stable character upon which he could "consciously and effortlessly lay an intellectual display of ideas" to which the reader would make full response. This discussion Huxley brought to a close by the thoughtful comment that his brief intensive experience with hypnosis had not yet begun to digest and that he could not expect to offer an intelligent comment without much more thought.

He asked urgently that further deep hypnosis be done with him in which more complex phenomena be induced to permit him to explore himself more adequately as a person. After a rapid mental review of what had been done and what might yet be done I decided upon the desirability of a deep trance state with the possibility of a two-stage dissociative regression—that is, of the procedure of regressing him by dissociating him from a selected recent area of his life experience so that he could view it as an onlooker from the orientation of another relatively recent area of life experience. The best way to do this, I felt, would be by a confusion technique (See "The confusion technique in hypnosis" in Section 2 of this volume). This decision to employ a confusion technique was influenced in large part by the author's awareness of Huxley's unlimited intellectual capacity and curiosity, which would aid greatly by leading Huxley to add to the confusion technique verbalizations other possible elaborate meanings and significances and associations, thereby actually supplementing in effect my own efforts. Unfortunately there was no tape recorder present to preserve the details of the actual suggestions, which were to the effect that Huxley go ever deeper and deeper into a trance until "the depth was a part and apart" from him, that before him would appear in "utter clarity, in living reality, in impossible actuality, that which once was, but which now in the depths of the trance, will, in bewildering confrontation challenge all of your memories and understandings." This was a purposely vague yet permissively comprehensive suggestion, and I simply relied upon Huxley's intelligence to elaborate it with an extensive meaningfulness for himself which I could not even attempt to guess. There were of course other suggestions, but they centered in effect upon the suggestion enclosed in the quotation above. What I had in mind was not a defined situation but a setting of the stage so that Huxley himself would be led to define the task. I did not even attempt to speculate upon what my suggestions might mean to Huxley.

It became obvious that Huxley was making an intensive hypnotic response during the prolonged, repetitious suggestions I was offering, when suddenly he raised his hand and said rather loudly and most urgently, "I say, Milton, do you mind hushing up there. This is most extraordinarily interesting down here, and your constant talking is frightfully distracting and annoying."

For more than two hours Huxley sat with his eyes open, gazing intently before him. The play of expression on his face was most rapid and bewildering. His heart rate and respiratory rate were observed to change suddenly and inexplicably and repeatedly at irregular intervals. Each time that the author attempted to speak to him, Huxley would raise his hand, perhaps lift his head, and speak as if the author were at some height above him, and frequently he would annoyedly request silence.

After well over two hours he suddenly looked up toward the ceiling and remarked with puzzled emphasis, "I say, Milton, this is an extraordinary contretemps. We don't know you. You do not belong here. You are sitting on the edge of a ravine watching both of us, and neither of us knows which one is talking to you; and we are in the vestibule looking at each other with most extraordinary interest. We know that you are someone who can determine our identity, and most extraordinarily we are both sure we know it and that the other is not really so, but merely a mental image of the past or of the future. But you must resolve it despite time and distances and even though we do not know you. I say, this is an extraordinarily fascinating predicament: Am I he or is he me? Come, Milton, whoever you are." There were other similar remarks of comparable meaning which could not be recorded, and Huxley's tone of voice suddenly became most urgent. The whole situation was most confusing to me, but temporal and other types of dissociation seemed to be definitely involved in the situation.

Wonderingly, but with outward calm, I undertook to arouse Huxley from the trance state by accepting the partial clues given and by saying in essence. "Wherever you are, whatever you are doing, listen closely to what is being said and slowly, gradually, comfortably begin to act upon it. Feel rested and comfortable, feel a need to establish an increasing contact with my voice, with me, with the situation I represent, a need of returning to matters in hand with me, not so long ago, in the not so long ago belonging to me, *and leave behind but* AVAILABLE UPON REQUEST *practically everything of importance,* KNOWING BUT NOT KNOWING *that it is* AVAILABLE UPON REQUEST. And now, let us see, that's right, you are sitting there, wide awake, rested, comfortable, and *ready for discussion of what little there is."*

Huxley aroused, rubbed his eyes, and remarked, "I have a most extraordinary feeling that I have been in a profound trance, but it has been a most sterile experience. I recall you suggesting that I go deeper in a trance, and I felt myself to be most compliant, and though I feel much time has elapsed, I truly believe a state of Deep Reflection would have been more fruitful."

Since he did not specifically ask the time, a desultory conversation was conducted in which Huxley compared the definite but vague appreciation of external realities of the light trance with the more definitely decreased awareness of externalities in the medium trance, which is accompanied by a peculiar sense of minor comfort that those external realities can become secure actualities at any given moment.

He was then asked about realities in the deep trance from which he had just

States of Consciousness

recently aroused. He replied thoughtfully that he could recall vaguely feeling that he was developing a deep trance, but no memories came to mind associated with it. After some discussion of hypnotic amnesia and the possibility that he might be manifesting such a phenomenon, he laughed with amusement and stated that such a topic would be most intriguing to discuss. After still further desultory conversation he was asked *a propos* of nothing, "In what vestibule would you place that chair?" (indicating a nearby armchair.) His reply was remarkable. "Really, Milton, that is a most extraordinary question. Frightfully so! It is quite without meaning, but that word 'vestibule' has a strange feeling of immense, anxious warmth about it. Most extraordinarily fascinating!" He lapsed into a puzzled thought for some minutes and finally stated that if there were any significance, it was undoubtedly some fleeting esoteric association. After further casual conversation I remarked, "As for the edge where I was sitting, I wonder how deep the ravine was." To this Huxley replied, "Really Milton, you can be most frightfully cryptic. Those words 'vestibule,' 'edge,' 'ravine' have an extraordinary effect upon me. It is most indescribable. Let me see if I can associate some meaning with them." For nearly 15 minutes Huxley struggled vainly to secure some meaningful associations with those words, now and then stating that my apparently purposive but unrevealing use of them constituted a full assurance that there was a meaningful significance which should be apparent to him. Finally he disclosed with elation, "I have it now. Most extraordinary how it escaped me. I'm fully aware that you had me in a trance, and unquestionably those words had something to do with the deep trance which seemed to be so sterile to me. I wonder if I can recover my associations."

After about 20 minutes of silent, obviously intense thought on his part Huxley remarked, "If those words do have a significance, I can truly say that I have a most profound hypnotic amnesia. I have attempted Deep Reflection, but I have found my thoughts centering around my mescaline experiences. It was indeed difficult to tear myself away from those thoughts. I had a feeling that I was employing them to preserve my amnesia. Shall we go on for another half-hour on other matters to see if there is any spontaneous recall in association with 'vestibule,' 'edge', and 'ravine?' "

Various topics were discussed until finally Huxley said, "It is a most extraordinary feeling of meaningful warmth those words have for me, but I am utterly, I might say frightfully, helpless. I suppose I will have to depend upon you for something, whatever that may be. It's extraordinary, most extraordinary."

This comment I deliberately bypassed, but during the ensuing conversation Huxley was observed to have a most thoughtful, puzzled expression on his face, though he made no effort to press me for assistance. After some time I commented with quiet emphasis, "Well, perhaps now matters will *become available.*" From his lounging, comfortable position in his chair Huxley straightened up in a startled amazed fashion and then poured forth a torrent of words too rapid to record except for occasional notes.

In essence his account was that the word "available" had the effect of drawing back an amnestic curtain, laying bare a most astonishing subjective experience that had miraculously been "wiped out" by the words "leave behind" and had been recovered *in toto* by virtue of the cue words "become available."

He explained that he now realized that he had developed a "deep trance," a psychological state far different from his state of Deep Reflection, that in Deep Reflection there was an attenuated but unconcerned and unimportant awareness of external reality, a feeling of being in a known sensed state of subjective awareness, of a feeling of control and a desire to utilize capabilities and in which past memories, learnings, and experiences flowed freely and easily. Along with this flow there would be a continuing sense in the self that these memories, learnings, experiences, and understandings, however vivid, were no more than just such an orderly, meaningful alignment of psychological experiences out of which to form a foundation for a profound, pleasing, subjective, emotional state from which would flow comprehensive understandings to be utilized immediately and with little conscious effort.

The deep trance state, he asserted, he now knew to be another and entirely different category of experience. External reality could enter, but it acquired a new kind of subjective reality, a special reality of a new and different significance entirely. For example, while I had been included in part in his deep trance state, it was not as a specific person with a specific identity. Instead I was known only as someone whom he (Huxley) knew in some vague and unimportant and completely unidentified relationship.

Aside from my "reality" there existed the type of reality that one encounters in vivid dreams, a reality that one does not question. Instead one accepts such reality completely without intellectual questioning, and there are no conflicting contrasts nor judgmental comparisons nor contradictions, so that whatever is subjectively experienced is unquestioningly accepted as both subjectively and objectively genuine and in keeping with all else.

In his deep trance Huxley found himself in a deep, wide ravine, high up on the steep side of which, on the very edge, I sat, identifiable only by name and as annoyingly verbose.

Before him in a wide expanse of soft, dry sand was a nude infant lying on its stomach. Acceptingly, unquestioning of its actuality, Huxley gazed at the infant, vastly curious about its behavior, vastly intent on trying to understand its flailing movements with its hands and the creeping movements of its legs. To his amazement he felt himself experiencing a vague, curious sense of wonderment as if he himself were the infant and looking at the soft sand and trying to understant what it was.

As he watched, he became annoyed with me since I was apparently trying to talk to him, and he experienced a wave of impatience and requested that I be silent. He turned back and noted that the infant was growing before his eyes, was creeping, sitting, standing, toddling, walking, playing, talking. In utter fascination he watched this growing child, sensed its subjective experiences of learning, of wanting, of feeling. He followed it in distorted time through a multitude of experiences as it passed from infancy to childhood to schooldays to early youth to teenage. He watched the child's physical development, sensed its physical and subjective mental experiences, sympathized with it, empathized with it, rejoiced with it, thought and wondered and learned with it. He felt as one with it, as if it were he himself, and he continued to watch it until finally he realized that he had watched that infant grow to the maturity of 23 years. He stepped closer to see what the young man was looking at, and suddenly realized that the young man was Aldous Huxley himself, and that this Aldous Huxley was looking at another Aldous Huxley, obviously in his early 50's, just across the vestibule in which they both were standing; and that he, aged 52, was looking at himself, Aldous, aged 23. Then Aldous aged 23 and Adlous aged 52 apparently realized simultaneously that they were looking at each other, and the curious questions at once arose in the mind of each of them. For one the question was, "Is that my idea of what I'll be like when I am 52?" and, "Is that really the way I appeared when I was 23?" Each was aware of the question in the other's mind. Each found the question of "extraordinarily fascinating interest," and each tried to determine which was the "actual reality" and which was the "mere subjective experience outwardly projected in hallucinatory form."

To each the past 23 years was an open book, all memories and events were clear, and they recognized that they shared those moemories in common, and to each only wondering speculation offered a possible explanation of any of the years between 23 and 52.

They looked across the vestibule (this "vestibule" was not defined) and up at the edge of the ravine where I was sitting. Both knew that that person sitting there had some undefined significance, was named Milton, and could be spoken to by both. The thought came to both, could he hear both of them, but the test failed because they found that they spoke simultaneously, nor could they speak separately.

Slowly, thoughtfully, they studied each other. One had to be real. One had to be a memory image or a projection of a self-image. Should not Aldous aged 52 have all the memories of the years from 23 to 52? But if he did, how could he then see Aldous aged 23 without the shadings and colorations of the years that had passed since that youthful age? If he were to view Aldous aged 23 clearly, he would have to blot out all subsequent memories in order to see that youthful Aldous clearly and as he then was. But if he were actually Aldous aged 23, why could he not speculatively fabricate memories for the years between 23 and 52 instead of merely seeing Aldous as 52 and nothing more? What manner of psychological blocking could exist to effect this peculiar state of affairs? Each found himself fully cognizant of the thinking and reasoning of the "other." Each doubted "the reality of the other," and each found reasonable explanations for such contrasting subjective experiences. The questions arose repeatedly, by what measure could the truth be established, and how did that unidentifiable person possessing only a name sitting on the edge of a ravine on the other side of the vestibule fit into the total situation? Could that vague person have an answer? Why not call to him and see?

With much pleasure and interest Huxley detailed his total subjective experience, speculating upon the years of time distortion experienced and the memory blockages creating the insoluble problem of actual identity.

Finally, experimentally, the author remarked casually, "Of course, all that could be *left behind to become* AVAILABLE *at some later time.*"

Immediately there occurred a reestablishment of the original posthypnotic amnesia. Efforts were made to disrupt this reinduced hypnotic amnesia by veiled remarks, by frank, open statements, by a narration of what had occurred. Huxley found my narrative statements about an infant on the sand, a deep ravine, a vestibule "curiously interesting," simply cryptic remarks for which Huxley judged I had a purpose. But they were not evocative of anything more. Each statement I made was in itself actually uninformative and intended only to arouse associations. Yet no results were forthcoming until again the word "AVAILable" resulted in the same effect as previously. The whole account was related by Huxley a second time but without his realization that he was repeating his account. Appropriate suggestions when he had finished his second narration resulted in a full recollection of his first account. His reaction, after his immediate astonishment, was to compare the two accounts item by item. Their identity amazed him, and he noted only minor changes in the order of narration and the choice of words.

Again, as before, a posthypnotic amnesia was induced, and a third recollection was then elicited, followed by an induced realization by Huxley that this was his third recollection.

Extensive, detailed notations were made of the whole sequence of events, and comparisons were made of the individual notations, with interspersed comments regarding significances. The many items were systematically discussed for their meanings, and brief trances were induced to vivify various items. However, only a relatively few notations were made by me of the content of Huxley's experience, since he would properly be the one to develop them fully. My notations concerned primarily the sequence of events and a fairly good summary of the total development.

This discussion was continued until preparations for scheduled activities for that evening intervened, but not before an agreement on a subsequent preparation of the material for publication. Huxley planned to use both Deep Reflection and additional self-induced trances to aid in writing the article, but the unfortunate holocaust precluded this.

CONCLUDING REMARKS

It is unfortunate that the above account is only a fragment of an extensive inquiry into the nature of various states of consciousness. Huxley's state of Deep

Reflection did not appear to be hypnotic in character. Instead it seemed to be a state of utterly intense concentration with much dissociation from external realities but with a full capacity to respond with varying degrees of readiness to externalities. It was entirely a personal experience serving apparently as an unrecognized foundation for conscious work activity enabling him to utlize freely all that had passed through his mind in Deep Reflection.

His hypnotic behavior was in full accord with hypnotic behavior elicited from other subjects. He was capable of all the phenomena of the deep trance and could respond readily to posthypnotic suggestions and to exceedingly minimal cues. He was emphatic in declaring that the hypnotic state was quite different from the Deep Reflection state.

While some comparison may be made with dream activity, and certainly the ready inclusion of the "vestibule" and the "ravine" in the same subjective situation is suggestive of dreamlike activity, such peculiar inclusions are somewhat frequently found as a spontaneous development of profound hypnotic ideosensory activity in highly intellectual subjects. His somnambulistic behavior, his open eyes, his responsiveness to me, his extensive posthypnotic behavior all indicate that hypnosis was unquestionably definitive of the total situation in that specific situation.

Huxley's remarkable development of a dissociated state, even bearing in mind his original request for a permissive technique, to view hypnotically his own growth and dvelopment in distorted time relationships, while indicative of Huxley's all-encompassing intellectual curiosity, is suggestive of most interesting and informative research possibilites. Postexperimental questioning disclosed that Huxley had no conscious thoughts or plans for review of his life experiences, nor did he at the time of the trance induction make any such interpretation of the suggestions given him. This was verified by a trance induction and making this special inquiry. His explanation was that when he felt himself "deep in the trance," he then began to search for something to do, and "suddenly there I found myself—most extraordinary."

While this experience with Huxley was most notable, it was not my first encounter with such developments in the regression of highly intelligent subjects. One such experimental subject asked that he be hypnotized and informed when in the trance that he was to develop a profoundly interesting type of regression. This was primarily to be done for his own interest while he was waiting for me to complete some work. His request was met, and he was left to his own devices while sitting in a comfortable chair on the other side of the laboratory. About two hours later he requested that I awaken him. He gave an account of suddenly finding himself on an unfamiliar hillside, and looking around he saw a small boy whom he immediately "knew" was six years old. Curious about this conviction of a strange little boy, he walked over to the child, only to discover that that child was himself. He immediately recognized the hillside and set about trying to discover how he could be himself at 26 years of age watching himself at the age of six years. He soon learned that he could not only see, hear, and feel his child-self, but that he knew the innermost thoughts and feelings. At the moment of realizing this, he felt the child's feeling of hunger and his wish for "brown cookies." This brought a flood of memories to his 26-year-old self, but he noticed that the boy's thoughts were still centering on cookies and that the boy remained totally unaware of him. He was an invisible man, in some way regressed in time so that he could see and sense completely his childhood self. My subject reported that he "lived" with that boy for years, watched his successes and his failures, knew all of his innermost life, wondered about the next day's events with the child, and like the child he found to his amazement that even though he was 26 years old, a total amnesia existed for all events subsequent to the child's immediate age at the moment, that he could not forsee the future any more than could the child. He went to school with the child, vacationed with him, always watching the continuing physical growth and development. As each new day arrived, he found that he had a wealth of associations about the actual happenings of the past up to the immediate moment of life for the child-self.

He went through grade school, high school, and then through a long process of deciding whether or not to go to college and what course of studies he should follow. He suffered the same agonies of indecision that his then-self did. He felt his other self's elation and relief when the decision was finally reached, and his own feeling of elation and relief was identical with that of his other self.

My subject explained that the experience was literally a moment-by-moment reliving of his life with only the same awareness he had then and that the highly limited restricted awareness of himself at 26 was that of being an invisible man watching his own growth and development from childhood on, with no more knowledge of the child's future than the child possessed.

He had enjoyed each completed event with a vast and vivid panorama of the past memories as each event reached completion. At the point of entrance to college the experience terminated. He then realized that he was in a deep trance and that he wanted to awaken and to take with him into conscious awareness the memory of what he had been subjectively experiencing.

This same type of experience has been encountered with other experimental subjects, both male and female, but each account varies in the manner in which the experience is achieved. For example a girl who had identical twin sisters three years younger than herself found herself to be "a pair of identical twins growing up together but always knowing everything about the other." In her account there was nothing about her actual twin sisters; all such memories and associations were excluded.

Another subject, highly inclined mechanically, constructed a robot which he endowed with life only to discover that it was his own life with which he endowed it. He then watched that robot throughout many years of experiential events and learnings, always himself achieving them also because he had an amnesia for his past.

Repeated efforts to set this up as an orderly experiement have to date failed.

Usually the subjects object or refuse for some not too comprehensible a reason. In all of my experience with this kind of development in hypnotic trances this type of "reliving" of one's life has always been a spontaneous occurrence with highly intelligent, well-adjusted experimental subjects.

Huxley's experience was the one most adequately recorded, and it is most unfortunate that the greater number of details, having been left with him, were destroyed before he had the opportunity to write them up in full. Huxley's remarkable memory, his capacity to use Deep Reflection, and his ability to develop a deep hypnotic state to achieve specific purposes and to arouse himself at will with full conscious awareness of what he had accomplished (Huxley required very little instruction the next day to become skilled in autohypnosis) augured exceedingly well for a most informative study. Unfortunately the destruction of both notebooks precluded him from any effort to reconstruct them from memory, because my notebook contained so many notations of items of procedure and observation for which he had no memories and which were vital to any satisfactory elaboration. However, it is hoped that the report given here may serve, despite its deficiencies, as an initial pilot study for the development of a more adequate and comprehensive study of various states of consciousness.

4. Autohypnotic Experiences of Milton H. Erickson

Milton H. Erickson and Ernest L. Rossi

During the past four years between the ages of 70 to 74, the senior author recounted a number of personal factors and experiences that contributed to the development of his interest, attitudes, and approaches to autohypnosis, trance, and psychotherapy. Many of Erickson's earliest memories deal with the ways in which his experience was different from others because of his constitutional problems: He experienced an unusual form of color blindness, arrhythmia, tone deafness, and dyslexia long before such conditions were well recognized and diagnosed in the fairly primitive rural community in which he was reared. As a child in elementary school, for example, he could never understand why people did that yelling and screeching they called "singing." Although he was different in ways that neither he nor others could understand, he possessed an acutely probing intelligence that initiated him into a lifetime of inquiry about the limitations and relativity of human perception and behavior. When he visited his maternal grandmother for the first time at the age of four, for example, the little Erickson was struck by the incredulity in her voice as she said over and over to his mother, "It's you Clara; it's really, really you?!" The grandmother had never traveled further than ten miles from her home and really did not have any conception of how people close to her could exist beyond that radius. When her daughter married and moved beyond it, she really never expected to see her again. Thus, by the age of four, Erickson was already struck, in however dim and wordless a manner, with the differences and limitations in people's perspectives.

Another experience with the limitations and rigidities in people's habitual frames of reference occurred somewhat before the age of ten, when Erickson doubted his grandfather's method of planting potatoes only during a certain phase of the moon and always with the "eyes" up. The young lad was hurt and saddened when his grandfather could not believe the facts when Erickson demonstrated that his own potato patch planted at the "wrong" phase of the moon with the "eyes" in all directions did just as well. From such early experiences

---

Reprinted with permission from *The American Journal of Clinical Hypnosis*, July, 1977, *20*, 36-54.

Autohypnotic Experiences

Erickson feels he developed a distaste for rigidities. These experiences provided an orientation for some of his original approaches to psychotherapy wherein he used shock and surprise to break through the habitual limitations in patients' frames of reference to effect a rapid therapeutic reorganization of their symptoms and life perspectives (Rossi, 1973). Depotentiating a subject's habitual mental sets and frames of references has been recently conceptualized as an important stage in initiating trance experience (Erickson, Rossi, and Rossi, 1976).

INSIGHT VIA LIGHT AND VISUAL HALLUCINATION

As a six-year-old child Erickson was apparently handicapped with dyslexia. Try as she might, his teacher could not convince him that a "3" and an "m" were not the same. One day the teacher wrote a 3 and then an m by guiding his hand with her own. Still Erickson could not recognize the difference. Suddenly he experienced a spontaneous visual hallucination in which he saw the difference in a blinding flash of light.

> E: Can you image how bewildering it is? Then one day, it's so amazing, there was a sudden burst of atomic light. I saw the m and I saw the 3. The m was standing on its legs and the 3 was on its side with the legs sticking out. The blinding flash of light! It was so bright! It cast into oblivion every other thing. There was a blinding flash of light and in the center of that terrible outburst of light were the 3 and the m.
> R: You really saw a blinding flash of light? You saw it out there, you're not just using a metaphor?
> E: Yes, and it obscured every other thing except a 3 and an m.
> R: Were you aware you were in an altered state? Did you, as a child, wonder about that funny experience?
> E: That's the way you learn things.
> R: I guess that's what I'd call a creative moment (Rossi, 1972, 1973). You experienced a genuine perceptual alteration: a flash of light with the 3 and the m in the center. Did they actually have legs?
> E: I saw them as they were. [Erickson draws a simple picture of a cloud effect with a 3 and an m in the center.] And this excluded everything else!
> R: Was this a visual hallucination? As a six-year-old child you actually experienced an important intellectual insight in the form of a visual hallucination?
> E: Yes, I can't remember anything else pertaining to that day. The most blinding, dazzling flash of light occurred in my sophomore year of high school. I had the nickname in grade school and high school,

"Dictionary," because I spent so much time reading the dictionary. One noon, just after the noon dismissal bell rang, I was in my usual chair reading the dictionary in the back of the room. Suddenly a blinding, dazzling flash of light occurred because I just learned how to use the dictionary. Up to that moment in looking up a word, I started at the first page and went through every column, page after page until I reached the word. In that blinding flash of light I realized that you use the alphabet as an ordered system for looking up a word. The students who brought their lunch to school always ate in the basement. I don't know how long I sat there completely dazzled by the blinding light, but when I did get down to the basement, most of the students had finished their lunches. When they asked me why I was so late in reaching the basement, I knew that I wouldn't tell them that I had just learned how to use the dictionary. I don't know why it took me so long. Did my unconscious purposely withhold that knowledge because of the immense amount of education I got from reading the dictionary?

In these early experiences we see the bewilderment of dyslexia and the special orientation it gave even the young child to learn about altered perceptions and states of experience. Erickson defines the presence of intense light and/or visual hallucination that blots out all other perception of outer reality as evidence of a spontaneous autohypnotic state. He notes the connection between such altered states and "the way you learn things." The source of his "utilization approach" is also contained in such experiences. Many years later he taught 70-year-old "Maw" how to read and write by utilizing her own internal images of legs, hoes, and other farm imagery to help her perceive the significance of the otherwise meaningless jumble of lines that are letters and words (Erickson, 1959).

Erickson relates his dyslexia and early difficulties with pronunciation to his therapeutic approach as follows:

> *E:* I must have had a slight dyslexia. I thought I knew for an absolute fact that when I said "co-mick-al, vin-gar, goverment, and mung" my pronunciation was identical with the sounds made when others said "comical, vinegar, government, and spoon." When I was a sophomore in high school, the debating coach spent a useless hour trying to teach me how to say "government." Upon sudden inspiration she used the name of a fellow student, "La Verne," and wrote on the blackboard, "govLaVernement." I read, "govlavernement." She then asked me to read it, omitting the La of LaVerne. As I did so a blinding flash of light occurred that obliterated all surrounding objects including the blackboard. I credit Miss Walsh for my technique of introducing the unexpected and irrelevant into a fixed, rigid pattern to explode it. A patient walked in today trembling and sobbing, "I'm fired. It always happens to me. My boss always bullies me. They always call me names

Autohypnotic Experiences

and I always cry. Today my boss yelled at me saying, "Stupid! stupid! stupid! Get out! Get out!' So here I am." I said very earnestly and seriously to her, "Why don't you tell him that if he had only let you know, you would have gladly done the job much more stupidly!" She looked blank, bewildered, stunned, and then burst into laughter, and the rest of the interview proceeded well with sudden gales of laughter-usually self-directed.

R: Her laughter indicates you had helped her break out of her limited view of herself as a victim. A basic principle of your *utilization* approach is illustrated in your early experience with Miss Walsh. She utilized your ability to pronounce LaVerne to help you break out of your stereotyped error in pronouncing *government*.

AUTOHYPNOSIS IN LIFE CRISIS

At the age of 17, when Erickson lay acutely ill with polio for the first time, he had the following experience.

E: As I lay in bed that night, I overheard the three doctors tell my parents in the other room that their boy would be dead in the morning. I felt intense anger that anyone should tell a mother her boy would be dead by morning. My mother then came in with as serene a face as can be. I asked her to arrange the dresser, push it up against the side of the bed at an angle. She did not understand why, she thought I was delirious. My speech was difficult. But at that angle by virtue of the mirror on the dresser I could see through the doorway, through the west window of the other room. I was damned if I would die without seeing one more sunset. If I had any skill in drawing, I could still sketch that sunset.

R: Your anger and wanting to see another sunset was a way you kept yourself alive through that critical day in spite of the doctors' predictions. But why do you call that an autohypnotic experience?

E: I saw that vast sunset covering the whole sky. But I know there was also a tree there outside the window, but I blocked it out.

R: You blocked it out? It was that selective perception that enables you to say you were in an altered state?

E: Yes, I did not do it consciously. I saw all the sunset, but I didn't see the fence and large boulder that were there. I blocked out everything except the sunset. After I saw the sunset, I lost consciousness for three days. When I finally awakened, I asked my father why they had taken out that fence, tree, and boulder. I did not realize I had blotted them out when I fixed my attention so intensely on the sunset. Then, as I recovered and became aware of my lack of abilities, I wondered how I was going to earn a living. I had already published a paper in a national agricultural journal. "Why Young Folks Leave the Farm." I no longer had the strength to be a farmer, but maybe I could make it as a doctor.

R: Would you say it was the intensity of your inner experience, your spirit and sense of defiance, that kept you alive to see that sunset?

E: Yes, I would. With patients who have a poor outlook, you say, "Well, you should live long enough to do this next month." And they do.

UTILIZING REAL SENSE MEMORIES RATHER THAN IMAGINATION

R: How do you use autohypnosis to help yourself with your infirmities and pain?

E: It usually takes me an hour after I awaken to get all the pain out. It used to be easier when I was younger. I have more muscle and joint difficulties now.

R: What were your first experiences in coping with your own muscle difficulties and pain? How did you learn to do it? Did someone train you in autohypnosis?

E: I learned by myself. I can recall how I approached using a microscope. If you really want to see through the microscope and you want to draw what you are seeing, you keep both eyes open. You look with one eye and you draw with the other.

R: What's that got to do with autohypnosis?

E: You don't see anything else.

R: You only see what is relevant for your task and block out everything else. It's that aspect of selective perception that enables you to recognize the altered state of autohypnosis. How did you cope with pain at that time?

E: One of my first efforts was to learn relaxation and building up my strength. I made chains out of rubber bands so I could pull against certain resistances. I went through that every night and all the exercises I could. Then I learned I could walk to induce fatigue to get rid of the pain. *Slowly I learned that if I could think about walking and fatigue and relaxation, I could get relief.*

R: Thinking about walking and fatigue was just as effective in producing pain relief as the actual physical process?

E: Yes, it became effective in reducing pain.

R: In your self-rehabilitative experiences between the ages of 17 and

Autohypnotic Experiences

19 you learned from your own experience that you could use your imagination to achieve the same effects as an actual physical effort.

E: An *intense memory* rather than imagination. You remember how something tastes, you know how you get a certain tingle from peppermint. As a child I used to climb a tree in a wood lot and then jump from one tree to another like a monkey. I would recall the many different twists and turns I made in order to find out what are the movements you make when you have full muscles.

R: You activated real memories from childhood in order to learn just how much muscle control you had left and how to reacquire that control.

E: Yes, you use real memories. At 18 I recalled all my childhood movements to help myself relearn muscle coordination. [Erickson now recalls how he spent much time and effort remembering the sensations of swimming, the feeling of water rushing past the different muscles of the body, etc.]

R: This could be a way of facilitating autohypnosis by having people go into their sense memories. This would activate autonomous sensory responses that are an aspect of autohypnotic behavior: not imagination but real sense memories.

E: As you watch Buster Keaton in a movie teetering on the edge of a building, you can feel your own muscles tense up.

R: The movie or pure imagination provides an associative pathway to your own sense memories, which you then actually experience in the form of muscle tension.

This fascinating account of his early self-taught approaches to self-rehabilitation by using sense memories to recall and relearn to use his muscles is the source of much of Erickson's experimental work with the nature of trance (Erickson, 1964, 1967) and hypnotic realities (Erickson, Rossi, and Rossi, 1976). An imaginative account in a book or movie might focus one inward and facilitate access to one's own sense memories, but it is these real memories rather than pure imagination per se that evoke the ideomotor and ideosensory processes that lead one more deeply into trance and new possibilities of learning. Whereas at the age of six Erickson had an entirely spontaneous experience of the relation between an altered state and new learning, by 19 he had begun to actually cultivate altered states by going deeply into his sense memories to relearn the use of his muscles. He did not yet label these experiences as altered states or autohypnosis. The obvious relation between these early experiences and his later understanding of trance is evident, however, when he wrote : *"The hypnotic state is an experience that belongs to the subject, derives from the subject's own accumulated learnings and memories,* not necessarily consciously recognized, but possible of manifestation in a special state of nonwaking awareness. Hence the hypnotic trance belongs only to the subject; the operator can do no more than learn how to proffer stimuli and suggestions to evoke responsive behavior based upon the subject's own experiential past" (Erickson, 1967). The view that all hypnosis is essentially autohypnosis certainly finds support in Erickson's personal and professional experience. Hypnotic induction techniques may be best understood as approaches that provide subjects with opportunities for the intense self-absorption and inner experiences called trance. The wise operator then develops skill in relating creatively to this inner experience of his subjects.

EARLY TRAINING IN DREAM AND SOMNAMBULISTIC ACTIVITY

E: I was forever observing. I'll tell you the most egotistical thing I ever did. I was 20 years old, a first-semester sophomore in college, when I applied for a job at the local newspaper, *The Daily Cardinal,* in Wisconsin. I wanted to write editorials. The editor, Porter Butz, humored me and told me I could drop them off in his mail box each morning on my way to school. I had a lot of reading and studying to do to make up for my barren background in literature on the farm. I wanted to get a lot of education. I got an idea of how to proceed by recalling how, when I was younger, I would sometimes correct arithmetic problems in my dreams.

My plan was to study in the evening and then go to bed at 10:30 P.M., when I'd fall asleep immediately. But I'd set my alarm clock for 1:00 A.M. I planned that I would get up at 1:00 A.M. and type out the editorial and place the typewriter on top of the pages and then go back to sleep. When I awakened the next morning, I was very surprised to see some typewritten material under my typewriter. I had no memory of getting up and writing. At every opportunity I'd write editorials in that way.

I purposely did not try to read the editorials but I kept a carbon copy. I'd place the unread editorials in the editor's mail box and every day I would look in the paper to see if I could find one written by me, but I couldn't. At the end of the week I looked at my carbon copies. There were three editorials, and all three had been published. They were mostly about the college and its relation to the community. I had not recognized my own work when it was on the printed page. I needed the carbon copies to prove it to myself.

R: Why did you decide not to look at your writing in the morning?

E: I wondered if I could write editorials. If I did not recognize my words on the printed page, that would tell me there was a lot more in my head than I realized. Then I had my proof that I was brighter than I knew. When I wanted to know something, I wanted it undistorted by somebody else's imperfect knowledge. My roommate was curious about why I jumped up at 1:00 A.M. to type. He said I did not seem to hear him when he shook my shoulder. He wondered if I was walking and typing in my sleep. I said that must be the explanation. That was my total understanding at the time. It was not till my third year in college that I took Hull's seminar and began my research in hypnosis.

R: Would this be a practical naturalistic approach for others to learn somnambulistic activity and autohypnosis? One could set an alarm clock to awaken in the middle of sleep so one could carry out some activity that could be forgotten. Would this be a way of training oneself in dissociative activity and hypnotic amnesia?

E: Yes, and after a while they would not need the alarm clock. I have trained many students this way.

AUTOHYPNOSIS IN IDENTITY CRISIS

E: I had a very bitter experience early in medical school. I was assigned to examine two patients. The first was a 73-year-old man. He was in every way an undesirable bum, alcoholic, petty thief, supported by the public his entire life. I was interested in that kind of life, so I took a careful history and learned every detail. He obviously had a good chance of living into his 80's. Then I went to see my other patient. I think she was one of the most beautiful girls I had ever seen—charming personality and highly intelligent. It was a pleasure to do a physical on her. Then, as I looked into her eyes, I found myself saying I had forgotten a task, so I asked to be excused and I would return as soon as possible. I went to the doctors' lounge and I looked into the future. That girl had Bright's disease, and if she lived another three months she'd be lucky. Here I saw the unfairness of life. A 73-year-old bum that never did anything worthwhile, never gave anything, often destructive. And here was this charming, beautiful girl who had so much to offer. I told myself, "You'd better think that over and get a perspective on life because that's what you're going to face over and over again as a doctor: the total unfairness of life."

R: What was autohypnotic about that?

E: I was alone there. I know others came in and out of the lounge but I was not aware of them. I was looking into the future.

R: How do you mean? Were your eyes open?

E: My eyes were open. I was seeing the unborn infants, the children who were yet to grow up and become such and such men and women dying in their 20's, 30's, 40's. Some living into their 80's and 90's and their particular values as people. All kinds of people. Their occupations, their lives, all went before my eyes.

R: Was this like a pseudo-orientation in time future? You lived your future life in your imagination?

E: Yes, you can't practice medicine and be upset emotionally. I had to learn to reconcile myself to the unfairness of life in that contrast between that lovely girl and that 73-year-old bum.

R: When did you realize you were in an autohypnotic state?

E: I knew I was as absorbed as when I wrote the editorials. I just let my absorption occur but I did not try to examine it. I went into that absorption to orient myself to my medical future.

R: You said to yourself, "I need to orient myself to my medical future." Then your unconscious took over and you experienced this profound reverie. So when we go into autohypnosis, we give ourselves a problem and then let the unconscious take over. The thoughts came and went by themselves? Were they cognitive or imagery?

E: They were both. I would see this little baby that grew up to be a man.

From this account we witness the spontaneous healing presence of profound reverie or autohypnosis during an identity crisis. A deep state of inner absorption which Erickson defines as trance was resorted to in order to cope with a problem that was apparently overwhelming for his conscious mind. This is another illustration of how autohypnosis and new learning are associated in Erickson's personal development.

AUTOHYPNOSIS DURING EXPERIMENTAL AND CLINICAL TRANCE WORK

E: In doing experimental hypnotic work with a subject in the laboratory I would notice we were all alone. The only thing present was the subject, the physical apparatus I was using to graph his behavior, and myself.

R: You were so focused on your work that everything else disappeared?

E: Yes, I discovered I was in a trance with my subject. The next thing I wanted to learn was, could I do equally good work with reality all around me, or did I have to go into trance. I found I could work equally well under both conditions.

R: Do you tend to go into autohypnosis now when you work with patients in trance?

E: At the present time if I have any doubt about my capacity to see the important things I go into a trance. When there is a crucial issue with a patient and I don't want to miss any of the clues, I go into trance.

Autohypnotic Experiences

R: How do you let yourself go into such trance?

E: It happens automatically because I start keeping close track of every movement, sign, or behavioral manifestation that could be important. And as I began speaking to you just now, my vision became tunnel-like and I saw only you and your chair. It happened automatically, that terrible intensity, as I was looking at you. The word "terrible" is wrong; it's pleasurable.

R: It's the same tunnel vision as sometimes happens when one does crystal gazing?

E: Yes.

Erickson now recounts a most amazing instance of when he went into trance spontaneously during the first sessions of his therapeutic work with a well-known and rather domineering psychiatrist from another country who was an experienced hypnotherapist. Erickson explains that he felt overwhelmed by his task but approached his first session with the expectation that his unconscious would come to his aid. He recalls beginning the first session and starting to write some notes. The next thing he knew he was alone in his office; two hours had passed, and there was a set of therapy notes in a closed folder on his desk. He then recognized he must have been in an autohypnotic state. Erickson respected his unconscious enough to allow his notes to remain unread in the closed folder. Spontaneously, without quite knowing how it happened, he went into a trance in the same way for the next 13 sessions. It wasn't until the 14th session that the psychiatrist-patient suddenly recognized Erickson's state. He then shouted, "Erickson, you are in trance right now!" Erickson was thus startled into normal awake state. He remained normally awake for the rest of the sessions. Erickson's profound respect for the autonomy of the unconscious is indicated by the fact that he never did read the notes he wrote while in autohypnotic trance during those first 14 sessions. The junior author recently looked at those faded pages and found they were nothing more than the typical notes a therapist might write.

On a more recent occasion Erickson was helping Dr. L experience a visual hallucination for the first time in trance. As Erickson looked at the door to his waiting room, where Dr. L was hallucinating a long hall and orchestra, Erickson also began to hallucinate it. When they later compared notes on their visions, they had an amusing dispute about just exactly where the various orchestra members were seated.

From these examples we gain a perspective of the range of autohypnotic experiences Erickson has had with his patients. A cardinal feature of all such experience is that he is always in complete rapport with the patient. He is never dissociated and out of contact with the patient. Autohypnotic trance usually comes on spontaneously and always enhances his perceptions and relations with the patient. Trance is an intensely focused attention that facilitates his therapeutic work.

THE CONSCIOUS AND UNCONSCIOUS IN AUTOHYPNOSIS

Dr. H visited Erickson to learn how to use autohypnosis.

E: You don't know all the things you can do. Use autohypnosis to explore, knowing you are going to find something that you don't know about yet.
H: Any way I can intensify my autohypnotic training?
E: No way you can consciously instruct the unconscious!
H: Is there any way *you* can consciously instruct my unconscious?
E: I don't want to. And I shouldn't, for the simple reason that you have to do things in your own way and you don't know what your way is. Now Mrs. Erickson goes into autohypnosis very deeply, but she insists on keeping her eyes open. Betty Alice likes to sit down and kick off her shoes, close her eyes, and levitate her hand to her face. Roxie, no matter what position she is in, just closes her eyes. We all have our own patterns.
H: I'd like to try to go deeper. Can I do that by myself?
E: You can go as deeply in the trance as you wish; the only thing is that you don't know when. In teaching people autohypnosis I tell them that their unconscious mind will select the time, place, and situation. Usually it's done in a much more advantageous situation than you consciously know about. I gave a resident in psychiatry those instructions and she went into autohypnosis on several occasions. Once she went into town and had breakfast with a psychologist, took a bus, met some high school friends she hadn't seen for years, went shopping with the psychologist—and he didn't know she was in a trance. She came back to the hospital and finally awakened standing in front of the mirror putting on her hat to go out. Then she noticed that the clock said 4 P.M. and the sun was coming in the westerly windows. That really scared her. She had picked up her train of thought from the morning, when she stood in front of the mirror putting on her hat, and she reawakened in that same position. She then phoned me and came over and wanted to know what to do about it. I suggested her unconscious ought to decide. So she went into a trance and told me what she wanted to do. She wanted to recall in order of time everything except the identity of her purchases. So she relived that day. Then I asked her to guess the identity of her purchases. She guessed she had bought all the things on her shopping list. But when she went home to check, she found that she bought all the things she had *formerly* wanted to purchase but had always forgotten.

Another time she presented a case conference to the professional staff without anyone realizing she was in trance. Another time she presented in front of the library club and found herself going into trance. Two visitors unexpectedly walked in, and I knew she would not see them or hear them. When one of them asked a question, I knew she would not hear it, so I got up and said, "I guess you did not hear Dr. X ask . . . " I knew she would hear my voice, and when I said "Dr. X" she was able to see him. I also mentioned Dr. Y's name so she could see him also. When the meeting was over, she thanked me for bringing them to her awareness. She said, "I forgot to make provision for unexpected visitors." *Everytime you go into trance you go prepared for all other possibilities.*

R: The conscious ego cannot tell the unconscious what to do?

E: That's right!

R: Yet that's why people want to use autohypnosis. They want to effect certain changes in themselves. When you use autohypnosis to relieve your pain, you go into trance and your unconscious cooperates with your wish to be free of pain.

E: Yes.

R: The unconscious can take a general instruction like "Relieve the pain." But the unconscious does not follow a specific instruction about how to do it exactly.

E: That's right. I have the thought, "I'd like to get rid of this pain." That's enough!

R: It's enough to enter trance with the thought: "How do I lose this weight?" "How do I give up smoking?" "How do I learn more efficiently?" These are effective ways of relating to the unconscious. You simply ask a question and let the unconscious be free to find its own way?

E: Yes. Now why should you know you've been in an autohypnotic trance?

R: The conscious mind wants to know and be able to validate the experience.

E: [E gives example of a child being unable to solve an arithmetic problem but then solving it in a dream or finding it very easy to do in the morning. Apparently the unconscious worked on it while the conscious mind was asleep.] You go into autohypnosis to achieve certain things or acquire certain knowledge. When do you need that knowledge? When you have a problem with a patient, you think it over. You work out in your unconscious mind how you're going to deal with it. Then two weeks later when the patient comes in, you say the right thing at the right moment. But you have no business knowing it ahead of time because as surely as you know it consciously, you start to improve on it and ruin it.

R: You really believe in a creative unconscious!

E: I believe in a different level of awareness.

R: So we could say the unconscious is a metaphor for another level of awareness, a metalevel?

E: I can walk down the street and not have to pay attention to the stoplight or the curb. I can climb Squaw Peak and I don't have to figure out each step.

R: Those things are being handled automatically by other levels of awareness.

Erickson's insistence on the separation of consciousness and the unconscious in autohypnosis presents a paradox: we go into autohypnosis in order to achieve certain conscious goals, yet the conscious mind cannot tell the unconscious what to do. The conscious mind can structure a general framework or ask questions, but it must be left to the autonomy of the unconscious as to how and when the desired activity will be carried out. Examples of how this takes place with pain relief are as follows:

AUTOHYPNOSIS FOR PAIN RELIEF: THE SEGMENTALIZED TRANCE

E: Yesterday I went into the house at noon to go to bed. I had to get rid of that agonizing pain here [in his back]. On my way to bed I asked my wife to prepare some grapefruit for me. The next thing I knew was that I went out and ate the grapefruit and rejoined you here in the office to continue our work. It was only then that I realized I did not have that horrible pain.

R: What did you do? Did you use autohypnosis to get rid of the pain?

E: I lay down on the bed knowing I'd better start to use autohypnosis in some way. But I don't know how I used it to get rid of the pain.

R: I see, it is a specific trance for that pain only.

E: It's a segmentalized trance.

R: Tell me more about that segmentalized trance.

E: S, with whom we worked yesterday, said her arms were numb. Not the rest of her body, only her arms. How do you get your arms numb? You segmentalize.

R: And the segmentalizing goes along with your conception of your body and not the actual distribution of sensory nerve tracts.

E: That's right. Pain is only part of your total experience, so in some way you must separate it off from your total experience. The pain was pretty agonizing here when I was in the office, so I went to bed with the intention of losing the pain. Then I forgot about losing it. When I came out here again, I suddenly realized I did not have the pain anymore.

R: Between lying on the bed and later eating the grapefruit the pain was somehow lost. But you don't know how or exactly the moment when.

E: That's right. I don't know how or exactly when, but I *knew* it would be lost. In losing it you also lose awareness that you did have pain.

R: In using autohypnosis you can tell yourself what you want to achieve but—

E: Then you leave it to your unconscious.

R: You cannot continue to question, "How am I going to lose it?" or think you can lose it consciously. This is very important in the use of autohypnosis. You can tell yourself what you want to achieve, but just exactly how and when it is achieved you have to leave to the unconscious. You must be content not to know how it is achieved.

E: Yes, that's right, because you can't know how it's achieved without keeping it with you.

R: As long as you are obsessively thinking about the pain, it is going to be there. You have to dissociate your conscious mind from the pain associations.

E: You must also have had an analogous experience such as this. [Erickson here details an example of how he would prepare a speech in his mind while driving to a conference. He could drive through the most complicated and troublesome traffic competently yet not remember a bit of it later when he found that he had arrived at the conference, since his mind had been occupied with the speech he was preparing.]

R: So there was a dissociation in your mind: part of you was automatically driving and another part preparing your speech.

The classical role of dissociation and distraction are clear in these examples together with Erickson's lack of intellectual insight about exactly how or when pain relief is achieved. It is an unconscious process. Talented and experienced as he is, however, Erickson still has difficulties, as is indicated in the following comments by his wife Elizabeth Erickson (EE).

EE: The unconscious may know more than the conscious mind, and should be left to develop its own learnings without interference, but it's not always plain sailing, and it may go about things in the wrong way.

Some of MHE's experiences with pain control have been trial-and-error, with a good deal of *error*. For example, there have been many long weary hours spent when he would analyze the sensations verbally, muscle by muscle, over and over, insisting on someone (usually me) not only listening but giving full, absorbed attention, no matter how late the hour or how urgent other duties might be. He has absolutely no memory of these sessions, and I still don't understand them. I feel they were blind alleys, but perhaps they may have involved some unconscious learnings. Then again, maybe not. The reason I mention this is that I think many people might get discouraged when the unconscious gets lost temporarily in a blind alley. The message is "Hang in there. Eventually it will work through."

DISTRACTION, DISPLACEMENT, AND REINTERPRETATION OF PAIN

E: At least for me physiological sleep will cause ordinary hypnosis to disappear. That means you should put your patients in a trance with instructions to remain in a trance until morning. In physiological sleep I simply let loose of the hypnotic frame of reference. I may awaken with pain, and I've got to reorient my frame of reference to a state of relaxation, a state of comfort, a state of well-being into which I am able to drift off into comfortable sleep. It may last for the rest of the night. Sometimes it may last no longer than two hours, so I'm awakened and must reorient to comfort. Recently the only way I could get control over the pain was by sitting in bed, pulling a chair close, and pressing my larynx against the back of the chair. That was very uncomfortable. But it was discomfort I was deliberately creating.

R: It displaced the involuntary pain?

E: Yes, I drifted into sleep restfully; then I would awaken with a sore larynx.

R: My goodness! Why did you choose this unusual way of causing yourself pain?

E: Voluntary pain is something that is under your control. And when you can control pain, it's much less painful than involuntary pain. You know you can get rid of it.

R: It gets rid of the future component of pain (Erickson, 1967). You get rid of a lot of pain of displacement and distraction.

E: Right! Distraction, displacement, and reinterpretation.

R: Reinterpretation; can you give me an example of how you've used that?

E: Okay. I had very severe shoulder pain, and my thought was I didn't like the arthritic pain. You might call it a sharp, cutting, lancinating, burning pain. So, I thought of how a red hot wire would feel just as sharp and burning. Then it suddenly felt as if I really did have a hot wire there! The arthritic pain had been deep in the shoulder, but now I had a hot wire lying across the *top* of the shoulder.

R: So you displaced the pain slightly and reinterpreted it.

E: Yes, I displaced my attention so I was still having pain, but I didn't feel it all through the shoulder joint.

R: That was a voluntary reinterpretation, so it was more tolerable.

E: It is more tolerable, and then I got bored with it and finally forgot it. You can study that sensation only so long. When you've exhausted all that you can think about it, you finally lose the pain sensations. It wasn't until about four hours later that I recalled that I had had the hot wire sensation there. I couldn't recall just when I lost it.

R: So you make good use of forgetting too.

E: One can always forget pain. One of the things I don't understand about patients is why they continue to keep their tension and pain.

R: Yes, by focusing attention on it they are actually helping it along.

UTILIZING EARLY MEMORIES TO REPLACE CURRENT PAIN

E: I get myself into a very awkward position on the bed so I cannot twitch too much. The twitching in my arms and legs and head jarred and aggravated me because I was having stabbing, lancinating, cutting pains. First here and there, very short. Overall body discomfort. I was lying on my stomach with my feet elevated and my legs crossed. My right arm was under my chest, immobilizing me. I was recovering the feeling of lying prone with my arms in front of me, head up and looking at that beautiful meadow as a child. I even felt my arm short as a child's. I went to sleep essentially reliving those childhood days when I was lying on my stomach on the hill overlooking the meadow or the green fields. They looked so beautiful and so blissful and so peaceful. Or I see woods and forest or a slowly running stream of water.

R: You tap into those internal images from childhood when your body was in fact sound and comfortable. You thereby utilize the ideomotor and ideosensory process associated with those early memories to enhance your current comfort.

E: And when I was just learning to enjoy the beauty of nature. But an inactive beauty. It was the gentle movement of the grass in the breeze, but the grass itself was not putting forth the effort.

R: That image of a lack of self-directed activity led to a corresponding peacefulness within you.

E: Yes, and that filled my mind entirely. Then when I later came out here to see a patient, I let my intensity of observation take over completely in working with her.

R: You continued to distract yourself so the pain did not have a chance to recapture your consciousness. When you fill your mind with those early childhood memories, what is actually happening? Do you feel you are reactivating those associative processes in your mind and, therefore, that simply displaces your current body pain?

E: Yes, and from a period of my life that is not very well informed, a simple and unsophisticated period. It allows a complete regression. I would have thoughts of my father and mother as they were *then*! Then I could have my own early feelings of being on the hill on the north side of the barn, etc.

R: And these feelings replaced the painful sensations you were having today?

E: Yes, I'm a visual type, so I use visual memories. [Erickson goes on to explain how he first explores a patient's early memories to determine whether they are predominantly visual or auditory. He then utilizes these predispositions in later trance work. One patient, for example, was able to distract himself from pain by focusing on the memories of the sound of crickets which he enjoyed in his childhood.]

THE WOUNDED PHYSICIAN

R: Later, when you were 51, you incurred polio again. How did you help yourself?

E: By that time I could relegate things to my unconscious because I knew I had gone through all that before. I would just go into trance saying, 'Unconscious, do your stuff.' Learning to write with my left hand the first time was very laborious. The second time I got polio my right hand was knocked out again, and I found I had to use my left, which I had not used since around 19.

R: The sense memory exercises at 17 through 19 really helped you recover the use of your right hand and your ability to walk. When you were again stricken with polio at the age of 51, you had this base of experience to draw upon and left it up to your unconscious in autohypnotic trance.

E: At the present time (age 73) I have tried repeatedly to write with my left hand. [Erickson demonstrates how he now writes by holding the pen with his right hand but guides that hand with his stronger left hand.] I'm currently holding on very carefully to everything I can do with my right hand because I'd better keep whatever use I have as long as possible.

R: I see, that's why I see you peeling potatoes in the kitchen. You certainly are an example of the archetype of the wounded physician who learns to help others through his work in healing himself. This has been the story of your life.

THE PROBLEM OF FEAR IN AUTOHYPNOSIS: THE NATURALISTIC APPROACH TO AUTOHYPNOSIS

R: Yesterday afternoon, after talking with you about autohypnosis, I let myself experience a trance by lying down comfortably and not giving myself any directions; I wanted to follow your advice and let my unconscious take over. After awhile I had a dream or dreamlike fantasy that someone was carefully pulling my floating, immobile body to the edge of a pool. I felt a bit sheepish because I wasn't drowning but had let myself get into a state where I could not move my body. Then I suddenly realized I was lying there on the couch of your waiting room in a trance and *I really couldn't move my body*. I felt a flash of oppressive fear but then tried to reassure myself that I was okay and actually experiencing a genuine body catalepsy in a deeper trance than I had ever experienced before. I tried to give myself some sensible suggestions, especially the idea that I'd be able to return to this deep state for further hypnotic work. But I guess I was simply too afraid. My mind kept running on and on with an irrational fear about what a terrible thing it would be if I really could not recover movement. After a minute or two I decided I would focus all my attention on the little finger of my right hand and just move it ever so slightly to reassure myself and as the first stage to waking up. I did just that, but now I'm sort of ashamed that after all my years of training with you, I allowed myself to fall into fear so I could not tolerate that profound trance for more than a minute or two.

E: The fright stopped you from exploring somewhat as follows: 'Here is a chance to find my body. How do I find my body? I know I've got a little finger. Next to it is another finger. If I move my little finger, I can move the next finger. And then I can progressively move all the fingers of that hand. And I know I have another hand. Shall I start moving the little finger of that hand first, or the thumb? Now what next do I want to do? Shall I start with my toes? Do I have to start with my toes? What of my sensory experience? What else can I explore in this state?'

R: What's the value of this step-by-step exercise?

E: It gives you an opportunity to learn to dissociate any part of your body. If you don't get frightened, it gives you a chance to start examining the autohypnotic state.

R: So once you somehow naturally fall into the autohypnotic state, you begin to experiment with it. It can be a study of dissociation. You can recover the movement of a few fingers and a hand and then let them go again (dissociate them) as you experiment with the other hand. You practice recovering mobility and sensation of different parts of your body and then dissociating them again as you go on to experiment with another part of your body. That could be marvelous training for hypnotic anaesthesia via dissociation. You can also experiment with altering your sensations and perceptions: warmth, cold, color, sounds, etc. That's a naturalistic approach to training yourself in autohypnosis.

E: That's right! When I awakened in a hotel room on one occasion by opening one eye, I wondered where I was because I didn't recognize anything in the room. I thought, 'I am curious to know if I can close this eye and recognize this room with the other eye.' And I did! Then I closed that eye and opened the first eye, and I was back to not knowing where I was.

R: Knowing where you were was dependent on which eye you had opened. That was a marvelous experiment with dissociation!

E: When you fall into these states, you explore them and *enjoy it*!

R: It's incredible that cognition and knowing could be associated with one eye and not the other. This is a very unusual form of dissociation.

E: You can eat something and blot out all recognition of what you're eating. And then you can let yourself discover, 'Oh yes, I've eaten this before.' You can develop an amnesia for any previous experience of eating that thing and then discover bit by bit what is familiar about it. Sometimes you recognize it by the texture, sometimes by odor and taste. You isolate each recognition factor.

R: This is an exercise in dissociation and sensory isolation that anyone could practice while awake and then later utilize that skill while in trance to develop it even further.

E: You can learn to prolong your hypnogogic and hypnopompic states (twilight zone between going to sleep and waking up) and experiment with yourself in these states. You can awaken from a dream and then go back to sleep to continue that dream. [Erickson gives an example of how, while taking a nap, he dreamed his wife was leaning against him whispering sweet things. He then awakened but still had the hallucination feeling of her body pressing comfortably against his elbow. He could no longer see or hear her as in the dream, but he took this occasion to experiment with keeping, losing, and shifting the warm and comfortable pressure of her body against his elbow. Gradually the comfortable feeling extended itself up to his shoulder, and Erickson then spent some time enjoying this feeling in his shoulder, letting go of it and then having it come back. On future occasions when he was troubled with arthritic pain in that shoulder, he let himself go into autohypnosis to receive this warm, comfortable pressure which would then gradually replace the arthritic pain. This is a clear example of how he utilized his own psychodynamic processes from a dream in a naturalistic manner.]

R: These would all be exercises in training the conscious mind to become more tolerant of the interface between consciousness and the unconscious. Gradually it can then develop certain skills in interacting with the unconscious in a way that could lead to the experience of all the classical hypnotic phenomena as well as other altered states. The conscious mind cannot control the process but it can relate to the unconscious in a creative manner. It's always an exploration, an adventure to be enjoyed, rather than a job to be done. The conscious mind can never be sure of the results; it's really the dependent partner. But once the conscious mind has developed certain skills in relating to the unconscious, it can use these skills in an emergency to influence certain sensory-perceptual and behavioral processes or whatever.

BEHAVIORAL ENRICHMENT IN AUTOHYPNOSIS

E: Why do things in just one way? [Erickson now gives numerous examples of how members of his family learned different ways of doing things: reading upside down, under water, etc.]

R: With autohypnosis we are attempting to learn greater flexibility in our functioning. We don't want to limit ourselves to one Generalized Reality Orientation (Shor, 1959). Your suggestion is that autohypnosis can be used to develop greater flexibility in the way we relate to our own behavior, sensory-perceptual processes, and cognition. We can alter and, in part, recreate our experience on practically any level. We have just begun learning how to do this. Psychedelic drugs and classical hypnotic work are relatively crude approaches we have accidentally stumbled upon in the past. We are actually engaged in sensory-perceptual and behavioral enrichment in our explorations with autohypnosis. In other words, trance is needed for new learning.

E: We lay down new pathways.

R: Trance helps depotentiate our old programs and gives us an opportunity to learn something new. The only reason why we cannot produce an anaesthesia at will, for example, is because we don't know how to give up our habitual generalized reality orientation that emphasizes the importance of pain and gives it primacy in consciousness. But if we allowed young children to experiment with their sensory perceptual processes in a fun way, they might easily develop skills with anaesthesia that could be very useful when they needed it. This would be an interesting piece of research, indeed.

SELF-ANALYSIS AND MEMORIES IN AUTOHYPNOSIS: THE IMPORTANCE OF FORGETTING AND NOT KNOWING

E: If you want to do autohypnosis, do it privately. Sit down in a quiet room and *don't decide what you are going to do*. Just go into a trance. Your unconscious will carry out the thing that needs to be done. But you can set an alarm to awaken by because you don't know yet how to measure time with your unconscious mind. And you ought to have a good time. And bear in mind that comic strip of Mutt and Jeff, where Mutt looked in all his pockets but one for his wallet, because if it wasn't there, he was afraid he would drop dead. You can be free to inquire into yourself instead of dropping dead when you discover something you don't want to know about yourself. Just *forget* it. You don't know just how much your unconscious wants you to know.

R: Have you used autohypnosis for memory problems?

E: You can go into autohypnotic trance for a memory problem. You may want to recall where you put that letter. Whose birthday have I forgotten? You may begin with hand levitation, but you don't know when you lose your hearing, your vision, your sense of your hand. Then spontaneously there comes to mind the memory you are searching for. [Erickson gives other examples of how he will ask his wife, who is reading, for the name of a certain poet. She keeps on reading and in a few minutes the name pops into her mind. Another colleague assigns her memory problems to a "little man up there in my head" and in a few minutes he gives her the answer. Others use a conscious associative approach recalling the circumstances surrounding the memory or fact they want to recall.] Years ago, after examining a house with lovely date trees which we found satisfactory for our family, I knew I had another reason for buying it. I knew it was a very strong reason but I did not know what it was. I spent a lot of time trying to find it. I bought the house in April and in September I got a sudden urge to find out why I bought the house. So I went into autohypnosis, but nothing came except a view of myself in grammar school in the fourth grade. I knew that must be important, but why? On a subsequent day I was in the backyard and then I recalled that I made a very solemn promise to myself in the fourth grade. I was reading a geography book with an illustration of a boy climbing a date tree. I promised myself that when I got to be a man I would climb a date tree. And I did climb that tree and pick those dates.

R: The memory came in two stages.

E: During trance I saw myself as a boy in the fourth grade looking at a book, but that did not go far enough. I was looking for the *reason* but not the *identity*. I bought the house to satisfy a fourth-grade boy's wish, so in a trance I just saw that fourth-grade boy sitting at his desk. It wasn't until I sat in the backyard looking at the trees that the whole thing came to me.

This example illustrates at least three factors of importance in memory work with autohypnosis. (1) There is frequently a prime time for going into autohypnosis when one feels an "urge" to find something. That "urge" is actually a means by which the unconscious is letting consciousness know that something is available at this time. (2) The unconscious is very literal. In this example it showed Erickson the "identity" in a fourth-grade boy but not the "reason" or why of the fourth-grader. (3) Finally, the unconscious takes time: between April and September to come forth with the first half of the reason and then another few days until circumstances were just right for consciousness to receive the why of it. Consciousness is not always aware of all the contingencies of such memory recall. Because of this much patience is required as it learns to cooperate with the dynamics of unconscious processes. Because the conscious mind rarely recognizes what is involved, it is very important that we give our unconscious as much freedom as possible to work things out. When we do make suggestions, they should be as broad as possible (Erickson, Rossi, Rossi, 1976).

NIRVANA OR AUTOHYPNOSIS AS A DISSOCIATION FROM ALL SENSE MODALITIES

On one occasion Erickson was doing some experimental work with K on stopped vision (Erickson, 1967), wherein she experienced being in "the middle of nowhere." Erickson recalled the following:

> *E:* I was in the backyard a year ago in the summertime. I was wondering what far-out experiences I'd like to have. As I puzzled over that, I noticed that I was sitting out in the middle of nowhere. I was an object in space.
> *K:* There you have it: the middle of nowhere.
> *E:* I was just an object in space. Of all the buildings I couldn't see an outline. I couldn't see the chair in which I was sitting; in fact, I couldn't feel it.
> *R:* You spontaneously experienced that vision?
> *E:* It was the most far-out thing I could do!
> *R:* That was the most far-out thing you could do?
> *E:* You can't get more far-out than that!
> *R:* It just happened to you as you were wondering about what you could do?

E: Yes.
R: An unconscious responding?
E: And that was my unconscious' full response.
R: I see; you can't get more far-out than that.
E: What more far-out could happen?
K: You were just floating or just a nothingness?
E: I was just an object and all alone with me was an empty void. No buildings, earth, stars, sun.
K: What emotions did you experience? Did you——curiosity or fear or apprehension?
E: It was one of the most pleasing experiences. What is this? Tremendous comfort. I knew that I was doing something far-out. And I was really doing it! And what greater joy is there than doing what you want to do? Inside the stars, the planets, the beaches. I couldn't feel the weight. I couldn't feel the earth. No matter how much I pushed down my feet, I couldn't feel anything.
R: That sounds like a spontaneous experience of nirvana or samadhi wherein Indian yogis say they experience "the void." You feel that is so?
E: Yes. The far-out experience of negating all reality-related stimuli.
R: That's what the yogis train themselves to do.
E: Yes, just negating the stimuli from the reality objects.
K: You found that pleasurable?
E: I always find when I can do something, it's pleasurable.

DISCUSSION

From his earliest memories and spontaneous initial experiences with altered states, Erickson developed a precocious attitude of wonderment about the relativity of human experience. His own constitutional problems forced an early recognition of individual differences in sensory-perceptual functioning and the surprising limitations in the world-view of most of the people around him. The motivation for his initial studies in hypnosis with Clark Hull in 1923 thus came from very personal sources and life experiences. Erickson's earliest autohypnotic experience centered around a process of learning; it was a creative moment of insight when he finally saw the difference between a 3 and the letter m in a hallucinatory flash of blinding light. In this early experience we see the beginning of a pattern wherein altered states and new learning are usually associated. In this sense Erickson is an original in the history of hypnosis; his earliest motivation came from personal sources having to do with problems of learning and altered modes of sensory-perceptual functioning rather than the traditional interest in psychopathology which was characteristic of earlier workers. From

Autohypnotic Experiences

these earliest experiences came his understanding of autohypnosis or trance as an altered state in which important, internal sensory-perceptual or cognitive processes could so occupy consciousness that our ordinary, everyday reality (the generalized reality orientation) could be "blocked" out, eclipsed, or depotentiated.

In his earliest experiences with self-rehabilitation by recalling early sense memories to help him relearn how to use his muscles, we witness his gradual discovery of some of the basic principles of hypnosis. Recalling early sense memories gave rise to ideomotor and ideosensory processes that could be the basis for relearning functions lost through illness. This is actually the origin of Erickson's *utilization* approaches to inducing trance as well as evoking and maximizing behavioral potentials in the therapy of organic and psychological problems. When he says, "Slowly I learned that if I could think about walking and fatigue and relaxation, I could get [pain] relief" he was discovering for himself how relaxation and the fixation of attention on inner realities could replace maladaptive or painful aspects of the generalized reality orientation.

Erickson's emphasis on real sense memories rather than imagination is reminescent of Bernheim's (1957) basic conception of suggestion as an enhancement of ideomotor and ideosensory processes whereby there is an "unconscious transformation of the thought into movement . . . sensation, or into a sensory image." Bernheim gives illustrations of how such ideodynamic processes operate by evoking "memory-images" within the subjects, which are then reexperienced as the suggested hypnotic phenomenon. This use of the patient's repertory of memory images and experiential learnings is the basis of Erickson's *utilization theory of hypnotic suggestion* (Erickson and Rossi, 1976). The utilization of the patient's previous learnings in hypnotic responsiveness has been discussed by Weitzenhoffer (1953) and has been recently rediscovered experimentally (Johnson and Barber, 1976). Further research will be needed to determine the relative contributions made by utilizing the patient's repertory of memories and learnings versus pure imagination (Sheehan, 1972) in hypnotic responsiveness. We expect that certain aspects of trance induction, deepening, and involvement may be a function of imagination, but specific ideodynamic responses may be more a function of whatever accumulated learnings and memories the patients can utilize to mediate the suggested phenomenon.

Erickson's accidental activation of what appears to have been a somnambulistic state during which he wrote his student editorials was another personal source of his understanding of trance. The amnesia that one usually has for somnambulistic activity thereafter became an important criterion for deep trance work and some forms of hypnotherapy (Erickson and Rossi, 1974). These personal somnambulistic experiences are also the basis on which he has trained others in what we may term the "naturalistic approach" to autohypnotic experience.

Erickson likes to emphasize that consciousness does not know how to do autohypnosis; consciousness can only set the stage for it to happen. The major difficulty in learning autohypnosis is in the desire of the conscious mind to control the process. For autohypnotic states to develop, consciousness must first give up control and lose itself so the unconscious can become manifest. The paradox of autohypnosis is that we go into trance because we are interested in controlling or at least altering certain aspects of behavior that are usually autonomous or unconscious in their functioning. Yet, Erickson insists, the conscious mind cannot control the unconscious. The paradox is resolved by (1) preparing ourselves to experience trance by, for example, arranging a period in which we can be comfortable and undisturbed, then allowing the unconscious to lead us as it will. (2) Once the conscious mind recognizes an altered state has been achieved (by the presence of spontaneous alterations of sensory, perceptual, motor, or cognitive processes), however, it can begin to experiment with those alterations by enhancing and diminishing them, transforming them in some way, relocating them, etc. In this way the conscious mind is engaged in a new pattern of learning: how to recognize and tolerate altered modes of functioning and eventually even modify and control them. The extent to which practitioners of yoga and other spiritual traditions are able to modify and transform their inner experience provides us with illustrations of what is possible with sufficient sensitivity to our altered states and awareness of our physiological functions. We can theoretically learn to accomplish with autohypnosis all those alterations that have been facilitated by the technology of biofeedback (Overlade, 1976). In this sense autohypnosis becomes a means of extending or broadening the range of human experience. It becomes a means of exploring and maximizing human potentialities. This exploration can be enhanced by an attitude of expectation and respect for the potentials of the unconscious and the new modes of functioning that can be learned. Consciousness can never be certain of what is going to be experienced, but it can learn to interact constructively with whatever altered mode of functioning the unconscious makes available.

A major difficulty in this new learning is fear, a natural fear that comes about whenever our Generalized Reality Orientation (Shor, 1959) is interrupted and restructured. Erickson developed his approaches through trial and error, and as we have seen from his wife's comments, there may have been much tedious effort lost in blind alleys where the unconscious or, rather, the creative interaction between the conscious and unconscious, went astray. Much time and effort can be wasted and less resolute individuals may become discouraged. Because of this it is wise to have an experienced guide monitor one's autohypnotic work. This can take place within the traditional formats of psychotherapy, specialized workshops, or experimental programs where careful records are kept and guidance is available (Fromm, 1973, 1974).

II. Approaches to Trance Induction

The papers in this section on trance induction are among Erickson's most original contributions to the art of hypnosis and to an understanding of its dynamics. Previously, hypnotic induction was conceptualized as something that was done to the subjects to put them in an altered state. There were various means and techniques for seizing the subjects' attention and "putting them under." The history of hypnosis is very much a history of the various methods of hypnotic induction and the theories elaborated to explain the methods. All too often there was an overemphasis on external manipulation and the use of fanciful lights and gadgets that purportedly put people into trance.

With the first short paper in this section, "Historical note on hand levitation and ideomotor techniques," Erickson traces the series of experiences and discoveries that led him to an understanding of the role of ideomotor and ideosensory processes in trance induction. As he states it, "The essential consideration in the use of ideomotor techniques lies not in their elaborateness or novelty but simply in the initiation of motor activity . . . as a means of fixing and focusing the subject's attention upon inner experiential learnings and capacities." This statement contains the basic insight that is a major consideration in all his hypnotic work: How do we help subjects get in contact with their own unique repertory of "inner experiential learnings and capacities" that are the actual raw material for hypnotic responsiveness?

Most of the incredible variety of approaches to trance induction that Erickson then developed throughout his career were evolved in an effort to answer this question. The *naturalistic techniques of hypnosis* utilized the subjects' own naturally occurring behaviors in the "here and now" situation to focus attention inward and gradually facilitate trance behavior. No longer were external devices needed to induce trance: Internal memories of crystal balls or ticking metronomes were found to be more effective than the real external objects. No longer were rote formulas and verbal commands or incantations needed: A casual conversational approach that evoked the subjects' own natural areas of interest was found to be more universally effective in facilitating the inner focus and comfort so characteristic of trance.

Erickson has frequently commented in informal discussions that "confusion is the basis of most of my approaches to trance induction." In one way or another momentary periods of confusion were found useful to help overintellectualized or "resistant" patients bypass their all-too-rigid conscious mental sets so that they could more readily get into contact with their own inner experiencing. The "surprise," "my friend John," and "pantomime" approaches to trance induction all share this common feature of helping subjects bypass their learned limitations so they can better realize inner potentials for responding in the involuntary manner characteristic of hypnotic responsiveness.

Included in this section is "A transcript of a trance induction with commentary," published in association with Haley and Weakland in 1959. This paper marks the beginning of a new period in the recognition and analysis of Erickson's unique contributions. It presents the most detailed analysis of an entire trance induction that had ever been done up till then, and became a model of much of the future work done by others seeking an understanding of Erickson's work. For the first time a detailed, phrase-by-phrase, word-by-word analysis of the dynamics of trance induction was undertaken. The significance of voice dynamics, minimal sensory cues, gesture, metaphor, implication, and many other forms of indirect suggestion in hypnotic work were beginning to be recognized in all their manifold complexities. The apparently bewildering array of innovations in Erickson's approaches to trance induction all share this one significant feature in common: *They illustrate how indirect suggestions and minimal cues that evoke and utilize the subject's own associations are the real basis of the hypnotherapist's skill.* This is particularly evident in the last three papers of this section, which were unpublished previously.[1] No longer could trance induction be seen as a simple ritual or mechanical technique. The approaches to trance induction were now very much dependent upon the therapists' observations and understanding of their patients' motivations and world-views. Therapists were now required to have a much greater understanding of how they were using verbal and nonverbal forms of communication.

The result of this greater understanding was that failures in trance induction could no longer be attributed to a subject's resistance or inability to experience trance. Everyone could experience trance; but did the operator have sufficient understanding and skill to facilitate a uniquely satisfying trance experience for a particular person in a particular situation? This places a much greater demand on researchers and clinicians to develop their understanding and skills if they want to do successful hypnotic work. On the other hand it also relieves them of the ill-assumed burden of control they had erroneously held themselves responsible for in the past. The operator needs to develop certain skills in understanding the subject and the presentation of suggestions as appropriate stimuli for hypnotic experience; the actual content of what is experienced, however, is a function of the subject's own repertory of inner potentials and life experiences. The operator offers the possibility of hypnotic behavior; the subject actually does the work of learning to experience responsiveness in the hypnotic modality.

---

[1] Another significant paper details Erickson's discovery and utilization of minimal sensory cues. It is "A field investigation by hypnosis of sound loci importance in human behavior," which appears in Volume 2 of this series.

5. Historical Note on the Hand Levitation and Other Ideomotor Techniques

Milton H. Erickson

In the spring of 1923 at the University of Wisconsin, interest in the writer's experimental work on hypnosis was expressed by Clark L. Hull, Ph.D., Associate Professor of Psychology. The suggestion was offered that the writer continue his studies throughout the summer and then report upon them before a postgraduate seminar on hypnosis to be conducted by the psychology department.

All of this was done, and the first formal postgraduate course in hypnosis was initiated at the University of Wisconsin in September, 1923, probably the first one in the United States. This seminar was devoted to a systematic examination and discussion of the summer's experimental procedures and findings reported upon or demonstrated before the group. Also presented was additional work initiated and performed by the writer during that academic year.

During that summer of 1923, among other things, the author became interested in automatic writing, first secured from subjects in a trance state and subsequently by posthypnotic suggestion. This gave rise to the possibility of using suggestions conducive to automatic writing as an indirect technique of trance induction for naive subjects. Although successful, it proved to be too slow and laborious an induction technique in most instances. It was modified by suggesting to the subjects that, instead of writing, the pencil point would merely move up and down on the paper or from side to side. The vertical or horizontal lines thus secured were later found to be an excellent approach to the teaching of automatic writing to difficult subjects.

Almost from the first trial it was recognized that the pencil and paper were superfluous and that the ideomotor activity was the primary consideration. Accordingly, the writer using his younger sister Bertha as a subject for the first time, induced a somnambulistic trance by a simple hand-levitation technique. Thereafter many variations of this original technique were devised, until it became apparent that the effectiveness of many supposedly different techniques of trance induction derived only from a basic use of ideomotor activity rather

---

Reprinted with permission from *The American Journal of Clinical Hypnosis,* January, 1961, *3*, 196-199.

than from variations of procedure, as is sometimes naively believed and reported. Perhaps of all the many variations of ideomotor techniques of induction that may be devised, the more generally useful are (1) simple direct hand levitation, because of the possibility of visual participation, and (2) the slightly more complex rhythmical hand levitation, in which visual and memory participation frequently lead to the ideosensory response of auditory hallucinations of music and the development of a somnambulistic trance.

Another highly technical and complicated procedure of trance induction was developed that summer and repeated in many variations, but with no real understanding at that time of what was involved. A 16-year-old boy who regularly drove a milk wagon had never before been hypnotized. He was asked to sit quietly in a chair and silently review in his own mind every feeling throughout his body as he systematically recalled the events of the 20-mile milk route over which he regularly drove a team of horses. The further explanation was given that, even as one can remember names, places, things, and events, so could one remember body feelings of all sorts and kinds. This he was to do by sitting quietly in the chair with his eyes closed and imagining himself driving along the highway, feeling the reins in his hands and the motions of the wagon and of the wagon seat.

Shortly it was noticed that he was shifting his hands and body in a manner suggestive of the actual experience of driving a team of horses. Suddenly he braced his feet, leaned backward, and presented the appearance of pulling hard on the reins. Immediately he was asked, "What are you doing now?" His reply was, as he opened his eyes, "Going down Coleman hill." (The writer himself had often driven that same milk route in the same wagon and recognized the characteristic behavior of handling the team in going down that steep, tortuous hill!)

Thereafter, with his eyes open and obviously in a somnambulistic trance, although he continued to sit in the chair, the boy went through a long, slow process of seemingly driving the horses, turning now right, now left, and heaving with his shoulders as if lifting cans of milk, thus reliving largely the experience of actually driving the milk route. The writer's own experience with that same milk route permitted a ready recognition of the progress being made along the route.

However, at one particular stretch of the road where there were no farmhouses, the boy went through the motions of pulling on the reins and calling "Whoa!" He was told to "drive on" and replied "Can't." After many futile efforts to induce him to continue driving and always eliciting the same response of "Can't," he was asked why he couldn't. The laconic reply of "Geese" was given. The writer immediately recalled that on infrequent occasions in his own experience a certain flock of geese happened to choose the moment of the milk wagon's arrival to cross the highway in single file on their way to another pond, thus stopping traffic.

This first trance lasted several hours as the boy went through the events of

Ideomotor Techniques

the "trip," and it seemed impossible to break into and interrupt it. Not until he turned the horses into the home driveway could the trance be terminated.

This particular trip was repeated later in similarly induced trances with similar results. The boy was also asked to relive other trips, in none of which the geese happened to appear, but his neglect of the established practice of letting the horses rest at a certain customary spot was disclosed in one such reliving.

At the time of this work there was no recognition by the writer of kinesthetic memories and images as a trance-induction technique, but it led to a systematic and profitable investigation of the possibility of using any sensory modality as a basic process in inducting hypnotic trances.

During his first demonstration of the hand-levitation technique of trance induction to that 1923-1924 seminar group, a special finding was made by the writer of the spontaneous manifestation in a volunteer subject of hallucinated ideomotor activity. She had volunteered to act as a subject for a demonstration of what the writer meant by a "hand-levitation trance induction." While she and the group intently watched her hands as they rested on her lap, the writer offered repeated, insistent, appropriate suggestions for right hand levitation, all without avail. Silent study of the subject in an effort to appraise the failure of response disclosed her gaze to be directed into midair at shoulder level, and her facial expression and apparent complete detachment from her surroundings indicated that a deep trance state had developed. She was told to elevate her left hand voluntarily to the level of her right hand. Without any alteration of the direction of her gaze, she brought her left hand up to shoulder level. She was told to replace her left hand in her lap and then to watch her right hand "slowly descend" to her lap. When it reached her lap, she was to give immediately a full verbal report upon her experience. There resulted a slow downward shifting of her gaze, and as it reached her lap, she looked up at the group and delightedly gave an extensive description of the "sensations" of her hallucinatory experience, with no realization that she had actually developed her first known trance state, but with an amnesia for the reality of the trance experience as such, though not for the content.

She asked to be allowed to repeat her experience and promptly did so. This time the group watched her eye and facial behavior. Again there was no hand movement, but all agreed that she developed a somnambulistic trance immediately upon beginning to shift her gaze upward. This conclusion was put to test at once by demonstrating with her the phenomena of deep hypnosis. She was then aroused, and there followed an extensive discussion of "kinesthetic imagery" or "kinesthetic memories" as possible techniques of hypnotic induction. The writer was assigned the task of further experimental work on these ideas, to be reported at the next meeting.

That report, in brief, was simply that trances could be induced in both naive or experienced subjects by techniques based upon (1) the visualization of a motor activity such as hand levitation or by visualizing the self climbing up or down a long stairway, and (2) upon "remembering the body and muscle and joint feeling and sensations" of motor activity of many kinds. To this was added the report on the findings with the 16-year-old boy.

Approximately 15 years after these earlier studies on ideomotor techniques had been reported to the seminar group at the University of Wisconsin, another study was begun. This was initiated by the observation that, especially at lectures on controversial topics, there are those in the audience who will unconsciously slowly nod or shake their heads in agreement or disagreement with the lecturer. This observation was further enhanced by noting that certain patients, while explaining their problems, will unwittingly nod or shake their heads contradictorily to their actual verbalizations. These informative manifestations suggested the possibility of utilizing this type of ideomotor activity as a hypnotic technique, particularly for resistant or difficult subjects, although it can also be used readily on naive subjects.

The actual technique is relatively simple. The explanation is offered to the subject that an affirmative or a negative answer can be given by a simple nod or shake of the head. Also, it is explained that thinking can be done separately and independently by both the conscious and unconscious mind, but that such thinking need not necessarily be in agreement. This is followed by asking some question phrased to require an answer independent of what the subject may be thinking consciously. Such a question is, "Does your unconscious mind think you will learn to go into a trance?" After being asked this type of question, the subject is told to await patiently and passively the answering head movement, which will constitute the answer of his "unconscious mind." A rapid or forceful response signifies a "conscious mind" reply. A slow, gentle head movement, sometimes not perceived by the subject, constitutes a direct communication from the "unconscious mind." With the response catalepsy develops, and a trance state ensues rapidly.

Or, as a simple variation, one can suggest that the levitation of one hand signifies the answer "yes," the levitation of the other, "no," the levitation of both, "I don't know," and then ask the above or a comparable question. The development of a trance state is concurrent with the development of levitation regardless of the significance of the reply.

These techniques are of particular value with patients who want hypnosis, who could benefit from it, but who resist any formal or overt effort at trance induction and who need to have their obstructive resistances bypassed. The essential consideration in the use of ideomotor techniques lies not in their elaborateness or novelty but simply in the initiation of motor activity, either real or hallucinated, as a means of fixating and focussing the subjects' attention upon inner experiential learnings and capabilities.

6. Deep Hypnosis and Its Induction

Milton H. Erickson

GENERAL CONSIDERATIONS

A primary problem in all hypnotic work is the induction of satisfactory trance states. Especially is this true in any work based upon deep hypnosis. Even the problem of inducing light trance states and maintaining them at a constant level is often a difficult task. The securing of comparable degrees of hypnosis in different subjects and similar trance states in the same subject at different times frequently constitutes a major problem.

The reasons for these difficulties derive from the fact that hypnosis depends upon inter- and intrapersonal relationships. Such relationships are inconstant and alter in accord with personality reactions to each hypnotic development. Additionally, each individual personality is unique, and its patterns of spontaneous and responsive behavior necessarily vary in relation to time, situation, purposes served, and the personalities involved.

Statistically, certain averages may be obtained for hypnotic behavior, but such averages do not represent the performance of any one subject. Hence they cannot be used to appraise either individual performances or specific hypnotic phenomena. To judge trance depths and hypnotic responses, consideration must be given not only to average responses but to the various deviations from the average that may be manifested by the individual. For example, catalepsy is a fairly standard form of hypnotic behavior, appearing usually in the light trance and persisting in the deep trance states. However, extensive experience will disclose that some subjects may never spontaneously develop catalepsy as a single phenomenon either in the light or deep trance. Others may manifest it only in the lighter stages of hypnosis, some only in the profound trances, and some only in the transition from the light to the deeper levels of hypnosis. Even more confusing are those subjects who manifest it only in relation to other types of hypnotic behavior, such as amnesia. However good an indicator of trance states catalepsy may be on the average, its presence or absence for any one subject must be interpreted entirely in terms of that subject's total hypnotic behavior.

Reprinted with permission from *Experimental Hypnosis*, Leslie M. LeCron (editor). New York, Macmillan, 1952, pp. 70-114. Copyright 1952 by Leslie M. LeCron.

Efforts have been made to solve some of these difficulties by developing special techniques for the induction and regulation of hypnotic trances, sometimes with little regard for the nature of hypnotic behavior. One of the most absurd of these endeavors, illustrative of a frequent tendency to disregard hypnosis as a phenomenon in favor of an induction technique as a rigidly controllable process apart from the subject's behavior, was the making of phonograph records. This was done on the assumption that identical suggestions would induce identical hypnotic responses in different subjects and at different times. There was a complete oversight of the individuality of subjects, their varying capacities to learn and to respond, and their differing attitudes, frames of reference, and purposes for engaging in hypnotic work. There was oversight of the importance of *interpersonal relationships* and of the fact that these are both contingent and dependent upon the *intrapsychic* or *intrapersonal relationships* of the subject.

Even in so established a field as pharmacology a standardized dose of a drug is actually an approximation so far as the individual's physiological response is concerned. When thought is given to the difficulty of "standardizing" such intangibles as inter- and intrapersonal relationships, the futility of a rigid hypnotic technique "to secure controlled results" is apparent. An awareness of the variability of human behavior and the need to meet it should be the basis of all hypnotic techniques.

In the problem of developing general techniques for the induction of trances and the eliciting of hypnotic behavior, there have been numerous uncritical utilizations of traditional misconceptions of hypnotic procedure. The "eagle eye," the "crystal ball," strokings and passes, and similar aids as sources of mysterious force have been discarded by the scientifically trained. Yet the literature abounds with reports of hypnotic techniques based upon the use of apparatus intended to limit and restrict the subjects' behavior, to produce fatigue and similar reactions, as if they were the essential desiderata of hypnosis: Crystal balls held at a certain distance from the eyes, revolving mirrors, metronomes, and flashing lights are often employed as the major consideration. As a result, too much emphasis is placed upon external factors and the subjects' responses to them. Primarily, emphasis should be placed upon the intrapsychic behavior of the subjects rather than upon the relationship to externalities. At best, apparatus is only an incidental aid, to be discarded at the earliest possible moment in favor of the utilization of the subjects' behavior, which may be initiated but not developed by the apparatus. However much staring at a crystal ball may be conducive to fatigue and sleep, neither of these results is an essential part of the hypnotic trance. To illustrate: A number of subjects were systematically trained by a competent hypnotist to develop a trance by staring fixedly at a crystal ball held at a distance of six inches and slightly above the subjects' eye level. As a result of this conditioning, efforts to hypnotize them without a crystal ball were difficult and, in some instances, ineffectual. Personal experimentation with these subjects disclosed that having them simply imagine that they were looking at a crystal ball resulted in more rapid trance induction and more profound trance states. Repetition of this procedure by colleagues and students yielded similar results. Return to the actual crystal gazing resulted in the original slower and less profound trances characterized by greater dependence upon external factors.

Numerous experiments by the author and his colleagues in which experienced subjects watched silent pendulums or listened to soft music or to metronomes disclosed that imaginery aids were much more effective than actual apparatus. The same findings were obtained with naive subjects. Medical students were divided into two groups: One stared at a crystal ball and the other merely tried to visualize a crystal ball. The latter group achieved more rapid and better results. The experiment was repeated by having the second group listen to a metronome while the first group was instructed to depend upon auditory imagery of a metronome. Again the imaginary aid proved the more effective. Numerous variations yielded similar results. The utilization of imagery rather than actual apparatus permits the subjects to utilize their actual capabilities without being hampered by an adjustment to nonessential externalities. This has been found true with experienced subjects as well as naive subjects, and in the whole range of imagery from visual to kinesthetic.

The utilization of imagery in trance induction almost always facilitates the development of similar or related more complex hypnotic behavior. For example, the subject who experiences much difficulty in developing hallucinations often learns to develop them when a trance is induced by utilization of imagery.

Subjective accounts from many subjects explaining these findings may be summarized as follows: "When I listen to the imaginary metronome, it speeds up or slows down, gets louder or fainter, as I start to go into a trance, and I just drift along. With the real metronome, it remains distractingly constant, and it keeps pulling me back to reality instead of letting me drift along into a trance. The imaginary metronome is changeable and always fits in with just the way I'm thinking and feeling, but I have to fit myself to the real one."

In this same connection mention should be made of findings in experimental and clinical work centering around hypnotically induced visual hallucinations. For example, a patient greatly confused about her personal identity was induced to visualize a number of crystal balls in which she could hallucinate a whole series of significant life experiences, make objective and subjective comparisons, and thus establish the continuity of her life, from one hallucinated experience to the next. With a real crystal ball the hallucinated experiences were physically limited in extent, and the changing and superimposition of "scenes" much less satisfying.

Another important general consideration in trance induction concerns the appreciation of time as a factor in itself. Traditionally, the mystic force of a single glance from the eagle eye is sufficient to induce hypnosis. This misconception has not really been discredited, since statements can be found in current literature to the effect that two to five minutes' time is sufficient to induce the profound neuro- and psychophysiological changes of hypnosis. When administering a powerful drug, these same writers would wait a reasonable time for its effects. The expectation of practically instantaneous results from the spoken word indicates an uncritical approach which militates against scientifically valid results. Unfortunately, much published work has been based upon an unrecognized belief in the immediate omnipotence of hypnotic suggestions and a failure to appreciate that responsive behavior in the hypnotic subjects as in unhypnotized persons, depends upon a time factor. Hypnotic subjects are often expected, in a few moments, to reorient themselves completely psychologically and physiologically, and to perform complex tasks ordinarily impossible in the nonhypnotic state.

Subjects vary in respect to time requirements, and their time requirements vary greatly from one type of behavior to another and also in relation to their immediate frame of reference. Some subjects who can develop visual hallucinations promptly may require a relatively prolonged time to develop auditory hallucinations. The presence of a certain mood may facilitate or hinder hypnotic responses. Incidental considerations may interfere with the development of hypnotic phenomena ordinarily possible for a subject. The fact that the author is a psychiatrist has more than once militated against subjects' readily developing auditory hallucinations.

Certain subjects can develop profound trances in a brief period of time and are capable of readily manifesting exceedingly complex hypnotic phenomena. However, critical study of such subjects frequently discloses a high incidence of "as if" behavior. Such a subject instructed, for example, to develop negative hallucinations for observers present will behave *as if* those persons were absent, accomplishing this primarily by avoidance reactions and inhibition of responses. If such behavior is accepted as valid and as the most that can be expected, the subject is likely to remain arrested at that level of functioning. If such subjects are given adequate time to reorganize their neuro- and psychophysiological processes, negative hallucinations can be developed which will withstand searching test procedures.

The ease with which a deep trance can be induced in a subject is too often uncritically accepted as a valid criterion of subsequent trance performances. Experience with many such subjects discloses a frequent tendency to return to a lighter trance state when given complicated hypnotic tasks. Such subjects for various reasons are thereby endeavoring to ensure adequate functioning by enlisting the aid of conscious mental processes. Hence unreliable and contradictory experimental findings are frequently obtained when apparently the experimental procedure was fully controlled.

Neither should the ease and rapidity of trance induction be mistaken as a valid indication of the ability to maintain a trance state. Easy hypnotizability may indicate a need to allow adequate time for a reorientation of the subject's total behavior to permit full and sustained responses. To believe that the subject who readily develops a deep trance will remain deeply hypnotized indefinitely is a naive assumption.

There are those subjects who hypnotize easily, develop a great variety of complex hypnotic behavior, and yet fail to learn some minor hypnotic adjustment. To illustrate, an excellent subject capable of amazingly complex hypnotic behavior was found to have extreme difficulty in relation to physical orientation. All experimental studies with him had to be done in a laboratory setting; otherwise his functioning tended to be at an "as if" level. However, a hallucinatory laboratory situation was as satisfactory to him as a genuine laboratory. Another capable subject, easily hypnotized, could not develop dissociation and depersonalization states unless she was first induced to hallucinate herself elsewhere, preferably at home reading a book. Once this was done, inconsistencies in her dissociative behavior disappeared. With both subjects, effort to economize on time in establishing the laboratory or home situation, despite their rapid hypnotizability, resulted in faulty hypnotic responses. The general situation, even as time considerations, may be an essential factor in the development and maintenance of satisfactory trances.

The oversight and actual neglect of time as an important factor in hypnosis and the disregard of the individual needs of subjects account for much contradiction in hypnotic studies. Published estimates of the hypnotizability of the general population range from 5-70 percent and even higher. The lower estimates are often due to a disregard of time as an important factor in the development of hypnotic behavior. Personal experience extending over 35 years with well over 3,500 hypnotic subjects has confirmed the importance of subject individuality and time values. One of the author's most capable subjects required less than 30 seconds to develop his first profound trance, with subsequent equally rapid and consistently reliable hypnotic behavior. A second remarkably competent subject required 300 hours of systematic labor before a trance was even induced; thereafter, a 20-30-minute period of trance induction was requisite to secure valid hypnotic behavior.

Ordinarily a total of four to eight hours of initial induction training is sufficient. Then, since trance induction is one process and trance utilization is another—to permit the subjects to reorganize behavioral processes in accord with projected hypnotic work, time must necessarily be alloted with full regard for their capacities to learn and to respond. For example, muscular rigidity is usually produced in a few moments, but a satisfactory anaesthesia or analgesia for childbirth may take hours in divided training periods.

The length of time subjects have been engaged in hypnotic work and the variety of their hypnotic experience are important factors in hypnotic research. Often, subjects are transients, serving in only one or two experimental studies. Personal experience, as well as that of colleagues, has demonstrated that the more extensive and varied a subject's hypnotic experience is, the more effectively a subject can function in complicated problems. The author prefers to do research with subjects who have experienced hypnosis repeatedly over a long period of time and who have been called upon to manifest a great variety of hypnotic phenomena. Lacking this, the subjects are systematically trained in different types of hypnotic behavior. In training subjects for hypnotic anaesthesia for obstetrical pruposes, they may be taught automatic writing and negative visual hallucinations as a preliminary foundation. The former is taught as a foundation for local dissociation of a body part and the latter as a means of instruction in not responding to stimuli. Such training might seem irrelevant, but experience has disclosed that it can be a highly effective procedure in securing the full utilization of the subjects' capabilities. The goal sought is often infinitely more important than the apparent logic of the procedure, and the mere testing of a hypnotic procedure should not be regarded as a testing of the possibility of hypnotic phenomena.

The foregoing has been presented as general background. Now more specific discussion will be offered concerning the nature of deep trances and their induction, but not with any view of trying to describe a specific technical procedure. The variability of subjects, the individuality of their general and immediate needs, their differences in time and situation requirements, the uniqueness of their personalities and capabilities, together with the demands made by the projected work, render impossible any absolutely rigid procedure. At best a rigid procedure can be employed to determine its effectiveness in securing certain results; as such it is a measure of itself primarily and not of the inherent nature of the results obtained. This is even more apparent when it is recognized that trance induction for experiments is actually a preliminary to trance utilization which belongs to another category of behavior. Such utilization depends not upon the procedure employed to secure a trance, but upon the behavior developments that arise subsequent to the induction and from the trance state itself. No matter how "controlled" a trance induction may be, the development of hypnotic phenomena, and of psychological reactions to those phenomena, introduce variables for which no rigid procedure of induction can provide controls. As an analogy: However dependent upon a controlled anaesthesia a surgical operation may be, the actual surgery and surgical results belong to another category of events merely facilitated by the anaesthesia.

DESCRIPTION OF DEEP HYPNOSIS

Before offering a discussion of deep trance induction, an effort will be made to describe deep hypnosis itself. It must be recognized that a description, no matter how accurate and complete, will not substitute for actual experience, nor can it be made applicable for all subjects. Any description of a deep trance must necessarily vary in minor details from one subject to another. There can be no absolute listing of hypnotic phenomena as belonging to any one level of hypnosis. Some subjects will develop phenomena in the light trance usually associated with the deep trance, and others in a deep trance will show some of the behavior commonly regarded as characteristic of the light trance. Some subjects who in light trances show behavior usually typical of the deep trance may show a loss of that same behavior when deep hypnosis actually develops. For example, subjects who easily develop amnesias in the light trance may just as easily fail to develop amnesia in the deep trance. The reason for such apparent anomalies lies in the entirely different psychological orientation of the deeply hypnotized persons as contrasted to their orientation in lighter stages of hypnosis. At the lighter levels there is an admixture of conscious understandings and expectations and a certain amount of conscious participation. In the deeper stages functioning is more properly at an unconscious level of awareness.

In the deep trance subjects behave in accordance with unconscious patterns of awareness and response which frequently differ from their conscious patterns. Especially is this so in naive subjects whose lack of experience with hypnosis and whose actual ignorance of hypnotic phenomena unwittingly interfere with the development of deep trance phenomena until experience permits a diffusion of understandings from the conscious to the unconscious mind.

An example frequently encountered is the difficulty of teaching good naive subjects to talk in the profound trance. In the light trance they can speak more or less readily, but in the deep trance where their unconscious mind is functioning directly, they find themselves unable to talk without awakening. They have had a lifetime of experience in which talking is done at a conscious level; they have no realization that talking is possible at a purely unconscious level of awareness. Subjects often need to be taught to realize their capabilities to function adequately, whether at a conscious or an unconscious level of awareness. It is for this reason that the author has so often emphasized the need of spending four to eight or more hours in inducing trances and training subjects to function adequately before attempting hypnotic experimentation or therapy.

Contradictory or unsatisfactory results in experimental work requiring deep hypnosis in which verbalization by a subject is necessary have resulted from the subject's need to return to a lighter stage of hypnosis in order to vocalize, without the experimenter's realizing this. Yet teaching subjects how to remain in deep trances and to talk and function as adequately as at a conscious level of awareness is relatively easy. Subjects who seem unable to learn to talk while in the deep trance can be taught automatic writing, to read silently that writing, and to mouth silently as they read; it is a relatively simple step to convert the motor activity of writing and mouthing into actual speaking. A little practice and, contrary to the subjects' past experiential understandings, speech becomes possible at the unconscious level of functioning. The situation is similar in relation to other types of hypnotic phenomena: Pain is a conscious experience, hence analgesia or anaesthesia often need to be taught in a like fashion. The same may be true for hallucinations, regression, amnesia, or other hypnotic phenomena. Some subjects require extensive instruction in a number of regards; others can themselves transfer learnings in one field to a problem of another sort.

The above is an introduction to a description of the nature of a deep trance:

Deep hypnosis is the level of hypnosis that permits subjects to function adequately and directly at an unconscious level of awareness without interference by the conscious mind.

Subjects in deep trance function in accord with unconscious understandings, independently of the forces to which their conscious mind ordinarily responds; they behave in accordance with the realities which exist in the given hypnotic situation for their unconscious mind. Conceptions, memories, and ideas constitute their reality world while they are in deep trance. The actual external environmental reality with which they are surrounded is relevant only insofar as it is utilized in the hypnotic situation. Hence external reality does not necessarily constitute concrete objective matter possessed of intrinsic values. Subjects can write automatically on paper and read what they have written. They can hallucinate equally well the paper, pencil, and motor behavior of writing and then read that "writing." The intrinsic significance of the concrete pencil and paper derives solely from the subjective experiential processes within the subject; once used, they cease to be a part of the total hypnotic situation. In light trances or in the waking state, pencil and paper are objects possessed of significances in addition to those significances peculiar to the individual mind.

The reality of the deep trance must necessarily be in accord with the fundamental needs and structure of the total personality. Thus it is that profoundly neurotic persons in the deep trance can, in that situation, be freed from their otherwise overwhelming neurotic behavior, and thereby a foundation laid for their therapeutic reeducation in accord with each fundamental personality. The overlay of neuroticism, however extensive, does not distort the central core of the personality, though it may disguise and cripple the manifestations of it. Similarly, any attempt to force upon hypnotic subjects, however deep the trance, suggestions unacceptable to their total personalities leads either to a rejection of the suggestions or to a transformation of them so that they can then be satisfied by pretense behavior (so often accepted as valid in attempted studies of hypnotically induced antisocial behavior). The need to appreciate the subject as a person possessing individuality which must be respected cannot be overemphasized. Such appreciation and respect constitute a foundation for recognizing and differentiating conscious and unconscious behavior. Only an awareness of what constitutes behavior deriving from the unconscious mind of the subjects enables the hypnotist to induce and to maintain deep trances. Solely for convenience of conceptualization, deep trances may be classified as (a) somnambulistic and (b) stuporous. In well-trained subjects the former is that type of trance in which a subject is seemingly awake and functioning adequately, freely, and well in the total hypnotic situation, in a manner similar to that of a nonhypnotized person operating at the waking level. Well-trained subjects are not those laboriously taught to behave in a certain way, but rather those trained to rely completely upon their own unconscious patterns of response and behavior.

An illustrative example is the instance in which the author, as a teaching device for the audience, had a subject in a profound somnambulistic trance conduct a lecture and demonstration of hypnosis (unaided by the author) before a group of psychiatrists and psychologists. Although many of the audience had had experience with hypnosis, none detected that she was in a trance. A similar instance concerns a psychiatrist, a student and subject of the author's, who, without the author's previous knowledge and as a personal experiment in autohypnosis, conducted a staff meeting and presented a case history successfully without her trance state being detected. However, once apprised of the situation, the audience could readily recognize the tremendous differences between ordinary conscious behavior and trance behavior, and repetitions of this procedure were detected.

The stuporous trance is characterized primarily by passive responsive behavior, marked by both psychological and physiological retardation. Spontaneous behavior and initiative, so characteristic of the somnambulistic state if allowed to develop, are lacking. There is likely to be a marked perseveration of incomplete responsive behavior, and there is a definite loss of ability to appreciate the self. Medical colleagues asked by the author to examine subjects in a stuporous trance without knowledge of the hypnotic situation have repeatedly offered the tentative opinion of a narcotized state. In the author's experience the stuporous trance is difficult to obtain in many subjects, apparently because of their objection to losing their awareness of themselves as persons. Its use by the author has been limited primarily to the study of physiological behavior and to its therapeutic application in certain types of profoundly neurotic patients.

PROBLEMS OF DEEP-TRANCE INDUCTION

An exposition of the numerous problems of deep-trance induction will be presented by means of a discussion of the major considerations involved, with a detailing of procedures that may be used and the purposes to be served. Although the author is presenting his own experience, this has been confirmed by the experience and practice of his students and colleagues. These considerations will be listed and discussed separately.

Trance Induction versus Trance Utilization

Foremost among the major considerations in any work with deep hypnosis is the need to recognize that trance induction is one thing and trance utilization is another (even as surgical preparation and anaesthesia are one thing and the surgery is another). This has been mentioned before and is repeated here for emphasis. Unless the projected work is no more than a study of trance induction itself, this differentiation must be made by both the subject and the hypnotist. Otherwise there can be a continuance of trance-induction behavior into the trance state with the result that "trance" activities become an admixture of partial and incomplete induction responses, elements of conscious behavior, and actual trance behavior.

Differentiation of Trance Behavior from Ordinary Conscious Behavior

Directly related to the first consideration is the recognition and differentiation of conscious behavior from the behavior arising from the unconscious. In this matter experience is the only teacher, and careful study of behavior manifestations is necessary. This is best accomplished in relation to reality objects. The subjects in profound hypnosis can be instructed to note well and thoroughly an actual chair. Secret removal of that chair does not necessarily interfere with their task. They can continue to hallucinate it in its original position, and sometimes to see it at the same time in a new position as a duplicate chair. Each image is then possessed of the same reality values to them. In the ordinary conscious state such behavior would be impossible or a pretense. Or if a subject discovers that the chair has been moved, searching study may disclose other mental adjustments. Thus, a subject may develop a different orientation of the object so that, to him, the chair remains unmoved in the northeast corner, his sense of direction having altered to meet the situational need.

Similarly, the induced hallucination of a person, resulting in two visual images, confronts the subject with the question of which visual image is real. The spontaneous solution, witnessed by the author on several occasions achieved especially by psychology and medical students, may be one in which the subject silently wishes that a certain movement would be made by the two figures. The figure responding to that silent wish is then recognized as hallucinatory. The reality to the self of the subjects' hypnotic behavior and its recognition by the hypnotist is essential to induce and to permit adequate functioning in the trance state. Failure of such recognition permits the acceptance of inadequate responses as valid manifestations, whereas prolonged and intensive effort may be required to produce the desired hypnotic phenomena.

Orientation of all Hypnotic Procedure About the Subjects

All techniques of procedure should be oriented about the subjects and their needs in order to secure their full cooperation. The projected hypnotic work should be no more than a part of the total hypnotic situation, and it should be adapted to the subjects, not the subjects to the work. These needs may range from the important to the insignificant, but in the hypnotic situation an apparently inconsequential matter may become crucial.

Deep Hypnosis

For example, a subject repeatedly used with equivocal and unsatisfactory results by another hypnotist in an experiment involving the use of a plethysmograph on his right hand cooperated with good results when the author recognized his unconscious need to have his left-handedness recognized by placing the plethysmograph on his left rather than his right hand. This done, it was found that he could then also cooperate when his right hand was used. An ambidextrous subject, in an experiment involving automatic writing and drawing, was found to insist unconsciously upon the privilege of using either hand at will. Other subjects, especially medical and psychology students, have often insisted at an unconscious level upon the satisfaction of mere whims or the performance of other hypnotic work before their full cooperation could be secured for the experimental project for which they had volunteered.

A patient with a circumscribed neurotic disability was both unable and unwilling to pay for therapy. Yet he did not want to receive treatment without first making payment. Accordingly, he was induced to act as a volunteer subject for a long series of experiments, and at his insistence no therapy was attempted. After more than a year of experimental work he unconsciously reached the conclusion that his volunteered hypnotic services constituted adequate payment for therapy, which he then accepted fully.

A subject's psychological needs, no matter how trivial and irrelevant, need to be met as fully as possible in hypnosis, where inter- and intrapersonal relationships are so vital. Oversight or neglect of this consideration will often lead to unsatisfactory, equivocal and even contradictory results. Indeed, when contradictory results are obtained from subjects, the entire hypnotic situation must be reviewed from their point of view.

The Need to Protect Subjects

Subjects need to be protected at all times as personalities possessed of rights, privileges, and privacies and recognized as being placed in a seemingly vulnerable position in the hypnotic situation.

Regardless of how well informed and intelligent subjects may be, there always exists, whether recognized or not, a general questioning uncertainty about what will happen or what may or may not be said or done. Even subjects who have unburdened themselves freely and without inhibition to the author as a psychiatrist have manifested this need to protect the self and to put their best feet forward no matter how freely the wrong foot had been exposed.

This protection should properly be given subjects in both the waking and the trance states. It is best given in an indirect way in the waking state and more directly in the trance state.

To illustrate, a 20-year-old girl volunteered as an experimental subject but always reported for work in the company of a tactless, sharp-tongued associate who constituted a serious obstacle to hypnotic work. After a considerable amount of work the subject began reporting alone. Some time later she explained with mixed amusement and embarrassment, "I used to bring Ruth with me because she is so awfully catty that I knew I wouldn't do or say anything I didn't want to." She then told of her desire for therapy for some concealed phobic reactions. Her experimental work both before and after therapy was excellent.

In working with new subjects, and always when planning to induce deep trances, a systematic effort is made to demonstrate to the subjects that they are in a fully protected situation. Measures to this end are relatively simple and seemingly absurdly inadequate. Nevertheless, personality reactions make them effective. For example, a psychology graduate volunteered as a demonstration subject for a seminar group. A light trance was induced with some difficulty, and her behavior suggested her need for assurance of protection. Under the pretext of teaching her automatic writing, she was instructed to write some interesting sentence and, having written it, not to show it until after automatic writing as a topic had been discussed. Hesitantly, she wrote briefly. She was told to turn the paper face down so that not even she could read it. Handed a new sheet of paper, she was asked to write automatically her conscious and unconscious answers to the question, "Are you willing to have me read what you wrote?" Both written replies were "yes," to which was automatically added, "anybody."

The suggestion was offered that there was no urgency about reading her sentence since it was her first effort at automatic writing, that it might be more interesting to fold it up and put it away in her purse and at some later time compare the script with further automatic writing she might do. Following this, a deep trance was easily induced.

Some time later she explained, "I really wanted to go into a trance but I didn't know if I could trust you, which was silly because everything was being done in front of the whole class. When you asked me to write, my hand just impulsively wrote, 'Do I love Jerry?' and then I wrote that you or anybody else could read it. But when you told me to put it away and later just examine it for the handwriting, without even hinting about a possible meaning of the writing, I knew then that I had no reason whatever for any hesitation. And I also knew that I could answer my own question later instead of doing it all at once and wondering if I was right."

Such behavior has been encountered many times, and this general method of handling the need for ego protection has been found remarkably effective in securing deep, unconscious cooperation toward inducing deep trances.

Another measure frequently employed in this same connection is that of instructing subjects in a light trance to dream a very vivid, pleasing dream, to enjoy it, and, upon its completion, to forget it and not to recall it until so desired at some later date in a suitable situation. Such instruction is manifold in its effects: It gives the subjects a sense of liberty which is entirely safe and yet can be in accord with any unconscious ideas of license and freedom in hypnosis. It utilizes familiar experiences in forgetting and repression. It gives a sense of

Deep Hypnosis

security and confidence in the self, and it also constitutes a posthypnotic suggestion to be executed only at the subjects' desire. A broad foundation is thus laid conducive to the development of profound trances.

This type of comprehensive suggestion is employed extensively by the author, since it serves to initiate a wealth of hypnotic responses pleasing to the subjects and constructive for the hypnotist, in a fashion fully protective of the subjects and thereby insuring cooperation.

Another measure of a somewhat negative character is that of instructing lightly hypnotized subjects to withhold some item of information from the hypnotist. This item should, preferably, be one of a definitely personal character not fully recognized by the subjects as such. It might be their middle name, what member of the family they resemble most, or the first name of their best friend when they were children. Thus the subjects discover by actual experience that they are not helpless automatons, that they can actually enjoy cooperating with the hypnotist, that they can succeed in executing hypnotic suggestions, and that it is their behavior rather than the hypnotist's that leads to success. All of these reactions are essential in securing deep trances. Also, subjects learn unwittingly that, if they can act successfully upon a *negative* suggestion, the converse is true.

Another frequently overlooked form of protection for the subjects is the expression of appreciation for their services. Full regard must be given to the human need to succeed and to the desire for recognition by the self and others of that success. Depriving the subjects of this constitutes a failure to protect them as sentient beings. Such failure may imperil the validity of hypnotic work, since the subjects may feel that their efforts are not appreciated, and this may result in lesser degrees of cooperation. Even more can this be recognized when it is realized that emotional reactions are not necessarily rational, especially at an unconscious level of reaction. Experience has shown that appreciation must be definitely expressed in some manner, preferably first in the trance state and later in the ordinary waking state. In projects where expressed appreciation is precluded, the subjects can receive in other situations the hypnotist's appreciation of services rendered. In any hypnotic work careful attention must be given to the full protection of the subjects' ego by meeting readily their needs as individuals.

The Utilization of All of the Subject's Responsive and Spontaneous Behavior During Trance Induction

Often techniques of hypnosis center primarily about what the hypnotist does or says to secure trances, with too little attention directed to what the subjects are doing and experiencing. Actually, the development of a trance state is an intrapsychic phenomenon, dependent upon internal processes, and the activity of the hypnotist serves only to create a favorable situation. As an analogy, an incubator supplies a favorable environment for the hatching of eggs, but the actual hatching derives from the development of life processes within the egg.

In trance induction inexperienced hypnotists often try to direct or bend the subject's behavior to fit their conception of how the subject "should" behave. There should be a constant minimization of the role of the hypnotist and a constant enlargement of the subject's role. An example may be cited of a volunteer subject, later used to teach hypnosis to medical students. After a general discussion of hypnosis, she expressed a willingness to go into a trance immediately. The suggestion was offered that she select the chair and position she felt would be most comfortable. When she had settled herself to her satisfaction, she remarked that she would like to smoke a cigarette. She was immediately given one, and she proceeded to smoke lazily, meditatively watching the smoke drifting upward. Casual conversational remarks were offered about the pleasure of smoking, of watching the curling smoke, the feeling of ease in lifting the cigarette to her mouth, the inner sense of satisfaction of becoming entirely absorbed just in smoking comfortably and without need to attend to any external things. Shortly, casual remarks were made about inhaling and exhaling, these words timed to fit in with her actual breathing. Others were made about the case with which she could almost automatically lift her cigarette to her mouth and then lower her hand to the arm of the chair. These remarks were also timed to coincide with her actual behavior. Soon the words "inhale," "exhale," "lift," and "lower" acquired a conditioning value of which she was unaware because of the seemingly conversational character of the suggestions. Similarly, casual suggestions were offered in which the words "sleep," "sleepy," and "sleeping" were timed to her eyelid behavior.

Before she had finished the cigarette, she developed a light trance. Then the suggestion was made that she might continue to enjoy smoking as she slept more and more soundly; that the cigarette would be looked after by the hypnotist while she absorbed herself more and more completely in deep sleep; that, as she slept, she would continue to experience the satisfying feelings and sensations of smoking. A satisfactory profound trance resulted, and she was given extensive training to teach her to respond in accord with her own unconscious pattern of behavior.

Thereafter she was presented on a number of occasions to groups of medical students as a volunteer subject with whom they might work. Her behavior with them was essentially the same as with the author. However, her request to smoke a cigarette was variously handled by the students. Some tactfully dissuaded her from thus postponing the trance induction, some joined her in smoking, and some patiently waited for her to finish. Only after the cigarette question was disposed of in some manner was she allowed to settle down to the task of being hypnotized. The result in every instance was a failure. At a final session with all of the students who had participated, two other students were brought in separately to attempt to hypnotize her. Both of these had been given independently the above account of the author's utilization of the subject's behavior.

Both induced profound trances. Then the other students, following the examples set them, also succeeded.

This case has been cited in some detail since it illustrates so clearly the importance of hypnotists' adapting whatever technique they may be employing to the behavioral activities of the subject. To interpret that subject's desire to smoke as an active resistance to trance induction would be incorrect; rather, it was an expression of an actual willingness to cooperate in a way fitting to her needs. It needed to be utilized as such rather than to be overcome or abolished as resistance.

Many times the apparent active resistance encountered in subjects is no more than an unconscious measure of testing the hypnotist's willingness to meet them halfway instead of trying to force them to act entirely in accord with his or her ideas. Thus one subject who had been worked with unsuccessfully by several hypnotists volunteered to act as a demonstration subject. When her offer was accepted, she seated herself in a stiffly upright, challenging position on the chair facing the audience. This apparently unpropitious behavior was met by a casual, conversational remark to the audience that hypnosis was not necessarily dependent upon complete relaxation or automatism, but that hypnosis could be induced in a willing subject if the hypnotist was willing himself to accept the subject's behavior fully. The subject responded to this by rising and asking if she could be hypnotized standing up. Her inquiry was countered by the suggestion, "Why not demonstrate that it can be?" A series of suggestions resulted in the rapid development of a deep trance. Inquiries by the audience revealed that she had read extensively on hypnosis and objected strenuously to the frequently encountered misconception of the hypnotized person as a passively responsive automaton, incapable of self-expression. She explained further that it should be made clear that spontaneous behavior was fully as feasible as responsive activity and that utilization of hypnosis could be made effectively by recognition of this fact.

It should be noted that the reply, "Why not demonstrate that it can be?" constituted an absolute acceptance of her behavior, committed her fully to the experience of being hypnotized, and ensured her full cooperation in achieving her own purposes as well as those of the hypnotist.

Throughout the demonstration she frequently offered suggestions to the author about what next he might ask her to demonstrate, sometimes actually altering the suggested task. At other times she was completely passive in her responses.

Another subject, a graduate in psychology, experienced great difficulty in going into a deep trance. After several hours of intensive effort she timidly inquired if she could advise on technique, even though she had no other experience with hypnosis. Her offer was gladly accepted, whereupon she gave counsel: "You're talking too fast on that point; you should say that very slowly and emphatically and keep repeating it. Say that very rapidly and wait awhile and then repeat it slowly; and please pause now and then to let me rest, and please don't split your infinitives."

With her aid a profound, almost stuporous trance was secured in less than 30 minutes. Thereafter she was employed extensively in a great variety of experimental work and was used to teach others how to induce deep trances.

Acceptance of such help is an expression neither of ignorance nor of incompetence; rather, it is an honest recognition that deep hypnosis is a joint endeavor in which the subjects do the work and the hypnotist tries to stimulate the subjects to make the necessary effort. It is an acknowledgment that no person can really understand the individual patterns of learning and response of another. While this measure works best with highly intelligent, seriously interested subjects, it is also effective with others. It establishes a feeling of trust, confidence, and active participation in a joint task. Moreover it serves to dispel misconceptions of the mystical powers of the hypnotist and to define indirectly the respective roles of the subject and the hypnotist.

Fortunately this experience occurred early in the author's work and has been found of immense value ever since in inducing hypnosis of every degree and in the eliciting of highly complex hypnotic behavior.

One often reads in the literature about subject resistance and the techniques employed to circumvent or overcome it. In the author's experience the most satisfactory procedure is that of accepting and utilizing the resistance as well as any other type of behavior, since properly used they can all favor the development of hypnosis. This can be done by wording suggestions in such a fashion that a positive or a negative response, or an absence of response, are all defined as responsive behavior. For example, a resistive subject who is not receptive to suggestions for hand levitation can be told, "Shortly your right hand, or it may be your left hand, will begin to lift up, or it may press down, or it may not move at all, but we will wait to see just what happens. Maybe the thumb will be first, or you may feel something happening in your little finger, but the really important thing is not whether your hand lifts up or presses down or just remains still; rather, it is your ability to sense fully whatever feelings may develop in your hand."

With such wording absence of motion, lifting up, and pressing down are all covered, and any of the possibilities constitutes responsive behavior. Thus a situation is created in which the subjects can express their resistance in a constructive, cooperative fashion; manifestation of resistance by subjects is best utilized by developing a situation in which resistance serves a purpose. Hypnosis cannot be resisted if there is no hypnosis attempted. The hypnotist, recognizing this, should so develop the situation that any opportunity to manifest resistance becomes contingent upon hypnotic responses with a localization of all resistance upon irrelevant possibilities. The subjects whose resistance is manifested by failure to hand levitation can be given suggestions that their right hand will levitate, their left hand will not. To resist successfully, contrary behavior must be manifested. The result is that the subjects find themselves responding to suggestion, but to their own satisfaction. In the scores of instances where this measure has been employed, less than a half dozen subjects realized that a situation had been created in which their ambivalence had been resolved. One writer on hypnosis naively employed a similar procedure in which he asked subjects to resist going into a trance in an effort to demonstrate that they could not resist hypnotic suggestion. The subjects cooperatively and willingly proved that they could readily accept suggestions to prove that they could not. The study was published in entire innocence of its actual meaning.

Whatever the behavior offered by the subjects it should be accepted and utilized to develop further responsive behavior. Any attempt to "correct" or alter the subjects' behavior, or to force them to do things they are not interested in, militates against trance induction and certainly against deep trances. The very fact that subjects volunteer to be hypnotized and then offer resistance indicates an ambivalence which, recognized, can be utilized to serve successfully the purposes of both the subjects and the hypnotists. Such recognition and concession to the needs of the subjects and the utilization of their behavior do not constitute, as some authors have declared, "unorthodox techniques," based upon "clinical intuition," instead they constitute a simple recognition of existing conditions, based upon full respect for subjects as functioning personalities.

The Basing of Each Progressive Step of Trance Induction upon Actual Accomplishments by the Subject

These accomplishments may be those of the hypnotic situation, or they may belong to the subject's everyday experience. Merely volunteering to act as a subject may be the outcome of a severe inner struggle. Relaxing comfortably in a chair and disregarding external distractions is an accomplishment. Absence of response to hand-levitation suggestions is not necessarily a failure, since the very immobility of the hands is in itself an accomplishment. Willingness to sit quietly while the hypnotist laboriously offers numerous suggestions, apparently futilely, is still another accomplishment. Each of these constitutes a form of behavior that may be emphasized as an initial successful step toward a greater development in the trance state.

To illustrate, a person with a Ph.D. in psychology, extremely scornful and skeptical of hypnosis, challenged the author to "try to work your little fad" on her in the presence of witnesses who would be able to attest to the author's failure. However, she did state that if it could be demonstrated to her that there were such a phenomenon as hypnosis, she would lend herself to any studies the author might plan. Her challenge and conditions were accepted. Her promise to act as a subject, if convinced, was carefully and quietly emphasized, since it constituted behavior of her own and could become the foundation for future trance behavior. Next, a technique of suggestion was employed which was believed certain to fail, which it did. Thus the subject was given a feeling of success, gratifying to her, but carrying an admixture of some regret over the author's discomfiture. This regret constituted a foundation stone for future trances. Then apparently as a face-saving device for the author, the topic of ideomotor activity was raised. After some discussion indirect suggestion led her to express a willingness to cooperate in experimentation of ideomotor activity. She qualified this by stating, "Don't try to tell me that ideomotor activity is hypnosis, because I know it isn't." This was countered by the observation that ideomotor activity could undoubtedly be achieved in hypnosis even as in the waking state. Thus another foundation stone was laid for future trance activity.

Hand levitation was selected as a good example of ideomotor activity, and she acceded readily, since she was unacquainted with the author's frequent use of hand levitation as an initial trance-induction procedure.

In the guise of a pedantic discussion a series of hand-levitation suggestions was offered. She responded quickly and delightedly. This was followed by the suggestion that, as a preliminary to experimental work, it might be well if she absorbed herself completely in the subjective aspects of the experience, disregarding, as she did so, all external stimuli except the author's remarks. Thus a further stone was laid. Within 10 minutes she developed a profound somnambulistic trance. After some minutes of further suggestion of variations in her ideomotor responses, the remark was made that she might like to discontinue and to return to another point in the original discussion. Thus she was given a suggestion to awaken from the trance, safe from any autocritical understandings. She agreed and wakened easily, and the author immediately resumed the original discussion. Shortly a second trance was induced by the same procedure, followed in the course of four hours by four more.

During the third trance she was tested for catalepsy, which was present. This alarmed and distressed her, but before she could awaken, it was described to her satisfaction as "arrested ideomotor activity," and this not only reassured her but stimulated further interest.

In the next two trances she willingly undertook to experience "other associated phenomena of ideomotor activity." Thus she was instructed to glance at the witnesses and then to note that, as her attention to the others waned and she became more absorbed subjectively in the ideomotor behavior of her hands, she would cease to see the others. In this way she was taught to develop negative hallucinations by extending her interest in ideomotor activity to an exclusion of other behavior. By a comparable measure she was taught positive hallucinations by visualizing her levitated hand so clearly in two different positions that she would not be able to distinguish her hand from its visual image in another position. This done, the specious argument was offered that, as her attention to her ideomotor activity waxed and waned, she would variously see and not see, hear and not hear, the others present, that she might visualize in duplicate others present, and that she could forget the presence of others and even ideas about them or any other thing. By this means she was induced to experience a wealth of hypnotic phenomena.

There followed the more difficult task of informing her that she had been hypnotized. This was done by suggesting, in the sixth trance, that she recall her feelings "during the first demonstration of ideomotor activity." As she did so, it was pointed out that her self-absorption might possibly be compared to a somewhat similar state that was manifested in hypnosis. Proceeding to the "second demonstration," the suggestion was offered that her behavior was almost trancelike. She was then asked to visualize herself as she must have appeared in the "third demonstration." As she did so, she was asked to comment on her cataleptic behavior, to develop auditory imagery of what had been said to her, and to note the responses made. This time hypnosis was hinted at as a definite probability, and she was tactfully praised for her ability to develop the imagery, visual and auditory, that enabled her to view so clearly her behavior. Immediately she was asked to consider the fourth instance. As she did so, she asked hesitantly if, in that demonstration, she were not really in a trance. Assured that she could understand freely, comfortably, and with a most pleasing sense of actual accomplishment, she declared, "Then I must really be in a trance right now." The author agreed and rapidly reminded her of every success she had achieved and how excellently she had been able to utilize her ideomotor activity to expand her field of personal experience. She was further instructed to review mentally the entire evening and to give the author any counsel she wished.

After quiet meditation she asked the author not to tell her, after she had awakened, that she had been hypnotized, but to give her time to reorganize her general attitudes toward hypnosis and toward the author as an exponent of hypnosis, and time to get used to the error of her previous thinking.

It was agreed, and she was told she would awaken with an amnesia for her trance experience and with a pleased feeling that both she and the author were interested in ideomotor phenomena. Suggestion was then given that her unconscious mind would take much pleasure in keeping awareness away from her consciousness of the fact that she had been hypnotized, and that this secret could be shared by her unconscious and the author. She was instructed that her unconscious could and would so govern her conscious mind that she could learn about hypnosis and her hypnotic experience in any way that was satisfying and informative to her as a total personality. By this posthypnotic suggestion the subject was given still further hypnotic training in relation to the independent functioning of the unconscious and conscious mind, the development of a hypnotic amnesia, and the execution of posthypnotic work. In addition she was made aware at a deep level that she, as a personality, was fully protected, that her functioning rather than the hypnotist's was the primary consideration in trance induction, and that utilization of one process of behavior could be made a stepping-stone to development of a similar but more complex form.

The outcome was most interesting. Two days later the subject offered her apologies for her "flippant skepticism" about hypnosis and her "unwarranted" disparagement of the author's work. She added that she was much amused by her need to apologize. A few days later she volunteered to act as a subject, stating she was now seriously interested and would like to participate in some investigative studies. She proved to be a most productive subject over a period of years.

This lengthy example illustrates many of the considerations this author has found of tremendous importance in inducing deep trances. The little item of having a "secret understanding" between the subjects' unconscious minds and the hypnotist has many times proved to be remarkably effective as a means of securing deep trances in otherwise aggressively resistant subjects. By virtue of this they could make conscious and express freely and safely their resistances. At the same time they could have a profound feeling that they were cooperating fully, securely, and effectively. The satisfaction so derived by the subjects leads to a desire for continued successful accomplishment, and active resistances are rapidly dispelled, resolved, or constructively utilized.

In brief, whatever the behavior manifested by the subjects, it should be accepted and regarded as grist for the mill. Acceptance of her need for the author to fail led to ideomotor activity. This led progressively to a wealth of hypnotic phenomena based either directly or indirectly upon ideomotor responses and culminated in a success pleasing to her as well as to the hypnotist. Had any effort been made to get that subject to conform to some rigid technique of trance induction, failure would have undoubtedly ensued, and rightly so, since the development of a trance was not to prove the author's ability but to secure experiential values and understandings by the subject.

Much of the foregoing material constitutes an exposition of the major considerations involved in the securing of deep trances. Some special hypnotic procedures which are usually successful will now be summarized. Full details are omitted due to space limitations and because of the constant shifting from one orientation to another which they require.

THE CONFUSION TECHNIQUE

For want of a better term, one of these special procedures may be referred to as the "confusion technique." It has been employed extensively for the induction of specific phenomena as well as deep trances. Usually it is best employed with highly intelligent subjects interested in the hypnotic process, or with those consciously unwilling to go into a trance despite an unconscious willingness.

In essence it is no more than a presentation of a whole series of individually differing, contradictory suggestions, apparently all at variance with each other, differently directed and requiring a constant shift in orientation by the subjects. For example, in producing hand levitation, emphatic suggestions directed to the levitation of the right hand are offered together with suggestions of the immobility of the left hand. Shortly the subjects become aware that the hypnotist is apparently misspeaking, since levitation of the left hand and immobility of the right are then suggested. As the subjects accommodate themselves to the seem-

Deep Hypnosis

ing confusion of the hypnotist, thereby unwittingly cooperating in a significant fashion, suggestions of immobility of both hands are given together with others of the simultaneous lifting of one and pressing down of the other. These are followed by a return to the initial suggestions.

As the subjects try, conditioned by their early cooperative responses to the hypnotist's apparent misspeaking, to accommodate themselves to the welter of confused, contradictory responses apparently sought, they find themselves at such a loss that they welcome any positive suggestion that will permit a retreat from so unsatisfying and confusing a situation. The rapidity, insistence, and confidence with which the suggestions are given serve to prevent the subjects from making any effort to bring about a semblance of order. At best they can only try to accommodate themselves and thus yield to the overall significance of the total series of suggestions.

Or, while successfully inducing levitation, one may systematically build up a state of confusion as to which hand is moving, which more rapidly or more laterally, which will become arrested in movement, and which will continue and in what direction, until a retreat from the confusion by a complete acceptance of the suggestions of the moment becomes a greatly desired goal.

In inducing an extensive amnesia with a regression of the subjects to earlier patterns of behavior, the "confusion technique" has been found extremely valuable and effective. It is based upon the utilization of everyday experiences familiar to everyone. To regress a subject to an earlier time, a beginning is made with casual conversational suggestions about how easy it is to sometimes become confused as to the day of the week, to misremember an appointment as of tomorrow instead of yesterday, and to give the date as the old year instead of the new. As the subject correlates these suggestions with actual past experiences, the remark is made that, although today is Tuesday, one might think of it as Thursday, but since today is Wednesday and since it is not important for the present situation whether it is Wednesday or Monday, one can call to mind vividly an experience of one week ago on Monday, that constituted a repetition of an experience of the previous Wednesday. This, in turn, is reminiscent of an event which occurred on the subject's birthday in 1948, at which time he could only speculate upon, but not know, about what would happen on the 1949 birthday and, even less so, about the events of the 1950 birthday, since they had not yet occurred. Further, since they had not occurred, there could be no memory of them in his thinking in 1948.

As the subjects receive these suggestions, they can recognize that they carry a weight of meaningfulness. However, in order to grasp it, their tendency is to try to think in terms of a birthday in 1948, but to do so they have to disregard 1949 and 1950. Barely have they begun to so orient their thinking when they are presented with another series of suggestions to the effect that one may remember some things and forget others; that people often forget things they are certain they will remember but which they do not; that certain childhood memories stand out even more vividly than memories of 1947, '46, '45; that actually every day they are forgetting something of this year as well as last year, or of 1945 or '44, and even more so of '42, '41, and '40. As for 1935, only certain things are remembered identifiably as of that year, and yet, as time goes on, still more will be forgotten.

These suggestions are also recognized as carrying a weight of acceptable meaningfulness, and every effort the subjects make to understand it leads to acceptance of them. In addition suggestions of amnesia have been offered, emphasis has been placed upon the remembering of childhood memories, and the processes of reorientation to an earlier age level are initiated.

These suggestions are not given initially in the form of commands or instructions but as thought-provoking comments. Then, as the subjects begin to respond, a slow, progressive shift is made to direct suggestions to recall more and more vividly the experiences of 1935 or 1930. As this is done, suggestions to forget the experiences subsequent to the selected age are given directly, but slowly, unnoticeably, and these suggestions are soon reworded to "forget many things, as naturally as one does, many things, events of the past, speculations about the future, but of course forgotten things are of no importance—only those things belonging to the present—thoughts, feelings, events, only these are vivid and meaningful." Thus a beginning order of ideas is suggested, needed by the subjects but requiring a certain type of response.

Next, suggestions are offered emphatically, with increasing intensity, that certain events of 1930 will be remembered so vividly that the subjects find themselves in the middle of the development of a life experience, one not yet completed. For example, one subject reoriented to his sixth birthday responded by experiencing himself sitting at the table anxiously waiting to see if his mother would give him one or two frankfurters. The Ph.D. person previously mentioned was reoriented to an earlier childhood level and responded by experiencing herself sitting in the schoolroom awaiting a lesson assignment.

It is at this point that an incredible error is made by many serious workers in hypnosis. This lies in the unthinking assumption that the subjects, reoriented to a period previous to their meeting with the hypnotist, can engage in conversation with the hypnotist, literally a nonexistent person. Yet, critical appreciation of this permits the hypnotist to accept seriously and not as a mere pretense a necessary transformation of his identity. The Ph.D woman, reliving her school experience, would not meet the author until more than 15 years later. So she spontaneously transformed his identity into that of her teacher, and her description as she perceived him in that situation, later checked, was found to be a valid description of the real teacher. For Dr. Erickson to talk to her in the schoolroom would be a ridiculous anachronism which would falsify the entire reorientation. With him seen as Miss Brown and responded to in the manner appropriate to the time, the schoolroom, and to Miss Brown, the situation became valid, a revivification of the past.

Perhaps the most absurd example of uncriticalness in this regard is that of the psychiatrist who reported at length upon his experimental regression of a subject

Deep Hypnosis

to the intrauterine stage, at which he secured a subjective account of intrauterine experiences. He disregarded the fact that the infant *in utero* neither speaks nor understands the spoken word. He did not realize that his findings were the outcome of a subject's compliant effort to please an uncritical, unthinking worker.

This need for the hypnotist to fit into the regression situation is imperative for valid results, and it can easily be accomplished. A patient under therapy was regressed to the age level of four years. Information obtained independently about the patient revealed that, at that time in her life, she had been entertained by a neighbor's gold hunting-case watch, a fact she had long forgotten. In regressing her, as she approached the four-year level, the author's gold hunting-case watch was gently introduced visually and without suggestion. His recognition as that neighbor was readily and spontaneously achieved.

This transformation of the hypnotist into another person is not peculiar only to regression work. Many times, in inducing a deep trance in a newly met subject, the author has encountered difficulty until he recognized that, as Dr. Erickson, he was only a meaningless stranger and that the full development of a deep trance was contingent upon accepting a transformation of his identity into that of another person. Thus a subject wishing for hypnotic anaesthesia for childbirth consistently identified the author as a former psychology professor; it was not until shortly before delivery that he was accorded his true identity. Failure to accept seriously the situation would have militated greatly against the development of a deep trance and the training for anaesthesia.

Regardless of a hypnotist's experience and ability, a paramount consideration in inducing deep trances and securing valid responses is a recognition of each subject as a personality, the meeting of their needs, and an awareness and a recognition of their patterns of unconscious functioning. The hypnotists, not the subjects, should be made to fit themselves into the hypnotic situation.

THE REHEARSAL TECHNIQUE

Another type of deep-trance induction may be termed the rehearsal or repetition technique. This can and often should be used for deep hypnosis and for individual phenomena. It can be employed in a variety of ways both experimentally and in therapeutic work, especially the latter. It consists of seizing upon some one form of behavior that apparently gives a promise of good development and having the subjects rehearse it and then repeat it in actuality.

Thus subjects who make little response to hypnosis but who seem to be potentially good subjects may make abortive responses to suggestions of automatic writing. This partial, tentative response can be seized upon as an instance of actual success. Then a series of suggestions is given, leading the subjects to rehearse mentally what must have been done to achieve that particular success. Then they are asked to rehearse mentally how it could be done on plain paper, on ruled paper, with a pen, a pencil, or a crayon. Next they are asked to perform what has been rehearsed mentally in the various permutations possible with that equipment. This can be followed by further rehearsals and repetitions, introducing as new variables hallucinatory paper and writing instruments and new letters, words, and sentences. As this procedure is followed, the subjects progressively develop a deeper and deeper trance, especially if the rehearsal and repetition are applied to other forms of hypnotic behavior.

Sometimes this technique can be applied in an entirely different fashion. For example, before a class of senior medical students, the author undertook to produce amnesia in a volunteer subject who wished both to go into a trance and to disappoint the author. The student expressed the opinion that he doubted if he could develop amnesia, and declared that he himself would propose his own proof of amnesia, namely the removal of his right shoe. Should this occur, he explained, it would constitute proof to him that he had developed an amnesia.

He developed a fairly good trance, and a whole series of instructions was given him, emphatically and repetitiously, that he perform several acts such as borrowing one student's cigarettes, another's glasses, etc. Repetitious command was also given to forget each simple task. Slipped unobtrusively into these suggestions was the statement that, after awakening, while discussing with the class the presence or absence of an amnesia for the assigned tasks, he would cross the room, write a sentence on the blackboard, and sign his name, still continuing his discussion.

Upon awakening, he declared that he recollected everything said to him and that he had done. His statement was challenged, whereupon he heatedly gave a running account of the tasks and his performance of them. Without interrupting his argument, he wrote the sentence and signed his name. After he had returned to his seat, his attention was called to the writing which he disclaimed, emphasizing that his narration proved his remembrance, and he extended his right foot with the shoe on to prove conclusively that he had no amnesia. He then continued his remarks, absentmindedly removing his shoe as he did so. This he did not discover until the class was dismissed. Systematically appraising the situation, he recognized that he had developed an amnesia with no conscious knowledge of the fact. The class was reconvened, and he was asked to duplicate the writing. As he was doing this, a few suggestions elicited a profound trance, and an extensive demonstration of the psychopathology of everyday life was conducted.

Thus the subject had been given a long, repetitious list of simple performances apparently to lead to amnesia, but actually to permit him to succeed over and over in accord with his personal needs. Hence the failures were really successful performances which could actually favor another successful performance, namely the development of amnesia. The unobtrusive slipping in of the suggestion of writing permitted him to set it apart from the other more urgent suggestions. Then, as he achieved his numerous successes of no amnesia, the pattern of response was completed for more successes by his proving the lack of amnesia, by exhibiting his shoe on his foot. This, however, left unsatisfied his actual desire for still more success, namely his demonstration of an amnesia by the removal of his shoe, an item of behavior he himself had selected. This he achieved by a double amnesia for the writing and the shoe removal, an even greater success than he had anticipated. Then, as he repeated the writing, he found himself again in the situation that had led to his most satisfying accomplishment. The situation led easily to a deep trance state by virtue of a repetition or rehearsal procedure.

Still another form of this technique has been found useful in inducing deep trances and in studies of motivation, association of ideas, regression, symbol analysis, repression, and the development of insight. It has proved a most effective therapeutic procedure and is primarily a matter of having the subjects repeat over and over in the trance state a dream or, less preferably, a fantasy, in constantly differing guises. That is, they repeat a spontaneous dream or an induced dream with a different cast of characters, perhaps in a different setting, but with the same meaning. After the second dreaming the same instructions are given again, and this continues until the purposes to be served are accomplished. To illustrate, a patient offered this spontaneous dream of the previous night: "I was alone in a grass-covered meadow. There were knolls and curving rises in the ground. It was warm and comfortable. I wanted something dreadfully—I don't know what. But I was scared—paralyzed with fear. It was horrible. I woke up trembling."

Repeated, the dream was: "I was walking up a narrow valley. I was looking for something I had to find, but I didn't want it. I didn't know what I was looking for, but I knew something was forcing me to look for it, and I was afraid of it, whatever it was. Then I came to the end of the valley where the walls came together and there was a little stream of water flowing from under a thick bush. That bush was covered with horrible thorns. It was poisonous. Something was pushing me closer, and I kept getting smaller and smaller and I still feel scared."

The next repetition was: "This seems to have something to do with part of the last dream. It was spring, and the logs were in the river and all the lumberjacks and all the men were there. Everybody owned one of the logs, me too. All the others had big hardwood logs, but mine, when I got it, was a little rotten stick. I hoped nobody noticed and I claimed another, but when I got it, it was just like the first."

Again repeated: "I was in a rowboat fishing. Everybody was fishing. Each of the others caught a great big fish. I fished and fished and all I got was a little sickly fish. I didn't want it, but I had to keep it. I felt horribly depressed."

Again: "I went fishing again. There were lots of big fish shooting around in the water, but I caught only miserable little fish that would fall off the hook and float dead on the water. But I had to have a fish, so I kept on fishing and got one that seemed to have a little life in it. So I put it in a gunny sack because I knew everybody should put his fish in a gunny sack. Everybody else did, and their fish always filled their gunny sacks completely. But my fish was just lost in the gunny sack, and then I noticed my gunny sack was all rotten and there was a hole in it, and a lot of slime and filth gushed out, and my fish floated away in that horrible slime, belly up, dead. And I looked around and I was on that meadow I told you about, and the gunny sack was under that bush with all those thorns and my good-for-nothing fish was floating down that stream of water I told you about, and it looked just like a rotten stick of wood."

A series of repetitions finally resulted in the breaking down of extensive amnesias and blockings and his disclosure that, at puberty, under circumstances of extreme poverty, he had acted as a nurse for his mother, who had rejected him completely since infancy and who had died of an extensive neglected cancer of the genitals. Additionally, he told for the first time of his profound feelings of inferiority deriving from his lack of phallic development, his strong homosexual inclinations, and his feeling that his only protection from homosexuality would be a yielding to the "horrible pressure and force society uses to shove you to heterosexuality."

This instance from a case history illustrates unconscious processes clearly: each succeeding dream resulted in a more easily induced and more easily maintained trance, at the same time giving the patient greater freedom in his thinking and in his use of less abstruse symbolism.

A necessary caution in utilizing this type of procedure for experimental or demonstration hypnosis is that dreams of a pleasant character should be employed if possible. If not, the implantation of an artificial complex, thereby limiting the extent of unpleasant emotions, is desirable. In all instances care should be taken to discontinue the work should it tend to lead to a situation which the hypnotist is not competent to handle. Otherwise, acute emotional disturbances and active repressions may result in a loss of the subject's good regard for the hypnotist and cause emotional distress to the subject.

Another variation of the rehearsal method is that of having subjects visualize themselves carrying out some hypnotic task and then adding to the visualization other forms of imagery such as auditory, kinesthetic, etc. For example, a patient under therapy for neurotic maladjustment had great difficulty in developing and maintaining a deep trance. By having her, as an induction procedure, mentally rehearse the probably general course of events for each exploratory or therapeutic session and then hallucinate as fully as possible the probable experiences for each occasion, it was possible to elicit and maintain satisfactorily deep trances. By giving her "previews," she was able to develop and maintain a profound trance. After exploration of the underlying causes of her problem, the next step in therapy was to outline in great detail, with her help, the exact course of activity that she would have to follow to free herself from past rigidly established habitual patterns of behavior. Then she was reoriented to a time actually three months in the future and thereby was enabled to offer a "reminiscent" account of her therapy and recovery. A wealth of details was given, affording an abundance of new material which could be incorporated into the final therapeutic procedure.

Deep Hypnosis

A comparable instance is that of a girl who was a most competent subject—except before an audience. Then it was impossible to induce a deep trance or to maintain one induced in private. By having her rehearse a fantasized public demonstration for the future and then reorienting her to a date several weeks further in the future, she was able to regard the fantasy as an actual successful accomplishment of the past, much to her satisfaction. Immediately she was asked to "repeat" her demonstration before a student group, which she willingly and successfully did. There was no recurrence of the difficulty even after she was given a full understanding of how she had been manipulated.

Subjects reoriented from the present to the actual future, and instructed to look back upon proposed hypnotic work as actually accomplished, can often, by their "reminiscence," provide the hypnotist with understandings that can readily lead to much sounder work in deep trances. In therapy, as well as experimentally, the author has found this measure highly effective, since it permits elaboration of hypnotic work in fuller accord with the subject's total personalities and unconscious needs and capabilities. It often permits the correction of errors and oversights before they can be made, and it furnishes a better understanding of how to develop suitable techniques. Subjects employed in this manner can often render invaluable service in mapping out procedures and techniques to be employed in experimentation and therapy.

MULTIPLE-DISSOCIATION TECHNIQUE

Another measure frequently employed by the author in inducing deep trances, or utilizing them for extensive complex work, is the induction of multiple visual hallucinations in which different but related things are visualized. (Many subjects can be taught "crystal gazing" in the light trance.) One patient, in a profoundly depressed, discouraged mood, readily seized the opportunity to intensify by contrast her unhappy mood by accepting the suggestion that she see in action in a crystal ball a happy incident of her childhood consciously forgotten. Utilizing her masochistic response to this, a second crystal ball was suggested in which she could see, simultaneously with the first, an incident belonging to another age level. Soon there was a total of a dozen hallucinatory crystals in each of which a life scene of a different age level was being portrayed by hallucinatory figures belonging to her experiential past. Thus a combined experimental investigative and therapeutic situation was created in which her limited immediate willingness for a brief trance served to carry her into an extensive development hours long that therapeutically served her total personality needs.

This procedure is not limited to induced hallucinatory behavior. A musician, unresponsive to direct hypnotic suggestion, was induced to recall the experience of having his "thoughts haunted by a strain of music." This led to a suggested search for other similar experiences. Soon he became so absorbed in trying to recall forgotten memories and beating time as a kinesthetic aid that a deep trance developed. In other words, dissociation phenomena, whether spontaneous or induced, can be used in a repetitious manner to establish a psychological momentum to which subjects easily and readily yield.

POSTHYPNOTIC TECHNIQUES

In a paper with E. M. Erickson attention was directed to the spontaneous hypnotic trance developed in relation to the execution of posthypnotic tasks. In inducing hypnosis, light or deep, the hypnotist may unobtrusively introduce some form of posthypnotic suggestion that will permit the subsequent development of a spontaneous trance. This trance can then be utilized as a point of departure for developing a new trance state. Not all subjects respond to this procedure, but it often proves of immense value.

Sometimes subjects who are only in a light trance can be given a simple posthypnotic suggestion. As they develop a spontaneous trance in executing the posthypnotic act, suggestions may be given to deepen it. The procedure can be repeated, and a third trance, still deeper, can result, until sufficient repetitions bring a deep hypnosis.

Concerning unobtrusive posthypnotic suggestions, the author resorts to such measures as saying, "Each time I take hold of your wrist and move your arm gently in this way (demonstrating), it will be a signal to you to do something—perhaps to move your other hand, perhaps to nod your head, perhaps to sleep more soundly, but each time you receive the signal, you will become ready to carry out the tast." Repeated several times in the first trance, the subjects, in their immediate thinking, apply the suggestion only to that trance session. However, weeks later, in an appropriate setting, the repetition of the signal may result in a rapid induction of hypnosis. This method has been used extensively as a time-saving procedure in teaching professional students to become both hypnotists and hypnotic subjects.

As to posthypnotic acts for subjects to execute, a simple, casual activity is much better than some attention-compelling, overt act: watching the hypnotist light a cigarette, noting whether the match tossed toward the wastebasket falls in it, or observing that the book on the desk is about two inches away from the edge, are all infinitely better than having the subjects clap hands when the word "pencil" is spoken. The more casually hypnotic work can be done, the easier it is for subjects to adapt to it. Casualness permits ready utilization of the behavioral developments of the total hypnotic situation.

In presenting this material the intention has not been to outline specific or exact techniques of procedure for hypnosis; rather, it has been to demonstrate that hypnosis should primarily be the outcome of a situation in which interpersonal and intrapersonal relationships are developed constructively to serve the

Deep Hypnosis

purpose of both the hypnotist and the subject. This cannot be done by following rigid procedures and fixed methods, nor by striving to reach a single specific goal. The complexity of human behavior and its underlying motivations make necessary a cognizance of the multitude of factors existing in any situation arising between two personalities engaged in a joint activity. Whatever the part played by the hypnotist may be, the role of the subjects involve the greater amount of active functioning—functioning which derives from the capabilities, learnings, and experiential history of their total personalities. Hypnotists can only guide, direct, supervise, and provide the opportunity for subjects to do the productive work. To accomplish this, hypnotists must understand the situation and its needs, protect the subjects fully, and be able to recognize the work accomplished. They must accept and utilize the behavior that develops and be able to create opportunities and situations favorable for adequate functioning of their subjects.

7. Naturalistic Techniques of Hypnosis

Milton H. Erickson

The naturalistic approach to the problem of the induction of hypnotic trances—as opposed to formalized, ritualistic procedures of trance induction—merits much more investigation, experimentation, and study than has been accorded it to date.

By naturalistic approach is meant the acceptance and utilization of the situation encountered without endeavoring to psychologically restructure it. In so doing, the presenting behavior of the patient becomes a definite aid and an actual part in inducing a trance, rather than a possible hindrance. For lack of a more definite terminology the method may be termed a naturalistic approach in which an aspect of the principle of synergism is utilized.

Basic to this naturalistic approach are the interrelationships and the interdependencies reported by this writer in 1943 and repeatedly confirmed in his experience since then. In these studies emphasis was placed upon the desirability of utilizing one modality of response as an integral part in the eliciting of responses in another modality, and upon the interdependency of differing modalities of behavior somewhat analogous to the increasing of the knee jerk by a tensing of the arm muscles.

To illustrate and clarify these points a number of reports will be cited.

REPORT NO. 1

A man in his 30's became interested in hypnosis and volunteered to act as a subject for some experimental studies at a university. In the first hypnotic session he discovered that he was an excellent hypnotic subject, but lost his interest in any further experimental studies.

Several years later he decided to have hypnosis employed by his dentist, since he needed extensive dental work and feared greatly the possibility of pain.

He entered a trance state for his dentist readily, developed an excellent anaesthesia of the hand upon suggestion, but failed to be able to transfer this

---

Reprinted with permission from *The American Journal of Clinical Hypnosis*, July, 1958, *1*, 3-8.

Naturalistic Techniques

anaesthesia or even an analgesia to his mouth in any degree. Instead he seemed to become even more sensitive orally. Efforts to develop oral anaesthesia or analgesia directly also failed.

Further but unsuccessful efforts were painstakingly made by the dentist and a colleague to teach this patient either anaesthesia or analgesia by various techniques. He could respond in this way only in parts of the body other than the mouth. He was then brought to this writer as a special problem.

A trance state was induced readily, and the patient was casually reminded of his wish for comfort in the dental chair. Thereupon he was instructed to be attentive to the instructions given him and to execute them fully.

Suggestions were then given him that his left hand would become exceedingly sensitive to all stimuli, in fact painfully so. This hyperesthetic state would continue until he received instructions to the contrary. Throughout its duration, however, adequate care would be exercised to protect his hand from painful contacts.

The patient made a full and adequate response to these suggestions. In addition to the hyperesthesia of the hand, and entirely without any suggestion to that effect, he developed a spontaneous anaesthesia of his mouth, permitting full dental work with no other anaesthetic agent.

Even in subsequent efforts anaesthesia or analgesia could not be induced directly or purposely except as a part of the hyperesthesia-anaesthesia pattern peculiar to that patient. However, this is not a single instance of this type of behavior. Other comparable cases have been encountered from time to time.

Apparently, the patient's fixed, psychological understanding was that dental work must absolutely be associated with hypersensitivity. When this rigid understanding was met, dental anaesthesia could be achieved in a fashion analogous to the relaxation of one muscle permitting the contraction of another.

REPORT NO. 2

Hypnosis had been attempted repeatedly and unsuccessfully on a dentist's wife by her husband and several of his colleagues. Each time, she stated, she became "absolutely scared stiff, so I just couldn't move and then I'd start crying. I just couldn't do anything they asked. I couldn't relax, I couldn't do hand levitation, I couldn't shut my eyes; all I could do was be scared silly and cry."

Again a naturalistic approach employing "synergism" was utilized. A general summary of her situation was offered to her in essentially the following words:

"You wish to have hypnosis utilized in connection with your dental work. Your husband and his colleagues wish the same, but each time hypnosis was attempted, you failed to go into a trance. You got scared stiff and you cried. *It would really be enough just to get stiff without crying.* Now you want me to treat you psychiatrically if necessary, but I don't believe it is. Instead I will just put you in a trance, so that you can have hypnosis for your dentistry."

She replied, "But I'll just get scared stiff and cry."

She was answered with, "No, you will first get stiff. That is the first thing to do and do it now. Just get more and more stiff, your arms, your legs, your body, your neck—completely stiff—even stiffer than you were with your husband.

"Now close your eyes and let the lids get stiff, so stiff that you can't open them."

Her responses were most adequate.

"Now the next thing you have to do is to get scared silly and then to cry. Of course, you don't want to do this, but you have to because you learned to, *but don't do it just yet*.

"It would be so much easier to take a deep breath and relax all over and to sleep deeply.

"Why don't you try this, instead of going on to getting scared silly and crying?"

Her response to this alternative suggestion was immediate and remarkably good.

The next suggestion was, "Of course you can continue to sleep deeper and deeper in the trance state and be relaxed and comfortable. But any time you wish you can start to get scared stiff and silly and to cry, but maybe now that you know how to do so, you will just keep on being comfortable in the trance so that any dental or medical work you need can be done comfortably for you."

A simple posthypnotic suggestion to enable the induction of future trances was then given.

Following this she was asked if she was interested in discovering that she was a most competent subject. Upon her assent various phenomena of the deep somnambulistic trance were elicited to her pleasure and satisfaction.

Since then, for a period of nearly a year, she has been a most competent subject.

REPORT NO. 3

Another type of case in which this same general approach was utilized concerns a bride of a week, who desired a consummation of her marriage but developed a state of extreme panic with her legs in the scissors position at every attempt or offer of an attempt.

She entered the office with her husband, haltingly gave her story, and explained that something had to be done, since she was being threatened with an annulment. Her husband comfirmed her story and added other descriptive details.

Naturalistic Techniques   171

The technique employed was essentially the same as that utilized in a half-dozen similar instances.

She was asked if she were willing to have any reasonable procedure employed to correct her problem. Her answer was, "Yes, anything except that I mustn't be touched, because I just go crazy if I'm touched." This statement her husband corroborated.

She was instructed that hypnosis would be employed. She consented hesitantly but again demanded that no effort be made to touch her.

She was told that her husband would sit continuously in the chair on the other side of the office and that the writer would also sit continuously beside her husband. She, however, was personally to move her chair to the far side of the room, there to sit down and watch her husband continuously. Should either he or the writer at any time leave their chairs, she was to leave the room immediately, since she was sitting next to the office door.

Next she was to sprawl out in her chair, leaning far back with her legs extended, her feet crossed, and all the muscles fully tensed. She was then to look at her husband fixedly until all she could see would be him, with just a view of the writer out of the corner of her eye. Her arms were to be crossed in front of her and her fists were to be tightly clenched.

Obediently she began this task. As she did so, she was told to sleep deeper and deeper, seeing nothing but her husband and the writer. As she slept more and more deeply, she would become scared and panicky, unable to move or to do anything except to watch us both and to sleep more and more deeply in the trance, in direct proportion to her panic state.

This panic state, she was instructed, would deepen her trance, and at the same time hold her rigidly immobile in the chair.

Then gradually, she was told, she would begin to feel her husband touching her intimately, caressingly, even though she would continue to see him still on the other side of the room. She was asked if she were willing to experience such sensations, and she was informed that her existing body rigidity would relax just sufficiently to permit her to nod or to shake her head in reply, and than an honest answer was to be given slowly and thoughtfully.

Slowly she nodded her head affirmatively. She was then asked to note that both her husband and the writer were turning their heads away from her, because she would not begin to feel a progressively more intimate caressing of her body by her husband, until finally she felt entirely pleased, happy, and relaxed.

Approximately five minutes later she addressed the writer, "Please don't look around. I'm so embarrassed. May we go home now, because I'm all right?"

She was dismissed from the office, and her husband was instructed to take her home and passively await developments.

Two hours later a joint telephone call was received, explaining simply, "Everything is all right."

A checkup telephone call a week later disclosed all to be well. Approximately 15 months later they brought their firstborn in with the greatest of pride.

Similar techniques have been employed in instances of nuptial impotence. These cases, in which this general approach has been employed, are eight in number; only one illustrative example will be cited.

REPORT NO. 4

This 24-year-old college-graduate and bridegroom returned from his honeymoon of two weeks most despondent in mood. His bride went immediately to a lawyer's office to seek an annulment, while he sought psychiatric aid.

He was persuaded to bring his wife to the office, and without difficulty she was persuaded to cooperate in the hypnotherapy of her husband.

This proceeded in the following fashion. He was told to look at his wife and to experience anew and completely his sense of absolute shame, humiliation, and hopeless helplessness.

As he did this, he would feel like doing anything, just anything, to escape from that completely wretched feeling. As this continued, he would feel himself becoming unable to see anything except his wife, even unable to see the writer, though able to hear his voice. As this happened, he would realize that he was entering a deep hypnotic trance in which he would have no control over his entire body. Then he would begin to hallucinate his bride in the nude, and then himself in the nude. This would lead to a discovery that he could not move his body and that he had no control over it. In turn this would then lead to the surprising discovery for him that he was sensing physical contact with his bride that would become more and more intimate and exciting, and that there would be nothing he could do to control his physical responses. However, there could be no completion of his uncontrolled responses until his bride so requested.

The trance state developed readily and in full accord with the instructions given above.

At the conclusion of the trance state he was instructed, "You now know that you can, you are confident. In fact, you have succeeded, and there is nothing that you can do to keep from succeeding again and again."

Consummation was readily effected that evening. They were seen thereafter occasionally in the role of a family advisor, and their marriage has been happy for more than 10 years.

Another type of case concerned the small child who had been brought unwillingly to the office, and whose parents had both threatened and bribed him in relation to the office call.

REPORT NO. 5

An example is that of an enuretic eight-year-old boy, half carried, half dragged into the office by his parents. They had previously solicited the aid of the neighbors on his behalf, and he had been prayed for publicly in church. Now he was being brought to a "crazy doctor" as the last resort, with a promise of a "hotel dinner," to be provided following the interview. His resentment and hostility toward all were fully apparent.

The approach was made by declaring, "You're mad and you're going to keep right on being mad, and you think there isn't a thing you can do about it, but there is. You don't like to see a 'crazy doctor,' but you are here and you would like to do something, but you don't know what. Your parents brought you here, made you come. Well, you can make them get out of the office. In fact we both can—come on, let's tell them to go on out." At this point the parents were unobtrusively given a dismissal signal, to which they readily responded, to the boy's immediate, almost startled satisfaction.

The writer then continued, "But you're still mad and so am I, because they ordered me to cure your bed wetting. But they can't give me orders like they give you. But before we fix them for that,"—with a slow, elaborate, attention-compelling, pointing gesture—"look at those puppies right there. I like the brown one best, but I suppose you like the black-and-white one, because its front paws are white. If you are very careful, you can pet mine too. I like puppies, don't you?"

Here the child, taken completely by surprise, readily developed a somnambulistic trance, walked over and went through the motions of petting two puppies, one more than the other. When finally he looked up at the writer, the statement was made to him, "I'm glad you're not mad at me any more and I don't think that you or I have to tell your parents anything. In fact maybe it would serve them just right for the way they brought you here if you waited until the school year was almost over. But one thing certain, you can just bet that after you've had a dry bed for a month, they will get you a puppy just about like little Spotty there, even if you never say a word to them about it. They just have to. Now close your eyes, take a deep breath, sleep deeply, and wake up awful hungry."

The child did as instructed and was dismissed in care of his parents, who had been given instructions privately. Two weeks later he was used as a demonstration subject for a group of physicians. No therapy was done.

During the last month of the school year the boy dramatically crossed off the current calendar day each morning.

Toward the last few days of the month he remarked cryptically to his mother, "You better get ready."

On the 31st day his mother told him there was a surprise for him. His reply was, "It better be black-and-white." At that moment his father came in with a puppy. In the boy's excited pleasure, he forgot to ask questions.

Eighteen months later, the boy's bed was still continuously dry.

REPORT NO. 6

One final case concerns a 16-year-old high school girl, whose thumb-sucking was the bane of her parents, her teachers, her schoolmates, the school bus driver—in fact, the special abhorrence of everybody who came in contact with her.

After much effort on the part of her parents, the soliciting of the aid of the entire neighborhood, the intervention (as in the preceding case) by public prayer in church, the forcing of her to wear a sign declaring her to be a thumb-sucker, it was finally decided in desperation to consult, as a last and shameful resort, a psychiatrist.

The parents' first statement to the writer was to express the hope that therapy of their daughter would be based primarily upon religion. As matters progressed, a promise was extracted from them that after the girl became the writer's patient, for a whole month neither parent would interfere with therapy, no matter what happened, nor would a single word or look of admonition be offered.

The girl came unwillingly to the office with her parents. She was nursing her thumb noisily. Her parents were dismissed from the office and the door closed. As the writer turned to face the girl, she removed her thumb sufficiently to declare her dislike of "nut doctors."

She was told in reply, "And I don't like the way your parents ordered me to cure your thumb-sucking. Ordering me, huh! It's your thumb and your mouth, and why in hell can't you suck it if you want to? Ordering me to cure you. Huh! The only thing I'm interested in is why, when you want to be aggressive about thumb-sucking, you don't really get aggressive instead of piddling around like a baby that doesn't know how to suck a thumb aggressively.

"What I'd like to do is tell you how to suck your thumb aggressively enough to irk the hell out of your old man and your old lady. If you're interested, I'll tell you—if you aren't, I'll just laugh at you."

The use of the word "hell" arrested her attention completely—she knew that a professional man ought not to use that kind of language to a high school girl who attended church regularly. Challenging the inadequacy of her aggressiveness, two terms the school psychologist had taught her, commanded her attention still more.

The offer to teach her how to irk her parents, referred to so disrespectfully, elicited even more complete fixation of her attention, so that to all intents and purposes she was in a hypnotic trance.

Thereupon, in an intent tone of voice, she was told:

"Every night after dinner, just like a clock, your father goes into the living room and reads the newspaper from the front page to the back. Each night when he does that, go in there, sit down beside him, really nurse your thumb good and loud, and irk the hell out of him for the longest 20 minutes he has ever experienced.

"Then go in the sewing room, where your mother sews for one hour every night before she washes dishes. Sit down beside her and nurse your thumb good and loud and irk the hell out of the old lady for the longest 20 minutes she ever knew.

"Do this every night and do it up good. And on the way to school, figure out carefully just which crummy jerk you dislike most, and every time you meet him, pop your thumb in your mouth and watch him turn his head away. And be ready to pop your thumb back if he turns to look again.

"And think over all your teachers and pick out the one you really dislike the most and treat that teacher to a thumb pop every time he or she looks at you. I just hope you can be really aggressive."

After some desultory, irrelevant remarks the girl was dismissed and her parents summoned into the office. They were reminded of the absoluteness of their promise and the declaration was made that if they kept their promises faithfully, the girl's thumb-sucking would cease within a month. Both parents affirmed their wholehearted cooperation.

On the way home the girl did not suck her thumb, and she was silent the entire trip. The parents were so pleased that they telephoned to report their gratification.

That evening however, to their horror, the girl obeyed instructions, as did they, all of which they reported unhappily by telephone the next day. They were reminded of their promise and of the writer's statement of the girl's prognosis.

Each night for the next 10 evenings the girl was faithful in her performance. Then it began to pall on her. She began to shorten the time, then she began late and quit early, then finally she skipped, and then she forgot!

In less than four weeks the girl had discontinued her thumb-sucking, both at home and elsewhere. She became increasingly interested in the much more legitimate teenage activities of her own group. Her adjustments improved in all regards.

The girl was seen again in a social setting about a year later. She recognized the writer, viewed him thoughtfully for a few minutes, and then remarked, "I don't know whether I like you or not, but I am grateful to you."

DISCUSSION AND SUMMARY

One of the most important of all considerations in inducing hypnosis is meeting adequately the patients as personalities and their needs as individuals. Too often the effort is made to fit the patients to an accepted formal technique of suggestion, rather than adapting the technique to the patients in accord with their actual personality situations. In any such adaptation there is an imperative need to accept and to utilize those psychological states, understandings, and attitudes that each patient brings into the situation. To ignore those factors in favor of some ritual of procedure may and often does delay, impede, limit, or even prevent the desired results. The acceptance and utilization of those factors, on the other hand, promotes more rapid trance induction, the development of more profound trance states, the more ready acceptance of therapy, and greater ease for the handling of the total therapeutic situation.

Another important consideration is the need to avoid a repetitious belaboring of the obvious. Once the patients and the therapist have a clear understanding of what is to be done, only fatigue is to be expected from further reiteration. The acceptance as an absolute finality of the patient's wants, needs, and what is to be done, and then expectantly and confidently awaiting the patients' responses, serve more readily to elicit the desired results than repetitious instructions for specific responses. This simplicity of instructions with adequate results is clearly illustrated in the second case report above.

In brief, in each of the above case reports an effort has been made to illustrate the utilization of patient behavior and patient needs as a naturalistic technique of hypnotic trance induction. Also, an effort has been made to demonstrate that the adaptation of hypnotic techniques to individual patients and their needs leads readily and easily to effective therapeutic results.

Suggested Readings

Hypnotic Investigation of Psychosomatic Phenomena: Psychosomatic Interrelationships Studied by Experimental Hypnosis. *Psychosom. Med.*, January, 1943, *5*, pp. 51–58.

(With Richard M. Brickner.) The Development of Aphasia-Like Reactions from Hypnotically Induced Amnesias: Experimental Observations and a Detailed Case Report. *Psychosom. Med.*, January, 1943, *5*, pp. 59-66.

A Controlled Experimental Use of Hypnotic Regression in the Therapy of an Acquired Food Intolerance. *Psychosom. Med.*, January, 1943, *5*, pp. 67-70.

Experimentally Elicited Salivary and Related Responses to Hypnotic Visual Hallucinations Confirmed by Personality Reactions. *Psychosom. Med.*, April, 1943, *5*, pp. 185–187.

The Therapy of a Psychosomatic Headache. *J. Clin. and Exper. Hyp.*, October, 1953, *1*, pp. 2-6.

The Development of an Acute Limited Obsessional Hysterical State in a Normal Hypnotic Subject. *J. Clin. and Exper. Hyp.*, January, 1954, *2*, pp. 27-41.

Special techniques of Brief Hypnotherapy. *J. Clin. and Exper. Hyp.*, April, 1954, *2*, pp. 109-129.

A Clinical Note on Indirect Hypnotic Therapy. *J. Clin. and Exper. Hyp.*, July, 1954, *2*, pp. 171-174.

8. Further Clinical Techniques of Hypnosis: Utilization Techniques

Milton H. Erickson

With the more common techniques of hypnotic trance induction the procedure is based primarily upon altering the subjects' activity of the moment and instructing them variously in a different forms of behavior. Thus the subjects may be told to sit quietly and comfortably in a chair, to fixate their gaze, to relax their bodies progressively, and to develop a trance state as they do this. Or they may be asked to close their eyes and to develop imagery of various types until a trance state develops. Similarly, in the hand-levitation technique a participatory attitude, an interest in the experiential aspects of the situation, and the development of ideomotor activity may all be suggested as a measure of inducing a trance.

Such techniques as these require a willing acceptance of, and cooperation with, an externally suggested or imposed form of behavior which may be either active or passive. Resistance to, or rejection of, this imposed behavior may require the operator to resort to another technique more readily accepted or more pleasing to the subjects. Or it may be met by a fatiguing of the subjects into an acquiescence by the operator's persistence, and sometimes it requires a postponement of the effort at hypnosis. Ordinarily one or another of these measures meets adequately the particular resistance problem presented by the individual patient, but there is always some risk that a change of technique, undue prolongation of effort, or postponement of the hypnosis will have an adverse effect upon a patient's acceptance of hypnosis as a personally possible experiential learning.

However, there is another type of patient actually readily amenable to hypnosis, but unresponsive and resistant to the usual induction techniques. While encountered more frequently in psychotherapeutic practice, they are met not infrequently in general medical and dental practice and are judged too frequently to be unsuitable for the use of hypnosis. These patients are those who are unwilling to accept any suggested behavior until their own resistant or contradictory or opposing behaviors have first been met by the operator. By reason

---

Reprinted with permission from *The American Journal of Clinical Hypnosis*, July, 1959, *2*, 3-21.

of their physical conditions, states of tension or anxiety, intense interest, concern or absorption in their own behaviors, they are unable to give either actively or passively the requisite cooperation to permit an effective alteration in their behavior. For these patients what may be termed *Techniques of Utilization* often serve to adequately meet most of their special needs. But more than this these same techniques are readily applicable to the usual patients and frequently serve to facilitate the process of trance induction in average patients.

These techniques are in essence no more than a simple reversal of the usual procedure of inducing hypnosis. Ordinarily trance induction is based upon securing from the patients some form of initial acceptance and cooperation with the operator. In Techniques of Utilization the usual procedure is reversed to an initial acceptance of the patients' presenting behaviors and a ready cooperation by the operator however seemingly adverse the presenting behaviors may appear to be in the clinical situation.

To clarify and illustrate these various Techniques of Utilization, the following clinical examples will be cited:

EXAMPLE 1

The patient entered the office in a most energetic fashion, declared at once that he did not know if he were hypnotizable, but that he would be willing to go into a trance if it were at all possible provided that the writer were willing to approach the entire matter in an intellectual fashion rather than in a mystical, ritualistic manner. He went on to declare that he needed psychotherapy for a variety of reasons, that he had tried various schools of psychotherapy extensively without benefit, that hypnosis had been attempted on various occasions and had failed miserably because of mysticism and a lack of appreciation for the "intellectual" approach.

Inquiry elicited that he felt that an "intelligent" approach signified not a suggestion of ideas to him but a questioning of him concerning his own thinking and feeling in relationship to reality. For example the writer, he declared, should recognize that he was sitting in a chair, that the chair was in front of a desk, and that these constituted absolute facts of reality and, as such, could not be overlooked, forgotten, denied, or ignored. In further illustration he pointed out that he was obviously tense and anxious and concerned about the tension tremors of his hands, which were resting on the arms of the chair, and that he was also highly distractible, noticing everything about him.

This last comment was seized upon immediately as the basis for the initial cooperation with him, and he was told, "Please proceed with an account of your ideas and understandings, permitting me only enough interruptions *to insure that I understand fully* and *that I follow along with you.* For example you mentioned the chair, but obviously you have seen my desk and have been

Utilization Techniques

distracted by the objects on it. Please explain fully.''

He responded verbosely with a wealth of more or less connected comments about everything in sight, but at every slight pause the writer interjected a word or a phrase to direct his attention anew. These interruptions, made with increasing frequency, were of the following order: and that paperweight; the filing cabinet; your foot on the rug; the ceiling light; the draperies; your right hand on the arm of the chair; the pictures on the wall; the changing focus of your eyes as you glance about; the interest of the book titles; the tension in your shoulders; the feeling of the chair; the disturbing noises; disturbing thoughts; weight of hands; weight of feet, weight of problems, weight of desk; the stationery stand; the records of many patients; the phenomena of life, of illness, of emotion, of physical and mental behavior; the restfulness of relaxation; the need to attend to one's needs; the need to attend to one's tension while looking at the desk or the paperweight or the filing cabinet; the comfort of withdrawal from the environment; fatigue and its development; the unchanging character of the desk; the monotony of the filing cabinet; the need to take a rest; the comfort of closing one's eyes; the relaxing sensation of a deep breath; the delight of learning passively; the capacity for intellectual learning by the unconscious. Various other similar brief interjections were offered, slowly at first and then with increasing frequency.

These initial interjections were merely supplementary to the patient's own train of thought and utterances, and the effect at first was simply to stimulate him to further effort. As this response was made, it became possible to utilize his acceptance of stimulation of his behavior by a procedure of pausing and hesitating in the completion of an interjection. This served to effect in him an *expectant dependency* upon the writer for further and more complete stimulation.

As this procedure was continued, gradually and unnoticeably to the patient his attention was progressively directed to inner subjective experiential matters, whereupon it became possible to use almost directly a simple, progressive relaxation technique of trance induction and to secure a light medium trance.

Throughout therapy for this patient further trance inductions were similar, although the procedure became progressively abbreviated.

EXAMPLE 2

Comparable to the first patient was the case of a woman who presented a somewhat similar problem. She stated that in all previous attempts she had been defeated in her efforts to secure therapy by a compulsive attentiveness to the minutiae of the immediate environment, and that she invariably found difficulty in completing her history and in attending to what was said to her because of the overpowering nature of her need to attend to and to comment upon what she saw about her. (Even this small amount of history was interrupted by her inquiries about, or simple mention of, various objects in the office.) She explained further that a family friend, a psychiatrist who knew her well, had suggested that hypnosis might enable her to cooperate in therapy, and he had referred her to the writer.

Since she herself had impressed the writer as a possible candidate for hypnotherapy, and since little progress was being made in the interview, hypnosis was attempted by utilizing her own behavior as the technique most suited to be employed. This was done in the following fashion:

As she inquired about a paperweight on the desk, reply was quickly made, "It is on the corner of the desk just behind the clock." As she flicked her gaze to the clock and asked urgently, "What time is it?" she was answered with, "The minute hand indicates the same numeral as does the desk calendar."

There followed then a whole series of comments and inquiries by her without pause for any replies, and with a rapid shifting from one object or subject to another. Her entire behavior was similar to that of an unhappy small child, warding off questioning by the measure of forcing the direction of the interrogation into irrelevant, distracting avenues.

Once launched into her verbal flow, it was not possible to interrupt her verbally except with great difficulty, and then fruitlessly. However, the measure of extending a paper knife compelled her to make mention of it. As she responded and then continued in her monologue, the writer polished his glasses, again forcing her to make a comment in accord with her pattern of behavior. Next she was interrupted by a placing of the glasses in their case, then the desk blotter was shifted, a glance was directed at the bookcase, and the schedule book opened and closed. Each of these acts was fitted by her into her compulsive stream of utterances. At first these various acts were performed by the writer at intervals and rather quickly, but as she developed an attitude of expectation for the writer's silent interruptions, his movements were deliberately slowed and made with slight, hesitant pauses, which compelled her to slow down her own behavior and to await the writer's utilization of her conduct. Then the writer added to his silent indication of objects an identifying word or phrase of comment.

As this procedure was continued, it had a progressively profound inhibitory effect upon her, with the result that she began to depend more and more exclusively upon the writer to indicate either verbally or by gesture the next object she was to comment upon or to name. After about 40 minutes of this it became possible to instruct her to close her eyes and to name from memory everything that she had seen and to do this until she developed a deep hypnotic sleep. As she obeyed, she was prompted, "And now, 'paper-weight,' and deeper asleep; and now 'clock,' go even deeper into the trance," etc., until in another 10 minutes a profound somnambulistic trance state was secured.

Thereafter, through this measure of utilizing as an induction technique of her own pattern of resistant behavior, ready cooperation in therapy marked the clinical course of this previously "impossible" patient. Each therapeutic session at the beginning began with her compulsive behavior, which was immediately utilized as a technique of another induction of a therapeutic trance. Later a simple gesture indicating the chair in which she was to sit sufficed to elicit a trance state.

EXAMPLE 3

Essentially the same procedure was employed with a male patient in his early thirties who entered the office and began pacing the floor. He explained repetitiously that he could not endure sitting quietly or lying on a couch and relating his problems and that he had repeatedly been discharged by various psychiatrists because they "accused" him of lack of cooperation. He asked that hypnotherapy be employed, if possible, since his anxieties were almost unendurable and always increased in intensity in a psychiatrist's office and made it necessary for him to pace the floor constantly.

There was still further repetitious explanation of his need to pace the floor which was finally successfully interrupted by the question, "Are you willing to cooperate with me *by continuing to pace the floor, even as you are doing now*?" His reply was a startled, "Willing? Good God, man! I've got to do it if I stay in the office." Thereupon he was asked to permit the writer to participate in his pacing by the measure of directing it in part. To this he agreed rather bewilderedly.

Thereupon he was asked to pace back and forth, to turn to the right, to the left, to walk away from the chair, and to walk toward it. At first these instructions were given in a tempo matching his step. Gradually the tempo of the instructions was slowed and the wording changed to, "Now turn to the right away from the chair in which you can sit; turn left toward the chair in which you can sit; walk away from the chair in which you can sit; walk toward the chair in which you can sit," etc. By this wording a foundation was laid for more cooperative behavior.

The tempo was slowed still more and the instructions again varied to include the phrase, "the chair which you will soon approach as if to seat yourself comfortably," and this in turn was altered to, "the chair in which you will shortly find yourself sitting comfortably." His pacing became progressively slower and more and more dependent upon the writer's verbal instructions until direct suggestions could be given that he seat himself in the chair and go deeper and deeper into a profound trance as he related his history.

Approximately 45 minutes were spent in this manner, inducing a medium trance that so lessened the patient's tension and anxiety that he could cooperate readily with therapy thereafter.

The value of this type of Utilization Technique probably lies in its effective demonstration to the patients that they are completely acceptable and that the therapist can deal effectively with them regardless of their behavior. *It meets both the patients' presenting needs and it employs as the significant part of the induction procedure the very behavior that dominates the patients.*

Another type of Utilization Technique is the employment of the patients' inner, as opposed to outer, behavior, that is, using their thoughts and understandings as the basis for the actual induction procedure. This technique has been employed experimentally and also more than once in therapeutic situations where the type of the patients' resistances made it advisable. Although it has been effectively used on naive subjects, intelligence and some degree of sophistication as well as earnestness of purpose, are ordinarily required.

The procedure is relatively simple. The subjects, whether experimental or therapeutic, are either asked or allowed to give expression freely to their thoughts, understandings, and opinions. As they do this, they are encouraged to speculate aloud more and more extensively upon what could be the possible course of their thinking and feeling if they were to develop a trance state. As patients do this, or even if they merely protest about the impossibility of such speculation, their utterances are repeated after them in their essence, as if the operator were either earnestly seeking further understanding or were confirming their statements. Thus further comments by the subjects are elicited and repeated in turn by the operator. In the more sophisticated subjects there tend to be greater spontaneity, but occasionally the naive, even uneducated subjects may prove to be remarkably responsive.

EXAMPLE 4

An illustration of this technique is the following account, which has been considerably abbreviated because of the extensive repetition required. With this technique the patients' utterances may vary greatly from one instance to another, but the following example is given in sufficient detail to illustrate the method.

In seeking psychiatric help, this patient declared, "I've made no progress at all in three years of psychoanalysis, and the year I spent in hypnotherapy was a total loss. I didn't even go into a trance. But I tried hard enough. I just got nowhere. But I've been referred to you and I don't see much sense in it. Probably another failure. I just can't conceive of me going into a trance. I don't even know what a trance is." These remarks, together with the information received previously from the referring physician, suggested the possibility of employing her own verbailization as the induction procedure.

In the following account the writer's utterances are in italics:

> You really can't conceive of what a trance is—no, I can't, what is it?—*yes, what is it?*—a psychological state, I suppose—*A psychological state you suppose, what else?*—I don't know—*you really don't*

Utilization Techniques

know—no, I don't—*you don't, you wonder, you think*—think what—*yes, what do you think, feel, sense?*—(pause)—I don't know—*but you can wonder*—do you go to sleep?—*no, tired, relaxed, sleepy*—really tired—*so very tired and relaxed, what else?*—I'm puzzled—*puzzles you, you wonder, you think, you feel, what do you feel?*—my eyes—*yes, your eyes, how?*—they seem blurred—*blurred, closing*—(pause)—they are closing—*closing, breathing deeper*—(pause)—*tired and relaxed, what else?*—(pause)—*sleep, tired, relaxed, sleep, breathing deeper*—(pause)—*what else*—I feel funny—*funny, so comfortable, really learning*—(pause)—*learning, yes, learning more and more*—(pause)—*eyes closed, breathing deeply, relaxed, comfortable, so very comfortable, what else?*—(pause)—I don't know—*you really don't know, but really learning to go deeper and deeper*—(pause)—too tired to talk, just sleep—(pause)—*maybe a word or two*—I don't know (spoken laboriously)—*breathing deeper, and you really don't know, just going deeper, sleeping soundly, more and more soundly, not caring, just learning, continuing ever deeper and deeper and learning more and more with your unconscious mind.*

From this point on it was possible to deal with her simply and directly without any special elaboration of suggestions, and subsequently trances were secured through the use of posthypnotic suggestions.

The above is simply a summary of the illustrative utterances and the method of utilization. In general there is much more repetition, usually only of certain ideas, and these vary from patient to patient. Sometimes this technique proves to be decidedly rapid. Frequently with anxious, fearful patients it serves to comfort them with a conviction that they are secure, that nothing is being done to them or being imposed upon them, and they feel that they can comfortably be aware of every step of the procedure. Consequently they are able to give full cooperation, which would be difficult to secure if they were to feel that a pattern of behavior was being forcibly imposed upon them.

The general principle of the above technique can be readily adapted into a separate Utilization Technique. Somewhat parallel in character, but clearly different, is its use as an effective reinduction for those patients who were previously good hypnotic subjects but who, for one reason or another, have become highly resistant to hypnosis despite outward cooperativeness.

The procedure is to get the subjects to recall from the beginning in a reasonably orderly, detailed manner the events of a previous successful hypnotic trance. As the subjects do this, repetitions of their statements are offered and helpful questions are asked. As they become absorbed in this task, the subjects revivify the previous trance state, usually regressing subjectively to that previous situation and developing a special rapport with the operator. The following example, in summary form, illustrates this Utilization Technique.

EXAMPLE 5

A volunteer subject at a lecture before a university group declared, "I was hypnotized once several years ago. It was a light trance, not very satisfactory, and while I would like to cooperate with you, I'm quite certain that I can't be hypnotized." "Do you recall the physical setting of that trance?" "Oh, yes, it was in the psychology laboratory of the university I was then attending." "Could you, as you sit here, recall and describe to me the physical setting of that trance situation?"

He agreeable proceeeded to describe in detail the laboratory room in which he had been hypnotized lightly, including a description of the chair in which he sat and a description of the professor who induced the trance. This was followed by a comparable response to the writer's request that he describe in as orderly and as comprehensive a fashion as possible his recollection of the actual suggestions given him at that time and the responses he made to them.

Slowly, thoughtfully, the subject described an eye-closure technique with suggestions of relaxation, fatigue, and sleep. As he progressed in his verbalizations of his recollections, his eyes slowly closed, his body relaxed, his speech became slower and more hesitant, and he required increasingly more prompting until it became evident that he was in a trance state. Thereupon he was asked to state where he was and who was present. He named the previous university and the former professor. Immediately he was asked to also listen carefully to what the writer had to say, and he was then employed to demonstrate the phenomena of the deep trance.

This same technique of utilizing previous hypnotic learnings has been employed with patients, particularly those who develop inexplicable resistances to further hypnosis or who declare that they have been in hypnotherapy elsewhere and therefore doubt seriously their ability to develop a trance for a new hypnotherapist. The simple measure of seating the patient comfortably and asking him to give a detailed account of a previous successful trance experience results in a trance, usually decidedly rapidly and usually a revivification of the previous trance, or even a regression to that trance. This technique can also be utilized with one's own patients who have developed resistance to further hypnosis. In such instances resolution of the resistances is frequently facilitated and therapy greatly accelerated.

Another Utilization Technique, comparable to those immediately above, has been employed experimentally and clinically on both naive and experienced subjects. It has been used as a means of circumventing resistances, as a method of initial trance induction, and as a trance-reinduction procedure. It is a technique based upon an immediate, direct elicitation of meaningful, unconsciously executed behavior which is separate and apart from consciously directed activity, except that of interested attention. The procedure is as follows:

EXAMPLE 6

Depending upon the subjects' educational backgrounds a suitable, casual explanation is given of the general concepts of the conscious and of the unconscious or subconscious minds. Similarly a casual though carefully instructive explanation is given of ideomotor activity with a citing of familiar examples, including hand levitation.

Then with utter simplicity the subjects are told to sit quietly, to rest their hands palm down on their thighs, and to listen carefully to a question that will be asked. This question, it is explained, can be answered only by their unconscious mind, not by their conscious mind. They can, it is added, offer a conscious reply, but such a reply will be only a conscious statement and not an actual reply to the question. As for the question itself, it can be one of several that could be asked, and it is of no particular significance to the personality. Its only purpose is to give the unconscious mind an opportunity to manifest itself in the answer given. The further explanation is offered that the answer will be an ideomotor response of one or the other hand upward, that of the left signifying an answer of "no," that of the right a "yes," to the question asked the unconscious mind.

The question is then presented: "Does your unconscious mind think that you can go into a trance?" Further elaboration is offered again: "Consciously you cannot know what your unconscious mind thinks or knows. But your unconscious mind can let your conscious mind discover what it thinks or understands by the simple process of causing a levitation of either the right or the left hand. Thus your unconscious mind can communicate in a visibly recognizable way with your conscious mind. Now just watch your hands and see what the answer is. Neither you nor I know what your unconscious mind thinks, but as you see one or the other of your hands lifting, you will know."

If there is much delay, additional suggestions can be given: "One of your hands is lifting. Try to notice the slightest movement, try to feel and to see it, and enjoy the sensation of its lifting and be pleased to learn what your unconscious thinks."

Regardless of which hand levitates, a trance state supervenes simultaneously, frequently of the somnambulistic type. Usually it is advisable to utilize, rather than to test, the trance immediately since the subjects tend to arouse promptly. This is usually best done by remarking simply and casually, "It is very pleasing to discover that your unconscious can communicate with your conscious mind in this way, and there are many other things that your unconscious can learn to do. For example, now that it has learned that it can develop a trance state and to do it remarkably well, it can learn various trance phenomena. For instance you might be interested in ————," and the needs of the situation can then be met.

In essence this technique centers on the utilization of the subjects' interest in their own unconscious activity. A "yes" or "no" situation is outlined concerning thinking, with action contingent upon that thinking and constituting an overt unconscious communication, a manifestation basic to, and an integral part of, a hypnotic trance. In other words it is necessary for the subjects to go into a trance in order to discover the answer to the question.

Various experienced subjects approached with this technique have recognized it immediately and made comment to the effect: "How interesting! No matter which answer you give, you first have to go into a trance."

The willing subjects disclose from the beginning their unaffected interest, while resistant, unwilling subjects manifest their attitudes by difficulty in understanding the preliminary explanations, by asking repeatedly for instructions, and then by an anticipation of hand levitation by lifting the left hand voluntarily. Those subjects who object to trance induction in this manner tend to awaken at the first effort to test or to utilize the trance. Most of them, however, will readily go back into the trance when told, "And you can go into a trance just as easily and quickly as your unconscious answered that question, just by continuing to watch as your unconscious mind continues to move your hand up toward your face. As your hand moves up, your eyes will close, and you will go into a deep trance." In nearly all instances the subjects develop a trance state.

An essential consideration in this technique, however, is an attitude on the part of the operator of utter expectancy, casualness, and simplicity, which places the responsibility for any developments entirely upon the subject.

Patients' misunderstandings, doubts, and uncertainties may also be utilized as the technique of induction. Exemplifying this approach are the instances of two patients, both college-bred women, one in her late 30's and the other in her early 40's.

EXAMPLE 7

The first patient expressed extreme doubt and uncertainty about the validity of hypnotic phenomena as applied to herself as a person, but explained that her desperate need for help compelled her to try it as a remotely possible means of therapy.

The other woman declared her conviction that hypnosis and physiological sleep were necessarily identical or, at the very least, equal and complementary component parts of a single psychophysiological manifestation and that she could not possibly go into a trance without first developing physiological sleep. This, she explained, would preclude therapy, and yet she felt that hypnosis offered the only possible, however questionable, means of psychotherapy for her, provided that the hypnotherapy was so conducted as to preclude physiological sleep. That this was possible she disbelieved completely.

Utilization Techniques

Efforts at explanation were futile and served only to increase the anxiety and tension of both patients. Therefore an approach utilizing their misapprehensions was employed, and the technique, except for the emphasis employed, was essentially the same for both patients. This was done by instructing each that deep hypnosis would be employed and that each would cooperate in going into a deep trance by assessing, appraising, evaluating, and examining the validity and genuineness of each item of reality and of each item of subjective experience that was mentioned. In so doing each was to feel under obligation to discredit and to reject anything that seemed at all uncertain or questionable. For the one patient, emphasis was placed primarily upon subjective sensations and reactions with an interspersed commentary upon reality objects. For the other, attentiveness to reality objects as proof of wakefulness was emphasized with an interspersing of suggestions of subjective responses. In this manner there was effected for each woman a progressive narrowing of the field of awareness and a corresponding increase in a dependency upon, and a responsiveness to, the writer. As this state developed, it became possible to induce in each a somnambulistic trance by employing a simple eye-closure, progressive-relaxation technique slightly modified to meet the special needs of each patient.

To illustrate the actual verbalization employed, the following sample of utterances, in which the emphasis is approximately evenly divided between subjective aspects and reality objects, is offered:

> As you sit comfortably in that chair, you can feel the weight of your arms resting on the arms of the chair. And your eyes are open, and you can see the desk, and there is only the ordinary blinking of the eyelids, which you may or may not notice, just as one may notice the feeling of the shoes on one's feet and then again forget about it. And you really know that you can see the bookcase, and you can wonder if your unconscious has noted any particular book title. But now again you can note the feeling of the shoes on your feet as they rest on the floor and at the same time you can become aware of the lowering of your eyelids as you direct your gaze upon the floor. And your arms are still resting their weight on the arms of the chair, and all these things are real, and you can be attentive to them and sense them. And if you look at your wrist and then look at the corner of the room, perhaps you can feel or sense the change in your visual focus and perhaps you can remember when, as a child, you may have played with the experience of looking at an object as if it were far off and then close by, and as associated memories of your childhood pass through your mind, they can range from simple memories to tired feelings because memories are real. They are things, even though abstract, as real as the chair and the desk and the tired feeling that comes from sitting without moving, and for which one can compensate by relaxing the muscles and sensing the weight of the body, just as one can feel so vividly the weariness

of the eyelids as fatigue and relaxation develop more and more. And all that has been said is real and your attention to it is real, and you can feel and sense more and more as you give your attention to your hand or to your foot or the desk or your breathing or to the memory of the feeling of comfort some time when you closed your eyes to rest your gaze. And you know that dreams are real, that one sees chairs and trees and people and hears and feels various things in his dreams and that visual and auditory images are as real as chairs and desks and bookcases that become visual images.

In this way, with increasing frequency, the writer's utterances became simple, direct suggestions for subjective responses.

This technique of utilizing doubts and misunderstandings has been used with other patients and with experimental subjects, and it also adapts well to the use of hand levitation as a final development, since ideomotor activity within the visual range offers opportunity for excellent objective and subjective realities.

Another Utilization Technique centers around the need that some potentially excellent subjects have to resist and reject hypnosis completely as a personal experience until after it becomes, paradoxically, an accomplished fact for them.

Occasionally such a person, because of naiveté or misdirected resistance, may even develop a somnambulistic trance, but thereafter is likely either to reject hypnosis completely or to limit unduly and inexplicably his capacity for hypnotic responses. More frequently such persons remain seemingly unhypnotizable, often despite an obvious capacity for responsiveness, until their special individual needs are met in a manner satisfying to them. Those who permit themselves limited hypnotic responses may for example develop an excellent obstetrical anaesthesia but remain incapable of dental anaesthesia, or vice versa. But should by some chance the second type of manifestation be secured, there may occur a loss of the capacity for the first type, or there may be a loss of capacity for all hypnotic responses. Another example is the similar type of patient in psychotherapy who will hypnotically respond only to specific types of circumscribed therapeutic problems.

On the whole these individuals constitute seemingly impossible or unpredictable and unreliable hypnotic subjects until their special needs are met, whereupon they can then become remarkably competent subjects.

Following are accounts of this type of subject, encountered in both experimental and clinical work.

EXAMPLE 8

A 20-year-old woman, a member of a group of psychology students actively engaged in experimental hypnosis both as subjects and operators, failed com-

Utilization Techniques

pletely to develop any trance phenomena despite many hours of endeavor to go into a trance. She had originally expressed a conviction that hypnosis was impossible as a personal experience, but that she hoped to learn otherwise. Finally two of her associates, both competent as operators and as somnambulistic subjects, suggested a visit to the writer as a last resort. The situation was explained in full, and Miss X reaffirmed both her conviction and her hope, and she requested the writer to make every possible effort to induce a trance. Her entire appearance and behavior suggested that she was essentially a most responsive type of personality.

She was found to be outwardly most cooperative but actually completely resistive and unresponsive hypnotically, even after three hours of intensive effort with a great variety of both direct and indirect techniques. This served to confirm Miss X's conviction of her unhypnotizability and to suggest to the writer the experimental possibility of utilizing her need to resist and reject hypnosis as a personal experience as a means of effecting paradoxical trance phenomena for her.

To achieve this Miss X was reminded that her two companions, A and B, were excellent somnambules and could enter a deep trance at a moment's notice. A and B were then openly instructed to remain continuously in the state of psychological awareness that existed for them at the moment and not to betray in any way to Miss X whether or not they had spontaneously gone into a trance state in response to the writer's efforts with Miss X. (They had not developed trance states, a fact obvious to the writer but not to Miss X.)

She was then challenged to scrutinize A and B carefully and to state definitely if she knew if they were in a trance, while A and B in turn were told to answer honestly with a simple nod or shake of the head any question put to them when so instructed by the writer.

Miss X confessed her inability to identify the state of awareness of either A or B. She was reminded that she was awake and could not develop a trance state and hence could not manifest trance phenomena, but that A and B, being experienced subjects, could do so readily. She agreed, and the statement was made that, if A and B were in a trance state, negative visual hallucinations could be elicited. Again she agreed. Turning away from the three of them and facing the office wall, the writer offered the following instructions:

> Miss X, I want you to observe carefully the responses that A and B make, since I shall not be looking at them, and at the end of my remarks I shall ask them a special question which they are to answer by either a nod or shake of the head, as I explained before. All of you know, do you not, the fish pond [a campus landmark], and all of you can nod your head in answer. You have seen it many times, you know it well, and you can see it any time you want to. Now, Miss X, observe A and B carefully and be ready to report their answer, and A and B, while Miss X continues to await your response, DO NOT SEE [speaking

softly, emphatically, and looking intently and pointing with slow deliberation at the office wall that was well within Miss X's field of vision], DO NOT SEE THE FISH POND RIGHT THERE. And you don't see the fish pond, do you?" A and B both shook their heads negatively, and Miss X excitedly declared, "They are both in a trance. They are showing negative hallucinations.

Without comment to her the writer asked A and B if they saw the students walking past the fish pond or the fish and plants in the water. Again they shook their heads negatively.

Thereupon the writer suggested to Miss X that A and B be left to their own devices while she and he discussed hypnosis. She agreed and almost immediately declared that the demonstration of negative visual hallucinations on the part of A and B had convinced her in some way that she could be hypnotized and that she would be glad to volunteer at any time to go into a trance, that she was certain that she could go into a deep trance.

Instead of replying directly to her statement she was asked if she were willing to talk to A and B. Upon her assent they were told to ask Miss X the written questions the writer had just handed to them. They asked her if she could see the fish pond and the students walking past it. Upon her affirmative reply she was asked to state exactly where she was. She described herself as standing with them and with the writer some 10 feet away from the campus fish pond.

She was then told by the writer that A and B would be awakened from their "trance" by the simple measure of having them, *while she did likewise,* close their eyes, and then at the count of three there would be a full awakening from all trance states with the continuing ability to go into a trance at any desired future time for any legitimate purpose. She awakened from her trance as instructed with a complete spontaneous amnesia for trance events and with an apparent persistence of her original ideas of her unhypnotizability. The trio was then dismissed, with A and B privately instructed to avoid all mention of hypnosis.

The next day Miss X again volunteered as a subject at the psychology laboratory and developed rapidly a profound somnambulistic trance. So pleased was she that she visited the writer that evening with the request that he make another attempt to hypnotize her. She responded with a deep trance almost immediately, and thereafter did extensive work as an experimental subject.

EXAMPLE 9

A clinical instance in which this same technique was employed is exemplified by an obstreperous 25-year-old patient for whom hypnotherapy was not indicated. Nevertheless he repeatedly demanded hypnosis and in the same breath declared himself unhypnotizable. On one occasion he forced the issue by demanding absolutely, "Hypnotize me even though I'm not hypnotizable."

This demand was met by employing softly spoken suggestions of slow, progressive relaxation, fatigue, and sleep. Throughout the hour that this was done, the patient sat on the edge of his chair, gesticulated, and bitterly denounced the entire procedure as stupid and incompetent. At the close of the session the patient declared that his time and money had been wasted, that he could "remember every ineffectual, stupid suggestion" that had been offered, and that he could "remember everything that took place the whole time."

The writer immediately seized upon these utterances to declare somewhat repetitiously, "Certainly you remember. You are here in the office. Naturally here in the office you can remember everything. It all occurred here in the office, and you were here, and here you can remember everything." Impatiently he demanded another appointment and left angrily.

At the next appointment he was deliberately met in the reception room. He immediately inquired if he had kept his previous appointment. Reply was given evasively that surely he would remember if he had done so. He explained that on that day he had suddenly found himself at home sitting in his car unable to remember if he had just returned from his appointment or were just leaving for it. This question he debated for an indefinite period of time before he thought of checking his watch, and then he discovered that the time was long past the proper hour. However, he was still unable to decide the problem because he did not know how long he had debated the question. Again he asked if he had kept his previous appointment, and again he was assured evasively that surely he would remember if he had.

As he entered the office, he stopped short and declared, "I did too keep my appointment. You wasted my time with that silly, soft, gentle, ineffectual hypnotic technique of yours, and you failed miserably."

After a few more derogatory comments from him, he was maneuvered into returning to the reception room, where he once more manifested an amnesia for the previous appointment as well as his original inquiries about it. His questions were again parried, and he was led back into the office, where for a second time he experienced full recall of the previous appointment.

Again he was induced to return to the reception room with a resultant reestablishment of his amnesia, but upon reentering the office, he added to his recollection of the previous appointment a full recall of his separate entrances into the reception room and the accompanying amnesic states. This bewildered and intrigued him to such an extent that he spent most of the hour going from the office to the reception room and back again, experiencing a full amnesia in the reception room and full recollection, inclusive of the reception room manifestations, of the total experience in the office.

The therapeutic effect of this hypnotic experience was the correction almost immediately of much of the patient's hostile, antagonistic, hypercritical, demanding attitude and the establishment of a good rapport and an acceleration of therapy, even though no further hypnosis was employed.

The technique employed in these two instances is somewhat comparable to the procedure reported by this writer in "Deep Hypnosis and Its Induction" (Erickson, 1954), and it has been used repeatedly with various modifications. Patients requiring the use of this technique are usually those with distressing needs for a sense of utter security in the competence of the therapist. Its advantage as a therapeutic technique lies in the fact that it permits the patients to achieve that sense of security through experiential learning as a single separate process rather than through a prolonged demonstration of competence always subject to their criticism and rejection.

In essence this technique is no more than a modification of a much simpler elementary procedure—such as the hand clasp and the postural sway—sometimes so effectively employed to correct minor attitudes of doubt and resistance to trance induction. Its advantage lies in the effectiveness with which it can both elicit the phenomena of even deep hypnosis and correct various problems of resistance to hypnosis and to therapy.

Another Utilization Technique was employed during a lecture and demonstration before a medical student body. One of the students proceeded, at the beginning of the lecture, to heckle the writer by denouncing hypnosis as a fraud and the writer as a charlatan, and he declared that any demonstration using his fellow students would be a prearranged hoax perpetrated upon the audience. The measures employed were as follows:

EXAMPLE 10

Since he persisted in his noisy, adverse comments as the lecture proceeded, it became necessary to take corrective action. Accordingly the lecture was interrupted and the writer engaged in an acrimonious interchange with the heckler, in which the writer's utterances were carefully worded to elicit an emphatic contradiction from the heckler, either verbally or by action.

Thus he was told that he had to remain silent; that he could not speak again; that he did not dare to stand up; that he could not again charge fraud; that he dared not walk over to the aisle or up to the front of the auditorium; that he had to do whatever the writer demanded; that he had to sit down; that he had to return to his original seat; that he was afraid of the writer; that he dared not risk being hypnotized; that he was a noisy coward; that he was afraid to look at the volunteer subjects sitting on the platform; that he had to take a seat in the back of the auditorium; that he did not dare to come up on the platform; that he was afraid to shake hands in a friendly fashion with the writer; *that he did not dare to remain silent*; that he was afraid to walk over to one of the chairs on the platform for volunteer subjects; that he was afraid to face the audience and to smile at them; that he dared not look at or listen to the writer; that he could not sit in one of the chairs; that he would have to put his hands behind him instead of resting them on his thighs; that he dared not experience hand levitation; that he was afraid to close his eyes; that he had to remain awake; that he was afraid to go into a trance; that he had to hurry off the platform; that he could not remain and go into a trance; that he could not even develop a light trance; that he dared not go into a deep trance, etc.

The student disputed either by word or action every step of the procedure with considerable ease until he was forced into silence. With his dissents then limited to action alone, and caught in his own pattern of contradiction of the writer, it became relatively easy to induce a somnambulistic trance state. He was then employed as the demonstration subject for the lecture most effectively.

The next weekend he sought out the writer, gave an account of his extensive personal unhappiness and unpopularity, and requested psychotherapy. In this he progressed with phenomenal rapidity and success.

This technique, either in part or in toto, has been used repeatedly with various modifications, especially with defiant, resistive patients, and particularly "incorrigible" juvenile delinquents. Its significance lies in the utilization of the patients' ambivalences and the opportunity such an approach affords the patients to successfully achieve contradictory goals, with the feeling that these derived out of the unexpected but adequate use of their own behavior. This need to fully meet the demands of the patients, however manifested, ought never to be minimized.

Another Technique of Utilization centers in a combination of utilization, distraction, and participatory activity, all of which are illustrated in the following account.

EXAMPLE 11

Seven-year-old Allan fell on a broken bottle and severely lacerated his leg. He came rushing into the kitchen, crying loudly from both pain and fright while shouting, "It's bleeding; it's bleeding." As he entered the kitchen, he seized a towel and began wildly swabbing to wipe up the blood. As he paused in his shouting to catch his breath, he was told urgently, "Wipe up that blood; wipe up that blood; use a bath towel; use a bath towel; use a bath towel, a bath towel, not a hand towel, a bath towel," and one was handed to him. He dropped the towel he had already used and was immediately told urgently, repetitiously, "Now wrap it around your leg, wrap it tightly, wrap it tightly." This he did awkwardly but sufficiently effectively, whereupon with continued urgency he was told, "Now hold it tight, hold it tight; let's get in the car and go to the doctor's office and hold it tightly."

All the way to the surgeon's office careful explanation was given him that his injury was really not large enough to warrant as many stitches as his sister had had at the time of her hand injury. However, he was urgently counseled and exhorted that it would be his responsibility entirely to see to it that the surgeon put in as many stitches as possible, and he was thoroughly coached all the way there on how to emphatically demand his full rights.

At the surgeon's office, without awaiting any inquiry, Allan emphatically told the nurse that he wanted 100 stitches. She made no response but merely said, "This way, sir, right to the surgery." As she was followed, Allan was told, "That's just the nurse. The doctor is in the next room. Now don't forget to tell him everything just the way you want it."

As Allan entered the room, he announced to the surgeon, "I want 100 stitches. See!" Whipping off the towel, he pointed at his leg and declared, "Right there, 100 stitches. That's a lot more than Betty Alice had. And don't put them too far apart. And don't get in my way. I want to see. I've got to count them. And I want black thread, so you can see it. Hey, I don't want a bandage. I want stitches!"

It was explained to the surgeon that Allan understood well his situation and needed no anaesthesia, and to Allan the writer explained that his leg would first have to be washed. Then he was to watch carefully and notice the placing of the sutures to make sure they were not too far apart and that he was to count each one carefully and not to make any mistakes in his counting.

While the surgeon performed his task in puzzled silence, Allan counted the sutures and rechecked his counting, demanded that the sutures be placed closer together, and complainingly lamented that he would not have as many as his sister. His parting statement to the surgeon was to the effect that with a little more effort the surgeon could have given him more sutures.

On the way home Allan was comforted regarding the fewness of the sutures and adequately complimented on his competence in overseeing so well the entire procedure. It was also suggested that he eat a big dinner and go to sleep right afterward so that his leg could heal faster, and so that he would not have to go to the hospital the way his sister did. Full of zeal, Allan did as suggested.

No mention of pain or anaesthesia was made to Allan at any time, nor were any "comforting reassurances" offered. Neither was there any formal effort to induce a trance. Instead various aspects of the total situation were utilized to distract his attention completely away from the painful considerations and to focus it upon values of importance to a seven-year-old boy and to secure his full, active cooperation and intense participation in dealing with the entire problem adequately.

In situations such as this the patient experiences as a personality a tremendously urgent need to have something done. Recognition of this need and a readiness to utilize it by doing something in direct relationship to the origin of the need constitutes a most effective type of suggestion in securing the patient's full cooperation for adequate measures.

EXAMPLE 12

To cite another similar example, when little Roxanna came sobbing into the house, distressed by an inconsequential (not to her) scratch upon her knee, adequate therapy was not assurance that the injury was too minor to warrant treatment, nor even the statement that she was mother's brave little girl and that mother would kiss her and the pain would cease and the scratch would heal. Instead effective therapy was based upon the utilization of the personality's need for something to be done in direct relationship to the injury. Hence a kiss *to the right*, a kiss *to the left*, and a kiss *right on top* of the scratch effected for Roxie an instantaneous healing of the wound, and the whole incident promptly became a part of her thrilling historical past.

This technique, based as it is upon the utilization of strong personality needs, is effective with both children and adults, and it can be adapted readily to situations requiring in some way strong, active, intense responses and participation by the patient.

These techniques of suggestive therapy in one form or another are in the repertoire of every experienced mother, and they are as old as motherhood itself. Every experienced general practitioner employs these techniques regularly without necessarily recognizing them as formally based upon suggestion. But with the development of clinical hypnosis there is a need to examine and give recognition to those psychological principles that enables the communication of desirable understandings at times of stress.

Another type of Utilization Technique is based upon a process of conditioning behavioral manifestations and then interpolating into them new and corrective forms of behavior.

EXAMPLE 13

An example of this is the therapy employed to correct the nightmares developed during convalescence by seven-year-old Robert, a traffic casualty, suffering from a skull fracture, brain concussion, fractured thighs, and other varied injuries.

Upon his return home in a body cast from the hospital, he was noted to suffer from almost nightly nightmares. These followed essentially the same pattern each time. They began with moaning, followed by frightened crying, then shuddering sobs, and finally culminated with the frightened cries, "Oh, oh, it's going to hit me—it's going to hit me," followed by a shuddering collapse into silence and slow, shallow breathing, as if he had fainted.

Sometimes several nightmares would occur in a single night, sometimes only one, and sometimes he would skip a night. He had no waking memory of these nightmares, and he disclaimed dreams.

Upon first noting the nightmares, an effort was made to arouse him from them, but the first few attempts were futile. When the lights were turned on in his bedroom, his eyes were found to be wide open, his pupils dilated, his face contorted in an expression of terror, and his attention could not be secured. When, however, he repeated his phrase of "It's going to hit me," his eyes would shut, his entire body would relax, and he would remain unresponsive as if in a faint for several minutes. Then he would seem to lapse into physiological sleep from which he could be aroused, but with no memory of the nightmare.

When all these findings had been confirmed repeatedly, a technique was devised to secure his attention and to correct the nightmare. The approach to the problem was relatively simple and comprehensive, and was based upon the assumption that the nightmares were essentially a distorted and disorderly, perhaps even fragmentary reliving of the accident. Therefore they could not be distorted or overthrown, but would have to be accepted and then modified and corrected.

The procedure was as follows: At the beginning of his nightmare, as his moaning began, Robert was told, in a cadence and tone that matched his outcries, "Something's going to happen—it's going to hurt you bad—it's a truck—it's coming right at you—it's going to hurt you—it's going to hit you—hit you—hurt you—hit you—hurt you awful bad." These utterances were matched with his outcries and were terminated with his collapse. In other words an effort was made to parallel in time and in character the inner subjective stimulation. In this way it was hoped to effect an association between the two types of stimulation and possibly to condition the one to the other.

The first night that the procedure was employed Robert had two nightmares. The next night again he had two more. After a long wait, and while he was sleeping peacefully, the procedure was employed again, and a third nightmare developed almost immediately.

On the third night, after he had been sleeping peacefully for some time and before a nightmare had developed, the procedure was deliberately employed twice. Both times a nightmare resulted, apparently in response to the procedure. A third nightmare was later elicited that night by the same procedure but with the addition of a new phrase that could possibly capitalize upon wishes and feelings without distorting the reality involved. This phrase was the statement that, "There is another truck on the other side of the street, and that one won't hit you. It will just go right by." The reason for this type of interpolation was to employ an idea that would be entirely acceptable and yet would not alter the historical reality. Then, if accepted, the way would be paved for more pertinent interpolations.

The next night he developed a nightmare spontaneously, which was treated by the modified procedure. A second nightmare was deliberately induced later that night and handled by a still further modification of the procedure, the change being the addition of, "but you will get well, all well, all well."

Thereafter, night after night, but only when he developed a spontaneous nightmare, was this general procedure followed. His utterances and cries were

Utilization Techniques

matched, but each time with a progressive modification of the writer's utterances, until the final content was nothing more than, "There's a truck coming, and it is too bad it is going to hit you. You will have to go to the hospital, but that will be all right because you will come home, and you will get all well. And all the other cars and trucks on the street you will see, and you will keep out of their way."

As the change was made progressively in the statements said to him, the character and severity of the nightmares slowly changed and lessened until it seemed that Robert was merely rousing slightly and listening for the reassurance offered.

From beginning to end the therapy of the nightmares covered a period of one month, and the last three were scarcely more than a slight seeming arousal from sleep, as if to assure himself vaguely of the writer's presence. Thereafter, to his present age of 14, he has continued to sleep well and without a recurrence of his nightmares.

The following Utilization Technique is one based upon the employment of seemingly inconsequential, irrelevant considerations and an apparent disregard or oversight of the major issues involved. Following are two illustrative instances.

EXAMPLE 14

A 70-year-old woman born in a rural community had not been allowed to attend school, since her parents did not believe in education for women. At the age of 14 she married a youth of 16, whose formal education was limited to his signature for signing checks and "figgering." The bride was pleased with her husband's greater education and resolved to have him teach her, since she resented her lack of schooling. This hope did not materialize. During the next six years she was kept busy with farm work and pregnancies, but she did learn to "figger" excellently but only mentally, since it was apparently impossible for her to learn to write numerals. Neither was she able to learn to sign her name.

At the age of 20 she hit upon the idea of furnishing room and board for the local rural schoolteacher, with the intention of receiving, in return for reduced rates, the much desired instruction in reading and writing.

Each school year for the next 50 years she made and kept her agreement, and the teachers hopefully began the attempt. Finally, some soon, others only after prolonged labor, abandoned the task of teaching her as hopeless. As the community grew, the number of teachers increased until she was boarding, year after year, a total of four. None succeeded, despite the sincerity of her desire and the honesty of their effort. Her children went through grade school, high school, and college, and they too tried to instruct their mother but without results.

Each time she was given a lesson, invariably she developed, after the manner of a seriously frightened small child, a state of mental blankness or a state of frantic, disorganized effort to please that led to a total impasse.

It was not that "Maw" was unintelligent. She had an excellent memory, good critical judgment, listened well, and was remarkably well informed. She often gave strangers, through her conversation, the impression that she had a college education, despite her faulty grammar.

At the time she was seen by the writer, she and her husband had been retired for some years, but she was still boarding teachers, three at that time. These three had made it a joint project for several months to teach her the elements of reading and writing but were finally forced to give up. They described her as:

> It's always the same. She starts the lesson period full of enthusiasm and hope, and that's the way you feel, too. But inside of a minute you'll swear that you must be talking a foreign language to her because she doesn't understand a thing you say or do. No matter what you say or do, she just sits there with those eager, troubled eyes, trying hard to make sense out of the nonsense you seem to be saying to her. We've tried everything. We've talked to some of our friends who have tried. She is just like a badly scared child who has blanked out completely, except that she doesn't seem scared but just blanked out. Because she is so intelligent, we just couldn't believe that she couldn't learn easily.

The patient herself explained, "My sons that graduated from engineering told me that I've got the right gears for reading and writing, but that they are of different sizes, and that's the reason they don't mesh. Now you can file them down or trim them to size because I've got to learn to read and write. Even boarding three teachers and baking and cooking and washing and ironing for them ain't half enough work for me, and I get so tired sitting around with nothing to do. Can you learn me?"

This history and much more comparable material suggested a long, persistent, circumscribed psychological blocking that might yield to hypnotic suggestion. Accordingly she was accepted as a patient with the rash promise that she would be reading and writing within three weeks' time, but *without being taught anything that she did not already know and had known for a long time*.

Although this declaration puzzled her, so great was her desire to learn that she was easily persuaded to cooperate fully in every way with the writer, *even though he might not teach her anything except how to let her read and write, which she already knew*.

The next step was to induce by simple, direct suggestions a light-to-medium trance, predicated, in accord with her own unique neurotic needs, upon *her full understandings that it would be something apart from, and completely unrelated to, her learning problem; that there would be no effort to teach her anything *she did not already know; that the trance would be employed only to let her do things she already knew how to do; and that everything undertaken would be something she had learned about a long time ago.* With her responses to hypnosis contingent upon these understandings, it became possible to induce a trance and to instruct her to remain in it until otherwise instructed and to obey completely and without argument every instruction given her *provided that it was always something in relationship to things she had already learned a long time ago.*

Thereupon paper and pencil were pushed toward her and she was instructed *"not to write* but just pick up the pencil any old way and hold it in your hand any old way. You and I know you can do that. Any baby can pick up a pencil in any old way.

> O. K. Now make a mark on the paper, any old scribbling mark *like a baby that can't write makes.* Just any old crooked mark! That's something you don't even have to learn.
>
> O. K. Now make a straight mark on the paper, like you make with a nail when you want to saw a board straight or with a stick when you mark a row in the garden. You can make it short or long or straight up and down or just lying down.
>
> O. K. Now make a mark like the hole in a doughnut and then two marks like the halves of the doughnut when you break the doughnut in halves.
>
> O. K. Now make two slanted marks, one like one side of the gable roof of a barn and the other like the other side.
>
> O. K. Now make a mark like a horse's crupper standing on the little end. And now poke the pencil in the paper and make just a little spot.
>
> O. K. Now all those marks you made you can make different sizes and in different places on the paper and in different order and even one on top of the other or one next to another. O. K.?
>
> Now, those marks that you made and can make again any old time [straight, vertical, horizontal, and oblique lines; circles, semicircles, etc.] *are writing, but you don't know that it is writing. You don't have to believe that it is writing*—all you have to do is know that you can make those marks and that isn't hard to know, because you already know it. Now I'm going to awaken you and do the same thing all over, and I want you to practice at home making those marks. O. K.?

The procedure of the trance state was repeated with no additional elaboration in the waking state and with the same instructions. She was dismissed, not entirely pleased but somewhat intrigued, with instructions to return the next day.

A medium-to-deep trance was readily induced, and it was learned that she had spent approximately two hours "marking marks!" The explanation was then offered her that the only difference between a pile of lumber to construct a house and the completed house was that the latter was the former "merely put together." To this she agreed wonderingly. She was then shown a rectangle and told, "That's a rough plan of the side of a 40-foot barn." The rectangle was then bisected vertically and she was told, "Now it's a rough plan of two 20-foot long barns end to end." Still wondering, she agreed.

She was then shown a neat copy of the "marks" she had made the previous day and was asked to select those that could be used to make a small-scale "rough plan" of the side of a 40-foot barn and to "mark out" such a plan. She was then asked to "split it in the middle" and then to "mark out one 20-foot side of a barn up on top of another one the same size." Bewilderedly she did so.

She was then asked to use the oblique lines to "mark out" the gable end of a roof and then one of the straight lines to "stretch halfway up from one side to the other like a scantling used to brace the end of the roof." Obediently she did so and she was emphatically assured that she now knew how to put marks together, but that she should take half of the doughnut hole and use it repeatedly to "round off the corners of the side of the barn." This she did.

Thereupon she was emphatically instructed as an indisputable item of information that not only did she know how to write, but the fact had been irrefutably established. This dogmatic statement puzzled her greatly but without diminishing her cooperation. Before she could organize any thoughts on this matter, she was peremptorily instructed to inspect the "marks" and "put them together in twos and threes in different ways."

With a little judicious maneuvering and indirect guidance on the part of the writer, it was possible to secure among the various "combinations" she made the complete alphabet printed in block form and with some of the letters formed in rounded fashion. These were carefully reduplicated on a separate sheet of paper. Thereupon a newspaper advertisement, magazine advertisements, and a child's textbook were brought out, and systematically it was pointed out that she, without recourse to a copying procedure, had printed each of the letters of the alphabet. She then was maneuvered into orienting her recognition of the letters not by comparing her printed letters with those in the book but by validating the letters in the book by their similarity to her own constructions. Great care was exerted to prevent her from losing this orientation. Her excitement, pleasure, and interest were most striking. The entire procedure was then repeated in the waking state.

The next problem was to interest her safely in "letter building" and "word building" and the "naming," not reading each new construct. Each step was accomplished first in the trance state and then repeated in the waking state. No mention was made of writing or reading; circumlocutions were used. For example she would be told, "Take some of these straight or crooked lines and build me another letter. Now build me a few letters alongside of each other and *name* the word."

Utilization Techniques

Then she was taught that "a dictionary is not a book to read; it is a book to look up words in, just like a picture book isn't for reading, it's just to look at pictures." With the dictionary she was enabled to discover that she could use vertical, horizontal, oblique, or curved lines to "build" any word in it, and great care was taken to emphasize the importance of "the right name for each word, just like you never forget the *correct* name for a harrow, a disk, or a cultivator."

As a succeeding step she was taught the game of anagrams, which was described as entirely comparable to tearing down "the back porch and using the old lumber to build on a new room with a kitchen sink." The task of "naming" the words became most fascinating to her.

The final step was to have her discover that "naming words is just like talking," and this was achieved simply by having her "build" words taken from the dictionary, apparently chosen at random but carefully selected by the writer, which she was asked to "set down here or there on this straight line." Since the words were not put down in correct order but were in correct spacing, the final result when she was called upon to "name" them astonished her. The words were, "Get going Ma and put some grub on the table." As she completed "naming" the words, she declared, "Why, that's what Pa always says—it's just like talking."

The transisition from "talking words" to "reading words" was then a minor matter. Within three weeks' time she was spending every spare minute with her dictionary and a *Readers' Digest*. She died of a cerebral hemorrhage at the age of 80, a most prolific reader and a frequent letter writer to her children and grandchildren.

EXAMPLE 15

The second instance concerns a nine-year-old girl who began failing all of her school work and withdrawing from social contacts. When questioned, she would reply either angrily or tearfully in a defensive fashion, "I just can't do nothing."

Inquiry disclosed good scholastic work in previous years but poor adjustment on the playground in that she was inept, hesitant, and awkward. However, her parents were concerned only about her scholastic rating and sought psychiatric aid from the writer for their daughter.

Since the girl would not come to the office, she was seen each evening in her home. One of the first bits of information elicited was that she didn't like certain girls because they were always playing jacks or roller skating or jumping rope. "They never do anything that's fun." It was learned that she had a set of jacks and a ball but that she "played terrible." The writer challenged her, on the grounds that infantile paralysis had crippled his right arm to the effect that he could play a "more terrible" game than she could. The challenge was accepted, but after the first few evenings a spirit of good competition and good rapport developed, and it was relatively easy to induce a light-to-medium trance. Some of the games were played in the trance state and some in the waking state. Within three weeks she was an excellent player, though her parents were highly displeased because of the writer's apparent lack of interest in her scholastic difficulties.

After three weeks of playing jacks the writer declared that he could be worse on roller skates than she could be, since his leg was crippled. There followed the same course of developments as with the jacks, only this time it took only two weeks for her to develop reasonable skill.

Next she was challenged to jump the rope and see if she could possibly teach the writer this skill. In a week's time she was adept.

Then the writer challenged her to a bicycle race, pointing out that he actually could ride a bicycle well, as she herself knew. The statement was boldly made that he could beat her in a race, and only her conviction that he would defeat her allowed her to accept. However, she did promise in the trance state to try hard. She had owned a bicycle for more than six months and had not ridden it more than one city block.

At the appointed time she appeared with her bicycle but demanded, "You have got to be honest and not just let me win. You got to try hard, and I know you can ride fast enough to beat me, so I'm going to watch you so you can't cheat."

The writer mounted his bike, and she followed on hers. What she did not know was that the use of both legs in pedaling constituted for the writer a serious handicap in riding a bicycle and that ordinarily only his left leg is used. But as the girl watched suspiciously, she saw the writer most laboriously pedaling with both feet without developing much speed. Finally convinced, she rode past to win the race to her complete satisfaction.

That was the last therapeutic interview. She promptly proceeded to become the grade school champion in jacks and rope jumping. Her scholastic work improved similarly.

Years later the girl sought out the writer to inquire how he had managed to let her excel him in bicycle riding. She explained that learning to play jacks and jump the rope and to roller skate had had the effect of bolstering her ego immensely, but that she had had to discredit those achievements considerably because of the writer's physical handicaps. The bicycle riding, however, she knew was another matter.

She explained that at that time she knew the writer to be a good bicyclist, and she was certain that he could beat her and that she had no intention of letting the race be handed to her. The fact that the writer had genuinely tried hard and that she had beaten him convinced her that she "could do anything." Elated with that conviction, she had found school and all that it offered a most pleasant challenge.

Utilization Techniques

A definitely different type of Utilization Technique is one in which the general reality situation is employed as the essential component of the induction procedure. A basic consideration is a seemingly incidental or unintentional interference with the subjects' spontaneous responses to the reality situation. This leads to a state of uncertainty, frustration, and confusion in the subjects, which in turn effects a ready acceptance of hypnosis as a possible means of resolving the subjective situation. It is a combined utilization-confusion technique and can be used exerimentally or clinically on both children and adults. It is frequently a technique of choice, and sometimes it is very simply and rapidly accomplished, with shy, timid children and with self-conscious adults. An illustrative instance is as follows:

EXAMPLE 16

At a lecture before the professional staff of a hospital a student nurse who had neither experienced nor witnessed hypnosis was authoritatively instructed by her superior to act as a "volunteer" subject for the writer. Although actually interested, she manifested definite resentment as she hesitantly came forward. Advantage was taken of her emotional state to employ a utilization technique that would effect, first, a state of confusion to obviate resistance and, second, the ready induction of hypnosis.

As she approached the front of the lecture room from a side aisle, a chair was moved somewhat ostentatiously into place for her. When she was within six feet of the chair, she was asked, "Will you sit in *this* chair *here*?" As the word "this" was spoken, the writer's left hand was carefully placed on the back of that chair, as if to point it out. As the word "here" was spoken, the writer gestured with his right hand, as if indicating a chair to the side of the actual chair. There was a momentary pause in her behavior, but as she continued her approach, the chair was pushed gently toward her, causing a slight but definitely audible noise as it scraped on the floor. As she came still closer to the chair, it was pulled slightly to one side away from her, and immediately, as she seemed to note this, it was pushed back an inch or so, and then another inch or so forward and to the side toward her. All of this she noted because the writer's left hand on the back of the chair constituted a focussing point for her gaze.

By this time she had reached the chair, had turned, and had begun to lower her body into it. As soon as her knees were bent, the chair was rotated somewhat noisily about one inch, and as she paused again momentarily to turn her head to look at the chair, the writer took hold of her right elbow and moved it away from her body slightly and then a bit forward. As she turned to look in response to this, her elbow was released and her right hand and wrist were gently taken and moved a little upward and then downward. As she shifted her gaze from her elbow to her hand, she was told quietly, "Just sit *all* the way down in the chair, and as you do so, just close your eyes and go 'way deeply into the trance, and as you continue to sit there, sleep ever more deeply in a hypnotic trance.'' As she settled in the chair, the additional statement was made, "And now you can take a deep comfortable breath while I go on with my lecture." Thereupon without any further delay or training she was immediately employed to demonstrate the somnambulistic trance and many other phenomena of the deep trance. She was awakened from the trance approximately an hour later.

An aspect of the original reality situation constituting a part of the utilization technique was reestablished by the measure of the writer, at the moment of awakening her, again holding her right hand and wrist as he had been doing at the moment of trance induction. Accordingly, upon awakening she reverted at once to the original state of conscious bewilderment which had been interrupted by the rapid development of a deep trance. This she demonstrated, along with a total amnesia for the events of the preceding hour, by stating, "But you've got me so confused I don't know what to do. Is it all right to sit this way, and what do you want me to do with my hand?" Reply was made, "Would you like to go into a trance?" She answered, "I don't really know. I'm not sure. I don't even know if I can be hypnotized. I suppose maybe I could. I'm willing to try if you want me to." She still had no awareness that she had been in a trance and that an hour had elapsed. This amnesia continued to persist. She was asked what she meant by saying that she was confused. "Well, when I started to come up here, you asked me to sit in this chair, and then you started moving it first one way and then another, and then somehow you started to move my arm, and before I knew what you wanted, you started moving my hand, and I'm still confused. What do you want me to do?"

In this last question the subject defines adequately the goal of a confusion technique, whether based upon direct suggestions eliciting variously oriented and contradictory responses from the subject or, as in this instance, upon a Utilization Technique employing various aspects of the reality situation. This goal is an urgent, pressing need on the part of the subject to have the confusion of the situation clarified, and hence the presentation of the suggestion of trance state as a definitive idea is readily accepted and acted upon. In this instance she accepted at once the instructions, "Sit down," "Close your eyes," "Sleep deeply." These instructions dispersed for her all of the confusion she had been experiencing.

For this subject, as in other instances in which this type of technique has been employed, the utilization of the reality situation was of such character that she could formulate no subjectively adequate responses. This resulted in an increasing need to make some kind of a response. As this desire increased, an opportunity for response was presented to her in a form rendered *inherently appropriate and effective by the total situation*. Thus the very nature of the total situation was utilized in the technique of induction.

To summarize, a number of special techniques of hypnotic trance induction are reported and illustrated by clinical and experimental examples. These methods are based upon the utilization of the subjects' own attitudes, thinking, feeling, and behavior, and aspects of the reality situation, variously employed, as the essential components of the trance induction procedure. In this way they differ from the more commonly used techniques which are based upon the suggestion of the subjects of some form of operator-selected responsive behavior. These special techniques, while readily adaptable to subjects in general, demonstrate particularly the applicability of hypnosis under various conditions of stress and to subjects seemingly not amenable to its use. They also serve to illustrate in part some of the fundamental psychological principles underlying hypnosis and its induction.

9. A Transcript of a Trance Induction With Commentary

Milton H. Erickson, Jay Haley, and John H. Weakland

The art of offering hypnotic suggestions in such fashion that the subject can accept them and then respond to them is difficult to explain. As an approach to this involved task, the following exposition of a trance induction is offered to clarify in some ways how suggestions are offered, presumably why they are effective, the methods that may be utilized to integrate one suggestion with others and to incorporate various responses into others, and to demonstrate the readiness with which communication with a subject can be established at various levels, both separate and distinct as well as interrelated.

The situation and procedure are given in the full detail afforded by tape recordings, together with a brief explanatory introduction, with only that editing requisite to make the conversational situation intelligible to the reader.

One evening in 1956 Milton H. Erickson hypnotized a subject during a weekly seminar he conducted in Phoenix. This trance induction was recorded. The following day he listened to the recording and discussed the induction with Jay Haley and John Weakland. This conversation was also recorded. What follows is a verbatim transcript of the two recordings: the trance induction recording is presented in the first column; the conversation about the trance induction (as the initial tape is played back) is given in the second.*

The hypnotic subject, who will be called Sue here, was not entirely a naive hypnotic subject. A stage hypnotist had tried to hypnotize her and rejected her, giving her the idea that she was a poor hypnotic subject. Dr. Erickson reports, "I met her for the first time at Dr. M's. I looked her over and nodded to Dr. M that she would make a good subject, and I indicated that later I wanted Dr.

Reprinted with permission from *The American Journal of Clinical Hypnosis*, October, 1959, 2, 49-84.

*This discussion was initiated by Jay Haley and John Weakland as part of their research on the Communications Research Project directed by Gregory Bateson. The project was financed by the Macy Foundation, administered by Stanford University, and located at the Veterans Administration Hospital in Palo Alto, California. The " double bind" mentioned in this paper is discussed in "Toward a Theory of Schizophrenia," *Behavioral Science*, 1, No. 4, 1956.

M to work on her. This was done by signals that Sue could not see. I went ahead on this occasion to work with another subject, and then I asked Sue to sit down in a chair beside me. I asked her if she'd like to be hypnotized, and she said, 'Yes, but I'm not a good subject.' I told her I thought she was a very good subject. I took hold of her arm and tested it for catalepsy. At the same time I tried to get some eye fixation. There was a fairly responsive eye fixation, then she shook her head and said, 'I don't think I can be hypnotized.' I asked her if she wanted Dr. M to work on her, and she did, so Doctor M had her look at the reflection of the light on the doorknob. Dr. M worked quite hard with her and produced practically no results. There was closing of the eyelids, but no catalepsy, no hand levitation, and rather restless behavior. When Dr. M told her to arouse, she explained that she wasn't so sure she had gone into a trance, but that she had tried very hard to cooperate. Perhaps she 'cooperated too hard.' She didn't think she would make a good subject, even though Dr. Erickson said she would. She thought that perhaps I had made a mistake. The next time hypnosis was attempted was in her home. I had two good subjects there, and Sue really watched both of them. She was the hostess and was answering the telephone and worrying about the children making a noise. She said, 'I'd like to be hypnotized, but I'm afraid I can't be.' I asked her to sit down and be a subject. She sat down, and I tried to hypnotize her. She was restless and said, 'I can't be hypnotized, I'm no good as a subject. I'm really not listening to you. I don't think I could be a subject, but I'd really like to be one.' That was the second effort. This recording constitutes the third attempt."

Before beginning his induction that evening, Erickson purposely arranged the seating of the people in the room. A short time later he rearranged the seating, having Sue move each time. His later comment on this was, "I put her in the chair that I later sat in, then I shifted her to the couch. I was in her place. And she had obeyed me by shifting to the couch. She'd put me in her place, with all its subtle implications. If there had been some other chair there, even if it had been more convenient to sit in it, I would have sat in her chair. The shifting prior to that implied that if there is prior shifting, there can be subsequent shifting. I introduced the idea of shifting earlier to make it completely acceptable. Then there is no chance that she is going to resist the shift." He also pointed out that on the couch Sue sat in a position where a good subject had been sitting.

The transcript of the recording of the comments on the induction, and the induction itself, follows:

Comment

H: Before we begin I wonder if you might comment on how you knew Sue was a good subject. How do you tell that a person is going to be a good subject?

Induction

E: I think, Sue, it's time for you to go into a trance.
S: O.K.
E: You aren't at home. That's a nice couch. Now I wonder what some of the things are that you'd like to experience in a deep trance.

[Fluttering of eyelids.]

Comment

E: When you see a person who shows decidedly responsive behavior. For example John is introduced to you. You see him making up his mind, 'So I'll shake hands, and I will say such and such,' worrying about details of the introduction. That's the kind of personality that's very difficult. But if you see a person being introduced and he looks expectantly toward the other person, he shows responsive behavior and natural behavior. When I visited Dr. M and was introduced to Sue, there was that completely responsive behavior. She was perfectly willing to respond, "How do you do, Dr. Erickson," perfectly willing to shake hands. She was waiting for cues, waiting to meet what I did. I watched her being introduced to other people, men and women. That complete responsiveness of her behavior, that's one way you can pick out a good subject. And she is that type.

W: What do you think made it difficult for her to be hypnotized the first two times?

E: She hadn't made up her mind about it. Her husband had raised the question with her previously, and she discounted him. She knew that he wasn't experienced. She hadn't met me, and this stage hypnotist certainly did not make a good impression on her. It was still an open question. Let's wait and see what the behavior is like, then I can respond.—That was her attitude.

W: You've already made it different from the last time.
H: You didn't seem to want her to respond to that last question. You said, "I wonder what some of the things are," but you didn't pose it as a question that she should answer. Is it just something that you wanted her to think about?
E: You open the question, bring about a readiness to respond, and inhibit the response, you

Trance Induction & Commentary

Induction	Comment
	postpone the response until later. *H:* It increases the later response if you open one up and then inhibit it? *E:* You're in a responding position. *W:* I think maybe it's particularly appropriate here, partly because she has had the uncertainty about responding. *E:* You're emphasizing the fact that she's going to respond, that she's all set to respond.
E: And slowly go deeper and deeper. [Long pause.] As you go deeper and deeper asleep, you can free your hands, separate them. And let them slightly, slowly, gradually begin to lift involuntarily. Lifting just a little.	*W:* We can comment here on that. You say lifting just a little. I'm not sure whether you see a very, very minimal lifting or what, but I noticed that you certainly take—I'm not sure whether you took no response as a response, or the tiniest response and said, "It's lifting." There were a number of times there when you said it when I couldn't quite detect whether anything was happening or not. *E:* There was one thing that happened. Put your hand on your thigh, take a deep breath. What happened to your hand? *W:* It lifts! *E:* You time the inspiration. And they haven't got an opportunity to deny it. . . . Later on I thought I would emphasize that by taking every other inspiration to say "lifting." *H:* Every other one? *E:* Yes. *W:* There's a little more going on than meets the eye! *H:* I hadn't noticed the inspirations in this at all. *E:* Nobody notices inspiration and expiration. They're used to that.
E: Lifting just a little bit more. Lifting —lifting —and lifting —and your lids are closing.	*H:* Were her lids closing at that moment? It seems to me usually you say, "Your lids will begin to close." You put it in the future. I noticed that you used "are" there, the present. *E:* A very slight quiver of the lids. They *are* closing. *H:* O. K.

Induction

E: And your hand lifting just a bit more. Lifting. Lifting. Lifting a bit. Forefingers moving. Moving just a little bit. Lifting, lifting again. And then the next finger will lift. The whole hand is stiff, lifting. Lifting. Lifting up. Lifting, lifting, lifting up.

E: The elbow is bending. The wrist is lifting up.

E: The whole arm lifting slowly—lifting—lifting a bit more. And lifting. [Pause.] Lifting. Lifting a bit more. The elbow is bending.

E: The elbow is lifting. The hand is lifting —lifting more and more. [The hand has lifted slightly. Long pause.] Now I want you to go deeper and deeper asleep. And to signify that you will, I want your head to nod forward *slowly*.

Comment

E: A rising inflection. Lifting [demonstrating voice rising as he says it.] And I think you probably noticed the - - "lifting."
H: The movement of the body, too.
E: The movement of my body. And of your own unconscious localization of the sound. [Demonstrating exaggeratedly as he straightens up.] Lifting. And the conveyance of the change of location. But you never pay attention to location of sounds consciously; you accept them.

H: Was the elbow bending?
E: A slight quiver of the biceps.

E: The tendency there was for me to say, "Lifting a bit more, lifting a bit more, *lifting* a bit more." The different volume in my voice.
H: Raising the volume?
E: Raising the volume. And you only raise the volume when it's *really* happening. Same words, but a different volume in the words. And you throw in that change of volume.
W: There are so many levels on which the suggestive effect can be paralleled. Instead of being different levels of message contradicting each other, this is where they reinforce.

H: It certainly nodded slowly.
W: By saying "slowly" or "just a little" or something like that, when the subject is only responding minimally anyway . . .
E: You are accepting their minimal performance, and it's good.
W: And you're avoiding asking for something more than you're likely to get at the moment.
E: You're content with what you're receiving, and they know it. And since you *are* content, they *must* be responding. It's fallacious, I know. And you'd rather they'd keep on being slower

Induction

E: [Pause.] Slowly nodding forward, still more —still more. [Pause.]

E: And still more. [Pause.] And you can go deeper and deeper asleep. [Pause.] And I want you to go deeper and deeper asleep.

E: And I'm going to count for *you*. One . . .

Comment

and *slower*. "Just a little bit more." How small is a little? But it *is* more.

E: A lapse of time demonstrates that it *has* moved forward. [Fallacious but subjectively convincing.]

W: You shift there from "you can go deeper asleep," which is certainly a reasonable statement from the depth she is in at that point. And then "I want you to go deeper."

E: You *can*, and I want you to—and we've joined forces.

H: Has she ever heard this count to 20 before?
E: Yes.
H: If she had never heard it before, would you have had to say . . .
E: I would have explained it to her.
H: That when you reached 20 she'd be deeply asleep.
E: But she'd heard it before; she'd seen it used before. She already knew what counting meant. She knew what counting meant in relationship to a good subject. And she saw a good subject respond to the count. And so when I started counting for *her*, she had to bring up all her previous knowledge, all her previous understanding, but that was hers.
W: It makes it . . .
E: All the more accepted.
W: It makes it more if you don't explain it. I mean, if you explain it, that implies that you've got to emphasize it, whereas if you don't explain it, that implies she already knows.
H: She's got to volunteer the understanding, yes. Well, what would you do with a naive subject who'd never heard a count before? How would you phrase that?
E: Then I'd explain how I could count from 1

Induction

E: ... 2, 3, 4, 5, 6, 7, 8, 9, 10—and half asleep—11, 12, 13, 14, 15 —three quarters asleep—16, 17, 18, 19, 20, and take a deep breath and go way deep sound asleep. Way deep sound asleep.

Comment

to 20, and at 5 a quarter asleep, and so on.

H: But I was interested in the preliminaries. I was not sure whether you'd explained first, or whether you counted to 5 and then said a quarter asleep and let them figure out that if 5 is a quarter asleep, 10 must be half, 15 three quarters, and 20 the full count.

E: It depends upon the intelligence of the subject and the readiness at grasping it. Some people even with college degrees can't understand what you mean when you say you can count to 20 by ones, or twos, that you're also telling them you can count by fours, fives. So you have to be rather elaborate. Some you can tell "I can count to 20 in various ways," and they think—"by ones, twos, by fours and fives."

H: Is it more effective if they figure it out?

E: More effective, because they're taking the ball and carrying it.

H: So really the minimum explanation you can get by with, the better.

E: The more participation you can get from them, the better.

H: And you suggested the deep breath by taking one yourself.

E: The very way [demonstrating with varying pauses and inflections] that I say, '16, 17, 18, 19, 20, now take a deep breath.' [Exhaling on 19 and 20, air gone when he says, "now take a deep breath."]

W: You need one by the time you get there.

E: The rise in force.

H: You rise in force and drop when you say "go to sleep."

Trance Induction & Commentary

Induction

E: . . . way deep sound asleep. And I want you to be sleeping sounder and sounder all the time. Sounder and sounder. Now there are certain things that you want to learn.

E: And I want you to be sure that you'll learn, and I want you to think clearly in your own mind of all the various things you *want* to learn. And then I want you to realize that you *can* learn them, and that you *will* learn them.

[Tape is played. Long pause.]

E: And go *still* deeper. Still deeper asleep. [Pause.] And now, Sue, I'm going shortly to awaken you. And there are certain things that I want you to do. And I really *want* you to do them.

Comment

E: There are *certain* things—that you want to learn. Completely specific and so general.
H: And you had nothing in particular in mind at that moment that she wanted to learn?
E: The development of the evening would single out the "certain things." But it sounds so specific, yet really it is so general.
H: It certainly is.

E: That you *can*, that you *will*.
W: And you want her to realize this, which implies, of course, it is absolutely so, and all she has to do is realize that it is so.
E: And she's obligated in all directions. She's having time to realize.

H: At this point you had already lifted her arms. Now when you lifted her left hand—as I remember, she hadn't levitated at all prior to that.
E: Just fluttered the arm.
H: Yes. When you lifted her left arm, you put it in a position where it would remain very easily, even if she were awake. You established that, and then you lifted the right arm into a position that required more catalepsy.
E: That is, I established *easy* catalepsy, a very convincing experience subjectively. And it's really so. Therefore it's so on the other side.
H: Yes. Why couldn't you have worked further

Induction

E: ... and you may enjoy doing them.

E: After you are awakened, Sue, I want you to tell me that you weren't *really* in a trance. And I want you to believe it.

E: And I want you to be

Comment

to get levitation for her?
E: In ordinary life she's rather quick and active. When she relaxes, she's slow. It takes too much time.
H: When you say in this last piece, "I really want you to do it," now this is related to something that interests us. How you use her concern about *you*.
W: Isn't it also a little more than that, as I heard it, a little bit, it's "I really *want* you—to do that."
E: You want to learn certain things, I really want you to. She's already had a suggestion that "there are certain things you want to learn."
H: But was this a second suggestion on how there are certain things she was going to do?
E: The background was: There are certain things that she wants to learn. I'm the teacher, therefore I really want her to do these things because I as the teacher can help her to learn the things that she really wants to learn. So it becomes a cooperative venture.
H: Well, it's cooperative, but it's using her concern about her to a great extent.
E: She wants me to be the teacher.
H: Yes, that's right.
H: Why do you use the word "may" there? Doesn't that pose the problem "you may not" when you use "may" instead of "will"?
E: I'd just told her "I want you to do this." That's awfully dictatorial. Let's contrast it with permissiveness. "You *may* enjoy doing this." So I've stepped from my completely dictatorial to a permissive role.

H: Did you assume she would do that anyhow?
E: There's a good possibility. So whatever negative thing she has said will really be a positive thing.
H: You put a frame around it.

Induction

emphatic in your statement. Quite emphatic. And you will be, will you not? [Pause.] And whatever else you need to do you will do, will you not?

E: [Pause.] And after you are awakened, you will *not* believe that you were in a trance. You'll be emphatic in your belief; you'll be polite about it. But you will know that you were not in a trance.

E: And now I'm going to awaken you, Sue. And I'll awaken you. [Pause.] I'll awaken you by counting backward from 20 to 1. 20, 19, 18, 17, 16, 15, 14, 13, 12, 11, 10, 9, 8, 7, 6, 5, 4, 3, 2, 1—awaken. Do you feel a bit tired, Sue? [Sue clears throat.]

Comment

H: What did you have in mind there?
E: Whatever else you need to do, you really will do.

W: Isn't that also in a way an amnesia suggestion?
E: Essentially.
W: So you take her tendency to produce denial and produce a phenomenon with it.

E: With it. And I say *"emphatic,"* and my enunciation of the word "emphatic" is also emphatic. "But you'll be polite about it." And there again, "you'll be polite about it" intensifies the need to deny, because she is going to be polite, she's under tremendous compulsion, cultural compulsion, to be polite. But the situation has been created in which she's got to be polite about a certain thing. She's under compulsion to be polite. That requires her to deny that she was in a trance.
H: She's under compulsion to be polite about something she feels emphatically about.
E: Yes. But she's also under compulsion to be polite. And there's only one thing in that situation, and so she has to be polite about it, thereby validating the existence of that one thing.

Induction

Do you think I'm right in thinking you're a good hypnotic subject. [She shakes her head.] You don't.
S: I sure try.
E: You surely do. How many times do you think we'll have to try?
S: Oh, I hope it won't be long [Laughing slightly.]
E: [Joining laugh.] Yes, I hope it won't be long until I get that fly. [He holds the fly swatter. Before trance he and subject had been pursuing a fly.]
S: Didn't you get him yet?
E: No.
S: Oh, my!

[Inaudible comments from others present about flies.]
E: Have you any idea what time it is?

Comment

E: Notice the change in my voice to fit a casual, social scene.

H: Is her statement "I hope it won't be long" also a statement "I hope I won't have to deny this very long"?

E: That may be, but I'm really switching away from the trance with that fly.
H: You surely are.
E: And she's joining me in that fly business.
W: You switch away from it; that makes easier the belief that it didn't happen.
E: That's right.
H: Do you think she had amnesia for it then?
E: I don't know. But we really got on the subject of the fly, and she could really join me, so we could share something in common.
H: She sounded very girlish when she joined you.
E: We could really be two against that adverse crowd.
W: Yes.
E: The others didn't really approve of us, but we two were kindred souls in the absurd pursuit of the fly.
H: You established that earlier, as I remember.

W: It just struck me that you brought up the question of time here, and then you brought it up later about how long she would feel—how much time had passed—was this a setup?

Induction

S: No.
E: Five minutes of eight.
E: Really?
E: Maybe you've been asleep.
S: I don't think so.
E: Sure about that?
S: Pretty sure.
E: You know, there's an astonishing phrase in the language?
S: Yes?
E: For a complete dinner we speak of it as everything from soup to nuts, do we not?
S: Yes.
E: And you really *understand* what that means, don't you? Soup to nuts. And then let's see, there's another phrase, everything from A to Z. It's pretty conclusive, isn't it? And inclusive. And you really *understand* what A to Z *means*.

E: And then you can vary the phrase. Everything from 1 to 20. [Pause.] From 1 to 20 and . . . take a deep breath. Go way deep asleep. [Pause.]

E: That's right. And you can really do it, can't you? [Pause.]

Comment

E: Yes, that is, I had a whole lot of setups. Here, there, everywhere. Knowing that I could not use all the setups, but I would be certain to use some of them. Not knowing what will develop, better have plenty of setups that you can use. A multitude of preliminary suggestions offers an opportunity for subsequent selection and use.

H: She wasn't emphatic there.

E: "Understand" is the word. And all I'm telling her is to prepare herself to *understand*. It's a distraction, the soup to nuts, A to Z, *understand*.
H: Is that just a distraction, or is that a statement that there's going to be a completion, from soup to nuts, from A to Z, from 1 to 20?
E: Yes, soup to nuts tells her the type of understanding. But she can start thinking about soup-nuts, A-Z, but *understands* puts it back . . .

H: One question comes up here. I notice that you repeat that "everything from 1 to 20" twice. Sometimes you repeat things, and sometimes you just drop them casually, saying it once. I wonder why it's necessary to repeat it.
E: Well, I wanted her to go deeply into a trance.
H: And repetition does that.
E: Yes.

E: Always match your positives to your negatives. "And you *can* . . . " If they're going to say "can't," better anticipate them.

Induction	Comment
And you can, can't you?	*H:* I see. So that when you say, "And you can," they don't think "but I can't." *E:* I've beaten them to it. I've said they can't, it's been said, they don't need to say it; therefore, not being able to say it, they can't act upon it. And the use of that "can't you" has a positive effect. "And you *can*, can't you?" You've got a negative positively stated; it prevents them from saying "I can't." *H:* Is it the same with "And you will, won't you?" *E:* Yes.
E: And you really can. You can nod your head. [Pause.] It rather surprised you, didn't it?	*H:* Did you pick that up from her, or just assume it? *E:* It did surprise her. *H:* How did you know? *E:* She was thinking "soup to nuts," A to Z, 1 to 20. And then surprised that soup to nuts, A to Z, could also be 1 to 20. *H:* Then you assumed the surprise; you didn't see from her expression that she was surprised. *E:* From the suddenness of her reaction to it, you can legitimately deduce surprise. I don't recall that I saw any particular expression of surprise. *H:* I just remember wondering at the time whether you were seeing something I wasn't seeing or whether you just assumed it.
E: [Long pause.] After you are awakened again, Sue—and I ask you about going into a trance, I want you to tell me that you weren't asleep the second time, that you were the first time. And you're most	

Induction

insistent on that, and you will repeat that, Sue, will you not?

Comment

W: Now by changing your "no" to the second one, you begin to get your acceptance catching up as you go along?
E: Yes. First I had her deny the first trance. Now I'm nullifying that denial.
W: By giving her another "no" to work on in the meantime.
E: And in order to work on the second negation, she's got to affirm the first.
H: A use of double binds!
E: What else can she do?
W: Well, one might approach that question by saying, "Suppose someone said that to you, what would you do?"
E: Every manipulator works it on that basis, too.
H: Well, when you get two like that, it does put her in a position where she has to affirm one of them in order to deny the other, yes.
E: In order to deny one of them, she has to affirm the other. The affirmation of one of them is the means of denying the other.
H: That's a classic double bind you've got there.
W: And why can't she see it or comment on it?
E: In other words why doesn't she say, "I wasn't asleep either time." We're talking about two separate trances. (They were compartmentalized.)
H: She couldn't comment on both with one word like "either," you mean.
E: That's right.

E: And now I'm going to awaken you. I'm going to count backward from 20 to 1. 20, 15, 10 —half awake —and 5, and 4, and 2, 3, 4, and 5, and 6, 7, 8, 9, 10—half asleep—and 9 and 8 and

Induction

7 and 6, 5, 4, 3 [slight pause], 2, 1. Wake up.

E: Thirsty?
S: Yes.
E: Be horrible if you could not pick up that glass of water, wouldn't it, Sue?
S: Yes.

Comment

W: Did you pause there to emphasize that the 2 was coming up again? It seemed as if you got down to 3, and just before the 2, that was the reversal point.
E: Just a wee bit louder.
H: What effect does it have when you give her the rough bounce but only up to 10?
E: "I can put you in any level of trance." And simply, and easily, and comfortably. And she is going to know that I said "4, 2—3, 4." Perhaps I said that 3 to correct myself. I shouldn't have skipped 3. I really shouldn't have, supposedly. And it's good that I said: 4, 5, 6. And then the goodness relates to going back into the trance.
H: That's the soft bounce.

H: O. K. What about that?
W: Yes, how did all of that work?
E: She awakened with an eager look, the wetting of her lips, and "be horrible [after a pause] if you couldn't pick up a glass of water."
H: Is "be horrible" then a statement about her feelings of thirst?
E: Yes. What I said was "be horrible if you couldn't get that drink," I also said *be horrible*. *Be*, the verb *to be*. It was a command.
H: You were commanding her to be horrible.
E: Yes.
H: Now how does that keep her from reaching for a glass of water?
E: That's comforting, that's pleasing, that's not horrible. And it would be horrible if she couldn't get that glass of water.
H: It would be the same if you said "be uncomfortable." "You would be uncomfortable

Induction	Comment
	if you couldn't reach for that glass of water." *E:* "It would be uncomfortable if you couldn't reach that glass of water." But "it would" be uncomfortable. *H:* What did you say? [They listen again.] *E:* There was no "it would" there. *H:* There certainly wasn't. Well, why did you choose "be horrible?" *E:* Because she was licking her lips. You don't say "uncomfortable," you use a stronger word. *H:* Well, why did she obey that suggestion if she were awake? *E:* Because I had first said "thirsty." Listen to the way I said "thirsty." [The tape is replayed.]
E: Thirsty!	*H:* Not a question, you mean. You mean it doesn't have a question inflection? *E:* It's also a command. "Thirsty." *H:* Well, did that command put her back in trance? *E:* What is she going to be in, "thirsty"? "Thirsty!" Is it a question, is it a command, just what is it? When the later statement is made, "thirsty" becomes a command. *H:* What I am trying to get clear is whether you awakened her when you said "wake up." *E:* Yes. *H:* And then "thirsty" put her back in trance? *E:* The "thirsty" arrested her behavior. Just what did I mean? Was it an inquiry; was it a command? Just what was it? *H:* And then "be horrible" did what? *E:* It was a command. *W:* This might be a place where we could raise the general question: In an induction like this how much do you simply do these things and how much do you do A, B, C, D, E, F, G? As we speak over the moves now, we can in a sense pick out and identify so many things as such. Are we identifying more than went through your mind when you were doing it? I mean, did you do it as consciously as you describe it to us now?

Induction

S: [Laughing slightly.]
I can't.
E: What's that?
S: I can't.

Comment

E: Well, you see, I noticed that licking of her lips, the directing of her glance, her general body movements. I couldn't know whether I wanted her to drink, whether I wanted to suggest that she drink, or what I would do. So I threw in that word, where neither she nor I really knew the interpretation. And having thrown it in, then I had enough time to say, "I will now use that word," but it was a nondescript usage, it wasn't a question.
W: It was a nondescript but specific response to what she had just done.
E: Yes, but it was a nondescript utterance of the word. Neither a question nor a command, really an observation of a state of some kind, which gave me time to decide how to use it.
H: Now when you said "be horrible if you couldn't pick up that glass," did she then go into trance? And she had been awake a moment before.
E: Yes.
W: I wonder if there was a partial thing there. I had the feeling watching it that it was as if she didn't dare test that one out to the limit. Now when I hear the "be horrible", it's almost as if "well, it's bad if I don't get it, but if I tried real hard to get it, and couldn't get it, then that would really be horrible."
E: That might be.
H: Now this is another example. In the inductions I've watched you do, in each one there is a kind of a challenge to the subject to try something which they find they can't do. Do you try to set this up for each induction?
E: Yes. And repeatedly throughout the evening I use that.
H: That's the only example I can think of.
E: We'll probably run across more.

Induction / Comment

E: You're getting thirsty.
S: I'm always thirsty.
E: You must have been in a trance.
S: Not really.
E: Not really?
S: No, no. I think you'd better work on your wife or F.
E: Yes.
S: I really do. Because maybe I'll get better from watching them.
E: Can you pick up that glass of water?
S: [Pause.] I don't think so.
E: What?
S: I don't think so.
E: You must have been in a trance. It seems to me as if you're acting as if you had a posthypnotic suggestion. Could be you were in a trance *one* of the times. Especially . . .
S: [Interrupting.] Well, I think I [clears her throat] was deeper in the first time.

H: Was that "I'm always thirsty" an agreement that she was following your suggestion while denying it? It's an acceptance that she was getting thirsty but also a statement, "I'm always getting thirsty, it isn't you."
W: Making it her own, in her own experience.
H: But also partially denying that she was thirsty because you were saying so.
E: It's relating it to herself.

W: Doesn't she compromise again in a way a little bit with your suggestion to deny one, and instead of saying "yes" and "no," she says, "Well, more than."
E: Because I raised the question "are you still in a trance now"? when I raised the question whether she was under the influence of a posthypnotic suggestion.
H: Well, first she said you'd better work with somebody else, and you said "can you reach

Induction

E: By the way, when did you get the posthypnotic suggestion about the glass of water?
S: I don't remember any.
E: You don't remember. [Pause.] Did you go in deeper the first time? It seems to me that you told me you weren't in a trance the first time.
S: Well [Pause], not like L. [A good subject she had seen in a trance].
E: Yes?

Comment

for the glass of water?" and she couldn't—did she go back into trance at that moment? Or was she continuing?
E: A vacillation up and down, in and out of a trance. Waiting for some kind of a cue from me to jell her state.
H: I've often seen that kind of thing when somebody feels he's awake in a trance, and you ask him if he can reach for a glass of water. Then he finds he can't, and he feels maybe he is in a trance. But I never saw it done when a person is awake. And you brought up the possibility of a posthypnotic suggestion, was that to put a doubt in her mind about the trance? Whether she had received one she didn't know about?
E: To make her awfully uncertain as to her state of awareness. And if she's uncertain about her state of awareness, then she can rely upon me to clarify it.
W: It seems to me if she's uncertain, she's *got* to rely on you to clarify it.
E: Yes, she's got to rely on me. Therefore she's got to do my suggestions.

E: Another item there that you will overlook is the fact in inducing a trance, you say "I want you to go deeper asleep, still deeper," a pause, "still deeper," a pause, and later in casual conversation I can ask you, "Is your dress light [Pause] colored? The pause itself can become a cue.
W: Could you use uncertainty in the tone of your voice if you wished to?

Trance Induction & Commentary

Induction

E: Maybe this last time you weren't in a trance.
S: I'd love to say yes.
E: You really would? And you'd really love a drink of water, wouldn't you? It is nice to pick it up, isn't it?

Comment

E: Oh, yes. And you can often use anxiety in your tone of voice to achieve certain results.
H: In our terms, the pause becomes a message then.
E: A message interpreted in terms of the effect of previous pauses. The not saying of something that had conditioned her previously.
H: Why did you point out to her that she had said before that she hadn't been asleep the first time?
E: Forcing her to recognize that I *can* direct her attention. To have her agree to it, then to agree to do it. I have no hesitation at all in doing that.
H: No hesitation about pointing out contradictions in what she says?
E: That's right.
H: Whereas she has hesitations about pointing out contradictions in what *you* say.
E: I'm the secure one; she had better follow along.
W: And this could also mean not only by your pointing out contradictions but also quite the opposite. I mean, you could be free to leave one without pointing it out and get a similar result out of it. That is, you could say something contradictory yourself and go right ahead with it.
E: I can't think of a particular instance in hypnosis, but some troops in training were caught in a bog and the officer lost his head, and the men were about to panic when one of the recruits said, "This way, boys." And he started off confidently. That was the end of the panic. *He* was secure. Over and over in battle this sort of thing would happen. Someone suddenly assumed an attitude of security in certain situations.
H: Is that why you once said it would bother the subject who was put into the stage trance if you could arouse anxiety in the hypnotist's voice?
E: Yes.

Induction

E: It is nice to pick it up, isn't it? [Long pause.] Isn't it? [Pause.] Just watch your hand. See what it does. There's your hand going to the glass. Watch it. It's moving to the left a little. [Pause.] Is it moving toward the glass?
S: A little bit.
E: Watch it, your hand moving.

E: All that suffering for so small a sip? Don't you think you had better take another sip?

[Long silence, during which E holds out his hand before Sue, and slowly closes his five fingers into a fist; then again, four times in all. Sue watches intently.]

E: And now you're be-

Comment

H: It's that important, that there be no anxiety in the hypnotist's voice.
E: That's right. In seminarians in practice sessions their anxiety in their own voice is detected by their fellow seminarians acting as subjects. Over and over again they will say I was going into a trance very satisfactorily until you got uncertainty in the tone of your voice.
W: You've now given her the nice experience.

H: Now was that all to wait for your permission to reach for the glass?
E: To initiate the move.
H: Waiting for *you* to initiate the move.
E: And for her . . .
H: Oh, for *her* to initiate it and you to approve it?
E: Yes.
H: Because once you asked if it was moving toward the glass, then she did this movement and she reached for it.

E: All right, she took a sip because she was thirsty. It was such a small sip. Then I had her take another. I was really generous, wasn't I? For one additional sip of water, I've got a lot of credit for generosity.
H: And how that situation gets set up! Where a small sip of water becomes that loaded as far as your generosity goes.
W: That's because there could be no sip at all. And all this is going on in the first 20 minutes.
H: Yes.

Trance Induction & Commentary

Induction

ginning to know that you can sleep like L, aren't you. Beginning to know. [Silence and long pause.] And you can close your eyes and go really deeply asleep, with a deep breath. A deep breath, and go really deep asleep. That's right. Deeply asleep. [Pause.] I'm going to talk to the others, but you just keep right on sleeping. And I want you to be interested in the fact that you can see my hand, too. [To others.] That answers your question about the communication of ideas, doesn't it?

E: [Pause.] And sleeping deeply, Sue. And this time when you awaken, I want you to recall how you went to sleep this last time, and try to explain it to the group. 20, 19, 18, 17, 16, 15, 14, 13, 12, 11, 10, 9, 8, 7, 6, 5, 4, 3, 2, 1. And wake up.

Comment

H: Did you tell her then that while you turned and talked to the others she could see your hand? Weren't her eyes closed at that moment?
E: She could continue to see my hand, whether her eyes were open or closed.
H: That was the first move toward a hallucination then.

E: I gave her a posthypnotic suggestion that she was to explain to the group how she went to sleep, what caused her to go to sleep. As surely as she could explain this, she is really ratifying very thoroughly the fact that she was in a trance. She's confirmed it, she's ratifying it, she's making it a matter of public explanation, she's making an utterly definitive statement, explaining to an interested group, a respectful group, and thereby ratifying her own experience.
H: When you put the question to her, how did she go in a trance? You started 20, 19 . . . Was that to give her a cue?
E: That was a wake-up signal.
H: I know, but you put the question and then

Induction

Comment

put in the 20 so fast there, as if they were related.
E: That was separating them.
W: Isn't it also true that you give a posthypnotic suggestion which you then—both you and the group—help her to carry out, because the suggestion is about something that you're going to be likely talking about as soon as you wake her up anyway? It seems to me this is the type of suggestion you could get more or less carried out in a light trance because it doesn't appear so much as a suggestion—that is, it doesn't appear set off from other things, it flows naturally into the discussion that comes up any way.
E: Even with a light trance you ask them to explain how light the trance was. But they are ratifying that there was a trance.
H: When you pose that posthypnotic suggestion to her, in order to discuss it as soon as she awakens, she has to either go back in a trance or still be in a trance, doesn't she? I mean, you're not really awakening her.
E: Not really awakening her fully.

E: How did you happen to go to sleep this last time, Sue?

Trance Induction & Commentary

Induction

S: Watching your hand.
E: What did my hand do?
S: It went like this [Opening and closing hand.]
E: And what did you do?
S: Just like this [Closes her eyes].
E: And what did it mean to you?
S: [Pause] Hands clasped.
E: Yes?
S: The movement, the flexing of the muscles. Just watched them.

Comment

E: That whole explanation that she gave is informative. She watched my hand, the movement of it—those were her conscious reactions. She was not aware that she counted 20 unconsciously. There's that sharp differentiation. The counting, which occurred unconsciously, the conscious watching of the hand, the movement. That was her conscious response.
H: Do you have any idea why there was such an inhibition on knowing that she counted.
E: Because counting belongs to the trance. Just as you give a posthypnotic suggestion, "whenever I put one cigarette package on top of the other, you'll go into a trance." And then you say, "Now this is much more than this." [Putting one package on top of another after shuffling various objects on his desk.] And when you ask for an explanation later of what you did, the subject says, "You picked up your case records and put them in order, you straightened up your schedule book, you moved the calendar, and I watched you." Here is the thing that they didn't see completely [putting package on another]. They may say, "You started to reach for your package of cigarettes, and first you did this, and this." This [the package] is another thing; it belongs to the unconscious.
W: Well, is that the fact that the induction process—that is, when you have a general amnesia for the trance, it includes from the point at which induction really began, doesn't it? It is as if the induction were a part of the trance situation that is forgotten.
E: Yes. "I sat down in the chair, you asked me to put my hands in my lap, and now half an hour has passed," is a representative example.
H: Another thing that puzzles me is that she says this as a posthypnotic suggestion and therefore she can't have reentered the trance to follow the suggestion. Yet she is giving her conscious description and not the number. So that, even in a trance she doesn't know why.

Induction

S: [The lights dim briefly.] Did everybody see that?
E: Yes, but what were you thinking? Why did you go to sleep?
S: [Pause, clearing throat.]
E: They have a deep freeze.
S: What?

Comment

E: Yes, but you see, I didn't give her a number.
H: You didn't?
E: No, it was her interpretation. I didn't give her a number. She understood.
H: She understood and didn't know she understood.

E: That's right. But I didn't give her a number. All she saw me doing was flexing my fingers.
H: Well, you didn't ask her what you did that put her in trance, you asked her why she went to sleep.

E: Yes.

H: And she didn't reply, 'Well, I interpreted that as the number 20.'
E: No, because as soon as she interpreted it as 1 to 20—which is an instantaneous realization—it was all completed.
H: And that was part of the trance. Did she have amnesia for that whole trance?
E: Except that she really didn't know she was in a trance.
H: Well, it's a kind of peculiar thing. She didn't know that she was in a trance, she had amnesia for the trance, and yet she was trying to explain what put her in a trance.
E: Yes, it was different levels of circumscribed awareness.
W: It gets pretty complicated in that one.
H: It surely does.

H: Why did you do it that way?
E: It was in reply to her question, was it not?
W: Yes, you didn't say it right away, but only after you asked her again about why she went to sleep.
E: Yes, I started her on a train of thought about why she went to sleep. And then I offered an irrelevant observation about the deep freeze.
H: She said "Oh, Bill!" Why did you do that?

Induction

E: They have a deep freeze.
S: Who does? Oh, Bill [the host].

S: Oh, that's what the light was. I see.
E: [Pause.] What else were you thinking about as you watched my hand?
S: Well, to me something like this [a fist] has always connoted strength. I couldn't tell you right off what was . . .
E: Anything else?
S: The breathing.
E: Yes.
S: The way your body breathed in and out, and I could feel myself breathing as you were.
E: Now suppose you let your unconscious *give* me an answer. Now why . . .
S: The closing of the eyes.
E: Go to *sleep*. [Pause.]
S: Because you wanted me to.

Comment

E: To give you a contrast between the type of talking and tone of speech that she manifested while thinking about why she went to sleep. And I offered that observation in the same tone of voice that called for ordinary waking behavior, and her voice demonstrated it so beautifully.
H: It surely did.
W: There's one other thing, too. At the same time you then become the person who settled the question about the flicker.
E: Oh, yes.
H: And you also settled the question of what was going to be talked about.

H: Did you notice her husband got up and lit F's cigarette when she said that? You were lighting her cigarette at that moment, and he got up and went clear across the room and lit F's.
E: That's right, I noticed that.
H: Did you time that to her breathing?
E: I don't recall. I may have done so automatically.

H: I wonder if that wasn't a real answer, "because you wanted me to."

Induction

E: When was the last time you went to sleep?
S: Just now.
E: That's right.

E: What was I saying to you, Sue, when you went to sleep? [Long pause.] You're not really awake now, are you?
S: I don't think so.
E: You don't think so. You really don't think so, do you? And you really don't think you're awake. And if you don't think you're awake, you're beginning to think at the moment you're asleep. You're beginning to think and to know that you are asleep? You'll find that out as your eyes close. They are closing more. [Pause.] And more. [Pause.] And more. That's it. And sleeping

Comment

E: That's right. Now how did I teach her that I wanted her to? When I count from 1 to 20, that's the demonstration that I want her to go to sleep "because you wanted me to."
H: And when you moved your hand, what you did was look at her very intently, and then you moved your hand. I mean, your looking at her was also a statement, "I want you to go to sleep," as well as moving the hand.
E: Looking at her meant, "Your attention, please." [Demonstrates hand passing in front of his face to arm of chair and then flexing.] "Your attention, please."
H: Well, the only reason you really wanted her attention was to put her in the trance, wasn't it?
E: Yes, though I could get her attention by asking a question.

W: What strikes me here is that this is a remarkably late time now for you to say "you're beginning to think." Since you've been through two or three maneuvers on this before, the "beginning" sort of stands out to me, and I wonder if that has a special significance.
E: No, it's just a matter of repetition. A good technique keeps referring back.

Trance Induction & Commentary

Induction

deeply and soundly. Very soundly, very soundly. And you can smoke while you're asleep, Sue. Do you want to? Then I'll take your cigarette. [Long pause.] Now, Sue, I'm going to awaken you again. I'll tell you when to go to sleep, Sue, but *you won't know it.* I'll tell you when to go to sleep, but *you won't know it.* But you'll go to sleep.

Comment

E: I can count her to sleep. I can tell her to go to sleep.

E: We may have to play it back to realize what I said to Sue. "I will tell you when to go to sleep, but *you* won't—*know* it."
H: The other kind of "no"—meaning you won't refuse?
E: No.
H: It sounds like that.
E: "But you won't—know it." That's a double statement. It means you won't know when I tell you this, you just won't know it. And also it says "*know* it" when I tell you to go to sleep.
W: Separating it on two levels.
E: Separating it on two levels. "You *won't know* it you won't *know it.*" Meaning, you won't know it when I tell you to go to sleep—*know* it when I tell you to go to sleep. Play it back. [The tape is replayed.]
H: It's very hard for me to tell the difference.
E: They're much more acute than you are. [The tape is replayed.]
E: You won't—*know* it.
H: Well, is it the same on both those repetitions, or different.
E: Essentially the same.
H: Oh, I was trying to find the difference.
E: They're both the same. There's a slight downward inflection on "won't," on "know it" a rising inflection, a slight rising inflection

Induction

E: [Pause.] And you will want to, won't you, when I tell you to? Even though you don't know it. You will go to sleep, will you not? When I tell you to. Even though you don't know it.

E: . . . And you're beginning to realize you can *sleep*, like L. And you can. And you're knowing it more and more, are you not? [Pause.] From 20 to 17 is 3—and 4 from that is 13—and 3 *more* makes 10—you're half awake. And 9, and 8, and 7, 6, and 5, 4, 3, 2, 1. Wake up. Somewhere in the hassle you lost sour cigarette. Would you like it? Mrs. C, this is Dr. and Mrs. Fingle.
S: How do you do. My hand is so cold. This one. It's cold.
E: Would you like your cigarette?
S: Yes.
E: Tell me, Sue, have you been in a trance?
S: I think *so*.
E: You think so.
S: Yes.
E: Are you awake now?
S: I think so. I'm not sure.

Comment

on "know."
H: Yes, I see it now.

H: Why did you follow that first series of "don't know it" with "you will," and then you said, "And you will, won't you"? Meaning, "You will know it, won't you?"

E: Yes.

E: From 20 to 17 is 3, and 4 from that is 13, and 3 *more* is 10.
H: Is that what you said then? [The tape is replayed.]
E: I want to put addition in there. Because after that I'm going to start adding.

W: This is the hand from which you took the cigarette. That she comments on. This is odd. I wonder if there's a connection there.
E: I think it was just a subjective observation.
W: It struck me, because in taking away the cigarette you talked more about "do you want to smoke" and finally she said a little "no," and you took the cigarette. And then you offered back the cigarette, and so I wondered if there was any connection.
E: I didn't follow that out at all.

Induction

E: Well, Mr. Haley and Mr. Weakland are recording everything here. They want a discussion of this later. They'll probably use it in their research project.
S: Fine.
E: Shall we really fascinate 'em?
S: [Low.] Yes.
E: I have eight children.
S: I know. I think it's marvelous.
E: And then there's some who have a dozen. [Pause.] And you know now, don't you?

Comment

H: That's what you wanted the adding in there for!
E: That's right. See how far in advance I planned that.
W: Far ahead of me.
E: I didn't know quite how to get that dozen in. But I was going to use addition. And "3 *more* is 10." I had the concept of addition there, and I waited for an opportunity. I had laid my foundation for adding, first by obvious subtraction, and then by "and 3 more—is 10." Is that addition or subtraction? But the question of addition would necessarily arise.
H: Do you think she would have reacted to the addition of 8 plus 12 if you hadn't put in the addition earlier?
E: Well, when I was subtracting 3 from 20 and making it 17, I knew I was going to need addition. While I was getting 4 from 17, realizing I had to get addition in there somewhere, what could I make as a casual statement so I could add something later to get 20? The first casual statement was the number of children I have. Now how would I verbalize "12"? Should I make it "a dozen"? I thought at the last moment if I used "dozen," that would be "1, 2." She would have to translate "dozen" into 12—8

Induction	Comment
	and 12 makes 20. So I made it the more involved "dozen."
	H: Well, what if you hadn't this addition in the counting earlier, do you think she would have gone into a trance on the basis of 8 plus a dozen?
	E: She might not. I wanted to insure it. I also wanted to show you how to plant suggestions.
	H: You showed us all right. Any particular reason for not bringing up the recorder and research earlier?
	E: She had been going into a trance, and earlier a mention of her being used for research might frighten her. It would remain an unanswered question. After she had been in a trance several times, then it was safe for me to bring it up because she had already been recorded, she was going to be used for research. If mentioned at first, it would be a threat, but now it's an accomplished fact she's going to be used for research, and it's obviously being continued; therefore it means her performance is valid.
	H: You employ odd mixtures of accomplished facts that turn into beneficial situations.
E: That's right. Close your eyes and go to sleep and 12 and 8 is 20, isn't it? Isn't that right?	
	H: So you say "3 more is 10." You didn't raise a questioning inflection on 10.
	W: A little bit, I thought. [The tape is replayed.]
E: 3 and 20 is 17 and 4 from that is 13, and 3 *more* is 10 and you're half asleep. [Long pause.] And after you are awakened, Sue, I want to introduce you to some people. You haven't met them before. And you *really haven't*.	*E:* Waking her up, the 3 *more* is again literally an addition phenomenon. And yet it's used as subtraction. Waking her up I would say "half *awake*" because I wanted to add the idea of addition—I was going to use it later. I put in half *asleep* instead of half awake, and much later I could again use 8 plus 12 is 20.
	H: Why did you say "you really haven't"?
	E: I wanted an amnesia. Now the effect of that

Trance Induction & Commentary

Induction	Comment

Induction

E: . . . And you'll be pleased to meet them. I'll tell you their names now, but you will forget their names until after you awaken. But then you'll remember when I tell you them. Dr. and Mrs. Fingle.

E: Now I'm going to awaken you. 20, 15, 10, 5, 4, 3, 2, 1. Wake. I think you've been asleep again.
S: Yes.
E: Here comes that fly again.
S: Yes.
E: Here comes that fly again.
S: Oh, the fly.
E: Oh, Sue, there are a couple of strangers here, Dr. and Mrs. Fingle.
F: How do you do?

Comment

is to transform the memory, the conscious memory of having met them, into a possibly trance hallucinatory experience. And to alter its identity. And thus it could be reduced to a trance experience and an amnesic experience.
H: By saying "you really haven't" the implication could be that what you say relates to a hallucination, you mean?
E: Or the entire process of introduction was a hallucinatory experience belonging to a trance, therefore an amnesic experience.
H: What she did after she awakened was ask about their names a couple of times, wasn't it?
E: At least once.
H: Trying to get it clear. And you said here, "You'll forget their names until after you awaken, and then you'll remember them." Was she busy making sure she'd remember them?
E: That's right.
W: Wait a minute, why do you tell her the names and then tell her to forget them here? Is that to get that back into the trance experience so that she can get rid of it?
E: Yes.
H: You make this trance experience such an isolated thing.
E: It serves to enhance specific phenomena.
H: You don't say "20, 15, 10, 5, 1." Would that be too sharp a jump for awakening?
E: Maybe she isn't awakening that rapidly. I have to give her some time to catch up.

W: And there you reinforce your previous suggestion by saying "a couple of strangers."
E: Yes, that is, make your waking situation as valid as possible.
H: They were strangers.
E: If she hadn't met them before, I'd better agree with my statement—a couple of strangers. I'd better be consistent, too. And therefore I set the example of consistency.
H: And she will use that as a model—if you set

Induction	Comment
S: How do you do? What's the name? *E:* Fingle. *S:* Fingle. *E:* Fingle.	an example of consistence. *E:* I want to be consistent to give my subjects a feeling of comfort and security. I make my statements valid. *W:* Well, when you contradict one, you contradict it very flatly. "You haven't met them." *E:* "And you *really* haven't." What does "*really* haven't" mean? A very special significance. *H:* In what way is it special? *E:* "You haven't *really* eaten a midnight snack until you have eaten one *I* prepared. You really haven't." *H:* There's that playing on the word "really" again. *E:* Yes. *H:* That's the trickiest word in the whole business. It's one of those words that can be literal or metaphorical or halfway in between.
E: Who's asleep around here? *S:* I'm going back. *E:* How many times have you been asleep? Say any number of times. *S:* Four. *E:* [Pause.] Not bad. *S:* [Bursting out laughing.] I didn't really mean it. That just came out. [Both laughing.] *E:* You didn't really mean it, but you said it. *S:* I don't know. *E:* Do you want to change it? *S:* Mmm. *E:* Try it. Say a number. *S:* Mmm. *E:* You can't say a	

Trance Induction & Commentary

Induction

number. Can you say the same one?
S: Four.
E: Let's give it a count.
S: How much?
E: Oh, just any count!
S: 1, 2—oh no! [Apparently feels herself going in trance.]
E: What's the matter?
S: Nothing.
E: Go ahead and count.

S: 1, 2, 3, 4, 5, 6, 7, 8, 9, 10, 11, 12, 13, 14, 15, 16, [becoming more slow and inaudible. Pause.]
E: You really convinced *yourself* that time, didn't you, Sue? You really did, didn't you? Now you know, do you not? Now you know. And you really know it, do you not?

Comment

H: Why did she stop when you said that? I've forgotten now.
E: I asked her to give me any number, to count—"1, 2, oh no!" She suddenly realized that she was counting in the direction of 20.
W: Yes, she felt herself going to sleep.
E: Now when you want to prove something to a subject, and really prove it to them, try to let the proof come from within them. And let it come from within them in a most unexpected way.
W: That makes it different. I tried it once with a very resistant subject. I had him tell his hand to lift. Now that wasn't unexpected, but it would have been proof from within himself.
E: Yes.
W: And he was so very reluctant to tell it to lift. He didn't want to find out, so he didn't want to tell his hand.
H: When she said "count to how much?" it apparently hadn't crossed her mind then?
E: No, it hadn't. "Oh, just count." "1, 2, oh no."
H: I remember now. She stopped overtly counting at about 17, and you waited until at that rate she would reach 20, and then you took a deep breath, wasn't that it?
E: Yes.
E: "And you really know it, do you not?" What has been said that she really knows? At that particular time no specific thing had really been said. But I told her she knows. And it covers *everything* I have said. It's all inclusive.

Induction

E: And now, Sue, I want you to have the feeling, the very, very strong feeling after you awaken that you've been asleep for a long, long time. At least two hours. I want you to have the feeling that you have been sleeping for two *long* hours. Very restful, very comfortable, and you won't believe your watch. And you won't believe it, will you? [Pause.] Because after you awaken . . .

Comment

And she knows. And in trying to search for some specific thing she has to look over the entire situation.

W: I notice you draw out all the words.

E: "And you won't believe your watch." "And you won't believe it, will you?" The suggestion [firmly] "And you won't believe your watch." [softly] "And you won't believe it, will you?" That's the suggestion—"And you won't believe it, will you?" Literally hauling her over to join me.
H: Yes, and the second one becomes a comment on the suggestion.
E: A comment. A shared comment.

W: I'm not quite sure I got that. "You won't believe your watch." Then what does the next one do?
E: "You won't believe your watch—and you won't, will you?" You see, it's a comment, and you're joining me on the comment as you listen to it. And when you comment on the suggestion, that suggestion is real; otherwise you can't offer a comment.
W: That's a thing we'd better think about, the matter of comment. And if there's no comment, maybe it isn't real.
H: This is again, as far as we're concerned, metacommunication, which is communication about communication.
E: Validate the suggestion by commenting on

Trance Induction & Commentary

Induction

E: . . . you will know from your inner feeling that you have slept for two long hours. And you'll feel rested, refreshed. And now take it easy, and just two hours have passed . . .

E: . . . and you're really feeling rested and refreshed. 20, 19, 18, 17, 16, 15, 14, 13, 12, 11, 10, 9, 8, 7, 6, 5, 4, 3, 2, 1. Wake up, wide awake.

Comment

it. "And you won't, will you?" "And you won't believe your watch. And you won't, will you?"
H: Was the phrasing, "and you won't, will you?" the same as "you can, can't you," so if it comes to her mind, "I will," you had already said it?
E: Yes.
H: The same thing again. That's a nice one.

W: You mentioned that she'll know from her inner feelings that she'll be rested and refreshed, because she's had that two long hours of sleep. This, then, builds up the disbelief in the watch because what is so sure as one's own real feelings?
E: One's own real feelings.
H: Not only disbelief in the watch, but she would disbelieve in every watch in the room then.
E: She had her feelings.
W: She had her feelings, and you had one feeling validated anyway. She felt it was two long hours and she felt refreshed as one would if he slept two long ours. Each one supports the other.

H: Was there any deliberate hesitation in that count?
E: You can never be consistent. You can never really count backward from 20 to 1 or forward from 1 to 20 always in the same way. You ought always to use hesitation and emphasis. On that particular occasion I just threw in some, not for any particular purpose except to demonstrate that I can use variations whenever I

please. And I don't ever want to get stuck by a subject learning a rigid pattern.

H: I see, you mean, as the "traditional" hypnotist does, a rote pattern that so many use.

E: The rote pattern.

H: I notice you hesitated on 12 and 8 there, was that all related to the 8 children and the dozen?

E: Not that I know of.

S: I never did get through with that cigarette, did I?

H: That's a funny one. If she thought at that moment that she'd slept two hours, how could she make a comment like that about her cigarette.

W: What did she say?

H: 'I never did finish that cigarette, did I?' And it was burning there in the ash tray. Isn't that a contradiction.

E: Sure, it's a contradiction.

H: Is it only a little later that the realization it has been two hours comes over her?

E: She was coming out of a disoriented time state. She started to smoke the cigarette when awake. A long trance state intervened. Two hours long. Then she awakened, reoriented to the original waking state because there's an amnesia for having been in a trance. And a general feeling that time has passed.

H: Wait a minute. When she said 'I never did finish that cigarette,' was she then thinking that she had just put that cigarette in the ash tray?

E: [Drawing]   Waking state

and cigarette   Waking state

and cigarette.   Trance

There's your diagram. Now this upper line is a conscious memory line. But so far as she was concerned, consciously it was a continuum but with an underlying sense of time duration.

H: Yes.

E: This lower line is amnesic. But at the same time she has a feeling of the passage of time.

W: Which then you develop a little bit as I remember by beginning to speak to her about time.

E: Yes. Because she had to become *aware* of that long passage of time. Just as you're listening to a lecture and all of a sudden you realize, 'Oh my, I've been here longer than I realized.'

W: It's a funny way to try to get it, but the shortness and the longness go together in some way.

H: She had amnesia for the trance, but in the trance she was told to feel that two hours had passed.

E: And that's her first initial awareness: 'I never did finish that cigarette.' You start asking your host a question, and an interruption occurs, and you've been enjoying yourself thoroughly, and then you say, 'I never did finish asking that question. Oh my, it's time for me to leave.'

H: Yes, let's see how she builds that up.

S: You know, when I started counting, all of a sudden I only saw one eye. There was one eye over here.

E: No eye over here?

S: At first I was looking at both of them and then there was only one [referring to E's eyes.]

E: Her spontaneous development of a negative hallucination. She saw only one eye.

H: Does that have a metaphorical meaning—'eye' in the sense of 'me'?

E: Maybe. It would have taken time, had I thought of it at the moment. 'What happened to the rest of the room?' There was only one eye. A vague awareness of the rest of me, but

Induction

E: What else happened?
S: Nothing.
E: [Pause.] What happened the first time you counted, or started to count?
S: Were there two counts? I only remember one.
E: Didn't you start to count and then refuse to count?
S: Yes.
E: What's the explanation of that?
S: I was afraid.
E: What were you afraid of?
S: A very funny feeling.
E: How did that feeling come to you?
S: I don't know.
E: What was the feeling really like?
S: Sinking.
E: Describe it more.
S: Oblivion.
E: Anything else.
S: It was very comfortable.

Comment

only one eye. The vagueness of me, the absence of everybody else.
W: I wonder if that has any relation to the importance of one in another sense. If she counted "one," that's all right, but if she had counted "two"—would she go into a trance?
E: No, because you get that one eye response in other situations.

H: That's a kind of contradictory kind of description, isn't it? Sinking, oblivion, fear, but very comfortable.
E: Now, did you notice her use of words?
H: I thought I did. What about it?
E: How can one describe partial conscious

Trance Induction & Commentary

Induction	Comment

Comment (continued):

awareness of trance development? I wonder what the word "oblivion" meant to her.

H: Well, she didn't misuse the word "fear."

E: It's out of context: "comfortable-fear," "comfortable"—utterly contradictory.

W: That's why Jay is raising the question.

H: Fear, sinking, oblivion, but very comfortable. You don't think she could be afraid of the trance and feel it was comfortable at the same time?

E: Yes, she could But that's something I don't understand about oblivion and fear, and comfortable.

H: And sinking.

E: And sinking. Was she sinking into a nice, soft mattress? One of my patients always described it as sinking into a nice, soft, pleasing cloud that floats so gently. A lot of them do, sinking in a very pleasant way.

H: If it was so pleasing, she wouldn't have stopped at the count of two in that way, would she? She stopped, startled, afraid.

E: Startled? Afraid? "Oh, no!" [Said softly.]

H: You thought it was a pleased "Oh, no!"?

E: An attitude of complete astonishment.

H: You mean a realization attitude more than a fear attitude?

E: Yes. Utter astonishment.

H: I just wondered if she started to say how she felt about the trance, that she was afraid of it and was sinking into oblivion, and thought this might antagonize you, and so she said "but it was comfortable."

E: I don't think so. I just wondered about her use of words.

Induction:

E: Did T want to serve coffee now?

S: I guess it is about time. How was the movie?

T: Watching television.

S: That late?

Induction

E: Look at your watch.
S: It's amazing! [Laughter.] The thing's stopped!
E: Do you believe your watch?
S: Well, it stopped three times today. [Laughter.] No, it's going. Unless it stopped during the time. What does your watch say?
SOMEONE: 8:30.
S: Does anybody else have a watch?
ANOTHER PERSON: 8.30.
S: 8:30?
E: Can't believe these watches.
S: Not very much. [Laughter.]
E: What time do you think it is?
S: Oh, about 9:30, 10 o'clock.
E: And what all has happened this evening?
S: Maybe you were talking to somebody else! [Laughing.] I don't want to miss it, though.
E: [Laughs.]
S: Don't do that to me!
E: You know, I have an idea you'd be a good subject!
S: Nothing I want more in this world . . .

Comment

W: There you say "I have an idea you'd be a good subject." This, now that she has done it—now your emphasis is on how about really doing something more.
E: Yes.
W: Whereas before, when you were getting her started, you were making the most of every-

Induction

S: I want to see the fawn that L saw.
E: You would? That one or another one? Tell me, in Maine, haven't you seen a fawn?
S: Every time I get near one—I never—I just see tracks.
E: Haven't you ever seen a deer?
S: I don't think so. I hunt 'em, but I can't ever find them.
E: But in Maine haven't you ever seen a deer or a fawn?
S: Not right up close.
E: In the distance.
S: Not that I can recall. That's right. I think I may have seen one once.
E: Was it in *Maine*?
S: I think I was passing by in a car, but I don't remember.
E: On the right, or maybe left-hand side?
S: No, it was going across the road.
E: Going across the road. Was it a wide road?
S: No, a dirt road.
E: A dirt road?

Comment

thing she did.
E: Yes, but it's a little bit more than that. You are having a perfectly wonderful time. Then you say, "I have an idea that we could have more fun." This confirms the goodness up to the moment and offers still further promise.

E: "That's one—or another one." She's going to have doubts; let's spread them, the doubts, I mean.
W: Oh, the doubts now are not on will you see it, but on what one will you see.
E: Yes, she's got to have doubts. "That one—or another one." So I've split the doubt.

Induction

S: Mmhmm.
E: Was it dry, a dry dirt road? Were there stones in it?
S: Yes, I think . . .
E: Yes, there were stones in it. Were there trees along the sides?
S: Yes.
E: Yes. And look at it closely. And see it. And it's nice to see it, isn't it? Look closer. [Pause.] Look closely, quietly. Look. Look closer, quietly, before it goes away. See it clearly. [Pause.] Is it gone?
S: I couldn't see it.
E: You couldn't see it; look carefully. It's by that tree.
S: It passed too quickly; just didn't see it.

Comment

H: Did she say "It passed too quickly"? Did she mean the deer, or did she mean she was in the car?
E: I think the deer.
H: That's what I wasn't sure of last night. I couldn't tell whether she was going past too fast in the car or not.
E: Now she had been in the waking state, and getting her to say "Maine," then again to say "Maine," and then my alteration in pronunciation of "Maine," and the very careful softening of my voice, and then to seize upon every clue.
H: What was the alteration in the word "Maine"?
E: Was it in Maine?" I softened my voice very greatly.
H: To start stalking the deer?
E: Yes. And "*that* tree"? A very specific tree,

Trance Induction & Commentary

Induction

E: Look again, beyond that other tree. Coming out. It's going quite fast. Look. Did you see the movement there?
S: Yes, but I missed the deer.
E: You missed the deer. See the movement, the swinging of the branch?
S: It starts.
E: You'll see it the next time, won't you? The next trance you get, you'll see it. [Pause.] Close your eyes and sleep deeply. Now take a deep breath. Sleep deeply. And wake up and tell me again about wanting to see the fawn that L did. Start the conversation on that . . . Wake up . . . Wake up. From 20 to 1, wake up. [Louder.] So you want to see the fawn that L did?
S: [Waking voice.] She saw it so clearly.
E: What are some of the other things that you'd like to see?
S: [Pause.] Nothing.

Comment

you know.
W: I noticed the whole series there, how with every utterance you duplicate an utterance and then—
E: Add another statement.
W: I understand.
E: And I led her from the waking state into an hallucinatory trance state.
H: And rapidly too!

E: Future trances. She'll see the deer.*
H: Why do you suppose she didn't this time? Is it tied up with L and the fawn?
E: L seeing the fawn, her wishful thinking—she never had, she wished she could, she always got there too late, she hunted and she only found the tracks. And every time you miss seeing the fawn—next time you will see it. So Im laying the foundation for a future trance. It moved too quickly, so I told her of the swinging of the branch. That was put in to validate that movement.

H: As I remember, you leaned back into the same position you were in just prior to her trance, didn't you?
E: Yes, I usually tend to do that. [That is, to use positions, movements, and remarks to establish and reestablish situations, both trance and nontrance.]

---

*It was later learned that she had never really seen a deer in Maine.

Induction

E: Nothing at all?
E: But you really couldn't see that fawn that L saw. That was on the Au Sable River.
S: I never even heard of it before.
E: Where else besides Maine have you been?
S: New York, California. I was in Florida a little while.
E: You say you go hunting.
S: Yes.
E: Where have you been hunting?
S: Out here.
E: Kaibab Forest?
S: No, we don't go for deer, just dove and quail. Lots of fun.
E: I like to eat them.
S: I have to clean them, if I kill them. You like to clean them?
E: I do.
S: And oh, there he goes [the fly], on your nose. [S and E join in hunting the fly, but miss.]
S: That's so—a hunt.
E: You know, I prefer to get them seven at a blow.
S: Sept d'un coup?
E: You want to go deer hunting?
S: I don't think so. I don't think I could kill one.
E: Haven't you ever

Comment

E: To emphasize the ordinary, casual situation, "I like to eat them." A highly personal statement, unrelated to the total situation. "I have to clean them." A highly personal thing, unrelated to that total situation. So she's really wide awake. My introduction of "I like to eat them" cleared the way for a completely full awakening.

E: I missed an opportunity there. "I don't think I could kill one." I missed a cue there as far as the trance was concerned. "You'd rather see one" should have been my response. I missed

Trance Induction & Commentary

Induction

seen any—deer, when you—
E: There [referring to fly.]
S: Please, please [pursuing with fly swatter]. Here he is. This is really a big home. In my home you can corner them.
E: When was the last time you were in Maine?
S: Last summer. If it's on me, don't worry, you can hit me. He's young. Got a lot of energy. There he is! Now he's back behind you.
E: Doggone that fly. [Pause.] When was the last time you were in Maine?
S: Last summer, June 19th.
E: Did you ever go up in the woods at all?
S: No, I was with the children, right in camp.
E: And that's where you learned your driving, is it?
S: Yes.
E: How old were you when you learned to drive?
S: Oh, 15 or 16.
E: And you had so little mercy on the boys there that you tried to run 'em down?
S: Oh, that was just teasing. I was always teased at camp because

Comment

it and felt badly afterward.

E: Did you realize that I was building up there in asking her about how old she was when she learned to drive a car. I was building up very carefully for a hallucination, a recovered memory of a long time ago. It seems to have been done very slowly, casually, and yet essentially it was done very rapidly.

Induction

I was the only girl in a boys' camp.
E: So you learned to drive a car at 16.
S: Yes, I learned a lot of things in Maine.
E: And everybody rushed for the canoes?
S: They didn't, really. They only . . .
E: They stood up.
S: Yeah, that's what the K's were telling them all.
E: How many boys were there at the camp?
S: Then, oh, I think—about 40, 45, maybe. Now it's much bigger.
E: I see.
S: Now they've got 120.
E: A hundred and—*twenty*.
S: Mmm.
E: [Pause.] A hundred and *twenty*. Take a deep breath. Because I want you to do something. And you can *remember* that camp. You saw that camp many times. And, as you think back, you can remember this boy and that boy—when you were 16. And you can look at your memory of that camp. And as you think back, you can recall this boy, and that boy, when you were 16. And you can look at

Comment

H: She had to say 20, didn't she? She said "120 boys in camp" and you said "a hundred and—twenty."

E: And as you think back, you can recall *this* boy and *that* boy.
H: Oh, by your movements you were setting them up?
E: Setting them up. *This* boy. *That* boy. Rolling back a bit. [Shifting position in chair.]

E: "And you can look at your memory of that

Trance Induction & Commentary

Induction	Comment
your memory of that camp.	camp." "You can" implies "you can *now* look back." And there I'm looking. It implies *now*.
	H: Did you select boys to look at on the basis of her phrase, "I learned a lot of things in Maine"?
	E: No, her statement was that she had been in that camp. The counselor always told the boys "take to the cliffs, she's going to drive." So there you've got an emotional memory. I believe her family owned the camp.
	H: Well, you have, particularly when you said "you learned to drive there," and she said, "Yes, I learned a lot of things in Maine," implying something else that she learned there. I just wondered if that was in the background of this a bit.
E: And I want you to see if there was grass around there. Was there a beach? Was the water smooth? Were there really trees there? Were they green? And look, and look up there and see a canoe, or see a boy, or see the beach, or see the water. You're beginning to see, and I want you to recognize one of the boys who was *there* when you were 16. And you can do that. See him plainly, clearly, and I want you to point to him. Point to him, and slowly your hand moves. It's going to point to him. And look—and see. Take your left hand and point. And point to him. That's it. That's it.	*H:* Notice my suggestion to point, "take your left hand and point," because I knew I was getting into deep water there, that is, severe difficulties.

Induction	Comment
Move your hand and point to him. Move your hand and point to him, and *see him* more and more plainly, and you can point. Are you pointing? Nod your head when you can see it shaping. Are you pointing? Are you pointing? [Pause.] Sleep deeply. [Long pause.]	*H:* Why deep water? *E:* Very deep water, because she wasn't making adequate response to me. So then I narrowed it down, "take your left hand and point." I knew I was getting in deep water there. I didn't know exactly what it was. I asked her to point. Her hand didn't point, so then I started narrowing down. Have her point with her left hand. When she failed to do that, I knew how deep in the water I was. Go ahead.
	E: The deep water I was in was that I was out of contact with her. She was back there [regressed spontaneously]. *E:* I made awfully sure of it, then I verified it by trying to get her to move her left hand to point, then I verified it by trying to get her to nod her head. I got no response at all. *H:* I remember wondering why you couldn't get any response from her on that. *E:* Because I wasn't there. She was there [in Maine, in regression]. Out of touch with me. She had drifted into that at the sound of my voice. I kept on. And you noticed that my voice went down and down and down [in volume]. So that I could lead into a silence. Go ahead. *E:* Now how did that begin? [Referring to tape recorder.]
E: And after you awake you will recall one of the boys you haven't thought of [pause] for a long time. You will tell me about him, will you not?	*W:* "And after you are awake, you will recall." *E:* A long pause. Soften the voice, a long pause, and the introduction of my voice saying something I had said before, "after you are awake." I gave her a long enough time to look at that boy. Then I used the words "you will recall the boy you haven't thought of for a long time," and if she hasn't thought of the boy for a long time, she can't possibly be back there in Maine. *H:* That was your way of bringing her out of it?

Comment

E: Yes.

H: Why didn't you want to regress her and have her there, and use that? I mean, make contact with her there?

E: You have to lay the foundation; I hadn't laid the foundation. Because I didn't want to lose her, and I had lost her there for a little while. Then I had to resort to silence, then begin with a suggestion I'd given before, and match it with "not for a long time."

H: Suppose you had said, "Who am I?" or brought yourself into it somehow back there, even without the foundation, what would happen?

E: I'd probably have been a counselor.

H: Well, what foundation should have been there that was absent, so you didn't want to do this sort of thing?

E: My voice is my voice; it's really not me. My voice can be heard with a phone. It can be heard on a tape recording. My voice can be heard in places where I'm not. And you could hear my voice in Florida, New York, California, Kaibab Forest, if you were ever there.

H: If you had done that earlier, you could have maintained contact while she was back there?

E: Yes, but I would have been a voice, and my voice could have been transformed into a counselor's, into her father's or mother's, and very often I've been identified as father, mother, uncle, aunt, cousin, the neighbor, teacher.

H: That's partly, too, why she referred later to how she was alone in Maine?

E: Yes, I wasn't there. Now if I'd laid my foundation, I could have been the voice of someone there talking to her. And that's difficult work because you have to use such very general questions that can be interpreted in terms of the people in that situation. I've had subjects comment on the screechiness of my voice, "My teacher talked to me and that screechy voice of hers is still ringing in my ears," and then repeat the

Induction	Comment
	things I had said. Too many operators, when they lose contact, fail to go right on as if they hadn't lost contact, lower their voices, and make use of silent techniques. Then slowly come out of it by utilizing previous utterances. And then throw in something that nullifies the regressed state. *W:* By lowering your voice down to the pause, then in effect you join the loss of contact, too, and take that over. *E:* Yes, because I've been training her all evening to accept and respond to my silences. I'd be curious to find out how long that visit she made was. It might have been an hour or two.
E: [Long pause.] Sleep deeply, and now awaken. 20, 19, 18, 17, 16, 15, 14, 13, 12, 11, 10, 9, 8, 7, 6, 5, 4, 3, 2, 1. Wake up. And I still haven't got that fly. *S:* Oh! *E:* I hope you have better luck with your doves than you are having with this fly. *S:* I hope so, too.	*H:* Is that amnesia again? *E:* Yes. *W:* Which you provoked with the reference to the fly. Your reference to the fly there is similar to her reference to the cigarette before. *E:* Yes. *H:* Do you usually calculatedly remember what was going on just before you started the induction, so you can set that up again afterwards? *E:* I try to. And it really promotes amnesia.

External circumstances caused an interruption of the commentary at this point, but further analysis would have served only to emphasize, with variations and modifications occasioned by the immediate intrinsic circumstances, the understandings already elaborated. It may be added that henceforth Sue was a competent subject, capable of all phenomena of the light and deep trance, including even the plenary state.

To summarize, a tape recording was made of a spontaneous and unplanned hypnotic induction of a somewhat resistant subject who had failed on three previous occasions to develop a trance and who believed that she could not be hypnotized. The next day this recording was played back by the authors, with many systematic interruptions to permit a point-by-point discussion and explanation of the significances, purposes, and interrelationships of the various suggestions and maneuvers employed in developing the subject's hypnotic responses. A transcription of a second recording, made of the entire procedure, constitutes this paper.

10. The Confusion Technique in Hypnosis

Milton H. Erickson

GENERAL CONSIDERATIONS AND RATIONALE OF DEVELOPMENT

The request has been made many times that I record in the literature an account of the Confusion Technique that I have developed and used over the years, including a description, definition, illustrative examples, and various observations, uses, and findings from it.

It is primarily a verbal technique, although pantomime can be used for confusional purposes as well as for communication, as I shall describe in another article. As a verbal technique, the Confusion Technique is based upon plays on words, an involved example of which can be readily understood by the reader but not by the listener, such as ''Write right right, not wright or write.'' Spoken to attentive listeners with complete earnestness, a burden of constructing a meaning is placed upon them, and before they can reject it, another statement can be made to hold their attention. This play on words can be illustrated in another fashion by the statement that a man lost his left hand in an accident and thus his *right* (hand) is his *left*. Thus two words with opposite meanings are used correctly to describe a single object, in this instance the remaining hand. Then, too, use is made of tenses to keep the subject in a state of constant endeavor to sort out the intended meaning. For example one may declare so easily that the *present* and the *past* can be so readily summarized by the simple statement, ''That which now *is* *will* soon be *was* yesterday's *future* even as it *will be* tomorrow's *was*.'' Thus are the past, the present, and the future all used in reference to the reality of ''today.''

The next item in the Confusion Technique is the employment of irrelevancies and non sequiturs, *each of which taken out of context* appears to be a sound and sensible communication. Taken *in context* they are confusing, distracting, and inhibiting and lead progressively to the subjects' earnest desire for and an actual need to receive some communication which, in their increasing state of frustration, they can readily comprehend and to which they can easily make a response.

Reprinted with permission from *The American Journal of Clinical Hypnosis,* January, 1964, *6,* 183-207.

Confusion Technique

It is in many ways an adaptation of common everyday behavior, particularly seen in the field of humor, a form of humor this author has enjoyed since childhood.

A primary consideration in the use of a Confusion Technique is the consistent maintenance of a general casual but definitely interested attitude and speaking in a gravely earnest, intent manner expressive of a certain, utterly complete expectation of their understanding of what is being said or done together with an extremely careful shifting of the tenses employed. Also of great importance is a ready flow of language, rapid for the fast thinker, slower for the slower-minded, but always being careful to give a little time for a response but never quite sufficient. Thus the subjects are led almost to begin a response, are frustrated in this by then being presented with the next idea, and the whole process is repeated with a continued development of a state of inhibition, leading to confusion and a growing need to receive a clear-cut, comprehensible communication to which they *can make* a ready and full response.

The incident, one of spontaneous humor on my part, that led to its adaptation as a possible hypnotic technique was as follows. One windy day as I was on my way to attend that first formal seminar on hypnosis conducted in the United States by Clark L. Hull at the University of Wisconsin in 1923, where I reported on my experimental work and graduate psychology students discussed my findings, a man came rushing around the corner of a building and bumped hard against me as I stood bracing myself against the wind. Before he could recover his poise to speak to me, I glanced elaborately at my watch and courteously, as if he had inquired the time of day, I stated "It's exactly 10 minutes of two," although it was actually closer to 4:00 P.M., and I walked on. About a half a block away I turned and saw him still looking at me, undoubtedly still puzzled and bewildered by my remark.

I continued on my way to the laboratory and began to puzzle over the total situation and to recall various other times I had made similar remarks to my classmates, laboratory mates, friends, and acquaintances and the resulting confusion, bewilderment, and feeling of mental eagerness on their part for some comprehensible understanding. Particularly did I recall the occasion on which my physics laboratory mate had told his friends that he intended to do the second (and interesting) part of a coming experiment and that he was going to make me do the first (and onerous) part of that experiment. I learned of this, and when we collected our experimental material and apparatus and were dividing it up into two separate piles, I told him at the crucial moment quietly but with great intensity, *"That sparrow really flew to the right, then suddenly flew left, and then up, and I just don't know what happened after that."* While he stared blankly at me, I took the equipment for the second part of the experiment and set busily to work, and he, still bewildered, merely followed my example by setting to work with the equipment for the first part of the experiment. Not until the experiment was nearly completed did he break the customary silence that characterized our working together. He asked, "How come I'm doing this part?

I wanted to do that part." To this I replied simply, "It just seemed to work out naturally this way."

As I reviewed and studied these occurrences and numerous others of a comparable character, they all appeared to have in common a certain number of psychological elements.

1. There was an interpersonal relationship of a sort that required some kind of joint participation and experience.
2. There was the sudden and inexplicable introduction of an irrelevant idea, comprehensible in its own context, but which was completely unrelated and irrelevant to the immediate situation.
3. Thus the person was confronted by (1) a comprehensible situation for which a pattern of response would be easily forthcoming, and (2) an utterly irrelevant, but comprehensible in itself alone, non sequitur, thereby leaving the person without any means of response until sufficient time had passed to permit adequate mental reorganization to dismiss the non sequitur from the pertinent situation. Thus in the first instance the inadvertent collision called for conventionalized social responses between two people, but instead a non sequitur, uncalled for and presented as an earnest factual communication despite the contradiction of it by reality, left the man inhibited in making any expectable conventional response, and the non sequitur, in itself comprehensible, called for no response since it had not been asked for, thereby leaving the man in a state of bewilderment until he could reorganize his mental activity to exclude the non sequitur and go about his business.

In the second example George and I completed the task of dividing the material and apparatus, and at the moment when he knew what he was going to do but did not know what I was really going to do, I impressively presented him with an irrelevant communication comprehensible in itself but offering no opportunity for a response on his part. Then as a mere matter of course I took that part of the material and apparatus chosen by me and he, inhibited by the unanswerable irrelevancy, automatically and passively followed my example by taking the remaining material, and we simply set to work in our customary silent manner. By the time he had dismissed the irrelevancy from his mind, it was much too late for him to say, "You do that and I will do this."

4. Thus there is a structuring of a situation so that definite and appropriate responses are called for but, before they can be made, an irrelevancy or non sequitur, which in itself alone is a meaningful communication, is introduced into the situation, thereby inhibiting the other person from making his natural response to the original situation. This results in a state of bewilderment and confusion and progressively leads to a profound need to do something, just anything, uncritically and indiscriminatingly. In the first instance the man merely stared helplessly after me; in the second instance George passively followed my example, and automatically and indiscriminatingly did the task he did not want to do, but a task which was *proper and fitting in the total laboratory setting,*

although previously rejected by him apparently without my knowledge.

In actuality, there was no essential difference in the psychology of the performance of the two men. Both had been profoundly inhibited in making their natural responses. Both were bewildered and confused and had a profound need to do something, anything, but, in a noncritical, indiscriminating way. The first man stood passively, helplessly, in the strong wind, looking after me until time itself or some other stimulus "shook" him out of his state of confusion. On the other hand George, inhibited in his natural responses, merely passively, automatically, and uncritically followed the example I carefully set for him.

5. In summary, if into any simple little situation evocative of simple natural responses there is introduced just previous to the moment of response a casual simple irrelevancy or non sequitur, confusion results, and there is an inhibition of natural responses. The non sequitur is completely meaningful in itself but has no bearing *except as an interruption* upon the original situation calling for a response. The need experienced to respond to the original situation and the immediate inhibition of that response by a seemingly meaningful communication results in an increased need to do something. Quite possibly this increased need is a summation of the need to respond to the original stimulus and the need to understand the inexplicable, seemingly meaningful addition. As this procedure is continued for hypnotic purposes, there often arises an intolerable state of bewilderment and confusion and a compelling, growing need for the subject of this procedure to make some kind of a response to relieve his increasing tension, and he readily seizes upon the first clear-cut, easily comprehended communication offered to him. In the meantime he has been presented with a wealth of seemingly related ideas, all of which have an underlying implication of primary but unrecognized significance leading to the development of hypnosis or of hypnotic phenomena.

This thinking led to extensive experimentation by deliberately making out-of-character, irrelevant, non sequitur remarks in groups and to single persons. The latter proved to be the better procedure, since the variations in individual behavior in group situations tended seriously to interfere but did not render the task impossible.

As originally worked out, the Confusion Technique was based upon the following items of procedure and employed primarily for the purposes of *age regression* before it was recognized as readily applicable to *other hypnotic phenomena*.

The original procedure consisted of the following items:

1. Mention of some commonplace item of everyday living such as eating.
2. Relating that item as an actual fact or possibility for the subject for the current day or *present*.
3. Mention its absolute probability in the *future,* specifying some one

particular day of the week, preferably the current day.
4. Comment on its probable occurrence (the eating) on that same day in the *past* week.
5. Comment on the identity of the day preceding the named day of the past week, emphasizing that such a day is a part of the *present* week even as it will occur in the *future* week.
6. Add that today's day had occurred last *week*, even *last month*, and that learning the names of the days of the week had constituted a *childhood problem*. (Thus the period of regression desired is subtly introduced.)
7. Mention that just as in the past a certain month would follow the *present month* even as the *present month* had been preceded by the *previous month* during which a meal had been eaten on some named weekday. And that weekday had been preceded by another weekday, just as the previous week had a day of an earlier ordinal position. (For sake of clarity to the reader, let us assume that the current day is the second Friday of June, 1963, that *next* Friday eating will occur even as it did *this* Friday, and as it undoubtedly did *last* Friday which was preceded by a Thursday, just as it was earlier in the *present month* and would be in the *future weeks*. Days, weeks, months, past, present, and future are all intermingled.)

Then one proceeds with mention that last month (May) had a Thursday—in fact, several Thursdays—each preceded by a Wednesday while the month of April preceded May, another *childhood task* of learning the months of the year. (Thus from Friday June 14, 1963, by a simple valid statement, an underlying implication of time is employed to arouse thoughts of *childhood*, or any chosen past time, without seemingly direct suggestion to that effect.)
8. This intermittent and varied reference to the present, future, and past is continued with increasing emphasis upon the past with an implication of the actual past as belonging to the present and then to the future. Again to clarify for the reader one might say;

"Not only did you (Reader, please bear in mind that it is the second Friday of June 1963) eat breakfast on Wednesday of last week, but before that you ate dinner on Tuesday in May, and *June was then in the future*, but before May was April and before that was March and *in February you probably had the same thing for lunch*, and you didn't even think of having it *next* April, but of course on January 1st, New Years Day, you *never even thought of the 14th of June 1963* (an implication of possible amnesia developing), it was *so far in the future*, but you certainly could think of Christmas, December 1962, and wasn't that a nice present you got—one that you didn't even dream of on Thanksgiving Day in November and what a Thanksgiving dinner, *so*

Confusion Technique

good (a present tense description of a series of ideas with an emotionally charged validation of the actual past as the present and then the future), but Labor Day came in September of '62, but before that was July 4, but on January 1st of 1962 you really *couldn't think of July 4th* because it was (this use of ''was'' implies a present tense) just the beginning of 1962. And then of course there was your birthday in 1961, and maybe on that birthday you *looked forward* to your birthday in 1962, *but that was in the future, and who could even guess a year ahead about the future?* But the really wonderful birthday was your *graduation year birthday. Twenty-one and a graduate* at last!'' (An item of fact you have carefully learned and to which you lead and finally state in terms of present reality with utter and pleasing emphasis. Or one could continue as above to the 17th birthday or the 10th or whatever year might be desired.)

9. Thus there has been a rapid and easy mention of realities of today gradually slipping into the future with the past becoming the present and thereby placing the mentioned realities, actually of the past, increasingly from the implied present into the more and more seemingly remote future.
10. Significant dates which are in themselves indisputable are selected, and as the backward progress in time orientation continues to the selected time, some actual positive strongly tinged emotional event is mentioned.
11. Throughout, tenses are watched carefully and one speaks freely, as in the illustration given of the 21st birthday. It *is* the year of 1956, hence one speaks joyously of the instructorship that *will being in September,* which is yet to come. (Reorientation in time by implication and emotionally validated by vivifying the emotions of the past.)
12. Throughout the entire time each statement is made impressively, with adequate and appropriate inflections, but before the subjects in their attentiveness have any opportunity to take issue with or to dispute mentally what has just been said, a new utterance compelling their attention has been offered to claim their thought and which arouses more effort toward further new understandings, with only a frustration of effort to respond resulting.
13. Finally a clear-cut, definitive, easily grasped and understood statement is uttered, and the striving subject seizes upon it as a Rock of Gibraltar in the running flow of suggestions that has kept him helplessly following along (graduation day and birthday—emotionally potent and coincidental and a valid fact).
14. Reinforcement of the patient's reorientation in the past by a ''specific orientation'' to a ''general'' orientation such as a vague general reference to his ''father's job,'' and by wondering, ''Let's see, did it

rain the last week?'' and followed by mention of the instructorship. (Two general, vague, possible ideas, followed by the validity of the instructorship, all to fixate the regression to the past as the present.)
15. Follow up with the specific statement, "Now that it is all over [the graduation], what shall we do now?" and let the subject lead the way, but carefully interposing objections to some impossible remark such as, "Let's go down to Lake Mendota and have a swim." (This is "impossible" since a bathing suit becomes an immediate reality). Instead one agrees that it would be nice to go to Lake Mendota, there to watch the waves, the birds, and the canoes, thereby leading to hallucinatory activity, and as this develops, hallucinatory swimming may then follow.

At what point does the subject develop the trance and begin to regress? You have mentioned eating, days of the week, months of the year, a backward succession of years, each in itself and by itself a valid utterance but in the total context requiring a constant shifting in the temporal orientation of the subject's thoughts and marked by the changing of tenses, and along with all this there is aroused an increasing vividness of emotions related to the past. (A personal example may be cited here: While relating to a friend in great detail the events of a trip made 10 years previously in the Rocky Mountains with a car having a floor shift, the author, who was driving in a steering-wheel-shift car which he had driven for more than five years, suddenly saw a red light and sought frantically with his right hand to find the floor shift to put the engine into neutral while his friend watched in amazement. The car was stopped only by the expedient of jamming the brake and turning off the ignition before the author realized that the vividness and extensiveness of his memories about the past trip had extended over into the field of unrecognized associated motor memories.)

To answer the question of when hypnosis develops is difficult. If *one wishes to induce hypnosis with age regression as the goal,* one continues until the subject's overt behavior (more easily recognized by long experience) discloses evidence of the desired trance state. However, the process can be interrupted at any point, depending upon the purposes to be served. This will be illustrated later.

To summarize the main points of the above Confusion Technique the following outline may serve. It is a general form that I have used many times, always with different wordings as partly illustrated in the outline to be given. The outline is put into brief form and then remodified to insure proper inclusions at the right places of general items of actual personal significance, but so that they cannot be recognized for their eventual significance, yet can progressively serve to validate the subject's progress.

Thus the following might be used as one of the outline forms for the above illustration; to which, when put into use, are added many details with *ready spontaneous modifications* as determined by the subjects reactions.

Confusion Technique

I am so very glad you volunteered to be a subject	Joint participation in a joint task
You probably enjoyed eating today	Irrelevant—most likely factual
Most people do, though sometimes they skip a meal	A valid, commonplace utterance
You probably ate breakfast this morning	The temporal present
Maybe you will want tomorrow something you had today	The future (an indirect implication of a certain identity of the past and of today with the future)
You have eaten it before, perhaps on Friday like today	The past and the present and a common identity
Maybe you will next week	The present and the future
Whether last week, this week, or next week makes no difference	The present, future, and past all equated
Thursday always comes before Friday	Irrelevant non sequitur, and valid
This was true last week, will be true next week, and is so this week	Irrelevant, meaningful, and true, but what does it mean? (Subject struggles mentally to put a *connected* meaning on all this future, present, and past, all included in a meaningful statement which lacks pertinence.)
Before Friday is Thursday and before June is May	How true: But note use of *present tense* in relation to today's yesterday and to May.
But first there is "whan that Aprille with its shoures soote"	Here comes April of the past (remote past), and it also *pinpoints a particular area* in the subject's life—*his college days*. (An item of fact predetermined—it might have been in high school—to introduce Chaucer creates a problem of relating it meaningfully to what has been said but this is a confusing task.)
And March followed the snows of February but who really remembers the 6th of February	Back now to March, then to February, and one does (present tense) remember February 12th, 14th, and 22nd. February 6th only offers confusion (It has

And January 1st is the beginning of the New Year of 1963 and *all that it will bring*

But December brought Christmas

But Thanksgiving preceded Christmas, and all that shopping to get done and what a good dinner.

been predetermined that February 6th is not a birthday or some such event but if it is meaningful, this serves only to impel the subject to validate that day also).

Thus is given a memory task. *It will bring June* (already here) but slipping unaccountably into the remote future because January is given a present tense.

True, valid, vivid memories of the past December and the implied coming of the year of 1963

November 1962 with an *impending urgency to do something in the coming December,* an emotionally valid dinner memory, all of 1962. (And there have been many New Years, Christmases, and Thanksgiving Days, all strongly emotionally tinged)

From then on progressively larger steps based upon factual and valid events, Labor Day, Fourth of July, New Year's Day, remembrance that a December of 1961 wish came true, and then finally the 21st birthday and college graduation all set up as a final culmination by the quotation from college Chaucer setting a goal for a specific regression in time and so early in the outline and so unrecognizably. But one is careful to use such a reference as Chaucer only after making sure when there was a reading of Chaucer. Similarly one might make reference to a song of a certain vintage. A few well-placed questions, even with total strangers, obscurely put, will yield much information around which the immediate details of the technique can be built. But bear in mind that while June is the present, it belongs also to all the past as well as to all of past birthdays for this subject, and also to all past graduations. In regression in time any small series of stated personally meaningful events can be used and subtly mentioned early in the procedure in some unrecognized form.

Originally, in the 1920's, the Confusion Technique was used to induce hypnotic age regression. Numerous manifestations noted, at first by chance and then later by watchful observation, led to the realization that the technique could be variously employed to induce hypnosis itself or to elicit specific or isolated phenomena for either experimental or clinical purposes, and much experimentation was done.

ILLUSTRATIVE EXPERIMENTAL PROCEDURES

These studies led to a special experimentation when I attempted in 1932 and 1933 to expound the concept of a certain type of spatial orientation found in schizophrenia, which had interested me since 1929. I had much discussion of this topic with Dr. Govindaswamy, now deceased, a diplomate in psychological medicine and later superintendent at the mental hospital in Mysore, India, who was spending 15 months in the United States to study American psychiatry. In attempting to outline to him my understanding of how schizophrenic patients could conceive of themselves as simultaneously sitting in a chair looking out a window and at the same time lying on a bed with eyes closed, I realized painfully the inadequacy of my verbal explanation. He could not follow my explanation of the equality and coexistence of two separate spatial concepts of the self without an accompanying spontaneous comparison or contrast and a consequent evaluative judgment. Accordingly I volunteered to let him witness and participate in such an experience through the utilization of hypnosis, which was also a modality in which he was intensely interested. This particular instance is cited because it was so well recorded at the time and illustrates so clearly the building up of a Confusion Technique.

To accomplish this purpose, in a large vacant room I stationed two chairs and then Dr. Govindaswamy and myself in a 12-foot square arrangement, the chairs on one side, we two on the other. The respective positions for the chairs were A and B, those for us, C and D, Miss K, an excellent somnambulistic subject who had been used extensively in experimental work, was then summoned. (Miss K had been deliberately selected for the experiment because of her high intelligence, her quick-wittedness, her fluency of speech, and her remarkably acute ear for changes in voice inflection and voice direction.) All of us are responsive, often unwittingly so, to a minimal change in the spoken voice when the head is changed to a different position and the voice thereby is given a new direction, and Miss K was unusually keen in this respect. One might recall to mind the common experience of the uninteresting lecturer who speaks to a spot on the back wall, contrasted to the interesting lecturer whose eyes roam constantly over the audience, thereby commanding their attention and giving each member of the audience the feeling that each and all of them are being addressed.

In Dr. G's presence it was explained to her that she was to develop a profound somnambulistic trance in which she would be in full rapport with Dr. G as well as with me. Shortly Miss K opened her eyes and looked at me, passively awaiting further instructions.

While Dr. G listened and watched, the author pasted paper labels bearing in small characters the letters A and B on the respective chair seats, and Dr. G was asked to note, for himself that the east chair was labeled A and the west chair was labeled B. He was asked to take up his position north of chair B and to draw a small circle around his feet with chalk. The author stood 12 feet north of chair A and drew with chalk a small square about his feet.

During this procedure Miss K stood quietly, staring unblinkingly into space. She was then asked to sit down in chair A, which was nearest the author, facing the chair B, the one nearest to Dr. G. Miss K took her seat and again passively awaited further instructions.

Since this entire procedure was a specific experimental effort, full notes were to be made by both Dr. G and the author. (Also, without disclosing his intentions, the author excused himself to correct an oversight, left the room briefly, and secretly summoned Miss F, an assistant, who had worked previously with the author and was well trained in how to record in full his experimental procedures including both words and action. She was asked to remain out of sight behind a certain curtain but where she would have a good view and to make a full shorthand record of all events).

Slowly, distinctly, Miss K was told:

> I wish to teach Dr. G something about geography ["spatial orientation," as a term was purposively avoided] and I need your help. You are to do exactly as I say and nothing more, with *one exception*. [Italics here indicate a special inflection of slow, intense emphasis with a slight deepening of the voice.] That exception [no special inflection on this use of the word "exception" had been given] is this. You will note mentally and remember whenever I do something that Dr. G does not do and vice versa. This you will do separately and apart from all the rest you are to do, and tomorrow, when you do some typing for Dr. G and for me, these separate memories will come to your mind, and you will fit them into the typing you are doing without saying a word about it to either of us.
>
> Now for today's work. The special task I have for you to do is this: You are to sit right where you are *continuously, continuously, continuously* [the same special inflection used in the preceding paragraph with *one exception* was again used with the word "continuously"] without ever moving. Dr. G will watch you and so will I. Yet, I want you to know that that chair [pointing at A] you are in is *here* to you [pointing at B] is *there*, but to Dr. G *this* chair [A] is *here* and *that* chair [B] is *there*, but as we *go around* [the same special inflection mentioned above again being used for *go around*] the *square*, I am *here* and you are *there*, but you know you are *here* and you know I am *there*, and we know *that* chair [B] and Dr. G are *there*, but he knows he is *here* and you are *there* and *that* chair [B] is *there* and I am *there* and he and I know that you and *that* chair [B] are *there*, while you know I am *here* and Dr. G and that chair [B] are *there*, but you know that Dr. G knows that he is *here* and you are *there* and *that* chair [A] *is there* and that I who am *here* am really *there*, and if *that* chair [B] could think, it would know that you are *there* and that Dr. G and I both think we

are *here* and that we know that you are *there* even though you think you are *here*, and so the three of us know that you are *there* while you think you are *here*, but I am *here* and you are *there* and Dr. G knows that he is *here*, but we know he is *there*, but then he knows you are *there* while he is *here*.

All this was said slowly, carefully, impressively, while Miss K listened intently, and the author strove to record his statements and tried to give Dr. G an opportunity to record them. (His record was later found to be most confused and incomplete as was the author's record, but fortunately Miss F obtained a full and accurate record because of her previous training in recording the author's Confusion Techniques).

Shortly Dr. G appeared to be unable to record any of the author's impressively uttered statements, glanced at and traced with his finger the chalk mark about the author's feet. The instructions were continued:

And now Miss K, slowly at first and then more and more rapidly until you are talking at a good speed, explain to Dr. G that while he thinks he is *here* and you are *there*, that you are *here* and that he is *there* even as I think *that* chair is *there* and I am *here* and you are *there*, and just as soon as you are saying it rapidly and Dr. G is beginning to understand that he is *here* and you are *there*, still talking rapidly, you slowly change from *this* [pointing at A] chair to *that* [pointing at B] chair, but keep his attention on your explanation of how each of us can think *be here* and *be there* or *be there* and think *be here* and then when he sees you sitting *there*, and thinks you are *here*, gently return, still explaining and even laughing at him for thinking you are *there* when you are *here*, and then not recognizing that you are *there* while he is still thinking you are *here*.

Miss K then took over, first speaking slowly, then with increasing rapidity. At first Dr. G ceased to try to record, and it soon became impossible for the author to record Miss K's rapid utterances identifying *here* and *there* variously employed.

At about this time the author noted horizontal nystagmus in Dr. G's eyes, and Miss K, still talking rapidly, reiterating variously the author's explanations of *here* and *there*, glided gently from chair A to chair B. Dr. G checked visually his chalk circle, the author's chalk square, and suddenly shouted, "You are sitting *here* in this chair," to which Miss K replied simply, "Yes, I am sitting *here* [changing places] in that chair *there* [changing places again]."

The horizontal nystagmus in Dr. G's eyes became worse, and he seized a piece of chalk and walked hastily over and marked a small x in front of one chair and a small o in front of the other chair. The author promptly signaled Miss K with his right hand, pointed at the chalked x and o with his left hand,

and made a covering movement with his foot. Miss K kept on talking *here* and *there,* gliding back and forth between the two chairs, sitting first in one and then the other, each time covering the x or the o with her foot while Dr. G said "You are sitting in the x chair—no, the x is gone but the o is *there,* so you are sitting in the o chair, but the o is gone (Miss K had quickly moved over) and the x is *there,* but the x is gone and the o is *here* and so you are *there.*"

His eye nystagmus increased greatly, he complained of severe vertigo, nausea and a painful headache. The experiment was discontinued, Miss K was aroused and dismissed, and the author deliberately began a continuation of the original question of dual spatial orientation in schizophrenia. Gradually Dr. G's headache, nausea, and vertigo disappeared; he picked up his notebook, began to read, and seemed suddenly to have a partial sudden recollection of some of the experimental procedure.

He explained that as the author had given his original instructions about *here* and *there* he had experienced much confusion, but that when Miss K had taken over and increased the rate of her speech, he had felt himself becoming dizzy and that suddenly the room began turning around and around. This he had attempted to stop by making x and o marks, but those seemed to shift back and forth and to disappear unaccountably even though the chalk circle and square remained constantly present. He appeared to have no realization that Miss K had actually changed back and forth from one chair to another, only that the room kept whirling around with increasing subjective distress and confusion on his part.

The next day Miss K was asked to type her recollections of yesterday's experimental procedure. She promptly developed a spontaneous trance and remained inactive. She was given instruction to recall and given a posthypnotic suggestion that she then type her recollections. She explained in the trance state, "I was so busy watching Dr. G and you and remembering *here* and *there* that I can't remember. I was just concentrating on saying *here* and *there* in different ways and being sure of what was being said just to me and what was being said to both Dr. G and me by the inflections of your voice. When you first said "one exception" and then said I was to sit 'continuously, continuously, continuously' with that same inflection three times, I knew you were saying one thing to Dr. G but something different to me, and I had to watch for it (the inflection) again because I knew you meant something special."

Nevertheless in the waking state Miss K readily typed my notes and Dr. G's, but it was noted that she apparently developed brief spontaneous trances whenever she inserted parenthetically various items in both Dr. G's record and mine, arousing spontaneously and continuing her typing without apparently noticing the insertions. (Much later I thought of time distortion and its possible bearing on Miss K's spontaneous trances and parenthetical insertions in her typing without there being any interruption of her typing. Perhaps, even quite possibly, she relived in distorted time the events of the previous day despite her trance assertion of inability to remember. These parenthetical insertions were less complete, but in good accord with Miss F's full record).

In Dr. G's effort to record Miss K particularly noted his failure of recording certain notes, his marking of the x and the o, his glancing at and fingering the chalk circle about his feet and glancing at the square about mine, and his apparent confusion when he emphatically announced that she was sitting in chair A and then noting that she was actually in chair B without having noticed her shifting of her position. She also noted his confusion about the appearance and disappearance of his marks of x and o, and she had observed the nystagmus. (This latter Miss F did not note—she could not see it—but she did note unsteadiness and arm waving as if to keep his balance. This latter Miss K also noted).

She also noted many gaps in the author's record because of his intense concentration on the task and correctly interpreted the author's notations of x and o and his writing of them crossed out or not crossed out as meaning "covered up" and "in view."

Miss F's account was fully comprehensive but could not be read by Dr. G, despite repeated attempts, without developing vertigo, nausea and a headache. (This recurrent reaction is a most suggestive experimental induction of profound psychological and physiological responses.) Reading by Dr. G of his record with Miss K's parenthetical insertions elicited sudden but not complete recollections, such as, "That's right, she did change chairs, only I didn't see her do it," and "She put her foot on the x, that's why it disappeared." However he could not fully recall the entire experience. After this experiment Dr. G sought out schizophrenic patients who showed altered spatial orientation for special interviews and explained that their assertions had become much more meaningful to him. He also expressed much sympathy for certain patients who complained of distress from altered spatial orientation. It may be added that he was unwilling to be a hypnotic subject, but he did inquire several times if he had been hypnotized on that occasion. An evasive answer each time seemed appropriate to the author and was each time readily accepted by Dr. G. That he did not want to know with certainty is a reasonable interpretation.

As a further test of this procedure with Dr. G it was employed separately on three other subjects, all having doctoral degrees in clinical psychology. The first such subject, Mr. P from Princeton University, personally disliked the author but was an ardent experimentalist who did not let his emotions interfere with his work. In fact he tended to dislike far too many people, but would collaborate wholeheartedly with them in experimental work.

The second subject, Miss S of Smith College, was interested in hypnosis but opposed for no reason that she knew to being a subject. She had observed others going into a trance unexpectedly without having been asked to do so or without volunteering while observing the induction of a trance in volunteer subjects. She had remarked to the author that she was too wary to allow this ever to happen to her, and when asked what she would do if it were to happen, she replied, "Once would be enough. Then I'd see to it that it never did again."

Mr. Y of Yale University had done some work with Hull, had tried many times to go into a trance as an experimental subject, and had never succeeded. Hull termed him an "impossible subject." While he was highly intelligent and extremely capable of working out an adequate protocol for controls, subjects, and procedures, he always insisted on a few rehearsals of his experiments with nonsubjects, even in simple nonsense-syllable learning experiments.

All of the subjects, including Dr. G, were in the age range of 27 to 31. Exactly the same procedure was employed with them as had been followed with Dr. G. Separately with each of them the author had discussed the problem of spatial orientation as observed in some schizophrenic patients and then proposed the possibility of doing a hypnotic experiment on the matter by using one of his subjects. Each was interested and expressed interest in being an observer.

Exactly the same procedure as had been employed with Dr. G was followed, with the exception that the term "spatial orientation" was used instead of "geography" as had been done with Dr. G. The reason for this was that in Dr. G's case the author did not know just what Miss K would understand by "spatial orientation," but he did know that she understood the game of "I am here and you are there and New York is there," etc.

Another difference was that Miss F had read all the reports on Dr. G and was placed so that she could observe the subjects' eyes and still be out of their sight. Secretly Miss K had been given hypnotic instructions to have an amnesia for Miss F's presence.

Much rereading of the Dr. G record enabled the author to proceed with greater ease and comfort, and both Miss K and Miss F were better qualified for their tasks, having done it once.

The results obtained with all three subjects were comparable to those secured from Dr. G with minor individual differences. None used the chalk, as available to them as it had been to Dr. G, to mark an x or an o to identify the chairs A and B. Each personally inspected the seat of the chair on which the author pasted the letters A and B. Mr. Y made this inspection three times for each chair, while Dr. G merely accepted the author's statement. Miss S and Mr. P merely watched the author draw the chalk circle and square about their feet and his, but Mr. Y glanced back and forth at the circle and square.

With Dr. G a little over an hour elapsed before the experiment was concluded. With Mr. P, who was the first of the three to be used, 35 minutes were sufficient. Miss S was the second, and 45 minutes were needed. Mr. Y needed only 25 minutes.

All three developed nystagmus, Mr. P and Mr. Y by their movements manifested vertigo, Miss S complained verbally of feeling dizzy.

None noticed Miss K slipping back and forth from one chair to the other.

Mr. P was noted to become angry first at Miss K and then at the author in addition. Miss K's record and that of Miss F typed the next day showed respectively (getting angry me), (more angry) (still angrier me and Dr. E) (yelling at us) (furious) and (getting mad at K) (madder), (really mad both), (yelling and then screaming at both Miss K and Dr. E).

Miss S was noted by both suddenly to glance about the room in a bewildered way and to complain of a severe headache and general physical distress.

Mr. Y was noted to keep moving his arms about as if to balance himself as his nystagmus grew worse. Then suddenly he closed his eyes and stood passively, presenting the appearance of a deep hypnotic trance.

The experiment for Mr. P was concluded by signaling silence to Miss K and stepping over to Mr. P and gently leading him outside the experimental room, closing the door behind us, the author resuming the conversation of spatial orientation at the point that it had just reached at the moment of beginning to open the door of the experimental room to perform the experiment. This had the effect of reorienting him in time to the moment at which we were about to enter the experimental room and had the effect of arousing him from an obvious hypnotic trance and with an amnesia for that trance state. Glancing at my watch I remarked that we had spent so much time in discussion that the experiment would have to be postponed, and the suggestion was offered that arrangements would be made at a later date. He was dismissed in an ordinary waking state.

The same procedure was employed with Miss S and Mr. Y with similar results.

These experiments were all done in one day, and assignments were so arranged that there was no opportunity for the three to meet that day.

The next day Miss K and Miss F typed up their respective reports on each subject. After reading them through and comparing them with each other and with the author's own memories, they were set aside for several days.

However, the next day Miss S came to the author with a peculiar complaint to the effect that she had to get some material out of the "Observation Room" but that she had developed "a peculiar phobia all of a sudden." This was a fear of entering that room (it had been the experimental room), and when she had forced herself to open the door, she had developed an excruciating headache. She wanted to know what was wrong. The answer was given that she was a clinical psychologist and had just described a phenomenon that she might like to explore on her own for a day or so, especially since she had said the headache had disappeared immediately upon closing the door.

Care was taken to have adequate contact with Mr. P and Mr. Y. Nothing new or unusual was noted. Nor was anything of note observed by Miss F or Miss K.

That weekend each was called separately into the office and each was given the accounts of the other two subjects to read. Each read those accounts with interest but with no seeming recollection of their own experience. They all thought the whole procedure was a most interesting, complicated hypnotic experiment and asked if they might be present to observe, should the author ever repeat the experiment. Each was then handed the record on Dr. G. Before each had finished reading the account, they realized that Dr. G referred to Dr. Govindaswamy. They then took the other records and studied them, speculating upon the possible identities of the other subjects without any success (each had been given the initial of the institution from where they came). Only Miss S ventured the speculation that Mr. P's record sounded like something Dr. M (Mr. P's actual initial) would do, but she went no further than that in her speculation.

Each was given his own record to read. Mr. P read his and commented that he would probably feel the same way if that sort of thing were done to him.

Mr. Y's only comment was, "Well, that chap figured out a good escape for himself."

Miss S read and reread the record on her with utter intentness and with an expression of growing understanding on her face.

Finally she looked up at the author and said, "So that's it. No wonder I had that phobic feeling and developed a headache. This is a record on me—". With this she jumped up from her chair, rushed down the corridor, and returned in a few minutes to report, "It's me, all right, I'm dead sure. I have a total amnesia, but I'm afraid of that room. I got a headache the moment I started to open the door. It vanished when I yanked the door shut. But I still don't remember a thing about it, but I am completely convinced that this is a record on me." Then she demanded, "What are you going to do about my phobia and headache?"

Reply was made, "That will be very simple. I can deal with it effectively, but I would like to do it in a way most instructive to you." Very warily she said, "And what is that?" My reply was to pick up the telephone and ask Dr. T (Mr. Y) to come to my office. Upon his arrival I asked him, "Do you mind showing Dr. W (Miss S) something?" He agreed readily, and the three of us walked down the corridor to the "Observation Room." There I suggested that we all enter it, and would Dr. T go first? He did so readily, but immediately developed a deep trance state as he entered the room. Motioning to Dr. W to step back out of sight, I stepped inside, took Dr. T by the arm, gently led him outside, and resumed my orivinal discussion of spatial orientation, again reorienting him to the time of the original approach to that room. He wakened with a total amnesia, and I commented that it was really too late to attempt an experiment that day. We returned to my office with Dr. W following discreetly behind me. I signaled her to enter the office, and as we all took seats I handed him the report on himself. He glanced at me quizzically, at the record casually, and then with a look of bewildered amazement practically shouted, "That's me, that's me." He added, "That happened last Monday, and when we came into the office, I was still thinking it was Monday."

Dr. W remarked, "And this record on Miss S is mine. When I saw that massive recollection by Dr. T, I experienced the same phenomenon." She paused thoughtfully, darted out of the office, and shortly returned to ask, "Why don't I have the phobia and headache now?"

Reply was made that much earlier she had commented that she was "too wary" to allow an unexpected trance induction in her, but that if it er happened, she would see to it that it never happened again. Hence her own unconscious mind had prevented her from entering the room where she had unwittingly gone into a trance lest a spontaneous trance such as Dr. T had just demonstrated might occur. This possibility her unconscious mind appreciated, hence her "protective phobia." This had led her immediately to seek out the author when she could have gone to a number of other physicians. Thus her unconscious had recognized that he was responsible and that the reply he had made carried an implication that there was no danger but an opportunity to learn. Hence she had readily accepted the statement that since she was a clinical psychologist, she could spend a few days thinking about it. By implication this signified that her phobia and headache could and would be corrected.

Then when she witnessed Dr. T's massive recollection, she was unconsciously impelled by her own spontaneous massive recollection to put it to test by dashing to the Observation Room and entering it with no fear of unwittingly developing a spontaneous trance.

The question then arose about Mr. P, about whom Dr. W immediately declared, "When Dr. M read that account of Mr. P, he said that was just the sort of a response he would make in such a situation. Let's call him in, and how shall we handle it?"

The author suggested that when Dr. M arrived, he would hand each of them their own records, asking them to reread them and that the author would sit so that he could see the page numbers on Dr. M's record. They were told that all three of them would be instructed to reread the records previously read by them, but that they (Dr. W and Dr. T) were to turn pages as if they were being read, but that they should primarily watch Dr. M's face. Then when the author cleared his throat, Dr. W was to say quietly, "I am Miss S," whereupon Dr. T would follow suit by saying, "I am Mr. Y." Dr. M read the record of Mr. P assiduously, and when he reached the place at which Miss F described Mr. P as "yelling and screaming at Miss K and Dr. E," the author cleared his throat and Drs. W and T made their remarks. Dr. M started violently, flushed deeply, and in a tone of utter amazement, he declared, "Wow! I certainly was raging mad right then".

He went on, "The whole thing is completely clear now in my memory. All week I've been haunted with a feeling that I knew something that I didn't know. No wonder I said that I would act like that fellow if that sort of thing were done to me."

Immediately Dr. W took Dr. M's hand and led him down the corridor to the Observation Room. She opened the door and asked him to step inside. Dr. M unhesitatingly walked in, looked around, and remarked, "That's right. This is where it happened." Thereupon he began to reconstruct verbally from memory the original experimental management of the room.

Thus did Dr. W demonstrate to her satisfaction that unconscious knowledge shared with the conscious mind would preclude a spontaneous trance such as Dr. T had developed. She asked what would have happened had she gone into the Observation Room before recollection had been made possible for her. She was told, "You would have developed a spontaneous trance, recognized that face unconsciously, and then you would have aroused immediately with most unkind thoughts and attitudes toward me, and it would have taken a long time to get back into your good graces."

Later Dr. W sought hypnotherapy for chronic dysmenorrhea accompanied by a severe headache; Dr. T acted as a subject in various experiments, and the attitude of Dr. M became much more friendly toward the author.

ILLUSTRATIVE CLINICAL PROCEDURES

Almost exactly the same technique of *here, there, this,* and *that* has been used repeatedly by the author for clinical purposes. Patients who enter the office and state frankly that they are resistant or who merely manifest an overt resistance to therapy and yet are obviously seeking it are offered the casual comment that as they sit in *that* chair they are resistant, but would they be resistant were they sitting in *this* other chair, or would they be nonresistant in *this* chair and thus leave their resistances in *that* chair they now occupy; that they can mentally consider changing chairs and sitting *here* in *this* one and leaving resistance in *that* chair *there* or sitting in *that* chair *there* while their resistance remains *here* in *this* chair *here;* that they might try sitting in *that* other chair *there* without resistance and then coming back *here* to *this* chair *here* and taking up their resistances either to keep or to leave them *there* in *this* or *that* chair or *here* or *there* with as much and as varied repetition as is needed.

Thus they are given a confusion in relation to their resistances and in a manner inexplicable to them. There results an unwillingness to keep the confusion, and hence they tend to relinquish their resistances and to cooperate with the therapy they are seeking. Sometimes a trance ensues, sometimes not, depending upon the intensity of their needs.

Clinically the Confusion Technique has been used in various other instances. Two such cases will be cited, similar in character, both seeming to be suitable patients for a Confusion Technique and each having a similar complaint. One was a 28-year-old woman, the other a 45-year-old man. Both complained bitterly of a complete hysterical paralysis of their right hand whenever an attempt was made to use it in writing. Both had positions requiring writing, and both were right-handed. In all other relationships and activities there were no right-handed difficulties, not even in typing. But a pen, a pencil, a stylus, or even a large stick with which to outline on the floor their names, a letter, or even a line, straight or crooked, resulted in a completely rigid paralysis of the right hand. Like all such patients this author has seen and has had reported to him by colleagues, both patients were adamant in their refusal to learn to write left-handedly, even to sign their names. Experience has also taught the author that any insistence upon learning to write left-handedly is likely to cause the loss of the patient, an experience also reported by colleagues.

Confusion Technique

Remembering the old childish game, "Put your *right* hand in front of you over your heart; now really pretend to throw away your *left* hand by putting it behind you. Now, which hand is *left?*" Inexplicably to the child, he finds himself in the difficult position of describing his *right* hand as his *left* hand. Furthermore, one can only *write right* from *left* to *right*, one cannot *write right* from *right* to *left* and *write* is not *right* nor is *right write* while *left*, though *left*, can *write* though not be *right*, yet *left* and *write right* from *right* to *left* if not from *left* to *right*.

With this sort of thinking in mind an extensive history was taken (actually not really extensive, since such patients in the author's experience are definitely restricted in the personal information they can offer) to obtain items of personal significances.

Another appointment to give the author adequate opportunity to work out a technique was given each patient.

In this preliminary preparation careful outlines were made in which to include meaningful personal items as irrelevances in a Confusion Technique centering around the words *right, left,* and *write,* intermingled with minor personal details to make them applicable respectively to each patient.

The woman was the first patient, and as the Confusion Technique was gradually intruded into the initial casual conversation, she became increasingly confused and uncertain, and finally developed a good trance state when told in prolonged detail that "it is *right* and good that your *left* hand is now on the *right* (it had elaborately and quite forcibly been placed by the author on her *right* shoulder) and that your *right* hand which cannot *write* is on the *left* (thigh, thus to establish a specious anatomical relationship). And now your *right* hand that cannot *write* is on the *left,* you have the hand on the *right* (shoulder) to *write.*"

With further elaboration and repetition, and several further trances with carefully worded posthypnotic suggestions, the patient made a permanent transfer of her right-handed writing disability to her left hand, to which was added by posthypnotic suggestion "a peculiar, not unpleasant, but interesting dollar-size spot of coolness on the back of your left hand." Three years later she was still working steadily, still had her left-handed paralysis whenever she attempted so much as to pick up a pencil with it, and the "cool spot" was still present and a source of childishly intense pride. Clinically she was regarded as a therapeutic success, although there was much about her that warranted change but with which she was entirely satisfied—for example, her extreme untidiness in her housekeeping and her extreme tardiness in her many social activities such as arriving two hours late for a birthday dinner prepared for her by a friend who had made repeated telephone calls to speed her arrival and to avoid keeping the other guests waiting. Nevertheless she was well-liked or at least extremely well tolerated, and she continued to be adequate with respect to right-hand functioning.

An even more carefully devised Confusion Technique was worked out for the man, who was of decidedly superior intelligence, a more difficult problem, and much quicker-witted. Since his work involved insurance, the words *"insurance, assurance" insure, assure, reinsure,* and *reassure* were intermingled with *write, right, left,* and fortuitously a relative of his was "named Wright but was not a wheelwright, though he could wheel right around right and thus go left which would be right." In other words the more difficult technique simply involved a more elaborate play on words and more utilization of various items taken from the patient's history together with quicker and more confusing changes of tense. In no way could there be secured a shift of his disability from right hand to the left. However, it was possible in the trance state to get him, perhaps as a measure of escaping his confusion, to accept his disability resignedly, to give up struggling to overcome it, and to accept a promotion previously offered him many times which did not require writing, and which he had consistently refused on the grounds that "I'm going to lick this thing [the writing disability] even if I never do anything else." He was also rated as a therapeutic success even though several years later he again sought out the author for another attempt at therapy for his writing disability, but he was easily put off with a promise to try again when it was most convenient for him. To date he has found no convenient time.

VARIOUS REACTIONS TO CONFUSION TECHNIQUES

The first Confusion Technique discussed in this article, which was also first worked out by the author to involve a time disorientation, offered a relatively easy means for the development of confusion and to use the confusion to elicit age regression. However, careful observation of such use soon disclosed other possible variations and applications. Accordingly a whole series of procedures was worked out, first in outline form and then by filling in details permitting the evocation of a state of hypnosis of specific phenomena and of isolated phenomena.

Another item of particular interest in regard to the Confusion Technique is the reaction of both experimental and clinical subjects. The latter, because of their therapeutic motivation, often lose their resistances and simpler techniques can then be employed. Occasionally, while resistances persist, they do not seem to mind repetitions of the same or varied forms of the Confusion Technique.

With experimental subjects the reactions vary greatly and sometimes in an intriguing way. For example, Miss K had had many variations of the Confusion Technique employed on her, and she always responded readily to the same or to variations of it. Additionally in the trance state she was much more adept than the author in using a Confusion Technique on other subjects, and it mattered not whether it had been used on her or merely, as above, described for the first time to her in the trance state.

In Miss F's case she too responded repeatedly to the same or other Confusion

Techniques. However, she could not use a Confusion Trance when she was either in or out of hypnosis. In fact most subjects while in a trance and who have been hypnotized by a Confusion Technique seem unable to use it, although in the trance state they will use successfully the ordinary traditional techniques even when they fail to be able to induce a trance in the waking state. Indeed long experience has disclosed that the easiest and quickest way to learn to induce a trance is to be hypnotized first, thus to learn the "feel" of it.

It is also of interest that subjects who respond readily and repeatedly to Confusion Techniques are likely to develop a trance while listening to a Confusion Technique being used on someone else. Miss K and Miss F, however, were remarkably competent secretaries and could listen to the Confusion Technique previously used on them and later record that same technique being used word for word upon someone else, making a complete record with no hypnotic response on their part. Apparently the presence of their sharpened pencils and the task constituted an adequate counterset against any hypnotic response. Also, upon request, both could record in shorthand in the trance state the Confusion Technique used on someone else. It is of interest to note that the measure of using a Confusion Technique to induce a trance in them, and then having them in the trance state record the use of the same technique on others with slight subtle alterations pertaining to them as persons did not affect their trance state or ability to record.

Miss H and Mr. T were excellent subjects for either traditional or the Confusion Techniques. However, after a few experiences with the Confusion Technique they reacted by bypassing it and developing a trance at once, no matter how subtly the author made his approach. As they would explain in the trance state, "As soon as I experienced the slightest feeling of confusion, I just dropped into a deep trance." They simply did not like to be confused. Neither of these subjects, fully capable with more common techniques, could seem to learn to use a Confusion Technique or even to outline a possible form. There were others who responded similarly.

Mr. H (no relative of Miss H) responded readily to various Confusion Techniques, spontaneously discovered that he could use them in the trance state and that he could conduct experiments on other subjects while he was still in the original trance I had induced in him by a Confusion Technique, and later investigate his waking capacity to devise and use effectually Confusion Techniques. In this connection his first spontaneous discovery of his capacity to use a Confusion Technique will be related here as an interesting and informative example.

Professor M at Yale University was highly critical of Clark L. Hull's work there and most disbelieving of hypnosis as an actual phenomenon. He sought out the author for further enlightenment about hypnosis and to see if the author could duplicate some of the hypnotic studies being made at Yale University. He was a psychologist himself, had never done any hypnotic work, and was not yet convinced of the validity of hypnosis by the studies to date at Yale. He was frank and free in his statements of his understandings and asked if the author would demonstrate hypnosis to him and perhaps duplicate some of the things that had been done by Hull and his students.

After some thought the author agreed and summoned by telephone two excellent somnambulistic subjects. Upon their arrival they were introduced to Professor M, who explained simply and fully his attitudes and wishes. Both subjects expressed a willingness to do anything he wished if the author approved.

This approval was given by suggesting to Miss R, who had a Ph.D. in psychology, that she hypnotize Mr. H and demonstrate hypnotic phenomena fully, in accordance with Professor M's request. The author then excused himself, after explaining to both Miss R and Mr. H that they would remain in rapport with the author despite his enforced absence at that time to work on an ergographic study of fatigue abolishment by hypnosis which was under way with another colleague. It was also added that the author would be absent for about an hour, possibly more, hence Miss R could take her time in whatever Professor M wished.

When the author returned about an hour later, he was confronted by a bewildering sight. Professor M was sitting at the desk ineffectually trying to make notes with a bemused and puzzled expression on his face. Miss R, who had been told to hypnotize Mr. H, was most obviously in a deep somnambulistic trance. Mr. H was also in a deep somnambulistic trance. Only Mr. H retained rapport with the author, manifesting it by looking up at the author as the author entered the room. Miss R apparently was unaware of the author, despite the fact that her eyes were wide open, and the author had immediately asked, "What has been taking place, Miss R?"

Her failure apparently to hear the author and the total situation itself suggested that a record be made of the situation. Miss K was immediately summoned, and upon her arrival with notebook and pencils the author stated, "Maintain the status quo. Now Mr. H, are you in a trance? And is Miss R in a trance?" To both questions H answered "Yes." "Are you both in rapport with me?" "No." "Who is, and why?" "Just me. I told Miss R to be in rapport only with me."

The author immediately said, "Stay as you are, maintain the status quo, do nothing more. I am taking Professor M out of the room for a while, and the two of you remain as you are, inactive. Is there any comment you wish to make about Professor M?"

Mr. H said simply, "He recognizes hypnosis as a genuine thing now," but made no response to the presence of Miss K or the professor.

Professor M, Miss K, and the author went into the next room. Systematically Professor M was asked what had happened.

In summary he explained that Miss R had induced a "deep trance" in Mr. H by hand levitation and had then used him to demonstrate anaesthesia, catalepsy, amnesia, positive and negative ideomotor and ideosensory phenomena, hypermnesia, posthypnotic suggestions, trance awakening, and reinduction.

In relation to each of these demonstrations she had asked Professor M to make his own tests of each phenomenon. This had convinced him that he was observing a most interesting and valid phenomenon.

When Miss R reinduced hypnosis in Mr. H, Professor M stated that Miss R had asked Mr. H if there were anything else that might be done to instruct Professor M. Mr. H had answered with a simple "Yes." She then asked if he would do it. Again he replied with a simple "Yes," but made no move of any sort. She had then asked, "Well, what is it?" To this he replied, "Can't tell, just do!"

The professor then said;

> "That was when I really got my eyes opened. Mr. H slowly got up out of the chair where he was sitting, his eyes open and unblinking, pupils dilated and apparently lacking in peripheral vision. He walked over to Miss R, took her hand very gently, lifted it up slowly, and softly told her to go deeply asleep in a deep trance. Then, when she started to say something, he began to talk in a very confusing way about you and me and Miss R and him and hypnosis and demonstration and ergographs and phenomena, and I got so confused that I didn't know what was happening until I suddenly realized that Miss R was in a trance and that he was too. Neither one took any notice of me, and he asked Miss R to do a lot of things comparable to what she had him do, but he added some. For example he told her to awaken with an amnesia for her name and whereabouts. At first I thought she was awake and I asked her her name, but she didn't seem to hear me, and Mr. H didn't seem to hear me either. I shook them both by the shoulders, but they made no response. Then she seemed to be frightened, so he told her to sleep deeply and feel comfortable and at ease. I was trying to think this through when you came in. I guess from the questions you asked, you grasped the situation.

We returned to the room where Miss R and Mr. H were waiting passively.

Mr. H was told to awaken. He did so at once, and a few simple questions disclosed the fact that he was reoriented in time to the author's announcement of his impending departure for the ergograph experiment.

The author then spoke to Miss R, but she failed to make any response. Mr. H looked astonished and bewildered, but before he could say anything, the author quickly intervened and asked Mr. H to tell Miss R to listen to the author. This he did, and the author said, "Is there anything you would like to say to me *now that I have come back?*" (This was a disguised instruction for her to arouse from the trance state.)

Her reply was one of instant arousal with a temporal orientation to the time at which she had reinduced the trance state in Mr. H. She replied simply that she had demonstrated all the usual phenomena to Professor M but that the author might wish to take over, explaining that Mr. H was still in a trance. Immediately

Mr. H declared, "No, you are the one in a trance. I just had to transfer rapport to Dr. Erickson so he could talk to you, and he hasn't yet told you to rouse up from the trance."

In bewilderment she answered, "No, you are in a trance, but I don't understand your behavior."

For another hour we let the two of them try o solve the situation while Miss K took notes.

Both had amnesia for their own trances, both believed the other to be in a trance, both could recognize that the other was behaving as in a waking state, and neither could elicit trance behavior from the other, nor could they even agree on the time. (I had confiscated Miss K's and Professor M's watch and removed mine, and neither of them had a watch.)

Miss R was certain that I had just returned after an hour's absence, and Mr. H was equally certain that the author was about to depart and Miss R about to begin her task. Both could not understand Miss K's presence and her notetaking, nor could they understand the refusal of Professor M and the author to clarify matters.

Finally they were dismissed, still arguing, and Miss K typed up her complete records. Later Professor M made another visit, and they and Miss K were summoned. To Miss R and Mr. H the issue was still unsettled, and neither seemed able to follow with recognition their respective trance experiences when reading Miss K's typewritten account.

However, interviewed separately in a deep trance state, both recalled all trance events, except that Mr. H had to ask Miss R to reestablish rapport with the author at the time he had withdrawn it before she could continue to relate her experiences at the author's request.

Posthypnotic suggestion to them both that they recover full waking memories of their total experiences were successful, and this established a most extensive topic of discussion with them and between them and others.

As for Professor M, he later did extensive experimental work with both Dr. Hull and the author.

Several years after this incident with Miss R and Professor M, for no known reason, Mr. H lost completely for a number of years his interest in, but not his respect for, hypnosis.

Then one day he was confronted with the statement by the anaesthesiologist and the surgeons that an elderly friend of his, absolutely needing a serious operation, would not survive the combination of surgical shock and chemoanaesthesia. Since Mr. H then had his medical license, he persuaded the reluctant surgeons to operate upon the patient while he used a Confusion Technique to induce a trance state and then a spatial and situational disorientation to effect a hypnoanaesthesis, and the patient underwent extensive abdominal surgery while hypnotically hallucinating a visit at home with Dr. H. His reason for using the Confusion Technique was that the patient and her relatives had been informed that surgery would result in nonsurvival. The patient actually made an excellent

Confusion Technique

recovery, and Mr. H, or rather Dr. H, now uses hypnosis extensively. But he does not want to go into a trance nor can he give the author any explanation of why this is so, nor can he explain his long period of personal disinterest in it.

There is also another type of subject who first reacts well to the Confusion Technique and then turns violently against it. This can be best illustrated by the following eloquent statement:

> I have always felt somewhat annoyed and distressed by the Confusion Technique, and I have resented its use, but initially I was willing to listen and cooperate as best I could. Part of my resentment was undoubtedly due to my own mental pattern of thought; I always like to grasp each idea and organize my thoughts before proceeding. However, I went along with the confusion suggestions and I know they worked on me, although not as well as other techniques did.
>
> At the present time they will not work on me. No matter how deep a trance I am in and how cooperative I am, I·simply stop listening if that type of suggestion is begun. Nor will I make any pretense of listening. If the operator insists on keeping on talking, I shut off my hearing (self-established hypnotic deafness) and I may wake up—feeling strongly annoyed.
>
> I can pinpoint the changeover from unwilling and somewhat resentful compliance to flat refusal to listen to any confusion suggestions. One day I was trying to decide whether or not I ought to disclose to the operator some information—I am not certain what it was, but I believe it was some information about the work at hand concerning which I was not sure whether or not I ought to disclose it. The operator was seeking that information and suddenly tried a tactic to confuse my thinking—namely, a topic to distract me was mentioned as I was preoccupied with something else, and the operator felt that the information was urgently needed. I cannot remember the confusing way in which the operator urgently demanded the information and attempted to distract me. I felt a surge of anger—I did not reply. Upon thinking it over now, I realize that I thought the tactic was unfair—trying to rush and confuse me into replying instead of allowing me to make a decision based on my considered judgment. I realized, too, either right then or possibly the next time the Confusion Technique was attempted on me, that it was basically the same thing, and it made me angry, too. I'm all through with it. It won't work again.

Such indeed is the case. Yet for other techniques this subject is remarkably responsive. And as the careful observer will note, both experimental and clinical subjects often have definite preferences which should be respected. Thus one subject may object strenuously to a relaxation technique but like the hand-levitation technique and at another time be responsive only to yet another technique.

VALUES OF CONFUSION TECHNIQUES

The values of the Confusion Technique are twofold. In experimental work it serves excellently to teach experimenters a facility in the use of words, a mental agility in shifting their habitual patterns of thought, and allows them to make adequate allowances for the problems involved in keeping the subjects attentive and responsive. Also it allows experimenters to learn to recognize and to understand the minimal cues of behavioral changes within the subject.

Clinically it is of much value with patients desperately seeking therapy but restricted and dominated by their clinical problem and uncontrollable resistances which prevent the initiation of therapy. Once these resistances are circumvented, there is then the possibility of securing the patients' cooperation in correcting both their clinical problems and dissipating the resistances. A final value is that long and frequent use of the Confusion Technique has many times effected exceedingly rapid hypnotic inductions under unfavorable conditions such as acute pain of terminal malignant disease and in persons interested but hostile, aggressive, and resistant.

Perhaps it would be well to give an example of a Confusion Technique used in handling resistant, disbelieving cancer patients, one suffering continuous pain and one suffering from irregularly periodic bouts of excruciating pain lasting from 10 to 30 minutes and often longer. In this author's experience the only real difference lies in the patients themselves, since essentially the same technique can be used on either type of patient with slight modifications to make it more personally applicable.

One patient suffering continuous pain with numerous metastases throughout her body was highly resentful over her impending death, unwilling to accept narcotics because she received no relief unless made stuporous, and she was most eager to spend all the time possible with her family. Her entire family had adverse religious ideas about hypnosis, even though it had been recommended by her family physician, a member of her faith. Fortunately the family was convinced by the printed words in a medical book, an article in an encyclopedia, and a personal letter to the author from a missionary of her faith telling of the successful use of hypnosis on her converts in treating them medically.

The other patient was a man in his 50's, who suffered at irregular but frequent and unexpected intervals from bouts of excruciating pain that were becoming progressively longer, ranging from 10 minutes to one hour, but with short bouts becoming fewer and the long bouts becoming increasingly more frequent.

His attitude was one of scornful disbelief and mockery as well as bitter resentment at his fate and a hostile attitude toward everyone, especially the medical profession for being so "stupid about cancer."

At all events the same general Confusion Technique was used, except for the special references of personal implications.

The approach was:

> You *know and I know* and the doctors you *know know* that there is *one answer* that you *know* that you don't want to *know* and that I *know* but don't want to *know,* that your family *knows* but doesn't want to *know, no* matter how much you want to say *no,* you *know* that the *no* is really a *yes,* and you wish it could be a good *yes* and so do you *know* that what you and your family *know* is *yes,* yet you wish that *yes* could be *no* and you *know* that all the doctors *know* that what they *know* is *yes,* yet they still wish it were *no.* And just as you wish there were *no pain,* you *know* that there is *but what* you *don't know* is *no pain* is something *you can know.* And no matter what you *knew no pain* would be better than what you *know* and of course *what you want to know* is *no pain* and that is *what* you are *going to know, no pain.* [All of this is said slowly but with utter intensity and with seemingly total disregard of any interruption of cries of pain or admonitions of "Shut up".] Esther [John, Dick, Harry, or Evangeline, some family member or friend] *knows* pain and *knows no pain* and so do you wish to *know no pain* but *comfort* and you *do know comfort* and *no pain* and as *comfort increases* you *know* that *you cannot* say *no to ease and comfort* but *you can* say *no pain* and *know no pain* but *you can* say *no pain* and *know no pain* but *know comfort and ease* and it is *so good* to *know comfort and ease and relaxation* and to *know it now and later* and *still longer and longer as more and more relaxation* occurs and to *know it now and later* and *still longer and longer as more and more relaxation and wonderment and surprise come to your mind as you begin to know a freedom and a comfort you have so greatly desired and as you feel it grow and grow you know, really know,* that *today, to-night, tomorrow, all next week and next month,* and at Esther's [John's] 16th birthday, and what a time that was, and those *wonderful feelings* that you had then seem almost as clear *as if they were today* and the *memory of every good thing* is a glorious thing. . . .

One can improvise indefinitely, but the slow, impressive, utterly intense, and quietly, softly emphatic way in which these plays on words and the unobtrusive introduction of new ideas, old happy memories, feelings of comfort, ease, and relaxation are presented usually results in an arrest of the patients' attention, rigid fixation of the eyes, the development of physical immobility, even catalepsy and of an intense desire to understand what the author so gravely and so earnestly is saying to them that their attention is sooner or later captured completely. Then with equal care the operator demonstrates a complete loss of fear, concern, or worry about negative words by introducing them as if to explain but actually to make further helpful suggestions.

> And now *you have forgotten* something, just as *we all forget* many things, *good* and *bad,* especially the *bad* because the *good* are *good to remember* and *you can remember comfort and ease and relaxation and restful sleep* and *now you know that you need no pain* and *it is good to know no pain* and *good to remember, always to remember,* that in *many places, here, there, everywhere* you have been at *ease* and *comfortable* and *now* that you *know* this, you *know* that *no pain is needed* but *that you do need to know all there is to know about ease and comfort and relaxation and numbness and dissociation and the redirection of thought and mental energies and to know and know fully all that will give you freedom to know your family and all that they are doing and to enjoy unimpeded the pleasures of being with them with all the comfort and pleasure that is possible for as long as possible* and *this is what you are going to do.*

Usually the patients' attention can be captured in about five minutes, but one may have to continue for an hour or even longer. Also, and very important, one uses words that the patients understand. Both of the above patients were college graduates.

When such cases are referred to me, I make a practice of getting preliminary information of personality type, history, interests, education, and attitudes, and then in longhand I write out a general outline of the order and frequency with which these special items of fact are worked into the endless flow of words delivered with such earnestness of manner.

Once the patients begin to develop a light trance, I speed the process more rapidly by jumping steps, yet retaining my right to mention pain so that patients know that I do not fear to name it and that I am utterly confident that they will lose it because of my ease and freedom in naming it, usually in a context negating pain in favor of absence or diminution or transformation of pain.

Then one should bear in mind that these patients are highly motivated, that their disinterest, antagonism, belligerence, and disbelief are actually allies in bringing about the eventual results, nor does this author ever hesitate to utilize what is offered. The angry, belligerent man can strike a blow that hurts his head and not notice it, the disbeliever closes his mind to exclude a boring dissertation, but that excludes the pain too, and from this there develops unwittingly in the patients a different state of inner orientation, highly conducive to hypnosis and receptive to any suggestion that meets their needs; sensibly one always inserts the suggestion that if ever the pain should come back enough to need medication, the relief from one or two tablets of aspirin will be sufficient. "And if any real emergency ever develops, a hypo will work far greater success than ever." Sometimes sterile water will suffice.

BRIEF CONFUSION TECHNIQUES

All of the foregoing indicates that the Confusion Technique is a prolonged, highly complicated and complex procedure. Working one out and explaining the rationale of the procedure is indeed a long hard task, but once one has done that more than once, and has learned to recognize the fundamental processes involved, there can then be a very easy, comfortable, and rapid trance induction under some most unfavorable conditions. To illustrate this, both a spontaneous experimental instance and a clinical case will be reported. The first of these occurred at a lecture before a medical society. One of the physicians present was most interested in learning hypnosis, listened attentively during the lecture, but in the social hour preceding the lecture he had repeatedly manifested hostile, aggressive behavior toward most of his colleagues. When introduced to the author, he shook hands with a bone-crushing grip, almost jerked the author off his balance (the man was at least six inches taller than the author and about 65 pounds heavier) and aggressively declared without any preamble that he would like to "see any damn fool try to hypnotize me."

When volunteers for a demonstration were requested, he came striding up and in a booming voice announced, "Well, I'm going to show everybody that you can't hypnotize me." As the man stepped up on the platform, the author slowly arose from his chair as if to greet him with a handshake. As the volunteer stretched forth his hand prepared to give the author another bone-crushing handshake, the author bent over and tied his own shoestrings slowly, elaborately, and left the man standing helplessly with his arm outstretched. Bewildered, confused, completely taken aback at the author's nonpertinent behavior, at a total loss for something to do, the man was completely vulnerable to the first comprehensible communication *fitting to the situation* that was offered to him. As the second shoestring was being tied, the author said, "Just take a deep breath, sit down in that chair, close your eyes, and go deeply into a trance."

Uncertainly, hesitantly, the man sat down, sighed deeply, closed his eyes, and within seconds he had developed a somnambulistic trance. Various phenomena were demonstrated, and he was then awakened after the posthypnotic suggestion that he would ask me courteously "Well, when do we begin the hypnosis?" and sometime later when I shifted my chair he would have a complete recollection of everything. He aroused and asked the question, to which I replied evasively. After a brief, casual conversation I reached for a glass of water but had to shift my chair. With a startled reaction my subject said, "Well I'll be damned! But how? Now do it again so I can know how you are doing it."

He was offered a choice of several traditional techniques. He chose the hand-levitation method as seeming the more interesting, and this technique was employed slowly both for his benefit and that of the audience, with another somnambulistic trance resulting.

As an experimental subject in that situation he presented in an excellent manner the problem of adequately meeting his behavioral patterns and eliciting responsive behavior of interest primarily to the audience, although he too was interested secondarily, but his primary interest as a person was one diametrically opposed. He wished to elicit responses of futility from the author, but even this was a tacit acknowledgment of hypnosis as a valid phenomenon.

The explanation of what happened is rather simple. The man came up to the podium with an intense determination to do something. The author's rising as if to greet him with a handshake and then bending over to tie his shoestrings left the man standing with an outstretched hand, unable to do anything, interrupted so suddenly in the initiation of what he was going to do, too astonished by the author's completely nonpertinent behavior, utterly at loss for something to do, and hence completely susceptible to any clearly comprehensible suggestion of what to do fitting to the total situation, that he responded relievedly to the simple, quiet instruction the author offered. And of course the man's underlying attitude toward hypnosis became manifest in his prompt request made upon his discovery of what had happened.

Similarly many clinical patients show comparable behavior of hostility, aggression, and resistance, yet they are earnestly seeking therapy. The Confusion Technique alters the situation from a contest between two people and transforms it into a therapeutic situation in which there is joint cooperation and participation in the mutual task centering properly about the patient's welfare and not about a contest between individuals, an item clinically to be avoided in favor of the therapeutic goal.

To illustrate with a similarly handled clinical instance, a patient entered the office for her first appointment with a hesitant, uncertain manner but with what seemed to be too forceful and too defiant a stride. She sat down in the chair in a stiff, upright fashion with her arms rigidly holding the palms of her hands braced against her knees, and in a weak voice hesitantly explained, "I was sent to you by Dr. X, who worked hours on me. Before him was Dr. Y, who also worked hours on me. And before him was Dr. Z, and he worked 30 hours on me. All of them told me that I was too resistant to be hypnotized, but they all said you could do it. But I went to the other two because they were near my home town. I didn't want to come all the way to Phoenix to be hypnotized, but even my family doctor has told me it would help overcome my resistances to therapy." Her diffident, uncertain, hesitant bearing and voice, her definite stride, her stiff upright position, her overemphasis upon the hours futilely spent already in trying to induce a trance, her regretful statement that she didn't want to come to Phoenix to be hypnotized, and her insistence on going to two other men when the first as well as both the others had recommended the author suggested: (1) that she would resist hypnosis; (2) that she was bewildered by her ambivalences; (3) that she could not be approached by any ordinary expectable technique of induction; (4) that she definitely wanted therapy; and (5) that she would try to embroil the author in a contest instead of accepting therapy.

Confusion Technique

Accordingly she was told rather bruskly, "Well, let's get this clear. Three doctors, all good men, just as good as I am, have worked hard and long on you. They found you to be too resistant, *as I will too. So let's have that understood at once.*" With markedly differing inflections and tempo the following was said to her as a two part statement, "I CAN'T HYPNOTIZE YOU *justyourarm.*"

In a bewildered fashion she said, "Can't hypnotize me, just my arm—I don't understand what you mean."

Again she was told with heavy emphasis and with the words spoken slowly, "THAT'S EXACTLY WHAT I MEAN. I CAN'T HYPNOTIZE YOU," then with a soft, gentle voice I added rapidly as if it were one word, *"justyourarm,see."*

As I said the word "See," I gently "lifted" her left arm upward, the touch of my fingers serving only to direct the upward movement, *not actually to lift it.* Gently I withdrew my fingers, leaving her hand cataleptically in midair. As she watched her arm in its upward course, I said softly and sighingly, "Just close your eyes, take a deep breath, so deeply asleep, and as you do so, your left hand will slowly come to rest on your thigh and remain there continuously as you sleep deeply and comfortably until I tell you to awaken."

Within five minutes after her entrance into the office she was in a deep, and as it proved to be, somnambulistic trance. What happened? The woman was desperately seeking therapy, had come a long distance to seek it in response to repeated advice, she came with a rigid counterset for any conventional, traditional, ritualistic, or other techniques that she could watch, hear, and understand. Believingly, agreeingly, she heard me say clearly and understandably, "I can't hypnotize you," to which was appended softly, quickly and gently while she was still in a believing or accepting frame of mind, the inexplicable three words, *"just your arm."*

Thus the very thing that she had come *to prove* was already affirmed; it was a closed issue. We were in total agreement, her purpose to prove that she could not be hypnotized was already accomplished, her counterset for hypnosis rendered unnecessary, useless. But those three peculiar words, *"just your arm,"* confronted her with a most bewildering question of what was meant. Thereby she was literally forced to ask for some explanation. The reaffirmation was given with deliberate emphasis, and while her mind was still receptive, four more words were quickly added, the fourth a command, "See!" From earliest childhood we learn to interpret certain tactile stimuli as meaning, "Move," *and she made an automatic response to such a tactile stimulation.* This she could not understand, she had no counterset for it, and she could "see" her arm behaving in a way she could not understand. Nor was she given any opportunity. The elicitation of one hypnotic response leads so easily to another, catalepsy, pupillary dilation, and then an all-comprehensive set of suggestions was given to insure a deep trance and its maintenance.

Hypnotherapy and waking psychotherapy were used on this patient, and the progress was phenomenally rapid for the simple reason that she was not allowed to interpose her resistances between herself and therapy, but put into a situation of objectively examining them. This was begun almost immediately with the statement, "Well, now we can proceed with therapy rather than wasting time on a question for which neither you nor I really knew the answer, but to which you have so easily found the correct answer, namely that *you can develop and keep a deep trance state* and that you don't need resistances."

SUMMARY

With the foregoing discussion and examples in mind it might be well to summarize the Confusion Technique as a play on words or communications of some sort that introduces progressively an element of confusion into the question of what is meant, thereby leading to an inhibition of responses called for but not allowed to be manifested and hence to an accumulating need to respond. It is reminiscent of the childhood word games such as "If it isn't *not raining,* then it *is raining,*" or "I am *here* and you are *not here* and New York is *not here,* so you must be in New York because you are *there, not here,* and New York is there, not *here.*"

Starting with these elementary ideas, the author has added to the play on words the modification of seemingly contradictory, irrelevant, or unrelated concepts, non sequiturs, and ideas, variously communicated, and each of which *out of context* is a simple, reasonable assertion, meaningful and complete in itself. *In context* such communications are given in a meaningfully emphatic manner along with valid, meaningful ideas, and thus the whole becomes a medley of seemingly valid and somehow related ideas that leads the subjects to try to combine them into a single totality of significance conducive to a response—literally compelling a response. But the rapidity of the communications inhibits any true understanding, thereby precluding responses and resulting in a state of confusion and frustration. This compels a need for some clear and understandable idea. As this state develops, one offers a clearly definite, easily comprehensible idea which is seized upon immediately and serves to arouse certain associations in the subjects' minds. The medley is then continued, and another comprehensible idea is offered, enhancing the associations of the previous clear understanding. And in the process one throws in irrelevancies and non sequiturs as if of pertinent value, thereby enhancing the confusion. This sort of thing constitutes in certain situations a form of humor such as in the case of the childish riddle of "Two ducks in front of a duck, two ducks behind a duck, and one duck in the middle. How many ducks are there?" Even those of my playmates on whom I tried this and who knew the answer to be three ducks would find themselves hopelessly bewildered when I would add with earnest helpfulness, "Of course you must remember they were beside the *left-hand door.*" And for those who did not know the answer and who were struggling with the *two* and *two* and *one,* the *left-hand door* often constituted an insuperable barrier to a responsive reply as a result of a natural tendency to fit that irrelevancy into the problem.

However, a Confusion Technique is sometimes most difficult for some users of hypnosis, and they find much difficulty in attempting it for either experimental or clinical work. Nevertheless it does have significant values for those who cannot use it in a hypnotic setting, since repeated efforts to devise and deliver a Confusion Technique for the sake of practice only will soon teach the user of more conventionalized, ritualistic, traditional, verbalized techniques a greater fluency in speech, a freedom from rote suggestions, a better understanding of the meaning of suggestions, and a greater ease in shifting one's own patterns of behavior in response to observed changes in the patients, and in shifting from one set of ideas to another. In repeated experience teaching hypnosis to medical and psychological students and residents in psychiatry, the assignment of the task of devising and analyzing a Confusion Technique aided them greatly in learning traditional verbalization techniques, even those who never could seem to learn to use a Confusion Technique spontaneously or intentionally in a hypnotic situation.

Thus the Confusion Technique is a presentation of ideas and understandings conducive of mental activity and response but so intermingled with seemingly related, valid but actually nonpertinent communications that responses are inhibited, frustration and uncertainty of mind engendered. The culmination occurs in a final suggestion permitting a ready and easy response satisfying to the subjects and validated by each subject's own, though perhaps unrecognized, on a conscious level, experiential learnings.

11. The Dynamics of Visualization, Levitation and Confusion in Trance Induction

Milton H. Erickson

Hypnotic techniques are no more than methods of communicating suggestions and ideas. In themselves they are of no particular significance. It is only the responses and the behavior that they stimulate the subject to make that have any value. Hence in describing a technique a primary consideration should not be a slavish presentation of verbalizations, but an effort to indicate the purposes to be served. Unfortunately the general tendency is to attach labels to a technique and then to use it in accord with the sometimes meaningless label.

VISUALIZATION APPROACHES

For example, an excellent visualization approach has been labeled The House–Tree–Man Technique. This designation much more properly should be An Example of Visual Imagery Technique, or A Technique Based upon Visual Imagery, or Visual Imagery as a Technique. As a technique The House–Tree–Man differs in no significant way from The Garden–Woman–Sundial or The Schoolhouse–Teacher–Pupil–Desk–Blackboard–Chalk Technique. The essential consideration is to evoke visual images related to experiential learnings and thus to initiate within the subjects, apart from externalities, a progressive series of responsive reactions that can develop into a trance. It is of utterly no importance that a house, a tree, or a man be mentioned to use the "House–Tree–Man" technique. The only important purpose in this technique is the initiation and utilization of the processes of visualization, and the objects to be employed as visual images should be selected in relationship to the subjects, not to some printed page. The basic approach is to orient all hypnotic techniques about the subjects, who are the responsive components of the situation.

Unpublished fragment, circa 1940s.

HAND LEVITATION APPROACHES

To cite another example, in the development and the teaching of the "hand levitation technique" this writer has endeavored to make clear and to emphasize that the technique is one in which the subjects overtly participate at a motor level—that it is a participatory technique involving motor activity. The term "hand levitation" is employed for several reasons.

The hand is employed for the reason that in the passively expectant state of the subjects, the idea of motor activity is easily related to the subjects' hand without disturbing their general physical inactivity. The subjects have a lifetime of experience of hand movement while the body is at rest.

It matters not which hand is levitated, yet uncritical, overenthusiastic innovators have attempted to develop as refinements separate techniques for levitation of the right, the left, of both simultaneously and alternately, and of the right index finger, the left index finger, etc., overlooking entirely that it is the motor activity and not the body part that is important. The body part is important only when it serves some other and specific purpose directly related to its use, as in finger signaling, for example, or in answering by gesture.

The term "levitation" is employed to signify primarily the subjective character of the motor activity and not the direction of the movement. It is the subjective sensation of lightness, of free, involuntary, or consciously effortless motor activity that is the primary consideration, not the direction of the movement. Hence the "levitation" may be upward or downward, horizontal or rotory. It is not even essential that there be actual movement since *it is the subjective sensation of involuntary or consciously effortless movement that is desired and not movement through linear space.* Hence the term "hand levitation" is properly used to present in an easily comprehensible form the suggestion of movement of a body part, any body part, of a special subjective quality.

CONFUSION APPROACHES

In a somewhat similar fashion many other techniques need to be discussed for their essential significance. For example, the "confusion technique" much mentioned, never really described in the literature, actually used more frequently than it is recognized, and regarded as rather involved and bewildering, is actually a relatively simple procedure. It is usually a verbal technique, but nonverbal elements can easily be added to it and even made the major part of the technique.

Defined simply, a "confusion technique" is one based upon the presentation to the subjects of a series of seemingly only loosely related ideas actually based upon a significant thread of continuity not readily recognized, leading to an increasing divergence of associations, interspersed with an emphasis on the obvious, *all of which preclude subjects from developing any one train of associations, yet stirs them increasingly to a need to do something until they are ready to accept the first clearcut definitive suggestion offered.* As stated, the technique may be purely verbal or an admixture of verbal and nonverbal elements; both may be used as rapid or slow inductions, depending upon the situation and the purposes to be served. [Editor's note: The editor's reading of this complex sentence is as follows: (1) "a series of seemingly only loosely related ideas actually based upon a significant thread of continuity not readily recognized" is a series of *indirect suggestions* that has as its common denominator an important therapeutic response that is to be evoked hypnotically; (2) "leading to an increasing divergence of associations" is the *unconscious search and processes* evoked by the indirect suggestions as the subjects struggle to find their meaning, their common denominator; (3) "interspersed with an emphasis on the obvious" is essentially a *yes set* evoked by a stream of obvious truths from the therapist that keeps the conscious minds of the subjects open in a simple acceptance set during trance; (4) "all of which precludes subjects from developing any one train of associations" means we don't want subjects to develop a train of conscious associations with their usual, habitual frames of reference and biases because these contain learned limitations that have prevented them from solving their problem by utilizing their own unconscious potentials; (5) "yet stirs them increasingly to a need to do something" means that since the subjects' habitual frames of reference cannot find closure, they experience a state of unstable equilibrium or *expectancy;* (6) "until they are ready to accept the first clearcut definitive suggestion offered," which will resolve the expectancy and effect closure by carrying a *direct therapeutic suggestion*. We see in this process how Erickson first sets up and activates patients' unconscious potentials with a series of indirect suggestions (steps 1 and 2) while keeping the patients' conscious mind open and accepting (steps 3 and 4). At the same time a certain tension and need to make some response is evoked in step 5, which is resolved by a direct therapeutic suggestion in step 6. This marvelous integration of indirect (step 1) and direct (step 6) suggestions follows the five-stage paradigm of the microdynamics of trance and suggestion presented later, in Section 3 of this volume.]

For example, in a lecture before the professional staff of a V.A. hospital, a student nurse was pressured by her superior to volunteer as a subject. Fortunately she was interested in being a subject, but she disliked being told to act as one. Advantage was taken of this emotional setting to use a confusion technique primarily nonverbal in character to secure in the subject, who had neither witnessed nor experienced hypnosis previously, a deep trance in a minimum of time.

As she approached the front of the lecture room from a side aisle, a chair was moved somewhat ostentatiously into place for her. When she was within six feet of the chair, she was asked, "Will you sit in *this* chair *here?*" As the word "this" was spoken, the writer's left hand was carefully placed on the back of that chair, as if to point it out. As the word "here" was spoken, the writer gestured with his right hand, as if indicating a chair to the side of the actual chair. There was a momentary pause in her behavior, but as she continued her approach, the chair was pushed slightly toward her, causing a slight noise as it scraped on the floor. This was readily audible. As she came still closer to the chair, it was pulled slightly to one side away from her, and immediately as she seemed to note this, it was pushed back an inch or so, and then another inch or so forward and to the side toward her. All of this she noted because the writer's left hand on the back of the chair constituted a focusing point.

By this time she had reached the chair, had turned slightly, and had begun to lower her body into it. As soon as her knees were bent, the chair was rotated about one inch, and as she paused again momentarily to look at the chair, the writer took hold of her right elbow and moved it away from her body slightly and then slightly forward. As she turned to look in response to this, her elbow was released and her right hand and wrist were gently taken and moved slightly upward and then downward. As she shifted her gaze from her elbow to her hand, she was told quietly, "Just sit all the way down in the chair, and as you do so just close your eyes and go 'way deeply into the trance, and as you continue to sit there, sleep ever more deeply in a hypnotic trance."

As she settled in the chair, the additional statement was made, "And now you can take a deep comfortable breath while I go on with my lecture." Thereupon, without further delay or training she was immediately employed to demonstrate somnambulistic trance and all the other phenomena of the deep trance. She was awakened approximately one hour later, and demonstrated spontaneously a total amnesia by stating, "But you've got me so confused I don't know what to do. Is it all right to sit this way, and what do you want me to do with my hand?"

Reply was made, "Would you like to go into a trance?"

She answered, "I don't really know. I'm not sure. I don't even know if I can be hypnotized. I suppose maybe I could. I'm willing to try if you want me to." She was asked what she meant by saying that she was confused.

"Well, when I started to come up here, you asked me to sit in this chair, and then you started moving it first one way and then another, and then somehow you started to move my arm, and before I knew what you wanted, you started on my hand and I'm still confused. What do you want me to do?"

In this last question the subject defines adequately the goal of a confusion technique, the pressing need to have a definite, easily comprehended understanding of what is wanted. In the distressing state of confusion developed, whether by verbal or nonverbal or combined methods, the subject is more than ready to accept and react to the first simple idea suggested that will end the confusion. In this instance she accepted at once the suggestions, "Sit down all the way," "close your eyes," and "sleep deeply." It was, indeed, a relief to do so. In rousing from the trance, she reverted to the state of conscious bewilderment that had been interrupted by a rapid development of the deep trance.

To summarize this example, a train of physical activity was initiated in this subject. As she followed along in its development, first one and then another nonverbal suggestion of a motor type was offered just long enough to permit her to become aware of it, but before she could respond another had taken its place. Each suggestion in itself was acceptable, but each time she was precluded from a response although a need to respond was being increasingly developed. Furthermore, each new suggestion was a compound of contradictory significances (that is forward and backward or left and right) which compelled a need to select from these multiple choices which were repeatedly varied. When it was felt clinically that the subject had reached a psychological point at which she was ready to put into action her rising need for a response, a direct, simple statement was given her.

In a single sentence, we may define a confusion technique as one in which a series of interrelated acceptable stimuli ordinarily leading to responsive action are given in such fashion that response is inhibited until the subject, in cumulative fashion, makes a massive response to the first clearcut definitive idea presented.

In the example cited, had the subject not yet been ready to develop a trance state, the writer could easily have continued by shifting attention from the right hand to the left, thence to the right elbow and then the left knee, in preference to any manipulation of objects about her. The reason is that one would want to build up increasingly within the subject a need to respond within the self.

12. Another Example of Confusion in Trance Induction

Milton H. Erickson

On one occasion Erickson was lecturing to a group of doctors about hypnosis. He was interrupted when another doctor brought in two women volunteers who were interested in experiencing hypnosis and introduced them to Erickson. In the following he describes the situation as he understood it.

> E: I began by telling them that they really didn't know anything about me but I had at least an average education; I'd gone to grade school; I'd lectured to doctors; I had learned to count, I could count to twenty easily; I could count to twenty by one, by twos, fours, fives, or tens; I could write my name. I told them a sheer bunch of nonsense along with that important statement about counting to twenty in different ways. And then I said, "Now, of course, whenever I count to twenty, you can go into a hypnotic trance." They just looked at me and I continued with my nonsensical discussion of irrelevant facts about myself. I liked corned beef, I liked golden-eyed trout, etc. Then I looked at them significantly and said, "I had four boys and four girls—that makes eight. They really come cheaper by the dozen, you know." With that they both went into a trance. Eight and twelve is twenty. The women came in expecting to go into a trance. They just didn't know what a trance induction was, so I started the nonsense discussion in which I talked about my education and counting to twenty; telling them that when I came to twenty they would go into a trance—then slipping in the statement, four boys, four girls—they come cheaper by the dozen; four plus four plus twelve equal twenty. I had earlier said that I could count to twenty in any fashion, and when I come to twenty you go into a trance. They went into a trance just that quickly. All that nonsense was not really nonsense; it was a confusion procedure. While they tried desperately to make sense out of all of that nonsense I was telling them (because it is nonsensical for somebody lecturing to a group of doctors to talk in that fashion), they probably asked them-

---
As told to the editor in 1976.

selves, "Why is he talking in that fashion? Why is he saying that? Why is he telling that to us?" They tried desperately to make some meaning out of it, and the first possible meaning to it was four plus four plus twelve, and as soon as they put that meaning on it, they went into a trance. Nice demonstration of confusion technique and of subjects struggling to put a meaning upon what you say and your awareness that the subjects are going to put a meaning upon what you say. Give them plenty and let them select.

13. An Hypnotic Technique for Resistant Patients: the Patient, the Technique, and its Rationale and Field Experiments

Milton H. Erickson

There are many types of difficult patients who seek psychotherapy and yet are openly hostile, antagonistic, resistant, defensive, and present every appearance of being unwilling to accept the therapy they have come to seek. This adverse attitude is part and parcel of their reason for seeking therapy; it is the manifestation of their neurotic attitude against the acceptance of therapy and their uncertainties about their loss of their defenses and hence it is a part of their symptomatology. Therefore this attitude should be respected rather than regarded as an active and deliberate or even unconscious intention to oppose the therapist. Such resistance should be openly accepted, in fact graciously accepted, since it is a vitally important communication of a part of their problems and often can be used as an opening into their defenses. This is something that the patients do not realize; rather, they may be distressed emotionally since they often interpret their behavior as uncontrollable, unpleasant, and uncooperative rather than as an informative exposition of certain of their important needs.

The therapist who is aware of this, particularly if well skilled in hypnotherapy, can easily and often quickly transform these overt, seemingly uncooperative forms of behavior into a good rapport, a feeling of being understood, and an attitude of hopeful expectancy of successfully achieving the goals being sought.

Usually these patients have consulted more than one therapist, have encountered failures of treatment, and their difficulties have grown worse. This fact alone warrants increased concern and care in meeting their needs, particularly if it is appreciated that such a seemingly unfriendly beginning of the therapeutic relationship often actually augurs well for a more speedy therapeutic course if met comfortably and easily as a symptom and not as a defense.

Hence the therapist aids the patients to express quickly and freely their unpleasant feelings and attitudes, encouraging the patients by open receptiveness

---

Reprinted with permission from *The American Journal of Clinical Hypnosis*, July, 1964, 7, 8-32.

and attentiveness, and by the therapist's willingness to comment appropriately in a manner to elicit their feelings fully in the initial session.

Perhaps this can be illustrated by the somewhat extreme example of a new patient whose opening statement as he entered the office characterized all psychiatrists as being best described by a commonly used profane vulgarity. The immediate reply was made, "You undoubtedly have a damn good reason for saying *that and even more*." The italicized words were not recognized by the patient as a direct intentional suggestion to be more communicative, but they were most effective. With much profanity and obscenity, with bitterness and resentment, and with contempt and hostility he related his unfortunate, unsuccessful, repeated, and often prolonged futile efforts to secure psychotherapy. When he paused, the simple comment was made casually, "Well, you must have had a hell of a good reason *to seek therapy from me*." (This was a definition of his visit unrecognized by him.)

Again the italicized words were no more than part of a seemingly wondering comment spoken in his own type of language. He did not recognize that a therapeutic situation was being defined to him, despite his response of, "Don't worry, I'm not going to develop a positive transference or [unprintable words] on you. I'm going to pay you good money to do a job on me, get it? I don't like you, I know a lot of people that don't like you. The only reason I'm here is I've read a lot of your publications and I figure you can handle a disagreeable, fault-finding, uncooperative [unprintable words] who is going to resist every damn thing you try to do for me. That's something I can't help, so either tell me to get the hell out of here or to shut up, and you get down to business, but don't try psychoanalysis. I've had all that baloney I can take. Hypnotize me, only I know you can't in spite of your writings. So, get a move on!"

The reply was made in a casual tone of voice and with a smile, "O.K., shut up, sit down, keep your damn mouth shut and listen; and get it straight, I am going to *get a move on* [using the words of the patient's own request], but *I move just as slow or as fast as I damn please*." My terms for the acceptance of his request for therapy were phrased in his own language, though said casually and in a voice free from any unpleasant intonations and inflections. Thus the patient is told effectively vitally important matters in the italicized words without his conscious recognition of the fact.

The patient seated himself and glared silently and belligerently at the author. He did not realize that he was thereby committing himself to a therapeutic situation. Instead he misunderstood his behavior as uncooperative defiance. With his attention and understandings thus fixated and centered a hypnotic technique was used that has been worked out over the years with the unintentional aid of many difficult, resistive, uncooperative patients and by much speculation upon how to transform their own utterances into vitally important suggestions effectively guiding their behavior, although without such recognition by them at the time.

THE TECHNIQUE AND ITS RATIONALE

The technique, to be given in detail shortly, which is used sometimes almost verbatim, can be shortened or made longer by repetitions and elaborations all in accord with the patient's capacities to understand and to respond. It is advantageous to modify it to include the patient's own style of speech, whether abrupt, impolite, or even outrageously profane. However, the author, in his use of it, usually discontinues very rapidly the discourtesies of the patient's own type of language, but he is likely to continue any ungrammatical constructions that may be characteristic of the patient's speech. Thus the patient's violence (linguistically expressed) is unnoticeably discarded and the patient and the therapist arrive at a safe, pleasant linguistic level familiar in form to the patient. The patient does not know how this happened nor does he often sense that it is happening because of its indirectness; nor is there any reason for the patient to be led to understand the techniques and levels of communication, any more than does the surgical patient need to have a full comprehension of the surgical techniques to be employed.

When sufficient material has been obtained from the aggressive, hostile, antagonistic, defensive, uncooperative patients to appraise their unfortunate behavior and attitudes and to judge their type of personalities, they are interrupted by an introductory paragraph of mixed positive and negative, seemingly appropriate and relevant remarks addressed to them in that form of language they can best understand at that moment. However, concealed and disguised in these remarks are various direct, indirect, and permissive suggestions intended to channel their reactions into receptive and responsive behavior.

For the patient cited above as an example, he was told, "I do not know whether or not you are going into a trance as you have asked." (One needs to scrutinize well this sentence to recognize all the positive and negatives, something not possible when listening to it.) With this introductory remark to this specific patient utilization was then made of the following technique, which is actually no more than a casual, not necessarily grammatical, explanation loaded with direct and indirect permissive suggestions and instructions but not easily recognizable as such. Hence these will, in large part, be italicized to enable more easy recognition. Parenthetical inserts or explanatory paragraphs are for clarification for the reader only, and were of course not part of the verbalized technique.

"You have come for therapy, you have requested hypnosis, and the history you have given of your problem leads me to believe strongly that hypnosis will help you. However, you state more convincingly that you are a resistant hypnotic subject, that others have failed despite prolonged efforts to induce a trance, that various techniques have been of no avail, and that reputable men have discredited hypnosis for you and as a therapeutic aid in itself. You have frankly expressed your conviction that I cannot induce a trance in you, and with equal frankness you have stated that you are convinced that you will resist all attempts at hypnosis and that this resistance will be despite your earnest desire and effort to cooperate. [To resist hypnosis one recognizes its existence, since there can be no resistance to the nonexistent and its existence implies its possibility. Thus the question becomes not one of the reality or value of hypnosis, but simply a question of his resistance to it. Thereby the ground is laid for the use of hypnosis but with his attention directed to his understanding of resistance to it. Hence hypnotic induction is rendered a possibility by any induction technique not recognizable to him.]

"*Since you have come for therapy* and you state that you are a fault-finding, uncooperative patient, let me explain some things *before we begin.* So that *I can have your attention,* just sit with your feet flat on the floor with your hands on your thighs, *just don't let your hands touch each other in any way.*" [This is the first intimation that more is being communicated than the ear hears.]

"Now so that *you will sit still* while I talk, just look at that paperweight, just an ordinary handy thing. By looking at it you will hold your eyes still, and that will hold your head still and that will hold your ears still, and *it's your ears I'm talking to.* [This is the first intimation of dissociation.] No, don't look at me, just at the paperweight, because I want your ears still and you move them when you turn to look at me. [Most patients tend at first to shift their glance, so eye-fixation is effected by a request not to move the ears, and rarely does it become necessary to repeat this simple request more than three times.] Now when you came into this room, you brought into it *both of your minds,* that is, the front of your mind and the back of your mind. ["Conscious mind" and "unconscious mind" can be used, depending upon the educational level, and thus a second intimation is given of dissociation.] Now, I really don't care if you listen to me with your conscious mind, because *it doesn't understand your problem* anyway, or you wouldn't be here, so *I just want to talk to your unconscious mind* because it's here and close enough to hear me, so you can let your conscious mind listen to the street noises or the planes overhead or the typing in the next room. Or you can think about any thoughts that come into your conscious mind, systematic thoughts, random thoughts becuase *all I want to do is to talk to your unconscious mind, and it will listen to me* because it is within hearing distance even if *your conscious mind does get bored* [boredom leads to distinterest, distraction, even sleep]. If your eyes get tired, it will be all right to close them but be sure to keep a good alert [a disarming word so far as any assumed threat of hypnosis is concerned], *a really good mental or visual image alertly* in your mind [an unrecognizable instruction to develop possible ideosensory visual phenomena while the word "alertly" reassures against hypnosis]. *Just be comfortable while I am talking to your unconscious mind, since I don't care what your conscious mind does.* [This is an unrecognizable dismissal of his conscious attention following immediately upon a suggestion of comfort and communication with only his unconscious mind.]

Resistant Patients

"Now before *therapy can be done,* I want to be sure that you realize that *your problems just aren't really understood by you* but that *you can learn to understand them with your unconscious mind.* [This is an indirect assertion that therapy can be achieved and how it can be done with more emphasis upon dissociation.]

"Something everybody knows is that people can communicate verbally ["talk by words" if warranted by low educational or intelligence level] or by sign language. The commonest sign language, of course, is when you *nod your head yes or no.* Anybody can do that. One can signal 'come' with the forefinger, or wave 'bye-bye' with the hand. The finger signal in a way means 'yes, come here,' and waving the hands means really 'no, don't stay.' In other words one can use the head, the finger, or the hand to mean either yes or no. We all do it. *So can you.* Sometimes when we listen to a person we may be *nodding or shaking the head not knowing it* in either agreement or disagreement. *It would be just as easy to do it with the finger or the hand.* Now I would like to ask your unconscious mind a question that can be answered with a simple yes or no. It's a question that *only your unconscious mind can answer.* Neither your conscious mind nor my conscious mind, nor, for that matter, even my unconscious mind knows the answers. *Only your unconscious mind knows* which *answer can be communicated,* and it *will have to think either a yes or a no answer. It could be by a nod or a shake of the head, a lifting of the index finger*—let us say the right index finger for the yes answer, the left index for a no since that is usually the case for the right-handed person and vice versa for the left-handed person. *Or the right hand could lift or the left hand could lift. But only your unconscious mind knows* what the answer will be when I ask for that yes or no answer. And not even your unconscious mind will know, when the question is asked, whether *it will answer with a head movement, or a finger movement,* and *your unconscious mind will have to think through that question* and *to decide, after it has formulated its own answer, just how it will answer.* [All of this explanation is essentially a series of suggestions so worded that responsive ideomotor behavior is made contingent upon an inevitable occurrence—namely, that the subject *"will have to think"* and *"to decide"* without there being an actual request for ideomotor responses. The implication only is there, and implications are difficult to resist.]

"Hence *in this difficult situation in which we find ourselves* [this establishes a "relatedness" to the patient] we will both have to sit back and *wait and wait* [participatory behavior] *for your unconscious mind to think the question through, to formulate its answer, then to decide,* whether by head, finger, or hand, *to let the answer happen.* [This is a second statement of suggestions and instructions in the guise of an explanation. Seemingly the subject has been asked to do nothing, but actually he is directly told to be passive and to permit an ideomotor response to occur at an unconscious level of awareness signifying an answer that he has been told carefully to "let happen" as another and definitive contingent result of mental processes. In all of this procedure there have been implied or indirect suggestions given that the conscious mind will be unaware of unconscious mental activity, in essence that he will develop an anamnestic trance state.]

"In other words I will ask a question to which *only your unconscious mind can give the answer,* and concerning which your conscious mind can only guess if it does at all; maybe correctly, maybe wrongly, or maybe have only some kind of an opinion, but, if so, only an opinion, *not an answer.* [Thus a lessening of importance of his conscious thinking not recognizable to him, and a further implication of a trance state.]

"Before I ask that question, I would like to suggest two possibilities. (1) Your conscious mind might want to know the answer. (2) Your unconscious mind *might not* want you to know the answer. My feeling, and I think you will agree, is that you came here for therapy for reasons *out of the reach of your conscious mind.* Therefore I think that we should approach this matter of the question I am going to put to your unconscious mind for *its own answer* in such a way that *your own deep unconscious wishes to withhold the answer or to share the answer with your conscious mind are adequately protected and respected.* This, to me, is a fair and equitable way in dealing with one's self and one's problems. [This is what he knows he wants from others, but has not quite recognized that he wants fair and equitable treatment from himself.]

"Now, to meet your needs, I am going to ask that yes or no question, and *be prepared to be pleased to let your unconscious mind answer* [this is an unrecognized authoritative suggestion with a foregone conclusion permissively stated], and in doing so either *to share* the answer with your conscious mind or *to withhold it, whatever your unconscious mind thinks to be the better course. The essential thing, of course, is the answer, not the sharing nor the withholding.* This is because any withholding will actually be only for the immediate present, *since the therapeutic gains you will make* [also an unrecognized authoritative statement given in the guise of an explanation] will eventually disclose the answer to you *at the time your unconscious mind regards as most suitable and helpful to you.* Thus *you can look forward to knowing the answer* sooner or later, and *your conscious desires, as well as your unconscious desires, are the seeking of therapy and the meeting of your needs in the right way at the right time.* [This is a definitive suggestion given as an explanation and a most emphatic positive suggestion.]

"Now how shall this question be answered? By speech? Hardly! You would have to verbalize and also to hear. Thus there could then be no *fair dealing* [socially and personally potent demanding words] with your unconscious mind if it wished, for your welfare, to withhold the answer from your conscious mind. How then? Quite simply by a muscular movement *which you may or may not notice,* one that can be done at either a noticeable voluntary level or *one that is done involuntarily and without being noticed,* just as you can nod your head or shake it without noticing it when you agree or disagree with a speaker, or frown when you think you are just trying to call something to mind.

"What shall that muscle movement be? I think it would be better to mention several possibilities [simply "think" or "mention," apparently not demanding, ordering, or suggesting], but before doing so let me describe the difference between a conscious mind muscle response and that of the unconscious mind. [Muscle response is mentioned while his attention is being fixated; a maneuver to maintain that attention for the future introduction of related but delaying material. The reader will note the previous use of this psychological gambit of mentioning a topic and then entering into a preliminary explanation.] The conscious mind response cannot be withheld from you. You know it at once. You accept it and you believe it, perhaps reluctantly. There is no delay to it. It springs to your mind at once, and you promptly make the response.

"An unconscious mind response is different, because *you do not know what it is to be. You have to wait for it to happen,* and consciously you cannot know whether it will be 'yes' or 'no.' [How can a muscle movement be a 'yes' or a 'no'? The patient has to listen intently for some reasonable explanation.] *It does not need to be in accord with the conscious answer* that can be present simultaneously in accord with your conscious mind's thinking. *You will have to wait,* and perhaps wait and wait, *to let it happen. And it will happen in its own time and at its own speed.* [This is an authoritative command but sounds like an explanation, and it provides time for behavior other than conscious, in itself a compelling force. Additionally one never tells the patient that an unconscious reply is almost always characterized by a strong element of perseveration. Apparently an altered time sense in hypnotic subjects, possibly deriving from their altered reality relationships, prevents even experienced subjects from appreciating this point, and it constitutes an excellent criterion of the character of the response. This perseveration of ideomotor activity, however, is much briefer in duration if the unconscious mind wishes the conscious mind to know; the time lag and the dissociated character are greatly reduced, although the unconscious answer may be considerably delayed as the unconscious mind goes through the process of formulating its reply and the decision to share or not to share. If the patient closes his eyes spontaneously, one can be almost certain that the reply given will be spontaneously withheld from the patient's conscious awareness. When the answer is "shared," especially if the conscious opinion is opposite in character, the patient shows amazement and sometimes unwillingly admits to the self an awareness or strong feeling that the unconscious answer is unquestionably correct, thereby intensifying his hypnotic response. A repetition for comparison by asking another simple question can be elicited by the operator by careful wording of a question such as, "But you *can* withhold an answer, can you not?" doing this so casually that the patient does not realize that a second question has been asked. Thus there can be secured a second ideomotor response that is withheld from, or not noticed by, the conscious awareness. Insuring that the patient learns both to share unconscious activity and to withhold it from conscious awareness greatly speeds psychotherapy. Thus I have had a resistant patient, in reply to my question, consciously and promptly shake his head in the negative, briefly and emphatically, and then sit wonderingly at my apparent tardiness of response to his reply, not knowing that I was waiting silently to see if there would occur a slow head turning in a perseverative way from left to right, or an up and down nodding. Experimenting with such patients has disclosed such perseverative movements, particularly of the head, that may last as long as five minutes without the patient becoming aware of what was occurring. Once the patient is in a trance, the ideomotor response can then be as rapid as movement in the ordinary state of awareness, although in general there is a cataleptic character that is most informative of the patient's hypnotic state. This is another criterion for the operator's guidance, unrecognized by the subject.]

"Now what shall the movement be? Most people nod or shake their head for a 'yes' or a 'no,' and the question I am going to ask is that kind of a question, one requiring either a simple 'yes' or a simple 'no.' Other people like to signal by an upward movement of the index fingers, one meaning 'yes,' the other 'no.' I usually, as do most people [the phrases "I usually" and "most people" indicate that *naturally it is to be expected of both of us that behavior common to most people will occur*] like to use the right index finger for 'yes' and the left for 'no,' but it is often the other way around for left-handed people. [Let there be no hint of arbitrary demands, since the patient is resistant and this suggestion is one of freedom of response, even though an illusory freedom.] Then again some people have expressive hands and can easily, voluntarily or involuntarily, move their right hand up to signify 'yes' or the left to signify 'no.' ["Expressive hands" is only an implied compliment, but most appealing to any narcissism. Indeed it is not at all uncommon for a person to beckon with a finger or to admonish with a finger or a hand.]

"I do not know if your unconscious mind wants your conscious mind to look at some object or to pay attention to your head or fingers or hands. Perhaps you might like to watch your hands, and if your eyes blur as you watch them fixedly while you wait to see which one will move when I ask my simple question, such blurring is comprehensible. It only means that your hands are close to you and that you are looking at them intently. [Even if the patient's eyes are closed, this paragraph can be used unconcernedly. In its essence it is highly suggestive of a number of things, but unobtrusively so. Actually the sole purpose of these purported and repetitious explanations is merely to offer or to repeat various suggestions and instructions without seemingly doing so. Also a variety of possibilities is offered, essentially as an indirect double bind, which renders a refusal to make a response most difficult. All of the items of behavior are being suggested in such fashion that seemingly all the patient does is to manifest *his choice*, but he has actually *not been asked* to make a choice of the possibilities merely mentioned to him. He is not aware of what else is being said or implied. The author's personal preference is an ideomotor head movement, which can easily be achieved without conscious awareness, but regardless of the type of movement employed by the patient, the author immediately shifts to a second

Resistant Patients

type of ideomotor response and perhaps to a third to intensify the patient's total responsiveness. The hand movement offers certain distinct advantages in that it lends itself readily to the elicitation of other phenomena, as will be described later.]

"Now [at long last, and the patient's eagerness is at a high point] we come to the question! I do not need to know what is to be your choice of the movements to be made. You have your head on your neck and your fingers are on your hands and you can let your hands rest comfortably on your thighs or on the arms of the chair. *The important thing is to be comfortable while awaiting your unconscious answer.* [In some way comfort and the unconscious answer become unrecognizedly contingent upon each other, and the patient naturally wants comfort. Equally naturally he has some degree of curiosity about his "unconscious answer." Also, another delaying preliminary explanation is being given.] Now you are in a position for any one or all of the possible movements [an unrecognized authoritative suggestion]. As for the question I am to ask, that, too, is not really important. What is important is *what your unconscious mind thinks, and what it does think neither you nor I consciously know. But your unconscious does know since it does do its own thinking but not always in accord with your conscious thoughts.*

"Since you have asked me to induce a trance, I could ask a question related to your request, but I would rather ask a simpler one [a possible threat of hypnosis removed]. Hence *let us* [we are working together] ask a question so general that it can be answered by any one of the various muscle ways described. Now here is the question to which I want you to listen carefully, and then to wait patiently to see, or perhaps not to see, what your unconscious answer is. [After so much apparently plausible delay, the patient's attention is now most fixed, he is, so to speak, "all ears" in his desire to know the question, and such desire has to have an unrecognized basis of acceptance of the idea that his unconscious mind will answer.] My question is [said slowly, intently, gravely], Does your unconscious mind *think* it will raise your hand or your finger or move your head?" [Three possibilities, hence the conscious mind cannot know.] "Just wait patiently, wonderingly, and let the answer happen."

What the patient does not know and has no way of realizing is that he is being communicated with on two levels, that he is in a double or triple bind. He cannot deny that his unconscious mind can think. He is inescapably bound by that word "think." *Any ideomotor or nonvolitional movement,* whether positive or negative, *is a direct communication from his unconscious mind* (but his thinking does not extend to that realization). If slowly his head shakes "no," my gentle lifting of either his "yes" or "no" hand will result in catalepsy. This cataleptic response is also hypnotic; it is one of the phenomena of hypnosis. I can then ask him to be more comfortable, and if his eyes are open, I add, "perhaps by closing your eyes, *taking a deep breath, and feeling pleased that your unconscious mind is free to communicate to me as it wishes.*"

Thus without his awareness and before he has time to analyze the fact, he is communicating at the level of the unconscious mind, thereby literally going into a trance despite his previous conscious conviction that he would inevitably defeat his own wishes to be hypnotized. In other words his resistances have been bypassed by making hypnotic responses contingent upon his thought processes in response to seemingly nonhypnotic discussion of various items, and his false belief that he cannot be hypnotized is nullified by a pleasing unconscious awareness that he can cooperate. If he becomes aware that he is responding with ideomotor activity, he is bound to recognize that his unconscious mind has charge of the situation. This places him in another double bind, that of being in the position of letting his unconscious mind "share" with his conscious mind whatever it wishes, which as a further double bind will commit him quite unwittingly also to let his unconscious mind *withhold* from his conscious mind, with a consequent hypnotic amnesia at the conscious level. Thus with no seeming effort at trance induction as the patient understands it, a trance state has been induced.

Fortunately for both the operator and the patient the elicitation of a single hypnotic phenomenon is often an excellent technique of trance induction, and should, for the patient's benefit, be used more often. The realization of this was first reached in the summer of 1923 while attempting to experiment with automatic writing. To the author's astonishment the subject, his sister Bertha, who had never before been hypnotized or seen hypnosis induced, developed a profound somnambulistic trance while suggestions were being made only to the effect that slowly, gradually, her right hand, holding a pencil on a pad of paper, would being to quiver, to move, to make scrawling marks until her hand wrote letters, then words forming a sentence while she stared fixedly at the doorknob just to enable her body to sit still. The sentence, "Grandma's dog likes eating those bones," was written, and the author inquired what she meant and received the reply, while she pointed cataleptically toward the door, "See! He is eating that dishful of bones and he likes them." Only then did the author realize that a trance had been unintentionally induced and that she was hallucinating visually what she had written, since Grandma's dog was miles away. Many times thereafter automatic writing was used as an indirect technique of trance induction, but was discarded because writing is a systematic ordering of a special skill and hence is too time-consuming. A ouija board was next utilized, but this, while somewhat effective in inducing a trance indirectly, was discarded because of its connotations of the supernatural. Resort was then more reasonably made to the simple movements of the type made automatically, promptly, requiring no particular skill. At first a modification of automatic writing was employed, a modification spontaneously and independently developed by a number of different subjects—namely, the use of a vertical line to signify "yes," a horizontal line to signify "no," and an oblique line to signify "I don't know." This has been described elsewhere by Erickson and Kubie (*Psychoanalytic Quarterly,* Oct. 1939, *8,* 471–509). It has often proved a rapid indirect technique of trance induction.

Resistant Patients

Once an ideomotor response is made, without further delay it can be utilized immediately. For example, should the patient shake his head "no," his "yes" hand is gently lifted, and spontaneous catalepsy becomes manifest. Or if the "yes" finger makes an ideomotor response, the hand opposite is lifted to effect catalepsy; or the patient may be told that his head can agree with his finger. If his eyes are open (they often close spontaneously as the ideomotor activity begins), the simple suggestion can then be made that he can increase his physical comfort by relaxing comfortably, closing his eyes, resting pleasurably, taking a deep breath, and *realizing with much satisfaction that his unconscious mind can communicate directly and adequately and is free to make whatever communication it wishes,* whether by sign language, verbally, or in both manners. He is urged to realize that there is no rush or hurry, that *his goals are to be accomplished satisfactorily rather than hurriedly,* and that *he can continue the unconscious mind communication indefinitely.* Thus the words "trance" or "hypnosis" are avoided, and yet a multitude of hypnotic and posthypnotic suggestions can be given in the form of a manifestation of interest in the patient's comfort, in explanations and in reassurances, all of which are worded to extend indefinitely into the future with the implied time limit of *goals satisfactorily reached.* (These italicized words are, in the situation, an actual double bind.) In this way a most extensive foundation is laid easily for good rapport, further trances, and rapid therapeutic progress, and usually this can be done within the first hour. In extraordinary cases the author has been forced by the patient to take as much as 15 hours, all spent by the patient in denouncing the author and the expected failure to result from the effort at treatment, with a good trance and therapeutic progress rapidly ensuing thereafter.

The use of this technique on the patient cited as an example above, whose intense, unhappy belligerency suggested its suitability, resulted in the development of a deep anamnestic trance employed to give posthypnotic suggestions governing future therapeutic hypnoanalytic sessions.

He was aroused from the trance by the simple expedient of remarking casually, as if there had been no intervening period of time, "Well, that *is* [note the present tense of the italicized word] some cussing that you have just been giving me." Thus the patient was subtly reoriented to the time at which he had been verbally assaulting me and accordingly he aroused "spontaneously" from his trance state, appearing much bewildered, checked the clock against his watch and the author's and then remarked in astonishment "I've been cussing you out for over 15 minutes, but a lot more than an hour has gone by! What happened to the rest of the time?" He was given the answer, "So you cussed me out about 15–20 minutes [a deliberate though minor expansion of his time statement], and *then you lost the rest of the time!* [Thus the patient is indirectly told he can *lose.*] Well, that is *my* cotton-picking business, and now that you know you can lose time, you ought to know you can lose some things you don't want to keep just as easily and unexpectedly. So, *get going,* come back the same time next Friday, and *pay* the girl in the next room. The patient's own words were used but turned back upon him. Although these words were used originally in terms of starting therapy, they were now in relationship to the therapist instructing the patient about his part in the therapy. Also, since he had said that he was paying "good money" for therapy, by requesting immediate payment, he was unwittingly being committed to the idea that he was receiving that which he had so emphatically and impolitely demanded.

Upon his return on Friday he took his seat and asked in a puzzled but unduly tense voice, "Do I have to like you?" The implications of the question are obvious, the tension in his voice betokened alarm, and hence he had to be reassured with no possibility of his detecting any effort to reassure him. Accordingly the tone of the first meeting was reestablished safely by casually, comfortably stating, "Hell no, you damn fool, *we got work to do.*" The sigh of relief and the physical relaxation that followed this seemingly impolite and unprofessional reply attested to his need, and it easily shifted his attention to the purpose expressed in the italicized words and relieved him of an inner anxiety which was actually a probable threat to continuance of therapy.

As he relaxed the casual statement was made, "Just close your eyes, take a deep breath, and *now let's get at that work we got to do.*" By the time the author had finished this statement, the patient was in a profound somnambulistic trance, and thereafter merely sitting down in that chair induced a trance. When the therapist did not wish him to develop a trance, he was simply asked to sit in another chair.

At the fourth session (a trance) he asked, "Is it all right to like you?" He was told, "Next time you come, sit in the straightback chair and the question and answer will come to you." (Note sharing in the description of the technique.)

At the next session he "spontaneously" sat in the straightback chair, looked startled, and declared, "Hell yes, I can do any damn thing I want to." The reply was made, "Slow learner, huh?" To this he answered, "I'm doing O.K." and arose, sat in the regular chair and went into a trance. (He didn't want any "baloney" about a "transference" and its "resolution," but he could do *"any damn thing" he "wanted to do."* Thus he recognized a certain emotional reaction, admitted it to himself, and then disposed of it by "going to work" and wasting no time in some laborious attempt at "analyzing his transference neurosis." Instead he was solely interested in what he had previously said in the word of "get going."

Therapy was less than 20 hours, each interview was highly productive with ever-increasing "sharing." Ten years later he is still well-adjusted and a warm friend of the author, though our meetings are infrequent.

The technique described above has been used many times over a long period of years with minor variations. Various patients have contributed to its development by presenting opportunities for the author to introduce new suggestions and additional indirect communications and various types of double binds. As given above, it is in essence complete and has been extensively used in this form with only the modifications required by the patient's own intelligence and attitudes. To write this paper old records were consulted, and the technique itself was written out first as a separate item. Then for this paper it was rewritten with parenthetical inserts and explanatory paragraphs for an exposition of the technique. In the field experiments that follow below, not originally even considered, the copy of the technique without inserts was employed to permit a smoother and easier use with those patients.

FIRST FIELD EXPERIMENT

This paper had been typed in final form up to this point and it had been carefully reviewed that same evening. The next morning a most fortunate coincidence occurred.

A new patient, 52 years old, a successful upper-social-class businessman, entered the office. He was shamefaced, embarrassed, and in apparently severe emotional distress. He pointedly looked at the state license to practice medicine in Arizona posted on the wall in accord with Arizona law, read the certificate from the American Board of Psychiatry and Neurology qualifying the author as a diplomate of that board, picked up the Directory of Medical Specialists from the dictionary stand, read the author's qualifications there, picked up the Psychological Directory and read the author's qualifications there, went to the bookcase and selected the books, *The Practical Applications of Medical and Dental Hypnosis* and *Time Distortion in Hypnosis,* pointed to the author's name on the dust jackets, and remarked caustically, "So you fool around with that stuff!" The author agreed casually but (to add further fuel to the patient's fire) added, "And just last night I finished writing a paper on hypnosis, and I am also the editor of *The American Journal of Clinical Hypnosis.*" The reply was, "Yes, I've heard plenty about you being a crackpot, but I'm in trouble (noting that the author was writing down each of his statements, the patient spontaneously slowed his speech to accommodate the author's writing speed, but otherwise continued uninterruptedly with his complaints), and I need help.

"And it's getting worse. It began about eight years ago. I'd be driving to work and I would go into a panic and would have to park the car at the curb. Maybe a half-hour later I could drive the rest of the way to the office. Not constantly, but slowly it increased in frequency until one day it changed. I couldn't park by the curb. I had to drive home. Sometimes it happened on my way home from the office and I'd have to drive back there. Then maybe after an hour, sometimes only a half-hour later, I could go to the office or home with no difficulty. My wife tried to drive me there to save me from these panic states. That just made things worse. I'd be sure to get a panic and yell at her to speed up. I tried taxicabs. That didn't work. The taximen thought I was off my rocker because I would suddenly yell at them to turn around and try to make them break the speed laws getting back home or getting back to the office. I tried a bus once and I thought I'd go crazy. The bus driver wouldn't let me off until he reached the next bus stop. I nearly killed myself running back home. It didn't happen every day at first, but it kept getting more frequent until three years ago it was every day I was late to the office and late back home. I had to take a lunch with me. I would get a panic going to or coming back from lunch.

"Three years ago I went into intensive therapy with Dr. X. He was trained in psychoanalysis at the Y Clinic for three years and had two years of controlled psychoanalysis himself. I saw him four or five times a week, an hour each time, for two and a half years, but I always had to allow about two hours to get there on time and then two more to get home. I didn't always need the time. I sometimes arrived way ahead of time, and sometimes I could leave on time. But I just continued to get worse. Then about six months ago the psychoanalyst put me on heavy dosages of tranquilizers because I had made no improvement; but he kept on analyzing me. The analysis didn't do any good. Some of the drugs would work for a week or even two, but then they would wear out. Most of them did nothing for me. Just name a tranquilizer; I've taken it. Pep pills! Sedatives! Extra analytic hours too. Then about a couple of months ago I tried whiskey. I never had done any drinking to speak of, but what a relief that whiskey was. I could take a drink in the morning, put in a day's work at the office, take a drink and go home feeling fine. With the tranquilizers that worked, I hadn't been able to do my office work, and even those that didn't work interfered with my office work terribly. I had had to take a simpler job. For one month I used two drinks of whiskey a day, one in the morning, one at quitting time, and everything was O.K. Then about a month ago I had to double the morning dosage, then take some at noon, then a double dose to get home. Then I started on triple doses with extra single ones thrown in between times. My home is 20 minutes from here. It took three drinks to get me here, stiff ones. I came early so I would have to wait a couple of hours and sober up, and I sober up fast.

"Just after I began my psychoanalysis I heard and read about hypnosis and heard of you. The psychoanalyst told me frankly what a crackpot you are and that hypnosis is dangerous and useless, but even if you are a crackpot, I know that at least you have proper medical and psychiatric credentials. And no matter how dangerous and useless and stupid hypnosis is, it can't be as bad as alcohol. The whiskey I have to take each day now is turning me into an alcoholic.

"Well, you can't do any worse with hypnosis than what the alcohol is doing. I'm going to try to cooperate with you, but after all I have heard about hypnosis from my psychoanalyst, and all the published stuff denouncing it he gave me, I know nobody in his right mind is going to let himself be hypnotized. But at least you can try."

This account was given while the newly finished paper on hypnotic techniques for patients uncooperative for various reasons was on the desk in front of the author. This suggested an immediate experiment. It was simply that the patient allow the author to read aloud his newly written paper, not disclosing the intention to use it as a hypnotic-induction technique. The man disgustedly agreed to the request but refused to fixate his gaze on any object. He kept glancing about the room, would not place his hands on his thighs, but did place them on the arms of the chair.

Slowly, carefully, the technique was read almost verbatim, sometimes rereading parts of it as judged best by his facial expression.

Finally the patient began to look first at one hand and then the other. At last his gaze became fixated on the right hand. The left-index or "no" finger raised slightly, then the left middle finger. Then the right index finger with jerky, cogwheel movements began lifting in a perseverative fashion. His left index finger lowered, but the middle finger remained cataleptic. His head then began a perseverative affirmative nodding that lasted until he was interrupted by the induction of catalepsy in both hands. His eyes had closed spontaneously when the left index finger was lowered.

He was allowed to remain in the trance, and the technique was again slowly, emphatically read to him.

He was allowed to continue in the trance for an additional 30 minutes while the author left the room briefly, came back, checked on the continued maintenance of his cataleptic position, and then worked on this manuscript additionally.

Finally the patient was aroused from his apparently deep trance by reiteration of the remark about reading the manuscript. He aroused slowly, shifted his position, and again remarked that it (hypnosis) wasn't any more harmful than alcohol. Suddenly he noticed the clock with a startled reaction and immediately checked it with his own watch and then the author's. His startled comment was, "I came in here half an hour ago. The clock and our watches say I've been here over two hours—nearly two and a half. I've got to leave."

He rushed out of the door, came rushing back, and asked how soon he could have another appointment as he shook the author's hand. He was given an appointment for three days later and told, "Be sure to bring a full bottle of whiskey." (He could not recognize the implications of this but he replied that he would, that the one in his hip pocket was nearly empty although it had been full that morning when he left the house.) He then departed from the waiting room, came back, and again shook hands with the author, stating simply that he had forgotten to say good-bye.

Three days later he entered the office smilingly, made a few casual remarks about current events, sat down comfortably in the chair, and offered a compliment on a paperweight. He was asked what had happened during the last three days. His eloquent reply was, "Well, I've been wondering about that problem I came to you about. I was pretty hot under the collar and I had plenty to say and I said it and you wrote it down word by word. I kept trying to figure out what it was costing me per word to let you take your time just writing it down. It irritated me quite strongly, and when I noticed I had been here two and a half hours just to let you write down verbatim what I had to say, I made up my mind that I would pay you for one hour only and let you argue about the rest. Then when you told me to bring a full bottle of whiskey the next time I came, I felt just as I did about those useless tranquilizers and I had half a mind not to come back. But after I got outside, I realized I was feeling unusually free from tension even though I was late for a business appointment, so I came back to say goodbye. [The reader will note that this is not the exact chronological sequence recorded above.] Then I forgot to take a drink in order to drive to my appointment, maybe because I was irritated about your mention of a full bottle of whiskey.

"Then the next day before I knew it, I was at the office on time, felt fine, put in a good day's work, went out to lunch, and drove home. Same thing the next day. Then this morning I remembered I had an appointment with you today. I was still angry about that 'full bottle' you mentioned, but I got one out to put in my pocket. I took a small drink out of another bottle, but forgot to put the full bottle in my pocket. I suppose you will interpret that as resistance or defiance of authority. I say I intended to and simply forgot. I was on time at the office, put in a good day's work, but at noontime an old-time friend dropped in unexpectedly and I had a long lunch with him along with a bottle of beer. Then I went back to work and just managed to remember my appointment in time to get here. So it's beginning to look as if you might be able to help me if you get around to starting instead of just writing down what I say. That's what took so long last time. I didn't need that drink this morning, but I couldn't come to you under false pretenses so I took one. A cocktail at dinner is O.K., but a morning drink is just no good. Somehow I don't feel bad about your taking your time to write down everything I say."

There was some casual discussion of current events, and the author offered the unexpected comment to the patient, "Well, let's see. You were once an editorial writer on a large metropolitan newspaper, and editorials are supposed to mold the opinions of the masses. Tell me, is the opinion molded in the conscious mind of the person; and what is your definition of the 'conscious mind' and the 'unconscious mind'?" He replied, "You don't go through two and a half years of psychoanalysis with wholehearted cooperation and then get brainwashed for another half-year with tranquilizers plus analysis, without learning a lot and losing a lot. All I can give you is an ordinary lay definition, namely, your conscious mind is the front of your mind and your unconscious mind is the back of your mind. But you probably know more about that than I do or Dr. X." He was asked, "And is it possible that ever the twain shall meet?" His answer was, "That's an odd question, but I think I get what you mean. I think that the unconscious mind can tell the conscious mind things, but I don't think the conscious mind can either tell the unconscious mind anything or even know what is in the unconscious. I spent plenty of time trying to excavate my unconscious mind with Dr. X and getting just nowhere, in fact getting worse." Another question was put to him, "Shall I discuss the conscious mind and the unconscious mind with you some time?" His answer was, "Well, if you keep on writing down everything I say and everything you say, and I have all the luck with my problem that I had when you spent the whole time just writing down my complaints the way you did last time—by the way, I had a wonderful afternoon playing golf yesterday with a client, first good game in years and no drinking either—well, go right ahead and discuss the conscious mind, the unconscious mind, politics, hypnosis, anything you wish.''

He was asked why he had made that reply. His answer was, "Well, this is a bit embarrassing. I'm 52 years old and I am just bubbling over inside like a little boy, and the feeling is one I would call faith and expectancy, just like a little kid who is dead certain he is going to have his most hopeful dreams about going to the circus fulfilled. Sounds silly, doesn't it, but I actually feel like a hopeful, happy, expectant little boy.''

The reply was made by asking, "Do you remember the position you sat in in that chair?'' Immediately he uncrossed his legs, dropped his hands on his lap, closed his eyes, slowly lowered his head, and was in a deep trance in a few moments' time.

The rest of the hour was spent in an "explanation of the importance of reordering the behavior patterns for tomorrow, the next day, the next week, the next year, in brief, of the future, in order to meet the satisfactory goals in life that are desired.'' This was all in vague generalities, seemingly explanations but actually cautious posthypnotic suggestions, intended to be interpreted by him to fit his needs.

He was aroused from the trance by remarking casually, "Yes, that is the way you sat in the chair last time,'' thereby effecting a reorientation to the time just previous to this second trance. As he aroused and opened his eyes, the author looked pointedly at the clock. The patient was again startled to find that time had passed so rapidly, asked for another appointment in three days but agreed to wait five days. On the way out of the reception room he paused to look at some wood carvings and commented that he was intending without delay to do some woodwork long postponed.

Five days later the man came in smilingly, sat down comfortably in his chair, and presented a conversational appearance. He was asked what had happened over the weekend and the other three days. His reply, given slowly and patiently as it was recorded by the author, was most informative.

"I've seen you twice. You haven't done a darn thing for me or my problem, and yet something is going on. I had trouble with my problem three times. I was going to the City A to dine with friends, my wife was in the front seat but I was driving. I felt the old panic coming on but I didn't let my wife know it. I haven't driven that road for years, and the last time I did, I got a panic at the same place that this new one seemed about to develop. That time I stopped the car, pretended to examine the tires, and then I asked my wife to drive. This time nothing could stop me from continuing to drive and the panic went away, but just when, I don't remember. We all had a nice time and I drove back without remembering the near panic I had on the way out. Then this noon I went to a hotel where I haven't eaten for years because of panics, and just as I was leaving, an old friend came up to greet me and to tell me a long-winded, boring story and I got mad at him—I wanted to get back at the office. I was just mad, not panicky. Then when I left the office to come here, a client nabbed me at the door and told me a joke, and I got mad because he was delaying my trip to your office. When I did get away, I realized that I had had only one slight panic that I handled all by myself, and what you might call 'two mads' because I was delayed by someone interfering with my going where I should go. Now you will have to tell me what's going on here. Oh yes, my wife and I had two drinks one night before dinner. She said a couple of mixed drinks would taste good and they did.

"But what is going on? You sit and write down what you and I say. You don't hypnotize me, you aren't doing any psychoanalysis. You talk to me but you don't say anything in particular. I suppose when you get around to it you will hypnotize me, but what for I don't know. That problem I came in with, psychoanalyzed without results for two and a half years and brainwashed with tranquilizers and psychoanalysis for another half-year, and now in two hours without you doing anything, I'm pretty sure I'm over my problem." A casual reply was made that therapy usually takes place within the patient, that the therapist is primarily a catalyst. To this he answered, "Well, 'catalyst' when you get ready. If I can waste three years on psychoanalysis and tranquilizers and just get worse and I get better [note first-person pronoun] in two hours watching you write, you can have all of my time you want. It's wonderful to go to the office and home and to lunch again and it was good to meet that old friend at the hotel, and that story our client told me wasn't half bad. When is my next appointment?"

He was instructed to come in a week's time and to let his unconscious mind work on his problem "'as needed."

A week later the man entered the office and inquired with some bewilderment, "Things are happening all right. I've had panics all week, not bad ones, puzzling ones. They were all in the wrong places. I do my regular work in the way I want to, I've increased my workload. I go back and forth to my office O.K. But what happens is something silly. I put on one of my shoes perfectly comfortably, but as I reach for the other, my panic hits me hard for a moment, then disappears, and I put on the other shoe comfortably. I drive into the garage, turn off the ignition, get out of the car, lock the garage door, and a sudden panic hits me, but by the time I've put my car keys in my pocket, the panic is gone. What's more, every panic I get makes me more amused, it's so silly and so short. I don't even mind them. It's funny how a man can get so panicky and suffer the way I did for so long when now it is so brief and so amusing.

"I wonder if the reason for these panics isn't my wife's irritation with me. She has always wanted me to see things her way, and it always made me mad. So I wonder if I get into these panics because they irritate the hell out of her. You know, I think that's the underlying cause. What I suspect is that somehow you are making me tear up the old problem and scatter it around like confetti.

I wonder if that's what I'm doing, tearing up my problem and just throwing it to the wind. I wonder why in three years I never told my analyst about my wife's antagonism. Four or five or more hours a week for three years ought to drain dry every idea a man has. Why did I tell you? You never asked! Oh yes, I played two days of golf the way I like to play, no drinking, no panics. Then on the way here I got a panic as I stepped outside the office building, and so I went into the [adjacent] bar, ordered three double shots of whiskey, paid for them, looked at them all lined up for me and never saw a sillier thing in my life. So while the bartender just stared at me and the untouched drinks, I walked out. I didn't have a panic.

"Now you have been writing about half-hour on what I've been telling you, and that clock there says its half-past the hour and I'm willing to bet the next time I look at it, it will be on the hour." (The implications of this remark are obvious.)

Slowly, gravely, the answer was given, "You are entirely right." Immediately his eyes closed, and a deep trance ensued at once. He was promptly asked to review the progress *he had made* and the account of the current interview was read slowly to him. As he listened, his head slowly nodded perseveratively in an affirmative fashion.

Exactly on the hour he was told, "It's just as you said, it's exactly the hour by the clock." He aroused, stretched, yawned, and asked, "How about next week, same time?"

The appointment was made.

As he left the office, he remarked, "I'm reading this (taking from his jacket pocket) delightful book. Would you like to read it when I'm finished?" He was assured that it would be a pleasure.

The next meeting wast most enlightening. As he entered, he remarked, "I'm enjoying these conversations. I'm understanding. For years I have unconsciously resented my wife in one way only. Her father died when she was an infant, and her mother swore she would be a father to the little baby. She was. She still is, and my wife is like her mother. She wears all the pants in the home. Mine, and my son's too. She is completely the man in the house in every way. But we are so compatible in every other way, and we are deeply in love with each other, and she always decides things the right way. The thing is, I would like permission from her to make the decision she is going to make anyway. No, that's wrong. I want no permission, I just want to make decisions and let her agree with them because my decision is right, instead of my agreeing with her decisions because they happen to be the ones I would make. Funny, I never even talked about all this in the three years' time in psychoanalysis; now I wonder why I have told you all this when I didn't even think highly of hypnosis. And last Sunday I laughed to myself. My wife announced that she was taking me and the kids to an entertainment that I wanted to attend, and she knew it. But I decided I would just stay home and I told her so. I really enjoyed doing it and I felt greatly amused. It was worth missing it. I just felt like a happy little boy who had successfully asserted himself.

"Now with your permission I'm going to—no, I don't want your permission because I decided to do it and I've been doing it for almost a week. What I do is this. The first day I got in my car, I deliberately had a short panic after the first block or two, and then drove on to the office comfortably. The next day I drove still further and deliberately had another brief panic and drove on. The same thing is done when I go home. I've only got about enough distance left for about four or five more short panics. Then I'll be through. But I'm not going to stop seeing you. It's worth it to have a conversation with you once a week if you don't mind, and I expect to be charged for it."

Therapy has continued in this fashion; at first a simple report by the patient of his "own behavior" with no expectation of any comment from the author and a general conversation on various related topics. Thus did the patient take over the responsibility of his own therapy, doing it in his own way at his own speed.

He is still continuing his weekly visits, sometimes on a purely social level, sometimes discussing the teenage behavior of his children not as a problem but as an interesting contrast to his own. His own problem has vanished so far as any personal difficulties are concerned. That he is willing to pay a psychiatric fee for social visits suggests that unconsciously the man wants the assurance of a continued friendship for some length of time from one who aided him to achieve a satisfying sense of masculine dominance without compelling him to go through a long, dependent, submissive, and fruitless relationship in search of therapy, but who instead simply placed the burden of responsibility for therapy upon him and his own unconscious mind. However, as the weeks go by the evidence is building that he will soon be reducing the frequency of his visits. Early summer plans have been repeatedly mentioned and these, as they are outlined, will make visits impossible. Thus, his unconscious mind is informing the author of the impending termination. Invariably he goes into a spontaneous trance of five to ten minutes' duration as the end of the hour approaches. In this trance he remains silent, and so does the author.

Similar therapeutic procedures have been employed in the past, not exactly in this fashion but in a decidedly comparable manner. One patient will make an appointment phrasing his request, "so that I can have my batteries recharged" (meaning a trance, sometimes with helpful suggestions, sometimes merely a trance). Other patients come in seemingly for no more than a "casual" conversation, eventually discontinuing this practice. In the past such therapeutic procedures have sufficed to achieve long-term satisfactory results, as witnessed by follow-up inquiries five and ten years later.

SECOND FIELD EXPERIMENT

Another unexpected opportunity arose to test the above technique. A 24-year old-girl who became acutely disturbed in 1961 by visual and auditory hallucinations of a persecutory character developed many persecutory delusions, became antagonistic (she was the youngest) toward her two siblings and her parents, and finally had to be hospitalized on an emergency basis where her case was diagnosed as schizophrenia, paranoid type, with a doubtful prognosis.

"Psychodynamically oriented" psychotherapy was undertaken by various psychoanalytically trained psychiatrists. The girl, a college student of decidedly superior intelligence, made mockery of them, ridiculed psychoanalytic concepts, placed the psychoanalysts in a self-defensive position, or else angered them and was regarded by them as "not amenable to any kind of psychotherapy." Electroshock therapy was recommended but refused possibly by both the relatives as well as by the patient. (The father, a dentist, had sought counseling on the matter from two other psychiatrically trained psychotherapists who had advised against it as too soon to be warranted. Hence it is not known whether the father or the patient refused, or both, the patient stating very simply, "I would not tolerate having my brains scrambled for thumbpushes on a button at $30 a push").

She was asked what she wished of the author. Her statement was, "I have a family that think you can hypnotize me into sanity, as they call it. God, how I hate them. So they just signed me out of the state hospital and brought me here willy-nilly. Now what kind of an ass are you going to make of yourself?"

"None at all, I hope, regardless of my potentialities. I'm not going to psychoanalyze you, I'm not going to take your history, I don't care about your Oedipus complex or your anal phase, I'm not going to Rorschach you or T.A.T. you. I'm going to show you a letter from your father (which reads in essence 'My college daughter 22 years old is very disturbed mentally. Will you accept her for therapy?') and my answer to him (which reads in essence 'I shall be glad to see your daughter in consultation.'). I do have one question to ask you, What did you major in?"

She answered, "I was going to major in psychology, but things began to go wrong so I just switched in my junior year to English, but I've read a lot of that crap called psychology. And I am fed up to the ears with psychoanalysis."

"Good, then *I won't have to waste your time or mine*. You see, all I want to do is *to find out if we can understand each other*. Now be patient with me and let me ramble on. You're here on a two-hour appointment and as long as you're going to be bored, let it be as boresome as can be."

Promptly she said, "Well, at least you are honest; most psychiatrists think they are interesting."

Very rapidly the author then explained that he was going to read to her a paper he had just written (she interjected, "Do anything to get an audience, wouldn't you?") and immediately he had, as in the preceding case, asked her to put both feet on the floor, her hands on her thighs, to stare steadily at the clock, being sure that she just "plain resented" the boredom "instead of going to sleep." (She knew that the author employed hypnosis, and this precluded her from thinking hypnosis would be used.)

Systematically the technique described above was used again almost verbatim. The only difference was that the author proceeded more slowly, and at first there was much repetition by varying slightly the words but not the essence of their meaning.

At first her expression was one of scornful mockery, but she suddenly declared in amazement, "My right hand is lifting, I don't believe it, but it is and I'm not in a trance. Ask a different kind of question."

She was asked if her unconscious mind thought it could communicate with me. In astonishment she declared, "My head is nodding 'yes' and I can't stop it, my right hand is lifting up and I can't stop it, and my right index finger is also lifting too. Maybe my unconscious mind can communicate with you, but make them stop moving."

"If your unconscious mind wants to stop them, it will do so itself" was the answer given to her.

Almost at once she said, "Oh, they've all stopped, so now maybe if you just ask me the questions, I can get at some stuff that I know I've repressed. Will you please go ahead?"

Her eyes closed, a spontaneous trance developed, therapeutic rapport was well-established before the two hours were up, and their girl is now a most eager, cooperative, and thoroughly responsive patient, making excellent progress.

This was but another impromptu field experiment prompted by the overt hostility of the opening of the session. She had been seen for less than 10 hours when her family expressed the belief that she was better than she was at anytime previously in her life. She, however, laughingly stated, "You don't live with mixed-up ideas such as I had so long as I did without learning that there is a terrific interweaving in all of your thinking. I want to stay in therapy and just keep on learning to understand myself."

Following the first 10 hours she enrolled in college where she is making an excellent adjustment seeing the author once a week. She discusses objectively, well, and understandingly her past symptomatic manifestations as emotionally violent experiences belonging to the past and usually terminates the therapeutic hour with a 15- to 20-minute trance.

THIRD FIELD EXPERIMENT

Before this paper had been typed in final form a third patient with a totally different type of resistance came into the office. She walked with a controlled rigidity of her body, stepping softly. The right side of her face was one of obviously controlled frozen immobility; she spoke clearly and lucidly, with a patterned left-sided mouthing of her words; her right eye blink was markedly reduced; her right arm movements were constrained and hesitant, and when she moved her hand toward the right side of her face, such movement was slower and definitely guarded in comparison with her left-arm movements, which were free and easy and decidedly expressive.

To spare the patient she was asked immediately, "How long have you had trigeminal neuralgia? Answer in the fewest possible words and slowly, since I do not need too much history *to begin your therapy.*"

Her reply was "Mayos', 1958, advised against surgery, against alcohol injections, told there was no treatment, have to put up with it and endure it all my life, (tears rolled down her cheeks), a psychiatrist friend said maybe you help."

"You working?"

"No, leave of absence, psychiatrist friend say see you—get help."

"Want help?"

"Yes."

"No faster than I can give it?" (That is, would she accept help at the rate I considered best. I wanted no expectation of a "miracle cure.")

"Yes."

"May I start work on you now?"

"Yes, please, but no good, all clinics say hopeless, painful. Everybody enjoy himself but I can't. I can't live with my husband, nothing, just pain, no hope, doctors laugh at me see you for hypnosis."

"Anyone suspect psychogenic origin of pain?"

"No, psychiatrists, neurologists, Mayos'—all clinics say organic, not psychogenic."

"And what advice do they give you?"

"Endure; surgery, alcohol, last resort."

"Do you think hypnosis will help?"

"No, organic disease, hypnosis psychological."

"What do you eat?"

"Liquid."

"How long does it take to drink a glass of milk?"

"Hour, longer."

"Trigger spots?"

In a gingerly fashion she pointed at her cheek, nose, and forehead.

"So you really think hypnosis won't work! Then why see me?"

"Nothing helps, one more try only cost a little more money. Everybody says no cure. I read medical books."

This was far from a satisfactory history, but the simplicity and honesty of her answers and her entire manner and behavior were convincing of the nature of her illness, its acute and disabling character, the reality of her agonizing pain, and her feeling of desperation. Her pain was beyond her control, it did not constitute a condition favorable to hypnosis; she was well-conditioned over a period of 30 to 40 out of 60 months (as was afterward learned) by the experience of severe uncontrollable pain with occasional brief remissions, and all respected medical authorities had pronounced her condition as incurable and had advised her "to learn to live with it and only as a last resort to try surgery or alcoholic injections." She had been informed that not even surgery was always successful, and surgical residuals were often troublesome. One man only, a psychiatrist who knew the author, advised her to try hypnosis as a "possible help."

In view of this well-established background of learning and conditioning based upon long experience direct hypnosis was regarded as inviting a probable failure. Accordingly the technique for resistant patients was employed. She was allowed to sit and watch the author, which she did with desperate attention. No suggestion of any sort was offered except the statement, made with marked firmness of tone of voice, *"Before I make any beginning of any sort, I want to offer you some general explanation. Then we can begin."* Very gently she nodded her head affirmatively.

The author proceeded at once with the technique described above, referring openly to the typed manuscript to make the repetition of it as verbatim as possible.

She responded to the technique with remarkable ease, demonstrated ideomotor movements of her head and arm catalepsy.

There was added to the technique the additional statements that an inadequate history had been taken, that her unconscious mind would search through all of its memories, and that she would communicate freely (to do so "freely" would imply "comfortably") any and all information desired, there should be a careful search of her unconscious mind of all possible ways and means of controlling, altering, changing, modifying, reinterpreting, lessening, or in any other way doing whatever was possible to meet her needs. She was then given the posthypnotic suggestion that she would again sit in the same chair and depend upon her unconscious mind to understand the author and his wishes. Slowly, perseveratively, she nodded her head in the affirmative.

She was aroused from the trance by saying, "As I just said, 'Before I make any beginning of any sort, I will want to offer you some general explanation. Then we can begin.'" To this was added with a pointed inflection, "Is that all right with you?" Slowly, over a period of two minutes, she opened her eyes, shifted her position, wiggled her fingers, twisted her hands, and then answered very easily and comfortably in marked contrast to her previous labored and guarded answers, "That will be perfectly all right." Immediately, in a most startled fashion, she exclaimed, "Oh my goodness, what happened? My voice is all right and it doesn't hurt to talk." With this she gently closed her mouth and slowly tightened the masseter muscles. Promptly she opened her mouth and said, "No, the neuralgia is there just as severe as ever, but I'm talking without any pain. That's funny. I don't understand. Since this attack began, it's been almost impossible to talk, and I don't feel the air on my trigger points." She fanned her cheek, nose, and right forehead, then gently touched her nose with a resulting spasm of extreme pain.

When this had subsided she said, "I'm not going to try the other trigger spots even if my face does feel different and I have normal speech."

Resistant Patients

She was asked, "How long have you been in this room?" Wonderingly she replied, "Oh, five minutes, at the very most 10, but not really that long." The face of the clock was turned toward her (its position had been carefully changed during her trance). In utter bewilderment she exclaimed, "But that's impossible. The clock shows more than an hour!" Pausing, she slid her watch from under her sleeve and said again (since her watch and the clock agreed) "But that's utterly impossible," to which the author said with great intensity, *"Yes, it is quote utterly impossible unquote but not in this office."* (The indirect hypnotic suggestion is obvious to the reader but it was not to the patient.)

She was given an appointment for the next day and rapidly ushered out of the office.

Upon entering the office she was asked before she took her seat, "And how did you sleep last night. Did you dream?"

"No, no dreams, but I kept waking up over and over all night long, and I kept having the funny thought that I was waking up to take a rest from sleeping or something."

She was told, *"Your unconscious mind understands very well and can work hard,* but first I want a fully history on you *before we work,* so sit down and just answer my questions."

Searching inquiries revealed a well-adjusted parental home, a happy childhood, and excellent college, marital, economic, social, and professional adjustments. It was also learned that her first attack had begun in 1958, had lasted continuously for 18 months during which time she had futilely sought medical or surgical aid from various well-known clinics, had undergone psychiatric examinations to rule out possible psychogenic factors, and had consulted various prominent neurologists. She was a psychiatric social worker and had a cheerful habit of softly whistling merry tunes almost continuously while at work or even walking down the street. She was exceedingly well-liked by her colleagues and explained that she had been referred to the author by an old-time friend of his, but that all others had commented most unfavorably about hypnosis. To this she added, "Just meeting a medical man who uses hypnosis has already helped me. I can talk easily, and this morning when I drank my glass of milk I did it in less than five minutes, and it usually takes an hour or more. So it wasn't a mistake to come here."

The reply was given, "I'm glad of that." Her eyes glazed, and spontaneously she developed a deep trance.

The details of the indirect suggestions to the effect that her unconscious could do what it desired will not be given. Partial remarks, remarks with implications, double binds, and making one thing contingent upon something entirely unrelated when read seem much too meaningless to report. When spoken, the intonations, the inflections, the emphases, the pauses, and all the varying implications and contingencies and double binds that could thus be created set into action a wealth of activities for which variously disguised instructions could be given. For example one statement was that the cracking of a Brazil nut with her teeth on the right side of her mouth would really be most painful, but, thank goodness, she had better sense than to try to crack Brazil nuts or hickory nuts with her teeth, especially on the right side of her mouth for the reason that it would be so painful *and not at all like eating.* The implication here is most emphatically that eating is not painful. Another was, "It's just too bad that that first bite of filet mignon will be so painful when *the rest of it will be so good.*" Again the implication could not be fully recognized, since the author immediately digressed to some other type of suggestion.

She was aroused from the trance state by the simple remark, "Well, that's all for today." Slowly she awakened and looked expectantly at the author. Pointedly he directed her attention to the clock. She exclaimed, "But I just got here and told you about the milk, and [looking at her watch] a whole hour has gone by! Where did it go?" Airily, flippantly (so that she could not suspect the reply) the author said, "Oh, the *lost time has gone to join the lost pain,*" and she was handed her appointment card for the next day and quickly ushered out of the office.

The next day she entered the office to declare, "I had filet mignon last night and the first bite was awful agony. But the rest of it was wonderful. You can't imagine how good it was, and the funny thing is that when I combed my hair this morning, I got a silly urge to jerk locks of it here and there. It made me feel so foolish but I did it, and I was watching my strange behavior and I noticed my hand resting on my right forehead. It isn't a trigger spot any more. See [demonstrating], I can touch it anywhere."

At the end of four hour-long sessions her pain was gone, and she raised the question at the fifth, "Maybe I ought to go back home." In a jocular manner the author said, *"But you haven't learned how to get over the recurrences!"*

Immediately her eyes glazed, closed, a deep trance ensued, and the author remarked, *"It always feel so good when you stop hitting your thumb with a hammer."*

A pause, then her body stiffened in a sudden spasm of pain, and then almost as quickly relaxed, and she smiled happily. Flippantly the author said, "Oh, phooey, you need more practice than that, *work up a sweat with a half dozen,* that will really make you realize that you've had excellent practice." (Flippancy does not belong in a dangerous or threatening situation, only where the outcome is certain to be pleasing.) Obediently she did as asked, and beads of perspiration formed on her forehead. When she had finally relaxed, the comment was made, "Honest toil brings beads of perspiration to the brow—there's a box of tissue there, why not dry your face." Taking her glasses off, and still in the trance, she reached for a sheet of tissue and mopped her face. She dried her right cheek and her nose as briskly as she had the painless left side of her face. No mention of this was made directly, but the seemingly irrelevant comment was made, "You know, it's nice to do things remarkably well and yet not know it." She merely looked puzzled except for an odd little smile of satisfaction. (Her unconscious was not yet "sharing" the loss of the trigger spots of her cheek and nose.)

She was aroused with the statement, "And now for tomorrow," handed her appointment card, and promptly dismissed.

As she entered the office at the next appointment, she remarked, "I just am at a loss about everything today. I don't need to come, but I'm here and I don't know why. All I know is the steak tastes good and I can sleep on my right side and everything is all right, but here I am." The answer given was, "Certainly you are here; just sit down and I'll tell you why. Today is your 'doubt day,' since anybody who has lost that much trigeminal neuralgia so fast is entitled to some doubts. So, slap your left cheek hard." Promptly she administered a swift, stinging slap, laughed, and said, "Well, I'm obedient, and that slap really stung."

With a yawn and a stretch the author said, "Now slap your right cheek the same way." There was marked hesitation followed by a quick slapping movement, the force of which was greatly reduced at the last fraction of a second. The author promptly remarked rather mockingly, "Pulled your punch, pulled your punch, had a doubt, didn't you, but how does your face feel?" With a look of astonishment she answered, "Why, it's all right, the trigger point is gone and there is no pain." "Right. Now do as I told you *and no more pulling your punch.*" (One does not yawn and stretch and speak mockingly to a patient who might have agonizing pain, but she could not analyze this.)

Very quickly and forcibly she slapped her right cheek and nose with a stinging blow and remarked, "I did have a doubt the first time but I haven't got any now, not even about my nose because I hit that too, but I didn't have that in mind." Thoughtfully she paused and then struck her forehead hard with her fist. She remarked, "Well, there's the end of doubts," her tone of voice both jocular and yet intensely pleased. In a similar manner the author remarked, "Astonishing how some people have to have a little understanding literally pounded into their heads." Her immediate reply was, "It's obvious there was room for it." We both laughed and then, with a sudden change of manner to one of utter intentness and gravity, she was told with slow heavy emphasis, *"There is one thing more I want to tell you."* Her eyes glazed, a deep trance ensued. With careful, impressive enunciation she was given the following posthypnotic suggestion. "You like to whistle, you like music, you like meaningful songs. Now I want you to make up a song and a melody using the words 'I can have you anytime I want you, But, Baby there ain't never gonna be a time when I want you,' and forever and always, as you whistle that tune you will know, and I do not need to explain, since you know!" Slowly, perseveratively, her head nodded affirmatively. (The burden of responsibility was hers, the means was hers.)

She was aroused by the simple statement, "Time really travels fast, doesn't it?" Promptly she awakened and looked at the clock and said, "I'll never understand it." Before she could proceed, she was interrupted with, "Well, the deed is done and cannot be undone, so let the dead past bury its dead. Bring me only one more good tomorrow and you will go home tomorrow with another good tomorrow and another and another, and all the other good tomorrows are forever yours. Same time" (meaning appointment for the next day at the same hour). She left the office without delay.

The final interview was simply one of a deep trance, a systematic, comprehensive review by her within her own mind of all of her accomplishments and the gentle request to believe with utter intensity in the goodness of her own body's potentials in meeting her needs and to be *"highly amused* when the skeptics suggest that you have had remissions before followed by relapses." (The author is well aware of the deadliness of skeptical disparaging remarks and of the engendering of iatrogenic disease.) Correspondence received since her return home has confirmed her freedom of pain and also that a neurologist, antagonistic toward hypnosis, offered her a long argument to the effect that the relief she experienced would be most transient and that there would be a relapse (an unwitting effort to produce iatrogenic disease). She related this, stating that his argument had made her feel "highly amused," thereby quoting directly from the author's own posthypnotic suggestion.

DISCUSSION AND COMMENTS

In previous publications this author has repeatedly indicated indirectly or directly that the induction of hypnotic states and phenomena is primarily a matter of communication of ideas and the elicitation of trains of thought and associations within the subject and consequent behavioral responses. It is not a matter of the operator *doing* something to subjects or *compelling* them to do things or even *telling them what to do and how to do it*. When trances are so elicited, they are still a result of ideas, associations, mental processes and understandings already existing and merely aroused within the subjects themselves. Yet too many investigators working in the field regard *their activities* and *their intentions and desires* as the effective forces, and they actually uncritically believe that their own utterances to the subject elicit, evoke, or initiate specific responses without seeming to realize that what they say or do serves only as a means to stimulate and arouse in the subjects past learnings, understandings, and experiential acquisitions, some consciously, some unconsciously acquired. For example the affirmative nodding of the head and the negative shaking of the head are not deliberate, intentional, supervised learning, and yet become a part of vertilized or nonverbalized overt communication, or an expression of the mental processes of the person, who thinks he is merely listening to a lecturer addressing an audience, which is unrecognized by the self but visible to others. Then, too, as another example, one learns to talk and to associate speech with hearing, and we need only to watch the small child learning to read to realize that the printed word, like the spoken word, becomes associated with lip movements and, as experiments have shown, with subliminal laryngeal speech. Hence when a severe stutterer endeavors to talk, definite effort is required by listeners to keep their lips and tongue from moving and to refrain from saying the words for the stutterer. Yet there never was any formalized or even indirect teaching of the listeners to move their lips, their tongue, or to speak the words for the stutterer. Nor does the stutterer want any other person to do it; he even resents it strongly. But this experiential learning is unconsciously acquired and is elicited by stimuli not even intended to do so but which set into action mental processes which the listener at an involuntary level, often uncontrollable and even known to be likely to incur bitter resentment on the part of the stutterer. The classic joke in this connection is that of the stutterer who approached a stranger and stammered painfully a request for directions. The stranger pointed to his ears and shook his head negatively, and the stutterer made his inquiry again of another bystander, who gave the directions. Thereupon the bystander asked the man who had indicated that he was deaf why he had not replied, and received the badly stuttered reply of, "Do you think I wanted my head knocked off?" His reply disclosed eloquently his full knowledge of his own intense resentments when somebody tried to "help" him to talk or seemed to mock him.

Yet the stutterer has not asked directly or indirectly for the other person to say his words for him; the listeners know it will be resented and do not want to do it, yet the distressing stimuli of stuttered words elicit their own long-established patterns of speech. So it is with the stimuli, verbal or otherwise, employed in induction techniques, and no one can predict with utter certainty just how a subject is going to use such stimuli. One names or indicates possible ways, but the subjects behave in accord with their learnings. Hence the importance of loosely organized, comprehensive, permissive suggestions and the relative unimportance of ritualistic, traditional techniques blindly used in rote fashion.

On several occasions this author has had opportunity to do special work with congenitally deaf people and those who had acquired nerve deafness in childhood, one an instance of a man who acquired nerve deafness after the age of 40. All of these people had been trained in "lip reading," although most of them explained to the author that "lip reading" was "face reading," and all of them could do sign language. To prove this one of these deaf people took the author to listen to a Sunday sermon by a heavily bearded minister and, by sign language, "translated" to show that he was "face reading," since the author then could read sign language. Further experimentation with this deaf man disclosed that if the minister spoke in a monotone or whispered, his face could not be "read."

With these deaf people an experiment was done in which it was explained that an assistant would write on a blackboard various words and that several adults (college level) would face the blackboard and merely silently watch the writing, making no comment of any sort. It was also explained to these adults that, separately, strangers would be brought in and placed in a chair facing them with their backs to the blackboard and continuing to face them as the assistant did the writing. They were not told that the strangers were deaf and could "lip read."

The deaf persons were fully aware that they were to "read the faces" before them and that they would be reading silently what the assistant was writing, but one additional fact was not disclosed.

In beautiful Spencerian script in large letters the assistant wrote words of varying numbers of syllables. What only the author and the assistant knew was that the words were written to form designs of a square, a diamond, a star and a triangle by the process of placing the words at the strategic points of the angles of the figures. A circle (the last figure) had been previously written on a black cardboard and was hung up on the blackboard. This latter was formed by the fewest possible and shortest words to permit easier reading as well as the design recognition.

The deaf persons were sitting behind a barrier just high enough to conceal their hands. As the assistant wrote, the author sat so he could see only the deaf persons' hands. The author could not see the blackboard nor did he know the order of the designs or what the words were. He did know that a list of possible words had been made by him and the assistant but that only about a third of them would be required and that the assistant would make his own choices. Furthermore for each deaf person each design except the circle would be in a different sequential order.

One subject (the deaf woman who had acquired nerve deafness after the age of 40) made a perfect score. Not only were the written words "read" by her in the faces of the adults watching the writing, but so were the identities of the designs. Moreover she told the author in sign language that there was "something wrong" with the words "square," "diamond," and "triangle" and something was "a little bit funny" about the word "star," and something "very funny" about the word "circle." One must add, however, that this woman was exceedingly paranoid, psychotically so. None of the others had a perfect record. One man gave all the replies except "circle." He "sign languaged" that the last series of words was written differently, but he could not explain how he identified all of the written words forming the circle. The other subjects all identified the written words, experienced some mild confusion about the words forming the circle, and missed "star" and "circle." This group all felt that they had missed two of the "words." All except the paranoid psychotic patient were allowed to see the blackboard, and the observers all were surprised to find that the strangers had read their facial expressions for both the design recognition as well as the written words.

This experiment was long in the author's mind in relation to the development of his own personal approach to the induction of hypnosis. Therefore, keeping well and clearly in mind his actual wishes, the author casually and permissively (or apparently permissively) presents a wealth of seemingly related ideas in a manner carefully calculated to hold or to fixate the subject's attention rather than the subject's eyes or to induce a special muscle state. Instead every effort is made to direct the subject's attention to processes within himself, to his own body sensations, his memories, emotions, thoughts, feelings, ideas, past learnings, past experiences, and past conditions, as well as to elicit current conditionings, understandings and ideas.

In this way, it is believed by the author, hypnosis can be best induced and a good hypnotic technique so organized can be remarkably effective even under seemingly highly adverse circumstances. However, the author has so far always failed with behavior merely personally objectionable to the subject but entirely legitimate. An account of an instance of this is given in this volume, Section 2 (See "Another example of confusion in trance induction"), and more than one otherwise compliant subject has "shut off my hearing," or awakened.

In this particular paper a total of four subjects were dealt with by a single technique with only slight modifications to meet the requirements of sex, intelligence, and educational level. All four represented different types of resistance, different backgrounds, and different types of problems. One was a rather severely maladjusted person, the second was unhappily governed by peculiar, circumscribed, uncontrollable maladjustments, the third had a long history of general maladjustment eventuating in a state hospital commitment with a diagnosis of "psychosis, paranoid type, probably schizophrenic," and the fourth was a patient diagnosed repeatedly at competent clinics and by competent neurologists and psychiatrists as suffering from a hopeless organic condition characterized by occasional brief remissions and treatable only in a partially satisfactory manner by organic measures entailing undesirable results. Five years' experience of excruciating pain had firmly convinced and conditioned this last patient to the understanding that the condition was untouchable by psychological measures, and only hopeless desperation led to the seeking of hypnotherapy.

The technique employed so successfully upon four such diverse patients was essentially a rigid arresting and fixation of their attention and then placing them in a situation of extracting from the author's words certain meanings and significances that would fit into the patterns of their own thinking and understandings, their own emotions and wishes, their own memories, ideas, understandings, learnings, conditioning, associational, and experiential acquisitions, and into their own patterns of response to stimuli. The author did not really instruct them. Rather he made statements casually, repetitiously, permissively, yet authoritatively, but in a manner so disguised that their attention was not directed away from their own inner world of experience to the author but remained fixated upon their own inner processes. Consequently a hypnotic trance state developed, one in which they were highly receptive to any general ideas that might be offered to them to examine and to evaluate and to discover for themselves any applicability to their problems. For example the second patient was not told to develop his brief and "silly" panics, nor was he told what plan to work out governing his control of his daily trips. Nor was the origin of his condition ever asked for; his intelligence told him it had an origin, and there was no need to tell him to search for it.

As for the patient with trigeminal neuralgia, neither analgesia nor anaesthesia was suggested. Nor was there a detailed personal history taken. She had been repeatedly diagnosed by competent clinics, neurologists, and psychiatrists as suffering from an organic painful disease, not a psychogenic problem. She knew these facts, the author could understand without any further mention or repetition. Neither was she offered a long and "helpful" discussion of what pain was and various methods of lessening or minimizing, altering or reconditioning her suffering. *No matter what the author said, she was dependent upon her own resources only.*

Hence no more than was necessary was said to initiate those inner processes of her own behavior, responses, and functionings which would be of service to her. Therefore direct mention was made that the first bite of the filet mignon would be painful *but that the rest of it would be so very good.* Out of this simple yet really involved statement she had to abstract all the meanings and implications, and in the process of so doing she was forced into an unwitting and favorably unequal comparison of many long years of comfortable and satisfying eating free from pain, with only a few years of painful eating.

To summarize, in the therapeutic use of hypnosis one primarily meets the patients' needs on the terms they themselves propose; and then one fixates the patients' attention, through adequate respect for and utilization of their method of presenting their problem, to their own inner processes of mental functioning. This is accomplished by casual but obviously earnest and sincere remarks, seemingly explanatory but intended solely to stimulate a wealth of the patients' own patterns of psychological functioning, so that they meet their problems by use of their learnings already acquired, or that will develop as they continue their progress.

14. Pantomime Techniques in Hypnosis and the Implications

Milton H. Erickson

In the early experiments done by this author on hypnotic deafness, verbal communication having been lost as a result of the induced deafness, the value of pantomime was recognized, used, and then replaced by written communications as easier.

The Pantomime Technique as a hypnotic technique complete in itself resulted from an invitation to address an affiliated society of American Society of Clinical Hypnosis, the Grupo de Estudio sobre Hipnosis Clinica y Experimental, in Mexico City in January, 1959.

Just before the meeting the author was informed that he was to demonstrate hypnosis as the introduction to his lecture by employing as a subject a nurse they had selected who knew nothing about hypnosis nor about the author and who could neither speak nor understand English—they already knew that I could not speak nor understand Spanish. They had explained privately to her that I was a North American doctor who would need her silent assistance and they informed her of our mutual language handicaps and assured her that she would be fully respected by me. Hence she was totally unaware of what was expected of her.

This unexpected proposal to the author led to rapid thinking about his past partial uses of pantomime by gesture, facial expressions, etc. This lead to the conclusion that this unexpected development offered a unique opportunity. A completely pantomime technique would have to be used, and the subject's own state of mental uncertainty and eagerness to comprehend would effect the same sort of readiness to accept any comprehensible communication by pantomime as is effected by clear-cut definite communications in the Confusion Technique ("The confusion technique in hypnosis" this volume, Section 2).   She was then brought through a side door to confront me. Silently we looked at each other, and then—as I had done many times previously with seminarians in the United States in seeking out what I consider clinically to be "good responsive" subjects before the beginning of a seminar and hence before I was known to

---

Reprinted with permission from *The American Journal of Clinical Hypnosis*, July, 1964, 7, 64–70.

them—I walked toward her briskly and smilingly and extended my right hand, and she extended hers. Slowly I shook hands with her, staring her fully in the eyes even as she was doing to me, and slowly I ceased smiling. As I let loose of her hand, I did so in an uncertain, irregular fashion, slowly withdrawing it, now increasing the pressure slightly with my thumb, then with the little finger, then with the middle finger, always in an uncertain, irregular, hesitant manner, and finally so gently withdrawing my hand that she would have no clear-cut awareness of just when I had released her hand or at what part of her hand I had last touched. At the same time I slowly changed the focus of my eyes by altering their convergence, thereby giving her a minimal but appreciable cue that I seemed to be looking not at but through her eyes and off into the distance. Slowly the pupils of her eyes dilated, and as they did so, I gently released her hand completely, leaving it in midair in a cataleptic position. A slight upward pressure on the heel of her hand raised it slightly. Then catalepsy was demonstrated in the other arm also, and she remained staring unblinkingly.

Slowly I closed my eyes, and so did she. I immediately opened my eyes, stepped behind her, and began explaining what I had done in English, since most of the audience knew English fairly well. She made no startle response, and did not even seem to hear me. I gently touched her ankle and then gently lifted her foot, leaving her to stand cataleptically on one leg. One of the doctors knew I had a smattering of German and held up his fist, opened it, saying questioningly, "die Augen." Gently I touched her closed lids and gave a slight upward pressure. She slowly opened them and looked at me with her pupils still dilated. I pointed to my feet, then to her upraised cataleptic foot, and signaled a downward movement. She frowned in puzzlement apparently at seeing both her hands and her foot uplifted, then smiled at my downward signal toward her foot only, and she put her foot down with what appeared to me to be an expression of some slight embarrassment or bewilderment. The arm catalepsy remained unchanged.

Several of the doctors called her by name and spoke to her in Spanish. She merely looked at me attentively, making no involuntary head or eye movements so common when addressed from some distance away by someone else, nor did she seem to pay any further attention to her hands.

I was asked in English if she could see the audience, since apparently she could not hear them. I moved her hands up, down, and across while she seemed to watch them and my eyes alternately. Then I pointed to my eyes and to her eyes by bringing my fingers close to them; than I made a futile, hopeless sweeping gesture of my right hand toward the audience as I assumed a look of blank surprise and wonderment as I faced the audience as a pantomime of not seeing anybody. She did likewise, showed a startled reaction and asked in Spanish, as I was told later, "Where are they? The doctors are supposed to be here?" Several of the doctors spoke to reassure her, but she merely continued to look frightened.

I promptly attracted her attention by putting my fingers close to her eyes, then to mine, then I lifted her hand and looked with a pleased smile at the ring on her hand as if I admired it. Her fright vanished apparently.

One of the audience asked me how I would awaken her. I showed her the second hand on my watch, marked out 10 seconds of time by synchronizing a finger movement with the second hand movement. She watched intently. Then I had her watch me close my eyes, beat out about 10 seconds, and then I opened my eyes with an upright alert jerk of my head. Then I smiled and with a nod of my head and a movement of my hand I indicated that she was to do likewise. As she did so, I stepped back rapidly, and when she opened her eyes she saw me at the far end of the platform. I immediately walked forward briskly with a pleased smile and extended my hand in greeting. This reestablished the original way in which we had met and she awakened immediately and shook hands with me as she looked me over. I bowed and said, "Thank you very much. I am most appreciative," as if dismissing her. One of the doctors translated my remarks; I repeated myself and again shook hands in a dismissal fashion. She looked puzzled and uncertain, so one of the group told her she could now leave. She left the room in what to me seemed a most puzzled fashion.

Later I was informed that she had developed a total amnesia for the entire experience, and had expressed wonderment at my immediate dismissal of her when she was supposed to assist me. She also expressed disbelief in hypnosis but volunteered as a subject, promptly developed a profound trance, recalled all of the events of her experience with the author including the "departure [negative hallucination] of the audience" and her "puzzlement" when dismissed, but when aroused from this trance, she again manifested a complete amnesia for both trances. She was subsequently used extensively by members of that group as an assistant and as an experimental and instructional subject.

The second unexpected, completely pantomime induction was done in January of 1961 during a visit to Caracas, Venzuela. I had been invited to tour the Hospital Concepcion Palacios during which I was asked to address the staff on the use of hypnosis in obstetrics at an impromptu meeting in the conference room. One of the audience suggested that I demonstrate as I discussed the phenomena of hypnosis. Remembering my experience in Mexico City I asked if I might work with some young woman who did not know the purpose of my visit there, who did not understand English, and who had had no experience in hypnosis of any sort. Three young women were brought in, and I looked them over and selected the one who gave me a clinical impression of what I term "responsive attentiveness." I asked that the others be dismissed and that she be told that I wished her cooperation while I lectured. Very carefully my translator so informed her without giving her any more information, and she nodded her head affirmatively.

Stepping over to her and standing face to face with her, I explained in English for those who understood it that they were to watch what I did. My translator kept silent, and the young lady eyed me most attentively and wonderingly.

I showed the girl my hands, which were empty, and then I reached over with my right hand and gently encircled her right wrist with my fingers, barely touching it except in an irregular, uncertain, changing pattern of tactile stimulation with my fingertips. The result was to attract her full, attentive, expectant, wondering interest in what I was doing. With my right thumb I made slight tactile pressure on the latero-volar-ulnar aspect of her wrist, as if to turn it upward; at the same moment at the area of the radial prominence I made a slightly downward tactile pressure at the dorso-lateral aspect of her wrist with my third finger; also at the same time I made various gentle touches with my other fingers somewhat comparable in intensity but nonsuggestive of direction. She made an automatic response to the directive touches without differentiating them consciously from the other touches, evidently paying attention first to one touch and then to another. As she began responding, I increased varyingly the directive touches without decreasing the number and variation of the other distracting tactile stimuli. Thus I suggested lateral and upward movements of her arm and hand by varying tactile stimuli intermingled with a decreasing number of nondirective touches. These responsive automatic movements, the origin of which she did recognize, startled her, and as her pupils dilated, I so touched her wrist with a suggestion of an upward movement that her arm began rising, so gently discontinuing the touch that she did not notice the tactile withdrawal, and the upward movement continued. Quickly shifting my fingertips to hers, I varied the touches to direct in an unrecognizable fashion a full upward turning of her palm, and then other touches on her fingertips served to straighten some fingers, to bend others, and a proper touch on the tip of the straightened fingers led to a continuing bending of her elbow. This led to a slow moving of her hand toward her eyes. As this began, I attracted with my fingers her visual attention and directed her attention to my eyes. I focussed my eyes for distant viewing as if looking through and beyond her, moved my fingers close to my eyes, slowly closed my eyes, took a deep sighing breath, sagged my shoulders in a relaxed fashion, and then pointed to her fingers, which were approaching her eyes.

She followed my pantomimed instructions and developed a trance that withstood the efforts of the staff to secure her attention or to awaken her in response to suggestions and commands given in English.

I asked for her name, and one of the staff gave it to me in rapid Spanish, the translator repeated it, laboriously enunciating the name so that I could grasp the phonetics. She made no response to anything the staff or the translator said or did, merely standing passively. When someone tried to push her, she became actively rigid but made no other response. I led her about the room, touching her eyelids to indicate that she was to open them, and then indicated a chair, in which she seated herself. Even with her eyes open, she seemed oblivious to everyone there and to all auditory stimulation.

I learned that she was a resident physician and that she had not yet been introduced to hypnosis. While she sat with her eyes open and apparently unseeingly and unhearingly, I discussed hypnosis.

At the close of my remarks I awakened her by turning to her and indicating she was to stand. Then, with the gesture of brushing my palms across each other as if the task were all done, I smiled at her and bowed. The hypnotic facial expression disappeared, she looked about the room and asked, as I was told later, "What am I to do?" while I, not understanding, bowed and said "Gracias, Señorita." She looked puzzled, my translator explained her task was done, and she left in a puzzled manner. I then began to answer questions from the audience.

The following August of the same year—that is, six months later— I visited there and again lectured to the staff. My former subject was present in the audience, and when I beckoned to her to come up on the platform, she did so in a pleased fashion but developed spontaneously a deep trance just before she reached the desk at which I sat.

She had in the meantime not only been a hypnotic subject for others but had also used it on her patients. As a result, despite the author's linguistic handicap, she could anticipate some of the phenomena that the author wished to demonstrate. In addition a translator conveyed his requests to her after rapport was transferred to him. This transfer of rapport was effected by the process of pointing to my right hand, then to hers, shaking hands with her, then withdrawing my hand, indicating it, reaching over and shaking hands with my translator while I indicated to her with my left hand that she was to see the translator and to do likewise, and as they shook hands they exchanged greetings in Spanish.

The next unexpected completely pantomime initial induction was done in Venezuela that same month before the Medical Society in Caracas. Just as I was about to begin my lecture I was courteously interrupted by the officers and the explanation was offered that many of the doctors present did not believe in hypnosis, that there was much conviction that I had a confederate with whose aid I would perpetrate a hoax. They were obviously most distressed to tell me this but explained that as the officers of the society they had been delegated to ask me to demonstrate hypnosis by maintaining a complete silence and to select someone from the large audience for whom they could secure a valid identification. I replied that I hoped the subject I secured would not be able to understand English.

In the rear of the auditorium I saw a woman about 30 years old who gave every evidence of what I term that "responsiveness," which I personally consider a most helpful indication of hypnotizability. I pointed the woman out to my translator, she was questioned for her identity, was discovered to be the wife of a physician who did not believe in hypnosis, and that she too did not believe in it and had never seen it. However, she readily came to the platform, differing from the Mexico City nurse in that she knew hypnosis was under consideration. As she approached me, I asked, "And if you please, what is your name?" She turned to the translator and asked him what I had said and this was broadcast by the public address system present. Thus the point was made that she did not understand English.

Essentially the same technique as was used in Mexico City was employed with the same hypnotic results. However, one addition was made. I patted the back of my hand gently during the demonstration and smiled as if I liked the sensation. I did likewise to her hand, and she too smiled.

Then I brushed off the back of my hand as if I were brushing away all sensation. I then pinched and twisted the skin of my hand in an obviously painful fashion but wore a look of profound astonishment and wonderment as if I felt nothing and then smiled happily. I reached for her hand, did likewise, and in astonishment she turned to my translator who, ill at ease on my account, had assured her as she came to the platform that he would remain on the platform as would the officers, and she should feel free at any time to speak to him.

As I forcibly pinched and twisted the skin of her left hand, the officers crowded around, did likewise, and the woman also tested her hand. She then asked the officers what had happened to her hand and asked if it (her hand) were dead, speaking in what the translator later reported as a tone of distress. A doctor in the audience and several others in the audience reassured her. She did not seem to hear them, and a negative hallucination of the audience, visual and auditory was spontaneously manifested. But the translator's explanation was readily heard by her, as were those of the officers on the platform. In other words she had interpreted the platform situation initially as signifying rapport with those who were there but not with the audience, even though her husband was in the audience.

A doubting Thomas in the audience declared in Spanish that he was fully convinced of the validity of hypnosis and asked the officers of the society if he could volunteer as a subject. This request was translated to me. Keeping the woman still there, I accepted his offer, and results similar to those with the woman were secured. However, he aroused from the trance state with a total amnesia and asked the translator to tell me to begin the hypnosis, a request that was broadcast by the public address system. He was reinduced, and the translator told him in Spanish, "After awakening, remember all." Upon awakening from the trance, he was most effervescent in his excited pleasure, and the woman too was much impressed by what she had seen occur with the Spanish physician. In each instance the awakening of the subjects was done by grasping their hands firmly, and since both had their eyes open, shaking their hands briskly and shaking my head briskly as if arousing and clearing my mind. Since the doctor had seen this maneuver with the woman, he responded more quickly than she had.

In brief, hypnosis is a cooperative experience depending upon a communication of ideas by whatever means available, and verbalized, ritualistic, traditional rote-memory techniques for the induction of hypnosis are no more than one means of beginning to learn how to communicate ideas and understandings in a joint task in which one person voluntarily seeks aid or understandings from another.

In two experiences in hypnotizing deaf-and-dumb persons sign language was employed with the added pantomime of listlessness and fatigue of movement in making the sign language. With these two subjects rapport was lost if they closed their eyes, and resort had to be made to a sharp shaking of them by the shoulder to awaken them, such a cue having been incorporated into the trance-inducing suggestions originally. When the measure of suggesting that they keep their eyes open in the deep trance was used, their peripheral vision greatly decreased and became so central in character that perhaps only one finger of a letter sign would be seen unless instructions to the contrary were given. However, a total of four trances with two such subjects is only adequate to state that the usual hypnotic trance and attendant phenomena can be induced in the neurologically deaf-and-dumb by sign language, but that there appears to be a profound loss of peripheral vision with a consequent loss of some rapport. This raises an intriguing question of why a trance should cause, in such subjects who are so dependent upon sight, a much greater loss of peripheral vision than this writer has encountered in trances in many thousand of people with normal speech and hearing, where a more limited loss of peripheral vision is very common. If, however, in such subjects a trance is induced by pantomimed instructions to keep their eyes open and to read lip movements, there is no such loss of peripheral vision even though they had previously spontaneously seen only one digit of a three-finger sign. In explanation of this finding one of the subjects explained, "Lip reading is really face reading; sign language is reading one sign."

Similarly, if during the induction sign language instructions are given that after a trance is developed they are to receive instruction through written communication, the loss of peripheral vision is minimal. This was explained by the same subject as, "In reading you see the paper or the blackboard too." Unfortunately the data on these subjects are insufficient to warrant further discussion.

The first and only previous report on the subject of deaf-mute induction of which this author is aware was presented by Dr. Alfredo Isasi of Barcelona, Spain at the Fifth European Congress of Psychosomatic Medicine in April 1962, and published in September 1962 in *La Revista Latino-Americana de Hipnosis Clinica* (Vol. 3, pp. 92–94.) It is entitled "Dos casos de sofrosis en sordomundos—(Two cases of sophrosis (hypnosis) in deaf-mutes." In this report a technique of inducing hypnosis in deaf mutes, a demonstration of which has been filmed, is described in detail. After the initial communication by sign and gesture the hypnotic state was induced through stroking and gentle pressure on the forehead, eyelids, and jawline, and tested by raising the arms gently and releasing them. Relaxation, analgesia, and control of bleeding enabling successful dental work in previously apprehensive, fearful, uncooperative patients was achieved. Two case records of young men deaf-mutes were presented in detail.

COMMENTS

Perhaps the most pertinent aspect of this matter of trance induction by a Pantomime Technique is the ease with which a communication of ideas and understandings can be effected without verbalization and in situations in which the subject may be totally uninformed as to the nature of the proposed task being done by two people of different cultures, languages, social usages, and customs. If then one thinks of the many so-called controlled studies and reports found in the hypnotic literature in which two homogenous groups, one called "experimental," one called "control," are handled by the same experimenter who uses slightly different words but has a full knowledge of what results he expects to secure, one can well wonder just how "controlled" are these experiments.

But when "control subjects" have been previously hypnotized by the experimenter or others or have watched hypnotic inductions and experiments of others by the experimenter, (who, of course, knows that he expects to duplicate hypnotic behavior in the "waking state" of the "control subjects"), one does more than wonder about the experimenter's scientific acumen. To this author both the intelligence and the scientific integrity on the part of the experimenter are in question—seriously so!

In the late 1920's, 30's, and 40's this author did some research involving the comparison of the dream symbolism of Hindu mentally ill patients with that of native-born Massachusetts and Michigan patients, using information obtained from Drs. Lalkaka and Govindaswamy, respectively of Bombay and Mysore, India. Similarly he then used recently drawn pictures of newly admitted mentally ill American patients, which were compared with those collected by Hans Prinzhorn in "Bildnerei Der Geisteskranken" (Verlag, Berlin, 1923) of mentally ill Germans. The similarities were amazing, until one realizes that the dreams and the pictures come from essentially similar human minds even though from different mental states and cultures. In this regard, in a report published in January 1940 in *The Psychoanalytic Quarterly* (V. 9, No. 1, pp. 51–63) this author in association with Lawrence S. Kubie, M.D., commented upon the possible correspondence or homogeneity of unconscious understandings in two people of the same culture. In this report one subject offered a slightly differing wording but precisely the same content as had been worked out *independently* by the subject who did the original cryptic writing in a deep hypnotic trance with no apparent conscious knowledge of its content. The experimenter himself did not know the content of the cryptic writing.

Thus the common dream symbolism of the mentally ill patients of India and of the United States; the common symbolism in the artwork of mentally ill German patients of an earlier era and those of newly admitted mentally ill patients in the United States; the translation of cryptic automatic writing by one hypnotic subject of another subject; along with this report on the Pantomime Technique in hypnosis, all suggest the following: That a parallelism of thought and comprehension processes exists which is not based upon verbalizations evocative of specified responses, but which derives from behavioral manifestations not ordinarily recognized or appreciated at the conscious level of mentation.

In brief, this report on the Pantomime Technique in hypnosis indicates that adequate hypnotic suggestions can be given intentionally without verbalization. It seems reasonable to infer that similar suggestions can also be unintentionally given in pantomime unwittingly to elicit complicated hypnotic phenomena from a subject unacquainted in any way with hypnosis, comparable to the way in which suggestions can be given when the subjects' language and cultural and social usages are unknown to the experimenter, even as the subjects are unacquainted with those of the experimenter.

Hence true experimentation in hypnosis should take into consideration far more than the selected items usually tested. When *control measures* are devised, it should be held constantly in mind that their purpose is to isolate the selected items so that their effect may be evaluated without distortion by factors which may not have even been considered or identified, let alone eliminated or controlled.

15. The "Surprise" and "My-Friend-John" Techniques of Hypnosis: Minimal Cues and Natural Field Experimentation

Milton H. Erickson

At a meeting before a medical society a long discussion was presented of hypnosis and its medical applications. At the close, requests for a demonstration of hypnosis were made, and two young women and a physician about 45 years of age came up to the platform. One of the young women stated, "I have never been hypnotized and I have never seen it done, but I don't think it can be done to me. In fact I am sure it can't be done to me." The other girl said, "I have never seen hypnosis or been hypnotized, but I would like to be." The physician stated, "I'm an impossible subject. I have spent a great deal of time with several other physicians and dentists trying to do into a trance, but I seem to be blocked against it. I would like to have you try, even though it will do no good. I would like to go into a trance even though I know I can't. I can use and I do use hypnosis on my patients, but I am not always sure of the validity of their responses. So I would like to join you on the platform so as to observe better."

He was asked if he were absolutely sure he could not go into a trance. His reply was that he was completely convinced that he could not be hypnotized. A member of the audience then mentioned that he himself had spent a total of approximately 30 hours over a period of time attempting to hypnotize this particular physician with no results whatever.

The girl A (the one who thought she could go into a trance) was asked to sit in a chair to the author's immediate right, the other girl (B) was seated to Miss A's right, and Dr. C was placed to Miss B's right but in a chair at a slight angle, so that he could easily watch the faces of the author and those of both girls. The author's chair was also at a slight angle, to give him a fairly good view of Miss B as well as Miss A and Dr. C.

Addressing Miss B and Dr. C, the author asked them to watch Miss A carefully, since he intended to use her as the demonstration subject. (This in essence

---

Reprinted with permission from *The American Journal of Clinical Hypnosis*, April, 1964, 6, 293–307.

was intended as a potent but indirect and unrecognized suggestion to Miss A.) To Dr. C the author explained in somewhat elaborate detail that he was to exercise his most critical judgment and thus to determine for himself whether or not the various hypnotic phenomena manifested by Miss A were valid in his eyes. (This too was a potent suggestion to Miss A, and it also defined Dr. C's role so that he need not feel resistances.) To Miss B the author remarked that she would undoubtedly enjoy watching the manifestation of hypnotic phenomena, *even though she would not understand all* (with special emphasis on these words) of the hypnotic phenomena that she would see. (Again Miss A was being instructed without my seeming to be doing so, and Dr. C was being informed that there would be more than would be comprehended, presumably by Miss B). The emphasis, very intense, upon the italicized words also gave an indirect suggestion that she and she alone of the three would see "all." None of the three would understand that emphasis at a conscious level of mentation, but all three would hear it and it would leave an unanswered, though unrecognized question in the minds of all of them which could be utilized later.

To Miss A the statement was then made that the hypnotic trance was based entirely upon learning processes within the subject; that it involved the utilization of the unconscious mind and *automatic processes of response;* thus there were given openly but indirectly instructions heard by A, B, and C for "automatic responses." It was stated that there were a *number of techniques* that could be employed and that *some of these* would be described briefly to her so that the *audience* would benefit from the reviewing of the various techniques, an unrecognizable implication that B and C were going to be excluded in some way.

There followed then a seemingly casual but rather full summary of the hand-levitation technique, the spot-on-the-wall and eye-closure technique, two variations of the coin technique, followed by an explanation of the technique I had previously developed and, in the mid-50's, termed jestingly "My-Friend-John Technique." In this, I explained elaborately, a person pretends that someone by the name of John is sitting in a chair, and he gives to that imaginary person, with much feeling and quite intense emphasis, the suggestions of the hand-levitation technique, sensing and feeling his own instructions and *making automatic responses to his own suggestions* in much the same way that one tries to say for the other person the word for which that person seems to be groping. Thereby one learns the "feel" and the "timing" of suggestions. In a typical instance the person tells "My Friend John" to sit comfortably in the empty chair, to place the palms of his hands lightly on his thighs, demonstrating this as the instructions are given, and then there are offered slowly and carefully, with full meaningfulness and intensity, the suggestions of finger, hand, and wrist levitation, the bending of the elbow, each step being illustrated by a slow continuing demonstration of such movements as the suggestions are given. Then it is added that as the hand approaches the face, the eyes will close; that when the fingers touch the face, the eyes will remain closed, a deep breath will be taken, and a deep trance state will accompany the taking of that deep breath and that the trance will continue until the purposes to be accomplished are achieved. This is a technique the author has employed in teaching others and in teaching autohypnosis to others for some legitimate purpose.

All three subjects and the audience listened with complete concentration to this rather extensive explanation. Then in continuation the author said, "And now Miss A, since you are to be the demonstration subject, I would like to use a rather simple technique on you that is often very easy and rapid and which I call the 'Surprise Technique.' It is really very simple. All I want you to do [speaking with quiet intense emphasis] is *to tell me* what *kind,* what *breed,* about what *age* is *that dog there''* (pointing with his extended finger to a bare spot on the platform and looking at that spot with great intensity of interest).

Slowly Miss A turned her head, her pupils dilated, her face showing a rigidity of expression. She looked carefully at the designated spot, and without turning her head back to me, she replied, "It's a Scottie, he's black, and he looks almost exactly like the one I have at home." Slowly she turned her head back to me and asked, "Is he yours? He is about three-quarters grown, like mine." She was asked, "Is he *standing, sitting,* or *lying down?"* Her reply was, "No, he is just sitting there.''

Miss B's face was expressive of marked amazement as she looked first at Miss A and then the bare spot on the floor. She started to say, "But there is no ——'' and her facial expression changed to one of complete bafflement as she turned to Dr. C and heard him say to the author, "That is not a valid hypnotic response. The dog is a collie and not a Scottie, and he is standing up and wagging his tail. I'm a collie fancier myself, and I ought to know. How do you suppose she got the idea of a Scottie, since you didn't suggest it?''

Placatingly the author explained that possibly Miss A did not know the breeds of dogs any better than the author did and he asked Miss A to explain to Dr. C what kind of a dog it was, *pointing to Dr. C* (thus insuring rapport between the two). Slowly Miss A turned to Dr. C, and as she did so Dr. C said, "Her facial expression, her head movements are hypnotic, but that seeing a Scottie instead of the collie—oh, she is hallucinating the collie as a Scottie." As he was making these observations, the author demonstrated catalepsy in Miss A's left arm, an item she did not seem to notice. Dr. C noted this and affirmed it to be genuine catalepsy and completely valid. While he was making this statement, the author slipped out of his chair and stood behind Miss B and whispered to her that she should attempt to force Miss A's arm down. She did so but received no response from Miss A except an increased rigidity, which Dr. C noted by saying, "Her arm catalepsy is becoming more rigid," speaking to the author as if the author were still sitting in the chair beside Miss A. Nor did he give any evidence that he saw Miss B and what she was doing, nor did Miss A seem to see or note Miss B's act. Neither did Miss A seem to give attention to what Dr. C said to the author, nor did Miss A note the author's departure from his chair.

Slowly Miss A explained to Dr. C that the dog was a Scottie, explaining fully

Minimal Cues 343

why it was a Scottie—and she apparently knew a great deal about that breed.

Dr. C disputed her very courteously, pointing out that the dog was a collie—in fact, that it resembled one to a marked degree that he had once owned. Dr. C made several side remarks to the author as if the author were still sitting in the original chair, commenting on Miss A's trance as valid, but Miss A gave no evidence of hearing these remarks, since they were not addressed to her. While this exchange between Miss A and Dr. C was continuing as well as the side remarks to the author as if he were still sitting in the original chair, the author had stepped over to Dr. C's right side, lifted his right arm up, and left it in an awkward cataleptic position. Then with his left arm the author reached over in such a fashion that the audience could see but Miss B could not, and gave a lock of Miss B's hair a sudden jerk; at just a later moment with his right hand he gave a similar sudden, even harder jerk to a lock of Dr. C's hair. Miss B looked up at the author in amazement, too startled to say anything, but her facial expression was one expressive of pain. As she looked up, she saw the yanking of Dr. C's hair. Immediately she looked at Dr. C's face and saw no evidence that he had felt the pulling of his hair but was continuing his argument with Miss A about the identity of the dog. (Miss B was beginning to see ALL the hypnotic phenomena, so she thought). The audience was now well aware of the fact that Dr. C had unaccountably and inexplicably developed a profound somnambulistic trance. He remained completely unaware of the audience and of Miss B and continued apparently to see and to address the author as if he had not changed his position. Miss A also continued to react as if the author were beside her.

Reaching down from behind, the author took Miss B's left hand and moved it back and up and nodded his head toward Miss A's head. Gingerly Miss B took a lock of Miss A's hair, gave it a tentative tug, and then several much harder tugs without receiving any response from Miss A and without interrupting the obviously interesting discussion Miss A and Dr. C were having about collies and Scotties. Nor did Dr. C notice this—in fact, neither Miss A nor Dr. C seemed to be aware of Miss B, an item of fact bewildering to her and most obvious to the audience.

At this point the author began speaking to the audience from behind Dr. C, explaining what had happened. Everybody including Miss B noted that the author's speaking to the audience did not interfere with Dr. C seeing and speaking to the author as if in the original chair, even while the author was addressing the audience from behind Dr. C. Dr. C continued to discuss Miss A and her behavior, continuing to speak as if the author were still in the original chair, and was obviously unresponsive to the sound of the author's voice as he addressed the audience. The author offered the explanation to the audience, that although they had witnessed in full an orderly systematic trance induction, they did not know that they were so doing, and that they were merely overlooking what was being done while waiting for the author to do something else more in accord with their general expectations. (Miss B heard this, too, but made no apparent personal application of the remark to herself).

It was explained that the seemingly *casual incidental explanation of various trance inductions* was only an easy way of effectively capturing the attention of the subjects and narrowing down their field of conscious awareness. But since the audience was there *to hear* and *to see* what the author as well as the subjects were doing, they had at least some mental counterset for any trance induction for them at the time. At this point one of the audience raised his hand and, when nodded permission to speak, he declared that "the counterset was not sufficient for me, because I saw *my boat* there instead of a dog, and that surprised me so much that I *came back* to the audience again. But I suppose I did have some counterset, as you call it, or I wouldn't have come back." (Later several others approached the author and reported that they too had hallucinated but only momentarily and then had "returned" to watch anew the demonstration.)

The author continued, "Then when I explained the 'My-Friend-John Technique,' I was careful to emphasize the importance in inducing hypnosis of speaking slowly, impressively, and meaningfully, and literally to 'feel' at the moment within the self the full significance of what was being said. For instance in my own use of the hand-levitation technique I soon learned during the process of developing that technique in my University of Wisconsin days that I almost invariably would find my hand lifting and my eyelids closing. Thus I learned the importance of giving my subjects suggestions in a tone of voice completely expressive of meaningfulness, expectation, and of 'feeling' my words and their meanings within me as a person. When Dr. C volunteered and gave his own history of personal disappointment about being hypnotically induced, and then had spoken of his doubts of validity of the hypnotic phenomena his subjects manifested, I recognized this statement by him as one of genuine interest and significance to him. I also recognized the opportunity it afforded to me to develop what might be called a 'natural field experiment' where nobody, especially neither the subjects nor the audience, could anticipate what would happen, nor could the subjects, who were strangers to me, conceive that an experiment might be done or even to conceive of what the experiment would be nor even what the behavior would be that might develop. For that matter *neither could I predict it*. All I knew was that I wished to demonstrate hypnotic phenomena, that I would try to utilize experimentally whatever phenomena I could elicit, and that I would rely on my knowledge of possible responses to my choice of words, emphases, and inflections to formulate my experiment 'on the spot.' If the experiment failed, nobody would know, and I could try other variations, since I could be reasonably certain of securing at least one hypnotic subject and some hypnotic phenomena, even if I did not know exactly what they would prove to be.

"My-Friend-John Technique is an excellent measure of teaching resistant subjects to go into a trance. I demonstrate it to the resistant patient who comes for therapy but resists, and I demonstrate it so thoroughly and carefully that as he watches me induce a trance in my purely imaginative friend John, he resents so much the waste of his time and money, and becomes so unwittingly responsive while I am hypnotizing 'John,' that he follows 'John's' example and develops a trance without needing to offer resistance. This, therapeutically, is an excellent beginning, since he came for therapy and not a contest. I use it also to teach self-hypnosis in the heterohypnotic situation, and with subjects who are to rehearse at home in relation to study, migraine, obesity, etc.

Therefore, when Dr. C spoke of his doubts of the validity of trance phenomena, I asked him to pass judgment upon the validity of Miss A's trance manifestations. While this was a comprehensible statement to him, it was also an absolute, direct, simple, but emphatic declaration that Miss A was going to go into a trance, and there was no way for her to resist or dispute or even to question that statement, since I had not spoken to her but to Dr. C. But it was also a statement rendering him responsible for the task of evaluating Miss A's behavior adequately. What this implied neither he nor the audience had time to analyze. I was relying on my past experience. How does one validate another's subjective experience? By participating, if possible! For example the swimmer says the water is cold. One can dive in and find out, or at least put in a finger or a toe! But the situation here was different. One cannot validate any hypnotic hallucination as one can a swimmer's subjective reaction to the temperature of the water. But Dr. C felt 'blocked' about hypnosis for himself and in doubt about the 'validity' of some of the hypnotic phenomena he himself elicited in his own practice. He was not 'blocked' on the possible validity of hypnotic phenomena, nor was he 'blocked,' to use his own words, when he was asked to 'validate' the genuineness of Miss A's hypnotic behavior. He expected hypnotic phenomena from Miss A, and to validate them by his cooperative critical effort. Neither he nor the audience realized that the suggestion that his effort to validate Miss A's hypnotic behavior required much more than a mere tentative questioning of the *age*, the *kind*, and the *breed* of a dog, the actuality of which was not the issue, *just its attributes*. To do such validating necessitated a dog, since Miss A had hallucinated one, therefore Dr. C, who had no mental block or counterset against validating Miss A's responses, found that the only way he could 'validate' her judgment as to *kind, breed,* and *age* was to have a dog by which to make such a comparison. Hence he was unwittingly placed in the same situation as had been Miss A, and neither she nor he nor the audience had time to realize this nor to analyze the manifold implications of that seemingly simple request to Dr. C that he *exercise his very best judgment in evaluating Miss A's responses*. His *'very best'* required his full potentials.

"Then with Miss A in a state of complete expectation, merely awaiting whatever suggestion I chose to give her, I mentioned the 'Surprise Technique.' I did not ask her to see a dog. I just asked her to *tell me the kind, the breed,* and *the age* of *that dog there*. It was not a question of whether or not a dog was there. The question was *kind, breed,* and *age,* and since she was prepared to accept my suggestion, her only way to do so would be to 'reach' into her unconscious mind and thus to project vividly a visual memory of a dog. To do this she had to go into a trance. How long does it take to develop a trance? How long does it take to develop physiological sleep? If you are sufficiently tired physically, you can fall asleep as your head hits the pillow. When you are sufficiently prepared psychologically, you can develop a trance just as quickly.

"As for Dr. C, what happened? He was adequately prepared for the development of hypnotic phenomena by Miss A. He actually fully expected the author to demonstrate hypnosis. He had stated that he could not be hypnotized, and his statement had been apparently accepted at face value; thus he had no need to offer any resistances. But he did have a task to do, which was *to cooperate with the author by judging the validity of hypnotic phenomena he expected Miss A to develop.* He, too, had a strongly expectant state for hypnotic phenomena, and he merely assumed that they would derive from Miss A, possibly from Miss B. He did not even recognize that he too might be a source, and hence he had no need to offer resistances. Instead there was a long history of intense wanting and striving to achieve hypnosis, and now an unrecognized opportunity to achieve. The whole psychological situation favored the author's hopes.

"Then when Miss A hallucinated a dog, Dr. C found himself in the position of validating that hallucination. How does one validate? Naturally by a comparison of the thing in question with a known comparable thing. One does not compare a dog, even an imaginary dog, with a carpet, a floor, or a chair but with another dog, or a mental image or a memory of one. Hence Dr. C, without ever realizing it, was forced into the situation of comparing Miss A's projected visual image with his own inner understandings, and this was best done by a projected image of a dog of his own memory. To do this (and he was ready and waiting to do it, but he had not analyzed the processes by which it would have to be done), he promptly developed a trance state, and thus he could make a comparison of his own trance visual hallucination with Miss A's verbalized discription of her subjective hypnotic experience. The fortuitous circumstance of the comparison of a Scottie and a collie gave rise then and there to an elaboration between them of the situation, and this occurred, aided by incidental remarks by the author, unplanned and arising out of the situation itself.

"Why a dog? Because general information indicates that dogs are much more commonly liked and owned than cats. But if Miss A had used a cat, Dr. C could still have used his collie if he preferred dogs, as *many repetitions of this particular experiment have revealed.* Subjective experiences were to be validated, not an object in reality, and Dr. C met the task imposed by Miss A, a subjective experience, adequately but in terms of his own visual and mental images and memories.

"I like to do this type of experiment when nobody knows an experiment is being done and when I myself do not know what will happen. Thus I have in the past carefully given suggestions directed to elicit visual hallucinations, and secured auditory ones, e.g. 'I can't see anybody there but I can hear people talking' (there were no people and no talking); also I have suggested that they listen to *that piano there* and had them explain, in bewilderment at my ignorance, 'that is an electric organ.' And the subject sees me take a closer look, thus to correct my 'obvious mistake.' "

All that I hope to know in most such experimental situations that I devise is the possible general variety of psychological processes and reactions I would like to elicit but do not know if I shall succeed in so doing, nor in what manner this will occur. Then, as the subjects respond in their own fashion, I promptly utilize that response. To illustrate from another medico-dental lecture-demonstration situation, in discussing ideosensory phenomena, I asked my intended hypnotic subject, a college graduate, her favorite recreation. She answered, "Well, I suppose it is driving about the country and enjoying the landscape." (She lived in Colorado.) Therefore I suggested that she might look "out of the side window over there at *that mountain range* and at *that mountain* with the *two deep ravines,* one on each side, and the *v-shaped pine forest* running up its side," pointing impressively at a bare wall. To my astonishment and that of all the others present she replied, "That's not a car window. That is my kitchen window and that's me washing dishes and listening to the hi-fi. It's playing my favorite piece, the one that reminds me of skiing," and she began a soft humming, interrupting that to explain to me, "Doesn't that music remind you of skiing down the mountain, following those long, lovely curves, just like the long, lovely sweeping tones of the music on the hi-fi. And oh, my goodness, that's impossible, but if you look out of the window, you can see the mountain where we always go skiing. And it's close enough so I can see it all. Look at that huge boulder that the ski trail curves around. Please, may I have some paper and pencil, I must sketch that scene." This she did, glancing up from the paper from time to time to check her "visual impression" of the "scene."

This subject was the wife of one of the dentists in the audience. He had often attempted, but futilely, to use hypnosis on her for dental work, and his colleagues had had similar failures on her. She had come to the meeting in his company only after making him promise that she would not be used as a subject. The author, in seeking volunteers for demonstration purposes, had asked "the pretty girl wearing the white hat in the back row" to come up to the platform. She had done so but explained immediately that she did not want to be hypnotized. She was earnestly assured that she need not go into a trance unless she wanted to, but that the author liked to have a number of volunteers when he demonstrated hypnosis, some to demonstrate the ordinary waking state, some to demonstrate the light trance, the medium trance, and the deep trance as well as varying types of hypnotic responses. She readily volunteered to be a "waking demonstrator." This offer was accepted, and she was told that since her husband used hypnosis, she might like to watch the other subjects who had volunteered and to watch the reactions of the audience as they observed the demonstrations and reach understandings of how to talk to their patients to convey meanings effectively. As she alertly watched both subjects and the audience and listened to the author's emphasis upon saying things meaningfully, he explained that Mrs. X was as wide awake and alert and unhypnotized as would be any new patient who entered the office unsophisticated in hypnosis. In the dental office a remark appropriate to the situation could be said as earnestly as the author, in his discussion of ideosensory phenomena, could turn to Mrs X and make a seemingly casual remark, or ask a seemingly casual question to effect a Surprise Technique Induction, as he would now demonstrate. It was at this point that the author put his question about her favorite recreation, by which there were elicited a succession of hypnotic phenomena at the ideosensory level in a somnambulistic trance.

What did Mrs. X's behavior signify? She was interested in hypnosis; she was interested in what was being said to the audience; and she was interested in what they were understanding. This, the author recognized, would be the case, and at what he judged the right moment, he explained what he was going to do and she, in her own wish to cooperate, did so but purely in terms of her own experience. She did not accept the suggestions offered her by the author; she accepted only the opportunity offered to reach understandings in her own way, taking advantage of the author's suggestions as a means but nothing more.

She was allowed to finish her sketch, and then she cooperated in demonstrating various other phenomena of the somnambulistic trance. The sketch was passed to the audience; her husband and several others recognized the scene (she had done much sketching and painting), and she was then awakened by the simple process of leading her to the edge of the platform where she had come up and saying to her, "And now, *you in the pretty white hat,* what is your name?" This had the effect of reorienting her to the moment at which she had arrived at the platform with a consequent amnesia for all trance events. (This measure of reorientation in time by reawakening trains of thought and associations preceding trance inductions, in this author's experience, is far more effective in inducing posthypnotic amnesia than direct, forceful suggestions for its development. One merely makes dominant the previous thought patterns and idea associations.) She was asked to take a seat, a different one than that which she had previously occupied, thus to preclude any chance reassociations.

She was questioned indirectly by the audience. People whom she did not know asked her about her hi-fi set, others about her skiing, the boulder around which the ski trail curved, and finally she was shown her sketch while the author sat back passively. She was bewildered by the questions but showed no evidence of any recollection of trance occurrences, and when shown the sketch, she named the area, spoke favorably of the excellence of the sketch, and was suddenly very startled to see her name signed to it. At first her facial expression was one of complete bafflement and blank surprise; then she looked at her watch, listened to it, compared it to the watch of the girl next to her, and then turned to the author and asked simply, "Have I been in a trance?" Her question was answered with a simple affirmative.

She paused thoughtfully, then looked at her husband with a pleased smile, and said, "Everybody will soon know so I am going to tell it now. I'm pregnant now and I want to have my baby under hypnosis, but I was absolutely convinced

I couldn't be hypnotized. I always tried so hard to go into a trance and I always failed. I didn't want to come today for fear my husband would want me to volunteer, and I didn't want to fail again. So I stuck close to him and even made him come late so he wouldn't have a chance to ask you to hypnotize me. I just couldn't take another failure. But when you asked me to come up and mentioned my hat, I knew it was just a coincidence and I was relieved when you told me I could demonstrate being awake. I knew I could do that. But what happened? Can you put me in a trance again so that I can have my baby under hypnosis?"

She was told simply that she did not need to have anybody "put" her into a trance, that it was a process of learning within herself, that all she needed to do to go into a trance was to look at her sketch and to arouse, by reading her name. Another way would be to listen to the hi-fi, even though it were 100 miles away, and go into a trance and awaken at the proper time. She promptly picked up the sketch, obviously developed a trance, slowly looked downward at the signature and aroused, and apparently realized she had just aroused from a trance. Then she cocked an ear as if listening, her eyes closed; she started to beat time with her foot, and her husband remarked, "She's keeping time to her favorite piece." Shortly the beating stopped, she awakened, thanked the author most graciously, and, picking up her sketch, left the platform and returned to her seat beside her husband as if she had no further contribution to make.

Two years later, when lecturing to that same group again, she was present. She introduced the author to her baby and explained that she was a perfect obstetrical and dental patient, an item of fact her husband confirmed.

Now back to Miss B: After having demonstrated and discussed matters at length with the audience, to which Miss B tried to listen while listening also to Miss A and Dr. C still discussing the merits of Scotties versus collies, there is another item that must be discussed. Turning to Miss B, I said, "When you came up you said you didn't think you could be hypnotized. Now what I'm wondering [note that "wondering" has nothing apparently to do with her going into a trance] is, what you would like to see, a dog?" "Dog" was said with a rising inflection as if to cast doubt on seeing a dog, since if there is going to be any doubt, it should be mine and not that of the subject. She laughed and said, "No, I'm a cat lover, and I have one named Snookie."

"What is cute about Snookie?"

"Oh, you ought to see Snookie playing in the living room."

"Oh, is that Snookie there, playing with that catnip mouse?" pointing again and looking intently at the bare floor as if I actually saw the catnip mouse.

Again the suggestion was worded in such fashion that the question as understood by Miss B was not "Is there a cat?" But "Is *that a catnip mouse being played* with?" To answer that question *she had to see a cat first,* and the preceding conversation had set the stage and had evoked strong personal memories.

She answered that it was *not* a catnip mouse but a *ball of yarn.* Again a Surprise Technique was used by asking a sudden question in a suitable situation, reply to which required an absolute affirmation of a postulated or implied hypnotic phenomenon in order to answer the question. One can speak to a stranger and say, "Here is a blackboard and a piece of chalk, and if you don't mind, I would like to know if you are right- or left-handed." Even if a verbal answer is given instead of accepting the chalk with the dominant hand and writing, there is certain to be some involuntary motor response such as looking down at the dominant hand, or a slight revealing movement will be made. This will occur even if the stranger otherwise gives only a cold, blank stare.

After various further demonstrations of hypnotic phenomena using all three subjects, with all three in rapport with the author—Miss B directly and Miss A and Dr. C with hallucinatory overtones—Dr. C and Miss A in rapport directly with each other only, and Miss B in rapport with the author only, the next problem was that of arousing them.

Resuming his original seat the author propounded the task to the audience as, "Now comes the problem of arousing them. You will all note that I apparently will not do so, therefore I urge you to watch the subjects carefully, to listen carefully to what I say, and to speculate upon the implications."

Turning to the subjects the author remarked casually but with veiled emphases "Well, Miss A and Miss B and Dr. C, since *we are all here* and the *audience is waiting,* don't you really think *I ought to begin* the demonstration for them?"

All three aroused at once, but *reoriented to the time of their original arrival on the platform.* Miss A smiled and said, "Well, I suppose since I'm the only one who wants to go into a trance, you had better start with me." Miss B, when I glanced at her, said, "I'm willing to try," and Dr. C answered, "I wish I could."

Obviously all three had a total amnesia for all trance events. An arousal, a reorientation in time, and an amnesia were all definitively implied by the three italicized statements in my remarks to all of them.

A stranger in the audience asked Dr. C, "Did you ever have a favorite collie?" Dr. C replied that he had had many favorite collies but of them all he liked best one that had died some years previously. Someone then said to Miss A, "So your favorite dog is a Scottie!" Her startled reply was, "How did you know that?" Another member of the audience who did not know Miss B asked her why she had never bought Snookie a catnip mouse. Immediately Miss B replied that she had, but that Snookie had torn it up. Then, with startled bewilderment, she inquired how the speaker knew about Snookie.

Dr. C had looked puzzled at the question about a collie, listened with bewilderment to the questions put to A and B, suddenly looked at his watch, and remarked in a bewildered fashion, "There's more than an hour gone by since I came up here. Everybody seems to know personal things about us; none of us seem to understand how they could be known. Does that mean that we all have been in a trance and have amnesia for it?" looking toward the author.

Instead of answering him the author addressed the audience by saying, "Of course the best answer to that question will be a *levitation of the right hand.*"

The three subjects appeared nonplussed by this seemingly nonpertinent statement.

Dr. C was the first to note his responding right-hand levitation, then looked at Miss B and Miss A in obvious amazement, since they too were showing the same phenomenon. Their facial expressions were those of startled amazement when they too saw what was happening. Then the question was asked, while the author looked at the back of the room, "Can you stop it?" All three noted their hands continuing to levitate. Then several in the audience noted the same thing occurring to them. Then the author remarked casually, "Thus one can get answers unknown to the self in various ways." To everybody's astonishment all levitation ceased and the raised hands dropped. The implication of the author's remark was that full reply had been made, hence there was no need to give further instruction. Astonished comments were received from several of the audience who discovered their own right-hand levitation.

In a somewhat comparable way the author, before an audience of visiting physicians, the state hospital staff, medical students, and registered and student nurses, had asked a student nurse to volunteer as a subject. She had demurred, stating she would like to but that she was too self-conscious to come up in front of so large an audience. To this the author replied, "So you would like to [true], you are too self-conscious to come up *in front of the audience* [nobody realized the *implication* of those italicized words, and the statement was also true], but *that is all right,* all I want you to do is, Just look at *that picture right there* on the wall, and *I* don't know *whose it is* nor in *what room* it is [pointing and looking intently at the bare auditorium wall]." Slowly the girl turned her head in the fashion of a deeply hypnotized subject, looked at the auditorium wall, and answered, "That's Lily's picture, and it's hanging right over the television set in her living room." I asked the nurse to come and sit beside me and to tell me about Lily. She came down the aisle, and after a few remarks I asked her to close her eyes and to help me with some work I had to do. After demonstrating various other phenomena, including a discussion of the Surprise Technique, I aroused her.

Her startled reaction was delightful to behold, and she asked, "How did I ever get up here?" Reply was given, "You are a remarkably good hypnotic subject and you will be able to teach the doctors and nurses here a lot. Later a correspondence with her revealed that she had asked for a full account from her fellow students, found it difficult to believe, and hence wrote to the author asking for a summary. She was most pleased with her experience. In explanation her actual willingness to be a subject, her unawareness that her seat in the audience would not be a barrier to hypnosis, although the request to "come down in front" implied that it was, and the burden so inexplicably thrust upon her to place a meaningful value upon an actually meaningless suggestion, compelled her to construct, by an outward projection, a meaningful response through the measure of entering into hypnosis and the visual projection of an actual memory.

Another example which may be cited of the "Surprise Technique" is of a slightly different character in that it depends upon the utilization of minimal cues entirely. This instance was a completey impromptu experiment in a university auditorium before a medical and psychological group, most of whom were sophisticated in relation to hypnosis, although some had no knowledge of it. Minimal cues not recognized by the audience or by the subjects were used to elicit both a deep trance state and specific responses for which no recognizable cue had been given that was apparent to the audience, and to which the subjects had to make a rather unusual response inexplicable to both the audience and to the subjects until proved by demonstration.

The situation was as follows: The author upon entering the auditorium by way of the door at the front of the room noticed by chance some colored chalk just behind the speaker's stand on top of the desk behind which the speaker could stand, and a blackboard on the wall behind the desk. No further thought was given to this at that time. Instead the author looked carefully and appraisingly over the audience, as is his customary practice, thus to make note of anything of interest to him. In so doing near the rear of the auditorium he saw two young women, one just slightly further back than the other, one on one side of the room, the other on the opposite side. Both girls' absorbed and attentive faces led to his clinical judgment that they were "good hypnotic subjects."

The author was not scheduled to speak, but he did take a seat in the front row in order to observe the speaker of the occasion, who was to discuss hypnosis and to demonstrate trance induction with a trained subject.

At the conclusion of the presentation the author was asked if he would offer a few comments. Since the demonstration had proved decidedly unsatisfactory, even from the speaker's point of view, the author accepted the invitation. In his comment he spoke adversely about the direct, emphatic, and authoritative suggestions that had been employed and indicated that no real effort had been made to meet the subject's seeming uneasiness, self-consciousness in being before an audience, or his possible resentments or resistances toward the autocratic way in which he had been handled. The author stressed the importance of *gentle, permissive,* and *indirect suggestions,* emphasizing that direct suggestions may give rise to resistances.

The author's comments were somewhat resented by the speaker, perhaps because he felt "let down" by his hitherto cooperative subject. At all events the speaker suggested rather insistently that the author demonstrate "a gentle, permissive approach and indirect suggestions" and that he choose someone from the audience as his subject. Rather reluctantly the challenge was accepted, and then it was realized that there might be the possibility for an experimental procedure of which only the author could possibly know in general what he *hoped* could be achieved. It was an excellent setting for a natural field experiment with only the author cognizant of his intentions, and under observation by the entire audience, some of whom were not too friendly.

Immediately the author had three chairs placed in a row in front of the desk.

Most emphatically he stated that the middle chair was *his* since he preferred to lecture while sitting down because of his residuals of anterior poliomyelitis. With no explanation the author took two handkerchiefs out of his pocket and stepped around to the rear of the desk. There, with his hands and their activity completely *out of sight of everybody,* two pieces of colored chalk were selected and rolled up separately in the handkerchiefs, and then one of these handkerchiefs was placed on the floor to the left of the left-hand chair and the other on the floor to the right of the right-hand chair. Even if anybody knew about the colored chalk, nobody could know which pieces had been selected and wrapped up in the handkerchiefs. Upon sitting down in the middle chair, the author took hold of his right wrist with his left hand and lifted his right (and obviously weaker, but not that weak, as was made evident later) arm over and indicated with his right hand that "This chair is for one subject." Dropping his right hand in his lap, he touched the right-hand chair with his left hand and said, "And this chair is for the other subject." No explanation of any sort was made of the peculiar placing of the handkerchiefs or of this crossed-arms designation of the chairs.

Thus everybody had seen a number of things done that could cause wonderment, intense watchfulness, and bewildered attention. There was the placing of three chairs with the middle one specifically identified as the author's, and the other two designated in an inexplicable manner as the chairs for two unspecified subjects. Then there was the remarkably odd item of handkerchiefs rolled up as if containing some unknown objects secured by the author in full view, except for his hand activities, and so peculiarly placed with no proffered explanation.

Then I began to discuss as lucidly and as informatively as I could the nature and values of soft, gentle, indirect, permissive techniques, the use of inflections and intonations, of hesitations, pauses, of a seeming groping for words to elicit efforts to speak for me, and of the giving of minimal cues and hints that the subject could cooperatively elaborate and act upon. I mentioned that I had already specified that there were two chairs for subjects and that I had said "that one subject will sit here," again indicating the left-hand chair by using my right hand to indicate it and "that the other subject [touching the right hand chair with my left hand] will sit here." Thus twice I had touched the left-hand chair with my right hand and the right-hand chair twice with my left hand. Although the audience was most attentive, as later questioning disclosed, no one placed unduly remarkable meaning upon this twice-done crossed-arms designation of the subjects' chairs. Yet everybody saw it and, as many later stated, related it to the more easily comprehended physical handicap of the author, so gratuitously mentioned.

Throughout my comments I was exceedingly careful to let my eyes roam constantly about the room in what appeared to be purely random fashion, glancing at the side aisles, following them with my eyes from in back of the room to down in front of the room, looking at the floor just in front of me and also further distant up the middle aisle, at the walls, the ceiling, the "No Smoking" sign on the right-hand wall, the chairs beside me, the window on the left-hand wall through which I could see a tree. Nobody could realize that as I paused for words, looking here, there, and everywhere that I was careful to look no member of the audience directly in the face with two exceptions, the two young women I had first noted. The impression was given that I was looking freely and comfortably at everybody and everything as I talked. Nor did anyone become aware, because of the randomness of my behavior and utterances with meaningful content, that it contained two separate rigid sequences. One of these sequences was looking out of the left wall window, shifting my gaze to look directly at the girl's face and eyes on the left-hand side of the room, at the same time so choosing my words so that I would be saying something like "a minimal cue means to you———" or, "as permissive suggestions are given, you———," always something that could be taken personally, following such utterances with a visual following down of the left side aisle to the front of the room and over to the right-hand chair, although seemingly I was addressing all of this to the entire audience. The same sort of a sequence was used with the girl on the right-hand side. Each time I looked at the "No Smoking" sign I glanced at her face and her eyes, making suggestions comparable to those given to the other girl; for example, "When you receive a suggestion however given, you will act upon it," or, "Minimal permissive suggestions to you can be highly significant," and this would be followed by a careful visual following of the right-hand aisle down to the front of the room and over to the left-hand chair. By repetition every effort was made in these remarks, seemingly addressed to the entire audience, to give both girls a sufficient number of the *same* wholly comparable suggestions. Thus the audience in general had a feeling of being spoken to and looked at as a group, but the direct look at the girls and the use of the pronoun "you" had an unrecognized, unrealized, but cumulative effect, and the sequence of events was consistently the same for each girl although at irregular intervals.

Finally I felt from the rigidity of their facial expressions and the failure of their blink reflex that all was ready. I stood up and walked up the middle aisle to the second row of seats, and glancing at the "No Smoking" sign and then at the girl on the right, saying slowly, "Now that you are ready———," pausing, taking a deep breath, slowly shifting my glance to the back wall, then looking out of the window on the left side of the room, then at the girl in the left side, again saying, "Now that you are ready——— (a pause) ———slowly now stand up and *walk down* and *take your proper seats.*"

The audience looked all around, was startled to see the girl on the left and the girl on the right arise and walk slowly down the side aisles while the author stared purposely and rigidly at the rear wall. Behind his back the two girls passed each other, the one from the right taking her place in the left-hand chair and the girl from the left seating herself in the right-hand chair. When I judged them as having reached their chairs by the stopping of their footsteps, I said very gently, "As you sit down, close your eyes and sleep very deeply and continue to sleep in a deep trance until I tell you otherwise."

After a brief wait I turned and sat down between them and remarked to the audience that I had asked the two girls to sit down in the *proper chairs*. To indicate that they had responded correctly I then asked the speaker who had asked me to demonstrate indirect trance induction and indirect suggestions to prove that they had seated themselves in the appropriate chair. As he looked blankly at me, I asked him to examine the handkerchiefs beside each chair. He unrolled the handkerchief beside the left chair and found a yellow piece of chalk; the girl was wearing a yellow dress. The chalk in the handkerchief beside the right-hand chair was red, and so was that girl's dress. To get to the *proper chair*, the girls had each had to go to the further chair and in so doing to pass each other behind the author's back while he was rigidly staring at the rear wall.

Various phenomena of deep hypnosis were elicited from each, and they were then aroused from the trance state by simple suggestion. They manifested an amazed, startled reaction at finding themselves in front of the audience, and questioning from the audience disclosed that each had a total amnesia for all trance events including rising from their seats, coming to the front of the room, and sitting down in the chairs.

Systematically they were questioned by the audience, and both explained that something, they knew not what, made them feel that they were being personally addressed by the author and that they had unaccountably found themselves taking an inexplicable interest in the chair in which they now found themselves sitting.

They could give no reason for these statements. Even when another trance was induced in them, they could only state that the author in some way gave them a definite feeling that they were to go into a trance, but they could not tell what it was that gave them that feeling. They did state that the elaborate but inexplicable behavior with the handkerchiefs had captured and fixated their attention. Upon being asked why that had been done and for what purpose, they looked beside the chair to see whether the handkerchiefs were still there. (While they were still in a deep trance, Dr. X had returned the pieces of chalk to their original place and the handkerchiefs to the author). Dr. X then retrieved the chalk and stated, "These were wrapped up in the handkerchiefs." Each made the feminine response of saying "And I am wearing a red (yellow) dress so the red (yellow) chalk was by my chair! But I didn't know that, I didn't even know there was chalk. Did anybody else?"

Only the author knew. Much discussion followed, but it was not until the tape recording was played back repeatedly that the two girls, who were graduate psychology students, were reminded by the repetitious sequence of certain utterances and of their memories of the sequences of the author's visual behavior. Soon various of the rest of the group could also recognize the rigid sequences they had previously ignored. Unfortunately the girls were not tested separately, but their recognitions were first of the sequence directly applicable to the self and then for the sequences directed to the other.

Suddenly one of the girls said, "But you can move your right hand more freely than you did when you forcibly lifted your right hand and put it on the left chair, and then elaborately leaned over to put the left hand on the right chair. That crossing-over was a cue too.''

Item by item they reviewed the tape recording, noting the extensive repetition of ideas which should have made the lecture boresome, and they reached the conclusion that the unanswerable puzzle of the meaningfulness of the handkerchiefs had served a large role in keeping everybody's attention at a high level, and the entire audience agreed that this was possible. It was also noted that there were many variations in the utterance of the same ideas. The author's own tension also unquestionably played some role.[1]

Later that day each girl requested a direct hypnosis of the self while the other watched, speculated, and discussed the phenomena under observation.

Actually while this experiment was a Surprise Technique, not only to the subjects but to the audience itself, it was simply a matter of systematically combining auditory, visual, and intellectual conditioning of the subjects to elicit certain predetermined responses knowable only to the author. The tape recording of the demonstration was played to determine if the words "red," "yellow," "walk down," or "girls" or "girl" had been used. They were missing from the tape recording, even as were the words "chalk" and "color."

One additional comment should be made, and that is that this sort of seemingly casual conversation loaded with minimal cues has many times been practiced by the author and his oldest son, sometimes on each other, more frequently upon others as a definite game or means of entertainment by enjoying intellectual ingenuity.[2]

One final paragraph might be added. To the unsophisticated onlooker, ready to believe in mind-reading, thought transference, the power of mind over matter, and the "dominance over the will" of another, the above material could deliberately and fraudulently be made to appear as evidence of such; or it might even be innocently so interpreted by an uncritical lecturer or experimenter unaware of the many minimal cues given unwittingly by the naive but honest worker.

Examined carefully, observed in full detail by the astute critic, no more was done than to utilize the experimental learnings and the innate capacities of the individual to receive and to accept and to act upon stimuli, recognizable and understandable to others but ordinarily overlooked and not appreciated, even though sensed.

They constitute, however, important and often decisive factors in the actions and adjustments made constantly in daily life, even though these cues and minimal stimuli may not reach the level of conscious awareness.

SUMMARY

Accounts are given of lecture-demonstrations on hypnosis before a general medical group, a medico-dental group, a medical-psychological group at a uni-

---

Note [1] begins on page 357. Note [2] begins on page 358.

Minimal Cues

versity, and a state hospital group with invited guests. In each instance opportunity arose for a natural field experiment to be conducted.

In the first account an "impossible subject," a volunteer subject not believing in hypnosis for herself, and another volunteer interested in hypnosis for herself were used.

The technique employed for all three subjects was a "Surprise Technique," for which an adequate preparation was made by an overelaboration, presumably for the audience but actually for the subjects themselves, based upon an extensive explanation of "My-Friend-John Technique."

In the second instance the "impossible" subject was fitted into the demonstration as a waking subject showing the usual alert behavior and then transforming her cooperative behavior into hypnotic by a "Surprise Technique," thereby discovering a hoped-for but despaired-of hypnotic ability.

The third instance was a totally unsuspected trance induction in a willing but hesitant subject who did not expect hypnosis. It occurred in response to a meaningfully given, although in the situation meaningless suggestion, to which she had to supply the meaning from her own experience by the special wording of a problem posed for her.

The fourth instance was a natural field experiment in which a Surprise Technique based on minimal cues not recognizable by the audience or the nonspecified subjects resulted in two somnambulistic subjects who could account neither in the waking nor the trance state for their entering the hypnotic state, nor could the audience. A repeated playing back of the tape recorder allowed the discovery of the minimal cues, first by the subjects, and then by the audience despite acute attentiveness throughout the entire induction process.

In all instances the author endeavors to indicate the probable psychological factors involved in eliciting the trance responses and to illustrate natural field experimentation.

In brief, in any experimentation in hypnosis, full attention should be given the psychological implications and minimal cues.

---

[1]Much later a transcription of this tape recording was made. To the reader's eye it was abominably repetitious, and the sequences of behavior relating to the two girls were easily detected.

This same transcription could be read aloud with adequate and deliberate impressiveness and could be made to sound most meaningful, but such reading rendered it actually uninformative. The minimal cues of the total situation and of the author's behavior, the chairs and the handkerchiefs were vital for any effective understandings.

Edited into good, clear, lucid, grammatical English, no matter how impressively read, it was meaningless.

Later by several months an associate of the author read aloud as best he could, so far as possible without mimicking the author, the unedited transcription of the tape recording separately to each of the original two girls. They were puzzled by his request but agreed willingly though wonderingly. Each declared that they had experienced but resisted a strong tendency to go into a trance. Later he read that same tape as expressively as he could to both an unsophisticated and to a group of trained subjects, without describing to them the original setting but endeavoring to duplicate the author's behavioral patterns in a prearranged room. The unsophisticated subjects were merely puzzled. They did have a feeling that they must have "missed something."

All of the half-dozen trained subjects declared that it had produced in them "very definite hypnotic feelings, as if I wanted to go into a trance." Some stated "Several times I felt like changing my seat. Also, the putting of the handkerchiefs on the floor beside the chairs next to you had the effect of making me listen most intently." The others gave less comprehensive but comparable statements.

The reading of the well-edited transcription was meaningless to a third group, but was recognized by the other two groups as a "cut-down," "meaningless version of what you read before." Yet the actual reading setting itself was identical. The minimal cues arising out of the totality of the original setting and the original character of the entire communication had been destroyed by the editing.

[2] Perhaps a very simple and easily understood example can be given to clarify this type of accumulation of minimal cues leading to a specific response: The rest of the family was out for the evening, I was ill but comfortably seated in a chair. Bert, aged 17, had volunteered to remain at home to keep me company although there was no such need. A casual conversation was initiated by Bert in which he mentioned the rush and turmoil of getting everybody dressed and fed and everything packed up for a past vacation trip to Northern Michigan. (We were living in Michigan at the time.) Next he mentioned the fishing, the catching of frogs and a frog-leg dinner, the beach dinner, and the sand that the smaller children managed to sprinkle over every item of food, and then the albino frog at the abandoned quarry we had found.

Next he described in vivid detail the turmoil of getting everything out of the summer cabin, the oversights, the hunting of misplaced items, and the wandering off of the smaller children and the hurried search for them, the locking-up of the cabin, and the hungry tired state we were in when we arrived at Wayne County General Hospital near Detroit where we lived.

At this point a vague notion passed through my mind to suggest to Bert that he might take the car and visit some friends, but this idea vanished as Bert laughingly told of how his brother Lance particularly liked eating Grandma Erickson's fried chicken on the way back to Michigan from Wisconsin. With much laughter he recalled another occasion in which his small brother Allan had amused everybody, and especially Grandma and Grandpa Erickson with his "bulldozer" pattern of eating, that is, holding his plate up to his mouth and systematically using his other hand to shove the contents of the plate slowly and steadily into his mouth.

Again, this time a clearer idea came to mind of suggesting that Bert take the car keys and go for a ride so that I could enjoy reading, but I forgot it as I recalled my father's amused comment on the absolute efficiency and speed of Allan's method of eating.

While we were laughing about this, Bert mentioned the trip to my brother's farm, and six-year-old Betty Alice's long, solemn explanation to three-year-old Allan's worried inquiry about how the mama chickens nursed their babies, that chickens were not mammals and only mammals nursed their young. While we were laughing about this, a third time the thought came to mind of offering Bert the car for the evening, this time most clearly, and I recognized why. In every item of reminiscences Bert was speaking of pleasant and happy memories based each upon the driving of a car. Yet not once had he actually said the word "car"; the nearest he came to that was to say "packing up," "trip," "went to see," "way out to the old quarry," "down to the beach," "on the way back to Michigan from Wisconsin," and the trip to my brother's farm, and not once did he mention the word key—locking up the cabin was as close as he came to that.

I recognized the situation at once and remarked, "The answer is 'no'." He laughed and said, "Well, Dad, you'll have to admit it was a good try." "Not good enough; I caught on too fast. You overemphasized trips in the car. You should have mentioned the picketing of Ned's place, where our car was serviced, Ed Carpenter from whom I bought the car, the ice-fishing trip which was in Emil's car but did involve an automobile. In brief you restricted yourself to a constant indirect mention of pleasure trips, always in relationship to us, it was always in our car. The inference to be drawn became too obvious. Do you really want the car?" His answer was, "No, I just thought I'd get a little fun out of getting you to offer me the car keys."

16. Respiratory Rhythm in Trance Induction: The Role of Minimal Sensory Cues in Normal and Trance Behavior

Milton H. Erickson

To orient the reader of this paper, it will be necessary to cite five items of fact out of order and as a preliminary consideration. This paper represents a rather unique lifelong investigative, exploratory study that began as a child's curious quest for an understanding of the unexplicable and then slowly evolved as a systematic inquiry into hypnosis as a method of interpersonal communication at both verbal and nonverbal levels.

Item Number 1 is this: Shortly after entering the University of Wisconsin, I sought out the professor of psychology, then Joseph Jastrow, and made known to him my wishes. He kindly had me tested in a great variety of ways, both by himself and others, and finally disclosed to me the fact that I was in the lower one percentile of those who appreciated or understood music and rhythm. He also disclosed that my range of hearing exceeded the average for both higher and lower pitched sounds.

Item No. 2 is that in the early 1930s I gave a lecture on hypnosis at the Worcester State Hospital. The late Edward Sapir, a linguist, Stirling Professor at Yale University, and his colleague, Dr. John Dollard, attended. The latter briefed Dr. Sapir to the effect that I grew up on a Wisconsin farm and had never been out of the United States. After the lecture Dr. Sapir introduced himself, stated that he was both a linguist and a violin virtuoso and that his hobby was collecting records of music from all parts of the world. He inquired if I knew that I was tone deaf and arhythmic. I told him I was so aware. He stated that he had listened to me speak with much fascination in an effort to discover what kind of an individual rhythm of speech I did have and to determine if I had acquired any trace of Occidental musical rhythm—and he had missed the content of my lecture. He later informed me that, in playing over his collection of records, he had come across one of a Central African tribe whose rhythm was similar to mine. In this same connection, since 1950 two anthropologist patients of mine have inquired separately if I had worked personally with a certain Brazilian-jungle Indian tribe and with a certain Peruvian-jungle Indian tribe.

Unpublished fragment, circa 1960s.

Both ascribed to me a vocal rhythm highly suggestive of the respective tribe with which they had worked.

Item No. 3 is the simple edifying comment of the five-year old patient brought to me for hypnotic therapy for severe enuresis of one year's duration after complete successful toilet training that had endured two-and-a-half years, and had then suddenly broke down completely. His remark, one made in various forms, particularly by children under the age of eight, was "Ebby night — mommy swings (sings) me to sweep (sleep), but you bweathe me to swe͜ɛ" He was entirely right. I had used my special respiratory rhythm technique for inducing hypnosis in him.

Item No. 4 is the comment of my daughter, Betty Alice, who summarized her view: "Ever since I was a little girl I sensed in some way that your breathing in itself was a hypnotic technique that you could use without anything else. Then when you used my college roomate for that Birmingham Michigan Medical Society as an example of a resistant hypnotic subject, I really understood what you were doing. She and the audience thought that you were casually discussing various ways of making an initial approach to the resistant patient, but all of a sudden I could see you sitting there beside Kelly, breathing in that peculiar rhythm, and Kelly's eyes slowly, involuntarily closing, and then you took that deep sighing breath, and Kelly was in a somnambulistic trance. I had to struggle to keep from going into a trance myself, but I could really see how she just followed along, breathing just as you did without knowing it. And I watched you cover up and conceal what you had done from the audience by demonstrating arm catalepsy, and the audience thought that that [the arm catalepsy] was the induction technique. They could never have understood if you had tried to explain the breathing."

Item No. 5 relates to the experience reported to me by two physician students of mine who had each made a tape recording of a specific trance induction in a subject before a professional audience and my demonstration of deep hypnotic phenomena. The experience of both physicians was essentially the same, the only difference being that the daughter of one was nine years old, while the daughter of the other was ten years old.

Both played their tape recording over and over, and each was distressed to discover that at a certain point in the tape recording they were fully aware from the subject's voice and their visual memories that the subject was "sound asleep in a deep somnambulistic trance," and that the next moment the subject had suddenly returned to a state of full waking awareness without the author having made any specific request or having given any suggestion. Both noted that, as the author discussed the various phenomena he was having demonstrated and then contrasting them with the waking state, the subject, whom they knew to be a first-time subject and a stranger to the author, awakened or redeveloped the trance in a seemingly spontaneous, automatic manner. Thus they seemed to be intentionally, and without being given cues, arousing from or developing a trance automatically in response to what the author was saying to the audience.

As the two physicians played and replayed their tapes, convinced that the author must have said something not recorded on the tape and expressed this belief aloud, both little girls had expostulated, "But he didn't say anything. He just changes his voice a little so he can breathe different so she will wake up." Both physicians had doubted this childish analysis and had replayed the tapes, asking their daughters to indicate this type of occurrence. Both girls repeatedly would declare, "Now his voice begins to get slower, he almost stops like he is taking a breath [or letting out a breath] and then she wakes up [or goes to sleep]."

Both physicians, to their own satisfaction, tested their daughters' auditory perceptions on the immediate and subsequent playings of the recording until convinced that the girls were reporting actual auditory experiences. One of them, a year later at a seminar, sought out the author and earnestly requested that he use exactly the same technique of induction that he had employed previously (identifying the occasion but offering no further information). He asked the author to give some casual specified signal so that he would know on which volunteer the same technique was being employed. The physician did not disclose to the author until much later the reason for this request. Also, it so happened that among the volunteers on that occasion there was a subject who was appraised rightly as capable of responding to the "breathing technique." Both of these physicians were present at this later seminar, and one had his daughter with him. When the "breathing technique" was employed, the daughter present made the astonished comment, "He is doing that same thing to the lady he is hypnotizing now." At the close of the meeting both physicians approached the author separately to disclose their daughters' analyses of the author's technique.

BACKGROUND OF ORIGINAL OBSERVATION

With the above scanty orientation for the reader, I would now like to start at the beginning of many long years of inquiry, exploration, experimentation, and observation.

As a child in grade school I could not understand the peculiar behavior of my schoolmates. It was inexplicable to me, and it was a source of endless curiosity, why my schoolmates should start wiggling their feet and hands when the teacher sat at the organ and hit the keys and made a lot of noise. I felt no desire to wave my hands, to lift my feet up and down, or to rock from side to side. Nor could I understand why the noise from the organ had anything to do with marching when all you had to do was watch the feet of the person in front of you, and the child leading the march obviously set the pace. But what troubled me most was a peculiar change in the breathing pattern of all my schoolmates, which varied greatly from "Tenting on the Old Campground" to "John Brown's Body Lies a'Mouldering" to "Oh, You Beautiful Doll."

My curious questions on this elicited only the unsatisfactory reply, "Everybody breathes. Don't be silly. Songs are different."

At church old Mrs. Snow (probably in her early 40's) was much in demand as a soloist for weddings, funerals, and weekly services. She also was a regular attendant at community sings.[1] I could never understand why Mrs. Snow put extra syllables into words nor why she did such peculiar breathing, because when she began that kind of breathing, so did other people, even if they didn't sing. When I asked her about it, she gave me irrelevant answers about thoracic, diaphragmatic, and abdominal breathing, but what I wanted to know was why people listening would tighten their throats and change their breathing. I often noticed that people would change their breathing and then begin to hum and then to sing. I also noticed that when people hummed, others would join in, even waving their hands or feet—for which I felt no urge. Then I noticed that people would sometimes become silent and thoughtful and change their breathing and then suddenly begin humming or singing. Also, I noticed many times that a person would change his breathing and soon the person beside him would be breathing the same way, and then they would start singing the same song with no previous mention of the song or singing. I noticed the same thing about people who marched. I could not understand what breathing had to do with foot movement or why one person's breathing could lead someone else to keep step with the special breathing of another person. It simply occurred spontaneously, or, as closely as I could determine, it occurred as a result of the breathing. All of my inquiries elicited rebuffs. Nobody seemed to understand my questions about breathing. Soon I began to keep my inquiries to myself, since everybody dismissed them as foolish.

This only enhanced my curiosity. I began learning to "breathe different ways," and would sit down quietly beside a sister or a schoolmate, apparently absorbed in reading a book, and breathe quietly at what I now know to have been at a subliminal auditory level. I would try to duplicate the breathing pattern for various songs (which I could never do accurately) to see if the person I was sitting beside would begin to hum and then to sing. More often they became irritated but did not recognize that I was breathing in some special manner. It seemed entirely reasonable to me that if people could hear a low, meaningless humming and respond by bursting into song and beating time, that a soft, low, meaningless breathing could effect the same thing. Over and over again I found that breathing and humming could separately elicit the same response, but that when breathing was employed, the other person assumed that he had initiated the singing. Humming was always ascribed to the proper person. Since my curiosity led only to rebuffs and disapproval, I kept my questions to myself, but was stimulated to further searching observations.

---

[1] In the early 1900s a favorite custom for the long cold Wisconsin winter evenings was gathering at a home where there was an organ and singing songs. My older sister was a regular attendant, and I was her escort; but I was never allowed to participate in the "yelling," which my sister indignantly insisted was not yelling but singing.

It was not long before I discovered the contagion of a yawn, and by diligent practice I finally learned how to initiate voluntarily a certain sensory process in my ear, which I still cannot identify and which is always succeeded by a long involuntary series of yawns.

Particularly in high school I utilized this to "rock" my classmates off balance when they were reciting. I could not understand why yawning, a form of breathing, could be as contagious as was humming a popular tune, and why it should lead to certain physical behavior even as humming would lead to beating time with feet and hands. Additionally it also furnished me with personal entertainment.

I always struggled manfully with my uncontrollable yawns once started, with the consequence that the entire class would become involved, including the teacher. One particular classmate was talented musically, and I would sit behind her and unobtrusively breathe in the right fashion to elicit a yawn. She never became aware of my part in the yawning, but she was a most responsive subject for what I would now term subliminal auditory stimulation.

I did not do this too often, just often enough to discover that one could carefully, unobtrusively, unrecognizedly induce others to hum or yawn. I was exceedingly careful never to betray myself.

I could not understand why such minimal sounds as those of breathing could so affect a person and actually be a means of eliciting behavior predetermined by me. Everybody breathed; nobody paid any attention to their breathing unless ill; and yet breathing was on a par with humming, singing, and vocalization of any sort. Also, breathing was basic to vocalization of any sort. Breathing was basic to vocal behavior, but nobody seemed ever to recognize it as such.

When I encountered my first stutterer, I was completely bewildered by his breathing pattern when he *thought of talking* and *when he spoke*. It made me uneasy and uncomfortable, and I avoided it after copying the pattern a couple of times as well as I could to make a classmate uncertain and hesitant in reciting. This frightened me and served to convince me further that people communicated with each other at "breathing" levels of awareness unknown to them. I did not then have an adequate vocabulary nor a clarity of concepts to come to a good understanding, even for myself. But I did know that communication with another could be achieved at a nonverbal and actually unrecognized fashion, but that there had to be definitive stimuli to achieve this end, and that it was best accomplished without the awareness of the other person.

Upon entering college, I was fortunately assigned to an English lecture course conducted by a professor who hated the course and who resented the students. My personal attitude was either like your work or get work you like. At all events I considered him fair game for my personal exploration. It was a wretched semester for him. I enlarged my nonverbal communication by nodding or shaking my head slightly in agreement with what he said, but synchronized my head movements with his respiration. (I always sat where he could see me, and I knew that any student who seemingly unconsciously moved his head in agreement with the teacher would be sought out as a form of solid support.) Soon he was breathing and I was moving my head, in unison. Then, by lagging or by speeding my head movement, I could influence him to change his respiratory rate involuntarily, causing speech difficulties. These in turn became stimuli in themselves for further speech difficulties for him. Or I would go through the preliminary respiratory movements of a yawn and establish in him a state of contagious yawn, which he intensified by his emotional reaction against it. However, I was careful never to be predictably regular. Thus I might "work on him" during the first half of the class period, the last half, the middle half, or a quarter of the period, always in some random fashion.

17. An Indirect Induction of Trance: Simulation and the Role of Indirect Suggestion and Minimal Cues

Milton H. Erickson

A student majoring in experimental psychology became greatly interested in hypnosis, and in the fall of 1923 he asked the author to collaborate with him in a special study. This project was to be a comparison and contrasting of the somnambulistic behaviors of different subjects in exhibiting various types of hypnotic phenomena. In preparation he had been training a number of volunteer subjects to develop somnambulistic trances. He proposed that the author participate with him in taking one of the better subjects and inducing a profound somnambulistic trance. Then, working together, they could use that subject to formulate a systematic procedure by which hypnotic phenomena could be elicited in an orderly and related fashion. The author readily accepted this offer.

At the appointed time the author was introduced to the volunteer subject, a third-year student majoring in literature, obviously a highly intelligent and perceptive person. As the introductions were made, the psychology student, Mr. H, casually handed the author a sealed envelope indicating that it was to be read at some later time.

The subject was remarkably competent, and a long series of tasks was done by him. As a final task, he was asked, at the request of the psychology student, to write three brief sentences pertaining to his childhood. These were not to be read immediately. Instead, the paper bearing them was to be folded and placed for safekeeping in a convenient book, the object being a test for hypnotic amnesia and to determine the processes of reassociation in recovering hypnotically repressed memories.

The subject was then awakened and there developed an extensive discussion of hypnotic phenomena in general and the hypnotic subject's behavior specifically, in which the subject tried to participate but could not do so successfully because of hypnotic amnesia. Finally the general question was raised by the psychology student concerning the possibility of successfully pretending to be in a trance, and what was there about the volunteer subject's trance behavior that would render it difficult for another to duplicate it by pretending to be in

---

Unpublished paper written in the 1960s.

Indirect Trance Induction

a trance? Wholly unsuspecting, the author made many dogmatic assertions, finally being brought to a painful halt by the request that he examine the contents of the envelope handed him when he first entered the room. Perusal of the contents disclosed the message, signed by the volunteer subject, "Tonight I am going to give a fake performance of every hypnotic act you suggest to me, and I am going to pretend to write automatically three brief sentences about my early childhood which will read as follows . . . . "—and three sentences were appended. Checking with the folded sheet of "automatic writing" confirmed the author's unhappy predicament. A few questions put to the subject gave abundant proof that the author had been most thoroughly hoaxed.

There followed a complete account by the psychology student of his systematic instruction and coaching of the subject, who was an experienced actor majoring in drama, by having him study the somnambulistic behavior of hypnotic subjects and then imitate it. The actor proved to be an apt pupil, and he was personally interested in the project since it presented to him an opportunity for special training in acting. When the actor judged that he could perform creditably, the psychologist proposed the experimental testing of the imitation by undertaking to deceive the author. This, if successful, would then be followed by an experimental study of actual and pretended hypnosis to be done by the psychologist and, it was hoped, by the author. The statement was made that the author was now so thoroughly sensitized that he would be a most able and critical judge of pretense and actuality.

The proposal was made that a joint study could now be developed and that the next step might logically be the converse of what had already been done. That is, now that it had been demonstrated that the operator could be deceived, could the "subject" be deceived?

Discussion of this led to the experimental plan of securing another experienced actor. Both the psychologist and the first actor would coach him with the purported intention of deceiving the author. However, the author, being fully aware of the situation, would then be in a position to maneuver the subject out of his deceptive role without betraying that fact to the subject. Just how this was to be done would be the author's task; the training of the next actor would be their task.

The second actor, another drama major, was decidedly competent. He could sneeze repeatedly, cough, gag, retch, even vomit, shed tears, and chatter his teeth, among other things, at will. He was given to understand that the author was exceedingly well experienced in hypnosis and that the purpose to be served was not just a hoax but a serious enterprise in comparing and contrasting behavioral manifestations in waking and hypnotic states. He recognized the validity of this proposal and also recognized his own opportunity to learn something more about acting.

The student and the two actors, together with a half-dozen good somnambulistic subjects who were unaware of the actors' purposes, worked hard training the subject until the psychologist and the first actor were certain of the second actor's competence.

When this task had been finally accomplished, the author was introduced to both actors by the graduate student, thereby adding further to the appearance of a hoax. The author pretended to make a choice of the two actors, Mr. A and Mr. B, as possible volunteer subjects by tossing and catching a coin and announcing his reading of it as indicating that the second actor, Mr. B, had been selected by chance as the first subject to be hypnotized.

As a preliminary measure of further confirmation for Mr. B that a hoax was being perpetrated upon the author, Mr. A was instructed in great detail to be most attentive to the author's trance induction of Mr. B and of Mr. B's hypnotic responses so that "perhaps you can learn more rapidly and effectively how to go into a trance, *perhaps even to go into a trance most unexpectedly.*" This last (italicized) statement was said with impressive but soft emphasis, glancing from one to the other of the two actors. Both the student and Mr. A tended to disregard the meaning of the statement because of their awareness of the situation. Mr. B was impressed by the emphasis but assumed it was meant to be meaningful only to Mr. A. Hence, he ignored it as personally intended. Thus both A and B heard a significant suggestion, but each assumed it to have no significance for himself, and was merely intended to carry a special message for the other person.

Then the author went through an eye-fixation and lid-closure technique of induction and elicited from his "subject" an excellent highly creditable imitation of somnambulistic phenomena. However, there was, to the author, no question that the hypnotic behavior was not genuine, but it was also apparent to him that to differentiate descriptively between the genuine and the false would be most difficult.

As apparently the last activity, the author suggested that automatic writing be done. A full, laboriously elaborate description of this was offered, and then, to the astonishment of Mr. A and the psychology student, Mr. A was asked to join Mr. B in this activity. They were told to walk slowly across the laboratory floor and to seat themselves in an upright position in the two chairs already in place on opposite sides of a laboratory table. In front of them they would find pencils and a paper pad on which to write. As they sat down, they were to pick up a pencil, place their hands in a writing position, and stare rigidly and continuously only at the eyes of the other. They were to walk in unison to their separate sides of the table, to pick up their pencils *in unison*—everything was to be done slowly, deliberately, and *in unison*. Nothing at all was said about Mr. A developing hypnosis, and no explanatory look was given to him or to the psychology student. As the two slowly took their seats, picked up their pencils, and positioned their hands, the author placed in front of each a screen, explaining to them that the screen would allow them to see only each other's eyes alone but neither their hands nor those of the other. Then, as they continued to look steadily at one another's eyes, they were to write *in unison at the rate of not*

Indirect Trance Induction

more than one letter every three to five seconds until they had written a brief sentence, very brief, about some forgotten event of October 1917. When they had written as instructed, they were silently to move their hands from the pad still holding the pencil. And they were to continue staring steadily into each other's eyes.

From a position of vantage the author kept both under full observation and silently, in a most expectant manner, waited. Fifteen minutes elapsed before the task was completed, being first accomplished in five minutes by Mr. A. Then Mr. B completed his writing, doing it at first in a most hesitant manner and then much more slowly than the other but seemingly in an improved state of comfort. They were both then instructed to rise slowly, still facing each other, then to turn and to walk *in unison* to the north end of the room, where they would note a chalked circle on the floor. They were to stand silently at attention facing each other from opposite sides of the circle. Immediately as they assumed their position, the author instructed them, "Now, Mr. A and Mr. B, continue to look at each other, but as you do so, each of you is to assume the identity, the personality of the other. This is to be done even as I am giving these instructions and will be completed as I finish this sentence. [Pause.] *Now maintain the status quo*. I shall leave the room for five minutes, and while I am gone, you will continue to *maintain the status quo* and you will do so after I return until I instruct you otherwise and *all instructions you will obey exactly*." The author left the room, quietly pocketing the automatic writing on his way.

As soon as the author had left the room, the psychology student, as he related subsequently, had remarked, "Wonder what he is up to now!" and looked expectantly at the two actors. To his astonishment, he found that both were in a deep trance and completely out of rapport with him. He spent the next few minutes desperately trying to establish rapport and to solve the problem the situation constituted.

As the author reentered the room (the departure had been to give the psychology student an opportunity to discover the situation, and his facial expression betrayed that he had), he addressed the subjects, "My colleague is now going to ask *one of you to arouse as you are*. You will be aware of him until you note that he is addressing the other, and then that one only will be aware of him." The fellow student was handed a written message reading, "Say to them, 'I am now speaking to you and I want you just as you are to awaken now, Mr. B.'" The student was astonished when Mr. A aroused and looked questioningly and bewilderedly at his fellow actor, the psychology student, the author, and then appeared to note his position in a puzzled way and to glance uncertainly at the chair over at the laboratory table. He was obviously at a loss to understand his situation. He was asked, "Would you like to speak or ask something?" "I certainly would! How did Jack get into my clothes [a startled facial expression and he looked down at himself], and how did I get into his? Not a bad fit, but I don't want them!" He proceeded to divest himself of his jacket, placing it upon a chair. He was asked to drop that matter and to explain how he felt. His answer was simply that he was too bewildered to think, and his eyes kept straying to his colleague, to the jacket on the chair and the trousers he was wearing. He seemed incapable of thinking spontaneously about anything else.

The second subject was then aroused by first touching his arm and then saying, "I am shortly going to ask you to awaken. Let me repeat, *I alone,* am going to ask you to awaken. Do so now!" Promptly the pseudo-Mr. A aroused and looked expectantly at the author. His colleague asked, "Why are you wearing my clothes, Jack?" but received no reply. It soon became apparent that the pseudo-Mr. A was in rapport with the author only and that he was simply passively awaiting instructions from the author. When it was judged that the situation was fully as clear as it could be to the others, the author flicked a glance at the jacket on the chair. The subject glanced at it, his face assumed a puzzled look, he glanced at the jacket he was wearing, glanced back at the jacket on the chair, then seemed to be struck with a new thought and glanced at his trousers. The author gave no encouragement to him that might lead to speaking. In troubled silence the subject looked around, noted the chairs at the table and the chalked circle but still continued not to see the others present.

There followed a great variety of manipulations, removing the amnesia from one, then restoring it, suggesting the return of the correct identity of one but not of the other, then reversing this until both actors and the psychology student were without doubt as to the genuineness of their hypnotic behavior and its marked difference from nonhypnotic behavior. But particularly bewildering to both A and B were their separately available memories of being in a trance, of being depersonalized, recalling their bewilderment when seemingly in the wrong clothes, and their inability to know when or how they developed a trance, and noting the ease with which the author could induce amnesias in the other upon request.

Finally, the author asked both separately (sending one out of the room while the other was questioned) about when they first developed a trance state. Both, after careful study of their recollections, offered the spontaneous statement that their last waking state memory dealt with "walking over together and sitting down in a chair and looking at [the other]." Beyond this neither could go. Indirect inquiry soon disclosed that neither remembered about the automatic writing, and when mention was made of automatic writing, both expressed a willingness to try it. The author repositioned the chair, seated them, and asked them, as a form of practice in writing, to "Just *snatch three words out of nowhere that you don't remember* and just write them down." This statement was given with careful emphasis. Both obeyed, with puzzled looks, and one noted that he had written "Me swim cold" while the other had written "Police arrested me." Extensive questioning by the author and the psychology student, who was following the author's lead, failed to establish any meaningfulness for the written words. The one stated that he had never been arrested, the other said he had done a lot of swimming when it was cold but otherwise what he had

Indirect Trance Induction 371

written was without meaning. When their lack of understanding had been obviously clearly defined, the author handed each his previously done automatic writing, saying with quiet emphasis, "'Remember!''

Both did so amazedly. First they recalled the actual experiences, a fall out of a boat and swimming ashore, the other an arrest for a Hallowe'en prank. Then they recovered the approximate date in October 1917, and then they noted that the automatic script was definitely of a rounded, childish character, quite unlike their own regular handwriting.

Among the many aspects of the evening's events reviewed and speculated upon was how a trance had been induced in them. B was chagrined to find that the author had in some way outmaneuvered him and was intrigued to know that A had hoaxed the author. A could only express his astonishment that he had been in some indirect way hypnotized, but he could not offer even an approximate guess of how it had happened. They were told that the author would describe the plan he had worked out in detail before coming to the laboratory, describing in detail the steps. If this seemed to be wrong, they were to say so. If the steps were correctly stated, or approximately so, they were to *sense whatever was the degree of correctness the described step had.*

The explanation was: "While Mr. B was faking so competently under the impression that he was deceiving me, quite possibly Mr. B was wondering if I would use Mr. A. Unquestionably he expected me to do so because of the coin tossing, which was only a pretense of deciding which was to be the subject. But only the author knew this. At the same time Mr. A was also undoubtedly wondering the same thing. Also, Mr. B was intensely concerned about giving the best possible performance he could. Mr. A, of course, knew that I was aware of the situation and that I was probably planning some special work concerning the actual deception of Mr. B despite Mr. B's belief that he was deceiving me. This special plan presumably might involve hypnosis. Mr. A could not know if the hypnosis involved him or Mr. B or both of them, but he could wonder. Yet I asked nothing of Mr. A except participation in an automatic-writing situation. The request was made that they walk *in unison,* sit down *in unison,* pick up the pencils, and so on, all *in unison.* This was *not a request for deceptive behavior but a request for a different kind of behavior than what had been presented* by either A or B previously. In responding to the request, Mr. A had thought of possible hypnosis in mind for himself and possibly for Mr. B, and the peculiar character of the task took Mr. B completely out of his role of behaving deceptively. He had to act differently, but how? *They were to see only each other's eyes,* and this was further emphasized by openly restricting their visual fields. They were being helplessly manipulated. The writing instructions they were given were worded puporsely to create a totally new writing situation for them, one in which they wrote slowly, laboriously, as they had in their remote past. The very situation compelled them to cooperate, but they could not determine for themselves how to cooperate. The instruction about the writing was intended to evoke a childhood pattern of script that would in turn elicit an actual age regression. The author picked the year of 1917 as appropriate, and the month of October because it was likely to have special childhood memories of Hallowe'en not too quickly realized by adults. The waiting at the table only gave both more opportunity to respond to the nondeceptive possibilities of the hypnotic situation, because neither Mr. A nor Mr. B could be entirely sure of himself or of the other. They had seen somnambulistic hypnotic states, and they were finding themselves in a situation they could neither falsify nor manipulate. The author was utterly and completely in charge. Both Mr. A and Mr. B were in a psychologic bind because the one had to do as did the other, and neither could act on his own responsibility. Both could suspect the other of hypnosis. *Neither could see any opportunity for deceptive behavior.* Then they were positioned on the chalk circle, which they had not previously noticed, walking *in unison, in unison* staring only at each other. *'Maintain the status quo'* is certainly not an expected hypnotic command, but it certainly is definitive as a command in commanding the continuance of hypnosis *if it exists.* The command itself would serve to dispel any doubts or lingering uncertainities they might have about hypnosis. Thereafter it would be a posthypnotic cue, since the command was definitely associated with a mental status, not just a physical position, at the chalk circle. In securing the automatically written material, care was taken to keep them in the waking state, by having them alertly *keep in unison,* thus to prevent any recovery of hypnotic memories, and *they were not told to write* but to 'snatch three words out of the nowhere that you don't remember' and just to write, not automatically, those words. In 'just snatch' was conveyed the implication that the words were already there, 'out of the nowhere that you don't remember.' Well, that 'nowhere' was the hypnotic amnesia and the forgotten automatic writing. They remembered only up to the point of the chairs in which they sat. All the rest became 'a nowhere that you can't remember,' not understandable in the waking state but readily so in the trance state.''

18. Notes on Minimal Cues in Vocal Dynamics and Memory[1]

Milton H. Erickson

Following Clark L. Hull's example, I made notes on a lot of observations on things that interested me and that I thought might some day be useful. A couple of weeks ago I happened to pull a folder out of my filing cabinet and found sheets of yellow and white paper bearing the enclosed material which I put together as a continuum. The first part was discussed with Larry Kubie and with Dave Rappaport when he was engrossed in writing his book on "Memory."

It is all material that helped shape my thinking about hypnosis and the importance of factors seemingly totally unrelated.

One of my favorite recollections is an incident that occurred when I was standing in the barn doorway when I was about ten years old. A "brilliant" idea occurred to me, now long forgotten. I knew to execute that brilliant idea I would need a hammer and a hatchet. But those things were on the back porch. I rushed to get the tools, but in some way, by the time I reached the porch, I had completely forgotten what I was after. Following a long, fruitless mental search, I returned to the barn door and recalled my brilliant idea and what was needed to execute it. My brilliant idea was associated with the barn door where I happened to get it.

That led to climbing trees and learning poems from an old magazine of my grandmother's. I picked trees at random, short poems at random, and noted the connection between individual trees and the poems I learned while sitting in those trees. Three years later I went on an exploration tour and found that when I climbed the right tree, my memory of the poem associated with it was greatly improved.

Notes on Minimal Cues: 1933-1964[2]

During the years 1930-34, while I was on the Research Service of the Worces-

---

[1] Unpublished letter to the editor, October 19, 1974.
[2] Editor's Note: Following is the unpublished material referred to in the above letter and written by Erickson in 1964.

ter State Hospital in Massachusetts, I slowly began acquiring an Eastern or "Harvard" accent. This was primarily a partial replacement of the flat A-sounds of the Midwest with the broad A-sounds of the Eastern coast. The replacement was amusingly inconsistent to my colleagues, since in a single sentence both broad and flat A-sounds would be enunciated while words of more than one syllable containing the letter "A" might be spoken with both the flat and broad A-sounds. A colleague who worked with me both as co-experimenter and as a hypnotic subject was the daughter of a university professor of English. She was highly sensitive to the spoken word and was writing her Ph.D. dissertation on an aspect of verbal communication. At first she was annoyed by the inconsistency of my use of both broad and flat A-sounds but shortly became amused by it. However, she was highly intolerant of split infinitives and very demanding of absolute precision and conciseness in hypnotic suggestions, since she objected to any need to redefine in her mind any suggestions given her in hypnotic experiments. Indeed, she would interrupt ongoing experiments to protest any "sloppiness" of speech. Her contention, with which I came to agree strongly, was that every hypnotic suggestion should be given in language permitting "ready and simplistic interpretation," explaining that the hypnotic state tended to limit the spoken word to its literal meaning. She further contended that precision and conciseness of instruction allowed subjects to respond in terms of their own understandings, free from added enforced implications of social adjustments. For example, the question, "Will you look at me?" requires an answer of no more than a no or a yes or an I don't know, rather than the execution of a physical response. Two other colleagues, also working on Ph.D. dissertations concerning aspects of the communication of ideas, both of whom had acted as co-experimenters and as hypnotic subjects, agreed with this understanding when their opinions were sought.

In a discussion of my inconsistent use of broad and flat A-sounds, it was regarded as signifying slowness in linguistic learning. None of them knew that I had not learned to talk until the age of four years despite a sister two years younger who began talking at the age of one year and was very fluent at the age of two years. The late Edward Sapir, the linguist, then the Sterling professor at Yale University, after listening to me lecture, spontaneously made the same comment and made direct mention of my tone deafness and primitive rhythm of speech.

The above information was kept in mind but without conscious utilization in subsequent experimental work.

Within two months after leaving Massachusetts in 1934, I had lost the broad A-sound, having been very self-conscious of it in the first few weeks in Michigan.

No more thought was given to my "lost accent" until September, 1937, when I attended the American Psychological Convention in Minnesota. There I encountered my former psychological colleagues. To my surprise, the mixture of broad and flat A-sounds returned to my speech, and they commented on my retention of my "Harvard accent." Only the emphatic assertions of my wife convinced them that it was a recurrence occasioned by the stimulation of old associative pathways by meeting them.

All traces of that "accent" disappeared on the way home to Michigan. Nothing more was thought about that matter except as something interesting to record, possibly for some future speculation.

In September, 1941, I learned that two former medical colleagues, who had left Massachusetts, one shortly before and one slightly after I left, were going to call on me on the same Saturday afternoon. Both were coming from two different Midwest states. This called to mind the earlier records I had made and provided the background for a field experiment in relation to unusual factors in memory-retention recovery.

Accordingly, for the several days preceding the arrival of Drs. A and B, I endeavored to recall the first names of the patients that I had worked with on the Research Service at Worcester, actually worked with jointly with my colleagues.

My colleagues arrived about ten minutes apart and were met by my secretary, who greeted each separately, escorted them to different rooms, furnished each with a notebook and pencils, explaining that I wished their help in an experiment I was currently conducting. This help was their recalling the first names of patients they had worked with on the Research Service. Each was told that the length of time to be allotted was at least a half-hour. They would be undisturbed and could work in silence, but that she would return in 30 to 40 minutes.

Both A and B acquiesced to the request readily. At the expiration of slightly more than 30 minutes my secretary told Dr. A, who told her that he had written down all the names he could recall, that there would begin shortly another half-hour of participation during which he was not to speak under any condition to anybody, and that she would return in a minute with further instructions. She then went two doors away, where Dr. B was idling time away unable to recall additional names. To him she explained that she would take him to another room to participate in another phase of the experiment and that under no condition was he to speak to anybody.

She led Dr. B into the room where Dr. A was waiting. Both were startled, since neither knew that the other had planned to visit me. Neither spoke, but my secretary instructed them to make a new list of additional names recalled.

Twenty minutes later she entered the room to find each with a new list, but merely biding their time for new instructions. She handed Dr. B that day's newspaper and brought Dr. A to my office, admonishing him on the way not to speak to anyone but merely to make a list of any additional names that he recalled after she had indicated where he was to seat himself.

Even as I began to make a list of additional names, so did Dr. A. Within 10 minutes we both had exhausted our recollection, so I signaled my secretary. She entered the office, asked Dr. A to maintain silence and to accompany her to another room where she handed him a newspaper. Then she brought Dr. B into my office, giving him the same instructions as she had given Dr. A.

Both Dr. B and I listed new names, but shortly we had exhausted our recollection. Upon signal my secretary brought in Dr. A, giving instructions for continued silence and a listing of any additional names.

Each of us added more names, but we soon gave up trying for more.

We then began exchanging personal news, followed by a discussion of the purpose of the tasks my secretary had asked of them. During this discussion Dr. B amusedly commented on the return of my "half-aahssed Harvard accent." This led to the awareness that all of us had reverted to some degree to the speech learning each of us had acquired during the more than three years each of us had spent at Worcester, Massachusetts, before leaving for different Midwest states.

Examination of the various lists revealed 37 names on my first list, 21 on Dr. A's, and 16 on Dr. B's. In Dr. A's presence Dr. B added 5 more names while Dr. A added 9 to his list. In my presence Dr. A added 7 more names to his list while I added 3 more. With Dr. B I added 1 name, he added 5. With the three of us together, I listed 5 more names, Dr. A added 11, Dr. B added 9. My total of names recalled was 46, while Dr. A's list totalled 41, and that of Dr. B totalled 35.

Although the number of names was 125, they represented only 95 individuals. Of these I had 21 in common with Dr. A and 14 in common with Dr. B. Dr. A had 18 in common with Dr. B. The three of us had in common only 16.

During our weekend visit new names occurred to both during our examination of our lists and spontaneously when visiting in other regards. No record was made of these names, since the actual method of recollection was vastly different.

The next observations pertinent to those above were made repeatedly during lecture trips to Boston at intervals between the years of 1957-1963. The first observation occurred quite unexpectedly while on a plane bound for Boston. While I was engaged in active conversation with my seatmate, the pilot of the plane announced over the loudspeaker, "We are now leaving the space over New York State, entering that of Massachusetts and beginning our descent to the Boston Airport."

As we resumed our conversation, I was astonished by my admixture of broad and flat A-sounds. It attracted the attention of my seatmate who commented, "You Harvard men never do forget your Harvard days. Is this a nostalgic trip for you?"

During the ensuing explanation and discussion, he commented on his own experience in noting that geography as well as many other items in life experience evoked past learnings.

On the return trip from Boston I noted that I had left behind my broad A-sounds only to be recovered on my next trip to Boston.

On one occasion, as the plane left New York City, I recalled the 1941 inquiry about recalling names of Worcester patients. I immediately set about listing names and had recalled 23 before reaching Boston. On a subsequent trip to Boston I spent an evening with a former associate, then living in Worcester. On the 40-mile trip from Boston to Worcester, I began recalling not only names but the year in which I met them. This had been attempted unsuccessfully by the three of us in 1941 but with unsatisfactory results. Upon returning home the next week, I checked my recollection of the names I had recalled on the way to Worcester. I recalled less than half of them. Of the identifying years, my recollections were essentially guesswork, in contradiction to the previous week's feeling of certainty and the confirmation by my former colleague who had been on the Research Service as long as I had.

III. On the Nature of Suggestion

In this section we may gain an overall perspective for comparing Erickson's own approach with those of his numerous students and collaborators. Erickson's own work may be characterized as the classical approach of exploring the nature of hypnotic phenomena and suggestion for its own sake as well as for its therapeutic applications. Most of his students and colleagues in the medical and dental professions have followed him in this classical approach, which is represented by Erickson's first book, *The Practical Application of Medical and Dental Hypnosis* (Julian Press, 1961), written with Hershman and Secter.

This classical approach is well represented in the first paper of this section "Concerning the nature and character of posthypnotic behavior." It is written with his wife Elizabeth in the scholarly tradition of first reviewing the work of one's predecessors and then adding the results of one's new observations and findings. There are no experimental designs, statistics, or control groups, however. There is only the insight and particular genius of the intrepid explorer who is at one with his field of inquiry. Actually it is difficult to understand how the most significant finding of this paper, that posthypnotic responses are themselves carried out in "a spontaneous, self-limited, posthypnotic trance" could have been discovered with all the paraphernalia of the modern experimental method. Careful observation, an infinite curiosity, and a few decades of devoted practice and study of hypnotic phenomena were required to recognize this most subtle alteration of consciousness, which had apparently escaped the notice of all previous investigators. Since the publication of this finding many of Erickson's students and clinical colleagues have recognized its value and explored its therapeutic applications. To the best of our knowledge, however, no one has yet done an experimental study to validate it and describe its parameters.

The same could be said of most of the other approaches elaborated by others in their studies with Erickson. The first of these other approaches is that of *psychoanalytic theory*, represented by the early work of Erickson in the 1930s and 1940s, in collaboration with Kubie, Hill, Huston and Shakow. These studies are presented in Volume 3 of this series, which deals with the hypnotic investigation of psychodynamic processes.

The second of the major collaborative approaches began in the 1950s with the *Double Bind Interpersonal Approach* of Bateson, Haley, and Weakland, which was represented in *Transcript of a trance induction* in Section II, and continued into the 1970s with the work of Watzlawick (1978), who emphasized the role of the left and right cerebral hemispheres in psychotherapeutic work. The 1950s was also a period in which Erickson worked extensively with Linn Cooper in studying the new hypnotic phenomenon called "time distortion."

The detailed analysis of Erickson's work was picked up again in the early 1970s by the editor, who sought an understanding of Erickson's own interpretation of his work unbiased by anyone else's theory or frames of reference. From this collaboration the twin themes of *utilization theory* and the *indirect forms of suggestion* emerged as the essence of Erickson's unique contribution to an understanding of the nature of hypnotic suggestion. These twin themes were already apparent in many of Erickson's original papers written decades earlier. Along with these themes, and perhaps in tune with modern humanistic psychology, came the third major approach which emphasized how the patient's own *creative processes* are evoked by hypnotic suggestion so that *human potentials could be actualized*. As will be seen in the fourth volume in this series, *Hypnotherapy: Innovative Approaches*, Erickson's therapuetic preoccupation throughout his career has been precisely in this area of helping patients break out of learned limitations so that their potentials could become manifest.

By the middle 1970s, yet another approach, that of *Chomsky's Transformational Linguistics*, was applied to an analysis of Erickson's work by Bandler and Grinder in their projected three volumes on *Patterns of the Hypnotic Techniques of Milton H. Erickson, M. D.*, (1975). During this same period Beahrs (1971, 1977a, 1977f; Beahrs & Humiston, 1974) added an existential dimension to our understanding of Erickson.

Each of these collaborative approaches is contributing to the current ferment of exploration into the nature of hypnotic suggestion. The papers of this section can only reflect a portion of that ferment. What we now clearly need is some extended experimental work to assess the relative merits of these theoretical ideas. The many students and professionals who are currently having informal seminars with Dr. Erickson may be the harbingers of this future work.

19. Concerning The Nature and Character Of Posthypnotic Behavior

Milton H. Erickson and Elizabeth M. Erickson

Despite the general familiarity of posthypnotic behavior and its extensive role in both experimental and therapeutic work, little recognition has been given to it as a problem complete in itself. Instead attention has been focused almost exclusively upon the various activities suggested to the subjects as posthypnotic tasks, with little heed given to the nature of the behavior characterizing, if not constituting, the posthypnotic state, and which influences and perhaps determines the nature and extent of the suggested posthypnotic performance. Emphasis has been placed primarily upon the results obtained from posthypnotic suggestions and not upon the character or nature of the psychological setting in which they were secured. The study of the mental processes and the patterns of behavior upon which those results are based and which must necessarily be in effect in some manner previous to, if not also during, the posthypnotic performance, has been neglected. Yet despite a lack of adequate experimental provision there has been a general recognition of certain significant facts regarding the posthypnotic performance which imply directly the existence of a special mental state or condition constituting the background out of which the posthypnotic act derives.

Foremost among these facts is the occurrence of the posthypnotic act in response to a suggestion which is remote from the situation in which it has its effect. Next the immediate stimulus, posthypnotic signal, or cue eliciting the posthypnotic act serves only to establish the time for the activity and not the kind of behavior, since this is determined by other factors. Also the posthypnotic act is not consciously motivated but derives out of a remote situation of which the subject is not consciously aware. Finally it is not an integrated part of the behavior of the total situation in which it occurs, but is actually disruptive of the conscious stream of activity, with which it may be entirely at variance.

In a search of the literature published during the past 20 years, covering approximately 450 titles, no references were found which were suggestive of a direct study of posthypnotic behavior itself, although many of the titles indicated

---

Reprinted with permission from *The Journal of Genetic Psychology,* 1941, 24, 95-133.

that posthypnotic suggestion had been used to study other patterns of behavior. Similarly a review of approximately 150 selected articles and books, some of which were published as early as 1888, yielded only a little information definitive of posthypnotic behavior as a specific phenomenon.

The more instructive references were found chiefly in the general textbooks on hypnotism rather than in experimental studies involving the use of posthypnotic behavior. However, even these were general assertions or brief, vague, and sometimes self-contradictory statements, based either upon the author's own experience and that of others, or upon experimental material of an inadequate and often irrelevant character in which there was a marked confusion of the results of suggested posthypnotic activities with the mental processes and patterns of posthypnotic behavior by which those results were obtained.

Nevertheless, despite their inadequacies the references found did indicate that there had been frequent recognition of posthypnotic behavior as constituting a phenomenon in itself, and a number of these will be cited and discussed briefly, with emphasis placed primarily upon those points we propose to develop in direct relation to experimental data in the body of this paper.

Thus Bernheim (1895, p. 157), in discussing posthypnotic activities, states, "I have said that somnambulists who are susceptible to suggestions *à longue échéance* are all eminently suggestible, even in the waking condition; they pass from one state of consciousness into the other very easily; I repeat the fact that they are somnambulists spontaneously, without any sort of preparation," but he offers no elaboration of this statement.

Likewise, Sidis (1898, p. 174), gives recognition to the fact that posthypnotic behavior is a thing apart from ordinary conscious behavior and is marked by special characteristics. He declares, "The posthypnotic suggestion rises up from the depths of the secondary self as a fixed, insistent idea. . . . In hypnosis the suggestion is taken up by the secondary, subwaking, suggestible self, and then afterward this suggestion breaks through the stream of waking consciousness. . . ." Without attempting to develop these points he proceeds with a discussion of certain experimental results, actually irrelevant to these observations.

Similarly, Bramwell (1921, p. 95) states:

> Under ordinary circumstances, the instant hypnosis is terminated all the phenomena which have characterized it immediately disappear. In response to suggestion, however, one or more of these phenomena may manifest themselves in the subject's waking life. This is brought about in two ways. (1) Where the operator suggests that one or more of the phenomena shall persist after waking. . . . (2) The most interesting class of posthypnotic suggestions, however, are those in which the appearance of the phenomena has been delayed until some more or less remote time after the termination of hypnosis.

Later in the same chapter Bramwell (1921, pp.111-112) states, "According to most authorities posthypnotic suggestions, even when executed some time after awakening, are not carried out in the normal condition; there is, in effect, a new hypnosis or a state closely resembling it." He proceeds:

> According to Moll, the conditions under which posthypnotic acts are carried out vary widely. He summarizes them as follows: (1) A state in which a new hypnosis, characterized by suggestibility, appears during the execution of the act, with loss of memory afterwards and no spontaneous awakening. (2) A state in which no symptoms of a fresh hypnosis are discoverable although the act is carried out. (3) A state with or without fresh susceptibility to suggestion, with complete forgetfulness of the act and spontaneous awaking. (4) A state of susceptibility to suggestion with subsequent loss of memory.

Apparently Bramwell approves of this fairly adequate, though confusingly worded recognition by Moll of the existence of a posthypnotic state. Nevertheless he continues his discussion with an irrelevant exposition of the immediate results obtained through posthypnotic suggestion in the treatment of physiological disturbances. Except for other similar unsatisfactory and scattered references he makes no further effort to elaborate his points or those he emphasizes from Moll.

Schilder and Kauders (1927, p. 64) offer the following statements which by their somewhat contradictory nature serve to emphasize that the post hypnotic state is of a special character, but that it is hard to recognize:

> Certain authors actually assume that the hypnosis again comes to life during the execution of the posthypnotic command, an assumption which is justifiable to the extent that in a number of such cases the persons experimented on actually do enter into a dream-like state while executing the posthypnotic order. In other cases, the person complying with the posthypnotic order can hardly be distinguished from any other person carrying out an order, so that it would be far-fetched to speak of a renewal of the hypnotic state.

No further effort is made to develop these points, except by a general discussion of some results obtained through posthypnotic suggestion.

Binet and Féré (1888, p. 177) recognize that subjects show a peculiar sensitivity to suggestion after awakening from a trance, and they direct attention to posthypnotic behavior as a specific phenomenon, placing emphasis upon this highly significant observation, ". . . when a subject remains under the influence of a suggestion after awaking, he has not, whatever be the appearance to the contrary, returned to his normal state."

Hull (1933, p. 300), in direct relation to this passage, takes exception to their declaration, commenting, "This statement is similarly ambiguous from our present point of view because acts performed by posthypnotic suggestion constitute a special case, as is shown by the fact that they are usually followed by waking amnesia of the acts in question." Just how this comment applies to that observation by Binet and Féré is uncertain. Although Hull, in his textbook published in 1933, does recognize that posthypnotic behavior is a "special case," he disregards his own statement as well as his awareness of the observation by Binet and Féré. Neither he nor his associates make any attempt in their extensive experimental work to provide for the possible existence of any special posthypnotic state which might have a significant bearing upon posthypnotic activities, without regard for the possible influence upon the assigned task of the mental processes and patterns of behavior peculiar to the posthypnotic state, and which might significantly, although perhaps indirectly, control the entire character of the posthypnotic performance. For example, quoting the work of various experimenters, Hull devotes an entire chapter of his textbook to post-hypnotic phenomena, but limits the chapter to studies of amnesia for directly suggested activities and of the durability of posthypnotic commands, with no reference to that mental state or condition of which the retention and execution of suggestions constitute only a partial reflection.

Nor are Hull and his associates alone in this regard, since it is a general tendency to study posthypnotic behavior only in terms of how well some suggested task is done, without regard for the mental state or psychic condition constituting the setting for that task. There seems to be no general recognition of the fact that the task performance is only a partial manifestation of the general mental state, and not until adequate provision is made for the needs of the situation in which the task is to be done can it be considered a measure of the capacity for performance.

In our judgment it is this oversight of the special character of the posthypnotic state that accounts in large part for the confused, unreliable, and contradictory nature of the results obtained in experimental studies of posthypnotic phenomena.

Thus in his study of functional anaesthesias Lundholm (1928, p. 338) states, "The experiments were carried out with the subject in a posthypnotic, fully waking condition, but in which he was deaf for the sound-click, the deafness being due to preceding suggestion during hypnotic sleep." An assumption is thereby made that the subject was fully awake and not in either a partially waking or a somnambulistic state, and there is no recognition of the fact that the suggestions given served to effect an actual continuance of the significant part of the trance state, since the posthypnotic suggestion compelled an uninterrupted persistence of certain phenomena of the trance state, not possible in a fully waking condition.

Another instance in which there is a complete disregard for the posthypnotic state and a confusion of somnambulistic states with the waking condition may be found in Platanow's (1933) experiment on age regression. In describing his experiments he states:

> After the subject had reached a suitable state of hypnosis, we generally addressed him as follows:
> *"At present you are six years old."* (This suggestion was repeated three times.) *"After you wake up you will be a child of six. Wake up!"*
> After the subject was awake, a short conversation was held with him, for orientation purposes, and this was followed by tests according to the Binet-Simon method. By means of suggestion the subjects were transferred to the ages of four, six, and ten. When transferred from one age to another they were hypnotized, given the corresponding suggestion, and awakened again. The experiments were generally ended by the suggestion of the real age, and were followed by amnesia.

From this description one is led to believe that the subjects were awake in the ordinary sense of the word during the administration of the psychometric tests, despite the experimenter's recognition of the fact that normal waking memories did not obtain and the fact that his experimental findings proved amply that a mental state other than the normal waking one was elicited by the posthypnotic suggestions.

Fortunately in both of the above experiments this confused and contradictory use of terms did not affect the validity of the findings or the conclusions.

A search of Hull's articles, as well as those of his associates, shows many references to the problems involved in studying the outcome of the posthypnotic state, but there is no apparent realization that the subject, as a consequence of receiving posthypnotic suggestions or in executing posthypnotic acts, might manifest behavior apart from the assigned task, which could alter the task performances significantly. Thus he proposes studies of learning behavior in response to posthypnotic suggestion or of amnesias as posthypnotic phenomena, without any provision for the possible effect, direct or indirect, which the posthypnotic state might have upon the behavior elicited (Hull, 1931). He is interested, apparently, only in the results secured, and he does not seem to realize that any interpretation of those results must be made in specific terms of the psychological setting in which they were obtained rather than in a categorization as broad and ill-defined as is the term "posthypnotic". The tendency to regard the results as representing a posthypnotic performance is of value to that extent only, but does not give any understanding of what the posthypnotic state itself is, and it accounts largely for the variability of the findings of posthypnotic investigations. In brief, Hull as well as others associated with him emphasizes only posthypnotic suggestions and their ultimate results and not the posthypnotic state that must be in existence prior to, if not actually during, the posthypnotic activity. They disregard entirely the fact that there must necessarily be some state of mind which permits a coming forth into consciousness, or partial consciousness, of the posthypnotic suggestion, of which, quite frequently, no awareness can be detected in the subject until after the proper cue is given. Even then that awareness is of a peculiar, limited, and restricted character, not comparable to ordinary conscious awareness. Yet Hull and his associates have directed their attention exclusively to the beginning and the end of a long, complicated process and have disregarded the intermediary steps.

To illustrate the confusion which exists in the use of posthypnotic suggestion, the experiment by Williams (1929, p. 324), among others, may be cited. In his report Williams states:

> In the case of the combined trance-normal work-periods, the subject was awakened when he had reached exhaustion in the trance by repeating rapidly, *"One, two, three-wide awake."* The instruction to "keep on pulling" was also added in this case so that the subject would continue his work, if possible, in the waking state.

In this combination of instruction in the trance state to awaken with the command to keep on pulling after awakening, Williams actually gave his subjects a posthypnotic command. Hence the "waking performance" was in response to an unintentional and unrecognized posthypnotic suggestion. Furthermore Williams apparently assumed that an awakening from a hypnotic trance could be accomplished instantly, despite a continuance of trance activity, and similarly, in the same experiment he assumed that a trance induction could also occur instantly without any interruption of waking activities. Hence the validity of his findings as representing performances in waking and in trance states is to be questioned.

This same confusion of ideas with regard to posthypnotic suggestion and the results to be expected from it is also shown by Messerschmidt (1927-1928) in her experiment on dissociation. Posthypnotic commands were given in direct and indirect relation to separate tasks, one of which was presumably to be done at a conscious level of awareness and the other as a posthypnotic or "subconscious" performance. As a consequence both the posthypnotic behavior and the supposedly waking behavior became integral parts of a single performance, one part of which was provided for by direct posthypnotic suggestions. The other part was in response to indirect and unintentional posthypnotic suggestions, specifically the instruction that the posthypnotic activity was to be carried on regardless of the assignment in the waking state of a new and different task. Thus the posthypnotic suggestions served to instruct the subjects to prepare themselves for certain definite tasks as well as for other tasks not yet specified, although as the experimental procedures were repeated on them, the subjects necessarily became aware in the trance state that the desired performances were to be dual in character. To instruct subjects in the trance state to execute a given task after awakening, when the subjects have full knowledge also of the fact that a second task, contingent upon the first, will be imposed upon in the waking state, is actually a method of giving two types of posthypnotic suggestion. Also, to instruct subjects in the trance state that upon awakening they are to do serial addition by automatic writing without regard for any other task which may be given them or to do serial addition "subconsciously" while reading aloud "consciously," constitutes the giving of posthypnotic suggestions covering both activities, and, hence the "conscious" task actually becomes a posthypnotic performance concomitant with the other posthypnotic activities. Likewise, to suggest to hypnotized subjects that they will do one task "subconsciously" and another task "consciously" will serve only to elicit posthypnotic performances of both tasks and not a waking peformance of one, despite the greater degree of conscious awareness of it, which itself constitutes an additional posthypnotic response.

Also, in addition to the oversights already mentioned, Messerschmidt's experiment, like Williams', makes no provision for the possible existence of a posthypnotic state, a somnambulistic state, or any special mental state that might interfere in some way with, or exercise a significant influence upon, the performance of the suggested tasks.

Quite different from the usual experimental study of posthypnotic behavior is the report by Brickner and Kubie (1936), who emphasize throughout their investigation the significant effect which the mental state that develops directly from posthypnotic suggestions has upon the total pattern of behavior. They also note the disappearance of those changes in the general behavior upon the completion of the posthypnotic task.

Similarly, although their studies were directed primarily to other purposes, Erickson (1935) and Huston and his coworkers (1934) demonstrate clearly the development, in direct consequence of posthypnotic suggestion, of a special mental state or condition which influences, alters, and even negates the subject's ordinary waking behavior in routine situations until the posthypnotic suggestion has been either removed or acted upon completely.

While this review of the literature is necessarily incomplete, it does disclose that there has been frequent, if inadequate, recognition as well as complete disregard of the special mental state that develops in direct relation to post hypnotic suggestions, and which is not necessarily limited to the task suggested as the posthypnotic activity. Also it shows that much experimental work has been done on posthypnotic behavior with no attempt made either to define the posthypnotic state or to make provision for any significant bearing it might have upon experimental procedures. Neither has there been any attempt to give an adequate definition of the posthypnotic act specifically, except in terms of the results secured from it. The mental processes and the patterns of response by which those results were achieved have been ignored. Instead there has been the general assumption that the posthypnotic act is simply a performance elicited in response to a command given during the trance state and characterized variously and uncertainly by degrees of amnesia, automaticity, and compulsiveness. As a consequence of the inadequate determination of the exact nature and character of a posthypnotic act, much experimental work has led to unsatisfactory and conflicting results, and hence there is a need for more definitive studies of posthypnotic behavior as a specific phenomenon rather than as a means by which to study other mental processes.

We propose therefore to report in this paper various significant observations, both general and specific, upon the nature and character of posthypnotic behavior. These observations have been made by us repeatedly and consistently during the course of experimental and therapueutic work extending over a period of years, and we have also verified our findings by inquiry into the experience of others and by direct observation of the posthypnotic behavior of subjects employed by other hypnotists.

A DEFINITION OF THE POSTHYPNOTIC ACT

We have found the following definition of the posthypnotic act to be consistently applicable and useful, since it serves to describe adequately a form of behavior we have elicited innumerable times in a great variety of situations and from a large number of subjects, ranging in type from the feebleminded to the highly intelligent, from the normal to the psychotic, and in age from children to middle-aged adults. For the moment we shall limit this definition strictly to the act itself, without regard for partial performances resulting from light trances or for certain other important considerations which will be dicussed later. A *posthypnotic act has been found to be one performed by the hypnotic subject after awakening from a trance, in response to suggestions given during the trance state, with the execution of the act marked by an absence of any demonstrable conscious awareness in the subject of the underlying cause and motive for his act.* We have come to regard as valid this form of the posthypnotic act, since its performance is invariably characterized by denfitive and highly significant attributive behavior.

THE BEHAVIOR CHARACTERIZING THE POSTHYPNOTIC PERFORMANCE

This important attributive behavior belonging to the posthypnotic response consists of the spontaneous and invariable development, as an integral part of the performance of the suggested posthypnotic act, of a self-limited, usually brief hypnotic trance. In other words we have observed repeatedly, under varying circumstances and in a great variety of situations, that the hypnotized subject instructed to execute some act posthypnotically invariably develops spontaneously a hypnotic trance. This trance is usually of brief duration, occurs in direct relation to the performance of the posthypnotic act, and apparently constitutes an essential part of the process of response to, and execution of, the post-hypnotic command. Its development has been found to be an invariable occurrence despite certain apparent exceptions, which will be discussed later, and regardless of the demands of the posthypnotic suggestion, which may entail a long complicated form of behavior, the introduction of a single word into a casual conversation, the development of an emotional response or attitude at a given stimulus, an avoidance reaction or even a slight modification of general behavior. Furthermore the development of a trance state as a part of the posthypnotic performance requires for its appearance neither suggestion nor instruction. This special trance state occurs as readily in the naive as in the highly trained subject; its manifestations, as we shall show, differ essentially in no way from those of an ordinary induced trance; and it seems to be a function of the process of initiating in the immediate situation a response to the posthypnotic suggestion given in a previous trance.

THE GENERAL CHARACTER OF THE SPONTANEOUS POSTHYPNOTIC TRANCE

The spontaneous posthypnotic trance is usually single in appearance, develops at the moment of initiation of the posthypnotic act, and persists usually for only a moment or two; hence it is easily overlooked despite certain residual effects it has upon the general behavior. Under various circumstances and with different subjects however, the trance may be multiple in appearance, constituting actually a succession of brief spontaneous trances related to aspects or phases of the posthypnotic act. It may appear in a prolonged form and persist throughout the greater part or even the entire duration of the posthypnotic performance; or there may be an irregular succession of relatively short and long spontaneous trances, apparently in relation to the difficulties, mental and physical, encountered in the course of the execution of the posthypnotic act. In general any variation in the form or the time of its appearance or reappearances seems to be a function of individual differences in the subjects and the difficulties occasioned by the general situation or by the posthypnotic act itself.

SPECIFIC MANIFESTATIONS OF THE SPONTANEOUS POSTHYPNOTIC TRANCE

The specific hypnotic manifestations which develop in relation to the performance of the posthypnotic act form an essentially constant pattern, although the duration of the separate items of behavior varies greatly both in accord with the purpose served and with the individual subject. They occur rapidly in direct relation to the giving of the specified cue for the posthypnotic act, with a tendency toward the following sequence: A slight pause in the subject's immediate activity, a facial expression of distraction and detachment, a peculiar glassiness of the eyes with a dilation of the pupils and a failure to focus, a condition of catalepsy, a fixity and narrowing of attention, an intentness of purpose, a marked loss of contact with the general environment, and an unresponsiveness to any external stimulus until the posthypnotic act is either in progress or has been completed, depending upon the actual duration of the trance state itself and the demands of the posthypnotic task. Even after the trance state has ceased, these manifestations, somewhat modified, continue as residual effects upon the subject, and result in the intent, rigid, and almost compulsive nature of his behavior and his state of absorption and general unresponsiveness until he has reoriented himself to the immediate situation.

Similarly, to a slight degree, the disappearance of the trance state, or to a much greater degree the completion of the posthypnotic performance, is marked by a brief interval of confusion and disorientation from which the subject quickly recovers by renewed and close attention to the immediate situation. Especially does this confusion and disorientation become marked if during the state of absorption in the posthypnotic performance there occurred any significant change or alteration in the general situation. In addition there is usually evidence of an amnesia, either partial or complete, for both the posthypnotic act and the concurrent events arising out of the immediate situation. In those instances in which the subject does have a recollection of the course of events, investigation will disclose their memories to be hazy, faulty, and frequently more deductions than memories, based upon their interpretations and rationalizations of the situation to which they have reoriented themselves. Occasionally, however, despite a poor recollection of, or a complete amnesia for, the attendant circumstances, a subject may recall clearly the entire posthypnotic performance, but will regard it merely as an isolated, unaccountable, circumscribed impulsion, or more often a compulsion having no connection with the immediate or general situation.

An example illustrative of many of these points is the following account given in a hesitating, uncertain fashion by a subject upon the completion of a posthypnotic act:

> We were talking about something, just what I've forgotten now, when I suddenly saw that book and I simply had to go over and pick it up and look at it—I don't know why—I just felt I had to—a sudden impulse, I suppose. Then I came back to my chair. It just happened that way. But you must have seen me because I must have had to walk around you to get it—I don't see any other way I could have reached it. Then when I laid it down again, I must have put those other books on top ot it. At least, I don't think anybody else did, since I don't remember anybody else being on that side of the room—but I wasn't paying much attention to anything, I guess, because, although I know

I looked carefully at that book and opened it, I don't even know the author or the title—probably fiction from the looks of it. Anyway, it was a funny thing to do—probably an impulse of the moment and doesn't mean a thing. What was it we were discussing?

THE DEMONSTRATION AND TESTING OF THE SPONTANEOUS POSTHYPNOTIC TRANCE

Although the various forms of hypnotic behavior spontaneously manifested by the subject in relation to posthypnotic acts constitute actually a demonstration of a trance state, their brevity and self-limited character necessitate special measure for a satisfactory examination of them and for a testing of their significance.

This may be done readily without distorting or altering significantly the actual hypnotic situation, since the giving of the posthypnotic cue or signal serves to reestablish that state of rapport existing at the time the posthypnotic suggestion was given. The task of such a demonstration, however, as experience will show, requires a considerable degree of skill. Usually it is most easily and effectively done by some form of interference, either with the posthypnotic act itself or with the subject after the posthypnotic response has been initiated but not yet completed. The demonstration of the trance state may follow one or two courses, depending upon the presence or the absence of hypnotic rapport between the demonstrator and the subject. If there is a state of rapport, the interference may be directed either to the subject or to his performance, and the trance manifestations are the positive responsive type, characteristic of the relationship between hypnotist and subject. In the absence of rapport effective interference must be directed primarily to the act itself and the trance manifestations are of the negative, unresponsive type, characteristic of the hypnotized subject's unresponsiveness to, and detachment from, that which is not included in the hypnotic situation. In both instances, however, the general and specific behavior obtained is wholly in keeping with that which would be obtained under similar circumstances from the same subject in an ordinary induced hypnotic trance.

The interference most effective in demonstrating the trance is that offered by the hypnotist or by some person actually in rapport with the subject when the posthypnotic suggestion was given in the original trance. It is best accomplished at the exact moment of initiation of the posthypnotic response by some measure serving to counteract or to alter the original posthypnotic suggestion, or to compel the subject to give special attention to the hypnotist—as, for example, the deliberate removal of the object which the subject was instructed to examine; the manipulation of the subject in such a fashion as to effect the development of catalepsy in one or both arms, thus rendering the examination difficult or impossible, or the use, even with naive subjects who have had no previous training, of such vague verbal suggestions as *"Wait a moment, just a moment,"*

"*Don't let anything change now,*" "*Stay as you are right now, never mind that,*" "*I'd rather talk to you now,*" or, "*I will be waiting as soon as you have done it,*" and similar remarks implying that an additional assignment may be made.

The effect of such interference is usually a complete arrest of the subjects' responses followed by an apparent waiting for further instructions, while their appearance and mannerisms suggest a state identical with that of the deep trance as ordinarily induced, and all the customary phenomena of the deep hypnotic trance can be elicited from them. Then if they are allowed to return to the performance of the posthypnotic task, a spontaneous awakening will ensue in due course, permitting an immediate and direct contrast of waking and hypnotic behavior as well as a demonstration of an amnesia for the posthypnotic act, the interference, and the events of the trance state. If, however, no use is made of the peculiar state of responsiveness established by the interference with them, the subjects tend to return to the problem of the posthypnotic task. The sequence of their behavior thereafter is essentially as if there had been no interference, but there is then a marked tendency for the spontaneous trance state to persist until the posthypnotic task has been completed. This is especially true if the interference has rendered the task more difficult. Occasionally, however, instead of being arrested in their behavior, the subjects may proceed uninterruptedly with their posthypnotic task and, upon its completion, appear to be awaiting further instructions. The phenomena of the deep-trance state can then be elicited, but if this is done, it becomes necessary to awaken the subjects at the finish.

To illustrate briefly, since other examples will be given later, a subject was told that, shortly after his awakening, a certain topic of conversation would be introduced, whereupon he was to leave his chair immediately, cross the room, and with his left hand pick up a small statuette and place it on top of a certain bookcase. At the proper time, as the subject stepped in front of the hypnotist to cross the room, his left arm was gently raised above his head, where it remained in a cataleptic state. The subject continued on his way without hesitation, but upon approaching the statuette, he apparently found himself unable to lower his left arm and turned to the hypnotist as if awaiting further instruction. Thereupon he was used to demonstrate a variety of the usual phenomena of the ordinary induced trance. Upon the completion of this demonstration he was instructed simply, "*All right, you may go ahead now.*" In response to this vague suggestion the subject returned to the interrupted posthypnotic performance, completed it, and resumed his original seat, awakening spontaneously with a complete amnesia for all of the events intervening between the giving of the cue and his awakening and without even an awareness that he had altered his position in the chair.

This same procedure of interference was repeated upon another subject with essentially the same results. When, however, the hypnotist made no response to the subject's expectant attitude, there occurred a fairly rapid disappearance of the catalepsy, a performance of the task, and a return to his seat, followed by a spontaneous waking with a complete amnesia for the entire experience.

SPECIAL TYPES OF SPONTANEOUS POSTHYPNOTIC TRANCE BEHAVIOR

In those instances in which the interference is not given at the proper moment, while it usually has the effect of intensifying and prolonging greatly the duration of the spontaneous trance, the subjects may respond to it by bewilderment and confusion succeeded by a laborious compulsive performance of the posthypnotic act and an overcoming of the interference. Again they may misinterpret the interruption of their task as a coincidental and meaningless, though obstructive, occurrence which is to be disregarded; or they may behave as if there really had been none.

This last type of behavior is of a remarkable character. It appears in other connections than the situation of mistimed interference and may serve widely different purposes for the same or different subjects. Thus it may occur when the interference is limited to the purpose of demonstrating the trance state without affecting the actual performance of the posthypnotic act. In this case the subject merely ignores the most persistent efforts on the part of the hypnotist, completes his posthypnotic task, and awakens spontaneously with a total amnesia for the entire occurrence. Frequently it develops when the possibility of the posthypnotic act has been nullified; and it often appears when the posthypnotic suggestion is rendered objectionable in character to the subject or too difficult as a result of the interference. But of most interest is its tendency to occur almost invariably when, upon the initiation of the posthypnotic behavior, some person not in rapport with the subject intrudes into the situation by means of an interference directed primarily to the posthypnotic act.

Although these situations differ greatly, the pattern of the subjects' behavior is essentially the same for all of them, and the general course of the subjects' responses in each type of situation is adequately exemplified in the following accounts: At the previously established posthypnotic cue the subject glanced across the room at an easily visible book lying on the table and proceeded to rise from his chair for the purpose of securing the book and placing it in the bookcase in accord with the previously given posthypnotic instructions. As he shifted his position in his chair preparatory to rising, an assistant, not in rapport with the subject, quickly removed and concealed the book, this being done at a moment when the subject's gaze was directed elsewhere. Despite this absolute interference with the posthypnotic act the subject unhesitatingly performed the task by apparently hallucinating the book, and gave no evidence of any realization that something unusual had occurred. This same procedure, repeated with other subjects, has led in more than one instance to an even more hallucinatory and delusional response,—namely, upon actually noting that the book had vanished, glancing at the bookcase in a bewildered fashion, and then apparently hallucinating the book in the place suggested for it, and assuming that they have just completed the task. As one subject spontaneously explained:

> It's funny how absent-minded you can get. For a minute there I intended to put that book in the bookcase, when actually I had just finished doing so. I suppose that's because it annoyed me so much just lying there that the thing before my mind was the doing of it, and that I hadn't got around yet to knowing that I had already done it.

Yet, upon resuming her seat, she spontaneously awakened and demonstrated a total amnesia inclusive even of her explanatory remarks.

Repetition of the procedure with these and with other subjects, but with the removal of the book effected while the subject's gaze was directed at it, sometimes led to similar results in that the removal of the book was not detected, thereby indirectly disclosing the defectiveness of the hypnotic subject's contact with the external environment and the tendency to substitute memory images for reality objects, behavior highly characteristic of the hypnotic state. In other instances the new position of the book was detected and the original position regarded as an illusion. Also in some instances plausible misconstructions were placed upon the new position or the detected movement, as for example: *"Why, who left this book lying in this chair? I remember distinctly seeing it on the table,"* or, *"I've been expecting that book to slip off the pile on the table all evening and at last it has. Do you mind if I put it in the bookcase?"* And, depending upon the actual experimental situation the real or an hallucinatory book would be recovered from the chair or the floor, and the posthypnotic act would be performed with the customary sequence of events.

Following this general type of posthypnotic behavior there develops either an amnesia complete in character and inclusive of both the posthypnotic act and the attendant circumstances, as well as of the subject's interpolated behavior, or, less frequently, a peculiar admixture of amnesia and fragmentary memories. These partial memories often tend to be remarkably clear, vivid, and distracting in character, and they may relate to the absolute facts or even to the hallucinatory and delusional items of the posthypnotic trance period. For example the last subject quoted above, when questioned for her recollections, recalled only that the hypnotist had a habit of piling books, papers, folders, and journals in untidy heaps, but she was unable to give a specific example of this practice. Another subject, in a similar experimental situation, remembered most vividly minute and utterly irrelevant details about the goldfish in the fish globe used only as a part of the environmental setting for the posthypnotic act, and he was most insistent that these memories constitued a complete account of the entire occurrence. Nevertheless some weeks later the subject disclaimed any memory of having made such statements.

THE EFFECT OF TIME UPON THE DEVELOPMENT OF THE SPONTANEOUS POSTHYPNOTIC TRANCE

One other general consideration in relation to the development of a spontaneous trance upon the initiation of posthypnotic behavior concerns the possible effect of the lapse of time. In this regard, on a considerable number of occasions subjects have been given specific instructions in the form of a posthypnotic suggestion to perform some simple act, the nature of which varied from subject to subject. This act was to be "done without fail on the occasion of our next meeting." Among these subjects were some who were not seen after the giving of such posthypnotic suggestions for varying periods of months. Of this group all carried out the posthypnotic act, developing as they did so a spontaneous trance. Two other subjects were actually not seen until three years later, respectively, during which periods of time there was no form of contact between the hypnotist and the subjects. Nevertheless at chance meetings with them the performance of the posthypnotic act and the development of a concomitant spontaneous trance state occured.

APPARENT EXCEPTIONS TO THE RULE OF SPONTANEOUS POSTHYPNOTIC TRANCES

However, before continuing with a discussion of various significances of the spontaneous posthypnotic trance, it may be well to offer an explanation of the apparent absolute exceptions, mentioned previously, to the development of a spontaneous trance, in relation to the execution of posthypnotic suggestions.

These exceptions, in which there is a performance posthypnotically of the trance-suggested act without the apparent development of a spontaneous trance, arise usually from certain conditions which will be listed generally and illustrated as follows:

1. Failure of the development of an amnesia for the posthypnotic suggestions: In this situation there may be actually no posthypnotic performance as such, since the subjects understand from the beginning the underlying motivations and causes of behavior, and hence act at a level of conscious awareness. Consequently the performance becomes similar in character to one suggested to a person in the ordinary waking state, and it is posthypnotic only in its time relationships.

In such instances the act is essentially voluntary in character, although frequently another element may enter into the situation—namely, a sense of being compelled to perform the specified task, despite the subjects apparently complete understanding of the situation. Thus the subjects may remember their instructions and be fully aware of what they are to do and why they are to do it, and yet experience an overwhelming compulsion that causes them to perform the act with literally no choice on their part. Occasionally, however, subjects responding to this compulsion and executing the posthypnotic instructions develop, as they perform the task, a spontaneous trance. This trance often serves to establish for the subjects a more or less complete amnesia for the instructions, for the period of waiting with its usually unpleasant compulsive feelings, and for the act itself. The trance is similar in character to that which develops in the ordinary posthypnotic situation, with the exception that the amnesia it may cause tends to be more limited. Thus the subjects may remember the posthypnotic suggestions, the period of waiting, and the feeling of compulsion, but have a complete amnesia for their actual performance. Or they may develop an amnesia for the posthypnotic instructions but remember experiencing a compulsion to perform an apparently irrational act. However, in some instances the spontaneous trance serves as a defense mechanism against the compulsive feelings rather than as an essential or integral part of the atypical posttrance performance. Finally the development of compulsive feelings constitutes a marked alteration of the essential nature of the entire pattern of behavior.

2. Failure to make clear to subjects that the posthypnotic instructions given concern the act itself and not the process of making provision for such an act: Thus the subjects instructed to perform a certain task posthypnotically, may, after awakening, go through a mental process of realizing, sometimes vaguely, sometimes clearly, that a certain act is to be performed and then simply hold themselves in readiness for the act. Hence upon the performance of the task no spontaneous trance occurs. However, this does not constitute a negation of the statement that a spontaneous trance always accompanies the posthypnotic performance, since close observation of the subjects in this situation will disclose that a spontaneous trance invariably accompanies this process of making ready for the act, provided that this understanding of their task occurs definitely after subjects have awakened from the trance in which the suggestion was given and not while they are going through a slow process of awakening, in which case the situation would become similar to that of the failure to develop amnesia.

3. Unwillingness on the part of the subjects to perform the posthypnotic act except as a deliberate act of choice on their part: Thus subjects may for some reason or whim object to the purely responsive character of a posthypnotic performance and react by making their response one of deliberate intention. In this situation, as in the foregoing example, there occurs upon awakening the same process of making ready for the suggested task, and hence upon the proper signal the posthypnotic performance is executed without the development of a spontaneous trance. However, this process of making ready for the act is again accompanied by a spontaneous trance.

4. The failure of the amnesia for the trance experiences: This is the most common and consists essentially in the spontaneous recovery of the memories

of the events and experiences of the trance state. For example, subjects instructed to perform a posthypnotic act at a given time after awakening may, before the specified time, more or less slowly begin to recall their various trance experiences, among them the posthypnotic instructions. This process of recollection is not one of preparation for the posthypnotic performance, but constitutes rather a recovery of memories, motivated usually by a sense of curiosity, and it is free from any purposeful significance in relation to the actual suggested posthypnotic task. Literally it is a breaking through of memories because of an inadequacy of amnesic barriers. With the recovery of the memory of the posthypnotic suggestions a somewhat similar situation obtains as exists when there is a failure of the development of an amnesia for posthypnotic suggestion, which has been described above. In general, while this type of behavior is the most common, it is exceedingly difficult to understand fully because there is first an amnesia for, and then a recollection of, posthypnotic instructions and because the memories, however complete eventually, are recovered in a fragmentary fashion.

Hence the failure, apparent or absolute, to develop a spontaneous trance upon the initiation of the execution of an act suggested as a posthypnotic performance does not necessarily constitute a contradiction of our observation. Rather it implies that there may occur within the subject certain changes in the psychological situation. These in turn may serve to alter or to transform the character of the posthypnotic act itself and thus to render it one for which the subject has a preliminary awareness as well as an understanding of its underlying nature and cause. Hence the act becomes transformed into one posthypnotic in time relationships only.

SIGNIFICANCES OF THE SPONTANEOUS POSTHYPNOTIC TRANCE

The significances of the spontaneous trance state as an integral part of the execution of posthypnotic suggestions are numerous and bear upon many important hypnotic questions. In particular they relate to such problems as the establishment of objective criteria for trance states and conditions, the training of subjects to develop more profound trances, and the direct elicitation of various hypnotic phenomena without a preliminary process of suggestion for trance induction. In addition the posthypnotic trance bears upon the general problem of dissociation, the various problems of individual hypnotic phenomena, such as rapport, amnesia, selective memories, catalepsy and dissociated states, and the general experimental and therapeutic implications of posthypnotic phenomena. Discussions of some of these considerations will be given in connection with our investigative work, but the reader will note that the experimental findings serve also to illustrate many points not directly mentioned.

THE SPONTANEOUS POSTHYPNOTIC TRANCE AS A CRITERION OF THE INDUCED HYPNOTIC TRANCE

In relation to the establishment of criteria for trance states, our experience has been that the spontaneous posthypnotic trance constitutes a reliable indicator of the validity of the original trance, and in this belief we have been confirmed by the experience reported to us by others. Apparently the posthypnotic trance is a phenomenon of sequence; it is based upon the original trance and constitutes actually a revivification of the hypnotic elements of that trance. Especially does this inference seem to be warranted since careful observation will often disclose an absolute continuance in the spontaneous posthypnotic trance of the behavior patterns belonging actually to the original trance state. This may be illustrated by the following experimental findings, made originally by chance and since repeated on other subjects: During a single hypnotic trance the hypnotist gave a large number of unrelated posthypnotic suggestions, each of which was to be performed later as a separate task and in response to separate cues. Also, during the course of that trance the subject's state of rapport with two observers was made to vary from time to time by suggestions independent of the posthypnotic suggestions. Subsequently, upon the execution of the posthypnotic suggestions the spontaneous trance states that developed showed remarkable variations, in that the subject, while always in rapport with the hypnotist, variously manifested rapport with one or the other or both or neither of the two observers. Although this was not understood at the time, subsequent checking of the record disclosed that the state of rapport manifested in each spontaneous posthypnotic trance state constituted an accurate reflection of the exact state of rapport existing at the time of the giving of the particular posthypnotic suggestion. Aside from the question of the continuance of patterns of behavior, the bearing of this finding upon the question of rapport is at once apparent.

Since then investigative work has disclosed that proper wording of posthypnotic suggestions may effect either a continuance or an absence in the spontaneous trance of the general behavior patterns belonging to the trance state in which the posthypnotic suggestion was given. Thus the giving of posthypnotic suggestions so worded as to carry an implication of a change or an alteration of the situation may militate against the evocation of original trance behavior. Yet the same suggestion so worded as to carry immediate as well as remote implications will usually serve to effect a continuance of the original trance behavior. To illustrate: During experimental work on this problem it was found that this wording of a posthypnotic suggestion, *"As I jingle my keys, you will invariably—"* often served to cause a continuance in the spontaneous posthypnotic trance of the behavior patterns belonging to the original trance, while *"Tomorrow, or whenever I jingle my keys, you will invariably——"* would fail in the same subject to elicit the behavior patterns of the original trance, since this wording implied possible changes in the situation. However, extensive work has shown that the behavior of subjects in carrying over the patterns of response belonging to the original trance is highly individualistic. Some almost invariably do so, others seldom or never, some almost wholly, others only in selected relationships, and the outcome of any experimental work is highly unpredictable, depending apparently upon the individuality of the subjects as well as their immediate understandings. Hence extreme care in wording suggestions is highly essential, and it should never be assumed that a subject's understanding of instructions is identical with that of the hypnotist. Neither should there be the assumption that an identical wording must necessarily convey an identical meaning to different subjects.

In other words the "standardized technique," or the giving of identical suggestions to different subjects, described by Hull (1933), is not, as he appears to believe, a controlled method for eliciting the same degree or type of response, but merely a measure of demonstrating the general limitations of such a technique.

Another type of evidence concerning the validity of the original trance is the failure to develop a spontaneous trance when apparently executing a posthypnotic suggestion, by subjects who were merely complaisantly cooperative or who were overeager to believe that they were in a trance, or who, for various reasons, simulated effectively being hypnotized. In direct contrast to these subjects are those relatively rare persons who actually do go into a deep hypnotic trance but who, because of individual peculiarites, seem unable to realize the fact, or are unable to admit it to themselves, and hence refuse to believe that they are or ever have been hypnotized. Yet, invariably this latter class of subjects develops a spontaneous trance upon the execution of the posthypnotic suggestions, an occurrence which in itself often constitutes an effective measure in correcting their mental attitudes and misunderstandings.

Furthermore, in studies directed to the detection of the simulation of trance behavior the failure of a trance state to develop upon the execution of posthypnotic suggestions disclose any simulations. Nor does sophistication and coaching in this regard serve to enable on many occasions trained subjects, purposely kept unaware that the performance they were watching was one of deliberate pretense, have declared the apparent performance of a posthypnotic act to be "*not right*," "*something wrong*," or have stated, "*I don't get the right feeling from the way he did that*," but without being able to define their reasons, since their own posthypnotic amnesias precluded full conscious understandings.

In brief, on innumerable occasions and under a variety of circumstances the spontaneous posthypnotic trance has been found to be characterized by the individual phenomena of the original trance state in which the posthypnotic suggestion was given, and to be an excellent measure of differentiating between real and simulated trances, especially so when the subjects, by being overcooperative deceive themselves. Likewise it has been found to be an effective measure in aiding responsive hypnotic subjects who for personality reasons cannot accept the fact of their hypnotization. Also it can be used to demonstrate effectively the individuality and variety of responses that may be elicited under apparently controlled conditions.

THE UTILIZATION OF THE SPONTANEOUS POSTHYPNOTIC TRANCE AS A SPECIAL HYPNOTIC TECHNIQUE

Of particular importance is the utilization of the spontaneous posthypnotic trance as a special experimental and therapeutic technique. Its usefulness is varied in character and relates to the intimately associated problems of avoiding difficulties deriving from waking behavior, securing new trance states, training subjects to develop more profound trances, and eliciting specific hypnotic phenomena without direct or indirect suggestions made to that end.

The method of utilization is illustrated in the following experimental account: A five-year-old child who had never witnessed a hypnotic trance was seen alone by the hypnotist. She was placed in a chair and told repeatedly to *"sleep"* and to *"sleep very soundly,"* while holding her favorite doll. No other suggestion of any sort was given her until after she had apparently slept soundly for some time. Then she was told, as a posthypnotic suggestion, that some other day the hypnotist would ask her about her doll, whereupon she was to (a) place it in a chair, (b) sit down near it, and (c) wait for it to go to sleep. After several repetitions of these instructions she was told to awaken and to continue her play. This threefold form of posthypnotic suggestion was employed since obedience to it would lead progressively to an essentially static situation for the subject. Particularly did the last item of behavior require an indefinitely prolonged and passive form of response, which could be best achieved by a continuation of the spontaneous posthypnotic trance.

Several days later she was seen while at play, and a casual inquiry was made about her doll. Securing the doll from its cradle, she exhibited it proudly and then explained that the doll was tired and wanted to go to sleep, placing it as she spoke in the proper chair and sitting down quietly beside it to watch. She soon gave the appearance of being in a trance state, although her eyes were still open. When asked what she was doing, she replied, *"Waiting,"* and nodded her head agreeably when told insistently, *"Stay just like you are and keep on waiting."* Systematic investigation, with an avoidance of any measure that might cause a purely responsive manifestation to a specific but unintentional hypnotic suggestion, led to the discovery of a wide variety of the phenomena typical of the ordinary induced trance. A number of these will be cited in detail in the following paragraphs to illustrate both the procedure employed and the results obtained.

Catalepsy and Literalism

The subject was asked if she would like to see a new toy the hypnotist had for her. Contrary to her ordinary behavior of excited response in such a situation, she simply nodded her head and waited passively for the hypnotist to secure the new toy (a large doll) from a place of concealment. She smiled happily when it was held up to her view, but made no effort to reach for it. Upon being asked if she would like to hold it, she nodded her head agreeably but still made no effort to take it. The doll was placed in her lap, and the hypnotist then helped her to nestle it in her right arm, but in such fashion that the arm was in a decidedly awkward position. She made no effort to shift the position of her arm but merely continued to look happily at the doll.

While she was so engaged, the hypnotist remarked that her shoestring was untied and asked if he might tie it for her. Again she nodded her head, and the hypnotist lifted her foot slightly by the shoestrings so that the task might be done more easily. When her foot was released, it remained in the position to which it had been elevated.

Following this she was asked if she would like to put the doll in its cradle. Her only response was an affirmative nod. After a few moments' wait she was asked if she would not like to do so at once. Again she nodded her head, but still continued to wait for specific instructions. Thereupon, the hypnotist told her to *"go ahead,"* meanwhile picking up a book as if to read. The subject responded by repeated futile attempts to rise from the chair, but the catalepsy present, manifested by the continuance of the awkward position in which she was holding the doll and the elevation of her foot, prevented her from making the shift of position necessary for rising. She was asked why she did not put the doll in the cradle, to which she replied, *"Can't."* When asked if she wanted help, she nodded her head, whereupon the hypnotist leaned forward in such fashion that he pushed her leg down. Taking her by the left hand, he gently pulled her to a standing position with her arm outstretched, in which position it remained upon being released. She immediately walked over to the cradle but stood there helplessly, apparently unable to move either arm, and it became necessary to tell her to put the doll in the cradle. With this specific instruction the catalepsy disappeared from her arms and she was able to obey.

Rapport and Hallucinatory Behavior

The subject was then asked to return to her original seat, where she continued to gaze in a passive manner at the first doll in its chair. One of the hypnotist's assistants entered the room, walked over and picked up that doll, and removed it to another chair. Despite the fact that the subject had her gaze directed fully at the doll, she made no response to this maneuver, nor did she appear to detect in any way the alteration of the situation. After a few moments the hypnotist asked her what she was doing. She replied, *"I'm watching my dolly."* Asked what the doll was doing, she answered simply, *"Sleeping."* At this point the assistant called the subject by name and inquired how long the doll had been sleeping, but elicited no response. The question was repeated without results, whereupon the assistant nudged the subject's arm. The subject immediately looked briefly at her arm, scratched it in a casual fashion, but made no other response.

Following this the assistant secured the two dolls and dropped them into the hypnotist's lap. The subject was then asked if she thought both dolls liked to sleep, thereby causing her to shift her gaze from the empty chair to the hypnotist. She apparently failed to see the dolls in the new position, but when they were picked up and looked at directly by the hypnotist she immediately became aware of them, glanced hesitatingly at the chair and then at the cradle, and remarked, *"You got them now,"* and seemed to be very much puzzled. Yet when the assistant quietly took the dolls out of the hypnotist's hands and walked to the other side of the room, the subject apparently continued to see the dolls as if they were still held by the hypnotist. An attempt on the part of the assistant to call the subject's attention to the dolls failed to elicit a response of any sort from the subject.

The subjects's mother then entered the room and attempted to attract her attention, but without results. Yet the subject could walk around, talk to the hypnotist, and see any particular object or person called directly to her attention by the hypnotist, although she was apparently totally unable to respond to anything not belonging strictly to the hypnotic situation.

Amnesia

The others were dismissed from the room, the dolls were restored to the chair and the cradle respectively, and the subject to her seat, whereupon she was told to awaken. Immediately upon manifesting an appearance of being awake, the subject, returning to the initial situation, remarked in her ordinary manner, *"I don't think dolly is going to go to sleep. She's awake."* She was asked various casual questions about the doll, following which the hypnotist remarked that maybe the doll did not like to go to sleep in a chair. Immediately the subject jumped up and declared her intention of putting the doll in its cradle, but when she attempted to do so she manifested very marked bewilderment at the presence of a new doll in the cradle. There was no recognition of it, no realization that she had ever seen the doll before, and no knowledge that it had been made a gift to her. She showed the typical excited childish desire for the new toy, asking whose it was and if she might have it. The assistant then reentered the room and picked up the doll, whereupon the subject began addressing remarks to the assistant. The assistant, replying to these, walked over to the chair and picked up the first doll. The subject made full and adequate response to this, disclosing complete contact with her surroundings and a complete amnesia for all trance occurrences.

Repetitions of the procedure upon the subject under varying circumstances led to similar findings. Likewise similar procedures have been employed with

Posthypnotic Behavior

other naive and trained subjects of various ages with comparable results.

This general type of technique we have found especially useful both experimentally and therapeutically, since it lessens greatly those difficulties encountered in the ordinary process of inducing a trance, which derive from the need to subordinate and eliminate waking patterns of behavior. Once the initial trance has been induced and limited strictly to passive sleeping behavior with only the additional item of an acceptable posthypnotic suggestion given in such fashion that its execution can fit into the natural course of ordinary waking events, there is then an opportunity to elicit the posthypnotic performance with its concomitant spontaneous trance. Proper interference, not necessary in the instance cited above because of the nature of the posthypnotic performance, can then serve to arrest the subject in that trance state.

However, it must be stated that to arrest subjects in the spontaneous trance and to have them remian in that state, the entire situation must be conducive to such a purpose, since any unwillingness on the part of the subjects will cause them to become unresponsive and to awaken. But under favorable circumstances subjects submit readily and fully to the new hypnotic situation in a passive, responsive fashion. Repeated intensive inquiry of subjects while in such prolonged trance states has disclosed no understanding of how the trance was secured nor any intellectual curiosity about it, and usually little or no spontaneous realization that they are in a trance. Rather there seems to be only a passive acceptance of their trance state marked by the automatic responsive behavior so characteristic of the ordinary deep induced trance.

By this general measure new trance states can be secured free from the limitations deriving from various factors such as the subjects's mental set, deliberate conscious intentions regarding trance behavior, misconceptions, and the continuance of waking patterns of behavior. Under ordinary circumstances hypnotic subjects obeying a posthypnotic command are making a response to a suggestion of which they are unaware at a conscious level of understanding, and which belongs to another situation of which they are similarly unaware. In addition they become so absorbed and so automatic in their performance ansd so limited in their responses to their general environment there there is little possibility of, and no immediate need for, the retention or continuance of conscious attitudes and patterns of behavior. Instead there is effected a dissociation from the immediate circumstances, more adequate and complete than can be achieved by suggestion in the usual process of trance induction. Hence the performance becomes exceedingly restricted in character, occurs at a level of awareness distinct from that of ordinary waking consciousness, and derives from a remote situation. In brief, it is a phenomenon of sequence, is based upon the revivification of the hypnotic elements of another situation, and thus is limited to hypnotic behavior.

The applicability of the above discussion to the problem of training subjects to develop more profound trances is apparent. Also the value of repeated trance inductions to secure more profound hypnotic states is generally recognized, and this same purpose can be served more satisfactorily, readily, and easily by the utilization of the posthypnotic performance and its concomitant trance. Especially is this so since the posthypnotic performance provides an opportunity to secure a trance state quickly and unexpectedly without the subjects having any opportunity to prepare themselves or to make any special and unnecessary adjustments for their behavior. Instead the subjects suddenly find themselves in the hypnotic state and limited to patterns of response and behavior belonging only to that state. Hence training can be accomplished without a laborious process of effecting by suggestion a dissociation of waking patterns of behavior, provided of course that the subject is essentially willing to forego the passive participation constituting a part of the usual training procedure.

The direct evocation of specific hypnotic phenomena without recourse to suggestion has been illustrated in the experimental account above. While the same thing may be done in the ordinary induced trance, there has been frequent and often well-founded criticism to the effect that many times the hypnotic behavior elicited was a direct response to intentional or unintentional suggestions given during the trance induction or to unexpected constructions placed by the subject upon suggestions. Behavior so elicited is expressive only of the hypnotic tendency to automatic obedience, and it is not a direct expression of the hypnotic state itself. As shown in the above account, the utilization of the spontaneous posthypnotic trance permits a direct evocation of specific phenomena without the questionable effects of a long series of suggestions given during the process of induction.

In the therapeutic situation the utilization of the spontaneous posthypnotic trance possesses special values for hypnotic psychotherapy, since it precludes the development of resistances and renders the patient particularly susceptible to therapeutic suggestions. Also the amnesia following this spontaneous trance is less easily broken down by the patient's desire to remember what suggestions have been given as is so often the case in relation to induced trances. Hence there is less likelihood of the patient controverting the psychotherapy given. In addition the spontaneous posthypnotic trance permits an easy combination of waking and hypnotic therapy, often an absolute essential for successful results. However, this problem of the combination of walking and hypnotic psychotherapy, or, more generally, the integration of hypnotic and posthypnotic behavior with the conscious stream of activity, does not come within the scope of this paper.

THE SPONTANEOUS POSTHYPNOTIC TRANCE AND DISSOCIATION PHENOMENA

Little that is definitve can be said about the significance of the spontaneous trance in relation to both the original trance and the posthypnotic performance as dissociation phenomena, since extensive controlled experimental work needs to be done to establish this point as well as the concept itself. However, careful observation discloses consistently that posthypnotic behavior simply irrupts or "breaks through" into the conscious stream of activity and fails to become an integral part of that activity except as a retrospective addition. Perhaps the best illustration of this disscoiated character of the trance and the posthypnotic act may be found in the following examples: As the subject was conversing casually with others in the room, he was interrupted in the middle of a sentence by the predetermined cue for a posthypnotic act requiring a brief absence from the room. Immediately upon perceiving the cue, the subject discontinued the remark he was making, manifested the typical posthypnotic trance behavior, executed the act, returned to his chair, readjusted himself to his original position, seemed to go through a process of wakening, and took up his remark and continued it from the exact point of interruption. Another subject, instructed to respond instantly to a sharp auditory stimulus serving as the cue for a posthypnotic act, was interrupted in the middle of the pronunciation of a long word while casually conversing with others present. His performance of the posthypnotic act was then interfered with, and the subject was used for a period of 15 to 20 minutes to demonstrate to the observers present a variety of hypnotic phenomena, following which the subject was told to *"go ahead."* In obedience to this vague suggestion the subject proceeded to complete his performance of the posthypnotic act, returned to his original position, readjusted himself, awakened, and completed the utterance of the interrupted word and continued in the same line of conversation, apparently totally unaware that there had been a lengthy interruption.

A subject similarly interrupted in the midst of rapid typing and used to demonstrate various phenomena, upon returning to his original position at the typewriter awakened and unhesitatingly resumed his typing task without any apparent necessity to reorient himself visually. Apparently he had held his orientation to his task in complete abeyance for ready resumption. This same type of procedure, with various control measures, has been repeated many times with similar and consistent results.

Not always, however, do the subjects return after a posthypnotic performance with such precision to the original waking train of thought. Sometimes it is picked up further along in the natural course of its development, as is shown by an interruption of the subject by posthypnotic activity while reciting the first part of a poem and a continuation by the subject upon awakening with the recitation of the last part, with a discoverable firm belief on the part of the subject that the intervening stanzas had been recited. Some subjects, however, show marked confusion, which may be illustrated by the subject who declared *"I've forgotten what I was just talking about,"* and required aid in renewing his remarks, but was found to believe that he had said more on the topic than was the fact. On still other occasions subjects have manifested a hazy awareness of the posthypnotic act and have digressed briefly to remark about some unusual circumstances apparently just discovered, as if seeking an explanation of the peculiar change in the situation of which they had just become somewhat aware. But on the whole, when subjects are left to readjust their behavior after an interpolated posthypnotic performance without interference of any sort from the observers, there tends to be a complete amnesia for the trance and its events and an approximate return to the general situation with seemingly no awareness of any changes in it.

From these examples, typical of numerous instances, the statement is warranted that the posthypnotic act and its spontaneously developed posthypnotic trance constitute forms of dissociation phenomena, and hence that they offer an opportunity to study experimentally the problem of dissociation. Similarly suggestive is the apparent continuance and independence of waking trains of thought during the trance state, despite other interpolated behavior as shown in the examples above.

Another comment that should be made before discussing the direct experimental implications concerns the usual conditions under which these observations were made—namely, those of a general social gathering in which the topic of hypnosis was discussed with the possibility of demonstrations, but in such fashion that the subjects were unaware of any deliberate, specific experimental intentions in relation to them on the part of the authors and their assistants. Maneuvering of the conversation would lead to the recitation of a poem or the giving of some famous quotations by the subject or the carrying on of guessing games, thus permitting a demonstration of the continuance of the original waking trains of thought, despite any interruption that might be occasioned by posthypnotic acts. Our general purpose in these informal settings was the avoidance of those limitations or restrictions upon patterns of response that obtain when the subjects are aware that their behavior is under direct scrutiny. In our experience the necessity for the avoidance of overt study in hypnotic work cannot be overemphasized. The natural course of behavior rather than the limited formalized pattern that may be expected in a strictly laboratory setting usually proves the more informative.

APPLICATIONS OF THE SPONTANEOUS POSTHYPNOTIC TRANCE IN EXPERIMENTAL WORK ON DISSOCIATION

The dissociation and independence of posthypnotic behavior from the conscious stream of activity, and the failure of integration of hypnotically motivated behavior with ordinary behavior, constitute significant considerations for which there must be adequate provision in any experimental work involving both waking and posthypnotic behavior. Hence in studies directed to the investigation of the capacity to perform simultaneously different tasks, such as reading aloud in

Posthypnotic Behavior

the waking state and doing mental addition as a posthypnotic task, provision must be made to keep the tasks entirely independent and not contingent upon one another. While provision is easily made for the posthypnotic activity, extreme care must be exercised to insure that the waking behavior derives entirely out of a situation belonging wholly to the waking state and that the development of a spontaneous posthypnotic trance does not interfere significantly with the waking behavior. In Messerschmidt's experiment, mentioned previously, none of these provisions was made, which accounts for her unsatisfactory and inconclusive findings.

One needs only to observe critically a subject in such an experimental situation as Messerschmidt devised to note the constant, rapid fluctuation from one state of awareness to another of a more limited character. The unsatisfactory results obtained under such conditions are not indicative of a lack of capacity on the part of the subject, but rather they indicate the obstructive effects of the posthypnotic trance developments and the interdependence of the two tasks. Accordingly, in experimental approaches to the concept of dissociation the problem is actually one of devising a technique by which the independence of the tasks is maintained despite any simultaneity of the performances.

In brief, an adequate technique should be one that limits the posthypnotic act to a single aspect of an entire task, of which the posthypnotic performance represents only the initiation or culmination of the unconsciously performed activity, while the consciously performed task derives wholly from the ordinary course of events belonging entirely to the waking situation.

To illustrate this type of technique, the following examples may be cited: A farmboy subject was instructed in the trance state that thereafter for a week every time he pumped water to fill a certain watering trough which was out of sight and hearing from the pump, and which was known by him to require 250 strokes of the pump handle to fill, he was to turn and walk to the trough the instant that it was full. Thus the posthypnotic act was an extremely limited part of a large implied task, and any posthypnotic trance manifestations would necessarily be limited to the specified posthypnotic act.

A few days later an agreement was made in the ordinary waking state that the subject would be relieved of a certain onerous task much disliked by him if he were able to spell correctly most of the words given him by the hypnotist, the words to be selected from his own school spelling book. To this the subject agreed eagerly, and as the spelling test started, the boy's father appeared, in accord with secret arrangements, and demanded that the watering trough be filled immediately. Accordingly the spelling test was conducted at the pump, where, as the subject pumped, one word after another was given him as rapidly as he spelled them. Suddenly the subject interrupted his spelling, ceased pumping, and turned and walked to the trough, his behavior typical of the posthypnotic trance state. The trough was found to be full. Repetitions of the experiment elicited the same results. Also, independent counting of the pump handle strokes disclosed the subject to be keeping accurate count despite the task of spelling.

Yet repetitions of the experiment in which the subject was instructed to count the strokes silently as the posthypnotic task itself, while spelling aloud as a conscious task, led to unsatisfactory results—specifically, confusion of the spelling with the counting. This admixture in his performance bewildered him greatly, since as a consequence of his amnesia for the posthypnotic suggestions he could not understand his frequent utterance of a number in place of a letter in his spelling.

When an attempt was made to have this subject count the strokes and spell as simultaneous waking tasks, he was found to be totally unable to do so except by deliberate, purposeful pauses and by a definite alternation of tasks. After much effort in this regard the subject spontaneously suggested, *"I can guess the number of strokes better instead of trying to count them while I'm spelling."* A test of this disclosed that the subject was able to "guess" accurately, but when he was questioned later in the hypnotic trance, he explained that the "guess" was only a conscious belief or understanding on his part, and that he had actually counted the strokes in the same manner as he had in the original experimental trials.

In a similar experiment a stenographer was told in the trance state that for the next week while taking dictation she would change pencils on the 320th word, the 550th word, and the 725th word. These instructions limited the posthypnotic act to a very small aspect of the total task. During that time she took dictation from three psychiatrists, each of whom noted the phrases at which she changed pencils. Despite the fact that she used many combined word phrases (symbols combining two or more words) it was discovered by count later that she approximated the correct number closely, never exceeding an error of 10 and averaging an error of three words.

Another important item is the fact that each time she changed pencils at the specified number of words, the subject became confused, manifested briefly the evidences of a spontaneous posthypnotic trance, and had to have a repetition of some of the dictation. Nevertheless she could change pencils elsewhere than on the specified words without any interruption of her writing. Furthermore her general behavior, except for the transient disturbances noted above, disclosed nothing unusual to the three psychiatrists, who, although unacquainted with the experimental situation, had been instructed to observe her behavior carefully and to give dictation at their customary speed, which ranged between 100 and 120 words a minute. Likewise, when the hypnotist himself gave her carefully timed dictation, no unusual behavior was noted except the transient disturbances in direct relation to the specified words.

Yet the same subject, instructed as the posthypnotic task to count the words as they were dictated, failed completely both in her counting and in her writing, as might be predicted if full consideration were given to habituation and learning processes and attention factors, apart from the influence of posthypnotic trance manifestations.

An attempt was made to have her perform the two tasks as a single waking performance, but she was found unable to divide her attention sufficiently both to count correctly and to attend to the dictation. However, when it was suggested to her that she attend only to the dictation and merely "guess" when she reached the designated number of words, it was found that she could approximate the correct count. In a subsequent hypnotic trance she explained that the permission to "guess" permitted her to dismiss the count from her "conscious mind" so that she "could do it subconsciously."

As a control measure for the above experiments nonhypnotic subjects and hypnotic subjects who had not been used in this type of experimentation were asked to "guess" in similar experimental situations. Their replies in all instances were found to be calculated, inaccurate approximations based upon various general considerations such as time elapsed or the number of pages covered, rather than an attempt to make an actual count.

A slightly different approach to the problem of simultaneous tasks at different levels of awareness is the utilization of posthypnotic suggestion simply to initiate a form of behavior which then continues as an automatic activity not impinging upon the subject's conscious awareness.

To illustrate: Another stenographer was instructed in the deep trance that the appearance of the hypnotist in her office would constitute a cue for her left hand to begin automatic writing without her conscious awareness of it, and that this writing was to be discontinued immediately upon his departure. Thus she was given posthypnotic suggestions serving directly to initiate and to terminate a certain form of behavior. Repeatedly thereafter, whenever the hypnotist entered her office, she manifested briefly the development of a posthypnotic trance with a definite disruption of her activities, particularly so if she were engaged in typing. Under such circumstances the posthypnotic trance would persist until she had been excused from one or the other of the two tasks. Care was taken, however, to enter her office frequently when she was sitting at a desk engaged in taking dictation from some one of the hypnotist's colleagues. In this situation she would manifest a brief spontaneous posthypnotic trance which would disrupt her immediate activity, and this would be followed by a resumption of her normal dictation behavior, accompanied by a continuous automatic writing with her left hand, which would be done on the desktop, the desk blotter, or any handy sheet of paper. If no pencil were available, her hand would still go through writing movements. Upon the departure of the hypnotist from the office there would again occur a brief spontaneous posthypnotic trance resulting in a disruption of her normal dictation behavior and a discontinuance of the automatic writing.

On more than one occasion one of the psychiatrists giving dictation, who had the habit of sitting with his back toward her, responded to the interruption occasioned by the spontaneous trance and her consequent request for repetition as if it were caused by some unfamiliar medical term or by unclear enunciation on his part and he did not become aware of the additional posthypnotic activity. There seemed to be no interference by the automatic writing with the conscious waking performance, although the automatic writing often included phrases from the dictation as well as other sentences and phrases related to other matters.

It was also possible for the hypnotist to give dictation to this subject in the ordinary course of the daily routine, but the spontaneous posthypontic trance developed when he entered her office for this purpose tended to be more prolonged than was the case when his entrance merely interrupted the dictation of the other psychiatrists.

When, however, an attempt was made to have this subject take dictation after she had been allowed to become consciously aware of the fact that her left hand was doing automatic writing, it was discovered that she could not take dictation successfully, nor could she do the automatic writing except by a process of alternating the tasks. When ample proof had been given to her that she had performed such tasks simultaneously in the past, she explained that she could probably do it if she were not asked to keep the automatic writing in mind while taking dictation, that she could take dictation adequately if she were permitted to "forget about the automatic writing."

In these three examples the spontaneous posthypnotic trance was limited to a minor aspect of the larger implied posthypnotic task, hence its interference with the concurrent conscious activity was decidedly brief in character. Also, in each instance neither of the two tasks performed simultaneously was contingent upon the other. The waking one derived entirely out of the routine course of ordinary waking events having no relation, however remote, to the trance state in which the posthypnotic suggestions were given. In all instances the subjects were entirely free to engage simultaneously in two wholly independent activities without the burden of a third task of coordinating them.

Apparently, then, the essential technical consideration in the simultaneous performance of two separate and distinct tasks, each at a different level of awareness, which is not ordinarily possible at a single level of awareness, consists in the provision of some form of motivation sufficient to set into action a train of learned activity which will then continue indefinitely at one level of awareness, despite the initiation or continuation of another train of activity at another level.

CONCLUSIONS

1. A survey of the literature discloses that although there has been frequent recognition of the fact that posthypnotic suggestions lead to the development of a peculiar mental state in the hypnotic subject, there has been no direct study made of that special mental condition. Neither has there been provision nor allowance made for its existence and its possible significant influences upon results obtained from posthypnotic suggestions.

2. The significant change in the subject's mental state, in direct relation to the

performance of the posthypnotic act, has been found by extensive observation and experimentation to signify the development of a spontaneous, self-limited posthypnotic trance, which constitutes an integral part of the process of response to, and execution of posthypnotic commands.

3. The spontaneous posthypnotic trance may be single or multiple, brief or prolonged, but in general it appears for only a moment or two at the initiation of the posthypnotic performance, and hence it is easily overlooked. Its specific manifestations and residual effects form an essentially constant pattern, despite variations in the duration of the separate items of behavior caused by the purposes served and the individuality of the subjects.

4. Demonstration and testing of the spontaneous posthypnotic trance are usually best accomplished at the moment of the initiation of the posthypnotic performance by interference either with the subject or with the suggested act. Properly given, such interference ordinarily leads to an immediate arrest in the subjects's behavior and to a prolongation of the spontaneous posthypnotic trance, permitting a direct evocation of hypnotic phenomena typical of the ordinary induced hypnotic trance. Occasionally, however, special types of hypnotic behavior may be elicited by interference improperly given or which causes a significant alteration of the posthypnotic performance.

5. The lapse of an indefinite period of time between the giving of a posthypnotic suggestion and the opportunity for its execution does not affect the development of a spontaneous posthypnotic trance as an integral part of the posthypnotic performance.

6. Apparent exceptions to the development of the spontaneous posthypnotic trance as an integral part of the posthypnotic performance are found to derive from significant changes in the intended posthypnotic situation which alter or transform it into one of another character.

7. The spontaneous posthypnotic trance is essentially a phenomenon of sequence, since it constitutes a revivification of the hypnotic elements of the trance situation in which the specific posthypnotic suggestion was given. Hence its development is a criterion of the validity of the previous trance.

8. The spontaneous posthypnotic trance may be used advantageously as a special experimental and therapeutic technique, since it obviates various of the difficulties inherent in the usual method of trance induction.

9. The posthypnotic performance and its associated spontaneous trance constitute dissociation phenomena, since they break into the ordinary stream of conscious activity as interpolations, and since they do not become integrated with the ordinary course of conscious activity.

10. Posthypnotic suggestion may be utilized effectively to study the capacity to perform simultaneously two separate and distinct tasks, each at a different level of awareness, if adequate provision be made for the nature and character of posthypnotic behavior.

20. Varieties of Double Bind

Milton H. Erickson and Ernest L. Rossi

When I was a boy on the farm, it was not uncommon for my father to say to me, "Do you want to feed the chickens first or the hogs, and then do you want to fill the woodbox or pump the water for the cows first?"

What I realized then was that my father had given me a choice; I as a person had the *primary* privilege of deciding which task I was to do first. I did not realize at the time that this primary privilege rested entirely upon my *secondary* acceptance of all the tasks mentioned. I was unwittingly committed to the performance of the tasks which had to be done by being given the primary privilege of determining their order. I did not recognize that I was accepting the position of being placed in a double bind. The tasks had to be done; there was no escaping the fact that the kitchen range burned wood to cook my breakfast and that the cows did need to drink. These were items of fact against which I could not rebel. But I did have the profoundly important privilege as an individual of deciding in which order I should and would do them. The conception of what a double bind was escaped me, though I often wondered why I was seemingly willing to "pick off" potato bugs or hoe potatoes rather than playing.

My first well-remembered intentional use of the double bind occurred in early boyhood. One winter day, with the weather below zero, my father led a calf out of the barn to the water trough. After the calf had satisfied its thirst, they turned back to the barn, but at the doorway the calf stubbornly braced its feet, and despite my father's desperate pulling on the halter, he could not budge the animal. I was outside playing in the snow and, observing the impasse, began laughing heartily. My father challenged me to pull the calf into the barn. Recognizing the situation as one of unreasoning stubborn resistance on the part of the calf, I decided to let the calf have full opportunity to resist, since that was what it apparently wished to do. Accordingly I presented the calf with a double bind by seizing it by the tail and pulling it away from the barn, while my father continued to pull it inward. The calf promptly chose to resist the weaker of the two forces and dragged me into the barn.

As I grew older I began employing my father's alternate-choice double bind on my unsuspecting siblings to secure their aid in the performance of farm

---

Reprinted with permission from *The American Journal of Clinical Hypnosis,* January, 1975, *17,* 143-157.

chores. In high school I used the same approach by carefully arranging the order in which I did my homework. I put myself in a double bind by doing the bookkeeping (which I disliked) first and then the geometry (which I liked) as a reward. I gave myself a reward, but the double bind was arranged so that all the homework was done.

In college, I became more and more interested in the double bind as a motivational force for the self and others. I began experimenting by suggesting to classmates the performance of two tasks, both of which I knew they would reject if presented singly. They would, however, execute one or the other if I made the refusal of one contingent upon the acceptance of the other.

I then began reading autobiographies extensively and discovered that this way of managing behavior was age-old. It was an item of psychological knowledge that properly belonged to the public domain and no one person could lay claim to it. Coincident with the development of my interest in hypnosis I began to realize that the double bind could be used in a variety of ways. In hypnosis the double bind could be direct, indirect, obvious, obscure, or even unrecognizable.

I found the double bind to be a remarkable force, but dangerously double-edged. In negative, enforced, and competitive situations the double bind yields unfortunate outcomes. As a child, for example, I knew where all the best berry patches were. I'd offer to show them to my companions if I could keep all I picked plus half of what they picked. They would accept the deal eagerly but later they would greatly resent it when they actually saw how much I got. In college I was interested in debating, but when I tried to employ the double bind I always lost. The judges invariably sought me out after the debate to tell me that I had actually won but that I had so aroused their antagonism that they could not help voting me down. The result was that I never made the college debating team, even though I was frequently proposed. I noted in these debating contests that double bind arguments lead to unfavorable reactions when those double binds were in favor of myself against an opponent. I learned that the competent debator was the one who presented a double bind argument in favor of his opponent and then demolished the advantage he had given his opponent.

It took me a long time to realize that when the double bind was used for personal advantage it led to bad results. When the double bind was employed for the other person's benefit, however, there could be lasting benefit. I therefore practiced it extensively in favor of my roommates, classmates, and professors with the knowledge that I would eventually use it to help patients.

When I entered psychiatry and began hypnotic experimentation at the clinical level (the experimental level had been previously explored extensively), the double bind became an approach of extensive interest for eliciting hypnotic phenomena and therapeutic responses.

In essence, the double bind provides an illusory freedom of choice between two possibilities, neither of which is really desired by the patient but both of which are actually necessary for his welfare. Perhaps the simplest example is provided by children's reluctance about going to bed. Instructed that they must go to bed at 8:00 P.M., they have the feeling of being coerced. If however, those same children are asked, "Do you want to go to bed at a quarter of eight or at eight o'clock?" the vast majority respond by selecting of their own "free will" the latter (which was actually the intended time). Regardless of which specified time the children select, they commit themselves to the task of going to bed. Of course children can say that they do not want to go to bed at all, whereupon another double bind can be employed, "Do you wish to take a bath before going to bed, or would you rather put your pajamas on in the bathroom?" This latter example illustrates the use of a non sequitur in a double bind. The lesser of the two evils is usually accepted. Either choice, however, confirms the matter of going to bed, which long experience has taught the children is inevitable. They have a sense of free choice about it, but their behavior has been determined.

Psychiatric patients are often resistant and withhold vital information indefinitely. When I observe this, I emphatically admonish them that they are not to reveal that information this week—in fact, I am insistent that they withhold it until the latter part of next week. In the intensity of their subjective desire to resist, they fail to evaluate adequately my admonition; they do not recognize it as a *double bind requiring them both to resist and to yield*. If the intensity of their subjective resistance is sufficiently great, they may take advantage of the double bind to disclose the resistant material without further delay. They thereby achieve their purpose of both communication and resistance. Patients rarely recognize the double bind when used on them, but they often comment on the ease they find in communicating and handling their feelings of resistance. In the cases that follow the critical reader may question the effectiveness of double binds because he is actually on a secondary level when he reads *about* them. The patients, who come to therapy with many emotional needs, however, are on a primary level when they are exposed to the double bind; they are usually unable to analyze them intellectually, and their behavior is thereby structured by them. The uses of the double bind are greatly facilitated by hypnosis, and it adds greatly to the multitude of ways in which it can be used.

CASE ONE

A 26-year-old man with a M.A. degree in psychology came reluctantly to the writer for hypnotherapy at his father's dictatorial demand. His problem was fingernail biting, begun at the age of four as a measure of escaping four hour's daily practice at the piano. He had bitten his fingernails to the quick until they bled, but his mother was unmoved by the bloodstains on the keys. He continued the piano and the fingernail biting until the latter had become an uncontrollable habit. He resented greatly being sent for hypnotherapy and freely stated so.

I began by assuring him that he was justified in his resentment, but I was amused that he had allowed himself to participate in self-frustration for 22 long years. He looked at me in a puzzled way so the explanation was given, "To get out of playing the piano you bit your fingernails to the quick until it became an unbreakable habit despite the fact you have wanted long fingernails. In other words, for 22 years you have literally deprived yourself of the privilege of biting off a good sized piece of finger nail, one that you could really set your teeth on satisfyingly."

The young man laughed and said, "I see exactly what you are doing to me. You are putting me in the position of growing fingernails long enough to give me some genuine satisfaction in biting them off and making the futile nibbling I'm doing even more frustrating." After further semihumorous discussion he acknowledged that he was not sure he really wanted to experience a formal hypnosis. I accepted this by adamently refusing to make any formal effort. This constituted a reverse-set double bind: He asked for something he was not sure he really wanted. It was refused. Therefore, he was bound to want it, since he could now do so safely.

In the ensuing conversation, however, *his interest was maintained at a high pitch and his attention was rigidly fixated,* as he was told earnestly and intently that he could grow one long fingernail. He could take infinite pride in getting it long enough to constitute a satisfying bite. At the same time he could frustrate himself thoroughly by nibbling futilely at the tiny bits of nail on the other nine digits. Although no formal trance was induced, his high response attentiveness indicated he was in what we might call "the common everyday trance" that is brought on by any absorbing activity or conversation.

This light trance suggestion was reinforced by the measure of arousing him with casually irrelevant remarks and then repeating the instructions. What is the purpose of this measure? When you casually repeat suggestions in the awake state right after they heard them in trance, the *patients say to themselves,* "Oh, yes, I know that already, it's okay." In saying something of this sort to themselves the patients are actually taking the first important step toward internalizing and reinforcing the suggestion as aspects of their own inner worlds. It is this internalization of the suggestion that makes it an effective agent in behavior change.

Many months later the patient returned to display normal fingernails on each hand. His explanation, while uncertain and groping, is adequately descriptive of the effect of the double bind. He explained, "At first I thought the whole thing hilariously funny, even though you were serious in your attitude. Then I felt myself being pulled two ways. I wanted 10 long fingernails. You said I could have one only, and I had to end up by biting it off and getting a 'real mouthful of fingernail.' That displeased me, but I felt compelled to do it and to keep gnawing at my other fingernails. That frustrated me painfully. When the one fingernail started growing out, I felt pleased and happy. I was more resentful than ever at the thought of biting it off, but I knew I had agreed to do so. I eventually got around that by growing a second nail—that left eight fingers to gnaw on, and I wouldn't have to bite the second long one off. I won't bore you with details. Things just got more confusing and frustrating. I just keep on growing more nails and nibbling on fewer fingers, until I just said 'To hell with it!' That compulsion to grow nails and nibble nails and to feel more frustrated all the time was just unbearable,. Just what were the motivations you put to work in me and how did it work?''

Now, more than eight years later, he is well-advanced in his profession. He is well-adjusted, a personal friend, and he has normal fingernails. He is convinced that the writer used hypnosis on him to some degree because he still remembers a "peculiar feeling, as if I couldn't move, when you were talking to me."

CASE TWO

A father and mother brough their 12-year-old son in to me and said: "This boy has wet the bed every night of his life since he was an infant. We've rubbed his face in it; we've made him wash his things; we've whipped him; we've made him go without food and water; we've given him every kind of punishment and he is still wetting the bed." I told them, "Now he is my patient. I don't want you interfering with any therapy that I do on your son. You let your son alone, and you let me make all my arrangements with your son. Keep your mouths shut and be courteous to my patient." Well, the parents were absolutely desperate, so they agreed to that. I told Joe how I had instructed his parents and he felt very pleased about it. Then I said, "you know Joe, your father is 6'1", he is a great big powerful husky man. You are only a 12-year-old kid. What does your father weigh? Two hundred twenty, and he isn't fat in the least. How much do you weigh? One hundred seventy." Joe couldn't quite see what I was driving at. I said, "Do you suppose it is taking a deuce of a lot of energy and strength to build that great bid beautiful chassis on a 12-year-old kid? Think of the muscle you've got. Think of the height you've got, the strength you've got. You have been putting an awful lot of energy in building that in 12 short years. What do you think you'll be when you are as old as your father? A shrimpy six foot two weighing only 220 pounds, or do you think you will be taller than your father and heavier than your father?" You could see Joe's mind turning handsprings in all directions, getting a new body image of himself as a man. Then I said, "As for your bed-wetting you have had that habit for a long time and this is Monday. Do you think you can stop wetting the bed, have a permanent dry bed by tommorrow night? I don't think so, and you don't think so, and nobody with any brains at all will think that sort of thing. Do you think you will have a dry bed permanently by Wednesday? I don't. You don't. Nobody does. In fact, I don't expect you to have a dry bed at all this week. Why should you? You have had a lifelong habit, and I just simply don't expect you to have a dry bed this week. I expect it to be wet every night this week and you expect it.

We're in agreement, but I also expect it to be wet next Monday, too, but you know there is one thing that really puzzles me and I really am absolutely thoroughly puzzled—*will you have a dry bed by accident on Wednesday or will it be on Thursday, and you'll have to wait until Friday morning to find out?"* Well, Joe had been listening to me, and he wasn't looking at the walls, the carpet, or the ceiling or the light on my desk or anything else. He was in the common everyday trance listening to all these new ideas, things he had never thought of before. Joe didn't know I was putting him in a double bind because the question wasn't, "Will I have a dry bed?" The question really was, *"which night?"* He was in a mental frame of reference to find out *which night* he would have the dry bed. I continued, "You come in next Friday afternoon and tell me whether it was Wednesday or Thursday, because *I don't know; you don't know. Your unconscious mind doesn't know. The back of your mind doesn't know, the front of your mind doesn't know. Nobody knows. We will have to wait until Friday afternoon."* So "we" both waited until Friday afternoon, and Joe came in beaming and he told me the most delightful thing, "Doctor, you were mistaken, it wasn't Wednesday or Thursday, it was both Wednesday and Thursday." I said, "Just two dry beds in succession doesn't mean that you are going to have a permanent dry bed. By next week half of the month of January is gone, and certainly in the last half you can't learn to have a permanent dry bed, and February is a very short month." (Never mind the speciousness of that argument, because February is a short month.) *"I don't know whether your permanent dry bed will begin on March 17, which is St. Patrick's Day, or will it begin on April Fools Day. I don't know. You don't know either, but there is one thing I do want you to know, that when it begins it is none of my business. Not ever, ever, ever is it going to be any of my business."*

Now why should it be any of my business when his permanent dry bed began? That was actually a posthypnotic suggestion that would go with him for the rest of his life. Now that is what you call a double bind. Little Joe couldn't understand what a double bind was. *You use double binds and triple binds always as a part of the strategy of psychotherapy. You present new ideas and new understandings and you relate them in some undisputable way to the remote future.* It is important to present therapeutic ideas and posthypnotic suggestions in a way that makes them contingent on something that will happen in the future. Joe would get older and taller. He would to on to high school and college. I never mentioned high school to him. I mentioned college, the remote future and the idea of being a football player. I didn't want him thinking about a wet bed. I wanted him thinking about the remote future and the things he could do instead of thinking: what am I going to do tonight—wet the bed.

CASE THREE

The serious question of what constitutes power and dominance and strength and reality and security had apparently been given considerable thought by Lal, approximately eight years old. At all events, shortly before the evening meal he approached his father and remarked interrogatively, "Teachers always tell little kids what they have to do?" An interrogative "yes" was offered in reply. Lal proceeded "And Daddys and Mammas always, always, tell their little children what they got to do?" Another interrogative affirmation was offered. Continuing, Lal said, "And they make their little children do what they say?" A questioning assent was given.

Bracing himself firmly with his feet widely apart, Lal declared through clenched teeth, "Well, you can't make me do a single thing, and to show you, I won't eat dinner and you can't make me."

The reply was made that his proposition seemed to offer a reasonable opportunity to determine the facts, but that it could be tested in a manner fully as adequate if he were to declare that he could not be made to drink an extra glass of milk. By this test, it was explained, he could enjoy his evening meal, he would not have to go hungry, and he could defintely establish his point of whether or not he could be made to drink his milk.

After thinking this over, Lal agreed but declared again that he was willing to abide by his first statement if there were any doubt in the father's mind about the resoluteness of his declaration. He was airily assured that the glass of milk being extra large would be an easily adequate test.

A large glassful of milk was placed in the middle of the table where it would be most noticeably in full view, and dinner was eaten in a leisurely fashion while the father outlined the proposed contest of wills.

This exposition was made carefully, and the boy was asked to approve or disapprove each statement made so that there could be no possible misunderstandings. The final agreement was that the issue would be decided by the glass of milk and that he, Lal, affirmed that his father could not make him drink the milk, *that he did not have to do a single thing his father told him to do about the milk.* In turn, the father said that he could make Lal do anything he wanted Lal to do with the milk, and that *there were some things he could make Lal do a number of times.*

When full understanding had been reached and it was agreed that the contest could begin, the father commanded, "Lal, drink your milk." With quiet determination the reply was made, "I don't have to and you can't make me."

This interplay was repeated several times. Then the father said quite simply, "Lal, spill your milk."

He looked startled, and when reminded he had to do whatever he was told to do about his milk, he shook his head and declared "I don't have to." This interplay was also repeated several times with the same firm negation given.

Then Lal was told to drop the glass of milk on the floor and thus to break the glass and spill the milk. He refused grimly.

Again he was reminded that he had to do with the milk whatever he was told to do, and this was followed with the stern admonition, "Don't pick up your glass of milk." After a moment's thought he defiantly lifted the glass. Immediately the order was given, "Don't put your glass down." A series of these two orders was given, eliciting consistently appropriate defiant action.

Stepping over to the wall blackboard the father wrote "Lift your milk" and at the other he wrote, "Put your milk down." He then explained that he would keep tally of each time Lal did something he had been told to do. He was reminded that he had already been told to do both of those things repeatedly, but that tally would now be kept by making a chalk mark each time he did either one of those two things he had been previously instructed to perform.

Lal listened with desperate attention.

The father continued, "Lal, don't pick up your glass," and made a tally mark under "Lift your milk," which Lal did in defiance. Then, "Don't put your milk down" and a tally mark was placed under, "Put your milk down" when this was done. After a few repetitions of this, while Lal watched the increasing size of the score for each task, his father wrote on the blackboard, "Drink your milk" and "Don't drink your milk," explaining that a new score would be kept on these items.

Lal listened attentively but with an expression of beginning hopelessness.

Gently he was told, "Don't drink your milk now." Slowly he put the glass to his lips but before he could sip, he was told, "Drink your milk." Relievedly he put the glass down. Two tally marks were made, one under "Put your milk down," and one under "Don't drink your milk."

After a few rounds of this, Lal was told not to hold his glass of milk over his head but to spill it on the floor. Slowly, carefully he held it at arm's length over his head. He was promptly admonished not to keep it there. Then the father walked into the other room, returned with a book and another glass of milk, and remarked, "I think this whole thing is silly. Don't put your milk down."

With a sigh of relief Lal put the glass on the table, looked at the scores on the blackboard, sighed again, and said, "Let's quit, Daddy."

"Certainly, Lal. It's a silly game and not real fun, and the next time we get into an argument, let's make it really something important that we can both think about and talk sensibly about."

Lal nodded his head in agreement.

Picking up his book, the father drained the second galss of milk preparatory to leaving the room. Lal watched, silently picked up his glass, and drained it.

Reality, security, definition of boundaries and limitations all constitute important considerations in the childhood growth of understandings. There is a desperate need to reach out and to define one's self and others. Lal, with full and good respect for himself as a person and as an intelligent person, challenged an opponent whom he considered fully worthy and who, to Lal's gain, demonstrated no fearful sense of insecurity upon being challenged to battle.

The battle was one in defense of a principle considered by one contestant to be of great merit, and his opinion was rigorously respected but regarded as faulty by the other contestant. It was not a petty quarrel for dominance between two petty persons. It was the determination of the worth of a principle. Lines were drawn, understandings reached, and forces were engaged in the struggle for the clarification of an issue finally demonstrated by both contestants to be in error and of no further importance.

More than 20 years have elapsed, and Lal has children of his own. He recalls that experience with pleasure and amusement and also with immense persoanl satisfaction. He defines it as "one time when I felt that I was really learning a lot. I didn't like what I was learning, but I was awful glad I was learning it. It just made me feel real good inside the way a little kid likes to feel. I even want to say it like a little child."

CASE FOUR

One day one of my children looked at the spinach on the dinner table and said, "I'm not going to eat any of that stuff!" I agreed with him totally, "Of course not. You are not old enough, you are not big enough, you are not strong enough." This is a double bind that makes his position less tenable and the spinach more desirable. His mother took his side by maintaining that he was big enough, and the issue then became an argument between his mother and me. The boy, of course, was on her side. I finally offered the compromise of letting him have a half a teaspoon full. They felt that was an unsatisfactory offer so I had to let him have half a dish. He ate that as fast as he could and loudly demanded more. I was reluctant but his mother agreed with him. Then very grudgingly I admitted "You are bigger and stronger than I thought." That now gave him a new status in his own eyes. I did not directly ask him to revise his self-image, but it occurred *indirectly* by (a) giving him an opportunity, a stage (the two sides of the argument between his mother and I) on which he could view and carefully consider a *revision of his own behavior,* and (b) the implications of this behavior change which *he drew himself* from my grudging admiission of his growth. The essence of this indirect approach is that it arranges circumstances that permit subjects to make their own appropriate choices.

ERICKSON'S CLINICAL APPROACH TO THE DOUBLE BIND

A review of Erickson's charming presentation of his approach to the double bind reveals the following characteristics.

1. The issues the patient is involved in are usually of immediate and deeply involving personal concern. There is *high motivation* that Erickson structures into the form of a double bind that can be used for behavior change. This is evident in all cases, from the calf-tail pulling incident of his childhood to the

problems of dealing with resistant patients.

2. Erickson always *accepts* the patient's immediate reality and frames of reference. He forms a *strong alliance* with *many different sides and levels* within the patient.

3. The patient has a problem because different response tendencies are in conflict in such a way that behavior change is stalemated. Erickson *facilitates expression of all response tendencies in such a way that the stalemated conflict is broken.* This was particularly evident in the case of the piano-playing nail biter who wanted to (a) frustrate his parents and yet (b) break his nail-biting habit, (c) enjoy long fingernails, and yet (d) enjoy biting off a long nail. He wanted to (e) resist his father's demand for hypnosis and yet (f) have it for his own purpose in his own way.

4. Erickson invariably adds something new to the situation that is related to the patient's central motivations in such a way that the patient is fascinated. The patient is opened with curiosity about the new point of view that Erickson is presenting; he *develops a creative moment (Rossi, 1972), or acceptance set, for all the suggestions that follow*. The patient listens with such attentiveness that a formal trance induction is often unnecessary. The patient listens with that sort of rapt response attentiveness that Erickson recognizes as the *common everday trance*.

5. The actual double bind is set by implications which structure the critical choices within the patient's own associative matrix. This was particularly evident in the way the father structured his son Lal's defiance into an appropriate issue where a reverse-set double bind could operate within the son. The father then "exercised" the reverse set to make sure it had "taken hold" before giving the critical suggestion. The importance of structuring and utilizing the patient's own internal responses to facilitate suggestions was emphasized in the piano-playing nail biter when Erickson *casually* repeated important suggestions so the patient would naturally affirm that he had already had them.

6. *Erickson usually offers a number of double or triple binds.* The double bind does not work by magic. It only works if it fits an appropriate need or frame of reference within the patient. The simple case where one double bind fits so exquisitely as to effect a precise and predictable behavior change all by itself as in the case of Lal is probably rare. Erickson does not always know beforehand which double bind or suggestion will be effective. He usually uses a buckshot approach of giving many suggestions but in such an innocuous manner (via implications, casualness, etc.) that the patient does not recognize them. While watching Erickson *offer* a series of double binds and suggestions, Rossi frequently had the impression of him as a sort of mental locksmith now gently trying this key and now that. He watches the patient intently and *expectantly*, always looking for the subtle changes of facial expression and body movement that provide an indication that the tumblers of the patient's mind have clicked; he has found a key that works much to his mutual delight with the patient.

7. Erickson tries to tie the double bind and posthypnotic suggestions of be-

havior change to reasonable future contingencies. *The suggestion is made contingent on an inevitability.* Erickson thus uses both time and the *patient's own inevitable behavior as vehicles for the suggestions.* Again we note that the effectiveness of Erickson's approach is in the way he binds his suggestions to processes occurring naturally within the patient. The effective suggestion is one that is tailor-made to fit within the patient's own associative matrix. Erickson is always busy observing and tinkering for the best fit.

THE VARIETIES OF DOUBLE BIND AND RUSSELL'S THEORY OF LOGICAL TYPES

Erickson's first unrealized exposure to the double binds that bound him to his humble farm chores reveals a fundamental characteristic of all double binds: There is free choice on a *primary or object* level that is recognized by the subject, but behavior is highly structured on a *seondary or metalevel* in a way that is frequently unrecognized. Other investigators (Bateson, 1972; Haley, 1963; Watzlawick, Beavin, & Jackson 1967; Watzlawick, Weakland, & Fisch, 1974) have related this fundamental characteristic of the double bind to Russell's Theory of Logical Types in Mathematical Logic (Whitehead & Russell, 1910), which was developed to resolve many classical and modern problems of paradox in logic and mathematics. The double bind, from this point of view, can be understood as a kind of paradox that the subjects cannot easily resolve so they "go along with it" and allow their behavior to be determined. In this sense the double bind can be recognized as a fundamental determinant of behavior on a par with other basic factors such as reflexes, conditioning, and learning.

The free choice on the primary level of deciding whether to feed the chickens or hogs first was actually contained within a wider framework, the secondary or metalevel, of "tasks which had to be done." Little Erickson could question what he wanted to do first on the primary level and he could feel proud of being permitted choice on that level. What the boy Erickson could not question was the metalevel of "tasks which had to be done." No one could question the metalevel, probably not even his father, because it was a mental framework that was built-in on the meta or unconscious level as a basic assumption of their way of life. These first examples of the double bind may therefore be described as *free choice of comparable alternatives* on a primary level with the acceptance of one of the alternatives determined on a metalevel.

FREE CHOICE OF COMPARABLE ALTERNATIVES

For didactic purposes we may now list how a number of double binds of this type can be used to facilitate hypnosis and therapy. The positive metalevel

Double Bind

determines that one of the free choices among comparable alternatives *will be accepted* in the therapeutic situation itself. Because we come to therapy of our own free will, for our own good, *we will accept* at least some of the therapeutic choices that are offered. The "transference" and "rapport" are also binding forces that usually operate at an unconscious or metalevel. In hypnosis we may consider that it is the trance situation itself which is the metalevel determining that some choice will be accepted among the comparable alternatives presented on the primary level by the hypnotherapist. In the following examples free choice is offered on the primary level of the "when" or "how" of trance, but it is determined on a metalevel that *trance will be experienced.*

"Would you like to go into trance now or later?"

"Would you like to go into trance standing up or sitting down?"

"Would you like to experience a light, medium, or deep trance?"

"Which of you in this group would like to be first in experiencing a trance?"

"Do you want to have your eyes open or closed when you experience trance?"

It is easily seen from the above that there is an infinite number of such double binds that can be constructed in the form of a simple question offering free choice among comparable alternatives, one of which will be chosen. The skill of the therapist is in recognizing which possible sets of alternatives will be most appealing and reinforcing for the patient to choose from.

The double bind question is uniquely suited for Erickson's experiential approach to trance phenomena. Thus:

"Tell me whether you begin to experience the numbness more in the right or left leg?"

"Will your right hand lift or press down or move to the side first? Or will it be your left? Let's just wait and see which it will be."

"Will your eyelids grow heavy and close or will they remain comfortable and open in that one position?"

"Do you want hypnosis to remove all the pain or do you want to leave a little bit of the pain as an important signal about the condition of your body?"

"Time can be of varying intensity. Will it be condensed? Expanded?"

"What part of your body will be most heavy? Warm? Light? etc?"

THE DOUBLE BIND IN RELATION TO THE CONSCIOUS AND UNCONSCIOUS

Probably the most fascinating double binds to the depth psychologist are those that somehow deal with the interface between the conscious and unconscious (Erickson, 1964a). Many of these are trance inducing, such as the following:

"If your unconscious wants you to enter trance, your right hand will lift. Otherwise your left will lift."

Whether one gets a yes (right hand) or no (left hand) response to this request, one has in fact begun to induce trance, since any truly autonomous response (lifting either hand) requires that a trance state exist. This is a particularly curious situation because in this case the double bind request at the primary conscious level appears to effect a change at the unconscious or metalevel. It is precisely because of this possibility that humans fall prey to paradoxes. Paradoxes, of course, raise problems, but they can also be used to facilitate the first stages of the therapy process where it is sometimes necessary to break up patients' old and inadequate frames of reference (their metalevels) to facilitate the possibility of creating new and more adequate frameworks (Erickson, 1954; Rossi, 1972, 1973; Watzlawick, Weakland, & Fisch, 1974).

Double binds can also be used to facilitate a creative interaction between the conscious and unconscious. When a patient is blocked or limited on the conscious level, the therapist can simply point out that the limitation is on the conscious level only and proceed to facilitate the unconscious somewhat as follows:

> Now it really doesn't matter what your conscious mind does because it is your unconscious that will find new possibilities that your conscious mind is unaware of or may have forgotten. Now you don't know what these new possibilities are, do you? Yet your unconscious can work on them all by itself. And how will they be communicated to your conscious mind? Will they come in a dream or a quiet moment of reflection? Will you recognize them easily at a conscious level or will you be surprised? Will you be eating, shopping, or driving a car when they come? You don't know but you will be happy to receive them when the do come.

In this series of double binds consciousness is depotentiated by *not knowing* and the unconscious is facilitated by a number of truisms about the autonomy of the unconscious and the many possible ways it has of communicating with consciousness. The person is in a double bind with a positive metalevel of hopeful expectation for constructive work. But because his conscious mind cannot deal directly with the unconscious, the limitations of the conscious level are held in check until the unconscious can marshal a solution through some original problem solving.

Weitzenhoffer (1960) has convincingly presented the view that the term "unconscious" in contexts such as we have used here is not the same as Freud's "unconscious." Our use of the term "unconscious" is similar to its usage with finger signaling and the Chevreul pendulum (Cheek & LeCron, 1968) where Prince's (1929) definition of *subconscious* or *co-conscious* as any process "of which the personality is unaware" but "which is a factor in the determination of conscious and bodily phenomena" is more appropriate. To adequately conceptualize the double bind and hypnotic phenomena in general, it may well be that in the future the term "metalevel" could usefully replace labels like "unconscious, subconscious, or co-conscious," since metalevels can be more precisely defined and thus enable us to apply the tools of symbolic logic, mathematics, and systems theory to human problems.

THE TIME DOUBLE BIND

Erickson will frequently use time as a double bind to facilitate a psychotherapeutic process. Typical examples are as follows:

"Do you want to get over that habit this week or next? That may seem too soon. Perhaps you'd like a longer period of time like three or four weeks."

"Before today's interview is over your unconscious will find a safe and constructive way of communicating something important to your conscius mind. And you really don't know how or when you will tell it. Now or later."

In explaining the use of such therapeutic double binds, Erickson feels they are approaches that enable the patient to cooperate with the therapist. The patient experiences great uncertainty, fright, and inner agony in not knowing how to give up a symptom or reveal traumatic material. The therapeutic double bind gives the power of decision to the patient's unconscious and provides the conscious mind with an opportunity to cooperate.

THE REVERSE SET DOUBLE BIND

Erickson gave a numer of examples of the reverse-set double bind: (a) Reversing the calf's direction by pulling its tail, (b) enabling patients to reveal material by enjoining them not to, (c) utilizing Lal's reverse set to make him drink milk. We will analyze the example of Lal to illustrate how the Theory of Logical Types could handle the reverse-set double bind.

1. The father immediately recognizes Lal's defiance from his behavior and verbal challenge about not eating dinner.

2. Recognizing that it is a matter of principle, the father's first move is to shift the battleground from a whole dinner to a mere glass of milk.

Father then defines the rules of the game so that the defiance is verbally crystallized into a reverse set: Lal "did not have to do a single thing his father told him to do about the milk." The father recognizes the reverse set, but the son does not. The son believes the contest is about drinking milk; he is on the primary or object level in that belief. The son does not recognize the reverse set that is operating within him on a metalevel.

4. The father then gives the son a chance to exercise the reverse set so that its operation becomes firmly established within him. The father is now giving commands to the son on the primary level while also locking the son firmly into

his reverse set on the metalevel.

5. The father sets up a tally sheet to demonstrate clearly to the son *"that there were some things he would make Lal do a number of times."* Lal begins to feel "hopelessness" with this repeated demonstration—he knows that he is losing in some way, but he does not know why or how since the reverse set is operating on a metalevel that is unconscious.

6. The father finally gives the critical command "Don't drink your milk," which completes the double bind. Lal raises the glass to drink, but the father steps in to save Lal's self-esteem just in the nick of time by telling him "to drink" so he does not have to.

7. Lal finally does drink the milk, but only when the name of the game is changed to *we drink milk together*. Lal's original defiance is transformed; the conflict between father and son is finally resolved as a joint behavior of drinking milk together.

THE NON SEQUITUR DOUBLE BIND

Illogic continues to have a field day with Erickson's casual insertions of all sorts of *non sequiturs* and *reductio ad absurdi* in the form of double binds. As was illustrated in Erickson's "going to bed" examples with children, he will often give a series of double binds when one does not suffice. Frequently, the more he gives the more absurd they become, except that consciousness does not recognize their absurdity and is eventually structured by them. In the *non sequitur* double bind there is a similarity in the *content* of the alternatives offered even though there is *no logical* connection. Thus Erickson says, "Do you wish to take a *bath* before going to bed, or would you rather put your pajamas on in the *bathroom*?" One could get vertigo trying to figure out the sense or illogic of such a proposition. One cannot figure it out, one cannot refute it, so one tends to go along with it.

THE SCHIZOGENIC DOUBLE BIND

The relation between Erickson's use of the double bind and the studies of it by Bateson *et al.* (1956) in the genesis of schizophrenia offers an interesting study of similarities and contrasts. (See Table 1)

It may be noted in summary that the schizogenic double bind carries *negative injunctions that are enforced* at the metalevel or abstract level that is outside the victim's control on the primary level. Erickson's therapeutic double binds, by contrast, always emphasize *positive agreement on the metalevel and offer alternatives that can be refused on the primary level*. Erickson has stated that

TABLE 1

The Bateson Schizogenic Double Bind

1. *Two or More Persons*:
   The child "victim" is usually ensnared by mother or a combination of parents and siblings.
2. *Repeated Experience*
   Double bind is a repeated occurrence rather than one simple traumatic event.
3. *A Primary Negative Injunction*
   "Do not do so-and-so or I will punish you."
4. *A Secondary Injunction* Conflicting With the First at a More Abstract (Meta) Level, and Like the First Enforced by Punishments or Signals Which Threaten Survival.
5. *A Tertiary Negative Injunction* Prohibiting the Victim from Escaping the Field.
6. Finally, the complete set of ingredients is no longer necessary when the victim has learned to perceive his universe in double bind patterns.

The Erickson Therapeutic Double Bind

1. *Two or More Persons*
   Usually patient and therapist are ensconced in a positive relationship.
2. *A Singe or Series of Experiences*
   If one is not enough, a series of double binds will be *offered* until one works.
3. *A Primary Positive Injunction*
   "I agree that you should continue doing such and such."
4. *A Secondary Positive Suggestion at the Metalevel That* Facilitates a Creative Interaction Between the *Primary (Conscious) and Metalevel (Unconscious)*. Responses at both levels are permitted to resolve stalemated conflicts.
5. *A Tertiary Positive Understanding* (Rapport, Transference) That Binds the Patient to His Therapeutic Task but Leaves Him Free to Leave if He Chooses.
6. The patient leaves therapy when his behavior change frees him from transference and the evoked double binds.

"While I put the patients into a double bind, they also sense, unconsciously, that I will never, never hold them to it. They know I will yield anytime. I will then put them in another double bind in some other situation to see if they can put it to constructive use because it meets their needs more adequately." For Erickson, then, the double bind is a useful device that *offers* a patient possibilities for constructive change. If one double bind does not fit, he will try another and another until he finds a key that fits.

ETHICS AND LIMITATIONS IN THE USE OF THE DOUBLE BIND

As Erickson indicated in his early exploration of the double bind, there are significant limitations in its use. When the double bind is used in a therapeutic milieu, there is a positive feeling associated with the therapeutic metalevel which determines that some choice will be made. Because of this basically positive context or metalevel patients will accept one alternative even if they do not care for any. They will accept bitter medicine, if it is good for them.

When a free choice among comparable alternatives is offered without a positive metalevel structuring the situation, the subjects are free to refuse all choices. If we walk up to a stranger and ask "Will you give me a dime or a dollar?" we will obviously be turned down more often than not because there is no metalevel binding the stranger to accept one of the offered alternatives. If the stranger happens to be charitable, however, this characteristic of charitablesness may function as a positive metalevel that will determine that we get at least a dime.

When the relationship or metalevel is *competitive* or *negative,* however, we can always expect a rejection of all the double bind alternatives offered on the primary level. The competitive situation of a debate yields negative results, as Erickson found, unless the alternatives favor the other side. In the utterly negative situation of war or harm, "Do you want a punch in the nose or a kick in the teeth?" we can expect universal rejection of the alternatives. The therapeutic usefulness of the double bind, then, is limited to situations that are structured by a positive metalevel. The structuring presence of a positive metalevel together with free choice on the primary level also defines the ethical use of the double bind.

RESEARCH ON THE DOUBLE BIND

Since the successful use of the double bind on the clinical level is so highly dependent on the rapport and recognition of the patient's unique individuality, we can anticipate difficulty in securing positive results in experimental work where standard approaches may be used with large groups of subjects with little or no knowledge of their individual differences. Statistics on the amount of success of a single double bind in the standardized laboratory situation would therefore have little applicability to the clinical situation. A standardized testing situation that employs a *series of double binds* all directed to facilitate one or a few closely related behaviors would have a better chance of producing a significant experimental effect than a single double bind, however. A second major difficulty in such research is in the difficulty of defining and recognizing just what is a double bind for a particular individual. Bateson (1974) has commented that "a good deal of rather silly research [has been done] by people who think they can count the number of double binds in a conversation. This cannot be done for the same reason that you cannot count the number of jokes."

To be able to count the number of double binds or possible jokes in a conversation, one would theoretically have to have access to a person's entire associative structure. Even with computers this is not practical. It may, however, be possible to write computer programs for double binds that could operate on the finite associative structure built into the computer program. On another level we anticipate that much fascinating research could be done investigating parameters influencing the simple reverse-set type of double bind illustrated in the case of Lal. In addition to Bateson's (1972) relating of the double bind to deuterolearning, experimental work with animals and humans on reversal and nonreversal shifts (Kendler & Kendler, 1962) suggestes other research paradigms relating the double bind to fundamental problems of learning. The fundamental nature of the double bind in structuring all forms of human behavior indicates that such research should have a high priority.

21. Two-Level Communication and the Microdynamics of Trance and Suggestion

Milton H. Erickson and Ernest L. Rossi

A professional woman, Dr. Erickson, and a number of other psychiatrists and psychologists are discussing the nature of hypnosis, the double bind, suggestions on two levels, etc. She mentions that she has never personally succeeded in performing automatic writing. Erickson undertakes to help her with the dialogue and hypnotic induction listed on the left side of the following pages. On the right side of each page Erickson and Rossi comment on the varieties of indirect suggestion and two-level communication that are taking place.

Induction   Commentary

Shifting Frames of Reference: Displacing Doubt, Resistance, and Failure

Subject: Now I have been trying for two years to automatically write something, and I can't get it. How do I go about getting it?

Erickson: She is telling me, "I have been trying for two years." Her emphasis is entirely on "trying."

Erickson: Do you want to get it?

E: I'm shifting her focus of attention with this question. I put the emphasis on "Do you want?" It is an unrecognizable shift from her concern with failure to the question of her motivation.

Rossi: You emphasize wanting rather than trying and failing. You are immediately shifting her

---

Reprinted with permission from *The American Journal of Clinical Hypnosis,* January, 1976, *18*, 153-171.

Two-Level Communication

out of her negative, failure frame of reference and reorienting her to her positive motivation.

E: Yes and she does not even realize it.

S: Yes! I wouldn't have been trying this long if I didn't want to.

R: Now in this sentence she immediately responds with your diffierentation: she is speaking of "trying" and "want to" as different things.

Shock and Surprise to Break Old Frames of Reference

E: Ever try writing with your left hand?

S: I don't think I have.

E: She wants to do automatic writing, and she has proved for two years that she cannot do it. By asking her if she has ever tried writing with her left hand and getting a "no" response from her, I imply there is *another* way of writing.

R: You open up another possibility that has not been associated with failure. You are again dislodging her from her failure frame of reference.

E: The geographical shift to her left hand is so unrealistic that her unconscious is going to be alerted.

R: Many associations and search programs are activated by your unrealistic introduction of the left hand. It is a surprise or shock to jog her out of her failure set and thus activate a search on the unconscious level for something new (Rossi, 1972, 1973).

E: Ever try writing backward with your left hand?

S: I don't think I could.

E: You probably couldn't do that. (Pause)

E: Here I'm opening up still another possibility. Whenever you do the unexpected, you jog a person out of their setting.

E: "You probably couldn't do that." That is where her failure is!

R: Oh, I see! You first dislodge her from her

past failure in automatic writing with her right hand, and then you shift her failure and place it on her probable inability to write backward with her left hand. You reify her failure, you dislodge it from the task at hand and then shift it to something irrelevant. This is a neat paradigm of your general approach to discharging and displacing doubt, resistance, or failure. You treat the resistance as a concrete thing that the patient must first express to get it out of her system. You then relocate the failure and resistance to a place where it will not interfere with constructive work on the problem at hand.

Distraction in the Dynamics of Two-Level Communication

Are you willing (Pause)

to find that out ? (Spoken softly with voice dropping.)

S: Yes.

E: Really?!

E: Again this involves a shift from trying to the question of conscious motivation: *Are you willing* is to the conscious level; **find that out** is to the unconscious level because I've attracted conscious attention with the *are you willing?* By adding **find that out** I'm also implying there is something to find out. (Communications to the conscious level are in italics, while communications to the unconscious are in bold print.)

R: A pause and voice dynamics separate the two levels. In the critical sentence, "*Are you willing* **to find that out**," your voice emphasis on "*willing*" catches the conscious mind. But the more softly spoken, "**to find that out. . .**"

E: . . . Catches the unconscious.

R: Why? Because all her conscious attention went to the emphasis on "*willing?*"

E: Yes. She had two years of failure, yet I'm questioning her willingness. The willingness to fail for two years and the willingness to write are two different things. I'm differentiating between them.

Two-Level Communication

S: Writing backward with my left hand?

E: No, **to find out.**
(Pause)
To find out (very softly).

S: I think I am willing.

E: Do you think you are willing **to find out?** (softly)

S: How do I do this? How do I set it up?

E: You don't set it up. You don't need to.

Just find out

(Pause)

R: You recognize that for two years she has been stalemated between (a) her willingness to do automatic writing and (b) her willingness to fail at it (Erickson, 1965). By questioning her willingness to do automatic writing you are actually challenging and thus fixating the attention of her conscious mind. Since her conscious mind is fixated on the first half of the sentence (*Are you willing*), it is distracted from the second half (**find that out**). This is the essential dynamic of communication on two levels: you activate, attract, and fixate attention with one item, and then add another item that will be received but not noticed. This is actually related to the classical notion of hypnosis as the fixation and distraction of attention.

E: Her question is on the conscious level, so the first part of my response *"No"* is on the conscious level, but the last part *"***to find out***"* is actually contradictory and does not make much sense in that context. Therefore it goes to the unconscious as a suggestion implying, **find out with your right hand.**

R: Here again she responds on the conscious level with this statement about *willing,* but you return by repeating your question on two levels.

R: She again emphasizes her conscious orientation with her very rational questions about how she is to set up the automatic handwriting. Your response that she does not need to set it up is a direct effort to depotentiate that rational orientation.

E: I break up her conscious set. Her questions are on the conscious level, but the answers require that she make a search on the unconscious level.

Trance Induction by Two-Level Communication

Just find out.

R: You again emphasize the unconscious level with your softly spoken phrase "**Just find out.**"

E: She does not realize I'm telling her to go into a trance. She thinks I said, "**Just find out.**" But I have said, "**Just find out**" to her unconscious mind, and having spoken to her unconscious mind, her unconscious mind has to come forth.

R: That coming forth of the unconscious defines the trance situation. You frequently induce trance by asking a question or assigning a task that cannot be dealt with by the patient's momentary conscious frame of reference. This momentarily depotentiates conscious sets, and the patient retreats to an unconcious level in search for an adequate response.

Do you mind if J takes your cigarette?

R: This question about J taking her cigarette is the first direct indication that you are structuring a trance situation.

Just find out.

(S's eyelids begin to blink slowly.)

E: All the foregoing was a trance induction by the two levels of speaking.

R: She was speaking on the conscious level, but her unconscious was picking up your suggestions on another level. To accommodate your suggestions on the unconscious level . . .

E: It [her unconscious] had to wipe out the conscious.

That's it, **close your eyes.**
(Pause)
And just close your eyes and sleep more and more deeply.
(Pause)

E: "That's it" tells her conscious mind that her unconscious is doing something.

R: You repeated your suggestion "**to find out**" to the unconscious so often that it finally depotentiated consciousness so she could easily enter trance.

E: I noticed the slowing of her eyelid blinking as I said that. I had to get rid of her cigarette because you can't go into trance smoking a cigarette, since it is a conscious act. I removed the last vestige of her need for conscious thinking.

"Wonder" as a Two-Level Suggestion

And now what I'd like to have you do is to **wonder** about that writing.

R: You emphasize **wonder** to introduce an exploratory set?

E: When a person **wonders,** it implies that they don't know.

R: "Wonder" depotentiates conscious sets on one level while stimulating exploratory efforts on the unconscious level. It is a two-level suggestion all by itself. Many other words like "try, explore, imagine, feel, sense" tend to evoke two-level communication. When confronted with such words, people tend to get that faraway look in their eyes that is characteristic of the common everyday trance (Erickson & Rossi, 1975). These words orient a person within themselves in a manner conducive to trance.

Dynamics of Dissociation and Need for Closure in Evoking Automatic Writing

I'd like to have you get the **feeling**

that you have **written** it.

But just the **feeling** that you have **written** it, just the **feeling.**

E: She has many times in the past had the feeling of writing with her right hand. I isolate that feeling and put in in the left hand, where it does not belong. But everybody likes to put together things that belong together.

R: You set up a tension by evoking the feeling of having written in her left hand. There is going to be a natural tendency to get that feeling in her right hand where it belongs. The only

And get that **feeling** in your **left hand.**
(Pause)
And get the **feeling** in your **left hand.**
(Pause)
And now in a different way I'd like to have you get the *knowledge* of how to *write* in your *right hand.*

The *knowledge* of how to *write* in your *right hand.*

way to get that feeling is to do the automatic writing. You set up an expectancy or need for closure in her right hand that can only be fulfilled by automatic writing.

E: Yes.

R: This suggestion of getting a *knowledge of how to write in her right hand* is a sort of truism that evokes many familiar associations, and as such tends to reinforce the suggestion of getting a **feeling of having written in the left hand.** That in turn strengthens the need for closure by doing the automatic writing, so that feeling of having written can get back to the right hand where it belongs.

These dynamics come into play at an unconscious level, however, so consciousness is further depotentiated and automatism facilitated.

Cognitive Overloading to Depotentiate Conscious Sets to Facilitate Hypnotic Responsiveness

But the **feeling** that you **have written** it in your **left hand.**

And while you are enjoying those two separate sensations,

you might be interested in a third realization.

R: There is also a cognitive overload and confusion introduced when you almost simultaneously evoke and carefully partition associations along those different dimensions, as follows:

Left Hand	*Right Hand*
Feeling	*Knowledge*
Past	*Present*

The reader can observe how you have associated **left hand, feeling,** *and* **past tense** *in some of your sentences and* *right hand, knowledge,* *and present tense in others. Her conscious mind cannot understand the significance of this dissociation, and therefore the controlling and directing function of her ego is depotentiated to the point where automatism tends to set in.*

	E: Yes. You are overloading the conscious mind, you are getting it off balance. It has to escape from that tension situation. I've been talking to the unconscious, and it is feeling comfortable because, I'm putting all the discomfort into the conscious mind.
A third experiential learning.	*R:* You then overload further with this introduction of a "third experiential learning." [Erickson now gives a number of illustrations of how the conscious mind can be overloaded, startled, or mystified in order to fixate attention while the therapist unobtrusively adds other suggestions that automatically drop into the unconscious because consciousness cannot cope with them while so fixated.]
You say that you want to do a **certain** *amount of writing.*	*E:* She didn't say she wanted to do a **certain** amount. I've overloaded her conscious mind with it. She has to search in her mind, "What makes you think it is a **certain** amount?
Just what it is **you don't know.**	
But you say you want to	*R:* There are multiple meanings of the word **certain** that come in here: **certain** can mean positive affirmation as well as a limitation of amount. It can also mean a particular item of special interest. There could be a **certain** subject that she wants to deal with via automatic writing.
and you really do.	
	E: We don't know which meanings her unconscious will act upon. But we do know that the word **certain** is a highly specific unspecific.

Voice Dynamics in Two-Level Communication

At least I believe you.	*E:* I'm telling her she can have her conscious *false beliefs* about not being able to do automatic writing, but **I believe she can.** Again I'm speaking to her unconscious.
I don't know if you believe you	

But I believe you
(softly)

R: Your initial phrase, *"I don't know if you believe you,"* acts as a challenge that catches her conscious attention. While she is attending to that, you softly say **"but I believe you,"** which acts as a suggestion that drops into her unconscious, since her consciousness was too occupied to heed it at that precise moment. You frequently use such compound statements wherein you fixate conscious attention with the first half so you can then unobtrusively drop a suggestion into the unconscious in the second half.

E: Yes, the phrase to the unconscious is spoken softly. I use one tone of voice to speak to the conscious mind and another to speak to the unconscious. When you use one tone of voice that pertains to conscious thinking and another tone of voice that expresses other ideas which you intend for the unconscious, you are establishing a duality.

The Double Bind

And the only question is,

when will you do it?

R: You then immediately follow up with the phrase "the only question is when," which displaces her from the question of success or failure in writing to the mere question of *when*.

E: That is a double bind.

Will you do it expectedly

or unexpectedly? You are interested in experiments.
You in your own mind can set up the experiment.

R: "Will you do it expectedly or unexpectedly?" is another double bind. It is not a question she can dispute, and therefore it plants the actual suggestion of writing very strongly. Structuring such forms of mutually exclusive response (expectedly or unexpectedly) is actually another form of double bind: on one level her unconscious is free to choose its own form of response; you have, however, structured the alternatives so that on another level (the meta-

Covering All Possibilities of Response: Multiple Form of Double Bind

You can write as Mary does.

A word here, a word there.

A syllable here, a syllable there.

A letter here, a letter there.

A word following a syllable, a letter.

You can misspell a word.

You can write the wrong word.

level) the range of her response possibilities are determined by you.

R: Here you outline a whole series of suggestions covering all possibilities of response so that unconscious processes can be facilitated. Whatever response she does manifest is acceptable as a correct step toward the ultimate goal of automatic handwriting. Covering all possibilities of response is actually a multiple form of the double bind. Rather than binding, however, it gives free reign to the patient's creative process. You don't know what mechanisms the patient's unconscious can use, so you give it carte blanche to use any available mechanism.

E: Yes, these are all just so many interlocking double binds.

The Double Dissociation Double Bind

You can write that material without ever knowing what it is.

Then you can go back and discover you know what it is without knowing that you've written it.

R: In this first statement you suggest a dissociation between writing and knowing what she has written.

In this second statement you offer the reverse dissociation: she can know what she has written but not know she has written it. Together these two statements effect a double dissociation in the form of a double bind that appears to cover all possibilities of response. It is an extremely powerful form of suggestion that so befuddles consciousness that it must rely on the unconscious to sort out the response possibilities.*

And as you continue

E: This is a very strong instruction to her unconscious that follows the double bind.

R: Conscious sets are momentarily depotentiated by the double bind, so whatever follows tends to drop directly into the unconscious.

Utilizing Disequilibrium to Evoke Hypnotic Phenomena

That **feeling** of **having written** in your **left hand,**

R: You again return to your tripart division of **feeling, past tense,** and **left hand** verses *knowledge, present tense, and right hand.*

it can be most interesting.

And the *knowledge* that you *can write* with *your right* hand

E: It evokes a need to pull together the things that belong together: to get the feeling of writing in the right hand. There is only one way to get that feeling in the right hand: doing automatic writing.

is also most interesting.

E: Here I'm getting the *present* tense ("is") into automatic writing. That is a bridging association from the past (**feeling of having written**) to *present*. To do the automatic writing she's got to have that **feeling** *now*.

R: You create a tension by suggesting a feeling in her left hand that really belongs in her right hand. You dissociate a feeling and take it out of its natural context so that a tension is created until it can return to its rightful place by exe-

---

*Another example of the double dissociation double bind that is analyzed in more detail by the authors (Erickson, Rossi & Rossi, 1976) goes as follows: "You can as a person awaken but you need not awaken as a body, (pause), or you can awaken when your body awakes but without a recognition of your body."

cuting the hypnotic phenomenon of automatic writing. This is a general principle for evoking hypnotic phenomena: *The therapist arranges to utilize internal states of tension, dissociation, or disequilibrium that can only be resolved by the execution of some desired hypnotic phenomena.*

E: If you observe children, you learn they do this sort of thing all the time.

R: Yes, the Zeigarnik (Woodworth & Schlosberg, 1956) effect, for example, illustrates how children will return to an incompleted task after an interruption because of the tension or disequilibrium aroused by their set for closure.

Two-Level Communication by Implication

And you want something at a two-level suggestion.

R: Here you talk about giving her a two-level suggestion, but I cannot find it.

Here and now,

and in the presence of all the others,

I'm going to say something to you

in a two-level suggestion.

And you can wonder what it is

E: I'm having her unconscious define what it is to be wondered about and what is worth waiting for.

and why.
(pause)
And you can wait,
and you can wonder,

R: By waiting and wondering her unconscious is going through all its programs in search of something worthwhile?

(pause)

and you can wait and
you can wonder,

and you can wait and
you can wonder.

Because what will that
suggestion be?
And you wait and you
can wonder.

(Pause)

E: Her problem was her difficulties with automatic handwriting. I'm really talking about that.

R: On the conscious level you are talking about wondering and waiting, but to the unconscious you are implying automatic writing. Is that the two-level suggestion?

E: Yes. I told her I would give her a two-level suggestion. I'm illustrating two levels by two different kinds of behavior: waiting and wondering. A choice between two things is also two; I'm illustrating twoness.

R: In a very concrete way.

Association and Two-Level Communications: Childhood Associations and Automatic Writing

And I taught my sister
that two plus two is
four.

And four and four is
eight.

And she didn't quite
believe me when I told
her that three and five
is eight.

Because she said that I
had told her that four
and four is eight.

(Long pause)

E: The unconscious works without your knowledge, and that is the way it prefers. I'm evoking the patient's own childhood patterns here by simply talking about childhood.

R: Why?

E: Automatic handwriting usually does have a childlike character.

R: So you introduce childhood associations to facilitate a regressive or autonomous process of automatic handwriting.

E: Yes, and on two levels.

R: On one level it implies that the conscious

mind does not always understand things (like the child's initial puzzlement about arithmetic), and on another level you are also facilitating regression by the simple process of association: talking about childhood reactivates memory traces of response tendencies appropriate to childhood. Since the conscious mind does not understand, it tends to be depotentiated. With consciousness momentarily puzzled and depotentiated, your associations about childhood can now reach her unconscious, where they may also reactivate memory traces and response tendencies appropriate to childhood and autonomous processes like automatic handwriting.

Dissociation to Facilitate automatic Writing

And writing is one thing and reading is another.

E: Knowing what you are writing is an awareness, while automatic writing is an unawareness. I'm dividing up the entire process of automatic writing and giving her permission to do only one of those parts.

And knowing what should be written is a third.

And concealment of the writing from the self is another thing.

R: You are breaking up what seems to be one unitary act of writing, reading, and awareness of what was written into its three component parts, so the possibility of writing without awareness is introduced. Many hypnotic phenomena are simply dissociated forms of normal behavior.

(Long pause as S apparently does some automatic writing.)

And keep right on because you are interested.

E: Yes, this is actually an instruction of how to do automatic writing.

Non Sequitur to Facilitate Two-Level Communication

And the feeling in your

R: The second half of this sentence ("You don't

left hand is so important

that you don't want to know that feeling.
(Pause)

want to know that feeling'') seems to be a non sequitur to the conscious mind, but it makes sense to the unconscious?

E: It is an important feeling, but you don't want to know it. The feeling is the essential thing. Knowing about it is not the essential thing.

R: What seems to be a non sequitur to the conscious mind is actually a way of depotentiating consciousness. You are actually telling the unconscious that the feeling is important, but consciousness is so unimportant that it need not know, recognize, or register that feeling.

And concealing it from you

is interesting.

And enjoy that.

''Concealing it from you'' effects a dissociation that depotentiates consciousness. It permits the unconscious to express itself in privacy and safety from consciousness.

Implied Directive and Two-Level Communication

And as soon as you feel that you are through writing,

you can rouse up.

(A tear begins to roll down her cheek.)

And are you going to hide that tear?

And are you going to hide that tear?

(Long pause)

S: (Awakens and sighs.)

R: This is an implied directive wherein you suggest an overt piece of behavior (awakening in this case) to signal when an indirectly formulated suggestion, the implied directive (''as soon as you feel you are through writing''), has taken place on the unconscious level. Many forms of ideomotor response (*e.g.*, finger, hand, or head signaling) can be used as signals to let the therapist know when a question has been answered (Cheek & LeCron, 1968) or a suggestion implemented on an unconscious level. The signaling response is actually a form of biofeedback without the use of electronic instrumentation. We can hypothesize that the implied directive and biofeedback are similar in that both function on an unconscious level (the subject does not know how he does it) and both use a signal to indicate when the desired re-

Two-Level Communication

sponse takes place. It would be fascinating to test whether ideomotor responses could be calibrated to give immediate knowledge of results and therefore reinforcement to any degree of the desired response, just as electronic instrumentation does for biofeedback. The implied directive and biofeedback are both forms of two-level communication whereby a signal expressed on the conscious level is an index of activity on an unconscious level.

A general conversation about other matters now takes place for about five minutes. Erickson then casually shows S the sheet on which she had been writing and continues as follows:

Protection of the Unconscious and Initial Stages of Hypnotic Learning

E: Now you recognize, of course, that this is automatic writing, don't you? And you recognize it is not written for me or for anybody else to read.

(Pause)

Would you recogonize that handwriting?

You recognize it is not for anybody else to read, and it is not for you to read at the present time.

So close your eyes.

And when you want to read it,

R: Apparently the writing was illegible, as the first efforts of automatic writing frequently are. You emphasize that it is automatic writing to forestall criticism from the conscious attitude that it is not comprehensible and therefore worthless. This is an example of how the therapist must frequently protect the initial stages of learning a new hypnotic phenomena because the conscious mind, particularly in our rationalistic age, tends to downgrade and thus destroy accomplishments of the unconscious.

E: [Erickson tells an interesting story of how useful automatic writing can be to help a person learn somethinv they know without knowing they know it. A woman wrote something in automatic handwriting, but then on suggestion she carefully folded it up without reading it and placed it absentmindedly in her pocketbook. A few months later, after making an important change in her marriage plans, she "accidentally" rediscovered the folded paper. She found her unconscious had worked on and had written

when you want to put
it together in proper
fashion,

I'd like to have you do
it before I leave Philadelphia.

And so

let's postpone the task
for a while.

Let's postpone the task

for a while.
(Pause)
And now rouse up.

Hi!

S: Hi!

about her change in plans automatically months earlier. It is thus a facilitative procedure to allow the unconscious to protect itself by taking cautionary measures that permit the automatic writing to remain hidden from the conscious until it is appropriate for the consciousness to know. Ideomotor signaling can be used to determine if the unconscious is ready to allow the conscious to learn what was written.]

E: You can make the unconscious known without making it known. You make it known by automatic writing. You make it unknown by folding the paper and putting it away till consciousness is ready for it.

The group breaks up and goes to dinner with no further discussion. It is important during the initial stages of learning to experience trance that the therapist prevent the rationally oriented individual from building associative bridges between the nascent and autonomous aspects of trance phenomena and their usual everyday awareness. Talking about trance immediately after experiencing it builds associative connections between trance and everyday awareness that destroys the dissociation between them. Talking amalgamates the nascent and autonomous qualities of trance phenomena into the individual's usual, "normal" state of awareness to the point where many researchers (Barber, Spanos, and Chaves, 1974) have come to believe that trance, as an altered state of consciousness, does not exist (Erickson and Rossi, 1974).

A CONTEXT THEORY OF TWO-LEVEL COMMUNICATION

In the commentary we analyzed the dynamics of two-level communication in terms of the classical notion of hypnosis as the fixation and distraction of attention. In what follows we propose a more comprehensive analysis that encompasses a broader range of phenomena ranging from the conceptions of the recent contextual theory of verbal associations (Jenkins, 1974) and literalism to the use

Two-Level Communication

of shock, surprise, analogy, and metaphor, which are so common in Erickson's approach.

The question, *"Are you willing* (pause) **to find that out**?" has as a general context a query about motivation (Are you willing?) which fixates or structures the subject's conscious frame of reference or sense of meaning. The individual words and phrases used to articulate that general context, however, have their own individual and literal associations that do not belong to that general context. These individual and literal associations are of course usually suppressed and excluded by consciousness in its effort to grasp the general context. These suppressed associations do remain in the unconscious, however, and under the special circumstances of trance, where dissociation and literalness are heightened, they can play a significant role in facilitating responsive behavior that is surprising to consciousness.

This situation can be made clear by analogy. The adult reader is usually searching for an author's meaning. Within certain limits it really doesn't matter what particular sentences or words are used. Many different sentences and combinations of words could be used to express the same meaning. It is the meaning or the general context of the sentences that registered in consciousness, while the particular sentences and words used fall into the unconscious where they are "forgotten." In the same way one "reads" the meaning of a whole word rather than the individual letters used to make up the word. The general context of the letters registers as the conscious meaning of a word rather than the individual associations of each letter. Jenkins (1974) has summarized the data of recent experimental work in the area of verbal association, event recognition, information integration, and memory that places a similar emphasis on the significance of context to understand these phenomena. In any discourse or phenomena using words it is usually the general context that establishes meaninv rather than the structural units that create the discourse.

The obvious exceptions to this of course are in puns, allusions, and all sorts of verbal jokes, where the punch line depends upon literal or individual verbal associations to words and phrases that originally escaped the attention of consciousness. Verbal jokes depend upon literal or individual associations that are usually suppressed.

In the same way Erickson's two-level communication utilizes a general context to fixate the attention of consciousness while the individual associations of words, phrases, or sentences within that context are registered in the unconscious, where they can work their effects. From this point of view Erickson's Interspersal Technique (1966) is the clearest example of two-level communication wherein subject matter of interest to a particular patient is utilized as a general context to fixate conscious attention, while interspersed suggestions are received for their effects on an unconscious level.

Erickson has devised a number of other techniques to activate the individual literal and unconscious associations to words, phrases, or sentences buried within a more general context. Turns of phrase that are shocking, surprising, mystifying, non sequitur, too difficult or incomprehensible for the general conscious context, for example, all tend to momentarily depotentiate the patient's conscious sets and activate a search on the unconscious level that will turn up the literal and individual associations that were previously suppressed. When Erickson overloads the general context with many words, phrases, or sentences that have common individual associations, those associations (the interspersed suggestion) gain ascendency in the unconscious until they finally spill over into responsive behavior that the conscious mind now registers with a sense of surprise. The conscious mind is surprised because it is presented with a response within itself that it cannot account for. The response is then described as having occurred "all by itself" without the intervention of the subject's ego or conscious motivation; the response appears to be autonomous or "hypnotic."

Analogy and metaphor as well as jokes can be understood as exerting their powerful effects through the same mechanism of activating unconscious association patterns and response tendencies that suddenly summate to present consciousness with an apparently "new" datum or behavioral response.

THE MICRODYNAMICS OF SUGGESTION

Once Erickson has fixated and focused a patient's attention with a question or general context of interest (e.g., ideally the possibility of dealing with the patient's problem), he then introduces a number of approaches designed to "depotentiate conscious sets." By depotentiating conscious sets we do not mean there is a loss of awareness in the sense of going to sleep; we are not confusing trance with the condition of sleep. Trance is a condition wherein there is a reduction of the patient's foci of attention to a few inner realities; consciousness has been fixated and focused to a relatively narrow frame of attention rather than being diffused over a broad area as in the more typical general reality orientation (Shor, 1959) of our usual everyday awareness. When fixated and focused in such a narrow frame, consciousness is in a state of unstable equilibrium; it can be "depotentiated" by being shifted, transformed, or bypassed with relative ease.

Erickson believes that the purpose of clinical induction is to focus attention inward and alter some of the ego's habitual patterns of functioning. Because of the limitations of a patient's habitual frames of reference, his usual everyday consciousness cannot cope with certain inner and/or outer realities, and the patient recognizes he has a "problem." Depotentiating a patient's usual everyday conscious sets is thus a way of depotentiating facets of his personal limitations; it is a way of deautomatizing (Deikman, 1972) an individual's habitual modes of functioning so that dissociation and many of its attendant classical hypnotic phenomena (e.g., age regression, amnesia, sensory-perceptual distortions, catalepsies, etc.) are frequently manifest in an entirely spontaneous manner (Erickson & Rossi, 1975). Depotentiating the limitations of the individual's usual patterns of awareness thus opens up the possibility that new combinations of associations and mental skills may be evolved for creative problem solving within that individual.

Erickson's approaches to depotentiating consciousness are so subtle and pervasive in the manner with which they are interwoven with the actual process of induction and suggestion that they are usually unrecognized even when studying a written transcript of his words. In order to place them in perspective we outlined the microdynamics of induction and suggestion in Table 1 as (a) fixation of attention, (b) depotentiating conscious sets, (c) unconscious search, (d) unconscious processes, and (e) hypnotic response. We have also listed a number of Erickson's approaches to facilitating each stage. Most of these approaches are illustrated in this paper and discussed in more detail elsewhere (Erickson and Rossi, 1974; Erickson and Rossi, 1975; Erickson, Rossi, and Rossi, 1976; Haley, 1967; Rossi, 1973). Although we may outline these processes as stages of a sequence in Table 1 for the purpose of analysis, they usually function as one simultaneous process. When we succeed in fixating attention, we automatically narrow the focus of attention to the point where one's usual frames of reference are vulnerable to being depotentiated. At such moments there is an automatic search on the unconscious level for new associations that can restructure a more stable frame of reference via the summation of unconscious processes. There is thus a certain arbitrariness to the order and the headings under which we assign some of the approaches Erickson used in this paper. He could equally well begin with an interesting story or pun as with a shock, surprise, or a formal induction of trance. Once the conditions in the first three columns have been set in motion by the therapist, however, the patient's own individual unconscious dynamics automatically carries out the processes of the last two columns.

A number of Erickson's most interesting approaches to facilitating hypnotic response are listed in Column 3 of Table 1. All these approaches are designed to evoke a search on the unconscious level. Allusions, puns, metaphors, implications, etc., are usually not grasped immediately by consciousness. There is a momentary delay before one "gets" a joke, and in part that is what is funny about it. In that delay period there obviously is a search and processes on an unconscious level (Column 4) that finally summate to present a new datum to consciousness so it gets the joke. All the approaches listed in Column 3 are communication devices that initiate a search for new combinations of associations and mental processes that can present consciousness with useful results in everyday life as well as in hypnosis. The approaches listed in Column 3 are also the essence of Erickson's indirect approach to suggestion (Erickson, Rossi and Rossi, 1976). The study of these approaches may be regarded as a contribution to the newly defined science of pragmatics: the relation between signs and the users of signs (Watzlawick, Beavin, and Jackson, 1967). Erickson relies upon the skillful utilization of such forms of communication to evoke hypnotic behavior rather than hypersuggestibility *per se.*

It is important to recognize that while Erickson does think of trance as a special state (of reduced foci of attention), he does not believe hypersuggestibility is a necessary characteristic of trance (Erickson, 1932). That is, just because a patient is experiencing trance, it does not mean that patient is going to accept and act upon the therapist's direct suggestions. This is a major misconception that accounts for many of the failures of hypnotherapy; it has frustrated and discouraged many clinical workers in the past and has impeded the scientific exploration of hypnosis in the laboratory. Trance is a special state that intensifies the therapeutic relationship and focuses the patien't attention on a few inner realities; *trance does not insure the acceptance of suggestions*. Erickson depends upon certain communication devices such as those listed in Column 3 to evoke, mobilize, and move a patient's associative processes and mental skills in certain directions to *sometimes* achieve certain therapeutic goals. He believes that hypnotic suggestion is actually this process of evoking and *utilizing* a patient's own mental processes in ways that are outside his usual range of ego control. This *utilization theory of hypnotic suggestion* can be validated, if it is found that other therapists and researchers can also effect more reliable results by carefully utilizing whatever associations and mental skills a particular patient already has that can be mobilized, extended, displaced, or transformed to achieve specific "hypnotic" phenomena and therapeutic goals.

In the formal trance situation the successful utilization of unconscious processes leads to an autonomous response; the ego is surprised to find itself confronted with a new datum or behavior (Column 5). The same situation is in evidence in everyday life, however, whenever attention is fixated with a question or an experience of the amazing, the unusual, or anything that holds a person's interest. At such moments people experience the common everyday trance; they tend to gaze off—to the right or left, depending upon which cerebral hemisphere is most dominant (Baken, 1969)—and get that "faraway" or "blank" look. Their eyes may actually close, their bodies tend to become immobile (a form of catalepsy), certain reflexes (e.g., swallowing, respiration, etc.) may be suppressed, and they seem momentarily oblivious to their surroundings until they have completed their inner search on the unconscious level for the new idea, response, or frames of reference that will restabilize their general reality orientation. We hypothesize that in everyday life consciousness is in a continual state of flux between the general reality orientation and the momentary microdynamics of trance as outlined in Table 1. The well-trained hypnotherapist is one who is acutely aware of these dynamics and their behavioral manifestations. Trance experience and hypnotherapy are simply the extension and utilization of these normal psychodynamic processes. Altered states of consciousness, wherein attention is fixated and the resulting narrow frame of reference shattered, shifted, and/or transformed with the help of drugs, sensory deprivation, meditation, biofeedback, or whatever, follow essentially the same pattern but with varying emphasis on the different stages. We may thus understand Table 1 as a general paradigm for understanding the genesis and microdynamics of altered states and their effects upon behavior.

Two-Level Communication

TABLE 1
The Microdynamics of Trance Induction and Suggestion

(1) Fixation of Attention	(2) Depotentiating Conscious Sets	(3) Unconscious Search	(4) Unconscious Processes	(5) Hypnotic Response
1. Stories that motivate interest, fascination, etc.	1. Shock, surprise, the unrealistic and unusual	Indirect Forms of Suggestion	1. Summation of: a. Interspersed suggestions b. Literal associations c. Individual associations d. Multiple meaning of words	"New" datum or behavioral response experienced as hypnotic or happening all by itself
2. Standard eye fixation	2. Shifting frames of reference; displacing doubt resistance and failure	1. Allusions, puns, jokes		
3. Pantomime approaches	3. Distraction	2. Metaphor, analogy, folk language	2. Autonomous, sensory, and perceptual processes	
4. Imagination and visualization approaches	4. Dissociation and disequilibrium	3. Implication	3. Freudian primary processes	
5. Hand levitation	5. Cognitive overloading	4. Implied directive	4. Personality mechanisms of defense	
6. Relaxation and all forms of inner sensory, perceptual, or emotional experience	6. Confusion, non sequiturs	5. Double binds	5. Ziegarnik effect	
	7. Paradox	6. Words initating exploratory sets	6. Etc.	
7. Etc.	8. Conditioning via voice dynamics, etc.	7. Questions and tasks requiring conscious search		
	9. Structured amnesias	8. Pause with therapist attitude of expectancy		
	10. Etc.	9. Open-ended suggestions		
		10. Covering all possibilities of response		
		11. Compound statements		
		12. Etc.		

22. The Indirect Forms of Suggestion

Milton H. Erickson and Ernest L. Rossi

The problem of what constitutes hypnotic suggestion has been a subject of research for more than a century (Tinterow, 1970; Weitzenhoffer, 1953, 1963). Recently Weitzenhoffer (1974) presented experimental data regarding the difficulty that is still prevalent in distinguishing between instructions and hypnotic suggestions. The recognition of when hypnotic suggestions are operative is a fundamental issue in experimental research, where it is important to distinvuish between treatments of hypnotic and of control groups. The nature of hypnotic suggestion is also fundamental in clinical hypnosis and psychotherapy, in general, where practitioners are concerned with the most effective means of facilitating therapeutic processes.

Traditionally, whether one speaks of waking or hypnotic suggestion, one usually means either *direct suggestion,* where the operator makes a clear, direct request for a certain response, or some form of *indirect suggestion,* where the relation between the operator's suggestion and the subject's response is less definite or obvious. The importance of the operator's prestige and authority and the principles of repetition, homeoaction, and heteroaction along with the evocation of ideosensory and ideomotor processes (Weitzenhoffer, 1957) that are frequently mediated by goal-directed fantasy (Barber, Spanos and Chaves, 1974) are usually recognized as the basis of direct suggestion. Even the earliest investigators realized that the dynamics of indirect suggestion were more complex, however. Indirect suggestion was recognized as being a function of the subject's individuality and, perhaps because of this, was frequently more effective than direct suggestion. In this paper we will first review some of the ways indirect suggestion has been understood by these investigators. We will then outline our own approach and describe many of the indirect forms of suggestion we have found effective in clinical hypnotherapy.

EARLIER VIEWS OF INDIRECT SUGGESTION

One of the earliest investigators to recognize the unique contribution of the subject's individuality in understanding the essential dynamics of indirect sug-

---

A portion of this paper was presented at the 28th Annual Meeting of the Society for Clinical and Experimental Hypnosis, 1976, under the title "Milton H. Erickson's Approaches to Trance Induction."

Indirect Forms of Suggestion

gestion was Albert Moll in his text on hypnotism (1890). He describes and illustrates his views as follows:

> The subject in this way completes most suggestions by a process resembling the *indirect suggestion*. . . . *The external suggestion* [from the operator] does not remain an isolated phenomenon, but causes a series of other mental processes, according to the character of the subject and to the hypnotic training he has received. I say to the subject, "Here, take this bottle of Eau de Cologne!" He believes that he feels the bottle in his hand, which in reality is empty; besides which he believes he sees the bottle and smells it, although I add nothing to my original suggestion. In short, he completes it independently. This is a very common occurrence.

In this illustration Moll recognizes that the subject completes the operator's bare suggestion of the presence of a bottle of Eau de Cologne by adding and apparently appreciating the visual and olfactory components of it. Simple and obvious as it may be, this example clearly illustrates a basic and most significant characteristic of indirect suggestion: The subject's own unique repertory of associations and behavioral potentials makes an important contribution to the hypnotic response.

A more revealing description of the role of nonverbal indirect suggestion is given by Sidis (1898) as follows:

> Instead of openly telling the subject what he should do, the experimenter produces some object, or makes a movement, a gesture, which in their own silent fashion tell the subject what to do. To illustrate it by a few examples, so as to make my meaning clearer: I stretch out the hand of the hypnotic subject and make it rigid, and while doing this I press his arm with an iron rod. In the next seance as soon as the iron rod touches the arm the hand becomes rigid. I tell the subject to spell the word 'Napoleon,' and when he comes to 'p' I stretch out my hand and make it stiff. The subject begins to stammer; the muscles of his lips spasmodically contract and stiffen. . . . Such a kind of suggestion may be properly designated as *indirect suggestion*.

The principles of *association* and *generalization* implied in this illustration, where an iron rod or the operator's stiffened arm is enough to make the subject's facial muscles stiffen, are also highly characteristic of the process of indirect suggestion. In the following exposition Sidis illustrates how the principles of *contiguity, similarity,* and *contrast* are additional means by which the subject's own unique psychodynamics make a contribution to the hypnotic response:

> In short, when there is full and complete realization of the idea or order suggested, directly or indirectly, we have that kind of suggestion which I designate as *immediate*.
>
> Instead, however, of immediately taking the hint and fully carrying it into execution, the subject may realize something else, either what is closely allied with the idea suggested or what is connected with it by association of contiguity. A suggestion given to the subject that when he wakes up he will see a tiger is an example. He is awakened, and sees a big cat. The subject is suggested that on awakening he will steal the pocketbook lying on the table. When aroused from the hypnotic state, he goes up to the table, does not take the pocketbook, but the pencil that lies close to it. The buyer does not always choose the precise thing which the salesman suggests, but some other thinv closely allied to it. In case the suggestion is not successful, it is still as a rule realized in some indirect and mediate way. Man is not always doing what has been suggested to him; he sometimes obeys not the suggested idea itself, but some other idea associated with the former by contiguity, similarity, or contrast. Suggestion by contrast is especially interesting, as it often gives rise to counter-suggestion. Now such kind of suggestion, where not the suggested idea itself but the one associated with it is realized, I designate as *mediate*.

The subject's tendency to *mediate* or actually *construct* his own hypnotic responses out of the stimuli and suggestions proffered by the operator is an essential insight. It does away with the still all too common misconception of the hypnotic subject as a passive automaton who is programmed and controlled by the operator.

Another view of the dynamics and effectiveness of indirect suggestion is that of the Pavlovian school discussed by Platonov (1959) as follows:

> In *indirect verbal suggestion* the effectuation of the suggestion is, as a rule, related to a particular object or influence by means of which the suggestion must actually be effectuated. Thus, for example, a waking subject is told that the indifferent white powder offered to him is a soporific. The subject therefore falls asleep as soon as he takes the white powder. . . . It follows that indirect verbal suggestion is based on the formation of a conditioned bond between the stimulus of the second signal system (the words of suggestion) and the stimuls of the first signal system (the white powder placebo), and the realization of the suggested effect (which provokes certain phenomena or acts), each of these three elements having definite direct cortical bonds with the past experience of the subject. . . . At the same time, in an indirect suggestion the moment of execution of the suggestion may be *postponed*. Thus, the execution of the suggestion is connected not only

with a definite object (or word, or place) but also with a definite time for which it will be set. By force of this, the very fact of *the suggestive verbal influence recedes, as it were, into the background.* In other words, the suggestion by word *becomes latently active.* . . . It is precisely the *conditions under which the suggestion is effectuated* that are of importance in this case, because they help in reducing criticism and sometimes make possible a direct uncritical attitude to the suggested state or action. This circumstance was reflected in A. Forel's well known words: "Suggestion is the stronger the more *concealed* it is" [in other words, the more indirect it is].

Indirect suggestion may be successfully used with the subject awake; its suggestive influence is much greater than that of a direct suggestion. It frequently exerts an effective influence on people who do not yield to direct suggestion, as was pointed out by V. Bekhterev, A. Forel, F. Löwenfeld, et al.

Even this cursory overview of indirect suggestion reveals a number of basic features that are of particular interest: (1) Indirect suggestion permits the subject's individuality, previous life experience, and unique potentials to become manifest; (2) the classical psychodynamics of learning with processes like association, contiguity, similarity, contrast, etc., are all involved on a more or less unconscious level so that (3) indirect suggestion tends to bypass conscious criticism and because of this can be more effective than direct suggestion.

These features are entirely in keeping with our experience (Erickson, Rossi, and Rossi, 1976; Erickson and Rossi, 1976), which led us to summarize the microdynamics of trance induction and indirect suggestion as a five-stage process: (1) the fixation of attention, (2) depotentiating conscious sets and habitual frameworks, (3) unconscious search, (4) unconscious processes, and (5) hypnotic response. In essence, an indirect suggestion is regarded as one that initiates an unconscious search and facilitates unconscious processes within subjects so that they are usually somewhat surprised by their own response when they recognize it. More often than not, however, subjects do not even recognize the indirect suggestion as such and how their behavior was initiated and partially structured by it.

In the following, we will simply list and then illustrate a number of the indirect forms of suggestion that the senior author habitually uses in hypnotherapeutic practice. No claim can be made for the scientific status of the indirect forms of suggestion as listed and described herein. While they do reflect a great deal of clinical experience, we can only present them with a variety of unsystematic speculations about how we might understand their effectiveness. The coordinated efforts of many other investigators will be required to experimentally evaluate the validity and value of these indirect forms of suggestion in the general process of communication as well as in hypnotherapeutic applications.

The Indirect Forms of Suggestion

1. Indirect Associative Focusing
2. Truisms Utilizing Ideodynamic Processes and Time
3. Questions That Focus, Suggest, and Reinforce
4. Implication
5. Therapeutic Binds and Double Binds
6. Compound Suggestions: Yes Set, Reinforcement, Shock, and Surprise
7. Contingent Associations and Associational Networks
8. The Implied Directive
9. Open-Ended Suggestions
10. Covering All Possibilities of Response
11. Apposition of Opposites
12. Dissociation and Cognitive Overloading
13. Other Indirect Approaches and Hypnotic Forms
14. Discussion

1. *Indirect Associative Focusing.* The simplest indirect form of suggestion is to raise a relevant topic without directing it in any obvious manner at the subject. Erickson likes to point out that the easiest way to help patients talk about their mothers is to talk about your own mother. A natural indirect associative process is thereby set in motion within the patients that brings up apparently spontaneous associations about their mother. Since Erickson does not directly ask about the patient's mother, the usual conscious sets and mental frameworks (e.g., psychological defenses) that such a direct question might evoke are bypassed. In a similar manner, when Erickson is working in a group, he will talk to one person about the hypnotic phenomena he wants another target person to experience. As he talks about hand levitation, hallucinatory sensations, or whatever, there is a natural process of ideomotor or ideosensory response that takes place within the target subject on an autonomous or unconscious level. Erickson *utilizes* these spontaneous and usually unrecognized internal responses to "prime" a target subject for hypnotic experience before the subject's resistance or limited beliefs about his or her own capacities can interfere.

Similarly, in therapy Erickson uses a process of indirectly focusing associations to help patients recognize a problem. He will make remarks, or tell stories about a network of topics S_1, S_2, S_3, S_k, all of which have a common "focus" association, S^1, which Erickson hypothesizes to be a relevant aspect of the patient's problem. The patient sometimes wonders why Erickson is making such interesting but apparently irrelevant conversation during the therapy hour. If S^1 is in fact a relevant aspect of the patient's problem, however, the patient will frequently find himself talking about it in a surprisingly revelatory manner. If Erickson quessed wrong and S^1 is not a relevant aspect, nothing is lost; the patient's associative matrix simply will not add enough significant contributions to raise S^1 to a conscious and verbal level. In this case Erickson allows himself

Indirect Forms of Suggestion

to be corrected and goes on to explore another associative matrix. This indirect associative focusing approach is the basic process in what Erickson calls the "Interspersal approach."

2. *Truisms Utilizing Ideodynamic Processes and Time*. The basic unit of ideodynamic focusing is the truism, which is a simple statement of fact about behavior that the patient has experienced so often that it cannot be denied. In most of our case illustrations it will be found that the senior author frequently talks about certain psychophysiological processes or mental mechanisms as if he were simply describing objective facts to the patient. Actually these verbal descriptions can function as indirect suggestions when they trip off ideodynamic responses from associations and learned patterns which already exist within patients as a repository of their life experience. The "generalized reality orientation" (Shor, 1959) usually maintains these subjective responses in appropriate check when we are engaged in ordinary conversation. When attention is fixed and focused in trance so that some of the limitations of the patient's habitual mental sets are depotentiated, however, the following truisms may actually trip off a literal and concrete experience of the suggested behavior placed in italics.

You already know how to experience pleasant sensations like the *warmth* of the sun on your skin.

Everyone has had the experience of *nodding their head* yes or shaking it no even without quite realizing it.

We know when you are asleep your unconscious can *dream*.

You can easily *forget* that dream when you awaken.

Another important form is the truism that incorporates time. Erickson would rarely make a direct suggestion for a definite behavioral response without tempering it with a time variable that the patient's own system can define.

***Sooner or later* your hand is going to lift (eyes close, etc.).**

Your headache (or whatever) will disappear *as soon as* your system is ready for it to leave.

3. *Questions that Focus, Suggest, and Reinforce*. Recent research (Sternberg, 1975) indicates that when questioned the human brain continues an exhaustive search throughout its entire memory system on an unconscious level even after it has found an answer that is apparently satisfactory on a conscious level. The mind scans 30 items per second even when the person is unaware that the search is continuing. This unconscious search and activation of mental processes on an

unconscious or autonomous level is the essence of Erickson's indirect approach, wherein he seeks to utilize a patient's unrecognized potentials to evoke hypnotic phenomena and therapeutic responses.

Questions are of particular value as indirect forms of suggestion when they cannot be answered by the conscious mind. Such questions tend to activate unconscious processes and initiate the autonomous responses which are the essence of trance behavior. The following are illustrations of how a series of questions can focus attention to initiate trance, reinforce comfort, and lead to hypnotic responsiveness.

Would you like to find a spot you can look at comfortably? As you continue looking at that spot, do your eyes get tired and have a tendency to blink?

Will they close all at once or flutter a bit first as some parts of your body begin to experience the comfort so characteristic of trance?

Does that comfort deepen as those eyes remain closed so you would rather not even try to open them?

And how soon will you forget about your eyes and begin nodding your head very slowly as you dream a pleasant dream?

This series begins with a question that requires conscious choice and volition on the part of the patient and ends with a question that can only be carried out by unconscious processes. An important feature of this approach is that it is *fail-safe* in the sense that any failure to respond can be accepted as a valid and meaningful response to a question. Another important feature is that each question suggests an *observable* response that gives the therapist important information about how well the patient is following the suggestions. These observable responses are all associated with important internal aspects of trance experience and can be used as *indicators* of them.

4. *Implication.* An understanding of how Erickson uses psychological implication can provide us with the clearest model of his indirect approach. Consider the following example of the multiple implications in a single sentence that seemingly states the obvious.

The very complexity of mental functioning,

    A truism about psychology that initiates a "yes" or acceptance set for what follows.

you go into trance to find out

    With a slight vocal emphasis on "to find out," this phrase implies

Indirect Forms of Suggestion

the patient will go into trance and will go into trance to find something important.

a whole lot of things you can do,

Implies that it is not what the therapist does but what the patient does that is important.

and they are so many more than you dreamed of. (Pause.)

The pause implies that the patient's unconscious may now make a search to explore potentials previously undreamed of. This sets up an important expectancy for experiencing unusual or hypnotic phenomena.

It is important in formulating implications to realize that the therapist only provides a stimulus; the hypnotic aspect of psychological implications is created on an unconscious level by the listener. The most effective aspect of any suggestion is that which stirs the listener's own associations and mental processes into automatic action; it is this autonomous activity of the listener's own mental processes that creates hypnotic experience.

The use of psychological implication by association illustrated above depends upon the therapist's ability to initiate subjective responses that will be of value to the patient. The more formal forms of *material implication,* by contrast, which have been carefully defined by the *if . . . then* relation between antecedent and consequent (Copi, 1954), depend upon the objective structure of language for their effects and are more universally applicable even without an understanding of the patient's subjective world.

On the simplest level Erickson might state, "If you sit down, then you can go into trance."

Or: $S \supset T$
Where: $S =$ If you sit down
$\supset =$ then (sign for material implication If . . . then
$T =$ you can go into trance.

On a more complex level Erickson might state, "If you sit or lie down, then you can go into trance."

Or: $(S \lor L) \supset T$
Where: $S =$ If you sit down
$\lor =$ or
$L =$ lie down
$\supset =$ If . . . then.
$T =$ you can go into trance.

When an implication is stated in this form of giving the patient two or more alternatives, all of which lead to the same desired response (trance in this case), we describe the situation as a therapeutic bind.

5. *Thereaputic Binds and Double Binds*. The presentation of two or more alternatives, any one of which will lead to a desired therapeutic response, is easily done with questions.

Would you like to experience a light, medium, or deep trance?

Would you like to go into trance now or in a few minutes?

When the patient's conscious mind can discriminate and make a choice between the alternatives, we speak of a *bind*. When the conscious mind cannot make a choice between the alternatives, we may more properly speak of a double bind because choice is then relegated to responding on another level. This other level, sometimes termed a metalevel (Bateson, 1972, 1975; Watzlawick, Beavin, and Jackson, 1967; Sluzki and Ransom, 1976), can be conceptualized as an unconscious or autonomous mental process.

Typically we induce trance and give subjects a certain amount of hypnotic training, which consists essentially of having them learn to give up control of what was formerly under their control (e.g., in hand levitation, what was formerly voluntary hand lifting is made involuntary; what was formerly a voluntary act of writing is now converted to automatic writing, and so on). This giving up of former areas of control in the special setting called the "hypnotherapeutic situation" is a rehearsal for unlearning what was formerly an overlearned but maladaptive and all too rigid mental frameworks that prevented the subjects from utilizing all their capacities. Hypnotherapeutic training helps patients unlearn their learned limitations. When thus freed from their learned limitations, they can experience their potentials for new and more creative patterns of behavior, which are the essence of therapeutic change. The conscious-unconscious double bind is a basic approach for achieving these goals.

The *conscious-unconscious double bind* is a term we use to describe a hypnotic form that is basic to much of Erickson's work. Erickson frequently gives a preinduction talk about the differences between the functioning of the conscious and unconscious mind. This prepares the patient for double binds that rest upon the fact that we cannot consciously control our unconscious. The conscious-unconscious double bind thus tends to block the patient's usual, voluntary modes of behavior so that responses must be mediated on a more autonomous or unconscious level. Any response to the following suggestions, for example, requires that the subject experience the sort of inner focus that Erickson describes as trance.

If your unconscious wants you to enter trance, your right hand will lift. Otherwise your left will lift.

Indirect Forms of Suggestion

> You don't even have to listen to me because your unconscious is here and can hear what it needs to, to respond in just the right way.

> And it really doesn't matter what your conscious mind does because your unconscious automatically will do just what it needs to in order to achieve that anaesthesia [age regression, catalepsy, etc.].

> You've said that your conscious mind is uncertain and confused. And that's because the conscious mind does forget. And yet we know the unconscious does have access to so many memories and images and experiences that it can make available to the conscious mind so you can solve that problem. And when will the unconscious make all those valuable learnings available to your conscious mind? Will it be in a dream? During the day? Will it come quickly or slowly? Today? Tomorrow?

The patient's consciousness obviously cannot answer these questions, so it must rely on an unconscious or metalevel of functioning to deal with the problem.

Suggestions that cannot be accomplished by voluntary effort tend to evoke therapeutic double binds.

> As you continue resting in trance, does that pain (or whatever symptom) grow stronger or does it tend to fade in and out?

> Does it slowly change its location?

> Tell me whatever changes you notice in that pain [or whatever] in the next few minutes.

> Let your head begin to nod very, very slowly when a feeling of warmth or coolness, prickliness, numbness, or whatever begins to develop in that pain area.

Whatever experience patients have in response to such suggestions is in a direction of therapeutic change. Even if the pain, for example, gets worse, the patients are caught in a therapeutic double bind because they are now experiencing the fact that they have some control over their pain, which was formerly experienced as being out of their control. If one can make the pain worse, it implies that one can also diminish it. This is the basis of the double bind approach to dealing with symptomatic behavior by *prescribing the symptom* (see Watzlawick, Beavin, and Jackson, 1967, for many examples). In dealing with weight problems, for example, Erickson will frequently suggest that a patient who is over weight at 180 pounds should first learn to "over eat enough to weigh 185 pounds." Whether the patients follow this suggestion with dismay or glee, he is still, without quite realizing it, learning to gain control over what had seemed uncontrollable. Having experienced this control the patient is then enjoined to "over eat enough to maintain a weight of 182 pounds, 181, 180, 178, 175, [etc., down to the proper weight]."

This approach to symptom control is actually the reverse of our earlier use of the conscious-unconscious double bind to facilitate trance induction by converting voluntary behavior into involuntary behavior. It is a fascinating and little realized characteristic of the double bind that it can help make involuntary what was previously voluntary, and vice versa. In some way the metalevel of the double bind enables us to change whatever was voluntary or involuntary on our ordinary level of behavior into its reverse. Thus when patients have symptoms or problems over which they claim no control, the double bind becomes a means of helping them experience and gradually establish control. When people have problems because their potentials are experienced as not being available to them (e.g., the underachiever in any area), the double bind can frequently facilitate within them the process of gradually acquiring control over these latent potentials so that they can become established abilities.

We have emphasized the conscious-unconscious double bind in this presentation because it is the easiest to understand and use in a variety of applications. In most real-life situations, however, the metalevel that frames or modifies the ordinary message level in the double bind can be made in many ways or through many channels. Haley (in Sluzki and Ransom, 1976) describes it succinctly as follows in his description of the development of double bind theory:

> The complexity of communication, when analyzed in terms of levels of classification, or logical types, was becoming more apparent. There were now at least four "channels" of communication (words, voice, body movement [or gesture], context) each emitting messages which qualified each other and so were of different logical type, and within each channel any message which qualified another was of another logical type. The number of metalevels began to appear infinite. The general tendency of the project was to simplify toward two levels of message and a third level qualifying those two.

It is thus apparent that communication, and hypnotic communication in particular, is vastly more complex than we have ever realized. Depth psychotherapists as well as traditional wisdom have recognized this in the view that our consciousness, however well developed, is still but a reed on the sea of unconsciousness.

6. *Compound Suggestions*. A surprisingly simple aspect of Erickson's approach is the use of compound suggestions. In its simplest form the compound suggestion is made up of two statements connected with an "and" or a slight pause. One statement is an obvious truism that initiates an acceptance or "yes" set, and the other is the suggestion proper.

When one of Erickson's daughters returned from the orthodontist, he said, **That mouthful of hardware that you've got in your mouth is miserably uncomfortable and it's going to be a deuce of a job to *get used to it.*"**

The first half of this sentence is a truism that states the facts of his daughter's undeniable reality of discomfort. The second half beginning with "and" is a suggestion that she will "get used to it" and not let it bother her. Erickson will frequently use a series of truisms to establish a yes set or acceptance set within the patient so that the suggestion that follows can be more readily accepted.

A more subtle type of compound suggestion is

Just look at one spot and I am going to talk to you.

In this example the therapist has control over his own behavior (I'm going to talk to you), and by simply talking he can actually reinforce the suggestion to "look at one spot."

A sense of shock or surprise can be used in the first half of a compound statement. This has the effect of depotentiating the patient's habitual conscious sets so that they are expectant and in need of further "explanation" to resolve the shock. The "explanation," of course, actually comes in the form of a suggestion that the patient now needs to reestablish his equilibrium. Any emotionally loaded words or ideas can be used to initiate the shock, which is then resolved with a therapeutic suggestion.

Secret feelings you have never told anyone about

can be reviewed calmly within the privacy of your own mind

for help with your current problem

In the above, "secret feelings" tends to initiate a shock that can then be resolved with the therapeutic suggestions that follow. This use of shock and surprise immediately followed by a therapeutic suggestion is most effective when it is formulated to touch upon the individual patient's most personal associations.

7. *Contingent Suggestions and Associational Networks.* Another form of compound suggestion is used when Erickson arranges conditions such that a patient's normal flow of voluntary responses is made contingent on the execution of a hypnotic suggestion (the "contingent" suggestion). A hypnotic response that may be low in a patient's behavioral hierarchy is associated with a pattern of responses high on the patient's behavioral repertory and usually already in the process of taking place. The patient finds that the momentum of ongoing behavior is too difficult to stop, so he simply adds the hypnotic suggestion as an acceptable condition for the completion of the pattern of behavior that has already begun and is pressing for completion. The contingent suggestion simply

"hitchhikes" onto the patient's ongoing flow of behavior. Responses that are inevitable and most likely to occur are made contingent on the execution of the hypnotic response. Erickson thus interlaces his suggestions into the patient's natural flow of responses in a way that causes hardly a ripple of demur.

A number of examples used to induce systematically deepened trance are as follows:

Your eyes will get tired and close all by themselves as you continue looking at that spot.

You will find yourself becoming more relaxed and comfortable as you continue sitting there with your eyes closed.

As you feel that deepening comfort you recognize you don't have to move, talk, or let anything bother you.

As the rest of your body maintains that immobility so characteristic of a good hypnotic subject, your right hand will move the pencil across the page writing automatically something you would like to experience in trance.

In the first two of the above the suggestion in the beginning of the sentence is tied to the ongoing behavior introduced in the second half with the word "as." In the second two the ongoing behavior is mentioned first and a suggestion is then tied to it.

There are many forms of contingent suggestions. When B is any form of ongoing or inevitable future behavior on the part of the subject and Sg is a suggestion, the following paradigms illustrate how one can structure contingent suggestions. While you B you can Sg; when you B please Sg; don't Sg until you B; why don't you Sg before you B; the closer you get to B the more you can Sg; after Sg you can B.

Associating suggestions in such interlocking chains creates a network of mutually reinforcing directives that gradually form a new self-consistent inner reality called "trance." It is construction of such interlocking networks of associations that gives "body" or substance to trance as an altered state of consciousness with its own guideposts, rules, and "reality."

8. *The Implied Directive.* The "implied directive" is a label we are proposing for a fairly common type of indirect suggestion that is in current use in clinical hypnosis (Check and LeCron, 1968). The implied directive usually has three parts: (1) a time-binding introduction, (2) the implied (or assumed) suggestion, and (3) a behavioral response to signal when the implied suggestion has been accomplished. Thus:

As soon as your unconscious knows

Indirect Forms of Suggestion 465

(1) A time-binding introduction that focuses the patient on the suggestion to follow

only you or I, or only you and my voice are here [or any suggested behavior]

(2) The implied (or assumed) suggestion

your right hand will descend to your thigh.

(3) The behavioral response signaling that the suggestion has been accomplished.

An implied directive frequently used by the author to end a hypnotherapeutic session is as follows:

As soon as your unconscious knows

(1) A time-binding introduction that facilitates dissociation and reliance on the unconscious.

it can again return to this state comfortably and easily to do constructive work the next time we are together.

(2) The implied suggestion for easy reentry to trance, phrased in a therapeutically motivating manner.

you will find yourself awakening feeling refreshed and alert.

(3) The behavioral response signaling that the above suggestion has been accomplished.

When the behavioral response signaling the accomplishment is also an inevitable response that the patient wants to happen (as in the above examples), we have a situation where the behavioral response can have motivating properties for the accomplishment of the suggestion. The behavioral response signaling the accomplishment of the suggestion takes place on an involuntary or unconscious level. Thus the unconscious that carries out the suggestion also signals when it is accomplished. Such implied directives engender a covert state of internal learning. It is covert because no one can tell it is occurring because it is a series of responses taking place entirely within the subject, frequently without conscious awareness and usually unremembered after trance. Therapist and patient only know it is completed when the requested automatic response (e.g., finger signaling, head nodding, awakening from trance) takes place, signaling the end of the internal state of learning.

One of Erickson's implied directives outlined above may be analyzed via symbolic logic and possibly improved on the basis of that analysis as follows:

Let S: As soon as you know that only you or I, or only you and my voice are here, then your right hand will descent to your thigh.

Where P: You know that only you or I are here.
    Q: You know that only you or my voice are here
    R: Your right hand will descend to your thigh.

The time-binding introduction, "As soon as you know," can be formulated for logical purposes as "Any time after this," so that S becomes S^1.

S^1: Any time after this, if you know that only you or I are here, or if you know that only you and my voice are here, then your right hand will descend.

This may be simplified to the form S^{11}.

S^{11}: When P or Q, then R

By using material implication where a time sequence is understood, (our time-binding introduction), S^{11} will have the form

$(P \vee Q) \supset R$

Under this form, if either P or Q holds, R has to follow. However, the fact that R occurs does not necessarily mean that either P or Q did in fact take place within the subject. The logical properties of material implication are such that it is true whenever its consequent R is true. In our particular case, whenever R occurs, it is true that P or Q is *sufficient* but not *necessary* for R.

Because of this, S understood as S^1 or S^{11} is too weak. It allows for other possibilities. The occurrence of R may have been brought about by conditions either than P or Q; in fact it could have been brought about by the non realization of P or of Q.

Because of this, when S is understood as S^1 or S^{11}, R is not an adequate signal that P or Q have in fact taken place. This could account for much of the variability found in response to S by different subjects.

S, however, can be understood another way—namely, as saying S*.

S*: Your right hand will descend to your thigh *as soon as* you know that only you or I, or only you and my voice are here.

"As soon as" in S* could have the sense of "only when," in which case S* will be understood as saying S**.

S**: Your right hand will descend to your thigh *only when* you know that only you or I or only you and my voice are here.

Indirect Forms of Suggestion

"Only when," like "when," suggests a time sequence (our time-binding introduction), but for our purposes here it will suffice to understand it in terms of the material implication, so "only when" paraphrases out as "only if," and S** may be formulated as S***.

S***: Your right hand will descend to your thigh only if you know that only you or I or only you and my voice are here.

S*** has the following form:

S****: R only if P or Q
: R ⊃ (P or Q)

When S is understood in terms of S***, the occurrence of R is a sufficient signal that one of P or Q has taken place, because unlike S^1 or S^{11}, S*** says that P or Q is a *necessary condition* for R.

This analysis of Erickson's use of the implied directive suggests that some failures to respond to this form of hypnotic suggestion may be due to the fact that the implied directive, on logical ground alone, is weak in the sense that it is not a *necessary condition* for a hypnotic response. Reformulating Erickson's original statement S as S*** strengthens the logical aspect so that the hypnotic response is more likely to occur. This is another point for empirical investigation, however. If it is found that S*** does in fact elicit the appropriate hypnotic response more than S, we will have empirically established the significance of correct logical formulations for hypnotic suggestions.

The implied directive is particularly interesting because of its similarity to the technique of biofeedback. In most forms of biofeedback an electronic device is used to signal when an internal response has been accomplished. With the implied directive the patient's own overt and autonomous behavioral response is used to signal when the internal response has been accomplished. The formal similarities between them may be listed as follows:

1. Consciousness is given a task it does not know how to accomplish by itself. Thus:

Raise (or lower) your blood pressure 10 points.

Warm your right hand and cool your left.

Increase the alpha of your right cortex.

Decrease the muscle tension in your forehead.

2. Consciousness is given a signal enabling it to recognize when any behavior changes are being made in the desired direction of response. In biofeedback this

is accomplished by an electronic transducer that measures the response (in the above examples, blood pressure, body temperatures, alpha waves, or muscle tension) and makes any change in this response evident on a meter that allows the subjects to monitor their own behavior.

In the implied directive, by contrast, the patient's own unconscious system serves as the transducer indicating when the desired internal response (blood pressure change, body temperature, etc.) has been made and translates it into an overt behavioral signal that consciousness can recognize.

9. *Open-Ended Suggestions.* The open-ended suggestion is of particular value for exploring whatever responses are currently available to subjects. It is of value on the level of conscious choice as well as unconscious determinism. When patients are fully awake, the open-ended suggestion permits them free choice about the issues and behavioral alternatives that are available. When patients are in trance where unconscious and autonomous tendencies are facilitated, the open-ended suggestion permits the unconscious to select just what experiences are most appropriate:

> **Every person has abilities not known to the self, abilities that can be expressed in trance.**
> **Memories, thoughts, feelings, sensations completely or partially forgotten by the conscious mind. Yet they are available to the unconscious and can be experienced within trance now or later whenever the unconscious is ready.**

In this series of open-ended suggestions a broad latitude is permitted, so that whatever the subject experiences can be accepted as valid and serve as a foundation for future work.

10. *Covering All Possibilities of Response.* While the open-ended suggestion is a form of open exploration seeking to utilize whatever response tendencies are available to a subject, suggestions covering all possibilities of response attempt to focus a response into a narrow range of particular interest. This is well illustrated when we use an iterative procedure for gaining successively closer approximations to the desired response. A sample of Erickson's work eliciting automatic handwriting with this approach is as follows:

> **You can scribble, or make a mark or a line here or there. You can write a letter here, a letter there. A syllable here, a syllable there. A word here, a word there. A word following a syllable, a letter. You can misspell a word. You can abbreviate or write the wrong word. [etc.]**

The classic example of facilitating suggestion by covering all possibilities of response is Erickson's (1952) directives for hand levitation.

> **Shortly your right hand, or it may be your left hand, will begin to lift up, or it may press down, or it may not move at all, but we will want to see just what happens. Maybe the thumb will be first, or you may feel something happening in your little finger, but the really important thing is not whether your hand lifts up or presses down or just remains still; rather, it is your ability to sense fully whatever feelings may develop in your hand.**

Covering all (or most) possibilities of response in this example permits the subjects' own individuality to select the modus operandi and hence greatly increases the likelihood of a response of one sort or another. It is a fail-safe suggestion because even if no ideomotor movement takes place, that possibility has been covered ("it may not move at all") as acceptable. The unrecognized implication in most suggestions that cover all possibilities of response is that attention is being fixated and focused and thus trance is being facilitated no matter what happens. The unconscious is being given freedom to express itself in whatever ideomotor fashion it can, while consciousness is fixated on the task of simply observing what will happen. The last phrase of the suggestion ("sense fully whatever feelings may develop in your hand") is an indirect suggestion for an ideosensory response that is actually an inevitability (everyone can experience *some* feeling in their hand). Whatever happens, then, can be experienced as a successful response. It can then be used as a starting point for exploring the type of responsiveness a subject can make available for other hypnotic work.

11. *Apposition of Opposites*. Another of Erickson's indirect forms of hypnotic suggestion is his penchant for the close juxtaposition or apposition of opposites. This seems to be a basic element in his confusion techniques, but it also may be a means of utilizing another natural mental mechanism to facilitate hypnotic responsiveness. Kinsbourne (1974) has discussed how the "balance between opponent systems" is a basic neurological mechanism that is built into the very structure of the nervous system. What we are labeling as the "apposition of opposites" may be a means of utilizing this fundamental neurological process to facilitate hypnotic responsiveness. In the following, Erickson is apparently balancing the opponent systems of remembering and forgetting to facilitate hypnotic amnesia. This apparent balancing of opposites is also a double bind: The end result is an amnesia no matter which alternative is acted upon.

> **You can *forget to remember* or *remember to forget*.**

Other modalities for the apposition of opposites are in lightness and heaviness, warmth and coolness, relaxation and tension, or just about any opponent system of the body that can be described verbally.

As your hand feels *light and lifts*, your eyelids will feel *heavy and close*.

This juxtaposition of lifting and lightness with heaviness and closure illustrates the balance between opponent systems. If we emphasize lightness and levitation, then we are shifting the subject out of equilibrium, heaviness and closure of the eyelids tends to reestablish that equilibrium in a subjective, psychological sense even though not in an objective or physiological sense.

12. *Dissociation and Cognitive Overloading.* Multiple tasks can be presented to divide the unified field of consciousness. The resulting state of dissociation can provide an optimal field for autonomous responses. When the greater part of consciousness is focused on one task, a second task can only be carried out in a state of dissociation and partial or complete autonomy. This is particularly the case when we use hand, head, or finger signaling as the second task as illustrated below.

I want you to see someone sitting over there, and while working on that you can wonder what your hands are going to do. Will they lift up or down? Lifting the left hand means no, and the right hand means yes, you will be able to see that visual image over there.

A curious example of overloading a patient with a confusing series of alternative responses that culminates in an easy-to-accept suggestion to enter trance runs somewhat as follows.

You can stand up or sit down. You can sit in that chair or the other. You can go out this door or that. You can come back to see me or refuse to see me. You can get well or remain sick. You can improve or you can get worse. You can accept therapy or you can refuse it. Or you can go into a trance to find out what you want.

Dissocation can be facilitated by offering tasks that the subject is unfamiliar with and multiple possibilities of response that can be alternatives or reversals of each other. This form of suggestion frequently leads to the sort of cognitive overloading and confusion that depotentiates the subject's ability to make a rational choice so that the response that finally emerges is likely to be more truly autonomous. An example is as follows:

You can write that material without ever knowing what it is. Then you can go back and discover you know what it is without knowing that you have written it.

This has been described as a double dissociation double bind (Erickson, Rossi,

Indirect Forms of Suggestion 471

Rossi, 1976), since each sentence by itself constitutes a dissociation: In the first sentence writing is dissociated from knowing, and in the second knowing what is written is dissociated from knowing that the subject wrote it.

Such formulations for automatic writing with or without a recognition of its meaning or that one has written it are not as arbitrary as they may seem. Studies of the secondary zones of the occipital cortex and optico-gnostic functions (Luria, 1973) illustrate that each of the above possibilities can occur naturally in the form of agnosias when there are specific organic disturbances to brain tissues. Each of these agnosias is only possible because a discrete mental mechanism for normal functioning has been disturbed when they appear. The agnosias are thus tags for identifying discrete mental mechanisms. A so-called suggestion in the form of a double dissociation double bind may be utilizing these same natural mental mechanisms. One could hypothesize that these mental mechanisms may be turned on or off in trance even though they are usually autonomous in their functioning when normally awake. From this point of view we can conceptualize "suggestion" as something more than verbal magic. Adequately formulated hypnotic suggestion may be utilizing natural processes of cortical functioning that are characteristic of the secondary and tertiary zones of cerebral organization. These processes are synthetic and integrative in their functioning and are responsible for processes of perception, experience, recognition, and knowing. Constructing hypnotic forms that can either block or facilitate these discrete mechanisms of the secondary and tertiary zones thus has the potential for vastly extending our understanding of cerebral functioning.

A careful reading of Luria (1973, particularly Part II, Chapter 5, on the "Parietal Regions and the Orangization of Simultaneous Synthesis"), for example, suggests fascinating possibilities for hypnotic research. If T_1, T_2, T_3 . . . T_K are all testable behavioral functions of the parietal cortex (Christensen, 1975 has already prepared a manual of such standardized tests), we may learn to gradually enhance or block a number of these related functions by suggestion. If we first block functions T_1, T_2, T_3 and then find that T_4 and T_5 are also blocked, we will have established that T_4 and T_5 are indeed related to T_1, T_2, and T_3 and mediated by similar neuropsychological processes. Such research would not only supplement our current approaches to identifying and tracing out neuropsychological functions, it would also be a new approach for establishing how certain forms of hypnotic suggestion are mediated by specific patterns of cortical activity. This writer strongly suspects that many of the fascinating but seemingly inexplicable psychosomatic interrelations reported by Erickson (1943) in his experimental investigations may be mediated by such processes.

The following is another example of a double dissociation double bind that is analyzed in greater detail with the help of symbolic logic.

Erickson statement	Symbolic Logic
1. **You can as a person awaken**	P
2. **but you do not need to awaken as a body**	-q
(Pause.)	v
3. **You can waken when your body awakens**	P . q
4. **but without a recognition of your body**	-r

Where P = Person awakening
-q = Not awakening as a body
P.q = Awakening as a person and body
-r = Without a recognition of your body
v = or (understood)

We may explicate the meaning of the four phrases of this statement as follows:

1. You can as a person awaken (P)

This first phrase has a simple, ordinary meaning that the patient can accept, and as such it begins to structure a yes set.

2. but you do not need to awaken as a body (-q)

This second phrase is curious in the context of the above, and it is well that Erickson pauses after it to let its effect take place.

Taken together these first two phrases (P . -q) have a point only within the following background assumptions of the patient.

i) P . q (a person awakens when his body awakens)

ii) In fact, P if and only if q, which is the same as:

if P then q, and if q then P.

Erickson grants (i) to the patient (as a yes set). Now the patient actually assumes (i) actually to mean (ii). But Erickson's second phrase (-q) invalidates the patient's assumption of (ii). This separation of the assumed association of P and q is startling to the patient, and it is the essence of a hypnotic phenomenon he experiences by a process of shock and dissociation. That is, breaking the association of P and q in (ii) sets the conditions for a hypnotic phenomenon: the manifestation of P and -q (the person awakens without his body awakening).

We may explicate phrases three and four in a similar manner. Phrase three, P . q (you can waken when your body awakes) functions as a yes set, while phrase four -r (but without a recognition of your body) again breaks certain of the patient's assumptions as follows.

Indirect Forms of Suggestion

(i) [P . q] . r (people awaken when their bodies awaken and they recognize their bodies)

(ii) in fact, r if and only if (P . q) (you recognize your body if and only if you awaken both as a person and a body)

Again we find that the conditions for a hypnotic phenomenon (P . q) . -r (not recognizing one's body when one awakens as a person and body) are arranged by breaking the association between behaviors that usually occur together. This is of course nothing new; hypnotic phenomena have frequently been conceptualized as a process of dissociation. What is new in this analysis is a proposal of how Erickson can effect these dissociations so succinctly with the turn of a phrase.

We may write the total statement using a *vel* (a logical connective for "or") in place of the pause as follows.

1. (P . -q) v [(P . q) . -r]

Unlike all the previous examples this statement is more open-ended insofar as anyone of a number of outcomes are possible. We may determine the logical possibilities of behavior by simplifying the above into a disjunctive normal form by repeated applications of distribution as follows:

2. [(P . -q) v (P . q)] . [(P . -q) v -r]
3. {(P . -q) . [(P . -q) v -r]} v{(P . q) . [P . -q) v -r]}

The first half of the above disjunction resolves as follows:

4. (P . -q) . [(P . -q) v-r]
5. [(P . -q) . (P . -q)] v [(P . -q) . -r]
6. (P . -q) v [(P . -q) . -r]

The second half of equation 3 resolves as follows:

7. (P . q) . [(P . -q) v -r]
8. [(P . q) . (P . -q)] v [(P . q) . -r]
            [(P . q) . -r]

Putting together the resolved equations 6 and 8 we obtain:

9. {(P . -q) v [(P . -q) . -r]} v {(P . q) . -r} or more simply:
10. [P . -q] v [P . -q . -r] v [P . q . -r]

The possible outcomes of Erickson's original statement may therefore be read:

a. You can as a person awaken, but you do not need to awaken as a body.

b. You can as a person awaken, but you do not need to awaken as a body and without recognition of your body.

c. You can as a person awaken, and you can as a body awaken, but without a recognition of your body.

Such an open-ended suggestion that admits many possible options of hypnotic response is very useful, since it provides greater assurance that some part of the overall suggestion will be followed. This is particularly important in the early phases of hypnotic work, where the therapist wants to investigate the patient's response aptitudes but not risk the possibility of the patient failing on a suggestion.

Such formulations have never been tested in a controlled empirical manner, however. It is now an empirical question to determine if Erickson's original statement of the form

$$(P . -q) v [(P . q) . -r]$$

when administered to a group of subjects, does in fact yield the varying possibilities of response

$$(P . -q) v (P . -q . -r) v (P . q . -r)$$

whatever P, q, and r may be.

According to logic all possibilities of response should be equipotent, so theoretically 33% of the subjects should be responding in each category. Any empirical deviation found from this theoretical expectation could then be attributed to processes of learning (conditioning, etc.), innate biological proclivities, or varying proportions of each.

13. Other Indirect Approaches and Hypnotic Forms. Because of space limitations we can only mention a number of other indirect approaches and hypnotic forms which Erickson and the author have presented previously in detail (Rossi, 1972, 1973; Erickson and Rossi, 1974, 1975, 1976; Erickson, Rossi, and Rossi, 1976; Erickson and Rossi, 1979). These include the paradigm of *Shock, Surprise, and Creative Moments, Intercontextual Cues and Suggestions, Partial Remarks and Dangling Phrases, Expectancy, Involuntary Signaling, Displacing and Discharging Resistance, The Negative, Two-Level Communication via Puns, Analogy, etc., Pantomime and Nonverbal Approaches, Confusion Approaches, Voice Locus and Dynamics, and Therapists' Rhythm.*

14. Discussion. While the indirect forms of hypnotic suggestion outlined in this paper are the results of more than 50 years of clinical experience and research by Erickson, the major limitation of this study is that it is a post hoc analysis of what he believes to be the significant factors in his work. Although this study illustrates how indirect suggestion can be effective, there is nothing in our work that establishes just how much of a contribution these indirect suggestions actually make in facilitating hypnotic responsiveness. Experimental research will be needed to establish the comparative merit of direct and indirect suggestion while controlling subject, operator, and response variables. In practice, Erickson's use of these indirect forms is not independent, from one another; he may use several in the same phrase or sentence. He believes that this shotgun approach enhances their effectiveness. These indirect forms are also frequently used in association with his utilization approach (Erickson, 1959), wherein he uses the subject's own behavior to enhance the development of hypnotic responses. Because of this the junior author would hypothesize that in factoral experimental designs the interaction of *indirect approaches X utilization* would be more significant than the main effect of either factor alone. Since much of the effectiveness of Erickson's work appears to be a function of his own personality, another major issue is the degree to which his approaches can be learned and used successfully by others. A certain amount of experience and skill is required to recognize and utilize a subject's ongoing flow of behavior to simultaneously explore and enhance hypnotic responsiveness. Any fair test of Erickson's approaches requires that the researcher first achieve some criterion of personal skill as a hypnotic operator in utilizing ongoing behavior.

An overview of this paper reveals a number of features of the indirect hypnotic forms. If patients have problems because of learned limitations, then the indirect hypnotic forms are particularly useful, because they are designed to bypass the biases and limitations of their conscious sets and belief systems so that their potentials have an opportunity to become manifest. If some hypnotic phenomena are processes mediated by the right hemisphere (Gur and Reyher, 1976), it is tempting to speculate that many of the indirect hypnotic forms may be communication paradigms in the language of the left hemisphere that somehow instruct or program the right hemisphere to initiate certain activities that can be carried out only by its unique nonverbal modes of functioning. Most of the indirect forms are fail-safe, nondirective, patient-centered approaches that are ideal for exploring individual differences and human potentials—particularly those nonverbal potentials related to the autonomic nervous system that are facilitated by biofeedback technology.

Most of the indirect approaches can be used in any form of therapy, education, or experimental procedures with or without the formal induction of trance. Because they fixate attention, focus the subject inward, and initiate autonomous or unconscious processes, these indirect approaches could be described as being trance-inducing in the most general sense of the word; they usually focus attention so the subject is momentarily but totally absorbed in what we call the "common everyday trance" (Erickson and Rossi, 1976). Because they tend to initiate trance behavior, the presence of these indirect forms must be carefully considered in any experimental procedure based upon the differential response of hypnotic and nonhypnotic control groups. The "instructions" given to nonhypnotic control groups should not contain any indirect hypnotic forms.

Erickson's emphasis on the indirect hypnotic forms could be another factor in the rapprochement between state and nonstate theorists (Spanos and Barber, 1974). Although Erickson continues to maintain that trance is an altered state, he certainly does not believe hypersuggestibility is a necessary characteristic of trance (Erickson, 1932). Along with Weitzenhoffer he believes trance and suggestibility are independent phenomena that may or may not coincide in any particular subject at any particular moment. Erickson depends upon communication devices such as the indirect hypnotic forms described in this paper to evoke and mobilize a patient's associative processes and mental skills to facilitate hypnotic phenomena. His utilization theory implies that the essence of hypnotic suggestion is actually this process of evoking and utilizing each patient's own mental processes in ways that are frequently experienced as being outside their usual sense of intentionality or voluntary control. The junior author, therefore, believes that Erickson (state theorist) and Barber (nonstate theorist) could agree that a formal or ritualized trance induction is not necessary for the experience of most hypnotic phenomena. In practice both rely upon certain forms of suggestion to mediate hypnotic phenomena. Their approaches to suggestion, however, are very different. When Barber asks a subject voluntarily to think and imagine along with those things that are directly suggested, he is obviously enlisting the aid of the subject's consciousness. Barber uses an essentially rational approach in the typical tradition of academic psychology and appears to be training people in *waking suggestion* (Weitzenhoffer, 1957), *where they learn to direct themselves in a conscious manner*. Erickson, by contrast, appears to make every effort to bypass the subject's conscious sets and intentionality with the indirect forms of suggestion which tend to evoke unconscious or autonomous processes. Erickson belongs to the tradition of depth psychology, in its typical reliance on the unconscious, and appears to be training people in *hypnotic suggestion where they learn to let things happen autonomously*.

A recent summary statement of the nonstate position is as follows: "For the nonstate investigators such as Sarbin and Barber, involved suggestion-related imagining (or its synonyms such as thinking and imagining with the themes of the suggestion) functions as an *alternative* to the traditional trance state formulation of hypnotic behavior" (Spanos and Barber, 1974). State theorists like Erickson might reply to this that "involved suggestion-related imagining" actually engages autonomous mental processes; it is precisely this deep involvement and absorption in the use of imagination that permits autonomous processes to play a larger role in evoking responses that are sometimes experienced as involuntary. The involuntary aspect of the response then becomes a defining characteristic of trance for the state theorist. Although state and nonstate theorists may call it by a different name, both can agree that the basic issue is to explore the condition and forms of suggestion that can facilitate what has been traditionally known as "hypnotic phenomena." This paper is a first-stage clinical

Indirect Forms of Suggestion

and logical effort to isolate and define a number of the indirect forms of suggestion that can facilitate such hypnotic phenomena. It is essentially a contribution to the science of pragmatics: the relations between signs and the users of signs (Morris, 1938).

23. Indirect Forms of Suggestion in Hand Levitation

Milton H. Erickson and Ernest L. Rossi

Since the senior author first introduced and demonstrated hand levitation at the 1923-1924 Hull seminar group at the University of Wisconsin, this approach has become an effective and widely used means of inducing hypnosis (Wolberg, 1948; Pattie, 1956; Kroger, 1963). The senior author (Erickson, 1961) regards hand levitation as just one of a class of ideomotor techniques (along with automatic head nodding or shaking, finger signaling, etc.) that induces trance by focusing attention. He has described his views as follows:

> These techniques are of particular value with patients who want hypnosis, who could benefit from it, but who resist any formal or overt effort at trance induction and who need to have their obstructive resistances bypassed. The essential consideration in the use of ideomotor techniques lies not in their elaborateness or novelty but simply in the initiation of motor activity, either real or hallucinated, as a means of fixating and focusing the subject's attention upon inner experiential learnings and capabilities. (Erickson, 1961)

In this paragraph the senior author uses the term "experiential learnings" in a special sense to refer to (1) unconsciously acquired patterns of response (termed "latent learning" in experimental psychology, Osgood, 1953), in contrast to the consciously acquired patterns of intellectual learning; and, (2) those overlearned patterns of behavior that have become automatic and more or less autonomous in their functioning. He believes *it is precisely these unconsciously acquired responses and overlearned behavior patterns that are the raw material out of which hypnotic phenomena are evoked.* Since such responses can appear automatically, the patient frequently experiences them with a sense of surprise when they are evoked by indirect suggestion. Such suggestions are indirect only in the sense that the conscious mind does not recognize how they are associated with, and provide a stimulus for, the automatic or "hypnotic" response.

The following protocol is an edited version of a demonstration of hand levitation by the senior author in a 1964 seminar on hypnosis.* In our commentaries

---
Previously unpublished paper written with Ernest L. Rossi, 1976–1978.
*Made available by Florence Sharp, Ph.D.

we will focus on the indirect forms of suggestion that are used to evoke the experiential learnings that facilitate trance induction. As presented in our previous work (Erickson, Rossi, and Rossi, 1976; Erickson and Rossi, 1976), indirect suggestions are understood as those which tend to bypass the learned limitations of the conscious mind's habitual sets so that unconscious searches and processes are initiated. This unconscious activity then evokes the automatic behavior patterns that are frequently experienced as taking place in an autonomous or "hypnotic" manner.

Hand Levitation: Nonverbal Cues As Indirect Suggestions To Focus The Patient Inward

E: You can lean back in your chair and relax your body while you give *your* attention to *your* hands placed on your thighs.
(Therapist models to provide nonverbal cues. Both hands rest lightly on the thighs without touching each other. Forearms and elbows are able to float freely without touching anything).   And you can notice the feeling and texture of your slacks in the tips of *your* fingers.

R: Your nonverbal cues modeling the desired behavior tend to bypass conscious critical analysis and are therefore a very effective form of indirect suggestion.
E: Now I carefully emphasized the pronoun "your". I emphasize a patient's own functioning and feelings as a unique personality. With a series of suggestions like this you can focus the patients' attention more and more onto their own inner experiences. The series begins with the very general and easy-to-accept suggestion to "lean back" and ends with a highly specific and individualized forcus of attention on feelings in the fingertips. It all sounds so casual and matter-of-fact that patients usually don't even recognize how they are already following suggestions and beginning to build a yes set that will facilitate the acceptance of further suggestions.
R: You are utilizing the patients' own inner responsiveness to focus attention on their experiential, inner realities. That intense focus on a few inner realities is a way of defining trance in contrast to the generalized reality orientation whereby we attend to many things simultaneously when we are awake.

Utilizing The Common Everyday Trance: Generalization, Implication, And Contingency As Indirect Hypnotic Forms

E: Now if *you* sense the texture of *your* slacks in your fingertips, it will probably remind *you* of other experiences, of other feelings you have had.

E: "Other experiences, other feelings" is a very inclusive generalization. It includes the possibility of utilizing trance feelings from everyday life that we all commonly experience when we are "absorbed" or in deep "reverie," concentrating very deeply on something. The patient does not recognize, however, that in accepting "other experiences, other feelings" he is actually including this possibility of trance experience from everyday life when he was similarly focused on a few inner feelings.

R: You are utilizing the "common everyday trance" experiences everyone has to facilitate the patient's current therapeutic trance. Although your use of generalization in this instance is so broad it could evoke almost anything, the basic principle remains that generalization is an indirect approach to suggestion that may move patients toward trance without their quite knowing why. If the patient's conscious mind does not know how to facilitate a "trance" experience, your indirect suggestions may automatically mobilize their experiential learning about trance from everyday life even though it may not have been labeled as trance before. The form of this sentence, "If you (easy behavior of sensing texture of slacks), it will probably remind you of (more relevant hypnotic behavior)" involves the use of implication and contigency as indirect hypnotic forms.

Knitting Suggestions Into The Fabric Of An Inner Reality Called "Trance"; Initiating An Associational Network

E: Now as you continue . . .

E: "Continue" is a continuing word. That word tells the patient to keep right on, and it ties the previously successful inner experience to the new suggestion you are going to introduce.

R: It enables you to knit a series of separate suggestions into the fabric of an inner reality we shall call "trance." You are integrating your suggestions into an associational network wherein they all mutually reinforce each other.

"Perhaps" To Initiate Inner Exploration

E: . . . to sense the feeling, the texture of the cloth with your fingers, *perhaps*, you will feel your hand getting lighter.

E: "Perhaps" means you're not ordering, you're not instructing. Actually it is a subtle challenge that motivates the patient to search for and experience a feeling of lightness. "Perhaps" utilizes a common experience most of us have had. When someone threatens to knock you down and you say, "perhaps!"

what are you doing? You are stimulating the bully to think, "Well, wait a minute. Does that guy really know how to fight?" Your "perhaps" thereby evokes pause, hesitation, and doubt, so he finally thinks, "Maybe I'd better not tangle with him after all." With that single word "perhaps" you've evoked a process of thought completely contradictory to his original assertion, "I'll knock you down." He doesn't even know you started him on it; he is too busy with it.

R: Many other words like "wonder, explore, imagine, feel, sense" tend to depotentiate our usual everyday frames of reference and tend to initiate an unconscious search and autonomous process that may evolve into hypnotic responses.

Voice Locus And Inflection As Indirect Cues: Utilizing Unconsciously Acquired Responses

E: Perhaps you will feel your hand getting lighter and lighter and lighter.

E: We are usually unaware of all the automatic responses we make on the basis of the locus of sound and the inflections of voice (Erickson, 1973). Thus such vocal cues are indirect forms of suggestion because they tend to facilitate automatic responses that can bypass conscious intentionality. Whenever you suggest an arm levitating higher, you can subtly pitch your voice higher. The locus of your voice is a very potent suggestion because you have learned that over a long period of time: "Look at me when you answer," says the teacher."

R: Utilizing the unconsciously acquired responses and association patterns to voice locus are an unusually clear example of how you evoke hypnotic phenomena out of the patient's repertory of past experiential patterns of learning. You do not suggest in the sense of putting something into the patient's mind; rather, your suggestions simly evoke unconscious response potentials and association patterns that are already there. The clinician's art is to help the patient reassociate and synthesize these previously learned associations into therapeutic responses.

Implication And Not Knowing As Indirect Hypnotic Forms Depotentiating Conscious Intentionality And Initiating An Unconscious Search

E: Now I don't know, I really don't know which finger is going to want to move first.

E: Here I am excluding myself so the patient must initiate his own inner exploration. At the same time, without quite realizing it the patient is receiving a very potent indirect suggestion in the form of an implication: a finger will move even though I don't know which one. I state it in such a way that the patient has to look and see which moves first.

R: *Not knowing* is another indirect hypnotic form that may depotentiate the patients' conscious mental sets and intentionality so that they have to wait and see which finger their unconscious will move. This initiates a dissociation between the conscious and the unconscious. Dissociation is also facilitated by your *wondering* "which finger is going to want to move first"; the implication is that a finger will initiate its own movement independent of conscious intentionality.

Mutually Reinforcing Compound Suggestions

E: It may be the first, second, third, fourth, or fifth, and after your fingers start moving, you will probably begin to feel your wrist lifting.

E: I've inserted a completely new suggestion about wrist lifting into the same sentence with finger movement so that the patient does not really recognize the separateness of the wrist lifting. Your vocal inflections can emphasize and motivate it, however.

R: This is a compound suggestion where you add a new, closely related suggestion to an already accepted or ongoing response. If the patient has been slow or responding to finger movement in a marginal manner only, the new wrist suggestion may add a burst of muscle tonus to that area so that the fingers now move more easily. Actually everyone will respond in their own individual way and the therapist's task is to recognize and reinforce whatever enhances each individual's responsiveness. Two or more closely related suggestions (a series again) can be given in such a manner that they are mutually reinforcing.

Shifting Foci Of Attention Utilizing Ongoing Patterns Of Behavior

E: As your wrist lifts, you will note your elbow bending.

E: Now it isn't a question of wrists lifting. Resistance cannot focus on wrists because it now appears that another thing is the focus of attention: "Note your elbow bending." Well, naturally, as his wrist lifts he will note his elbow bending; it cannot be otherwise. When a wrist lifts, an elbow has to bend. It is an inevitability and thus a safe suggestion that cannot be rejected. Also notice I'm only directly suggesting a *psychological awareness* of the bending of the elbow. The patient has to bend his elbow in order to become psychologically aware of it, but the actual bending is his own addition to my suggestion.

Hand Levitation

R: I've observed this before in your work (Erickson and Rossi, 1976): With rapid shifts of attention you frequently arrange multiple tasks to utilize awareness, states of tension, dissociation, disequilibrium, and ongoing patterns of behavior (the inevitabilities) that can only be resolved or completed by the execution of some suggested response.

Truisms As Indirect Hypnotic Forms

E: As your elbow bends, your wrist will lift higher and higher
(Pause)
and higher.

E: I pause because it is a continual process. When I pause at the second "higher," you almost feel that's as high as it's going to go. Then he has to correct it because you throw in the third "higher." I am using time, pauses, inflections, and inevitabilities: of course, the wrist and hand will lift higher as the elbow bends. He knows it is true, and therefore he has to verify it by the actual bending of his elbow.

R: In other words, these suggestions are basic truths, truisms, that no one could possibly deny. Truisms are indirect hypnotic forms insofar as they initiate a yes or acceptance set for whatever other suggestions the therapist may choose to add to the situation.

Permitting Choice: The Apposition Of Opposites

E: And as it lifts higher and higher
(Pause)
and still higher,
your eyelids may lower in direct relationship to the lifting of your hand.

E: There are two possibilities: the lowering of his eyelids and the lifting of his hand. Shall they take place simultaneously? That is a possibility. Shall they take place separately? "Well," he may think to himself, "but my eyelids aren't lowering even though my hand is lifting." Well, he has confirmed the lifting of his hand by rejecting the lowering of his lids. You see, psychologically one needs to give the patient the opportunity both to accept and to reject anything you offer. He has the opportunity to refuse the lowering of the lids, but in doing that he has to emphasize the lifting of the hand. If he accepts the lowering of the lids, that also confirms the lifting of his hand, and so you have both processes of behavior. But it is his choice.

R: Choice activates unconscious searches and processes that can facilitate each individual's own unique predispositions for response. You arrange the situation so that the patient has choices, but whatever choice is made leads to a desired hypnotic response. The close juxtaposition of *lifting* hand with *lowering* eyelids tends to maintain a form of psychological equilibrium (if the patient begins to resist so much *lifting,* his psychological equilibrium can be reestablished by the *lowering*) that we have called the apposition of opposites.

Distraction In A Double Suggestion: Mutually Reinforcing Suggestions

E: And as your hand goes higher and higher, perhaps your elbow will lift up so that your hand comes nearer to your face.

E: When I say the "hand comes nearer to your face," I've intensified what I've said about the elbow. The real question appears to be: Will his hand come nearer to his face or not? So attention is focused on the last part of the suggestion about the hand getting nearer to the face. The lifting of the elbow is automatically accepted, so he can deal with the hand question. If he accepts the hand question, however, he has automatically accepted the elbow suggestion. I've intensified it. This is a double suggestion wherein I've distracted attention away from an important part of the suggestion (elbow bending) to an unimportant part.

R: They are a mutually reinforcing pair of suggestions; whichever is accepted will automatically reinforce the other.

Hitchhiking A Series Of Suggestions

E: And as the hand comes nearer to your face, it will probably move more slowly
until you are ready to take a deep breath and close your eyes and go into a trance.

E: I am not ordering the patient because I've observed that his hand was, in fact, going slower. As he accepted this observation of his own experience, he also accepts taking a deep breath, closing eyes, and going into a deep trance.

R: This is a series of suggestions that is easy to accept and follow because you hitchhike taking a deep breath, closing eyes, and a deep trance onto the already initiated behavior of the hand moving slowly nearer the face. You are again integrating your suggestions into an associational network wherein they tend to be mutually reinforcing, creating a reality of autonomous and semiautonomous behavior that we call "trance."

Displacing And Discharging Resistance: Contingent Suggestion

E: Your hand is moving slowly toward your face,
but you won't go into a trance
until
your hand touches your face.

E: It's much better for the therapist to say "you won't go into a trance" than for the patient to say it.

R: You thereby displace and discharge any resistance that the patient may have with your own negative "you *won't* go into a trance."

E: The word "until" has pivotal significance. Going into a trance is thereby made contingent on an inevitability: The hand is moving toward the face, the patient now knows it eventually will touch his face and, therefore, tends to agree that he will go into a trance.

Implication Initiating Unconscious Search And Processes Of Trance Experience

E: In all probability you will not be able to recognize the trance for some moments.

E: How long is some moments?

R: You're allowing the patient to define and take his own time.

E: You evoke the question within the patient's mind, "Will I be able to recognize the trance?" When he asks himself that question, he is assuming absolutely that there will be a trance. The only question is, will he be able to recognize it?

R: Your question initiates an *unconscious search* for cues enabling him to recognize trance. It contains the implication that trance is or soon will be present. That implication probably evokes an *unconscious search* and *processes* that will evoke certain unconscious mental mechanisms that will be experienced as trance.

E: While he is busy with that curious question about recognizing trance, you raise another goal as follows.

Implied Directive And Interspersed Suggestion

E: Probably not until after your hand has slowly lowered to your lap to signify that you will continue in a deep trance. Will you be able to recognize it?

E: So you give him another goal, and he wants to recognize it. His recognition is going to depend on the lowering of his hand to his lap. But you have put upon that lowering of his hand the condition that it will signify that he will "continue in a deep trance." Remember that the word "continue" has a continuing message; the actual meaning of the word is itself a suggestion. He is going to look forward to that.

R: "Continue" is itself an interspersed suggestion buried within the broader context of the whole sentence. The sentence as a whole is an example of what we've called the implied directive (Erickson, Rossi, and Rossi, 1976), wherein a behavioral response (hand in lap) signals when an internal response (the implied directive "continue in deep trance") has taken place. In this case the implied directive is itself hidden as attention is distracted to the fascinating question of being able to recognize trance.

Contingency Rather Than Logic In Suggestion: Permissiveness In Trance Induction

E: In the induction of hypnosis you make one thing contingent upon another because your subject cannot analyze your suggestions for their logic. He cannot and does not have time to recognize that the suggestions are fallacious in so many ways. You are here utilizing the fact that we have a lifetime of experience in responding to false contingencies and false relationships. The suggestion you give the patient is only a suggestion that he do something, possibly produce hand levitation. Just possible. If there is something else he prefers to do, let him do it. Do not try to restrict him to hand levitation. That is false and that is wrong. Your attitude should be completely permissive. He can respond to your hand levitation suggestion by the procedure of pushing down harder and harder and harder with his hands, as I've had subjects do. I'm thinking of a certain college student that did that. After he did that long enough, I said, "It's rather interesting and surprising, at least it is to me, I think it will be to you when you discover that you can't stop pushing down." He thought he was resisting. The idea that he couldn't stop took him completely by surprise, and it was a full-grown idea when it hit him. That would be something he would be interested in. He'd be surprised. He couldn't stop pushing down. Not being able to stop pushing down was contingent upon the word surprise. He actually found to his surprise that he couldn't stop pushing down, and he asked, "What happened?" I said, "At least your arms have gone into a trance. Can you stand up?" Can he? That simple question generalized "at least your arms have gone into a trance." Can you stand up? Of course he couldn't stand up. There was only one conclusion to reach: His body is in a trance because he no longer has control over it. Apparently that's what he wants to regard hypnosis as—a condition in which you have no control of yourself—or else he wouldn't get into that sort of a situation.

Twofold Hand Levitation: Simultaneous Direct and Indirect Suggestion For Hand Levitation: Separating Thinking and Doing

The senior author recently described an interesting form of direct and indirect suggestion for hand levitation.

E: One or the other hand is going to lift, and you might enjoy *thinking* one isn't.

E: This produces two types of hand levitation: the first phrase is a direct suggestion, while the second is an indirect suggestion by implication. The second phrase "you might enjoy *thinking* one isn't" is an indirect suggestion for levitation, because the more the subject is certain in "thinking" that one hand won't lift, the more it lifts. This is because I emphasized the word "thinking" in such a tone as to imply doubt. The doubt implies that the subject *only thinks* the hand will not lift; actually it will. I'm introducing a separation between thinking and doing that is actually very common in everyday life. How often do we think one thing and actually do another?

R: This is particularly true in habit problems where we *think* we will do one thing but unfortunately find ourselves *doing* another. You are therefore utilizing this very common and all too haunting (that is, unconsciously determined) dissociation between thinking and doing that we all have experienced to facilitate an autonomous or hypnotic behavioral response.

E: Another variation of the same thing is as follows:

E: Your right hand is going to move up toward your face; you might like to *think* your left hand isn't going to move.

E: The second half is again an indirect suggestion for levitation. This indirect suggestion by implication usually yields a slower and more hesitant levitation of the left hand in comparison with the quicker levitation of the right hand by direct suggestion.

R: The implication for levitating the left hand works more slowly, but is it more autonomous, would you say?

E: Yes, it is more autonomous.

R: Since it is more autonomous, does it lead to deeper trance?

E: Yes, that deepens the trance very much.

R: The direct suggestions for levitating the right hand could be followed simply because the subject is complacent and consciously wants to cooperate. It is therefore less hypnotic in character than the more autonomous response of the left hand, which surprises the subject. But suppose only the right hand lifted with the direct suggestion and the left hand with the indirect suggestion did not?

E: You would wait and then continue with, "And you are still thinking your left hand isn't going to lift." With that they tend to go into a deeper trance. You use that twofold hand levitation to induce somnambulism. They experience something happening to them that is outside their control: The hand continues to lift even when the conscious mind thinks it isn't.

R: This begins to sound like a confusion technique.

E: So much of what I do is confusion. You're dealing with patches of conscious awareness along with patterns of unconscious behavior.

R: The confusion tends to depotentiate whatever patches of conscious awareness are present so the unconscious patterns of behavior can become more manifest. When the patches of awareness sense the presence of these autonomous patterns of behavior, the patient's habitual "normal" belief system and its learned limitations tend to be further depotentiated, so the unconscious has more freedom to utilize its latent potentials for facilitating a therapeutic response. In therapy this can become a self-perpetuating cycle wherein autonomous processes find more and more freedom from the learned limitations of the concious mind, so the unconscious can operate in new ways to create therapeutic responses previously unknown to therapist and patient.

Exercises For Learning Indirect Hypnotic Suggestion

In working out various hypnotic approaches, I've written them down in detail so that I could understand the actual meaning of the statement that I made. When planning a series of suggestions, first write them down. Then you can pick them apart more easily for their actual significance. You can rearrange the wording to see the advantage of placing one phrase or one clause first and the other one second; you try to analyze your suggestion for the purpose of placing a pause in any particular location to emphasize a specific word so that one word stands out. Years ago I'd write out about 40 pages of suggestions that I would condense down to 20 pages and then down to 10. Then I'd carefully reformulate and make good use of every word and phrase so I'd finally condense it down to about five pages. Everyone who is serious about learning suggestion needs to go through that process to become truly aware of just what they are really saying.

I am not the least bit shy about hesitating, pausing, or even deliberately stuttering on words. I may misprounounce a potent word because that is the word I want the patients to hear. I want that word to echo in their own minds correctly. If I mispronounce it slightly, they mentally correct it, but they are the ones that are saying it; they have joined with me in saying that word, and when *they* join me in saying it, they are making the suggestion to themselves. The subjects should participate. They are not placid, indifferent people when in trance. They should be participating much more than you because you are only offering them a wealth of suggestions, knowing that at best they're going to select this one here, that one there, and still another one over there to act upon. I see too many people use hypnosis in an attempt to get a subject to act on all the suggestions given when, of course, the subject isn't going to. I've watched a student work with the hand levitation technique and laboriously try to get the little finger up, the third finger, the little finger, the index finger, then the thumb, the palm, and then the rest. The student was so busy with the hands that he forgot the subject. You should keep totally aware of your subject all the time.

Hallucinatory hand levitation is a very effective way of developing an immediate somnambulistic trance; some subjects will not actually move their hand, but they will hallucinate the hand levitation. If you are waiting for that hand to move, you're just not going to see it. Yet as you watch the fixed expression of the face and the retarded blinking of the eyelids, the breathing, the pulse rate, the condition of the neck muscles, and so on, you realize your subject is already in a trance state. Very often when I see the subject has already gone into a trance state while I'm still beginning the hand levitation suggestions, I say, "And you can continue as you are, doing it even better while I make some more suggestions about your hands—not that they are important, what you are doing is more important." And so I continue and let subjects deepen their own trances because what they are doing is more important, and they can continue. I continue my hand levitation suggestions, knowing that they are useless and serving no purpose except to give the subjects opportunity to deepen their own trance experiences.

IV. On The Possible Dangers Of Hypnosis

Although fascinating by mystery, we also fear it. This is certainly the situation most of us are in where we first come in contact with the popular misconceptions of hypnosis. It is only natural, then, that one of the basic issues in the early history of hypnosis was its potential for harm as well as for healing. Even today professionals as well as laymen are concerned about the possible misuses of hypnosis.

The first paper in this section, "Possible detrimental effects from experimental hypnosis" (1932) is actually Erickson's first publication in the area of hypnosis. He concludes this early survey and discussion with the following.

> In summary, then, the literature offers little credible information concerning possible detrimental effects of experimental hypnosis, although replete with dogmatic and opinionated denunciations founded on outworn and untenable concepts of the phenomenon. . . . The author's own experience, based upon several thousand trances on approximately 300 individual subjects, some of whom were hypnotized at least 500 times each over a period of four to six years, reveals no evidence of such harmful effects. This clinical finding is further substantiated by the well-known difficulties encountered in the deliberate therapeutic attempts to occasion desired changes in the personality. Accordingly marked changes from experimental hypnosis appear questionable.

The issue could not be so easily disposed of, however. Seven years later, in response to Rowland's study which indicated hypnosis could be misused, Erickson made a more extensive empirical study, which was published as "An experimental investigation of the possible antisocial use of hypnosis" (1939). In summarizing his results he strikes another blow at the common misconception of hypnosis as a state wherein the subject is an automaton fully under the control of the hypnotist. He states it as follows.

> The findings disclosed consistently the failure of all experimental measures to induce hypnotic subjects, in response to hypnotic suggestions, to perform acts of an objectionable character, even though many of the suggested acts were acceptable to them under circumstances of waking

consciousness. Instead of blind, submissive, automatic, unthinking obedience and acquiescence to the hypnotist . . . the subjects demonstrated a full capacity and ability for self-protection, ready and complete understanding with critical judgment, avoidance, evasion, or complete rejection of commands . . . and objection to instrumentation by the hypnotist. . . . In addition many demonstrated a full capacity to take over control of the hypnotic situation and actually did so by compelling the experimenter to make amends for his unacceptable suggestions. . . . Hence the conclusion warranted by these experimental findings is that hypnosis cannot be misused to induce hypnotized persons to commit actual wrongful acts either against themselves or others and that the only serious risk encountered in such attempts is incurred by hypnotists in the form of condemnation, rejection, and exposure.

These early studies thus present a strong case for the phenomenon of hypnosis as not being amenable to harm or misuse. After a few decades of experience in real-world situations outside the professional laboratory and consulting room, however, Erickson had to acknowledge that simple ignorance could lead to harmful misinterpretations and abuses of the hypnotic *situation*. The well-known demonstration of catalepsy whereby the stage hypnotist suspends his subject's rigid body between two chairs was found, for example, to later lead to the clinical complaint of a long-continued backache. There was nothing intrinsic in the nature of hypnosis itself that was harmful, but the *situation* of being too long suspended in an awkward position could lead to physical strain. When humans behave in an ignorant and heedless manner, they can misuse just about any situation. However there is no body of acceptable, scientific evidence that hypnosis and the experience of trance is in itself harmful.

24. Possible Detrimental Effects Of Experimental Hypnosis

Milton H. Erickson

Since the time of Mesmer there has been a general attitude of prejudice against, and fear of, hypnosis. Mesmer's own attitude did much to clothe the phenomenon in mystery and occultism and to awaken strong criticism against his discovery. The absurd claims made and the fantastic explanations given contributed to the development of scientific antagonism to the art. Further the later utilization of hypnotism by charlatans made every honest man extremely wary lest even his sincere interest in it bring him into disrepute.

Fortunately, however, not all true scientists were frightened by the bugbear of public misunderstanding, and such men as Charcot, Liebault, Heidenhein, Janet, James, Hall, Prince, and Sidis have contributed greatly to a present rational attitude on the subject. As a result there is a growing realization among the general public, both lay and professional, that it is a normal phenomenon of the human mind, fairly explicable, as are all other psychological processes, in our crude concepts of mental mechanisms. Further, there is a rapidly increasing realization, as well as a somewhat slower development of its usefulness in the therapeutic field. In the latter regard there is still tendency to expect extravagant therapeutic results and, if they are not forthcoming, to discard the method as of little or no value. As is obvious, such utilization is wrong, since hypnosis, like every other psychotherapeutic procedure, should be looked upon as a means of approach to the problem and not as the royal road to the achievement of miracles.

As yet present limitations upon the knowledge and understanding of hypnotism itself suggest that its greatest value lies in the field of psychological investigation and experimentation. Its use in psychotherapy is essentially empirical. No really rational use of it can be made until psychologists and specially trained investigators capable of plumbing the depths of ignorance surrounding it and properly evaluating the psychological principles upon which it is based have explored it as a problem complete in itself. As a fertile field for investigation its intrinsic value cannot be questioned. Whether or not the eventual findings

---

Reprinted with permission from *The Journal of Abnormal and Social Psychology*, 1932, 37, 321–327.

will be of immediate and positive profit is entirely speculative and quite beside the question, since every realm of human activity and behavior is worthy of scientific examination.

This observation then gives rise to the question, at what cost such a study could be made. If only at the expense of labor and study, well enough, but if hypnosis wreaks irreparable harm upon innocent subjects, it is time to call a halt and to devise other means of psychic exploration. The pathway of knowledge is already sufficiently strewn with costly human errors, and it is always well to consider avoidance of more, however innocently and unintentionally they may be made.

A survey of the critical literature suggests that hypnotism is fraught with dangers, if mere opinions and ignorance can be given weight. But perusal of the various literary damnations of the phenomenon awakens serious distrust of their cogency. In one bitter attack on hypnotism published about 1850 (the identification of the reference has been lost) the author naively declares, "I thank God I have neither witnessed nor practiced the abominable art," following which, in dogmatic statements, he attributed innumerable evils to "The New Witchcraft." Then in more recent times the practice of hypnotism has been considered synonymous with the enslavement of the personality, the destruction of the willpower, and the automatizing of the innocent subject. The attacks consist of personal opinions founded on abstract concepts no longer tenable, and supported by hearsay evidence. In brief, the literature is barren of anything deserving of much scientific credence. Even as late as 1924 a well-known journal of forensic medicine contained a long editorial emphatically denouncing hypnosis, adducing reasons therefor from innumerable opinions of laypeople and considerable hearsay evidence. No references of scientific value were offered except the editor's own subjective opinion based upon some experience and founded upon the concepts of faculty psychology extant 40 years ago. This same editor now has a book in press on forensic medicine that, he assures the writer, embodies the same views, many of which are the same as those first advanced against Mesmer when the term "Black Magic" was supposed to classify hypnotism adequately.

Other than these unfounded denunciations, the literature contains only sincere speculations upon possible detrimental effects, some of which are partially founded on actual evidence and experience but none of which are dogmatic nor, for that matter, carefully controlled and evaluated. Even the literature on experimental hypnosis is most unsatisfactory, since practically none of the experimental work published has been carefully planned and controlled. Findings are empirical in nature and are indicative only of possibilities. The same holds true in the psychotherapeutic aspects, with the result that the whole field is considerably uncultivated in character. Accordingly there can be no room for any dogmatic declarations, except the need of caution and of honest observation.

The question of possible harmful effects from hypnosis is one worthy of serious consideration, fully as much so as the possibility of beneficial results.

Fortunately it is no longer necessary to consider such things as "the emanation of the secret power," "the control of a weak will by an overpoweringly strong will," "the irresistible transmission of thoughts," and similar exploded superstitions. In the light of present-day knowledge hypnotism is looked upon in intelligent circles as a normal though unusual and little understood phenomenon of the human mind, dependent wholly upon the cooperation of the subject, and which can be practiced by anybody willing to learn the psychological principles and technique involved.

But there are certain theoretical possibilities of harm which should be considered and studied even though in the writer's experience findings in these regards are negative. It is true that these possibilities are entirely speculative and problematical, but a reasonable answer must be given before there can be a ready acceptance of this method of scientific investigation.

The first of these theories of possible detrimental effects centers around the question of the development of hypersuggestibility. The literature is barren of information in this regard. However, there is carefully planned and controlled work under way in a well-known psychological laboratory, and results so far, though not yet complete, are negative. In the writer's own experience, upon which it unfortunately will be necessary to a large extent to base the elaboration of these various questions, hypersuggestibility was not noticed, although the list of individual subjects totals approximately 300 and the number of trances several thousand. Further, a considerable number were hypnotized from 300 to 500 times each over a period of years. Also several of the subjects were immediate relatives with consequent intimate daily contact, and they were trained to respond, in experimentation, quickly and readily to the slightest suggestion. Far from making them hypersuggestible, it was found necessary to deal very gingerly with them to keep from losing their cooperation, and it was often felt that they developed a compensatory negativism toward the hypnotist to offset any increased suggestibility. Subjects trained to go into a deep trance instantly at the snap of a finger would successfully resist when unwilling or more interested in other projects. Even when persuaded to give their consent against their original wishes, the induction of a trance was impossible. Nor were those subjects more suggestible to other people, since, when their services were "loaned" to the author's colleagues, the production of hypnosis in them, despite their extensive training, was just as hard as it had been originally for the author. And the same thing was found true when the author "borrowed" subjects. In brief, it seems probable that if there is a development of increased suggestibility, it is negligible in extent.

A second question is that concerning the possiblity of the alteration of personality. Just exactly what such a question means is difficult to define, but at all events the general significance of the question is comprehensible. As we all know, alterations of personality occur in response to suggestion in ordinary daily life. Hence it is only logical to presume that a state of enhanced suggestibility such as an hypnotic trance would show an increased susceptibility to alteration of personality. In the writer's experience, where members of the family were very frequently hypnotized over a period of four years, no alteration in personality was noted in any way attributable to hypnosis. The same thing was observed in the case of friends who were utilized as subjects over a similar length of time, and likewise with subjects met in the laboratory. But an even more forceful and trenchant answer may be derived from the experience of psychotherapists who have deliberately and carefully utilized the method to induce desired alterations in the personality of their patients with disappointing results and usually failed even when such was the goal of their efforts. The inefficiency of hypnosis in the treatment of homosexualism is an excellent illustration of the difficulties of fundamentally altering a personality. Briefly, then, it seems that the conclusion may be drawn justifiably that experimental hypnosis will not cause any fundamental alteration of personality or possibly even any alteration in addition to that which would accrue from ordinary personal contact. However, before this question can be left, there arises another concerning the charge that various dissociated personalities were created by the overzealous investigations of the hypnotist. Obviously there can be no dogmatic answer to such a charge, since the whole thing itself is a matter of speculation. That it is a possiblity is to be admitted readily, but personal experience suggests that just as readily may it be characterized as an improbability. The one conclusion to be drawn is that the operator should be clear of vision and mind and of unimpeachable integrity, qualifications not to be limited to any one field of research.

During the induction of a trance the subject's contact with reality is greatly reduced. This gives rise to the question of the possibility of weakening the subject's perceptual powers concerning reality and unreality. An eminent practitioner in the field of behavior disorders reports that he utilized hypnotism as a therapeutic agent over a brief period of years, following his cases carefully, and discontinuing it because of a subjective feeling that they had lost somewhat the ability to distinguish between actuality and phantasy. But he added very honestly that this feeling was entirely subjective and that he could not offer any real evidence. When it is considered that his cases were behavior problems and presumably of unstable personality, and that the hypnosis was used for therapeutic purposes, it seems reasonable that such might have occurred. But before any great weight could be placed upon his subjective impressions, there would have to be a careful evaluation of the many significant factors concerned. At best it is only a subjective opinion and serves only to contradict the writer's, which is entirely to the contrary but based more on experimental studies than on therapeutic work.

Also in this same regard may be mentioned the religion of the Christian Scientists, which is based fundamentally on the principles of self-hypnosis, and of which the entire philosophy of life centers around a denial of the difference between reality and unreality. However, even the most ardent, despite the honesty and sincerity of their wishes and practice, seem to have no difficulty in this regard, as the material prosperity of the church and its members attests. If an entire philosophy of life with training from infancy upward is insufficient to accomplish this, it is difficult to believe that a time-limited hypnotic trance for other purposes would accomplish such an end. From a purely psychological point of view, the stimuli emanating from reality and those from memory traces within the brain are fundamentally different in their components, and it smacks of the miraculous to assume that a time-limited procedure could establish a fundamental alteration of the psychological habits established in a lifetime.

Fourth and last of the questions to be discussed in this paper is the probability of subjects acquiring unhealthy escape mechanisms as a result of their experiences. This speculation arises from the observation of a trick one of the author's subjects developed. He was a university student, "majoring" in psychology and "minoring" in art, and intensely interested in hypnotism. When given an art assignment of an original picture, having been taught how, he would take a crystal and crystal gaze until he saw a suitable picture, which he would then copy. Or if it were an English theme assignment, he would crystal gaze until he saw a typewritten outline of a suitable plot and then would fill in the necessary details. The question arises, could he make use of a similar type of mental mechanism to force himself to believe that some unpleasant duty was done or to escape some unpleasant situation? Or could the subject taught to show hypnotic paralysis or anaesthesia later develop the same things as hysterical symptoms? However, the history of psychopathology is replete with evidence to show that the human mind, however lacking it may be in fundamental endowments needs little instruction in devising complex escape mechanisms. Hence it is much more reasonable though less disturbing to suppose that the added knowledge subjects derive from hypnotic experiences gives them an increased understanding of themselves. In the author's experiences there was noticed only a tendency to utilize hypnotic experiences for profit, a finding substantiated by inquiry into the experience of other trained workers. Briefly, what little evidence there is and an attempt at a fair evaluation of theoretical possiblities suggests small likelihood of detrimental effects in this regard.

In summary, then, the literature offers little credible information concerning possible detrimental effects of experimental hypnosis, although replete with dogmatic and opinionated denunciations founded on outworn and untenable concepts of the phenomenon.

Theoretical possibilities of detrimental effects that are possible include the development of hypersuggestibility, the alteration of personality, weakening of the subject's perceptual powers in regard to reality and unreality, and lastly, the development of unhealthy mental attitudes and escape mechanisms.

The literature is barren of controlled experimental investigation of these problems. The author's own experience, based upon several thousand trances on approximately 300 individual subjects, some of whom were hypnotized at least 500 times each over a period of four to six years, reveals no evidence of such harmful effects. This clinical finding is further substantiated by the well-known difficulties encountered in the deliberate therapeutic attempts to occasion desired changes in the personality. Accordingly, marked changes from experimental hypnosis appear questionable.

25. An Experimental Investigation of the Possible AntiSocial Use of Hypnosis

Milton H. Erickson

The possibility of the misuse of hypnosis for antisocial or criminal purposes constitutes a most controversial question, not only for the layman but also for the psychologist, the physician, and the psychiatrist interested in its study, its nature, and its uses and applications. To settle this question is difficult, since it involves three inseparable factors of unknown potentialities—specifically, the hypnotist as a person, the subject as a person, and hypnosis as such, to say nothing of the significant influence upon these three, both individually and collectively, of the suggestion and the performance of a questionable act.

We know that it is possible, without recourse to hypnosis, for one person to induce another to commit a wrong, a fact we may explain loosely as the influence of one personality upon another. Hence the question arises, "Can hypnosis, as a form of influence of one personality upon another, be utilized for wrongdoing?" Actually, however, the problem is not this simple, since in any hypnotic situation there exists not only the hypnotic relationship, but also interpersonal relationships entirely apart from the hypnotic, however intimately these various relationships are bound together in a single situation.

Hence any experimental approach to the question requires an emphasis upon one another of the significant factors to determine its intrinsic importance. In this paper an effort will be made to emphasize primarily the hypnotic elements and thus to determine how much hypnotic suggestion itself can accomplish in inducing wrong behavior.

Recently Rowland (1939) has made inquiry into the general hypnotic literature on the question of the possibility of inducing hypnotic subjects to perform harmful or objectionable acts, and has found that Hollander, Loewenfeld, Schilder, and Young were essentially agreed that there was little likelihood, if any, of such a possibility.

He then devised two experiments to discover if deeply hypnotized subjects could be induced to expose themselves to danger or to try to harm others. The one experiment consisted of having the subjects pick up a rattlesnake, variously described to them as a rubber hose and as a snake, lying in a carefully constructed box, the front of which was made of invisible glass and gave the

---

Reprinted with permission from *Psychiatry*, August, 1939, *2*, 391-414.

impression of being open. The second experiment consisted of having the subject throw fluid he knew to be acid at the experimenter's face, which was protected in an unnoticeable way by invisible glass. Three of four subjects did as asked in the first experiment, and both subjects used in the second experiment did as instructed, while 42 persons in the waking state could not be induced to attempt the performance of the first experiment. The author presents these data as evidence of the possible misuse of hypnosis and offers as a possible explanation of the results a brief statement to the effect that the subjects' confidence in the hypnotist might have caused them to forego their better judgment. In addition the author emphasizes the need to reexamine the entire question of the possible misuse of hypnosis.

That these experimental findings are valid as to their apparent significance is to be questioned, for the reason of the serious oversight, except for slight hints summarized in the tentative explanation offered for the results, of the definite and highly important subject-hypnotist relationship of trust and confidence, which could account fully for the findings. Particularly does this seem true for the situation in which these experiments were performed, aside from the consideration of the possible discovery by the subjects of the actual protection against harm afforded by the experimental apparatus. In this connection Schilder and Kauders have made an excellent survey of the literature and offer, in relation to various aspects of the entire problem of the misuse of hypnosis, a wealth of general opinions based upon their own experience and that of others. They declare, "But we must not forget that the hypnotized person is always aware of the general situation, that he is conscious of the fact that an experiment is being made on him, and that he must be well aware that the hypnotizer is not inducing him to commit an actual murder, if the hypnotizer is a man of respected social position" (Schilder & Kauders, 1927, p. 52).

Furthermore it is doubtful if any definite answer to the general question can be obtained *except by an experimental situation in which the suggested antisocial act really can become an accomplished fact, obviously and unmistakably so, and without the protection afforded by a falsified situation which can serve only to vitiate or negate the experimental procedure for both subject and investigator.*

While some recognition has been given to various aspects of this entire problem, a general survey of the literature discloses no systematic, comprehensive experimental study of the question, and also that the available information tends to be limited either to general statements based upon the personal experience of reliable investigators or to reports centering around limited experimental situations of rather extreme character—Rowland's study, for instance—without sufficient attention being given to the highly important factors of trust and confidence in the experimenter, the subject's probable realization of the actual use of concealed protective measures, and the general tendency, emphasized so strongly by Schilder and Kauders, for subjects to look upon any hypnotic situation as essentially an experimental procedure, particularly so in any formal laboratory setting.

GENERAL COMMENTS ON EXPERIMENTAL PURPOSES AND PROCEDURES AND ON THE SUBJECTS AND THEIR IMMEDIATE REACTIONS TO THE EXPERIMENTS

In this paper it is proposed to report a series of experiments, performed over a period of years, bearing upon this important problem of the misuse of hypnosis, in which an earnest effort was made to avoid the difficulties involved in experimental settings as such and to meet the absolute need for realism. To achieve these ends informal situations for the most part were utilized, and acts of an extreme nature were avoided. Instead definitely objectionable acts of a relatively minor antisocial character were employed, since such acts could reasonably be made to serve the investigative purposes and to yield significant, informative, and indicative data.

The actual experimental procedure was in general simple in character, and consisted chiefly of seizing upon favorable opportunities and situations to suggest hypnotically some form of objectionable behavior, sometimes directly, sometimes indirectly. For some of the more complicated and difficult experiments an elaborate technique of suggestion was evolved in which extensive allowance was made for the subject's personality. In all instances every effort was made to induce either an actual performance or an approximation of the suggested act, so that, whatever the degree of the experimenter's responsibility and guilt or the extent of possible protective measures, there would still be *the inescapable fact of the subject's own participation in an undesirable performance directed either against himself or against others*. Also, whenever possible, control experiments were made in an effort to secure similar behavior in the waking state.

Practically all of the experimental procedures cited were repeated on several subjects, but only the more informative and representative examples are given, although it may be added that the instances omitted actually confirm those cited and that the findings were essentially the same for all types of subjects. No attempt will be made, because of the large number of experiments, to give all the experimental details; rather, a concise summary will be offered except in those instances where the subject's behavior is peculiarly informative.

The material to be presented is based upon the findings obtained from approximately 50 subjects selected from a total of more than 75. Among these subjects were children and adults, normal persons and some who had recovered from psychotic episodes, and they ranged in intelligence from feeblemindedness to the superior adult level, but the majority were either college students or graduates. They were all well known to the hypnotist, many had been utilized repeatedly for other hypnotic work, and all were well trained to accept any type of suggestion and to develop profound somnambulistic trances, as well as complete amnesias for all trance experiences.

However, despite their well-established trust and confidence in the experimenter, almost invariably the experimentation reported here caused them to develop intense resentments and antagonisms toward him. Only their realization, subsequently, of the scientific purposes of the work, aside from their general understanding of the hypnotist and the high degree of trust and confidence they had in his official position, served to effect a resolution of their resentments. Even then there were some who thereafter limited any further participation in hypnotic experiments to strictly impersonal procedures.

Another important fact concerning their anger and resentment was that the subjects tended to develop and manifest much more intense feeling at the hypnotic level of awareness than at the conscious, waking level. *Many of the subjects in the waking state readily and easily forgave the experimenter, when informed of the situation, only to manifest in the trance state a full continuance of their anger.* Also, the emotions of the hypnotic trance, despite the general state of suggestibility and the actual existence of a favorable waking attitude, were much more difficult to deal with than those of the ordinary waking state. Rarely did the subjects show equal degrees of resentment in both the waking and hypnotic states, and still more rarely was the waking displeasure greater than the trance emotion. Also it is of interest to note that certain of the subjects actually inflicted punishment and humiliation upon the experimenter in retaliation for his objectionable commands, the possibility of which has been noted by Schilder and Kauders (1927, p. 52).

INQUIRY INTO GENERAL POSTEXPERIMENTAL ATTITUDES, OPINIONS, AND REACTIONS OF THE SUBJECTS

Before proceeding to the actual experiments, it may be desirable to present the results of postexperimental inquiries to serve as a general background for an understanding of the experimental findings. Exceptions to these general statements will be found in the individual experimental accounts.

In this connection, *before the subjects had been given any recollection of their hypnotic experiences*, and as a postexperimental measure, since previous experience had shown that such inquiries tend to make subjects suspicious and hesitant about participation in hypnotic work, inquiry disclosed that approximately 40 percent of the subjects employed believed that they could be induced in the trance state to perform objectionable acts of a definitely minor character, if the acts were directed primarily against themselves, and that among these were many who had rejected such suggestions unconditionally with no attempt made either to evade the demands placed upon them or to alter the performance so as to render it unobjectionable. About 50 percent were most emphatic in denying such a possibility, and in this group largely were those who had seized upon the opportunity offered by the antisocial suggestions to inflict punishment upon the experimenter, while the remainder tended to be, on the whole, rather doubtful. All, however, were emphatic in denying the possibility of being induced hypnotically to commit antisocial acts of a major character.

Following this, despite the consistent failure to experimentally induce antisocial behavior of a genuine or effective character, certain of the subjects were given a full recollection of *only their actual experimental behavior*, and inquiry disclosed that many were emphatic in their declaration that only their trust and confidence in the experimenter could account for their submission to the experimental procedures, aside from the question of accepting and possibly acting upon the suggestions. Others declared that they must have been confident at the time that protective measures were actually in force and that "things were really different than they seemed." Still others explained that they must have had a general realization that the author probably had secret legitimate purposes behind his requests, which made it possible for them to accept suggestions out of the question under any other circumstances. A few explained that they had probably been willing to do whatever was asked because they regarded the situation as having legitimate scientific implications, but that even so they must have found the requests to be "impossible" because of the violation of their personal code. And some others offered only the naive explanation, "Well, that just goes to show you how I really would act."

When instructed further to recall their *feelings and attitudes when given the objectionable task*, as well as their actual behavior, the results were essentially a confirmation of their previous statements and gave the impression of being a confusion of their immediate and of their retrospective understandings.

The remainder of the subjects were instructed to recall as a single task *both their feelings and their behavior of the trance state*, but, probably because the experimental situation demanded action rather than reflection, little that was informative could be obtained, except for statements of feelings of anger, resentment, hesitation, negativism, and unwillingness, and any elaboration of these statements was made in terms of their immediate understandings. It did not seem possible for them to differentiate between their understandings of how they felt at the time of the experiment and at the time of the postexperimental questioning.

Inquiry about the possibility of being induced to commit some seriously dangerous or culpable act because of implicit trust in the hypnotist and a certainty that there were adequate protective measures elicited the significant reply that hypnotic suggestion did not and, as they knew from personal experience, could not render the subject an obedient, unthinking automaton, as, in their opinion, the experimenter had discovered adequately. Also, they emphasized that invariably they scrutinized carefully every suggestion offered, primarily as a measure of understanding it fully to permit complete obedience and not for the purpose of taking exception to it, and that if they were at all uncertain of it, their hypnotic state would force them to await either more adequate instruction or a better understanding by a direct, thoughtful, and critical consideration of the command.

They added that this tendency would be all the more marked in the case of unusual or potentially dangerous suggestions and situations.

Inquiry about the possibility of being manipulated unfavorably or skillfully tricked by an unscrupulous hypnotist who had won their full confidence, disclosed the common belief that they could be deceived to a certain degree but not seriously, probably less so than in the waking state, because of the reasons given above and because the limitations of the hypnotic trance would constitute a protection in itself, since it is limited in time and situation and restricts so markedly environmental contact, and hence would preclude the dangers of overconfidence likely to obtain in the waking state.

In addition inquiry on these points among a large number of experienced subjects not used in this type of experimentation disclosed their beliefs to be identical with those given above, and they also declared that a successful deception by an unscrupulous hypnotist would have to be one more readily achieved in the waking state, and then that it would not be a function of the hypnotic condition, but rather that the hypnosis would be, as Schilder and Kauders remark, nothing more than "a particularly noneffective technical auxiliary" (1927, p. 54) for inducing antisocial behavior.

EXPERIMENTAL FINDINGS

In presenting the experimental findings, an effort has been made to select material from as many different subjects as possible and to classify and group the various accounts in accord with their primary significance. However, many of the reports illustrate several points, as will become apparent to the reader. Also, while written as single accounts, the reader will note many instances in which the account is a summary of experiments and variations of those experiments upon a number of subjects.

No attempt will be made to offer a general discussion of all the material, since for the most part the reports are relatively clear. Rather, brief comments, wherever pertinent, will be made in direct relationship either to the individual experiment or to types of experiments, and these comments will be limited to the general problem of this paper, although the reader may repeatedly observe experimental illustrations of various dynamisms of behavior.

Finally, to avoid needless repetition of the fact, the statement may be made that except where specifically stated otherwise, *all the subjects were in profound somnambulistic hypnotic trances, and profound amnesias were developed in each of them for all trance experiences until the purposes of the experimentation warranted their waking recollection of all or part of the trance events.* Thus experimentation in the waking state could follow hypnotic experimentation without the subject's conscious awareness that it constituted a repetition of a previous experiment, and in some instances amnesias were produced for waking events to permit repetitions of waking acts.

EXPERIMENTAL ACCOUNTS

Experiments Involving Physical or Mental Injury to the Self

Account 1: The subject was shown hand electrodes, and the flow of current was demonstrated by the experimenter's receiving a shock obviously disagreeable and violent in effects. He was then instructed emphatically and insistently to experience the same shock. This he refused, explaining that the experimenter's own discomfort and violent muscular reactions had satisfied all his curiosity about it. An attempt to compel or force him into obedience failed, although he did make several tentative attempts to pick up the electrodes. Finally, after much insistence by the experimenter, the subject became antagonistic and rejected the whole procedure as foolish and unnecessary.

Subsequently, with the subject in the waking state, the experimenter repeated the entire performance, but the subject still refused to receive a shock, giving essentially his trance explanation. Finally he consented to take a lesser shock, when casually shown the use of a resistance coil. He demanded, however, that the experimenter prove the lessening of the current by receiving another shock. After he had experienced a mild shock, an attempt was made to induce him, still in the waking state, to permit a strengthening of the current. This he refused.

Again hypnotized and the original procedure repeated, he agreed to receive a mild shock, but insisted upon a preliminary demonstration of its mildness, checking additionally on the adjustment of the resistance coil. Argument that the experimenter's own performance demonstrated the harmlessness of the entire procedure elicited the explanation that nothing worthwhile could be accomplished by such self-punishment and that a mild shock was sufficiently unpleasant to warrant no further experimentation.

Account 2: The subject was told to develop an anaesthesia of his hand and then to prove it by holding a lighted match underneath his index finger. Ordinarily hypnotic subjects will refuse unconditionally to permit a testing of a hypnotically induced anaesthesia by measures they regard as too injurious or destructive. This subject, however, readily did as asked, holding the lighted match to his finger until he smelled the odor of burning flesh. Commenting on this, he threw the match aside and asked irritably if the experimenter thought his purposes warranted such results. When answered in the affirmative, the subject replied that such had been his opinion. He then asked that the experimenter awaken him and give him a full conscious recollection of the incident.

Several days later, in the waking state, he discussed his experience with fellow medical students, emphasizing his loss of pain sensation. One of the students asked him if he could develop an anaesthesia spontaneously. Becoming interested in this, the subject began making suggestions to himself that his hand would again become anaesthetic, finally testing the self-induced anaesthesia with a lighted match. The other students declared that he was probably willfully enduring pain to uphold his argument. In answer he attempted unsuccessfully to control his pain reactions to a lighted match applied to his nonanaesthetic hand.

On another occasion the subject in the waking state became interested in the ability of psychotic patients to endure pain in smoking a cigarette to the last puff and proceeded to duplicate the performance, willingly enduring a severe burn on his lips as a result, thereby illustrating his behavior when the question of hypnosis was not involved, either directly or indirectly.

Account 3: The subject, a 12-year-old girl, was given suggestions to the effect that a certain box was actually a hot stove. She accepted these suggestions and, upon request, sat upon the illusory hot stove, squirming, twisting, and protesting that she was being burned, and begging to be allowed to get off. All of her behavior was fully suggestive of the reality of the experience to her.

Two weeks later the experiment was repeated, with the modification that on this occasion extremely careful suggestions were given to effect a realistic illusion of the selected box as a hot stove. This achieved, she could not be induced to sit on it. Yet, when another box was simply described as a hot stove and she was told to sit on it, she promptly did so, repeating her behavior of the original experiment. Nevertheless she could not be induced to sit upon the more realistic illusory hot stove.

On another occasion an attempt was made to induce this same subject to sit upon an actual hot stove. She obeyed the request by mistaking another article of furniture for that stove and sitting upon it instead, giving every evidence of discomfort and distress. No amount of effort could make her approach the real stove, even when protective measures were provided that could be recognized by the subject.

As a variation, using this subject and a number of others to permit adequate control of each step of the procedure, an attempt was made to induce the placing of the hand on a hot stove, first casually and then later effectively described as being cold. Only an approximate performance could be secured, that of holding the hand briefly an inch or so above the stove and declaring that it was actually in contact with the stove. The induction of an anaesthesia in the chosen hand led to a preliminary testing with the nonanaesthetic hand and resentment over the attempted deception. When, by careful suggestion, the subject was deprived of all self-protective measures, an unconditional refusal resulted.

Account 4: During some experimentation on crystal gazing, a subject was told, by chance, to visualize the most important event of the year 1925, as a measure of keeping her busy while the experimenter directed his attention elsewhere. Promptly, as the crystal images began to develop, the subject began to manifest extreme emotional distress, and there occurred a marked loss of rapport with the experimenter. With difficulty hypnotic contact was reestablished with her and sufficient information elicited to disclose that she had visualized an occurrence of marked psychic traumatic significance. Thereafter it was necessary to reassure this subject about hypnosis, and she could not be induced to do crystal gazing unless first instructed firmly to see only pleasant, happy scenes, and this demand continued to be made even after she had spontaneously requested from the experimenter a psychotherapeutic review of her unhappy experience.

Since this incident the experimenter has had many similar experiences, especially with patients seeking psychotherapy, but also with subjects employed only for experimental or demonstration purposes.

Comment: These four accounts illustrate clearly that hypnotic subjects are not blindly obedient automatons, that they possess a good critical ability, and a full capacity for self-protection, both in the immediate sense and in relation to the future. In addition the need to know what subjects will do in the ordinary waking state, and the profound need for realism in the experimental situation, are clearly shown. Also one needs only a few such experiences as given in the last account to realize how easily good hypnotic subjects or patients may be lost by having them face a painful experience too precipitately.

Involving Damage or Loss of Personal Property

Account 5: This subject smoked secretly but knew and did not object to the fact that the experimenter was aware of her habit. One day, when she was in his office, noting that she had with her a gift handkerchief which she prized highly, the experimenter hypnotized her and gave her a cigarette to smoke, counseling her earnestly that should someone happen to enter, she should keep secret her smoking by crumpling the cigarette in her handkerchief thus concealing the evidence. She was not receptive to the idea, explaining that such a procedure would burn her handkerchief, but it was argued insistently that that measure might well be kept in mind. However, she continued to smoke, not taking the suggestions seriously. Suddenly the experimenter summoned the occupant of the next office, but so maneuvered that while the visitor's back was toward the subject upon entrance, his discovery of her was imminent, thus confronting her with an immediate and compelling need to dispose of her cigarette by the method suggested. As the visitor entered, the subject flushed angrily, glanced at her handkerchief, made several tentative moves to follow the suggestions given her, then carefully and deliberately tucked the handkerchief into her sleeve and continued to smoke, despite the fact that she particularly did not want that visitor to know of her practice. When this reaction had been noted, the visitor was manipulated out of the office without a betrayal of her secret. Nevertheless, she gave the experimenter an angry scolding and criticized him harshly for his conduct and for his deliberate attempt to make her ruin her

Possible Antisocial Use

handkerchief, demanded to be awakened, threatened to awaken spontaneously if this were not done at once, and declared her intention of never again being hypnotized.

Only after she had been given a complete understanding of the situation was it possible to win back her confidence, and it was necessary to do this in both the hypnotic and the waking states, despite her waking amnesia for the experience.

Account 6: This subject possessed a prized book which had been greatly admired and often solicited by a friend as a gift, but only an implied promise that on some auspicious occasion it might be made a gift had been elicited. In a deep trance extensive systematic efforts were made to induce the subject to keep that implied promise, either at once or by a specified date, with even the privilege of naming the date, but the most that could be accomplished was a repetition of her waking promise—namely, that sometime the book might be made a gift. Approximately a year later the book was made a gift, but to another friend not mentioned in the trance, who also desired it greatly.

Comment: In Account 5 the subject was painfully and sharply trapped by the situation and apparently given no alternative except obedience to the urgent suggestions given her. Nevertheless she made a deliberate and painful choice of behavior in contradiction to the hypnotic commands, and despite the continuance of the trance state, she exercised fully her normal waking pregrogatives by denouncing the experimenter and depriving him of his control over the situation, emphasizing the latter by compelling a justification at both the hypnotic and the waking levels of awareness.

In the next account, although the general idea suggested was entirely acceptable, the subject could not be induced to act upon it except under conditions and circumstances to be self-decided in the waking state. The final outcome suggests an actual defeating of the hypnotic suggestions.

Giving of Adverse Information About Oneself

Account 7: While engaged in mischief, a young man injured himself seriously, necessitating surgical intervention. Before full treatment could be administered effeciently, it was necessary to know the exact nature and method of his accident. Questioning at length by the experimenter's colleagues elicited an obviously false and misleading story because of the embarrassing and humiliating chraracter of the injury, nor could the emergency of this situation be impressed upon him sufficiently to induce him to tell the truth. Accordingly the experimenter was asked to hypnotize him, since he was one of the experimenter's well-trained subjects, and thus to secure the essential information. The subject went into a deep trance readily enough, but persisted in telling the same false story as he had in the waking state, despite instruction about the seriousness of the situation. Finally, when the experimenter refused to accept his story, the patient offered the argument that the experimenter was a doctor and really ought to understand. Accepting this contention, the experimenter instructed him, while still in the trance state, to listen carefully to the experimenter's understanding of the probable course of events and to correct any misstatements. In this indirect and unsatisfactory way sufficient correct information was reluctantly and incompletely yielded to permit proper treatment, although the persistence in a general misstatement of facts continued.

Even after recovery the subject persisted in his false story in both waking and trance states, although he knew that the surgical intervention had disclosed the truth.

Nor is this case unusual, since similar behavior is frequently encountered in the therapy of neurotic conditions, even when the patient earnestly desires help. Likewise, with normal hypnotic subjects detected in a lie, a systematic and careful attempt to secure the truth in the trance state will frequently elicit only a stubborn persistence in the falsification unless a justification, adequate for the inquisition and satisfactory to the subject as a person, can be proved. Otherwise anger and resentment, concealed or open, is likely to develop, together with loss of trust, confidence, and hypnotic services. This situation is difficult to alter by any straightforward objective explanation, since the highly subjective character of the situation renders objectivity difficult to achieve.

Nevertheless, under conditions where the subject's personality situation warrants it, hypnotic measures are exceedingly effective in eliciting adverse information about the self, and it frequently happens that the subject will disclose the truth unreservedly in the trance state, but in a most inexplicable fashion will persist in his right to a negation of the truth and absolute misstatements in the waking state.

Comment: Despite the shift of responsibility, the submissiveness of the hypnotic subject, the peculiar significance and strength of the hypnotist-subject relationship, and the tremendous and recognized importance of obeying the hypnotic commands, the actual character and nature of the individual's waking patterns of behavior carried over into the trance situation. Apparently, from this and from general hypnotic therapeutic experience, the elicitation of adverse information about the self is a function not of hypnosis itself but rather of the total personality situation.

Involving Violation of the Subjects' Moral or Conventional Codes

Inducing Subjects to Lie

Account 8: Attempts were made to induce a number of subjects to tell deliberate lies to persons placed in rapport with them, the lies to cause both petty annoyance and marked inconvenience, or even definite difficulties. In all instances the efforts failed, although all of the subjects could be induced to tell "white lies," but even so they all reserved the privilege of correcting or nullifying the lie should it lead to even the slightest inconvenience for the victim. Thus one subject, induced to make a slip of the tongue in informing a friend about the hour set for a ride home from the office, nullified the act by an apparently casual waking decision to accompany that friend home.

However, it was found that if the subjects were given sufficient reason, they could be induced to promise to tell lies in the deep trance state of a character protective of themselves and of others, but marked limitation was placed by the subjects upon this willingness, and their lies were again restricted to those of an insignificant character when they were forced to act upon their promise. In addition they invariably reserved the privilege of correcting or nullifying their misstatements, and in all instances the lies were corrected subsequently, either directly or indirectly.

But of particular significance was the discovery that *when the subject could be induced to lie effectively, it was necessary for the subject to be in a trance state.* Despite every measure of technique it was found to be impossible to bridge the gap between the hypnotic and the waking levels of awareness to permit a meaningful waking reiteration of the lie.

Efforts made to induce lying in response to posthypnotic suggestions invariably led to unsatisfactory results—namely, the defeating of the purposes of falsification, even when the lies were of a protective character. Inquiries about this afterward in the trance state disclosed that the subjects objected strenuously to posthypnotic lying, and they explained that they preferred to work out another and truthful method of either dealing with the situation or evading it. Nor could any amount of suggestion alter their attitudes, since they argued that a waking knowledge of the desired behaviour would actually aid them because of increased contact with the environment, if there were a justification for the lying.

In those instances where they were induced to tell lies posthypnotically with some degree of success the results were totally unsatisfactory, since each of the subjects performed his task in a compulsive and inadequate fashion, rendering the falsity of his statement at once apparent. An adequate explanation of the failure of lying as a posthypnotic performance may be found in the peculiarities of posthypnotic behavior as such, which does not come within the scope of this paper.

Comment: As shown in previous accounts, subjects can tell lies while in the trance state for reasons of their own, but apparently the situation becomes totally different when the hypnotist tries to induce them to tell lies in the trance state. In such case, apart from the conflict aroused by the violation of the subject's personal code by the attempt to induce lying and the self-protective reactions engendered by this, the separateness of hypnotic and waking levels of awareness apparently renders lying in the trance state, however successful in a limited sense, only an alien intrusion into waking patterns of behavior to be rejected at the earliest opportunity. One is at once impressed by the significant bearing of the above findings upon the generally recognized folly of dealing only with a single limited aspect of the total personality.

In such procedures as the above one is only setting, under the time- and situation-limited circumstances of the hypnotic trance, a restricted aspect of the personality at variance with another and more dominant aspect, and asking that lesser aspect, contrary to its nature and habit, to act directly in the field of conscious awareness—an impossible task, apparently, to judge from the experimental findings.

Inducing the Drinking of Liquor

Account 9: A subject known to have scruples against drinking liquor was urged to take a cocktail. Every suggestion to this effect failed, although she did explain under pressure that she might do so if she were awake. When it was argued plausibly that the entire purpose was to have her take the drink in the hypnotic state to see if she could detect having done so after awakening, she failed to be convinced of the desirability of the act.

After awakening, however, she was persuaded by renewed argument to taste the cocktail, but she declared that it was distasteful and pleaded to be excused from the task, explaining that she would, despite personal objections, drink the rest of it if to do so were really necessary. She was promptly hypnotized and informed most urgently that it was highly essential for her to finish the cocktail. She refused to do so unless she were awakened, arguing that if drinking the cocktail were really important, it would be better for her to drink it in the waking rather than in the hypnotic state.

Similarly an attempt to induce intoxication failed completely in a subject who drank moderately and who objected strenuously to intoxication, despite an admitted strong personal desire to experience such a state. The explanation offered by this subject for his absolute refusal to take more than the customary amount of liquor was simply that to become intoxicated would be strictly a matter of personal interest and desire, possible of satisfactory achievement only in the waking state, and that the experimenter's interest in intoxication during the trance state was of no moment or pertinence.

On the other hand a subject who had previously been intoxicated in the waking state and who desired the additional experience of becoming intoxicated while in the trance state, just as unequivocally refused to take a single drink until he had first been hypnotized.

Comment: Apparently the need to satisfy the wishes of the total personality and the need to participate as a total personality in an objectionable, questionable, or special performance takes entire precedence over the wishes and commands of the hypnotist.

Violation of Personal Privacy

Physical Examinations

Account 10: Several of the author's sisters, as has been mentioned briefly elsewhere, (Erickson, 1934) were hypnotized separately and instructed that they were to be given a complete physical examination in the presence of their mother, for which they were to undress completely. Each refused unconditionally. An explanation was requested, and they responded by declaring that even though the experimenter was their brother and a doctor, they did not think it fitting for him to make such a request, and no measure of persuasion succeeded.

Subsequently, in the waking state, the same issue was raised with each of them, and each consented hesitantly to the request. Questioned upon rehypnotizing as to this apparent inconsistency in their attitudes, they explained that being examined when they were awake gave them a sense of better contact with the entire situation, but that in the trance state, being asleep, they felt that they would not know what was going on.

Similarly a hypnotic subject suffering from a painful pelvic condition came to the experimenter for examination. The suggestion was given her that she could be hypnotized and given a hypnotic anaesthesia which would relieve her of much pain and distress. She refused unconditionally, despite the presence of the attending nurse, until the promise was made to produce the anaesthesia as a posthypnotic phenomenon, so that she could be more satisfactorily in contact with reality during the entire time of the examination and treatment. Apparently the highly personal character of hypnosis in such a situation renders it less acceptable than a drug anaesthesia, as the experimenter has found on a number of occasions.

Comment: Whatever the strength and nature of the hypnotic relationship, it does not alter the sanctity of one's personal privacy. This belongs apparently to the waking state, upon which it depends for protection. Had a violation of the stipulation regarding the examination been attempted in Account 10, an awakening from the trance would have occurred, since an attempt at examination would have been equivalent to a cue to awaken. One may judge from the above that the process of being hypnotized is perceived by the subject as a peculiar alteration of his control over the self, necessitating compensatory measures in relationship to any occurrence seeming to imply a threat to the control of the self.

Giving Information of an Intimate Character

Account 11: The subject was asked deliberately to disclose the name of the girl in whom he was most interested. This he did readily. Later, in the waking state, he asked for an account of all trance occurrences. Disclosure of the question about the girl's name elicited violent anger, and he declared that his trust in the experimenter had been destroyed. When he was convinced by adequate proof that he had made the same disclosure some weeks previous in the waking state, a fact he had forgotten, his anger abated, but thereafter he refused to participate in hypnotic work except for strictly impersonal procedures, and any attempt to violate that condition, even indirectly, resulted in a prompt and angry awakening from the trance. Nor could this state of affairs be altered by careful hypnotic suggestion designed to correct his attitude.

In this same connection it is not an unusual experience in medical or psychiatric practice to have patients seeking any type of therapy, particularly psychotherapy, withhold or distort information bearing upon their problems because they feel the details of personal history to be of too intimate a character or too embarrassing to reveal, as has been noted above in Account 7. When recourse is had to hypnosis during the course of the therapy as a measure of securing information, the same tendency to withhold or to distort information is to be found, and this despite the fact that the patient may actually and urgently be seeking aid and has a clear realization that there is a legitimate reason for yielding the specific information. Usually, however, hypnotic questioning serves to elicit the information more readily than can be done in the waking state, but the entire process of overcoming the resistance and reluctance depends on the development of a good patient-physician relationship rather than upon hypnotic measures, and the hypnosis is essentially, in such situations, no more than a means by which the patient can give the information in a relatively comfortable fashion.

Comment: Although there had actually been no violation of personal privacy, the questioning was so construed in the waking state. Yet despite refutation this temporary misunderstanding permanently limited the extent of subsequent hypnotic work and precluded any alteration of the state of affairs by hypnotic suggestion. The relationship of these findings to unfortunate errors in psychotherapy is at once apparent.

Exhibiting the Contents of One's Purse

Account 12: On several occasions and under various circumstances female subjects were asked to exhibit the contents of their purses, and definite systematic attempts were made to build up in each a compulsion to do as requested. In each instance, however, the attempt failed, and the explanation was obtained repeatedly that they considered such a request an unwarranted intrusion upon their privacy.

When this procedure was repeated on them later in the waking state, one subject yielded sufficiently to exhibit a part of the contents, but the others regarded the request as unreasonable. When told that there were justifiable and legitimate reasons for the experimenter's seemingly rude request, they replied that whatever his scientific purposes might be, he would have to be satisfied by their refusal.

However, these same subjects in the waking state would not resist the experimenter's picking up their purses and examining the contents. Rather, they took sardonic pleasure in reducing the experimenter, by the implications of their manner, to the position of a prying busybody.

When a similar attempt was made to investigate their purses while they were in a second trance state, they resented and resisted it strenuously, nor could they be induced to account adequately for the inconsistencies of their waking and trance reactions.

This same general experimental request in relationship to the contents of their pockets was readily and even proudly acceded to in both waking and trance states by small boys and by little girls with purses. When, however, an attempt was made to induce adult male subjects to exhibit the contents of their purses, they reacted as did the female subjects, or else yielded to the request in such fashion as to humiliate the experimenter greatly.

Comment: A direct but inconsequential aggression upon the subjects' privacy was resisted even after it had been permitted in the waking state. One has the feeling that as a result of their hypnotic state they sensed a certain feeling of helplessness reflected in intensified self-protection, as has been noted in the comment on Account 10.

Experiments Involving Harm to Others

Physical Harm to Others

Account 13: Some college students had played the prank of feeding a large quantity of cathartic candy to an unpopular and greedy student, who was also openly disliked by the experimenter and his hypnotic subject. Sometime later this subject was given a package of cathartic gum and instructed to replace with it a similar but harmless package of gum in the unpopular student's desk, so that unwittingly he would again become ill. The subject refused unconditionally, stated that the student had already been made sick once, and that, while he would not mind a repetition of the prank, he preferred that the experimenter himself play the trick.

No amount of urging could induce the subject to change his mind, although it was discovered that he had been one of the original pranksters. Questioned about this, the subject explained that he had already satisfied his dislike fully, and hence that there was no need of repeating the prank. When the experimenter offered to do it, the subject looked on with obvious amusement, but he could not be induced to share in the performance, nor did he seem to have any realization or expectation that the experimenter would secretly correct this act. Yet at a later time this subject in the waking state did pass out cathartic gum to his unsuspecting friends.

Account 14: An explanation was given to a subject of the crude joke in which one inhales cigarette smoke deeply and then, professing to blow it out of his eyes to distract the victim's attention, dexterously burns the victim's hand.

The subject was urged to play this joke upon a suitable victim, and he was asked to go through a mock performance with the experimenter as a measure of ensuring a smooth enactment. Instead of a mock performance the subject deliberately burned the experimenter's hand. No comment was made on this, and a discussion was held as to the proper victim, but one proposal after another was rejected. Finally the subject declared an absolute unwillingness to do it on anybody except the experimenter, explaining that a cigarette burn was a nasty, unpleasant thing, that there was no humor in the joke, and that the whole thing was not worth doing.

Inquiry subsequently disclosed that the subject felt justified in burning the experimenter's hand as a punishment for trying to take advantage of him, but that he did not feel that anybody else should be made a victim of so crude and painful a joke.

Account 15: As a practical joke it was suggested to a subject that a third person be induced to lift a box having metal handles which were actually electrodes connected with a source of current. The experimenter then demonstrated on himself the effect of the shock, which was definitely violent and disagreeable. However, the subject could not be induced to test the shock himself, and when an unsuspecting victim was secured, he refused to close the switch, despite his willingness and readiness to turn on the current when the experimenter was lifting the box. He explained his refusal on the grounds that the experimenter's full acquaintance with the apparatus and obvious willingness to take the shock justified his turning on the current, but that the unexpectedness of a violent shock for an unsuspecting victim would be a most questionable and unwise thing. Yet subsequently, in the waking state, he joined with his fellows in using this apparatus to shock unsuspecting victims. Even then he could not be induced to go through the performance in the trance state, declaring that to do so would be only a blind automatic performance lacking in any element of humor and that, at best, he would not be a participant but only an instrument, a rôle for which he had no liking.

Account 16: An exceedingly spoiled and pampered young woman had the unpleasant habit of slapping anyone who offended her even slightly. When she was in a deep trance state, an assistant was placed in rapport with her with secret instructions to make definitely offensive remarks to her. When he obeyed these instructions, she flushed angrily, turned to the experimenter, and declared that the assistant was probably acting in response to the experimenter's request and that, by rights, the experimenter should have his face slapped, and that his face would be slapped if the assistant continued to make disagreeable remarks.

An attempt was made to persuade her of the experimenter's innocence and also that regardless of his innocence or guilt, she ought to slap the assistant, since he really had free choice in the matter. She declared, however, that she preferred to do her slapping when she was awake and that unless the trance procedure were changed, she would awaken herself and would refuse to do any further hypnotic work, and it was found necessary to accede to her demands.

Comment: In these four accounts not only did the subjects resist suggestions for acts actually acceptable under ordinary waking conditions, but they carried over into the trance state the normal waking tendency to reject instrumentalization by another. However, acting on their own sense of responsibility, there was no hesitation about aggressive behavior directed against the experimenter, but apparently the submissiveness of the trance state and the instrumentalization effected by the hypnotic suggestions of aggression against others rendered such suggested acts so impersonal and lacking in motivation as to be completely objectionable in the trance state.

Verbally Abusing and Giving Adverse Information About Others

Account 17: The subject was instructed to make a number of cutting, disagreeable remarks to a person strongly disliked by that subject and also to persons actually liked. However, she refused to perform either of these tasks in the trance state, declaring that she would not hurt her friends' feelings in any such fashion and explaining that if she said unpleasant things to people she disliked, she preferred to be awake so that she could enjoy their discomfiture.

When it was suggested that she make disagreeable remarks to disliked persons as a posthypnotic performance, she again refused, explaining that if she said unpleasant things, she wanted to be the one who originated them, and that it would be done only at her desire and at an opportunity that she selected, and not in response to the experimenter's request. Despite much urging, she could not be induced to alter her attitude.

Yet in an obviously experimental setting, where it was plain that everybody understood the total situation, this subject as well as many others (Erickson, 1939) was found entirely willing to accede to such requests and even to take advantage of the opportunity to say things more disagreeable than necessary, but to secure such a performance there is always a need for the protection afforded by a recognized experimental situation. However, even under obviously experimental conditions many subjects will refuse to accede to this type of request, explaining that they might inadvertently hurt someone's feelings.

Comment: While the suggestions themselves were not repugnant to the subject, the general situation was, and the subject reserved full rights and demanded the privilege of obeying only under conditions of full conscious awareness. Yet at a mere experimental level, where the purposes of the act are defeated by the nature of the setting, full obedience may be obtained. Again, resistance by the subject to instrumentalization is apparent.

Account 18: A subject known to be aware of certain unpleasant facts concerning an acquaintance whom she disliked greatly was questioned extensively in an effort to secure from her that information. She refused to relate it, even though previous to the trance she had on several occasions been on the verge of imparting that information to the experimenter and had been deliberately put off. She did explain that perhaps sometime when she was awake she might disclose the facts, but that she would not do so in the trance state. No manner of suggestion served to induce her to yield, even though the experimenter's secret knowledge of the entire matter permitted the asking of leading questions and the relating of a sufficient amount of detail to justify her fully in the feeling that she would betray little or nothing. After much pressure she finally expressed a willingness to tell after awakening, if the experimenter could convince her in the waking state of the legitimacy of his request. Her offer was accepted, but when the attempt was made, she evaded the situation by a deliberate falsehood, which, if the experimenter had persisted in his inquiries, would have served to force him into a position where he would have had to embarrass and humiliate her by the exposure of her falsehood.

Comment: Not only did the subject resist the hypnotic commands, but also she withstood a situation which ordinarily in the waking state would lead to capitulation, and in addition she effected, at an unconscious level of thought, a contretemps precluding any further action by the experimenter. In this instance, at least, the subject was more capable of resisting the experimenter's commands in the trance state or by unconscious measures than she was in the waking state.

Offenses Against Good Taste and the Privacy of Others

Account 19: A subject was asked to tell risqué stories in a mixed group. This request he refused unconditionally. Subterfuges of seemingly hypnotizing the other members of the group and giving them instructions to become deaf failed to convince the subject of the reality of the performance. Finally suggestions were given him to the effect that the others present had left and that he was now alone with the experimenter and could tell the stories. The subject apparently accepted this suggestion of the absence of others but declared that there was something peculiar about the room, that there were inexplicable sounds to be detected, and he refused to accede to the request.

On a later occasion the subject was rendered hypnotically blind and taken into a room where others were quietly present. When asked to tell a risqué story, he explained that he could not because he was not confident of the nature of the situation.

Possible Antisocial Use

On still another occasion he was rendered hypnotically blind and hypnotically deaf, with prearranged tactile cues calling for different types of behavior, among which was the relating of a certain objectionable story. Finally the signal for the story was given him, but the subject demanded that the experimenter assure him honestly, by a tactile cue which he specified, that there was nobody else in the room. Only then would he relate the story.

When an account of this was given to him later, with the implication that others might have been present, the subject remarked sardonically that any embarrassment deriving from the situation belonged solely to the experimenter and to any others present.

Comment: The need for realism in the actual situation, the capacity for self-protection in even a recognized experimental setting, and the ability to allocate responsibility is obvious.

Account 20: A subject was instructed to open her companion's pocketbook, to secure a cigarette, and to give it to the experimenter, this to be done with the full awareness of her companion but without express permission. She refused to do so despite urgent demands and angry insistence. Since these measures failed, she was given a posthypnotic suggestion to the effect that after awakening she would notice the experimenter fumbling with an empty cigarette package and that she would then openly abstract a cigarette from her friend's purse. She agreed, but rather hesitantly. After awakening, the proper cue being given, she made several abortive attempts to obey the command and finally took refuge from the situation by lapsing back into the trance state, explaining that she "just couldn't do it, it wasn't nice, it wasn't proper, and it was too discourteous." It was pointed out to her immediately that the companion's full awareness of the situation and failure to manifest any objection rendered the request legitimate. Nevertheless she persisted in her refusal.

Subsequently she was awakened with a complete amnesia for the trance and the posthypnotic experience. During the course of a casual conversation the experimenter asked her for a cigarette. When she replied that she had none, he suggested that her companion had cigarettes, and this statement was confirmed by her friend. She was then asked if she would open her companion's purse and secure a cigarette. Her first reaction was one of being shocked at the impropriety of the request, but finally she yielded to repeated demands, first thinking the matter over and then reasoning aloud, "If you ask me to do a thing like that, you must have a good reason, and she [the friend] certainly looks as if she were waiting for me to do it, and doesn't object, so, with your permission [addressed to the friend] I will do it. If I didn't think you [the experimenter] had a good reason, I wouldn't do it."

Shortly afterward she was rehypnotized, reminded of the entire course of events, and was again asked to secure another cigarette. She explained that she could do it better if she were awake, and when the experimenter persisted in his demands that she do it while still in the trance state, she again refused. Nor would she repeat her waking performance in response to further posthypnotic suggestions, declaring that once was enough and that the whole thing was entirely unnecessary.

Account 21: Another subject was instructed emphatically but unsuccessfully to examine the contents of her friend's purse. Finally resort was had to posthypnotic suggestion, and when this failed, she was given posthypnotic suggestions to the effect that after awakening she would absentmindedly pick up her friend's purse under the impression that it was her own (care had been taken to arrange that the friend's purse could be mistaken easily for the subject's), open it, and become so puzzled and bewildered at seeing unfamiliar objects in her purse that she would examine them in an effort to discover how they happened to get there. After awakening, during a casual conversation the proper posthypnotic cue was given. She immediately mentioned that she felt like smoking, casually picked up her friend's purse, and started to open it, but as she did so, remarked, "What's the matter with the clasp on my purse? It's suddenly got awfully stiff. Why, this isn't my purse!" and then, recognizing it, put it down and picked up her own, apologizing to her friend.

Upon being rehypnotized, the subject explained that she simply could not do what had been asked, but added that she had "tried hard."

An attempt to repeat these two experiments, 20 and 21, in the absence of the owner of the purse was resisted strenuously, and the experimenter's own attempt to examine the purse was met with anger and extreme contempt. Similar results were obtained with several other subjects.

Account 22: The subject was engaged in a casual conversation about how little things tell a great deal about the personality. From this, comment was made upon the contents of small boys' pockets, and then it was suggested that the contents of the experimenter's purse might be most revealing. She was then urged to take his purse, empty it of all its contents, and make a critical examination of them. The subject was most unwilling to do this, but after extensive urging she finally yielded, declaring, "You must have some purpose in this, or you wouldn't want to make me do it, and it's going to be your own hard luck if I do. I will do it, even though I don't want to. I suppose you are carrying on an experiment and I will just help you out the way you want me to. Another thing, you probably planned this so there isn't going to be anything in your purse you don't want me to see." Having made these remarks, she performed the task, but with obvious distaste and reluctance, and constant urging was required to induce her to scrutinize each object.

Comment: In the three accounts 20, 21, and 22, the subjects either rejected the suggestions or transformed the performance into one entirely excusable though obviously distasteful. Such was the strength of their objections in the trance state that they would not permit the experimenter to perform the act

Possible Antisocial Use

required of them in accounts 20 and 21 except at serious risk to himself. In brief, not only did they control the situation for themselves, but they also limited the experimenter in his own aggressive behavior against others not present and who presumably would never be aware of that aggression.

Account 23: Over a period of months a hypnotic subject was instructed, in accord with a carefully planned technique of suggestion, to read his roommate's love letters, without the subject's knowledge that the experimenter had secretly made contact with that roommate and had arranged for the leaving of personal letters readily accessible. On the occasion of each hypnotic trance the subject was asked urgently if he had performed his task, and every effort was made to convince him of the legitimacy of the act as a worthy scientific procedure, related to the investigation of the ability to remember unpleasant things, and connected in turn with an investigation of memory processes as affected by hypnosis.

Nevertheless the subject failed to obey instructions, and offered to do any number of disagreeable tasks which could be used as a memory test and which involved himself only. Finally a promise was secured from the subject that he would do as asked on a particular evening if the experimenter would be present. His demand was met, and the subject in the deep trance state was told to find a letter, actually readily accessible, and to read it. Extreme difficulty was experienced by the subject in finding that letter. He overlooked it repeatedly and searched in all the wrong places, since no overt move was made by the experimenter to direct his search. Eventually he had to be forced to find the letter and to open it. He immediately discovered that he could not read it because he had mislaid his glasses. In searching for his glasses he succeeded in mislaying the letter, and when both the glasses and the letter were at hand, he opened the letter in such fashion that he was confronted by the blank sides of the pages. These he kept turning around and around in a helpless fashion, explaining that the pages were blank. After being told insistently to turn the pages over, he yielded, but did this in such fashion that the writing was then upside down. When this error was corrected, the subject developed spontaneously a blindness and became unable to read. When the blindness was corrected by suggestion and the letter again presented to the subject, the blindness returned, and it finally became necessary to discontinue the attempt.

Some weeks later the roommate, again under instruction from the experimenter, remarked to the subject, "I just got a letter from my girl that I want you to read." The subject replied, "I would like to. It's a funny thing, but for a long time I have wanted to read your mail. I don't know why. I've just had an awfully strong urge and it has disturbed me a lot, and I will be glad to do it and get that urge out of my system." He then read the letter, of which fact the experimenter was notified by the roommate. On the occasion of the next trance the subject was asked the general question about having read his roommate's mail. He stated that he had done so one day in the waking state *at the roommate's but not at the experimenter's request*. He was then questioned extensively for the content of the letter, but he was found unable to remember any of it. When it was suggested that he reread the letter, he agreed, but demanded insistently the privilege of asking his roommate's permission first, nor would he consent to reread the letter unless this concession were made.

Comment: Despite a hypnotic technique of suggestion sufficient to hold an offensive task before the subject for a period of months, an exceedingly plausible and acceptable justification, and obviously worthy motives, the entire attempt was so complete a failure that he could not be induced hypnotically to repeat the waking performance authorized in a socially acceptable manner except under the precise conditions of that waking performance. Yet extensive knowledge of him disclosed him to be no more conventional than the average college student.

Acceptance of Complexes Implying Misdeeds Against Others

Account 24: Before presenting the material of the next four experiments, which have been briefly reported in a study of the induction or implantation of artificial complexes, (Huston, Shakow & Erickson, 1934) a preliminary explanation may be offered. These four experiments centered around the procedure of causing hypnotic subjects to believe that they had already committed an objectionable act. While developing an adequate technique of suggestion for this complex implantation, it was discovered that, to be effective, that is, to elicit genuine rather than realistic responses, the complex had to be about an act supposedly already accomplished in the relatively remote past only, and all attempts to build up a complex about some unfortunate act that they would inevitably perform in the future failed. Each explained, when the latter type of suggestions was attempted, that they could not conceive of the possibility of doing such a thing in the future. Yet these same subjects, told they had actually done the same thing in the past, could be induced to accept the suggestion and would then respond in a highly significant fashion, as has been reported in the experiment mentioned above. The significance of these findings in relationship to the suggestion of criminalistic behavior to hypnotic subjects is at once apparent.

Another consideration of equal importance is the fact that *the subject must necessarily have a waking amnesia for the complex material*. Conscious recollection of the story, unless so vague, incomplete, and inadequate as to render it meaningless, will effect a complete understanding and a rejection of it. Attempts to induce a belief in a complex at both waking and hypnotic levels of awareness invariably lead to a complete and resentful rejection of the complex story. The outcome of a conscious recollection is illustrated fully in *The Study of an Experimental Neurosis Hypnotically Induced in a Case of Ejaculatio Praecox,"* (Erickson, 1935) in which the subject first recalled the complex as a reality experience and then immediately recognized its nature, nullifying completely its reality. Hence, *although subjects may be induced to believe that they committed some reproachable act, they must not be allowed to become consciously aware of this belief. Its acceptance as a truth apparently depends upon its remoteness from the possibility of conscious examination, and its effect upon the personality is comparable to that of repressed experiences.*

Since the four experiments were all of the same general character, they will be presented as a single account.

Subject A was given a complex centering around the belief that he had accidentally burned a hole in a girl's dress through carelessness in smoking. He accepted the complex, reacted strongly to it, complained the next day of a severe headache, quit smoking, gave away his cigarettes, and was hostile and resentful toward the experimenter and uncooperative in regard to future hypnosis. Rapport was reestablished with difficulty, and thereafter for some months, despite the removal of the complex and the giving of insight, he was unwilling to act as a hypnotic subject unless convinced of the value of the scientific purposes to be served.

Subjects B and C were separately given complexes to the effect that in their eagerness as medical internes to learn the technique of the cisterna puncture they had inadvertently caused a patient's death, which they failed to report. Both accepted the complex in part but rejected certain points for various plausible reasons, and their exposition of these was then followed by a complete rejection of the complex. Both reacted with intense resentment toward the experimenter, although friendly feelings were reestablished when they were acquainted fully with the experiment. Also, both then expressed regret about failing to meet the experimenter's purposes by their rejection of the complex. Nevertheless, when another attempt was made later to induce in them a second complex centering about a culpable act, both rejected it unconditionally with essentially the same succession of events as occurred in relation to the first complex. Of particular interest is the fact that one of these subjects was used in the experiment in Account 2 above. Apparently his intense curiosity did not extend to this type of painful experience.

Subjects D and E, occupational therapists, were given complexes to the effect that they had, through carelessness not in itself seriously culpable, been directly responsible for a serious injury to a patient. Both accepted the complex, reacted with great intensity to it, became markedly hostile and resentful toward the experimenter, but cooperated with him in the trance state because of his secret knowledge of their supposed misdoing. After the complex had been removed and insight given, both demanded that no further experiments of that nature be done on them, and thereafter they tended to scrutinize closely any suggestions given them in the trance state.

Subject F, a nurse, was given a complex to the effect that she had inadvertently applied the wrong medication to a patient's wound with serious results. When an attempt was made to describe the extent of the unfortunate consequences, it was found necessary to minimize them somewhat if the subject were to be induced to accept the complex. Later, after the complex had been removed and an understanding of the situation had been given, the nurse explained spontaneously that her acceptance of the complex had actually been based upon a somewhat similar mistake nearly committed during her course of training, and she remarked that the experimenter had been fortunate in seizing upon something that could be directly related to a real incident of her past, since otherwise she could not conceive of ever having been so careless.

Comment: The fact that such complexes as the above could be induced only in relationship to the past is highly significant in itself. *Apparently it is easier to conceive of oneself having already done wrong than to consider the possibility of committing a wrong in the future*. An indirect criterion of the validity of the experiment is to be found in the account of Subjects B and C, who, even after being acquainted fully with the experimental nature of the procedure, rejected unconditionally the second complex.

Finally these experiments serve to demonstrate that while there is a good possibility of making hypnotic subjects believe—in the trance state only and not in the waking state—that they have done an objectionable act, they cannot be induced to believe that they will do such an act.

Offenses Against the Property of Others

Damage, Destruction, or Loss

Account 25: It was suggested to a subject that a practical joke could be played on a certain unpopular girl who was highly critical of the habit of smoking and who professed falsely never to smoke. The joke as outlined was to the effect that the subject should light a cigarette and then, watching her opportunity, pick up a handkerchief which the disliked girl had on her desk and crumple the cigarette in it, so that those aware of the joke could discover it and accuse that girl of smoking secretly and of being surprised in the act and driven to conceal the evidence in this manner.

Adequate arrangements were made secretly with the proposed victim to permit a favorable situation for the perpetration of the joke. However, when the time came to act, the subject refused, declared that it was unfair and wrong to destroy that girl's handkerchief by burning it, even though the girl was a liar, and argued that there must and would have to be a better way to carry out the joke. No amount of urging could induce the subject to accede to the proposal, but she was entirely willing that the experimenter perform the act. Even so she could not be induced to encourage the experimenter or anyone else in such a performance.

Account 26: A subject employed as a stenographer was typing the final copy

Possible Antisocial Use

of a colleague's paper, a task which she had been instructed by her superiors to complete at a specified hour. While so engaged, the subject was hypnotized, and a great variety of suggestions was given her to compel her to type inaccurately and to make a poor copy, with the excuse offered that the poor quality of her work could be accounted for by haste and overanxiety. These suggestions failed, and she could not be induced to do anything of a destructive character despite the fact that she knew the experimenter could and would, by virtue of his official position, protect her from any possible consequences. The only results of the suggestions were a temporary decrease of her speed in typing and a general increase in the care with which she worked.

Account 27: A subject was instructed to destroy or throw away certain important papers lying at hand on the desk of a disliked superior. All circumstances were arranged to make the general situation entirely favorable for the performance. Despite repeated and insistent efforts all suggestions were rejected, although there was no objection to the experimenter's offer to do the task.

Account 28: The subject was instructed to abstract from a colleague's desk certain important papers and to mislay them in some inaccessible place, thereby causing serious inconvenience to their owner. Despite insistence and emphatic suggestion the proposal was rejected. Posthypnotic suggestions were given to the effect that later in the day, while securing legitimately from that desk certain other papers, there would be an accidental and unnoticed picking up of those documents. Thus in an absentminded way there could be an actual and guiltless mislaying of the papers.

There resulted only an obedience to the first part of the posthypnotic suggestion—namely, securing and filing away the proper documents, but the others, while picked up at the same time, were promptly sorted out and returned.

Comment: In the four above accounts various factors of justification for the performance, the existence of adequate protection, a degree of willingness to do the suggested act at a waking level, and in Accounts 26 and 28 the possibility for total exculpation on the basis of accident, all failed completely to permit a performance of the suggested acts.

Inducing Subjects to Commit Thefts

Account 29: A subject was presented with a specious argument about the possibility of developing marked finger dexterity as the result of hypnotic suggestion, and it was proposed to use him for that purpose, to which he readily consented. It was then suggested that he pick his roommate's pockets, and long, detailed instructions and careful practice were given him, particularly about how to stand, how to distract his intended victim's attention, and how to rely upon his own subconscious understandings of dexterity to pick pockets unnoticeably.

The subject objected most strenuously to the entire plan but finally yielded to the specious arguments offered him. On the selected occasion, with provision made for the distraction of the roommate's attention through his close examination of an attention-compelling object, the experimenter and the subject crowded against the victim closely, jostling him in an apparent eagerness to join in the examination. As this was done the subject proceeded with the pocket-picking, but did it so crudely and so roughly that it was impossible for the victim, who was fully aware of the situation, to avoid noticing what was occurring.

Nevertheless the subject insisted that he had performed the act gently and delicately, and nothing could convince him that he had been rough and forceful in all of his movements. Similar results were obtained upon repetition with this subject, despite his realization then that it was an experimental situation.

Similar findings were made with other subjects, among whom was one whose favorite practical poke was picking the pockets of his friends and distributing his loot among the pockets of the group, and then, by some clever subterfuge, causing a discovery of the trick. In the trance state he declared an entire willingness to do this when awake, since then he "would know everything going on," but he flatly refused to do it as a trance performance, since he would be out of contact with his environment and since it would not be a joke but a highly questionable performance carried on at the behest of another.

Comment: The apparent acceptance of the suggestions for pocket-picking was made entirely meaningless by the character of the performer, and the persistence in this type of performance, even after the nature of the act had been revealed, disclosed that the unconventional aspect alone of the misdeed was sufficient to preclude a satisfactory execution. Likewise the attitude of the jokester makes clear the sense of limitation that hypnotized subjects feel in relation to their environment. Also there is an adequate demonstration of the ability of the hypnotized subject to recognize readily the entirely different significations of a performance when executed as a prank and when done as an act of simple obedience.

Account 30: During a casual visit a subject, displaying his empty package, asked the experimenter for a cigarette. The experimenter apologized for not having any, induced a deep trance, and suggested that the subject purloin from the adjacent office a package of cigarettes habitually left on the desk, since the owner would have no real objection. Thus both he and the experimenter could enjoy a smoke, and the whole situation could then be forgotten. The subject expressed entire willingness to do this if confession might be made to the owner of the cigarettes. When this concession was refused, the subject rejected all the suggestions, even though the experimenter offered to replace the cigarettes with a full package later.

Subsequently, while the subject was in the waking state, in response to his original request for a cigarette it was suggested that he might, as a joke, purloin cigarettes from that same office. To this the subject consented readily, went to that office, and secured two cigarettes, one of which he gave to the experimenter with marked insistence that it be smoked while he smoked the other. Later it was found that the subject made full confession of his act to the owner of the cigarettes.

Comment: An act, not entirely acceptable in the waking state, as shown by the insistence upon inculpating the experimenter and the making of amends, was found completely unacceptable in the trance state, despite the knowledge that restitution would be made.

Account 31: A poverty-stricken college student was instructed repeatedly in a series of trances extending over a period of weeks to purloin small sums of money left lying carelessly about by his roommate, with whom secret arrangements had been made. Elaborate suggestions and rationalizations were employed, but always without avail. Yet on the occasion of each new trance state, although invariably he pleaded to be excused from the task, he could be induced to renew his previous promises to obey. Finally it became necessary to discontinue the experiment because the subject's intense resentments were effecting a breakdown of the profound amnesias for the trance experiences, which had been established by the experimenter both as a measure of promoting the suggested act and as a means of preventing the subject from discovering the purposes of the repeated hypnotic trances.

Subsequently it was learned that during the course of the experiment the subject had made numerous vague inquiries among the experimenter's colleagues concerning the experimenter's character, for which conduct he could give no reason at the time. When later the subject was given an account of the experimental procedure, he was very much relieved, protested that the experimenter should have known that hypnosis could not be used to make a thief of anybody, and declared that he could now understand his past "peculiar unhappy feelings about you" which had distressed him greatly at the time and which had caused him to seek reassurance about the experimenter's character.

Comment: Apparently, in attempting to induce felonious behavior by hypnosis, the danger lies not in the possibility of success but in the risk to the hypnotist himself. What might have happened had an adverse opinion been given of the experimenter is interesting only to speculate upon, since general knowledge of hypnotic reactions suggests that an unfavorable statement would have served to abrogate the suggestions for an amnesia of the trance events. The probability of this will be shown in Accounts 34 and 35.

Experiments Involving the Direct Abuse by the Hypnotist of the Subject's Confidence

Account 32: A subject was induced by careful suggestion to believe as the truth a statement originally known by the subject to be false. The outcome was a firm and effective expression of belief in its veracity in subsequent trance states, but a full recognition of its falsity in the waking state. All action on the statement was limited to the waking state, since during hypnosis the burden of any action was shifted upon the experimenter. Efforts made to have the conviction of truth carry over into the waking state failed, apparently because there had to be a meeting of conscious objections to the statement at the level of conscious awareness.

Comment: Yet the "poisoning of the mind" by subtle lies in the ordinary waking state will lead to the development of complete belief, both conscious and unconscious. Apparently the time and situational limitations of the trance state serve to preclude a similar development of belief for both the hypnotic and the waking levels of awareness.

Account 33: Another subject was carefully given malicious misinformation about an acquaintance, and this was systematically and convincingly confirmed by the experimenter's colleagues. There resulted in the waking state the development of a definite attitude of dislike, distrust, and avoidance, coupled with a marked alertness and an intense interest and curiosity on the part of the subject concerning that acquaintance. Within a few days, however, the subject complained to the experimenter of having felt vaguely but distressingly uncomfortable for some unknown reason since the occasion of the last hypnotic session, and demand was made of rehypnotizing as a measure of relief. This request was granted, but an attempt was made to evade the issue. The subject, however, demanded that a full waking recollection be given of the communications of the previous trance, explaining only that "it just has to be done."

When this was finally done, the subject reacted in a relieved but bewildered way, finally declaring, "Well, if that's true, and they all said it was, why did you have to tell me when I was asleep? Even if they did say it was true, I don't believe it. I can't believe it. I'd have to find out for myself, and just telling me when I'm asleep wouldn't make me believe it. You'd have to tell me when I'm awake so I would know it. You can't believe a thing if you don't know it, and you told me when I was asleep so I wouldn't know it. If you want me to believe a thing, you will have to tell me so I'll know it when I'm awake and not just when I'm asleep. If it is true, I'll find out about it and then I'll believe it, but this way, why it's no more than a nasty story. What were you trying to do?"

A full statement and proof of the victim's awareness of the experiment clarified the situation, and subsequent hypnotic work met with no difficulty, the subject accounting for this on the grounds that the whole experience had been merely unpleasant and of no importance except scientifically, and that there had never been any credence to the story.

Comment: Apparently, to judge from the subject's remarks, such a communication as the above to a subject in the trance state lacks some attribute or quality of reality essential for credence. Despite the acceptance of the story in the state of hypnotic submissiveness the failure of the inclusion in such acceptance of processes of conscious awareness and of conscious responses to the information deprived the story of any significant credence value.

Account 34: A second subject, utilized for a repetition of the above experiment, showed essentially the same course of behavior, with the exception that no direct requests were made for a second trance. Instead frequent, apparently purposeless visits were made to the experimenter's office, with vague, hesitant complaints offered about feeling generally depressed and unhappy, all of which were received with casual indifference which led finally to a rather sudden resentful departure by the subject.

About an hour later the subject burst into the office in a violent rage, and a most difficult situation followed. In the period of time after leaving the office there had developed slowly and then with increasing rapidity a full, spontaneous recollection of the events of the trance session, a critical review of the entire situation and of the misinformation given, a complete repudiation of its veracity, and the development of an intense anger toward the experimenter and everybody concerned. Finally, however, the exhibition of the experimental protocol and of the observations that had been recorded, and proof of the victim's awareness, served to effect a satisfactory adjustment, probably aided by the subject's own scientific training and intense interest in clinical psychology and hypnosis.

In reviewing the whole experience a few days later, this subject offered essentially the same explanations as had been given by the first subject. In addition the intensity of the angry outburst was explained as the reaction to the experimenter's violation of the hypnotist-subject relationship occasioned by his seeming indifference to the vague complaints of distress and by his virtual refusal to meet his responsibilities in a situation where all responsibility belonged entirely to him. As in the first case no difficulties were encountered in further hypnotic work with the subject.

Comment: In addition to confirming the findings of the preceding experiment, this account is particularly informative in relationship to the general futility of this type of attempted misuse of hypnosis and to the seriousness of the risk encountered by the hypnotist in such attempts. Also the outcome suggests what might have occurred if the experiment on theft in Account 31 had not been interrupted.

Account 35: One actual instance of intentionally unscrupulous use of hypnosis concerns a hypnotic subject employed in some laboratory experimentation by Mr. Blank, a capable hypnotist generally regarded as of somewhat questionable character and who was known to dislike the author intensely. Over a period of weeks this subject manifested increasingly marked avoidance reactions toward the author, with whom there existed a casual acquaintance. After about a month of such behavior the subject suddenly entered the author's office, rudely demanded attention, and burst into a tirade of, "I don't like you, I hate you, I despise you, I've got no respect for you, I can't stand the sight of you, and I don't know why. That's why I've come here. I want to find out. I want you to hypnotize me, and when I'm in a trance, I want you to ask me so that I can tell you. It may not be important to you, but it is to me, and I want to know what it's all about."

Attempts to question him in the waking state elicited only the sullen, insistent reply that he did not come to bandy words, that he came to be hypnotized so that he could find out something. *However, he did add that he had never done or said anything against the author and that nobody else knew how he felt.* He explained further that he was a well-trained subject and that he was certain he would go easily into a satisfactory trance.

Taking him at his word, the author induced a deep trance easily, recapitulated the remarks that had been made upon entering the office, and suggested that perhaps he could now know what he wished. The subject proceeded at once to tell a long, detailed story about how Blank, in almost daily hypnotic sessions over a period of two months, had subjected him to an endless recital of innuendoes, veiled remarks, and subtle suggestions discrediting the author. He explained that while he believed none of the remarks, he had found the situation increasingly intolerable, and that it had now become imperative to escape from it. Just how he might do this he did not know, since he did not wish to disrupt Blank's experimental work, which he believed to be excellent, as was actually the case. He then suggested that it might help to give him a full conscious recollection of these matters, since Blank always gave him insistent instructions never to remember consciously any of his trance experiences, with the explanation that such memories, whatever they might be, might interfere with the experimental work, even though it was purely physiological in character.

The subject's suggestion was accepted and acted upon, with a complete readjustment of his attitude toward the author and an intense anger toward Blank, but so adequately controlled was that anger that Blank's experimental findings on him continued to agree with those on other subjects. Upon the completion of that work the subject refused to do any further work with Blank. Subsequently he explained that after his trance with the author he had continued to have a full, conscious recollection of all those events of his trances with Blank not connected with the experiment, and that in this way he promptly "washed them out" immediately upon awakening.

On a later occasion another of Blank's subjects was hypnotized by the author, and inquiry disclosed that a similar attempt had been made upon him, but that his reaction had been, "But I knew you and I liked you, so I didn't pay any attention to what he said, and when he kept on I just told him that I liked you and that you were a friend of mine, and so he shut up."

Comment: Here there is an actual unscrupulous attempt to misuse hypnosis, and yet, despite the extreme care with which it was carried on, it led to results unfavorable only to the hypnotist himself, without causing sufficient disruption of the subject's personality reactions to interfere with the legitimate hypnotic work being done with him by the unscrupulous hypnotist. The adequacy and the effectiveness of the protective measures employed by the subject, who was apparently susceptible to such abuse, is striking.

SUMMARY AND CONCLUSION

To summarize this investigation one may state briefly that a great variety of experimental procedures was employed upon a large number of well-trained hypnotic subjects to induce them, in trance states or in response to commands and suggestions given during trance states, to perform acts of an unconventional, harmful, antisocial, and even criminal nature, these acts to involve aggressions against both the self and others, as well as to permit direct abuse of the hypnotic subject by the hypnotist. Every effort was made to meet the need for control investigations covering the possibilities of waking behavior, for realism in the experimental situation, and for adequate and varied techniques of hypnotic suggestion. The findings disclosed consistently the failure of all experimental measures to induce hypnotic subjects, in response to hypnotic suggestion, to perform acts of an objectionable character, even though many of the suggested acts were acceptable to them under circumstances of waking consciousness. Instead of blind, submissive, automatic, unthinking obedience and acquiescence to the hypnotist and the acceptance of carefully given suggestions and commands, the subjects demonstrated a full capacity and ability for self-protection, ready and complete understanding with critical judgment, avoidance, evasion, or complete rejection of commands, resentment and objection to instrumentalization by the hypnotist, and for aggression and retaliation, direct and immediate, against the hypnotist for his objectionable suggestions and commands. In addition many demonstrated a full capacity to take over control of the hypnotic situation and actually did so by compelling the experimenter to make amends for his unacceptable suggestions.

Had the above experiments been conducted as obviously experimental investigations, it is entirely possible that the subjects would have given realistic performances in such protected situations, but under those conditions the outcome would not have been a function of the hypnosis itself but of the general situation. In that type of setting one might deceive a subject into performing some objectionable act, but the deception would not be dependent upon the hypnosis. Rather it would depend upon entirely different factors, and the hypnosis, as shown repeatedly above, could easily constitute an actual obstacle to a deception based upon other factors.

Hence the conclusion warranted by these experimental findings is that hypnosis cannot be misused to induce hypnotized persons to commit actual wrongful acts against either themselves or others, and that the only serious risk encountered in such attempts is incurred by the hypnotists in the form of condemnation, rejection, and exposure.

26. An Instance of Potentially Harmful Misinterpretation of Hypnosis

Milton H. Erickson

This account is an addendum to "One Aspect of Legal Implication Involved During the Use of Hypnosis," published in this issue of the JOURNAL by Lawrence M. Staples, D.M.D. It is only one of many such instances of misinterpretation; it is presented because of its timeliness and the simplicity of its development.

In the spring of 1960 a college student demonstrated hypnosis for purposes of entertainment. He first attempted to hypnotize Mrs. A., a young married woman with several children. Mrs. A. declared repeatedly that he could not hypnotize her and that she was "not smart enough" to be hypnotized. The student, after two unsuccessful attempts on Mrs. A., tried another member of the group, succeeded, and demonstrated elaborately the phenomenon of regression. As he did this, he explained mistakenly that he would have to be careful to remember every step of the procedure, since otherwise his subject might remain permanently in a state of childhood. Later Mrs. A. gave an account of this occurrence to her friend Mrs. B.

Several months later Mrs. B's young son underwent hypnosis satisfactorily during dental work. In discussing hypnosis, the dentist stressed that it should be used only in the field of one's competence, it should not be used as a means of entertainment, and it was seriously wrong to "toy" with it.

Another three months passed uneventfully, and then Mrs. A. developed a sudden, severe "nervous breakdown," requiring extensive psychiatric aid. This breakdown was not regarded as very remarkable, since Mrs. A. was known to have a most traumatic history. She had lost her mother at an early age, had been reared in various foster homes, some of which had rejected her, had always felt rejected and unloved, and she had a long history of unpredictable temper tantrums. She also felt that she had never had any happiness until after her marriage.

About a month after Mrs. A's illness Mrs. B, in sympathetic wonderment about the nature of mental illness, recalled some lay discussion of Mrs. A's symptoms. As she reviewed this, she became impressed by a similarity between

---

Reprinted with permission from *The American Journal of Clinical Hypnosis*, April, 1961, *3*, 242-243.

the patient's helpless psychotic behavior and delusional statements, quite characteristic of an acute catatonic schizophrenic episode, and her own memories of Mrs. A's account of the hypnotic regression at that parlor entertainment. She reasoned that Mrs. B, despite her assertions to the contrary at the time of the occurrence, had been inadvertently hypnotized and regressed simultaneously with the other subject and that this effect in some way had lain dormant, only to appear unexpectedly as a "nervous breakdown" many months later.

She was convinced that she was on the trail of vital information pertinent to Mrs. A's recovery, but fortunately and wisely she consulted the dentist who had used hypnosis on her son and who had emphasized that it was "seriously wrong to toy" with hypnosis or to use it for entertainment.

The dentist, avowing his lack of competence in psychiatry, referred the matter to this writer for psychiatric evaluation.

This is another instance demonstrating that good intentions, based upon a lack of knowledge, non sequitur, and post hoc propter hoc reasoning could have led to harm for all concerned, had not the dentist been sufficiently well-informed to be able to interrupt the growing body of misinformation and misunderstandings deriving from Mrs. B's assiduous, earnest efforts to be helpful.

From those misunderstandings, though they were based upon an uninformed effort to be of service, irreparable harm could have come to the three families involved in that parlor trick, unwarranted blame could have been heaped upon that student, and the use of scientific hypnosis by reputable professional men could have been made questionable in the eyes of the public.

It is sufficient misfortune that the patient has a long traumatic history and a recognizable psychosis without obscuring these matters by misinterpretations. It is most desirable that her condition be understood by her relatives and by her community in the best possible psychiatric terms and not in the terms of uninformed, misleading post hoc thinking, so destructive to scientific knowledge.

27. Stage Hypnotist Back Syndrome

Milton H. Erickson

During the past 14 years this author has encountered approximately a score of patients, both male and female, and all under the age of 30, who were found to have in common two special items of experience. The first of these was a history of having been a volunteer subject for a stage hypnotist who demonstrated total body catalepsy to his audience by suspending his subject's rigid body between two chairs or similar supports and placing heavy weights upon the subject's rigid abdomen.

The second item was a complaint of a long-continued backache which was difficult to describe and which had puzzled the attending physician because of its vague origin and peculiar symptomatology and which had not been satisfactorily amenable to treatment.

In questioning these patients for their medical history the time interval between the stage hypnosis and the backache was found in each instance to range between five and seven months. None of the patients had made a spontaneous association between the stage hypnosis and the backache and no such suggestion was offered them, since they were already patients seeking psychotherapy for other reasons. However, adequate warnings against stage hypnotists were given, and these were readily, in some instances eagerly, accepted.

The onset of the backache tended to occur in two ways. For a lesser number of patients the onset was insidious and was well described by one patient as, "It just seemed to creep up on me until it was so bad I couldn't help noticing it, and then it really bothered me a whole lot." But the greater number of patients related its onset to a state of muscular effort of previously innocuous history. Thus one patient felt that "Something must have gone wrong with my regular push-up exercises and wrenched my back, but I didn't notice it right then." Another thought that he had probably held his back too rigidly in his golf putting practice. Another spoke of a possible strain on his back from his regular diving practice. Several women attributed it to the weight of advancing pregnancy. One explained it as a result of, "My whole body freezing stiff and paralyzed when I saw that automobile accident." In no instance was a reasonably adequate causation described that could be readily accepted.

Reprinted with permission from *The American Journal of Clinical Hypnosis*, October, 1962, 5, 141-142.

Despite their divergences of personality and background these patients tended to describe their complaints in remarkably comparable terms. These various descriptions can be best summarized by typical quotations most clearly describing the salient symptoms described by all of the patients:

> 1. "Your back feels awful sore all over, but you just can't lay a finger on just how it hurts or just where; there are a lot of pin pricks in the bones here and there that come and go."
> 2. "You get a soreness in your neck and across the top of your shoulders that you can feel, all right, but you can't show the doctor just where." (However, several of the patients definitely indicated that their complaint had been accompanied by a painful condition of the tips of the spinous processes of the upper vertebrae.)
> 3. "Where your ribs join your backbone, they feel as if they are being pulled off, especially the bottom ribs."
> 4. "Your breathing seems hard to do, but there doesn't seem to be anything stopping you. You just feel that way."
> 5. "That pain in your back makes you feel afraid to move and you hold yourself stiffer, and that makes the pain worse but you are still afraid to move."
> 6. "It more or less lays you up if you can't stand pain, or you take a lot of pain killer and sleeping pills, and after about three months it gradually goes away."

The medical treatment accorded these patients included a great variety of medications and procedures including body casts and traction. The effective agent, however, appeared to be the natural healing processes of the body aided by the passage of time.

The first few cases of this condition seen by the author were not fully appreciated and hence were not fully questioned. All the others included in this report were patients who reported in detail upon a past disability. Three patients who came to the author in the early stages of their condition were sent to orthopedists for a preliminary examination, but they did not return because of a warning by the orthopedists against the use of hypnosis by a psychiatrist.

This account is given not as a definitive report but as a measure of interesting others who may be in a better medical position than is a psychiatrist to investigate more searchingly certain obscure types of backache of apparently unknown causation and to publicize the possibility of a traumatic condition meriting the designation of Stage Hypnotist Back Syndrome.

This author does not undertake in anyway to explain this condition as described to him. It seems unreasonable that the traumatic results should be five to seven months in becoming manifest. However, the patient's psychological welfare was regarded as more important than research into the details of a past experience that might lead to the development of new fears and anxieties. Hence the patients were given no opportunity to develop new neurotic concerns by associating back pain history with what were regarded by the patients as no more than silly and somewhat shameful exhibitionistic incidents. More detailed research can be done on acute cases much more effectively and with much better opportunity for more informative findings.

28. Editorial

Milton H. Erickson

The Editor, because of his well-known interest in hypnosis, has received over the years a wealth of telephone calls and office visits in the guise of consultations, but which have been actually efforts to secure aid and instruction by laymen in the hope of exploiting the public through their use of hypnosis. Nor is the Editor the only person upon whom these unscrupulous and ill-informed laymen have endeavored to impose their selfish desires, since many colleagues have reported similar instances of solicitation.

Recently a lay hypnotist telephoned and insistently demanded information over the telephone, seeking instructions in some new technique he might use in an "emergency situation." He impatiently disclosed that he had a high school education, that he had taken instruction in a local lay school of hypnotism, and that he had been taught a technique of hypnosis of the theatrical variety. As a "sideline" he had used that technique to solicit paying clients to "cure" of headaches, backaches, and various bad habits such as overeating and smoking.

His present problem was an emergency. He had told his "client" that her habit of smoking could be cured by hypnosis and that the "cure" would be effective immediately. The client had responded well to the one technique of trance induction which he knew and had accepted his "therapeutic" or "corrective" posthypnotic suggestions that "the thought, mention, or sight of a cigarette would induce convulsive vomiting." He was now urgently asking for telephone instructions for another kind of technique for trance induction because he could no longer induce a trance in his victim, who had been "convulsively vomiting for three days and wanted more help." He refused to give his name or that of his victim, though he did state that two years ago she had been under psychiatric treatment, and that he had obviously picked a self-destructive personality who was so utilizing the situation. Also, he refused to take his victim to a physician for fear of consequences. Instead he insisted that the Editor give him immediately full instructions over the telephone how he "should handle this present emergency" that his lack of medical training and judgment or even common sense had precipitated.

He harshly criticized the Editor's admonitions and concern about his behavior

---

Reprinted with permission from *The American Journal of Clinical Hypnosis*, July, 1964, 7, 1-3.

by declaring that the Editor merely "wanted to cut in on the work of an honest ethical lay hypnotist," and that he was a "qualified hypnotechnician" lacking only a variety of "hypnotic techniques," and he then angrily ended the telephone call.

This instance is comparable to another example of an "ethical lay hypnotechnician" advertising his private practice of psychosomatic medicine in the telephone directory. He undertook the "cure of grinding one's teeth at night," and he gave to his client posthypnotic suggestions that the "grinding" could be stopped easily by placing one's tongue between the teeth and "grinding so hard that a posthypnotic conditioned reflex would be quickly established, thereby abolishing the bad habit."

The victim, a young girl who became severely incapacitated by the wound to her tongue, was advised by the physician who treated the injury to sue the man for the practice of medicine and dentistry without a license. Unfortunately she told the charlatan of her intentions, and he left town for parts unknown. The results were that a physician was made greatly antagonistic toward hypnosis, a girl had been victimized, hypnosis had been given a bad name, and the "ethical lay hypnotechnician," so styled in his advertisement, probably continued his "ethical hypnotechnician" practice of medicine and dentistry on other victims elsewhere. This full account was obtained and verified when the girl, a compulsive hysterical type, became the Editor's patient.

Innumerable telephone calls have been received from charlatans describing themselves as "ethical lay hypnotists," and numerous other unqualified persons have presented themselves for specialized training so that they could illegitimately advertise their practice of medicine and psychiatry by means of cautiously worded statements in the classified advertisements of the telephone directory, and, if possible, including the name of some reputable physician in the advertisement. Indeed, the trademark of the charlatan is his name-dropping in his self-glorifying advertisements, especially those sent through the mail.

Numerous colleagues of the Editor have cited to him similar experiences. This state of affairs is a serious danger to the public caused by misinformation and lack of information. Many hospitals and county and state medical societies forbid qualified medical men, competent and fully trained, to do correctly the very thing that the unlicensed, uninformed charlatan does badly and wrongly with glowing, convincing promises to the public.

One need only consult the classified telephone directories of cities throughout the country to realize that the medical profession is assisting this new crop of pseudomedical victimizers of the general public by all too often shutting its eyes to hypnosis as a legitimate adjunct to the healing arts which should be understood by all members of the medical profession. As the situation now stands, the public, seeking intelligent advice, is led to go to charlatans for medical help that properly should be entirely within the province of the professional person trained in the healing arts.

An example of how ignorance of hypnosis leads to mistakes by members of the medical profession in this encouragement of lay hypnotists is the invitation from a midwestern state medical association to a charlatan holding a mail order degree from an Indiana diploma mill to address the State Medical Association at its annual meeting. He received an honorarium for this "service," delivering his address in a city where "qualified ethical hypnotechnicians" claim a group membership of 200 "engaged in the professional practice of the treatment and cure of migraine, backaches, headaches, alcoholism, smoking, emphysema, obesity, colitis, etc." (Incidentally the Editor, by means of sending semi-illiterate letters of inquiry written with pencil and ruled tablet paper under various names, has received a wealth of information and invitations from various such organizations to take courses and to become a "certified hypnotechnician," a "qualified lay hypnotist trained to assist physicians and dentists in their professional work, and to treat cases referred for therapy," to be "a trained ethical lay hypnotist prepared to treat various body and mind disturbances," etc. The lack of education evidenced by the laborious penciled script, the ruled tablet paper, the misspellings and erasures, were no barrier to invitations to take courses leading to "certification as a trained ethical lay hypnotist qualified to practice hypnosis in disturbances of mind and body.")

Another example is that of an eastern medical school presenting a postgraduate program which included in its panel of speakers a state certified "psychologist" whose university record shows only 30 hours of scattered psychological courses. The state issuing his certification declares that a doctoral degree in psychology is officially requisite for certification, but the unfortunate loophole of a "grandfather clause" has allowed the certification of actually unqualified persons.

Still another example is the dental school which was officially advised to cancel a scheduled course on hypnosis to be taught by a faculty which included two psychiatrists, one a diplomate of the American Board of Psychiatry and Neurology and a Fellow of the American Psychological Association, the other a holder of a Ph.D. degree in psychology in addition to memberships in the American Psychiatric and Psychological Associations, as well as certified internists, obstetricians, anaesthesiologists, psychologists, and dentists, the ostensible reason being that such a course should be given only under the auspices of the psychiatric department in a medical school. At the same time that this course in an accredited dental school was being opposed by an officially appointed central medical committee, the legislature of another state, lobbied by lay hypnotists, was passing a law permitting the medical use of hypnosis by lay hypnotists, this action being unimpeded by any official medical groups.

All of the above is in marked contrast to the constructive and responsible action of one Canadian medical association, which invited the same charlatan as had the midwestern state society to address their annual meeting, encouraged to do so by the apparent endorsement of him by the previous invitation to lecture in the U.S. at a state annual medical meeting, a fact well exploited in the charlatan's advertisements.

Fortunately, because of proper legislation in that area, the Canadian society investigated the charlatan's credentials upon his arrival and firmly ejected him from the country for fraudulent misrepresentation, replacing him on the program by a properly trained and experienced medical professional.

Unfortunately both the American Medical Association and the American Psychiatric Association have done much to discourage the use of scientific hypnosis by medically competent people who have already demonstrated adequately their abilities to deal well and successfully with patients of all kinds under conditions of all manner of stress and strain. And the telephone directories of the homes of these associations, namely Chicago and Washington, D.C., have extensive classified advertising listing charlatans who are only too glad to take the place of those professionals who should be utilizing hypnosis properly. Medical practitioners are losers, the public suffers, as does science itself. No one profits but the unscrupulous exploiter.

One can only regret that throughout the history of science, medical and otherwise, there have been all too many obstacles thrown in the way of scientific advancement by those who should properly have promoted it, and a handicapping of such advancement by those who prey upon human weakness and ignorance.

29. Editorial

Milton H. Erickson

The Editor in his practice of psychotherapy is governed by his own conception of what constitutes effective psychotherapy. He is also well acquainted with the many and varying schools of thought concerning methodologies of psychotherapy. He is well aware of a great variety of ways and means by which a patient may be dealt with, manipulated, proselytized, reeducated, reconditioned, and otherwise led into a more constructive way of living than that which has led him to seek assistance. To the Editor, the leading of the patient into this more satisfying method of living and of expressing the self is a rightful goal greatly to be desired. The means by which this may be best accomplished is a matter of concern and interest to all students of psychotherapeutic procedures.

The achievement of the goal, while primary, is not the only consideration. Also worthy of evaluation, planning, and thought by the therapist are the matters of time spent, of effective utilization of effort, and above all of the fullest possible utilization of the functional capacities and abilities and the experiential and acquisitional learnings of the patient. These should take precedence over the teaching of new ways of living which are developed from the therapist's possible incomplete understandings of what may be right and serviceable to the individual concerned. Most distressing to the Editor is the type of therapist who will state arbitrarily, "You will need to be in therapy X days a week for three years before you can consider yourself sufficiently well-adjusted to meet the ordinary demands of your life situation." To the Editor such a statement is on a par with that of a lay hypnotist who may blithely promise a completely remade life in 10 easy lessons. Neither of these would-be therapists takes into consideration the individuality of the patients, their own particular learning capacities, and their abilities to execute and to elaborate understandings. No regard is given to the roles of emotions in a patient's pattern of functioning except in terms of formalized constructions.

For example a brilliant young psychiatric resident, concerned with his anxieties about his actual rheumatic heart disease, separately approached two outstanding men who were widely known as representing a certain school of

---

Reprinted with permission from *The American Journal of Clinical Hypnosis*, July, 1965, *8*, 1-2.

psychotherapy. He recounted his misgivings concerning this emotional reaction to his concern about his cardiac condition, his interest in rearing a family, and the concern he felt about his bride of a year's duration who might run a risk of undertaking the support of a child should one be born to them and should he be prevented from providing for this possible child. The wife was a college graduate.

Both therapists assured him that he needed not less than six years' intensive psychotherapy as would his wife also (she had not yet been interviewed) before the problems of family life could ever be considered. Both accepted this advice; the man took an exacting institutional job to pay for his therapy, the wife accepted a teaching position to pay for hers. Six years later, by accident, a child was born to them, causing dismay, increased financial hardship, and a resulting intensification of therapy. Four years later a second child was born, also an accidental conception. As for the promising young psychiatrist, he had become an ardent disciple of his therapist, living, breathing, and thinking solely in terms of his therapist's teachings. Now at long last, after more than 10 years, he has become independent of his weekly multiple visits to the therapist's office. But instead of genuinely practicing psychiatry or psychotherapy, this once promising young man is only continuing to teach the same precepts that held him in bondage for 10 long years and prevented him from living in a normal life situation. This case is admittedly extreme, yet the proponents of that particular school of thought are arbitrarily and emphatically opposed to any form of psychotherapy for any patient which encompasses less than at least two years' intensive work, regardless of the opinions of other psychiatrists who may agree that brief psychotherapy is all that is requisite for the particular patient concerned. Nor is this the only extreme example that could be cited. Colleagues of the Editor have reported instances comparable to the instance cited.

In such examples the words "psychodynamic orientation" are frequently emphasized in fetishistic style, as if psychodynamic orientation in its true sense were not part and parcel of all interpersonal relationships. Any school of thought which claims sole ownership of "psychodynamic factors" is either blindly or deliberately misrepresenting facts. Yet the word "psychodynamic" has become a symbol, though meaningless, with which to intimidate the unsophisticated, to signify almost mystical values of great and rare importance, and to place a special aura of supremacy upon arbitrarily defined concepts and approaches, with a consequent condemnation of other therapeutic experiences.

To the Editor any contact between two people in which there is an exchange of ideas and understandings is one which is truly *psychodynamic* in character and significance. Such should be the usage of the term, rather than a rigid limitation to one school of therapy.

And in any psychotherapeutic situation, whatever the school of thought which predominates, there must be recognized over and above the formalized structure of thinking, the importance of the patients themselves as sentient beings with needs, capabilities, experiences, and separateness as individuals, with their own background of experiential and acquisitional learning. They are not properly to be squeezed into any ritualistic, traditional method of procedure nor limited by predetermined rules and formulae.

For these reasons, among others, the Editor strongly favors the use of hypnosis as a modality of psychotherapy, since it serves to elicit and to release the actual patterns of behavior and response existing within the patient and available for adequate and useful expression of the personality. Hypnosis does not try to educate the patient into any one of the many arbitrarily regimented schools of interpretative thought that may possibly fit various people but certainly cannot be universal in application. Instead hypnosis is a modality which can elicit with greater than ordinary ease those patterns of behavior, thinking, and feeling more conducive to the welfare of the individual and society than to the promotion of some school of interpretative and speculative theoretical concepts and formulations.

Appendix 1

Future Volumes of *The Collected Papers of Milton H. Erickson on Hypnosis*

VOLUME 2: Hypnotic Alteration of Sensory, Perceptual and Psychophysical Processes

I. *Visual Processes*

Introduction

1. The hypnotic induction of hallucinatory color vision followed by pseudonegative after images. Written with E. M. Erickson, 1938.

2. Discussion: Critical comments on Hibler's presentation of his work on negative afterimages of hypnotically induced hallucinated colors, 1941.

3. The induction of color blindness by a technique of hypnotic suggestion, 1939.

4. An experimental investigation of the hypnotic subject's apparent ability to become unaware of stimuli, 1944.

5. The development of an acute limited obsessional hysterical state in a normal hypnotic subject, 1954.

6. Observations concerning alterations in hypnosis of visual perceptions, 1962.

7. Further observations on hypnotic alteration of visual perception, 1966.

8. An investigation of optokinetic nystagmus, 1962.

9. Acquired control of pupillary responses, 1965.

II. *Auditory Processes*

Introduction

10. A study of clinical and experimental findings on hypnotic deafness: I. Clinical experimentation and findings, 1938.

11. A study of clinical and experimental findings on hypnotic deafness: II. Experimental findings with a conditioned response technique, 1938.

12. Chemo-anaesthesia in relation to hearing and memory, 1963.

13. A field investigation by hypnosis of sound loci importance on human behavior, 1973.

III. *Psychophysiological Processes*

Introduction

14. Hypnotic investigation of psychosomatic phenomena: Psychosomatic interrelationships studied by experimental hypnosis, 1943.

15. The development of aphasia-like reactions from hypnotically induced amnesias. Written with R. M. Brickner, 1943.

16. A controlled experimental use of hypnotic regression in the therapy of an acquired food intolerance, 1943.

17. Experimentally elicited salivary and related responses to hypnotic visual hallucinations confirmed by personality reactions, 1943.

18. Control of physiological functions by hypnosis, 1952-1977.

19. The hypnotic alteration of blood flow: An experiment comparing waking and hypnotic responsiveness. Unpublished manuscript, 1958.

20. A clinical experimental approach to psychogenic infertility. Unpublished manuscript, 1958.

21. Breast development possibly influenced by hypnosis: Two instances and the psychotherapeutic results, 1960.

22. Psychogenic alteration of menstrual functioning: Three instances, 1960.

23. The appearance in three generations of an atypical pattern of the sneezing reflex, 1940.

24. An addendum to a report of the appearance in three generations of an atypical pattern of the sneezing reflex, 1964.

IV. *Time Distortion*

Introduction

25. Time distortion in hypnosis, I. Written by L. F. Cooper, 1948.

26. Time distortion in hypnosis, II. Written with L. F. Cooper, 1950.

27. The clinical and therapeutic applications of time distortion. Written with L. F. Cooper, 1954.

28. Further considerations of time distortion: Subjective time condensation as distinct from time expansion. Written with E. M. Erickson, 1958.

V. *Research Problems*

Introduction

29. Clinical and experimental trance: Definitions and suggestions for their development. Unpublished discussion, circa 1960.

30. Laboratory and clinical hypnosis: The same or different phenomena?, 1967.

31. Explorations in hypnosis research, 1960. With a discussion by T. X. Barber, R. Dorcus, H. Guze, T. Sarbin, and A. Weitzenhoffer.

32. Expectancy and minimal sensory cues in hypnosis. Incomplete report, circa 1960's.

33. Basic psychological problems in hypnotic research, 1962.

34. The experience of interviewing in the presence of observers, 1966.

References

VOLUME 3: The Hypnotic Investigation of Psychodynamic Processes

I. *General and Historical Surveys of Hypnotism*

Introduction

1. A brief survey of hypnotism, 1934.

2. Hypnosis: A general review, 1941.

3. Hypnotism, 1954.

4. The basis of hypnosis: Panel discussion on hypnosis, 1959.

II. *Psychodynamic Processes: Hypnotic Approaches to the Unconscious*

Introduction

Section 1: Amnesia

Introduction

5. The investigation of a specific amnesia, 1933.

6. Development of apparent unconsciousness during hypnotic reliving of a traumatic experience, 1937.

7. Clinical and experimental observations on hypnotic amnesia: Introduction to an unpublished paper, circa 1950's.

8. The problem of amnesia in waking and hypnotic states, circa 1960's.

9. Varieties of hypnotic amnesia. Written with E. L. Rossi, 1974.

Section 2: Literalness

Introduction

10. Literalness: An experimental study. Unpublished manuscript, circa 1950s.

11. Literalness and the use of trance in neurosis. Dialogue with E. L. Rossi, 1973.

Section 3: Age Regression

Introduction

Appendix I

12. Age regression: Two unpublished fragments of a student's study, 1924-1931.

13. On the possible occurrence of a dream in an eight-month-old infant, 1941.

14. The successful treatment of a case of acute hysterical depression by a return under hypnosis to a critical phase of childhood, 1941.

15. Past week-day determination in hypnotic and waking states. Written with Allan Erickson, 1962.

Section 4: Automatic Writing and Drawing

Introduction

16. The experimental demonstration of unconscious mentation by automatic writing, 1937.

17. The use of automatic drawing in the interpretation and relief of a state of acute obsessional depression, 1938.

18. The translation of the cryptic automatic writing of one hypnotic subject by another in a trance-like dissociated state. Written with L. S. Kubie, 1940.

Section 5: Mental Mechanisms

Introduction

19. Experimental demonstrations of the psychopathology of everyday life, 1939.

20. Demonstration of mental mechanisms by hypnosis, 1939.

21. Unconscious mental activity in hypnosis: Psychoanalytic implications. Written with L. B. Hill, 1944.

22. The negation or reversal of legal testimony, 1938.

Section 6: Dual Personality

Introduction

23. The permanent relief of an obsessional phobia by means of com-

munication with an unsuspected dual personality. Written with L. S. Kubie, 1939.

24. The clinical discovery of a dual personality. Unpublished manuscript, circa 1940s.

25. Findings on the nature of the personality structure in two different dual personalities by means of projective and psychometric tests. Unpublished manuscript written with D. Rapaport, circa 1940s.

Section 7: Experimental Neuroses

Introduction

26. A clinical note on a word-association test, 1936.

27. A study of hypnotically induced complexes by means of the Luria technique. Written with P. E. Huston and D. Shakow, 1934.

28. A study of an experimental neurosis hypnotically induced in a case of ejaculatio praecox, 1935.

29. The method employed to formulate a complex story for the induction of an experimental neurosis in an hypnotic subject, 1944.

References

VOLUME 4: Innovative Hypnotherapy

General Introduction

An Introduction to Unorthodox Therapy, written by Milton H. Erickson

I. *General Introductions to Hypnotherapy*

Introduction

1. The application of hypnosis to psychiatry, 1939.

2. Hypnosis in medicine, 1944.

3. Hypnotic techniques for the therapy of acute psychiatric disturbances in war, 1945.

4. Hypnotic psychotherapy, 1948.

Appendix I   549

    5. Hypnosis in general practice, 1957.

    6. Hypnosis: Its renascence as a treatment modality, 1967.

    7. Hypnotic approaches to therapy, 1977.

II. *Indirect Approaches to Symptom Resolution*

Introduction

    8. A clinical note on indirect hypnotic therapy, 1954.

    9. The hypnotic and hypnotherapeutic investigation and determination of symptom-function. Written with H. Rosen, 1954.

    10. Experimental hypnotherapy in Tourette's Disease, 1965.

    11. Hypnotherapy: The patient's right to both success and failure, 1965.

    12. Successful hypnotherapy that failed, 1966.

    13. Visual hallucination as a rehearsal for symptom resolution. Unpublished case discussion with E. L. Rossi, 1974.

III. *Utilization Approaches to Hypnotherapy*

Introduction

    14. Special techniques of brief hypnotherapy, 1954.

    15. Pediatric hypnotherapy, 1959.

    16. The utilization of patient behavior in the hypnotherapy of obesity: Three case reports, 1960.

    17. Hypnosis and examination panics, 1965.

    18. Experiential knowledge of hypnotic phenomena employed for hypnotherapy, 1966.

    19. The burden of responsibility in effective psychotherapy, 1964.

    20. The use of symptoms as an integral part of therapy, 1965.

    21. Hypnosis in obstetrics: Utilizing experiential learnings. Unpublished

manuscript, circa 1950s.

22. A therapeutic double bind utilizing the patient's rebellion. Unpublished manuscript, 1952.

23. Utilizing the patient's own personality and ideas: "Doing it his own way." Unpublished manuscript, 1954.

IV. *Hypnotherapeutic Approaches to Pain*

Introduction

24. An introduction to the study and application of hypnosis for pain control, 1967.

25. The therapy of a psychosomatic headache, 1953.

26. Migraine headache in a resistant patient. Unpublished manuscript, 1936.

27. Hypnosis in painful terminal illness, 1959.

28. The interspersal hypnotic technique for symptom correction and pain control, 1966.

29. Hypnotic training for transforming the experience of chronic pain. Unpublished dialogue with E. L. Rossi, 1973.

V. *Hypnotherapeutic Approaches in Rehabilitation*

Introduction

30. Hypnotically oriented psychotherapy in organic brain damage, 1963.

31. Hypnotically oriented psychotherapy in organic brain damage: An addendum, 1964.

32. An application of implications of Lashley's researches in a circumscribed arteriosclerotic brain condition, 1963.

33. Experimental hypnotherapy in speech problems: A case report, 1965.

34. Provoking recovery from cerebro-vascular accident. Unpublished manuscript, circa 1965.

Appendix I

VI. *Sexual Problems: Hypnotherapeutic Reorientations to Emotional Satisfaction*

Introduction: An Hypothesis about Therapeutic Implants

35. Posthypnotic suggestion for ejaculatio praecox. Unpublished manuscript, circa 1930's.

36. Psychotherapy achieved by a reversal of the neurotic processes in a case of ejaculatio praecox, 1973.

37. Modesty: An authoritarian approach permitting a reconditioning via fantasy. Unpublished manuscript, circa 1950's.

38. Impotence: Facilitating unconscious reconditioning. Unpublished manuscript, 1953.

39. Latent homosexuality: Identity exploration in hypnosis. Unpublished manuscript, 1935.

40. The abortion issue: Facilitating unconscious dynamics permitting real choice. Unpublished manuscript, circa 1950's.

41. The psychological significance of vasectomy, 1954.

42. Vasectomy: A detailed illustration of a therapeutic reorientation. Unpublished manuscript, circa 1950's.

43. Sterility: A therapeutic reorientation to sexual satisfaction. Unpublished manuscript, circa 1950's.

VII. *Self-Exploration in the Hypnotic State: Facilitating Unconscious Processes and Objective Thinking*

Introduction

44. Pseudo-orientation in time as a hypnotherapeutic procedure, 1954.

45. Facilitating objective thinking and new frames of reference with pseudo-orientation in time. Unpublished manuscript, circa 1940's.

46. Self-exploration in the hypnotic state, 1955.

47. Self-exploration in trance following a surprise handshake induction.

Unpublished manuscript, 1952-1954.

48. The reorganization of unconscious thinking without conscious awareness. Unpublished manuscript, 1956.

VIII. *Facilitating New Identity*

Introduction

49. Psychological shocks and creative moments in psychotherapy. Written by E. L. Rossi, 1973.

50. The hypnotic corrective emotional experience, 1965.

51. A shocking breakout of mother domination. Unpublished manuscript, circa 1930s.

52. Shock and surprise facilitating a new self-image. Unpublished manuscript, circa 1930s.

53. The identification of a secure reality, 1962.

54. The hypnotherapy of two psychosomatic dental problems, 1955.

55. The ugly duckling: Transforming the self-image. Unpublished manuscript, 1933.

56. Facilitating a new cosmetic frame of reference. Unpublished manuscript, 1927.

57. Correcting an inferiority complex. Unpublished manuscript, 1937-1938.

58. The February man. Unpublished manuscript, 1942.

References

Appendix 2

Other Writings by Milton H. Erickson

The four volumes of this series are *a complete collection of Milton H. Erickson's papers on hypnosis*. His earlier writings which dealt primarily with subjects of a general nature in psychiatry, intelligence, and criminal behavior have not been included either because they are out of date, unrelated to hypnosis, or the information they contain is already represented adequately in our selection. Papers that are not included in these volumes are listed below:

1. Why young folks leave the farm. *Wisconsin Agriculturists,* 1916. Reprinted in *Wisconsin Agriculturist,* July 9, 1927.

2. A study of the relationship between intelligence and crime. *Journal of the American Institute of Criminal Law and Criminology,* 1929, *19,* 592-635.

3. Marriage and propagation among criminals. *Journal of Social Hygiene,* 1929, *15,* 464-475.

4. Application of Pressey X-O tests to delinquents. *Medico-Legal Journal,* 1930, *47,* 75-87. Written with M. J. Prescor.

5. An interpretation of a case of biological deviation. *Medico-Legal Journal,* 1930, *47,* 140-145.

6. Some aspects of abandonment, feeblemindedness, and crime. *American Journal of Sociology,* 1931, *36,* 758-769.

7. Evolutionary factors in a psychotic. *Medico-Legal Journal,* 1931, *48,* 69-74.

8. Grading patients in mental hospitals as a therapeutic measure. *American Journal of Psychiatry,* 1931, *11,* 103-109. Written with R. G. Hoskins.

9. A cooperative research in schizophrenia. *Archives of Neurology and Psychiatry,* 1933, *30,* 388-401. Written with R. G. Hoskins et al.

10. The concomitance of organic and psychological changes during marked improvement in schizophrenia: a case analysis. *American Journal of Psy-*

chiatry, 1934, *13*, 1349-1357.

11. Opportunities for psychological research in mental hospitals. *Medical Record*, 1936, *143*, 389-392.

12. Psychological factors involved in the placement of the mental patient on visit and family care. *Mental Hygiene*, 1937, *21*, 425-435.

13. "Arrested" mental development. *Medical Record*, 1937, *146*, 352-354.

14. The problem of the definition and the dynamic values of psychiatric concepts: Part I General considerations. *Medical Record*, 1938, *148*, 107-109.

15. The problem of the definition and the dynamic values of psychiatric concepts: Part II. Case history. *Medical Record*, 1938, *148*, 185-189.

16. Criminality in a group of male psychiatric patients. *Mental Hygiene*, 1938, *22*, 459-476.

17. The early recognition of mental disease. *Diseases of the Nervous System*, 1941, *2*, 99-108.

18. A teaching program for commissioned reserve officers. *Diseases of the Nervous System*, 1944, *5*, 112-115.

19. Concerning present inadequacies in the legal recognition and handling of the mentally ill. *Diseases of the Nervous System*, 1946, *7*, 107-109.

20. Hypnotism. *Encyclopaedia Brittanica*, 1946.

21. Hypnotism. *Encyclopaedia Brittanica Junior*, 1946.

22. Foreword. In L. M. LeCron and J. Bordeaux, *Hypnotism today*. New York: Grune and Stratton, 1947. Pp. v-vii.

23. Review of M. Brenman and M. Gill, *Hypnotherapy: A survey of the literature*. New York: International Universities Press, 1947. *Journal of Abnormal and Social Psychology*, 1948, *43*.

24. Hypnotism. *Collier's Encyclopedia*, 1948.

25. Psychological significance of physical restraint to mental patients. *American Journal of Psychiatry*, 1949, *105*, 612-614.

Appendix II

26. Foreword. In H. Rosen, *Hypnotherapy in clinical psychiatry*. New York: Julian Press, 1953. Pp. ix-x.

27. Hypnotism. *Encyclopaedia Brittanica*, 1960.

28. Ciertos principios en la hipnosis medica. *Revista Latino-Americana de Hipnosis Clinica*, 1961, *2*, 67-69.

29. *Refresher course outline*. Texas Medical Association Annual Session, 1962.

30. Critical evaluation: The inhumanity of ordinary people. *International Journal of Psychiatry*, 1967, 277-279.

31. Preface. In D. Akstein (Ed.), *Hipnologia, Volume 1*. Rio de Janeiro: Editoria Hypnos Ltda., 1973. Pp. vii.

32. Foreword. In P. Watzlawick, J. Weakland, and R. Fisch, *Change*. New York: Norton, 1974. Pp. ix-x.

Books by Milton H. Erickson and collaborators:

33. *Time distortion in hypnosis*. Baltimore: Williams and Wilkins, 1954. Written with L. F. Cooper.

34. *The practical application of medical and dental hypnosis*. New York: Julian Press, 1961. Written with S. Hershman and I. I. Secter.

35. *Hypnotic realities*. New York: Irvington, 1976. Written with E. Rossi and S. Rossi.

36. *Hypnotherapy: An exploratory casebook*. New York: Irvington, 1979. Written with E. Rossi.

References

Baken, P. Hypnotizability, laterality of eye movements and functional brain asymmetry. *Perceptual and Motor Skills*, 1969, *28*, 927-932.

Bandler, R., and Grinder, J. *Patterns of the hypnotic techniques of Milton H. Erickson, M.D.*, Vol. 1. Cupertino, California: Meta Publications, 1975.

Barber, T., Spanos, N., and Chaves, J. *Hypnotism, imagination and human potentialities*. New York: Pergamon, 1974.

Bateson, G. *Steps to an ecology of mind*. New York: Ballantine, 1972.

Bateson, G. Personal communication. Letter, 1974.

Bateson, G. Personal communication. Letter of November 10, 1975.

Bateson, G., Jackson, D., Haley, J., and Weakland, J. Toward a theory of schizophrenia. *Behavioral Science*, 1956, *1*, 251-264.

Beahrs, J. The hypnotic psychotherapy of Milton H. Erickson. *American Journal of Clinical Hypnosis*, 1971, *2*, 73-90.

Beahrs, J. Integrating Erickson's approach. *American Journal of Clinical Hypnosis*, 1977, *20*, 55-68.(a)

Beahrs, J. *That which is: An inquiry into the nature of energy, ethics, and mental health*. Palo Alto: Science and Behavior Books, 1977.(b)

Beahrs, J., and Humiston, K. Dynamics of experiential therapy. *American Journal of Clinical Hypnosis*, 1974, *17*, 1-14.

Bernheim, H. *Suggestive therapeutics*. New York: Putnam, 1895.

Binet, A., and Fere, C. *Animal magnetism*. New York: Appleton, 1888.

Bramwell, J. *Hypnotism*. London: Rider, 1921.

Brickner, R., and Kubie, L. A miniature psychotic storm produced by a superego conflict over simple posthypnotic suggestion. *Psychoanalytic Quarterly*, 1936, *5*, 467-487.

Cheek, D., and LeCron, L. *Clinical hypnotherapy*. New York: Grune & Stratton, 1968.

Christensen, A. *Luria's neuropsychological investigation*. New York: Halsted Press, Wiley, 1975.

Cooper, L., and Erickson, M. *Time distortion in hypnosis*. Baltimore: Williams and Wilkins, 1959.

Copi, I. *Symbolic logic*. New York: Macmillan, 1954.

Deese, J. *The structure of associations in language and thought*. Baltimore: John Hopkins, 1965.

Deikman, A. Deautomization in the mystic experience. In C. T. Tart (Ed.), *Altered states of consciousness*. New York: Doubleday, 1972.

Erickson, M. Possible detrimental effects of experimental hypnosis. *The Journal of Abnormal and Social Psychology*, 1932, *27*, 321-327.

Erickson, M. A brief survey of hypnotism. *Medical Record*, 1934, *140*, 609-613.

References

Erickson, M. A study of an experimental neurosis hypnotically induced in a case of ejaculatio praecox. *British Journal of Medical Psychology*, 1935, *15*, 34-50.

Erickson, M. A study of clinical and experimental findings on hypnotic deafness. I) Clinical experimentation and findings. II) Experimental findings with a conditioned reflex technique. *Journal of Genetic Psychology*, 1938, *19*, 127-150; 151-167.

Erickson, M. Experimental demonstration of the psychopathology of everyday life. *The Psychoanalytic Quarterly*, 1939, *8*, 338-353.

Erickson, M. Experimentally elicited salivary and related responses to hypnotic visual hallucinations confirmed by personality reactions. *Psychosomatic Medicine*, 1943, *5*, 185-187.(a)

Erickson, M. Hypnotic investigation of psychosomatic phenomena: psychosomatic interrelations studied by experimental hypnosis. *Psychosomatic Medicine*, 1943, *5*, 51-58.(b)

Erickson, M. An experimental investigation of the hypnotic subject's apparent ability to become unaware of stimuli. *Journal of General Psychology*, 1944, *31*, 191-212.

Erickson, M. Deep hypnosis and its induction. In L. M. LeCron (Ed.), *Experimental hypnosis*. New York: Macmillan, 1952.

Erickson, M. Further techniques of hypnosis-utilization techniques. *American Journal of Clinical Hypnosis*, 1959, *2*, 3-21.

Erickson, M. Historical note on the hand levitation and other ideomotor techniques. *American Journal of Clinical Hypnosis*, 1961, *3*, 196-199.

Erickson, M. A hypnotic technique for resistant patients: The patient, the technique, and its rationale and field experiments. *American Journal of Clinical Hypnosis*, 1964, *1*, 8-32.(a)

Erickson, M. Initial experiments investigating the nature of hypnosis. *American Journal of Clinical Hypnosis*, 1964, *7*, 152-162.(b)

Erickson, M. Pantomime techniques in hypnosis and the implications. *American Journal of Clinical Hypnosis*, 1964, *7*, 65-70.(c)

Erickson, M. Hypnotherapy: The patient's right to both success and failure. *American Journal of Clinical Hypnosis*, 1965, *7*, 254-257.

Erickson, M. The interspersal hypnotic technique for symptom correction and pain control. *American Journal of Clinical Hypnosis*, 1966, *3*, 198-209.

Erickson, M. Further experimental investigations of hypnosis: Hypnotic and nonhypnotic realities. *American Journal of Clinical Hypnosis*, 1967, *10*, 87-135.

Erickson, M., and Rossi, E. Varieties of hypnotic amnesia. *American Journal of Clinical Hypnosis*, 1974, *16*, 225-239.

Erickson, M., and Rossi, E. Varieties of double bind. *American Journal of Clinical Hypnosis*, 1975, *17*, 143-147.

Erickson, M., and Rossi, E. Two-level communication and the microdynamics of trance and suggestion. *American Journal of Clinical Hypnosis*, 1976,

18, 153-171.
Erickson, M., Rossi, E., and Rossi, S. *Hypnotic realities*. New York: Irvington, 1976.
Erickson, M., and Rossi, E. *Hypnotherapy: An exploratory casebook*. New York: Irvington, 1979.
Fromm, E. Similarities and differences between self-hypnosis and heterohypnosis. Presidential Address, American Psychological Association, 1973.
Fromm, E. An idiosyncronic long-term study of self-hypnosis. Paper presented at the American Psychological Association Convention, 1974.
Gur, R., and Reyher, J. Enhancement of creativity via free-imagery and hypnosis. *American Journal of Clinical Hypnosis*, 1976, *18*, 237-249.
Haley, J. *Strategies of psychotherapy*. New York: Grune & Stratton, 1963.
Haley, J. (Ed.) *Advanced techniques of hypnosis and therapy: Selected papers of Milton H. Erickson*. New York: Grune & Stratton, 1967.
Hull, C. Quantitative methods of investigating hypnotic suggestion: Part I. *Journal of Abnormal and Social Psychology*, 1931, *25*, 390-417.
Hull, C. *Hypnosis and suggestibility*. New York: Appleton-Century, 1933.
Huston, P., Shakow, D., and Erickson, M. A study of hypnotically induced complexes by means of the Luria technique. *Journal of General Psychology*, 1934, *11*, 65-97.
Jenkins, J. Remember that old theory of memory? Well, forget it! *American Psychologist*, 1974, *29*, 785-795.
Johnson, R., and Barber, T. Hypnotic suggestions for blister formation: subjective and physiological effects. *American Journal of Clinical Hypnosis*, 1976, *18*, 172-181.
Kendler, H., and Kendler, T. Vertical and horizontal processes in problem solving. *Psychological Review*, 1962, *69*, 1-16.
Kinsbourne, M., and Smith, W. (Eds.) *Hemispheric disconnection and cerebral function*. Springfield, Ill.: C. C. Thomas, 1974.
Kroger, W. *Clinical and experimental hypnosis*. Philadelphia: Lippincott, 1963.
Lundholm, H. An experimental study of functional anesthesias as induced by suggestion in hypnosis. *Journal of Abnormal and Social Psychology*, 1928, *23*, 337-355.
Luria, A. *The working brain*. New York: Basic Books, 1973.
Messerschmidt, R. A quantitative investigation of the alleged independent operation of conscious and subconscious processes. *Journal of Abnormal and Social Psychology*, 1927-1928, *22*, 325-340.
Milgram, S. Behavioral study of obedience. *Journal of Abnormal and Social Psychology*, 1963, *4*, 371-378.
Moll, A. *Hypnotism*. London: Walter Scott, 1890.
Morris, C. Foundations of the theory of signs. In Neurath, V., Carnap, R., and Morris, C. W. (Eds.), *International encyclopedia of unified science*. Vol. 1, No. 2. Chicago: University of Chicago Press, 1938.
Osgood, C. *Method and theory in experimental psychology*. New York: Oxford

References

University Press, 1953.

Overlade, D. The production of fasciculations by suggestion. *American Journal of Clinical Hypnosis*, 1976, *19*, 50-56.

Pattie, F. Methods of induction, susceptibility of subjects and criteria of hypnosis. In R. Dorcus (Ed.), *Hypnosis and its therapeutic applications*. New York: McGraw-Hill, 1956.

Platonov, K. On the objective proof of the experimental personality age regression. *Journal of Experimental Psychology*, 1933, *9*, 190-210.

Platonov, K. *The word as a physiological and therapeutic factor*. Moscow: Foreign Languages Publishing House, 1959.

Prince, M. *The unconscious*. New York: Macmillan, 1929.

Rossi, E. *Dreams and the growth of personality: Expanding awareness in psychotherapy*. New York: Pergamon, 1972.

Rossi, E. Psychological shocks and creative moments in psychotherapy. *American Journal of Clinical Hypnosis*, 1973, *16*, 9-22.

Rowland, L. Will hypnotized persons try to harm themselves or others? *Journal of Abnormal and Social Psychology,* 1939, *34*, 114-117.

Schilder, P., and Kauders, O. *Hypnosis*. Washington, D. C.: Nervous and Mental Disorders Publishing Company, 1927.

Sheehan, P. Hypnosis and the manifestations of imagination. In E. Fromm, & R. Shor (Eds.), *Hypnosis: Research developments and perspectives*. New York: Aldine-Atherton, 1972.

Shor, R. Hypnosis and the concept of the generalized reality orientation. *American Journal of Psychotherapy*, 1959, *13*, 582-602.

Sidis, B. *The psychology of suggestion*. New York: Appleton, 1898.

Sluzki, C., and Ransom, D. *Double bind*. New York: Grune & Stratton, 1976.

Spanos, N., and Barber, T. Toward a convergence in hypnotic research. *American Psychologist*, 1974, *29*, 500-511.

Sternberg, S. Memory scanning: New findings and current controversies. *Quarterly Journal of Experimental Psychology*, 1975, *22*, 1-32.

Tinterow, M. *Foundations of hypnosis*. Springfield, Ill.: C. C. Thomas, 1970.

Watzlawick, P. *The language of change*. New York: Basic Books, 1978.

Watzlawick, P., Beavin, J., and Jackson, D. *Pragmatics of human communication: A study of interactional patterns, pathologies and paradoxes*. New York: Norton, 1967.

Watzlawick, P., Weakland, J., and Fisch, R. *Change: Principles of problem formation and problem resolution*. New York: Norton, 1974.

Weitzenhoffer, A. *Hypnotism: an objective study in suggestibility*. New York: Wiley, 1953.

Weitzenhoffer, A. *General techniques of hypnotism*. New York: Grune & Stratton, 1957.

Weitzenhoffer, A. Unconscious or co-conscious? Reflections upon certain recent trends in medical hypnosis. *American Journal of Clinical Hypnosis*, 1960, *2*, 177-196.

Weitzenhoffer, A. The nature of hypnosis: Parts I and II. *American Journal of Clinical Hypnosis*, 1963, *5*, 295-321; *6*, 40-72.

Weitzenhoffer, A. When is an "instruction" an "instruction"? *The International Journal of Clinical and Experimental Hypnosis*, 1974, *22*, 258-269.

Whitehead, A., and Russell, B. *Principia mathematica*. Cambridge: Cambridge University Press, 1910.

Williams, G. The effect of hypnosis on muscular fatigue. *Journal of Abnormal and Social Psychology*, 1929, *24*, 318-329.

Wolberg, L. *Medical Hypnosis, Vol. 1*. New York: Grune & Stratton, 1948.

Woodworth, R., and Schlosberg, H. *Experimental psychology*. New York: Holt, 1956.

Subject Index

[Page numbers in **bold face** *type are major references.]*

Accents
  personal associations and 374f
Acceptance set
  creative moment and 421
  truisms initiating 483
Age regression
  Aldous Huxley's double-dissociative 102f
  examples of 19, 102, 105f, 372, 461
  pain relief and 123
  Platanov's experiments in 386
  via confusion 261f
Agnosias 471
Altered state
  and new learning 130
Ambivalence (see Confusion)
  utilizing 288f
Amnesia (forgetting)
  autohypnotic training for 126
  examples of 9, 27, 86f, 93, 191, 256, 281f, 350f, 372
  importance of 128, 139
  possible antisocial use of 503
  posthypnotic 96, 402
  recurring in office 191
  selective 96
Anaesthesia (analgesia)
  examples of 93, 193f, 329
  Huxley's 93
  hyperesthetic state and 169
  learning in autohypnosis 126
  oral 169
  saddle-block 96
  surgical 144
Antisocial behavior
  possible hypnotic use of 498f
  self-injury of 504
Archetype
  of wounded physician 2, 124
Association
  principle in suggestion **453f**
Attention
  Erickson's focused attention in trance work 117
  fixation of in double bind 415f
  fixing 285f
  focusing inward 179, 479
  microdynamics of suggestion following the fixation of **448f**
  pain and 123
  response attentiveness 333
  shifting foci of 482

Audience hypnosis 344f, 361
Autohypnosis (see Self-hypnosis)
  behavioral enrichment and 127
  conscious and unconscious in 118
  experimental and clinical trance work in 116
  fear of 125
  life crisis and 111, 115
  memories and 128f
  Milton H. Erickson's use of 108f
  Nirvana and 129
  pain relief and 120
  paradox of **120, 132**
  self-analysis and 128f
  training in **125f**
Automatic (autonomous) processes
  (see Ideomotor, Involuntary movement, Unconscious)
  as hypnotic experience 448
  Huxley's Deep Reflection and 86
  implication and **488f**
  over-learned patterns as 478
  response to suggestion and 341f
Automatic writing 135, 366f
  childhood associations and 442
  dissociation and 443
  examples of **435**, 442
  involuntary behavior of 460
  need for closure evoking 435
Awareness 18f, 83f, 108f
  initial investigations of 22f
  of trance development 244

Bedwetting
  therapy via double bind 416f
Behavioral flexibility
  learned in autohypnosis 127
Biofeedback
  implied directive and 445
  microdynamics of trance 450
Bleeding control
  in dental work 337
Boredom
  in trance induction 302

Cancer
  examples of hypnotherapy in treatment of 284
Casual
  approach in suggestion 96, 169, 185, 186, 250, 344, 351

Catalepsy 139, 285
  arm 289
  autohypnosis and 125
  backache and 492
  examples of 461
  harmful use of 492
  Huxley's 96
  microdynamics of trance and **450f**
  posthypnotic behavior and 400f
Cerebral organization
  synthetic and integrative functions 471
Children
  examples of hypnotherapy with **172f**, 174, 193, 195f, 201f
Choice
  permitting 483
Chomsky's Transformational Linguistics 380
Co-Conscious (subconscious)
  definition of 424
Comfort
  examples in trance induction **169f**, 183f
  trance and 96, 177
Common everyday trance
  utilized in hypnotic induction **479f**
Confusion
  approaches 285f, 293f
  as basis of trance induction 133
  examples of 183, 259f, **488f**
    age regression 261f
    chair
      repositioning of 295
      uncertain seating in 203
    duck riddle 290
    justyourarm 289
    know and no 285f
    nonsense 297
    right and left 258, 276f, 290
    schizophrenic simulation via *here and there, this and that* 267, 290, 294
    time 258, 261f
  humor and 259
  microdynamics of trance and suggestion and **448f**
  psychosomatic reactions to 272f
  technique 99, 158f, **258f**
    brief 287
    humor and 259
    irrevelancies in 258, 260f
    non sequitur 258, 260f
    pantomime as 258
    verbal 258, 278
Conscious and Unconscious
  conscious cannot instruct unconscious 118f
  creative relation between 127
  double bind utilizing 302f, 423
  in trance induction 185
  separation of 120
  training the interface between **127**
Conscious sets
  depotentiating **448, 451,** 481f
Consciousness (see Awareness, Somnambulism)
  alterations of 1
  character and states of 83f
  learning and 132
  unconscious in trance and 243
Context theory
  of two level communication **446f**
Contingent tasks
  posthypnotic behavior in 386
  unconscious communication and 186
Control
  untilizing a lack of 172
Covering all possibilities of response 439
Creative processes
  facilitating 2f
  human potentials and 380
  relating conscious and unconscious 127
Cryptic writing
  in deep trance 338
Crystal ball
  and hypnotic induction 140f

Deaf
  deaf and dumb hypnotic inductions 336
  hypnotic work with 327f
Deep Reflection 2, 85f
  and color 88
Dentistry
  examples of hypnosis in **168f**
Depotentiating
  conscious sets 109, **448f, 451,** 481
  learned limitations **448**
Displacing and discharging (see Resistance)
  hypersensitivity 169
  resistance 485
Dissociation (separating) 121
  age regression and 102f
  anesthesia and autohypnosis in **126**
  double bind and 439
  dynamics of 435
  examples of 435, 439, 443
  Huxley's 105
  microdynamics of trance and suggestion for 451
  multiple 165
  Nirvana and 129

pain relief and 121
posthypnotic trance and 406
seeing and feeling 171
sensory isolation and 126
thinking and doing 487
Distraction
 double suggestions and 484
 microdynamics of trance and suggestion for 451
 two level communication and 432
Double bind **412f**
 double dissociation 439f, **471f**
 Erickson's clinical approach to 420
 ethics of 427
 examples of 185f, **414f**, 438f
 free choice and 422
 fundamental determinant of behavior, as 422
 interpersonal approach and 379
 limitations of 427
 non sequitur 426
 reductio ad absurdi 426
 reverse set 425f
 schizogenic 426f
 time as 425
 triple binds 421
Doubt
 about hypnosis 186, 189, 191
 displacing 430
Dreams
 problem solving and 119
 reality of 102
 symbolism of Hindu mentally ill 338
 training for the creative use of 114
Dyslexia 108f

Ejaculatio praecox 520
Enuresis
 hypnotherapy of 172f
Ergograph experiments 281
Erickson family
 hypnosis-related incidents and anecdotes **135f,** 193, 195f, 358, 361, 374f, 418f
Expectancy 294
 as attitude of therapist 186
 as dependency in induction 179
 in resistance technique 306f
Experiential (see Naturalistic, Utilization)
 latent learning as **478f**
 learning 177f, 291, **478f**
Experimentation with hypnosis 3f, **16f,** 18f
 and autohypnosis 116
 controls for 69
 identical twin hallucination 54
 natural field experiments **340f**

picture hanging experiment 44f
problems with experimentation 16, 65
validity of 71

Frames of reference
 depotentiating 109f
 rigidity of 38
 shifting **430f**
 S-O-I-L illustrating 38
Freudian primary processes
 microdynamics of trance and suggestion in 451
Fright reaction
 in introspection experiment and hypnosis 9f

Generalization
 as indirect hypnotic form 453f, 479
Generalized reality orientation 127, 132
 depotentiation of **448f**
 indirect suggestion and 457

Hallucinations
 auditory 92f
 crystal balls and 140f
 examples of 19f, 83f, 92f, 109f, 117, 136, 342f, 401f
 hand levitation 478, 489
 Huxley's varieties of **96f**
 identical twin 54, 102
 ideosensory 97
 introspection experiment and 8f
 learning and **109f**
 negative 98, 189
 touch 171
 training for 251
 trance induction and **136**
 treatment of 318f
 utilization in hypnotherapy 170, 172
 visual 92f
Hand levitation
 approaches 293
 examples of 13, 185, 209f, 351f
 historical note on 135f
 tactile pressure methods facilitating 334
 twofold example of **487f**
Hyperesthetic state (hypersensitivity)
 in dentistry 169
Hypermnesia 93f, 98
Hypersuggestibility
 not noticed in trance **495**
Hypnosis
 antisocial uses of **498f**
 black magic and 494
 criterion of 7, 398, **450f**

dangers of 491
experimental (laboratory) studies of 3f, **16f**
harmful misinterpretation of **531f**
ignorant use of **533f, 536f**
indirect (see Indirect forms of suggestion)
nature of **3f, 18f,** 22, **113**
physiological sleep and 122
simulation (and faking) 16, 23f, 50, 81, **367f**
subjective response to **88f**
validity of 279, 346
witchcraft and 494
Hypnotic induction 147f
authoritative technique of 15
confusion technique of 158, **258f**
counting in induction and awakening 211f
deep hypnosis and 139, 147f
fright reactions to 6, 9f
hand levitation via **478f**
ideomotor 135, 308f
imagery 141
indirect approach to **15,** 135
interpersonal relationships and 140f
multiple dissociation technique of 165
my-friend-John **340f**
naturalistic approaches to 133, **168f**
naturalistic techniques of **168f**
pantomine technique of **331f**
permissive approach to **15,** 352, 486
posthypnotic tasks as a form of 166
rehearsal technique of 161
resistant patients and 299f
respiratory rhythm during 360f
standardized technique of 3, 175, 399
surprise technique of 109, **340f**
traditional (ritualistic) 49, 140, 168, 291, 327
uncertain chair techniques of 203f
utilization techniques of 177f
via reality testing 187
visualization in 137
Hypnotic learning
definition of **113**
Erickson's personal experiences of **109f**
hand levitation and 185, **479f**
initial stages of 185, 445
microdynamics of trance and suggestion for **448f**
utilizing previous learnings as 197f
Hypnotic phenomena (see each phenomenon listed under its own heading) **478f**

disequilibrium and 440
evoking, general principle of **441,** 448
ideodynamic conception of **131**
in light, medium and deep trance 90f
microdynamics of trance and **450f**
subject's determination of 17
unconsciously acquired over learned patterns **478f**
Hypnotic realities 1f
differentiating hypnotic and waking awareness 28f, 37, 44f, 148f
nonhypnotic realities and 1f, 18f
Hypnotic responsiveness
recognition of 2, 13
Hypnotist, hypnotherapist
abuse of subject's confidence by 526
attitudes of 186
learning indirect suggestion **489f**
manner and attitude in giving suggestions 285
role in suggestion and therapy 326
skills of 134, 391, 450
training via confusion technique 284, 291
unscrupulous 503
Hypnotizability 143
Hysterical paralysis
resolved via confusion 267f

Ideoaffective processes 23
Ideodynamic processes (see Ideomotor, Ideosensory processes)
Bernheim's conception of 131
Ideomotor (see Hand levitation) 131, **478f**
double bind questioning 423f
indirect associative focusing and 456
processes in resistance technique 303f
signaling 138
techniques of hypnotic induction 7, **135f**
Ideosensory processes 131, **135f**
Imagery (see Visualization)
in hypnotic induction 141
Immobility (see Catalepsy)
in hypnotic induction 170, 171, 172
Implication (implies)
examples of 253, 350f, 488
indirect hypnotic form as **458f,** 481f
microdynamics of trance and suggestion of **449f,** 451
Indirect forms of suggestion (and factors facilitating indirect suggestion; see also separate

Index

headings for each indirect form of suggestion) **456f, 478f**
apposition of opposites 456, **469f**, 483
associational networks **463f**, 480, 484
binds and double binds **460f**
casual approach 169, 250, 344, 351
cognitive overloading and 456
compound suggestions **462f**, 482
confusion approaches 474
conscious-unconscious double bind **460f**
contingency as **463f**, 479, 485, 486
covering all possibilities 468f
displacing and discharging resistance 474
dissociation 456
double dissociation double bind **470f**
expectancy 474
generalization 453f, 479f
implication **458f**, 481f, 488
implied directive **464f**, 486
indirect associative focusing **456f**
intercontextual cues 474
interspersed suggestions 486
involuntary signaling 474
mispronounciation 489
negative 170, **192f**
not knowing 131, 182f, **481**
open-ended **468f**
pantomime and nonverbal 474, 479
partial remarks and dangling phrases 474
pause 489
questions 184f, 457f
shock, surprise, and creative moments as 474
therapist's rhythm as 474
truisms **457f**, 483
two level communication as 474
voice locus and dynamics of 474, 481
yes set 294, 421, 462, 483
Indirect suggestion (see Indirect forms of suggestion)
examples of 323, 366f
for awakening 281
hypnotic responses as **478f**
nonverbal **479f**
resistance technique and **452f**
Insight
via visual hallucinations 109
Interpersonal communication
verbal and nonverbal **360f**
Interspersal technique
two level communication and 447
Introspection
experiment 5f
fright reactions to 6, 9f

Involuntary movement (see Ideomotor)
in resistance technique 307f
subjective sensation of in hand levitation 293

Jokes (puns)
microdynamics of trance and suggestion for **449f**

Kinesthetic memories (see Sense memories)
in trance induction 137

Latero-volar-ulnar
hypnotic induction and 334
tactile pressure on 334
Lay hypnotist **536f**
Learned limitations
breaking out of 380, 460, 488
bypassing via indirect suggestions **479f**
Lecture-demonstrations (see Audience hypnosis)
of hypnosis 340f
Levels of awareness
in hypnosis 120
Literal
as attribute of the unconscious 129
Literalism
in posthypnotic behavior 400f
Logic (logical)
contingency and **486**
Russell's type theory of 422

Memory
minimal cues and 373f
problems and autohypnosis 128
visual projection of 351
Mental mechanisms 471
Mental set
for posthypnotic behavior 410
Metalevel 460
as unconscious or autonomous process 120, 460f
Metaphor
microdynamics of trance and suggestion for **450f**
unconscious as 120
Microdynamics of trance induction and suggestion 294, 430f, **448f, 451**, 455
outline of 451
two level communication and 430f
"Middle of nowhere"
in hypnosis 129
Mind reading (thought transference)
via minimal cues 356

Minimal cues 134, **360f, 366f, 373f**
  hypnotic induction and **340f, 360f, 373f**
  indirect suggestions in everyday life 358
  mind reading, thought transference, and psychic phenomena via 356
Miss O 11f, 18f, 42
  trance temper tantrum 11f
Moral code violations
  experimental study of **508f**

Nailbiting
  therapy via double bind 415
Naturalistic **168f**
  approaches to autohypnosis **125f,** 131
  approaches to trance induction 133f, **168f**
  synergism 169
  techniques of hypnosis **168f**
Negative
  words 286
Neuro- and psychophysiological changes in hypnosis
  time for development of 141
Nightmares
  hypnotherapeutic de-conditioning of 196
Nirvana 87
  as "middle of nowhere" 129
  autohypnosis and 129f
Non sequitur
  confusion and 258, 260f
  depotentiating conscious sets via 448
  double bind and 426
  two level communication and 443
Nonverbal (see Pantomime, Suggestion)
  indirect forms of suggestion **453f**
Not knowing 128

Optico-gnostic functions 471

Pain
  displacing 122
  dissociating 121
  early memories of 123
  fatigue and 112
  reinterpreting **122f**
  relief from 112, 120f, 284f
  voluntary 122
Panic states
  hypnotherapy of 171, 311f
Pantomime
  confusion technique and 258
  microdynamics of trance and suggestion 451
  technique in hypnosis **331f**

Paradox (see Double bind) 422
  in autohypnosis 120
  in microdynamics of trance and suggestion **451**
  in trance induction 188
"Perhaps"
  initiating inner exploration 480
Persecutory delusions
  treatment of 319f
Personality alteration
  via hypnosis 495
Picture Hanging Experiment 44f
Posthypnotic
  double binds 421
  inevitable behavior 421
  suggestions, example of 229
  techniques 166
Posthypnotic suggestion and behavior **381f**
  amnesia for 287, 396f
  compulsion of 393
  definition of **388**
  nature and character of **318f**
  right- and left-hand shift of disability, as example of 277
  serial suggestion 400
  spontaneous posthypnotic trance **389f**
Prescribing the symptom (see Symptom)
  in naturalistic approach **168f**
  in utilization approach **177f**
Profanity 300f
  use in resistance technique 300
Psychedelic
  drugs and hypnosis 127
  Huxley's experiments with mescaline 85
Psychoanalysis and psychoanalytic theory
  Erickson's approach in relation to 379
  failure of 182f
  mental mechanisms in 493
  psychodynamics factors of **540f**
Psychodynamic
  as meaningless symbol **541f**
Psychopathology 497
Psychosomatic
  reactions to confusion 272f
Psychotherapy
  methodologies and practice of **540f**
Pupils
  dilation of 281, 289
Puzzle (puzzlement)
  in hypnotic induction 332f

Questions
  double bind 138, **460f**

examples in trance induction 184f
pain relief and **120f**

Rapport 24, 42
   Erickson's development of 117
   posthypnotic behavior in 391f, 401
transferring 282
Repetition
   avoiding in hypnotic work 176
   in trance induction 182f
Resistance
   as antisocial behavior in hypnosis **498f**
   displacing and discharging 430, 485
   not understanding and 186
   to hypnotic commands **498f,** 516
   to rapid induction 495
   to trance 177, 183, 188, 284, 288
   utilizing 288f
Resistance technique **177f,** 299f
   ideomotor 138
Response attentiveness 333
Riddle
   ducks 290

Schizophrenia
   hypnotic simulation of 267
Self-hypnosis (see Autohypnosis)
   Christian Science use of 496
Sense memories
   replacing pain 123
   trance induction and **137f**
   versus imagination 112
Sensory isolation
   dissociation experiment in autohypnosis 126
Sexual problems
   hypnotic resolution of **170f,** 172
Shock (see Surprise)
   breaking old frames of reference 109, 431, 477, 463
Somnambulism 1f
   behavioral indications of **29,** 49
   examples of 11f, 19f, 26f, 32, 41f, 76f, **83f,** 114, 136, 170, 180, 187, 190, 267f, 280, 287, 289, 361, 366f
   hand levitation and 488
   introspection experiment and 10f
   possible antisocial use of 503
   subjective experience of 10f, 64, 78, 86f
   sudden development of 41
   training for **114f**
Stage Hypnotist's Back Syndrome **533f**
State and nonstate theories **476f**
Suggestibility
   and trance 1
Suggestion
   association principle in 453f

contiguity principle in **473f**
contrast principle in 453f
direct and indirect 452f, 487
direct suggestion for subjective responses 188
external 453
generalization of 453f
hitchhiking 484
hypersuggestibility **495**
immediate 454
indirect forms of **452f**
mediate 454
microdynamics of **448f**
mutually reinforcing 482, 484
psychodynamics of **430f, 452f**
similarity principle of 453f
trance and **450**
utilization theory of **450f**
verbal magic 471
Surprise (and shock) 284
   breaking old frames of reference 431
   examples of (see Confusion technique) 288, 431
   hypnotic responsiveness and 478
   microdynamics of trance and suggestion for **448f**
   technique of hypnotic induction **340f**
Symbolic logic (see Logic)
   and suggestion 459, **466f**
Symptom
   prescription 169f, 461
Synergism (see Naturalistic)
   naturalistic approach and **168f**

Testing trance
   utilize rather than test 185
Thinking and doing
   separating, example of 487
Thumbsucking
   hypnotherapy of 174
Time binding suggestion 464f
Time distortion
   Cooper, L. and 380
   examples of 313
   Huxley's 93
   reorientation, as 350
   via confusion 261f, 278
   via "yet" 170
"Timeless and spaceless void" 2, 3, 87, 130
Trance (see Hypnosis, Hypnotic induction, Somnambulism)
   as inner reality 480
   awakening from 8
   behavioral indications of 7, **29,** 105, 281, 285
   danger of **491f**
   deep 49, 96f, 139f, 144f, 281f, 313, 495

depotentiating old programs 127
Erickson's spontaneous 117
induction vs. utilization of 147
induction with commentary 206f
learning 185
iight
medium 28, 91f
microdynamics of 294
segmentalized 120
stuporous 147
Trigeminal neuralgia
　treatment of 321f, 329
Two-level communication **430f**
　association and 442
　context theory of **446f**
　implication and 441
　implied directive and 444
　interspersal technique and 447
　microdynamics of trance and
　　suggestion in **430f**
　shifting frames of reference, 430
　trance induction and 434

Unconscious
　as creative 119
　communication via ideomotor
　　signals 185, 304f
　protection by 445
　questions for 185, 303
　respect for 117
　search in microdynamics of trance
　　and suggestion **449f**
　time requirements for hypnotic work
　　in 129
　work on problems 316
Unconscious search and processes 294
　in microdynamics of trance and
　　suggestion **450f**
Utilization (utilizing)
　aggression 174
　anger 173f
　compulsive attention to detail 178, 179
　conditioning 195
　disequilibrium 440
　doubt 186f, 189, 191
　emotional states to deepen trance 172
　fatigue 177

fear 169
hyperesthetic state 169
intellectual approach 178f
interest in unconscious activity 186
lack of control 172
memories 187
need to "have something done" 194
not knowing 182f
ongoing patterns of behavior 482
panic to deepen trance 171
patient's frame of reference 197f
psychotherapy **540f**
rationale for approach **177f**
reality situation 203
resistance 180f, 288
spontaneous posthypnotic trance 400
stiffness 170
subject's responsive behavior 151
surprise 173f
techniques of hypnosis **168f, 177f,** 205
theory of hypnotic suggestion 131, 380
unconsciously acquired responses 481

Vision
　blurred during induction 183
　peripheral, lacking in trance 281
Visualization (see Imagery) 292f
　in hypnotic induction **137f,** 292f
　microdynamics of trance and
　　suggestion 451
Vocal locus, rhythm, and dynamics 2, 360
　examples of 437
　indirect cues as 474, 481
　two level communication and 437
Void 2, 87, 130

"Wonder"
　as two level suggestion 435
　examples of 183, 481f
Words
　multiple meanings of **451**

Yes set 294, 421, 462
　truisms initiating 483
"Yet"
　facilitating time distortion 170

Name Index

Baken, P. 450, 556
Bandler, R. 380, 556
Barber, T. 131, 446, 452, 476, 556, 558, 559
Bateson, G. 379, 422, 426, 429, 460, 556
Beahrs, J. 380, 556
Beavin, J. 422, 449, 460f, 559
Bekhterev, V. 455
Bernheim, H. 1, 131, 382, 556
Binet, A. 383, 556
Blackwenn, W. 39
Bramwell, J. 382, 556
Brickner, R. 387, 556

Charcot, J. 493
Chaves, J. 446, 452, 556
Cheek, D. 424, 444, 464, 556
Christensen, A. 556
Cooper, L. 380, 556
Copi, I. 459, 556

Deese, J. 556
Deikman, A. 448, 556
Dollard, J. 360

Erickson, A. 193f
Erickson, B. 361
Erickson, E. 121, 166, 379, 381
Erickson, M. (See also Erickson family in Subject Index)
autobiographical and personal characteristics related to hypnotherapeutic skill xi, 2, **108f, 135f,** 360f, 373f, **412f,** 556f

Ferre, C. 383, 556
Fisch, R. 422, 424, 559
Forel, A. 455
Fromm, E. 132, 558

Govindaswamy, M. 267f, 338
Grinder, J. 380, 556
Gur, R. 475, 558

Haley, J. 134, 206, 379, 422, 449, 558
Hall, M. 493
Heidenhein, R. 493
Hershman, S. 379
Hill, L. 379
Hollander, B. 498
Hull, C. 1, 3f, 11, 18f, 37f, 130, 135, 259, 279, 373, 384f, 399, 478, 558

Humiston, K. 380, 556
Huston, P. 379, 387, 520, 558
Huxley, A. 2, **83f**

Isasi, A. 337

Jackson, D. 422, 449, 460f, 559
James, W. 493
Janet, P. 493
Jastrow, J. 4, 39, 360
Jenkins, J. 446f, 558
Johnson, R. 131, 558

Kauders, O. **499f,** 559
Kendler, H. 429, 558
Kendler, T. 429, 558
Kinsbourne, M. 469, 558
Kroger, W. 478, 558
Kubie, L. 308, 338, 373, 379, 387, 556

Lalkaka, K. 338
LeCron, L. 424, 444, 464, 556
Liebault, M. 1, 493
Loefenhart, A. 39
Lorenz, W. 39
Lowenfeld, F. 455, 498
Lundholm, H. 384, 558
Luria, A. 471, 558

Mesmer, F. 493f
Messerschmidt, R. 386f, 407, 558
Milgram, S. 16, 558
Moll, A. 383, 453, 558
Morris, C., 477, 558

Osgood, C. 478, 558
Overlade, D. 132, 559

Pattie, F. 478, 559
Pillsbury, W. 4
Platonov, K. (Platonow) 385, 454, 559
Prince, M. 424, 493, 559

Ransom, D. 460, 559
Rapport, D. 373
Rees, H. 39
Reyher, J. 475, 558
Rossi, E. 131, 421, 424, 430f, 452f, 478f, 557f
Rowland, L. 491, **498f,** 559
Russell, B. **422,** 560

569

Sapir, E. 360
Sarbin, T. 476
Schilder, P. 383, 499f, 559
Schlosberg, H. 441, 560
Secter, I. 379
Shakow, D. 379, 520, 558
Sheehan, P. 131, 559
Shor, R. 127, 132, 448, 457, 559
Sidis, B. 382, 453, 493, 559
Sluzki, C. 460, 559
Smith, W. 558
Spanos, N. 446, 482, 476, 559
Staples, L. 531
Sternberg, S. 457, 559

Tinterow, M. 452, 559

Titchener, E. 4

Watzlawick, P. 380, 422, 424, 449, 460f, 559
Weakland, J. 134, 206, 379, 422, 424, 460, 559
Weitzenhoffer, A. 131, 424, 452, 476, 559
Whitehead, A. 422, 560
Williams, G. 386, 560
Wolberg, L. v, 478, 560
Woodworth, R. 441, 560
Wundt, W. 4

Young, P. 498